# Free Companion CD

YOUR **FREE** CD CONTAINS three programs that are specially designed to help you get the most out of this book and enhance your studies for your CNA credentials. With the help of this CD, you are sure to find success in your NetWare education.

This CD contains *The Clarke Tests*, a Windows-based, interactive learning system (copyright ©1994–1995 LearningWare); WireRIP, a GUI for the World Wire on-line service (copyright ©1993–1995 World Wire); and McAfee Virus Protection (copyright ©1991–1995 McAfee).

For more detailed descriptions of the files on the CD, consult the introduction to this book.

D0932509

# The CNA
# Study Guide

# INTRODUCING NETWORK PRESS™

You *can* judge a book by its cover.

Welcome to Network Press™, the new and expanded successor to **Sybex's** acclaimed **Novell Press**® book series. If you liked our Novell Press books, you'll be impressed by the improvements we've made in the books that replace them. With **Network Press**, you'll find the same quality from a truly independent and unbiased viewpoint. You'll also find full coverage of not only Novell, but Microsoft and other network environments.

Building on a 20-year history of technical and publishing excellence, **Network Press**™ is dedicated to providing you with the fullest range and depth of networking information available today. You'll find the same commitment to quality, contents, and timeliness that you have come to expect from Novell Press books by Sybex. All previously released Novell Press titles remain available from Sybex.

---

**Network Press** books continue to offer you:

- winning certification test preparation strategies
- respected authors you know and trust
- all new titles in a wide variety of topics
- completely updated editions of familiar best-sellers
- distinctive new covers

Our leadership approach guarantees your ongoing success in managing every aspect of your network's software and hardware.

---

Look for these **Network Press** titles, available now at your local bookstore:

*The CNE Study Guide, Second Edition,* by David James Clarke IV
    (Revised and updated edition of *Novell's CNE Study Guide*)
*The Network Press Dictionary of Networking*, by Peter Dyson
    (Revised and updated edition of *Novell's Dictionary of Networking*)
*The Complete Guide to NetWare 4.1,* by James E. Gaskin
*Managing an Inherited NetWare Network*, by Michael J. Miller
*The CNE Update to NetWare 4.1,* by Michael Moncur

**For more information about Network Press, please contact:**

Network Press
2021 Challenger Drive
Alameda, CA 94501
Tel: (510) 523-8233/(800) 227-2346
Fax: (510) 523-2373/Email: info@sybex.com

# The CNA<sup>CLM</sup> Study Guide

## Second Edition

The first edition of this book was published
under the title *Novell's CNA Study Guide*.

**David James Clarke, IV**

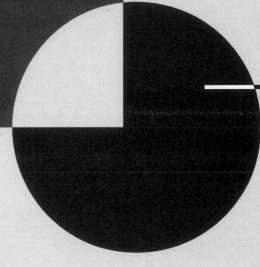

San Francisco ■ Paris ■ Düsseldorf ■ Soest

Acquisitions Manager: Kristine Plachy
Developmental Editors: David Kolodney and Guy Hart-Davis
Editors: Armin Brott and Abby Azrael
Technical Editor: Mark D. Hall
Book Designer: Seventeenth Street Studios
Technical Artist: Cuong Le
Desktop Publisher: London Road Design
Proofreader/Production Assistant: Ron Jost
Indexer: Lynn Brown
Cover Designer: Archer Design
Cover Photographer: Greg Probst

Screen reproductions produced with Collage Plus.

Collage Plus is a trademark of Inner Media Inc.

Network Press and the Network Press logo are trademarks of SYBEX Inc.

SYBEX is a registered trademark of SYBEX Inc.

TRADEMARKS: SYBEX has attempted throughout this book to distinguish proprietary trademarks from descriptive terms by following the capitalization style used by the manufacturer.

Every effort has been made to supply complete and accurate information. However, SYBEX assumes no responsibility for its use, nor for any infringement of the intellectual property rights of third parties which would result from such use.

The first edition of this book was published under the title *Novell's CNA Study Guide* copyright © 1994 SYBEX Inc.

Library of Congress Card Number: 95-70851
ISBN: 0-7821-1819-4

Manufactured in the United States of America

10 9 8 7 6 5 4 3 2

# Warranty and Disclaimer

## Warranty

SYBEX warrants the enclosed CD-ROM to be free of physical defects for a period of ninety (90) days after purchase. If you discover a defect in the CD during this warranty period, you can obtain a replacement CD at no charge by sending the defective CD, postage prepaid, with proof of purchase to:

SYBEX Inc.
Customer Service Department
2021 Challenger Drive
Alameda, CA 94501
(800) 227-2346
Fax: (510) 523-2373

After the 90-day period, you can obtain a replacement CD by sending us the defective CD, proof of purchase, and a check or money order for $10, payable to SYBEX.

## Disclaimer

SYBEX makes no warranty or representation, either express or implied, with respect to this medium or its contents, its quality, performance, merchantability, or fitness for a particular purpose. In no event will SYBEX, its distributors, or dealers be liable for direct, indirect, special, incidental, or consequential damages arising out of the use of or inability to use the software, even if advised of the possibility of such damage.

The exclusion of implied warranties is not permitted by some states. Therefore, the above exclusion may not apply to you. This warranty provides you with specific legal rights; there may be other rights that you may have that vary from state to state.

## Copy Protection

None of the programs on the CD is copy-protected. However, in all cases, reselling or making copies of these programs without authorization is expressly forbidden.

*I dedicate this book to the human race for never ceasing to amaze me.*

# Acknowledgments

S
O MANY PEOPLE TO thank, and so little time. What a cliché, but it's true. I believe we are all molded by our past and present experiences. With this in mind, I would like to take a moment to thank the sculptors of my personality. It all started with my family—literally. My wife, Mary, deserves the most credit for supporting my work and bringing a great deal of happiness to my life. Thanks! To Leia—my new daughter—this book pales in comparison to her grand arrival. Thanks for providing my life with much-needed perspective.

I owe a tremendous amount to my parents for their unending support and devotion. They were very active artists in molding my life. I couldn't have done any of this without their help. In addition, my sister, Athena and her new family, Ralph and Taylor, deserve kudos for supporting me through the crazy times. Thanks to my second family for opening their hearts to me: Don and Diane for their kindness and Keith and Bob for their wisdom. In addition, I owe a great deal to Dr. James Buxbaum and Rene Mendoza—my mentors and extended family.

Speaking of virtual family, I would like to thank all of the frightfully talented students who have shared their dreams with me over the past five years. Talk about molding...thanks to the Wednesday night therapy crowd at Clarity, weekend Jack and the heart attacks, the beta classes from DVC, and all the curious night owls at Las Positas College. Let's not forget the Irvine Valley classes and their wonderful sense of humor. It's safe to say that my students have had a profound effect on my life. Draw your own conclusions!

There are numerous friends to thank. Lori Jorgeson, for her relentless help and timely editing. We make a great team. Armin Brott, for his remarkable editing talent and creative abilities. Thanks for polishing the personality of my book. Mark Hall for his technical expertise and valuable input. Abby Azrael for spearheading the project, the SYBEX production team for putting the book together, and Lynn Brown for a wonderful index. Thanks to Altima for an incredible notebook and Tears for Fears for musical therapy. Finally, thanks to David Foster and K. C. Sue at Novell Education for their support and contribution.

Probably the most important architects of *The CNA Study Guide* are Rose Kearsley, Peter Jerram, and David Kolodney—they are great friends. Thanks

Rose, for your friendship, enthusiasm, and support; Peter for your wisdom and ideas; and David for your exceptional guidance. I owe a great deal to all of you for banding around a common idea and bringing this book to life. What a great team.

I saved the best for last. Thanks to YOU for caring enough about your NetWare career to buy this book. You deserve a great deal of credit for your enthusiasm and dedication—this education can change your life. Good luck with NetWare, and enjoy the book!

*Welcome to your life, there's no turning back!*

*Tears for Fears*

# Contents at a Glance

# Table of Contents

# Introduction

## The README.NOW File

So you want to be a Certified Novell Administrator—a noble proposition! Life as a CNA is both exciting and rigorous. It is an obstacle course of unpredictable network challenges—connectivity problems, user complaints, security violations, and so on. But just like the aim in doing any obstacle course, the goal is to finish in one piece. Don't worry, you'll do great.

In this book, we will journey through the pitfalls and triumphs of NetWare system management—together. You will acquire a NetWare "Utility Belt" filled with wondrous CNA tools, including Novell resources, advanced management techniques, security procedures, and sample login scripts. In addition, we will learn about NetWare directory structures, drive mapping, security, menu utilities, printing, network management, and LAN optimization. Wow!

To aid you on this noble journey, *The CNA Study Guide* is filled with valuable learning tools: icon-oriented text, 3-D graphics, laboratory exercises, technical tips, crossword puzzles, and most importantly, a bank of new, original CNA test sample questions on CD-ROM. The goal is to walk with you through the entire CNA program, presenting it in an effective, entertaining manner. I think you'll like it.

Before we get started, let's warm up with a brief preview of what's ahead. We'll start with an overview of the similarities and differences between NetWare 2.2 and NetWare 3.12. Then, we will explore the layout of the land—icons, exercises, CD-ROM, and that sort of thing. Then we'll take a look at where you can go for some additional HELP, and wind down with The Bottom Line. Every book should have one.

---

# NetWare 2.2 vs. NetWare 3.12

*Never invest in anything that eats or needs repairing!*

*Billy Rose*

NetWare 2.2 and 3.12 represent Novell's seventh and eighth generations of their best-selling NetWare network operating system. NetWare 2.2 is a complete 16-bit solution that meets the needs of small businesses, professional offices, workgroups, and departments. It is a nonmodular "rock" of technology that provides excellent file and printing services, but no support for multiple protocols or interconnectivity. NetWare 3.12, on the other hand, is a fully modular 32-bit operating system that supports simultaneous access from DOS and non-DOS workstations. In addition, NetWare 3.12 takes full advantage of the 32-bit file server architecture by providing nearly unlimited access to shared disk storage, memory, and interconnected LANs.

NetWare 2.2 is Play-Doh—rigid and moderately useful. NetWare 3.12 is Legos—modular, robust, and fun. Let me explain. Play-Doh is flexible at first. It can be easily molded into any shape. But once it dries, it becomes an inflexible rock—no changes. Similarly, NetWare 2.2 is flexible at first. But once the operating system has been installed and the NET$OS.EXE file has been configured, the system manager is pretty much stuck with the design.

Legos, on the other hand, can be easily assembled into a beautiful palace and then dismantled and reassembled into a race car. This level of modular versatility is evident through NetWare 3.12's NetWare Loadable Module (NLM) architecture. With this design, all LAN facilities can be loaded and unloaded at will. NetWare 3.12 consists of three components: the NetWare file system, the system executive, and NLM software bus. With the right imagination, the system manager can build any type of network—small, medium, or large.

# Two Books in One!

*Some books are to be tasted, others swallowed, and some few to be chewed and digested.*

*Francis Bacon*

Novell offers CNA 2.2 and CNA 3.12 certifications. In an effort to be both clear and complete, I have broken this material into two parts—Part 2: The NetWare 2.2 CNA Program and Part 3: The NetWare 3.12 CNA Program. The 2.2 CNA program is designed for system managers who work primarily with NetWare 2.2 LANs. The 3.12 CNA program is slanted toward the more advanced NetWare 3.12 platform. The trick is to cover both programs completely without too much repetition. I chose to approach each version autonomously; that is, each program is covered completely in its own half of the book. I avoid repetition because NetWare 2.2 and 3.12 differ dramatically in their approach to system management. Each CNA program has its own unique focus. Think of it as getting two books in one—what a deal!

The first step towards becoming a Certified Novell Administrator is a clear understanding of NetWare basics. It all begins with Part 1: CNA Fundamentals. In Chapters 1 and 2, I will lay the foundation for the NetWare CNA program—Microcomputer/DOS Fundamentals and NetWare Basics. NetWare 2.2 system management is comprehensively detailed in Part 2: The NetWare 2.2 CNA Program. Part 2 compares the CNA's role to that of manager of an apartment building—with rooms, tenants, security, and a LAN laundry room. Chapter 3 starts the NetWare 2.2 CNA program with a discussion of Net-Ware directory structures and drive mapping. Security is next, with an outline of NetWare 2.2's multilayered security model. Chapter 5, NetWare 2.2 Utilities, introduces you to some of NetWare's most useful and productive CNA tools. Chapter 6, NetWare 2.2 Network Management, provides an in-depth discussion of the CNA's key system management responsibilities—login restrictions, login scripts, user interface, and backup. Finally, the NetWare 2.2 CNA program ends with a journey into the world of printing installation and management.

The exciting journeys of NetWare 3.12 CNAs are chronicled in Part 3: The NetWare 3.12 CNA Program. In Part 3, you will assume many management roles within a big, luxurious hotel: You will wear the hats of the hotel architect, handyman, house detective, and interior decorator. Chapter 8 explains

NetWare directory structures and drive mapping. Security, Chapter 9, delves deeply into the maze of login restrictions and access rights. In addition, the security chapter provides you with some easy-to-follow models for high and low levels of NetWare 3.12 security. Chapter 10, NetWare 3.12 Utilities, focuses on the tools available for NetWare 3.12 CNA system management—menu utilities, command-line utilities, supervisor utilities, and console commands. Chapter 11, NetWare 3.12 Network Management, provides an in-depth discussion of the NetWare 3.12 CNA's key system management roles and responsibilities. It begins with a peek at system management strategies, and then dives into login scripts, user interface, multiprotocol management, backup, and the remote management facility. Chapter 12 focuses on NetWare 3.12 printing installation, management, customization, and troubleshooting. Finally, the NetWare 3.12 CNA program ends with a journey into the world of NetWare 3.12 performance management. This is a special chapter that explains NetWare's performance management components and provides a checklist of strategies for monitoring and customizing NetWare 3.12 server performance. What a way to end!

Next, you will find a variety of valuable appendices. Appendix A is a comprehensive overview of Novell's education strategy. Warning: information contained in this appendix could change your life. Appendices B and C include rare NetWare 2.2 and 3.12 installation and management worksheets. These forms lay the foundation for your all-important NetWare Log. Appendix D is filled with detailed answers to all of the lab and case exercises, and Appendix E is a dictionary of the acronyms used throughout the book. Don't ignore the appendices—they're full of valuable CNA resources.

# Are We Having Fun Yet!?!!

*All animals except man know that the principal business of life is to enjoy it.*

*Samuel Butler*

I couldn't have said it any better myself—so I won't.

The main goal of this book is to take the reader through a magic carpet ride of CNA responsibilities, tools, and technologies—nobody said it couldn't be fun! To accomplish this monumental task and cover the enormous wealth of NetWare knowledge, I have incorporated a variety of learning tools: text and graphics, exercises, icons, and diskettes. Let's take a quick look.

## Text and Graphics

The majority of the information is in the text. The format is interesting and I have made every effort to provide you with an enjoyable level of readability. Learning doesn't have to be torture. In addition, I have included "pull-quotes" to highlight key concepts and milestones. These pull-quotes provide a whole new level of speed reading. Also, there are over one hundred clear and concise graphics to illustrate major technical points.

## Lab Exercises

Some of these exercises call for written answers, but most are hands-on. These exercises are designed to provide the reader with "real-life" experience in implementing important CNA responsibilities. In addition, they help you to practice with CNA tools you have learned to use. Note—most of the Lab Exercises assume that you have access to a NetWare LAN. If you don't, we have made an on-line lab available to you through LAN*imation*—refer to the Help! section of this introduction for more details.

**Case Exercises**—this is as real as it gets. You will manage, maintain, and troubleshoot an existing NetWare 3.12 LAN for Snouzer, Inc.—a fictional doggie fashions company.

**Matching Exercises**—test your skills against four matching exercises—covering topics such as Microcomputer Fundamentals and Performance Management Components.

**Crossword Puzzles**—have fun with three challenging puzzles—covering Part I, Part II, and Part III.

The answers to all of the exercises are included in excruciating detail in Appendix D.

### Icons

The icons are my pride and joy. These quips provide instant information in the form of Tips, Quotes, and Knowledge tidbits. Here is what they look like—

*Tips highlight time-proven management techniques and action-oriented ideas.*

*Quotes add flavor from people more dazzling than myself.*

*David Clarke*

*Knowledge icons point out critical theories, concepts, and/or delectable facts.*

Refer to the icons throughout the text for additional information and added value. This strategy provides another level of speed reading.

## CD-ROM

A special CD-ROM has been included with *The CNA Study Guide* to enhance and support your NetWare education. Inside you will find three exciting surprises. Let's take a closer look.

**THE CLARKE TESTS** With help from LAN*imation* and NUI, I have developed a whole new way of studying for CNA tests. *The Clarke Tests* is Windows-based software that offers more than just sample test questions. It is an interactive learning system! In addition to valuable CNA test questions, the software offers interactive clues, graphics, page references to Novell-authorized courseware, and various study paths. But the real stars are the interactive answers. Each question includes a full page or more of explanation and study material. These challenging test questions and interactive answers are an invaluable study tool for passing the Certified Novell Administrator exams. Give this demo version a try.

Refer to the README.CLK file for installation instructions. It can be found in the D:\CNA\CLARKE subdirectory on the CD-ROM. Begin Microsoft Windows and choose File ➤ Run. Then type D:\CNA\CLARKE\SETUP in the input window and click OK. Note: If your CD-ROM drive letter is something other than D, type in that letter instead of D. Once the demo of the Clarke tests has been installed, you can walk through the interactive testing system using the special tutorial program. It's never been so easy to study. Remember, the Clarke tests are just a learning tool for the actual Drake certification exams. They are not the real CNA tests.

**WIRERIP** WireRIP is the graphical user interface for World Wire. World Wire is a new, exciting on-line service specifically designed for networking professionals. It includes technical information, downloadable files, forums, and an on-line shopping mall. But the feature that sets it apart is the on-line lab. The World Wire LAB gives you full access to NetWare 2.*x*, 3.1*x*, and 4.*x* servers. You can complete CNA exercises, try out new management configurations, or just get comfortable with NetWare's many command-line and menu utilities. WireRIP uses a menu-driven interface with built-in phone directories and support for almost all modems. In addition, WireRIP was specially designed to optimize performance in the World Wire LAB. Refer to the C:\CNA\README.CNA file for installation instructions.

**MCAFEE VIRUS PROTECTION** Throughout this book, we will explore the deadly nature of computer viruses. We will discuss strategies for preventing and destroying them. One of the best solutions is provided by McAfee

Associates, the leader in virus-protection technology. To save your LAN from infection, I have included McAfee's latest workstation and server virus-prevention products on the CD-ROM. It's up to you to use them. Refer to the C:\CNA\README.CNA file for installation instructions. Also, there are McAfee documentation files in the VIRUS subdirectory. Refer to these text files for more information. Please follow my networking tools motto: Use it or lose it!

There really is no substitute for personal, live training. But we have done everything we can to make this study guide almost as interesting. Some say this book has a mind of its own!

## Help!

*An ounce of action is worth a ton of theory.*

*Friedrich Engels*

Inevitably, you are going to want to apply this great NetWare knowledge to some physical structure—a LAN perhaps. One assumes you will *act* on this book's CNA concepts, theories, methods, and procedures. It would be very irresponsible of me to abandon you at the very point you need the most help—real life! So in an attempt to provide you with the most complete assistance possible, I have created an organization called LAN*imation*. LAN*imation* is a team of CNEs, students, authors, and networking professionals who have banded together to offer NetWare assistance to readers of this book. We currently use a variety of different resources, including CompuServe, Internet, and World Wire. If you are interested in joining LAN*imation* or just need some help, contact us at any of the following locations:

| | |
|---|---|
| Electronic Mail | CompuServe at David James Clarke, IV—71700,403 |
| Phone | LAN*imation* at (510) 254-7283 |
| Physical Mail | LAN*imation* at 140 Stein Way Orinda, CA 94563-3431 |
| World Wire (explained next) | (510) 254-1193 or local access number |

In addition to LAN tips and answers, LAN*imation* supports a remote on-line NetWare LAN for readers who don't have a network of their own. You can use the system to complete the lab exercises, Snouzer case studies, or just practice what I preach. The system is called World Wire, and it requires a PC, modem (14.4 baud supported), and any communications software (see Chapter 2). A graphical user interface can be downloaded for free. Give it a try.

## Bottom Line

*The longer the island of knowledge, the longer the shoreline of wonder.*

*Ralph W. Sockman*

The bottom line is this: *The CNA Study Guide* covers all of the CNA and most of the CNE/CNI system management objectives.

If you are interested in obtaining any of these three NetWare certifications, you should definitely attend Novell-authorized courses. This book is designed to supplement Novell's traditional education methods. But it can also be used to supplement your practical knowledge and NetWare LAN experience. The information provided in this book is comprehensive, accurate, and Novell-compatible. Certification is within your grasp. In this book, we will cover three certification versions: NetWare 2.2, 3.11, and 3.12. The NetWare 3.11 and 3.12 material is covered together in the NetWare 3.12 CNA section, because 3.11 and 3.12 are nearly identical. They differ only in workstation software, documentation, NCP packet signature, menu software, backup, electronic mail, and alloc short term memory. In each of these cases a Tip is used to point out the differences.

Have a great time and good luck with NetWare. Enjoy the book!

# CNA
# Fundamentals

PART

S O YOU WANT TO be a Certified Novell Administrator. A noble proposition. Life as a CNA is both exciting and rigorous. It is an obstacle
course of unpredictable network challenges: connectivity problems,
user complaints, security violations, and so on. But just like with any other
obstacle course, the goal is to finish in one piece. Don't worry, you'll do great.

In this book, we'll walk through the pitfalls and triumphs of NetWare system
management—together. You will acquire a NetWare utility belt filled with wondrous CNA tools, including Novell resources, advanced management techniques,
security procedures, and sample login scripts. In addition, we'll learn about Net-
Ware directory structures, drive mapping, security, menu utilities, printing, network
management, and LAN optimization. Wow!

To aid you on your journey, *The CNA Study Guide* is filled with valuable learning
tools: icon-oriented text, 3-D graphics, laboratory exercises, sample computer-
based training, simulations, Q & A, and—most importantly—a bank of NEW CNA
test questions. The goal is to present a superset of Novell's CNA program in an
effective, entertaining manner. I think you'll like it.

Novell offers three CNA certifications—2.2, 3.12, and 4.0. In an effort to be
both clear and complete, we have broken this book into two programs—2.2 and
3.12. The 2.2 program is designed for system managers who work primarily with
LANs running NetWare 2.2. The 3.12 program is slanted toward the more advanced 3.12 platform. Each program corresponds with the appropriate 2.2 or 3.12
CNA certification. The trick is to cover both programs completely without too
much repetition. We chose to approach each version autonomously—with each
program covered completely in its own half of the book. We avoid repetition because NetWare 2.2 and 3.12 differ dramatically in their approach to system management. Each CNA program has its own unique focus. Think of it as getting two
books in one—what a deal.

Before we dive into the first CNA program, NetWare 2.2, we need to spend
a few minutes reviewing LAN fundamentals. The first two chapters of this book
cover the basics of microcomputers/DOS and NetWare. Chapter 1, Micro-
computer/DOS Fundamentals, provides a quick system management review of

microcomputer and DOS concepts. Chapter 2, NetWare Basics, focuses on the fundamentals of LAN management and NetWare hardware/software basics. These early fundamentals will provide you with a holster for your NetWare system management tools. Once you acquire your NetWare utility belt, you will be ready to fill it with valuable CNA tools.

Let's begin with Microcomputer/DOS fundamentals.

# Microcomputer/ DOS Fundamentals

BEFORE WE DIVE INTO the glamorous pool of NetWare system management, we must put on our swimming suit of microcomputer/DOS basics. A fundamental understanding of microcomputers and DOS (Disk Operating System) is necessary to make the transition from the shallow end of stand-alone computing to the deep waters of network management. After all, you don't want to be swallowed by the Ethernet whitewash or devoured by the mainframe sharks.

In this chapter we will explore the basics of microcomputer hardware and DOS software. We will focus on how these components affect local area network (LAN) connectivity and NetWare system management. The most important thing to get out of this chapter is an appreciation for the complex relationship between file server hardware (Intel-based microcomputers) and workstation software (DOS). Let's begin with microcomputers.

# Understanding Microcomputers

SINCE ITS INTRODUCTION in 1977, no other electronic component has altered the course of humanity's future more than the microcomputer. Its presence is evident in every aspect of our lives—our homes, our schools, our jobs, and our books. The microcomputer is also the basis of our local area networks—workstations and file servers.

*The most impor-
tant thing to get out
of this chapter is an
appreciation for the
complex relationship
between file
server hardware
(Intel-based micro-
computers) and
workstation software
(DOS).*

The microcomputer architecture follows the same fundamental concepts as earlier computers. The basic functions of any computer, whether it's a micro-, mini-, or gigantic mainframe computer, can be summarized into four basic operations:

- input

- processing

- storage

- output

Figure 1.1 graphically displays the relationship of these basic computer operations. Input is the process of feeding a computer raw data. Input tools include keyboards, mice, trackballs, and scanners. Some microcomputers even have voice-recognition systems that will allow users to input data by simply talking to their machines. This technology opens a whole new arena for psychiatrists and counselors.

Once data has been fed into the system, it waits in a buffer until the microprocessor is ready to process it. Data processing is performed by a critical computer component called the Central Processing Unit (CPU). The CPU consists of two components—the control unit and arithmetic/logic unit (ALU). We will discuss the details of microcomputer processing later in the chapter.

*Processing includes a variety of different computer operations—classifying, sorting, calculating, recording, summarizing, combining, and separating. In reality, all of these complex operations are accomplished by seven simple arithmetic/logic tasks—addition, subtraction, multiplication, division, less than, greater than, and equal to. At the most elementary level, these seven tasks are the only things a computer can do!!*

Once data has been input and processed, it becomes useful *information*. Information has three different places to go:

- It can be sent to an external output device—monitor, printer, plotter, etc.

- It can be written to a temporary or permanent storage location. Computer storage involves recording the information as electronic bits on a magnetic media such as a hard disk, floppy disk, or magnetic tape.

**FIGURE 1.1**
The computer model

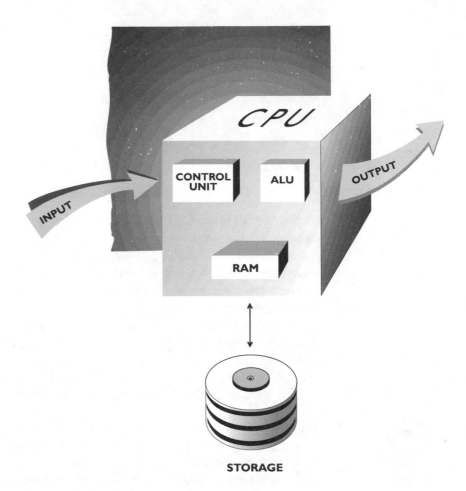

*All of these internal computer gyrations are made possible by electronics. The electronics of a microcomputer operate like a light switch—on or off.*

▪ Processed information can be returned to the microprocessor as input. In this case, the information becomes data for a secondary computer operation.

All of these internal computer gyrations are made possible by electronics. The electronics of a microcomputer operate like a light switch—on or off. This is called *binary* operation. Microcomputers represent binary data as digits of information. An ON condition is represented by the digit 1 and an OFF condition is a logical 0. The computer's binary digits—0s and 1s—are called *bits*. Bits are further organized into logical words called bytes—8 bits make a *byte*.

Unfortunately, most humans don't understand bits and bytes. The real trick is to translate microcomputer electronics into something understandable—like characters of the alphabet, for example. One such translation code is called ASCII, or American Symbolic Code for Information Interchange. The ASCII code takes a combination of 8 bits and translates them into an ASCII character. Most of the ASCII characters are recognizable— letters, numbers, and so on—but some are reserved as graphic symbols. Standard ASCII consists of 128 characters of 7 bits per byte whereas the extended ASCII set has 256 characters in 8 bits per byte.

While all of this techno-babble is fascinating to some, it doesn't mean a hill of beans to many LAN users because it represents information as non-tangible components. It's very difficult to touch an electronic bit (but if you do, watch out—they've been known to cause some very serious hair). Our discussion of microcomputer fundamentals is not going to focus on the electronics of the computer. Instead, we will explore the microcomputer's relationship with NetWare and the components that create LAN work-stations and file servers.

*You can lead a boy to college, but you cannot make him think.*

*Elbert Hubbard*

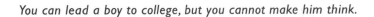

In this chapter, we will explore six fundamental microcomputer components:

- microprocessor

- data bus

- memory

- disk

- video display

- input/output

These components work together in synergy to bring form and function to NetWare LAN hardware. The first component is the microprocessor, or CPU. The CPU communicates with other internal components over the data bus pathway. Memory is required for the CPU to carry out its function and performs a temporary storage role for CPU instructions and software. Disks are permanent storage for NetWare files and workstation operating systems. Video display provides a colorful graphic output for users, and input/output components provide a facility for the integration of external peripherals and other hardware components.

Let's begin our discussion with the details of the microprocessor.

## Microprocessors

As mentioned above, the microprocessor is the brains of the microcomputer. Microprocessors are miniature wafers of silicon with tiny integrated circuits and intelligent transistors. Silicon provides a semi-conductive surface for electronic communications and a semi-insulated surface for decreased friction. Silicon closely resembles carbon on the periodic table.

As mentioned earlier, microprocessors are functionally organized into two primary components: a control unit and arithmetic/logic unit (ALU). The control unit handles internal operations and directs the software instructions to the proper elements of the ALU. The arithmetic/logic unit performs the real "computing"—add, subtract, multiply, divide, less than, greater than, and equal to.

*The microcomputer brain is composed primarily of silicon, a versatile, durable element that closely resembles carbon. Many scientists have theorized that a computer made of carbon could literally think like a human being. Ironically, the human brain is made entirely out of carbon and water. It makes you think, doesn't it?*

*The world of microprocessors has united around two manufacturers—Intel and Motorola.*

The world of microprocessors has united around two manufacturers—Intel and Motorola. The Intel-based microprocessors are powerful and arithmetic-oriented. They perform complex mathematic calculations and excel with spreadsheet and database software. Intel microprocessors are the foundation of IBM-compatible microcomputers. The Motorola-based microprocessors are also powerful, but in a different way. They are designed to perform complex display operations for engineering, artificial intelligence, and advanced graphics. The Motorola microprocessors are the foundation of Apple Macintosh, Silicon Graphics, and NeXT microcomputers. The following is a brief discussion of Intel and Motorola microprocessors.

### Intel Microprocessors

Intel introduced its first microprocessor in 1978. Over the past fifteen years Intel has produced eight unique microchip generations and is currently working on numbers nine and ten. The Intel chip has been the mainstay of the microcomputer revolution as it spawned the IBM PC line of microcomputers and clones. It uses a relatively simple, yet effectively open architecture. Here are descriptions of each of Intel's eight microchip generations.

**8086**  The 8086 was Intel's first chip. It surprised everybody by using a 16-bit architecture (the standard at that time was 8-bit). Unfortunately for Intel, nobody could use the chip—it was simply too advanced. So they returned to the proverbial drawing board and created an 8-bit version of the 8086, which they called the 8088.

*Data communications within the microcomputer is analogous to lanes on a freeway. The more lanes, the faster the traffic. Hence, the more bits allowed through the computer, the faster the data communications. For example, a 16-bit microprocessor can handle 16 bits of information simultaneously— a significant improvement over the earlier 8-bit architecture.*

**8088**  The 8088 chip was Intel's compromise in 1979. The 8088 was basically the same as the 8086, except it used 8-bit data communications, which was necessary to support the 8-bit hardware of that era. The 8088 became the foundation of IBM's original IBM PC. In addition, this chip featured 20-bit memory addressing (up to 1MB RAM) and clock speeds of 4.77 to 10 megahertz (MHz). A MHz represents one million clock cycles per second. A clock cycle is required for each fundamental microprocessor task. The more MHz, the faster the microcomputer.

**80286**  In 1984, Intel introduced a revolutionary advancement beyond the 8086—the 80286. The 80286 chip's 16-bit architecture became the foundation of IBM's new AT class of microcomputers. The new 16-bit microprocessor boasted numerous enhancements over its predecessors. Here's a brief list:

- The 80286 could simulate a large amount of internal real memory as virtual memory. Virtual memory is disk space that appears as random access memory (RAM). The 80286 was capable of 1GB of virtual memory.

*The 80386 is currently the most popular microprocessor in the world and it represents a significant advancement over the earlier chips.*

- The 80286 supported hardware multitasking. Multitasking allows the computer to entertain multiple programs simultaneously. Unfortunately, Intel didn't create any multitasking programs to take advantage of this feature. The multitasking capabilities laid dormant for years until Microsoft caught up and introduced the first multitasking program—Windows/286.

- The 80286 supported two modes of operation—real and protected mode. In real mode, the 80286 simulated an 8086/8088 for DOS compatibility. In protected mode, the 80286 supported multitasking and program protection against lockups and system failure. In addition, the 80286 supported 16MB of memory and clock speeds up to 20MHz.

**80386**    The 80386 represents a significant advancement over earlier chips. The 80386 uses 32-bit communication lines within the chip and on the external data bus. The 32-bit architecture provides enhanced flexibility and unparalleled speeds. Some of the most notable improvements are:

- The 80386 can switch between real and protected mode without resetting the system.

- In addition to real mode and protected mode, the 80386 offers *virtual real mode,* which allows multiple real mode sessions simultaneously. This requires a software manager.

- The 80386 supports a variety of different clock speeds—16, 20, 25, and 33 MHz. Also, the new 32-bit architecture supports 4GB of real memory and 64TB (Tera-bytes—1,000 GB) of virtual memory. Wow!

The only problem with the 32-bit chip was compatibility with existing 16-bit expansion cards. While the 80386 supported the cards, many thought it was a waste of 32-bit resources. In response, Intel released a cheaper version of the 80386 chip that included a 32-bit internal chip and 16-bit external data bus. It was called the 80386SX. The original 80386 was then renamed 80386DX.

**80486**    The leap to the 80486 microprocessor wasn't nearly as big as that from the 80286 to the 80386. The 80486 chip is simply a turbo-charged version of the 80386. In addition, the 80486 includes an internal memory cache controller. The 80486DX has a math coprocessor built-in (which provides additional functionality for complex mathematic calculations and computer-aided design operations.) Earlier chips required an extra math chip on the motherboard. Intel also offers an 80486SX that is a full 80486DX without the built-in math coprocessor. The 80486 also offers 8 KB of internal memory caching. This feature directs CPU operations through special high-speed memory that is part of the microchip. The end product is faster processing and better ALU throughput.

*Intel has jumped on the coat tails of the 80386SX by offering a cheaper, less powerful version of the 80486 (also with an SX designation). The irony is that the chip is exactly the same as the 80486DX except the math coprocessor functionality has been turned off. When users upgrade to an 80486DX, Intel sends them another full 80486 chip with everything turned off except the math coprocessor functionality. The end product is a machine with two partially functioning full 80486 microprocessors.*

The 80486 uses the same 32-bit communications path as the 80386, so its specifications are identical. The 80486 clock speeds, however, are greatly enhanced over the 80386. This speed is due to a feature called "clock doubling." Clock doubling allows the chip to process two tasks for every clock cycle, thus doubling the processing throughput of the microprocessor. The clock doubling chip is referred to as the DX2. The 80486DX at 25MHz becomes an 80486DX2 at 50MHz. Amazing!

*Processing capabilities of Intel microchips have become so advanced that scientists are now using mainframe measurements to gauge performance. A typical mainframe processing benchmark is MIPS, or millions of instructions per second. Early Intel chips were capable of less than one MIP, compared to minicomputers and mainframes that could process in the 50–100 MIP range. But Intel microprocessors quickly caught up, and now the Pentium surpasses most minicomputers and a good number of mainframes.*

*The latest and greatest Intel chip is the Pentium, or 80586. The Pentium represents a quantum leap ahead of earlier Intel chips.*

**PENTIUM**  The latest and greatest Intel chip is the Pentium, or 80586. The Pentium was so named to distinguish Intel's microprocessors from those of the increasing number of clone manufacturers. The Pentium represents a quantum leap ahead of earlier Intel chips. The Pentium includes two 80486-type CPUs for true dual processing, independent access to multiple internal data cache (8KB each), backward compatibility to the 80386, over 120 MHz speeds, a 64-bit wide internal interface, and 3 million transistors. In addition, the Pentium features a super-scalar design that uses a mix of RISC (Reduced Instruction Set Computing) construction and CISC (Complex Instruction

Set Computing) orientation. The redesigned FPU (Floating Point Unit) uses mathematical firmware to achieve a 300% improvement in geometric computations. Simply stated, this is one HOT microchip!

Here is a brief look at the evolution of microprocessor MIPS:

| | |
|---|---|
| 8086/8088 | 0.33 MIPS |
| 80286 | 3 MIPS |
| 80386 | 11 MIPS |
| 80486 | 41 MIPS |
| Pentium | over 100 MIPS |

## Motorola Microprocessors

The first Motorola microprocessor was introduced in 1979. The chip was the MC68000 and it spawned the Apple line of personal computers. The Motorola architecture is more sophisticated than the Intel chip, but it lacks pure processing power and speed. The Motorola chip is better suited for advanced graphic operations and multitasking. Following are descriptions of Motorola's five microchip generations.

**MC68000**   The MC68000 was Motorola's first chip. It offered a startling 24-bit internal architecture and a 16-bit data bus. The MC68000 supported 16MB of internal memory and up to 16MHz clock speed. Motorola's first offering was comparable to Intel's 80286, but it lacked virtual memory addressing and protected mode. The MC68000 is the brains for the following Apple Macintosh computers:

- Macintosh 128K

- Macintosh 512K

- Macintosh 512Ke

- Macintosh Plus

- Macintosh SE

- Macintosh Classic

- Macintosh Portable (uses the MC68HC000, a low-powered version of the chip)

*In the beginning, Motorola chips were regarded as highly superior to the Intel microprocessors. The MC68000 offered more flexibility and a highly specialized architecture. In fact, Novell used the MC68000 microchip as the brains of its first NetWare server. But Motorola signed agreements with other companies who favor closed architectures—Apple and NeXT. Meanwhile, Intel opted for a more open approach and quickly gained the lion's share of the microprocessor market. Today, the debate continues—Intel or Motorola, IBM or Apple, Coke or Pepsi.*

**MC68020**  The MC68020 was the first full 32-bit microprocessor. It offered 32-bit communications within the CPU and 32-bit communications throughout the data bus. In addition, the MC68020 supported 4GB of real memory, 16MHz clock speed, and an additional math coprocessor. The MC68020 is the brains for the following Apple Macintosh computers:

- Macintosh LC

- Macintosh II

**MC68030**  The MC68030 was the third generation of Motorola microprocessors and became the foundation for the NeXT computer revolution. It offered a unique approach to microcomputing—two buses. The MC68030 supported two independent 32-bit data buses that could service the microprocessor twice as fast. This revolutionary new chip represented the first attempt to multiprocess within a microcomputer. In addition, the MC68030 offered internal memory caching, a math coprocessor, and clock speeds up to 40MHz. The MC68030 is the brains for the following Apple Macintosh computers:

- Macintosh SE/30

- Macintosh IIx

- Macintosh IIcx

- Macintosh IIci

- Macintosh IIsi

- Macintosh IIfx

**MC68040** The latest Motorola microprocessor is the MC68040. This evolutionary chip builds on the advancements of the MC68030. It offers 64-bit communications and faster multiprocessing capabilities. The MC68040 is the brains of the Apple Macintosh Quadra computer.

*Every great advance in science has issued from a new audacity of imagination.*

*John Dewey*

The microcomputer revolution is in full swing. As you can see from the previous pages, there have been some major technological advancements over the past 15 years. Table 1.1 below summarizes the differences between the different Intel and Motorola microprocessors. By the time you are finished reading the table, it will already be obsolete.

| **TABLE 1.1** Comparing the Capabilities of Intel and Motorola Microprocessors | MICRO-PROCESSOR | INTERNAL | DATA BUS | CACHE/MATH | MAX MHZ |
|---|---|---|---|---|---|
| | Intel 8086 | 16-bit | 16-bit | No/No | 8 or 10 |
| | Intel 8088 | 16-bit | 8-bit | No/No | 8 or 10 |
| | Intel 80286 | 16-bit | 16-bit | No/No | 20 |
| | MC68000 | 24-bit | 16-bit | No/No | 16 |
| | Intel 80386SX | 32-bit | 16-bit | No/No | 20 |
| | MC68020 | 32-bit | 32-bit | No/Extra | 16 |
| | Intel 80386DX | 32-bit | 32-bit | No/Extra | 33 |
| | Intel 80486SX | 32-bit | 32-bit | Yes/Extra | 33 |
| | MC68030 | 32-bit | 32-bit | Yes/Yes | 40 |
| | Intel 80486DX | 32-bit | 32-bit | Yes/Yes | 66 (DX2) |
| | MC68040 | 64-bit | 64-bit | Yes/Yes | 64 |
| | Pentium | 64-bit | 32-bit | Yes/Yes | 120 |

*Table 1.1 is your friend. Use it to learn the different specs of each microprocessor evolution. Also, learn which Motorola CPU each Macintosh model uses.*

# The Data Bus

*The microcomputer data bus provides a pathway for communications between the intelligent CPU and external system components—memory, disks, video, and peripherals.*

*Recently, there has been a movement toward 32-bit bus channels. The 32-bit architecture offers a substantial improvement over earlier designs in performance of key components such as memory, the CPU, and expansion cards.*

If the microprocessor is the microcomputer's brains, then the data bus is its nervous system. The microcomputer data bus provides a pathway for communications between the intelligent CPU and external system components— memory, disks, video and peripherals. This pathway exists as an internal electronic circuit that transfers tiny bits of data from one component to another. Figure 1.2 shows for an illustration of the internal microcomputer architecture.

The data bus connects all of the system components. The speed and physical method that govern data transfer are dictated by the type of data bus you use. Earlier we talked about the 8-bit, 16-bit, and 32-bit processors that use internal and external parallel channels. External processor channels define the microcomputer data bus. In this discussion, we will explore five different data bus architectures and learn how their electronic throughput affects the performance of microcomputer workstations and file servers.

Besides the microprocessor and memory, the most important component of the data bus architecture is expansion slots. These slots typically support 8-, 16-, or 32-bit channels and communicate directly with the microprocessor and memory. Expansion slots allow the system to accommodate external peripherals and sub-components, including video, disk controllers, modems, parallel ports, sound cards, additional memory modules, and of course, one of the most important components to us, the network interface card. The expansion bus architecture of the original IBM PC used the simplest design and minimal support circuitry. In 1981, however, this was considered quite advanced. The IBM XT bus was 8 bits wide and it used an 8088 Intel microprocessor. The next generation, in 1984, was called the Advanced Technology, or AT Bus. It offered numerous improvements over the IBM XT—a 16-bit data bus, access directly to the 80286 microprocessor, and backward compatibility with earlier 8-bit expansion cards.

Recently, there has been a movement towards 32-bit bus channels. The 32-bit architecture offers a substantial improvement over earlier designs in performance of key components such as memory, the CPU, and expansion cards. For example, new 32-bit cards have been introduced for all facets of

**FIGURE I.2**
Inside the microcomputer

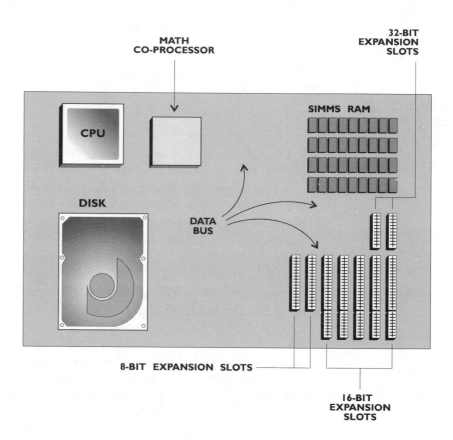

microcomputing—32-bit network interface cards, 32-bit disk controllers, and 32-bit video.

The world of microcomputer data buses is broken into four main standards: ISA, EISA, VESA, and MCA. We'll discuss each of these in some depth and give you an understanding of how they differ and which is ideal in a workstation or file server format.

## ISA

Industry Standard Architecture, or ISA bus, was the first standard introduced in 1979 and quickly became the mainstay of the IBM XT and AT microcomputers. With its 8-bit or 16-bit data/expansion bus, the ISA bus is the most common format. ISA bus communications are based on the same parallel model we discussed earlier—multiple paths working together to simultaneously transmit 8, 16, or 32 bits of data. The ISA bus is ideal for workstations and low-end file servers. Keep in mind that the 16-bit ISA bus doesn't take advantage of the 32-bit processing capabilities of the 80386 microprocessor. Incidentally, most of the standard clones—Compaq, AST, Dell, etc.—use the ISA bus.

## EISA

The EISA bus, which stands for Extended Industry Standard Architecture, was developed to provide 32-bit throughput over the standard ISA architecture. EISA was developed in September, 1987 by a consortium of PC makers in response to the IBM dominance of that era. This particular organization, known as the Gang of Nine, included Compaq, AST, Epson, Hewlett-Packard, NEC, Olivetti, Tandy, Wyse, and Zenith. EISA did not replace the AT bus, it simply expanded on it. EISA offered backward compatibility, 32-bit throughput, and auto-configuration. The typical EISA motherboard includes two 32-bit EISA slots and six 16-bit ISA slots. The EISA architecture is ideal for NetWare file servers when it is combined with a 32-bit disk controller and 32-bit network interface card. This configuration optimizes server disk throughput and network communications.

## VESA

The VESA standard is an enhanced EISA design that provides a dedicated 32-bit line directly from the VESA slot to the microprocessor. This technology is called *local bus* because it treats the VESA components as part of the native data bus. VESA throughput is dramatically improved over EISA and ISA. Some industry experts say that a VESA local bus system is in the neighborhood of ten times faster than the ISA standard. NetWare file servers respond very favorably to the excellent throughput and performance of VESA disk controllers and NICs.

While EISA and VESA are expensive, they're not extravagant. The increase in speed and communications performance is justified for NetWare file servers. EISA and VESA for a workstation is harder to justify. Workstations don't process the multiple disk and communication requests that file servers do. They simply handle their own specific load.

### MCA

MCA, Micro Channel Architecture, was developed by the IBM Corporation in 1987 to provide a proprietary, 32-bit alternative to ISA. MCA provided several improvements over the existing ISA architecture—32-bit throughput and auto-configuration. On the downside, MCA is truly proprietary (no compatibility with ISA or EISA). This becomes a really big problem with component swapping and file server upgrades. IBM's isolationist approach with Micro Channel has caused many system managers to shy away from the technology, no matter what they think of it.

The Micro Channel architecture is the basis of IBM's second generation microcomputer, the PS/2, or Personal System 2. While the PS/2 line became synonymous with Micro Channel, not all PS/2 models have the Micro Channel architecture. The model 25 and 30 machines are built around the ISA bus. Most machines with the 80386 microprocessor have the MCA bus—models 50, 60, 70, 80, and 90/95 (which are 80486s). The models 50 and 60 use a 16-bit version of the MCA bus while the models 70, 80, and 90/95 use 32-bit Micro Channel.

*The term MCA was recently withdrawn by IBM after the Music Corporation of America, also known as MCA, filed a lawsuit. This architecture is now simply known as Micro Channel.*

While 90% of the microcomputers made today use one of the four data bus standards described above, there are two other architectures that warrant some discussion here—Compaq's FLEX standard and the NuBus design of the Apple Macintosh.

*Also, learn about the "oddball" data bus architectures (FLEX and PDS) for the test.*

The FLEX architecture, designed by Compaq Computer Corporation, was the first extension of the ISA design. It was intended to provide direct access from memory to the processor by packing megabytes of information across a dedicated line. This particular design was based on a solution called DMA, or Direct Memory Access. The FLEX architecture is no longer being designed in its original form, although variations of this design are built into EISA and VESA microcomputer architectures.

Apple Macintosh data bus designs differ dramatically from the IBM-compatible standards we are used to. Designed by Texas Instruments and adopted by Apple, they're built around what is called the NuBus architecture. NuBus relies on one proprietary processor slot called the Processor Direct Slot, or PDS. The PDS slot gives direct access to the processor from one expansion card. While PDS expansion has performance advantages, the card must be processor-specific. This means that a card from a Motorola 68030 Processor Direct Slot won't work in a new 68040 machine. In some cases, the NuBus data bus architecture and the Processor Direct Slot are mutually exclusive. That is to say, most Macintosh II computers are built around the NuBus design and do not use the Processor Direct Slot. The Mac SE, on the other hand, has no NuBus, but it uses the Processor Direct Slot architecture. The exceptions to this rule are the Mac II FX and some of the new Quadra machines, which use six NuBus slots and one Processor Direct Slot. I'm confused.

*Apple Macintosh data bus designs differ dramatically from the IBM-compatible standards we are used to.*

*Perplexity is the beginning of knowledge.*

*Kahlil Gibran*

## Configurations

As you can see from our discussion of data bus standards, this is quite a complex system. High-speed communications between multiple expansion cards, memory, and the CPU can pose some interesting configuration problems. It is important to have an organized, effective method for controlling these communications. The key is to avoid component interference. The microcomputer industry has settled on three methods for controlling component configuration:

- interrupts
- memory addressing
- I/O addressing

The interrupt configuration method describes a dedicated pathway from microcomputer hardware to the central CPU. Each of the computer's internal components—disk controller, network interface card, keyboard, memory, printer card, and so on—use the interrupt configuration as a pathway and the I/O address as a door for microcomputer communications. The memory address reserves a special place in microcomputer RAM for buffering CPU requests.

Data bus configurations are defined using a variety of different elements. In this section, we will take a moment to review the three different configuration concepts and the five popular elements that define them.

**CONFIGURATION CONCEPTS** Communications between microcomputer hardware and the CPU are based on the interrupt model. When a hardware device requests processing from the CPU, it sends a signal through the interrupt line to the CPU. The CPU will stop whatever it's doing and pay attention to that device for a fixed period of time. This interrupt line is called the IRQ, or Interrupt Request line. Each time the CPU receives a request from hardware to perform an operation, it goes to memory and recalls a hardware-specific routine of instructions called the Interrupt Service Routine. The CPU keeps track of the host hardware device by noting its IRQ. The IRQ number determines which interrupt service routine to perform. Another important function of the IRQ is that it allows each of the components to coexist without interrupting each other or stepping on each other's toes. Since each device must have its own dedicated IRQ line, it is imperative to configure the microcomputer hardware correctly. If two components share the same IRQ, one of them will not function—first come, first serve. See Table 1.2 for some sample microcomputer hardware interrupts.

The second configuration methodology for expansion board communication is memory addressing. The memory address is similar to the IRQ in that it provides a dedicated line to the CPU for data communications. The difference is that the IRQ is used for a device communication and memory is used for instruction set communications. Let me explain what this means. The primary function of memory is to provide a buffer for instructions to the CPU. When a device uses the IRQ line to interrupt the CPU for some service, the CPU uses the IRQ number to find a corresponding memory range in RAM. The CPU uses this range as the source for this particular device's operation instructions. It's very important to match a device's IRQ with the memory address it needs to store the instructions for that process.

The final, and third, configuration methodology is I/O address, or Input/Output addressing. The I/O address controls device handling by providing a hardware door to the CPU. In analogy, the IRQ is a dedicated hallway to the CPU. The I/O address is a door upon which the device knocks when it wants to enter and place a request.

*Think of the microcomputer as a restaurant—McDonald's, for example. The CPU is the kitchen, servicing our request for a Big Mac. The IRQ is the line you stand in (each person is in a separate one). The memory address is the cash register, which marks down all of your requests and sends them back to the kitchen. The cashier itself would be the I/O address. Hungry yet?*

Table 1.2 shows a list of basic hardware components and their default configurations. Now, if you understand the concepts of configurations and why interrupts, memory addressing, and I/O addressing are so important, let's move on to the actual hardware elements that define these different configurations.

*Table 1.2 is your friend. It's important to understand the general concepts of IRQ and I/O, but it's imperative to understand the practical implications of using them on your LAN. Besides, they'll test you on it.*

| TABLE 1.2 | DEVICE | IRQ | I/O |
|---|---|---|---|
| Common Microcomputer Hardware Configurations | Serial Port 1 | 4 | 3F8 |
| | Serial Port 2 | 3 | 2F8 |
| | Parallel Port 1 | 7 | 378 |
| | Parallel Port 2 | 5 | 278 |
| | Default NIC* | 3 | 300 |
| | Tape Controller | 5 | 280 |
| | Mouse Card* | 5 | 280 |
| | E.G.A. Adapter | 2 | 3C0 |
| | Internal Modem* | 3 | 2F8 |
| | Sound Card* | 7 | 220 |

* = typical

**CONFIGURATION ELEMENTS**  Configuration elements are important because they provide us with a way of enforcing configuration concepts. Configuration elements consist of hardware and software devices that provide a methodology for defining specific configuration values. These hardware and software devices include dip switches, jumpers, terminating resistors, CMOS, and drivers. Here's a detailed description of the five most popular microcomputer configuration elements.

**Dip switches** (Dual In-line Package) are used to customize hardware device options on expansion boards or the motherboard itself. They are used on expansion boards—NICs for example—to define the existence of a PROM (Programmable Read Only Memory) chip or to configure the appropriate port for Ethernet connections. Dip switches are used on the motherboard to configure the status of internal hardware components—type of video, amount of memory, number of disk drives, and so on. There are two different types of dip switches: the rocker switch and the slide switch. Each switch has two states: on or off. You can use a bank of dip switches in combination to define multiple options. For example, a bank of eight dip switches would provide $2^8$ or 256 possible options. This is quite common.

**Jumpers** are also used to configure microcomputer hardware devices. Jumpers are much more common in network interface cards for setting IRQ, memory addresses, and I/O addresses. Jumpers exist in two states: jumped or not jumped. The jumper consists of two pins that stick up out of the expansion board. A jumped state is achieved by attaching a metal jumper to both pins and creating an electronic contact between them. A not jumped state is achieved by leaving the contact open. Most jumpers work in banks. For example, a bank with five jumpers would provide a variety of different options—jumper 1 set, jumper 2 set, jumper 3 set, jumpers 2 and 5 set, and so on. One good application of this approach is used by the popular NE2000 NIC (Network Interface Card). The existence of jumpers on certain pin numbers defines IRQ and I/O address—IRQ 3 and I/O address 300H (default setting), for example.

**Terminator Resistors,** or terminators, are used to terminate the end of cable systems. This is important for two very popular types of cabling systems: SCSI disk drives and Ethernet coaxial trunks. SCSI stands for Small Computer System Interface. These large disk drives actually work in parallel of each other, daisy-chained together. Terminators are required at the end of the chain or else the signal will reflect back on itself and cause collisions. The same thing happens with Ethernet cabling trunks, which

*C MOS (Complementary Metal Oxide Semiconductor) is the most common setup program or setup configuration option on microcomputers. The CMOS Firmware is built into the computer's BIOS, or Basic Input/ Output System.*

incidentally are used to connect network interface cards together on a LAN. Ethernet signals travel at very high speeds over the cable. When they reach the end of the cable, they must be terminated or else they will bounce back and collide with other signals. This can cause such serious problems as data loss, corruption, or hardware failure.

**CMOS** (Complementary Metal Oxide Semiconductor) is used for the most common setup program or setup configuration option on microcomputers. The CMOS firmware is built into the computer's BIOS, or Basic Input/ Output System. The BIOS is a chip on the motherboard that keeps track of critical system setups, including date, time, the amount of memory you have, the type of video adapter you're using, whether you have a math co-processor, the type of disk drive you have for floppy A, floppy B, or hard disk C, whether you want the memory test to continue upon boot up, the boot sequence, and so on. These global configurations are stored in the BIOS using the CMOS chip. The CMOS is configured using a special BIOS setup routine. This routine is typically activated by pressing the Del key during bootup.

**Drivers** are special software routines that communicate between the operating system and internal hardware devices. Drivers are important because hardware must have a way of communicating what it's doing when the time comes for the user to request a service. LAN drivers, for example, provide a communications pathway between NetWare and internal network interface cards.

That completes our discussion of the data bus and its configurations. The next critical hardware component is memory. If you remember from our earlier discussion of the microprocessor and the data bus, the microprocessor needs to have instructions loaded in memory before it can process any instructions. Memory provides data buffering services and acts as a holding cell for key CPU instructions.

*Memory is the cabinet of imagination, the treasury of reason, the registry of conscience, and the council chamber of thought.*

*Saint Basil*

## Memory

Memory, busiest of the microcomputer components, is a key player in almost all operations. Figure 1.3 shows a basic microcomputer layout of the CPU, memory, and expansion bus. If you were to follow the steps of data as it traveled through the microcomputer forest, you would find that memory played a very important role. Let's say, for example, this particular figure shows a file server servicing a user's request for data.

There are twelve steps from the point the internal NIC receives the request until it sends the data back to the user. Let's follow these steps:

1. The request is received by the network interface card. The NIC is not intelligent, so it says, "Gee, I don't know what to do with this." The first thing it does is send it to memory.

2. Before anything can happen, the request is held in memory until the CPU can be interrupted.

3. During step three, the request is sent from memory over a specific interrupt request line—the NIC IRQ—to the CPU where it enters a specific

**FIGURE 1.3**
The microcomputer layout and twelve steps for processing data

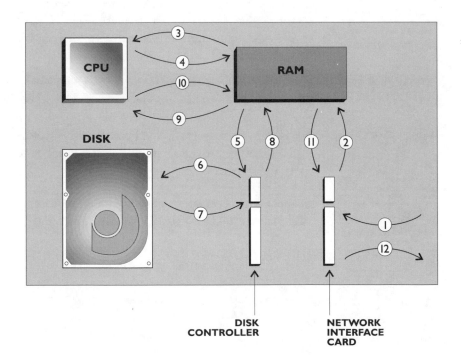

I/O door (the NIC I/O address). The CPU knows this is a NIC request because it monitors the IRQ and I/O address. The CPU assumes this is most likely a request from a user for a network resource. It processes the request and says, "Oh, this is a request for data." The processor goes to NetWare and says, "This is a request for data. What should I do with it?" NetWare says, "Oh, well, here's the Directory Entry Table and the File Allocation Table." These two tables tell the system where on the hard disk to look for the data. The CPU takes that information and sends it back to the disk controller.

4. The data request and disk addresses are sent back to memory where they wait to be shuffled off to the disk controller.

5. The data request and disk addresses are shuffled over the expansion bus to the disk controller on a specific IRQ line—the disk controller's IRQ. The disk controller takes a look at the location on the disk where the data resides and goes to get the data.

*All the steps to this point have taken place on the data bus. That's because we've been transferring requests and processing information. Steps six and seven involve the transferring of data to and from the server disk. This process does NOT take place on the data bus because the data bus is not capable of handling large amounts of data. Data transfer takes place through a special ribbon cable that connects the disk controller to the hard disk.*

6. The file server hard disk retrieves the data that corresponds to the addresses that were provided by the disk controller.

7. The user data is sent back to the disk controller over a specialized parallel ribbon cable that connects the disk controller and the disk. Because the disk controller is unintelligent, it doesn't know what to do with the data and sends it back to the CPU for instructions.

8. The data is transferred from the hard disk to memory. Memory holds the request until the CPU can be interrupted.

9. The request is sent from memory over a specific interrupt request line (the disk controller IRQ) to the CPU, where it enters a specific I/O door (the disk controller I/O address). The CPU knows this is data because it monitors the IRQ and I/O address. The CPU says, "Oh yeah, I remember this data. What should I do with it?" The CPU asks NetWare, and NetWare says, "Send it back to user Q."

10. The answer is sent back to memory where it rejoins the data and waits for a trip to the NIC.

11. The data is shuffled off to the network interface card over the NIC's unique IRQ line.

12. A reply packet is generated with user Q's address and the data is attached to it. The reply packet with the data attached is sent to the user over network cabling.

As you can see, there's a lot going on inside the file server when you make a simple request. I hope this scenario has given you a new appreciation for the complex relationship among memory, CPU, expansion cards, the data bus, and LAN cabling.

Memory played a key role in the above scenario. Memory is the only component that touched the request every time it moved from one component to another. This is because RAM acts as a holding tank for the CPU. Also, memory stores the software instructions that the CPU needs for processing (NetWare, for example, was in memory).

## Types of Memory

The file server memory from our example is called Random Access Memory, or RAM. RAM is volatile; when you turn off the power to your computer, the information stored in memory goes away. RAM is also very fast—one hundred times faster than disk access. That's a 10,000% increase in performance! In addition to RAM, there is Read Only Memory, or ROM. ROM is semipermanent—it keeps information once power is lost, but doesn't store it in a permanent, disk-like format. ROM simply holds the information in a memory buffer on firmware—otherwise known as software on a chip. ROM is much smaller than RAM. It stores special system configurations like BIOS information and remote booting instructions.

Let's spend a moment discussing the two types of memory, and then move on to a more detailed discussion of RAM and how it is used in a typical microcomputer workstation or file server.

**RAM** RAM is the memory used by programs, the CPU, and special expansion cards. There are two different types of RAM in a microcomputer: Dynamic RAM (DRAM) and Static RAM (SRAM). The most popular and most common is DRAM. DRAM contains hundreds of tiny capacitors that store information in bit format—0s and 1s. A 1 is represented by an electrically charged capacitor. If the capacitor is discharged, it is a 0. On the downside, the amount of charge is so small that it dissipates very quickly. This means that DRAM needs to be continually refreshed.

SRAM differs from DRAM in that it's not electronic (instead, it's made of thousands of tiny electronic switches). The switches are either set on (representing a 1) or off (representing a 0). SRAM is very fast, but it tends to be much more expensive than DRAM. SRAM is not very popular these days and is typically used for cache memory.

Both types of RAM are temporary and require power from the computer. They also need to exist in large amounts so programs and large computer software instructions can function properly. RAM performance is typically measured in nanoseconds. Some of today's most common memory has access times of 60 to 70 nanoseconds. Most microcomputer RAM exists in SIMMS modules, or Single In-line Memory Modules. The SIMMS module is a small card that stores 1-, 4-, 16-, or 32-megabyte chunks of RAM. The SIMMS card slides into a small SIMMS slot on the motherboard. There are typically 8 SIMMS slots—two banks of 4—which provide the capacity for 256 MB of DRAM on the motherboard.

**ROM**  ROM, on the other hand, stores programs permanently so they can be recalled during system boot up. ROM is reserved for global system-type configurations. You cannot add or subtract the amount of ROM a system has. Microcomputers are designed to have a certain amount of ROM on the motherboard and that's it! ROM BIOS, Basic Input/Output System, is the most common type of ROM. This is where the boot procedures and operating system instructions exist for activating the microcomputer environment. ROM memory is programmed at the factory and is virtually impossible to change. There are two types of ROM chips, however, that *can* be changed: PROM (Programmable Read Only Memory) and EPROM (Erasable Programmable Read Only Memory). But changing them is difficult and it's not a good idea to mess around with your system ROM.

*Hardware is the type of computer component you can touch. Software, on the other hand, is typically made of electronic information that you can't touch. ROM is known as* firmware *because it's software that's been programmed onto a hardware chip. What will they think of next?*

### System Memory

The discussion so far has focused on the fundamentals of what RAM and ROM are. What does this really mean? How does it affect the user? Why do I care? In this section, we will discuss the fundamentals of system memory as it applies to the user. We will focus on how memory—primarily RAM—affects application programs and a user's ability to perform his/her duties.

When the first IBM PC was introduced, the 8088's ability to address 1MB of memory was very exciting. 640K of that memory was directly accessible as conventional memory. Figure 1.4 shows a breakdown of system memory into its multiple components (conventional memory at the bottom, followed by 128K of video memory and 256K of ROM memory for a total of 1024K, or 1MB).

*The 640K conventional RAM barrier was originally created because at that time, most microcomputers had a system memory limitation of 64K. The DOS designers figured that a ten-fold increase would be more RAM than anybody could ever use. Boy, do they have egg on their faces! Just as an example, NetWare or Windows NT requires in excess of 12MB of memory just to run the operating system.*

**FIGURE 1.4**
The components of
system memory

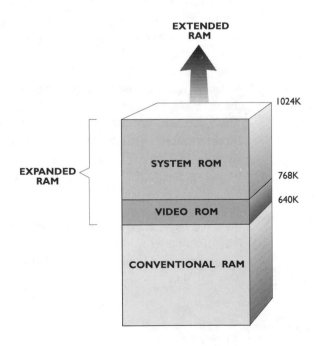

As more complex CPUs came along, they provided 16-bit addressing instead of 8-bit addressing and the amount of addressable memory rose dramatically. The 80286 supports 16MB of system memory while the 32-bit 80386 supports up to 4GB of addressable RAM. Besides conventional memory, there are two other memory categories: expanded and extended. Expanded memory uses the top 256K of 1MB as a temporary swapping pool for system programs—we'll talk about this in just a second. Extended memory is any RAM above 1MB. So if you had 16MB of memory, the first 640K would be conventional, the middle 384K, including the video memory, would be expanded and the 15MB above the 1MB barrier would be extended memory.

*They'll definitely test you on conventional, expanded, and extended memory. The question is—who's they?*

Let's take a look at conventional, expanded, and extended memory and see how NetWare and other operating systems use them.

**CONVENTIONAL MEMORY**  Conventional memory is the only memory DOS can directly address. NetWare can address all memory, but DOS can only address this 640K conventional RAM. If you're running Windows, for example, Windows will address expanded and extended memory, but it will first have to run your DOS programs in conventional memory. This poses a problem. You might have 128MB of memory, but only 640K can be used by your DOS programs. This is why some programs run out of memory even if you have plenty of expanded and extended RAM.

**EXPANDED RAM**  Expanded RAM is memory that is not directly addressable by the CPU or DOS. Expanded memory requires a special software driver called EMS, or Expanded Memory Specification. If you use EMS in conjunction with expanded memory, it allows you to break the 640K barrier. The latest EMS software, LIM EMS 4.0, incorporates a technique called bank switching to swap different banks of expanded memory in and out of this reserved area. This is how it works: the 256K ROM area that we talked about earlier is reserved for PC memory addressing. It is addressable by the CPU. You can swap programs in and out of this area in 16K or 64K pages from extended RAM. In effect, although you're only addressing 256K of memory at one time, you can address 32MB by swapping it back and forth from the extended memory area. The problem with this is that it's very, very slow.

*The LIM EMS and LIM XMS standards are named after the three companies that developed them—Lotus, Intel, and Microsoft. While it's hard to imagine cooperation among these three industry giants, it's amazing what can be accomplished with a little teamwork.*

**EXTENDED MEMORY** Extended memory is memory beyond the 1MB barrier that is addressable to the CPU. To use it, you must run a special software driver called XMS, or Extended Memory Specification. In the past, extended memory has gone primarily unused. Now there are new operating systems that can directly address extended memory—OS/2, UNIX, Windows NT, and NetWare. Microsoft Windows, for example, is probably the most popular memory management software. It's not an operating system, but a memory management software program. Windows allows you to directly address extended memory and will use the RAM for processing Windows-based programs. Other memory management software programs also allow you to activate extended memory in DOS—QEMM, for example. In addition, DOS has its own memory management drivers that provide support for applications that use extended memory.

*Experience is a comb that life gives you after you lose your hair.*

*Judith Stern*

This completes our discussion of memory. It's important that you understand the difference between RAM and ROM. Also, be aware that RAM is the only memory we're concerned with in a network environment. For the most part, the NetWare file server uses all the memory it can to load the network operating system, run programs, and perform internal file caching (explained in the next chapter).

If you're a workstation, you'll most likely be using DOS. If that's the case, you're going to need some memory management software to address memory above the 640K barrier. Windows has become the most popular. If you're using another workstation operating system such as OS/2, UNIX, or Windows NT, you'll be able to address extended memory directly and not have to worry about using any memory management software.

# Disks

*Without a doubt, the most important resource on the LAN is the file server disk. After all, the file server's main function is to serve files.*

Earlier, we talked about the CPU and how it processes information using the data bus. We also described how the data bus shuffles requests from the CPU to other internal components. We talked about memory and how it's a holding cell for CPU requests. The last and most important component from a data storage standpoint is of course the disks—floppy and hard.

If you think about the file server and its primary purpose for a moment, you get an overwhelming feeling that the disk is pretty important. After all, the file server's main function is to *serve files*. Without a doubt, the most important resource on the LAN is the file server disk. Outside of the LAN, an argument can be made for floppy disks. Floppy disks are important because they provide a way of transporting files from one microcomputer to another—assuming, of course, that you don't have a network.

Both floppy and hard disks use the same means of recording data—small electronic bits on a magnetized recording medium. Incidentally, this technology is almost identical to the technology used by audio or video tape. Here's how it works: a recording head, or read-write head, magnetizes small particles of electronic information on some specially coated recording media—tape or disk. The magnetized spots represent 1s and the demagnetized spots represent 0s.

Again, this ties back to the way memory stores data. Before a disk can be used to store data, it must be formatted. Formatting a disk enables the computer to place data in a specific place and then be found again. Formatting entails logically dividing the disk into two small patterns: circles and slices. The circle divisions consist of concentric circles (called tracks) that encircle the disk. The slice divisions consist of pie slices (called sectors) throughout the circular disk. Each location on the disk is then represented as a cross section between a track and a sector (Figure 1.5).

The more sectors and tracks you have, the more data you can store. There are four different types of floppy disks (5¼" high density, 5¼" low density, 3½" high density, and 3½" low density) and many different types of hard disks.

*A new series of hard disks is emerging for notebook computers. They have the same storage capacities as the larger ones, but are housed in a 2" frame and can be balanced on the tip of your finger.*

Let's take a closer look at floppy disks.

**FIGURE 1.5**
The layout of
magnetic disks

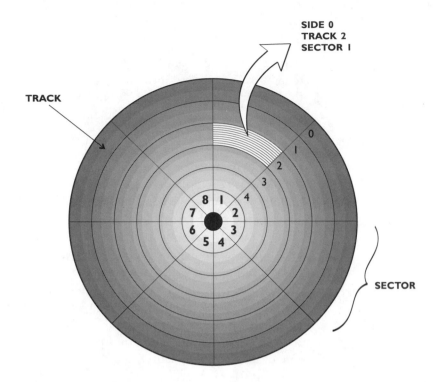

## Floppy Disks

As we mentioned above, floppy disks come in two sizes: 5¼" and 3½". Most of today's microcomputers use the 3½" floppy because its harder encasing provides a little more durability. Both sizes come in two flavors—low and high density. The 5¼" floppy disk provides slightly less capacity (360K and 1.2MB respectively) than the 3½" disk (720K and 1.44MB respectively). The floppy disk itself is enclosed in a vinyl or hard plastic cover. The protective cover keeps the disks from harmful exposure—to sunlight, water, electronics, magnetic fields, and so on. Also, there's a metal slider at the bottom of the 3½" disk that protects the write area from accidental exposure. It's not a good idea to get these disks near any magnetic fields, because direct exposure to any magnetic field will completely remagnetize your disk—no data!

Disk drive compatibilities are very important for floppy disks. Make sure that when you're formatting a particular floppy disk you use the right density drive. Later in the DOS section of this chapter, we'll discuss the format command and how to specify which density you're formatting. Keep in mind that if you have a 5¼" high density disk, you must format it with a 5¼" high density drive. A 5¼" high density disk cannot be read by a low density drive. The reverse, however, is not true (a high density drive can in fact read a low density disk). The same goes for 3½" disks.

*A new floppy disk technology has emerged that combines the read/write flexibility of magnetic media with the storage capacity of optical media. These new floppy disks (called* floppticals) *can store 21MB on one 3½" disk.*

That just about does it for floppy disks. Now let's take a detailed look at hard disk technology.

## Hard Disks

Hard disks are the foundation of the network—especially from the file server's point of view. Hard disks differ from floppy disks in many respects and are probably the most important resource on the LAN. The hard disk obviously has a much larger capacity than the floppy disk and is non-removable. It's also much faster than the floppy disk because it moves at much higher rpms (revolutions per minute).

The physical structure of the hard disk also differs from that of the floppy—it's not made of floppy mylar. Instead, the hard disk is made of aluminum and coated with a magnetic recording material. This disk itself is called a platter. Most hard disks are made of five platters, each with two sides. The platters are stacked inside a vacuum-sealed container to keep out dust and other contaminant particles. The read-write head is also sealed inside the vacuum, and reads the data as it travels from the outside to the inside of the disk. The platters revolve clockwise at 3600 rpm to 7200 rpm for newer hard disks.

The hard disk is organized exactly the same way as the floppy disk—concentric circles (tracks) and pie slices (sectors). In addition to tracks and sectors, hard disks have *cylinders*, which are tracks that span parallel platters. Cylinders provide the capability of reading data from multiple platters as well as multiple sectors and tracks.

Hard disk performance is measured by random access time. The random access time of a hard disk is a measurement of the amount of time required for the drive to deliver data after the computer sends a request to the disk controller. Most of today's quality disks have access times in the range of 10–20 milliseconds.

*The hard disk is organized in exactly the same way as is the floppy disk—concentric circles (tracks) and pie slices (sectors). In addition to tracks and sectors, hard disks have cylinders, which are tracks that span parallel platters.*

The hard disk has two components that the floppy disk will never have: partitions and interfaces. Hard disk partitioning is the process of dividing the disk into logical pieces for alternative operating systems and files. Interfaces define the mode of communications between the disk controller and the disk. The following is a brief discussion of hard disk partitioning and interfaces.

**HARD DISK PARTITIONING** Hard disk partitioning refers to the process of preparing a hard disk for formatting. Hard disks are formatted in the same way as are floppy disks except they're much larger, so they must be prepared or partitioned before they're formatted. Typically, partitioning takes place for a variety of different reasons. An operating system such as DOS 3.3, for example, allows a maximum partition of only 32MB. This limitation is unacceptable for most microcomputer applications, so you are forced to create multiple 32MB partitions. Also, you can use multiple partitions to support multiple operating systems on one hard disk. For example, in NetWare 3.12, the file server is booted from a DOS partition. The server then moves to the NetWare partition and stores all data files there. NetWare 2.2, incidentally, requires that the entire hard disk be partitioned for NetWare. In DOS, partitioning is performed using the FDISK utility. In NetWare, partitioning is performed using the INSTALL utility.

**HARD DISK INTERFACES** The hard disk interface describes a communications methodology for data transfer between the disk controller and hard disk. This is the language the disk controller uses for transferring data between the disk and the microcomputer data bus. It is essential that the hard disk interface be designed so that it's compatible not only with DOS but also with NetWare. There are four major hard disk interfaces that are currently accepted, each with its own advantages and disadvantages. Let's review them.

**MFM/RLL** interfaces were developed by Seagate Technologies in the late '70s. Typically known as the ST506 interface, this particular technology describes a data transfer rate of 5 megabits per second and uses a data encoding method called Modified Frequency Modulation, or MFM. RLL was created a few years later as an enhancement to MFM and it used a data encoding method called Run Length Limited. RLL supports a data transfer rate of 7.5 megabits per second. On the downside, these encoding methods cannot be interchanged. This means that a disk controller created for an MFM disk cannot be used with an RLL drive. MFM and RLL are common with older drives in the 20MB and 40MB range. These standards have been replaced by faster, more sophisticated technologies—namely, ESDI, SCSI, and IDE.

*Another big differ-
ence between ESDI
and SCSI technology
is that SCSI is not
just a drive interface,
it's a system inter-
face. As a general
system interface, SCSI
supports additional
storage components
beyond just disks—
including CD-ROMs,
tape back-up drives,
read-write optical,
and so on.*

**ESDI** is an enhanced version of the ST506 interface that was developed by a consortium of disk drive manufacturers in the mid-1980s. It is now accepted as a standard by ANSI (American National Standards Institute). The data transfer rate for ESDI is around 10 megabits per second, but some faster controllers can operate as quickly as 15 megabits per second. ESDI is well understood and accepted as a reliable technology for mid-sized drives—100 to 340 MB. On the downside, ESDI has a tendency to break down in high load environments, because the technology is in the controller, not the drive.

**SCSI** (Small Computer System Interface—pronounced "scuzzy") is a very high speed interface that was developed as an enhancement to ESDI and ST506. The key difference is that SCSI uses parallel communications—the other interfaces use serial communications for data transfer (one bit after another). The parallel SCSI interface is much faster and more reliable than the other serial technologies. Also, SCSI controllers speak the same language as the data bus, thus enhancing microcomputer data transfer rates.

Another big difference between ESDI and SCSI technology is that SCSI is not just a drive interface, it's a *system* interface. As a general system interface, SCSI supports additional storage components beyond just disks—including CD-ROMs, tape backup drives, read-write optical, and so on. The SCSI technology allows you to daisy chain up to 7 devices from one controller. Just make sure to terminate the final device with a terminating resistor. The SCSI standard provides a very fast data rate, reliability, and high storage capacity. It's an excellent choice for large file server disks in excess of 300MB.

**IDE** (intelligent drive electronics) was developed by Western Digital Corporation in the mid- to late 1980s. IDE is similar to SCSI in that the intelligence is on the drive itself, not on the controller board. IDE controllers are relatively inexpensive, but the drives are a little more expensive than ESDI. IDE differs from SCSI in that it's a drive interface, not a system interface. On the downside, IDE drives use RLL encoding, which is an older type of encoding that operates at 1 to 5 megabytes per second. IDE is extremely flexible and it has excellent capacity and reliability for smaller workstation drives—under 340MB.

*There are many alternative technologies that enhance the hard disk environment. Caching controllers, for example, combine DRAM chips with the disk controller to provide memory buffering for hard disks. This combination can*

*increase hard disk access time performance more than 10,000%. Another technology involves EISA motherboards and 32-bit disk controllers. In addition, some operating systems—NetWare 4.0 and MS-DOS v6.0 for example—provide built-in data compression, which can effectively increase the storage capacity of a 340MB hard disk to almost 1GB!*

## Video Display

The video display component is an important piece of the microcomputer puzzle because it defines a critical interface between the user and the computer. The two most important interface components for the user are input (keyboard) and output (display). Output is defined in two different ways: softcopy and hardcopy. Softcopy output includes the temporary pictures that appear on the screen. Hardcopy output, on the other hand, includes the permanent printed pages that create reports, memos, and books. In this section, we will focus on softcopy output and the display standards that define a user's environment.

*Men are born with two eyes, but with one tongue, in order that they should see twice as much as they say.*

*Charles Caleb Colton*

Although the terms *display* and *monitor* are often used interchangeably, they are not the same thing. The display is the device or the technology that produces the image on the screen. The monitor is the entire package, which includes the display electronics as well as the display itself. Monitor operation is very similar to a television set, and uses CRT, or cathode ray tube technology. While this technology is common for most large monitors, laptops and notebook computers use a more advanced technology known as liquid crystal or gas plasma display. Some of the more advanced notebooks today use what's called an active matrix gas plasma display, which produces a very high resolution color signal over a thin small screen. CRT technology uses either a digital or analog signal in producing the video image. Digital signals are more similar to the other computer components, but they don't produce very vivid colors or high resolution. Remember, digital signals are limited to only two states—on or off. This system is ideal for most computer operations. With display, however, you want as much variation as possible. Analog CRT monitors produce a much higher resolution image with a greater variety of colors, but they are typically more expensive.

In this section, we will discuss the display elements that define video and the standards that have been adopted to define resolution, color, intensity, and so on. Let's start with display elements.

### Video Display Elements

There are two basic modes of display operation: text and graphics. The text mode is used to display simple basic—ASCII—characters. The graphics mode, on the other hand, defines a much more complex signal that provides a variation of colors as well as three dimensional images. There are three basic display elements that define the graphics mode: quality, resolution, and color. Each of these elements works in synergy to define the interface that the user spends time staring at all day. It is important that these elements work together in creating a quality picture that can be viewed both accurately as well as without eyestrain.

**QUALITY**  Display quality is vital because the user is going to be spending the day staring at the computer screen. Also, quality dramatically affects productivity. A good, clear, quality display provides much more clarity and reduces eyestrain.

**RESOLUTION**  Resolution is important because it affects the quality of the display. Also, poor resolution can affect the accuracy of softcopy and hardcopy output. Resolution is measured in pixels, or picture elements. Pixels are dots that combine to create images on the screen. One of the main differences between the various graphic systems available is the number of dots per square inch the screen supports. The more dots, the better the resolution and the clearer the picture.

**COLOR**  Multiple colors can provide more accurate softcopy output. This typically equates to better user productivity. There are two different types of display color: monochrome (one color) and color (a larger variety of colors). Monochrome displays come in a variety of different configurations: green on black, amber on black, or black on white. Green monochrome is the most popular, but amber is better for the eyes. Monochrome displays are common for applications that produce simple, text-based output. Color displays,

*Although the terms display and monitor are often used interchangeably, they are not the same thing. The display is the device or the technology that produces the image on the screen. The monitor is the entire package, which includes the display electronics as well as the display itself.*

on the other hand, are very useful for applications that produce complex, graphical output. Color also reduces eye stress and makes the screen easier to look at. If you have to stare at a screen all day, you might as well enjoy what you're looking at.

This concludes our discussion of video display elements. As you can tell, these different elements play a key role in the quality, resolution, and effectiveness of the video output. These display elements have been combined into a variety of different standards that define resolution, quality, color, and so on. In the next section, we will explore the five most popular display standards and describe the specifications of each.

## Display Standards

The display monitor interfaces with the microcomputer through an expansion card called a *video adapter*. Most video adapters are specifically created to support a standard specification—resolution, color, and so on. Users purchase video adapters to match the capabilities of their monitor. There are five different standards that define the quality and effectiveness of video adapters and monitors:

- monochrome

- RGB

- CGA

- EGA

- VGA

*Learn the display resolution specs. It's for your own good. Especially focus on CGA, EGA, and VGA.*

Let's take a quick look at these five different display standards.

**MONOCHROME**   As you remember, we described monochrome as a single color on a black background. There are four different monochrome standards: TTL, Composite, VGA, and Multiscanning. TTL monochrome is the original display offered by IBM on its first PC computer. It was a digital signal generated by what's called transistor logic. This is a family of integrated circuits that creates a boxy, low-resolution, green-colored display on a black background. Composite monochrome is the lowest resolution of all monochrome monitors. It has the same resolution as CGA (Color Graphics Adapter), but without the color. Composite monochrome is very inexpensive and it can be plugged into any of the low-end video adapters. VGA is a very high resolution standard. It uses an analog signal to produce a high-quality image. VGA monochrome normally is not compatible with color VGA devices. Multiscanning monochrome describes a very flexible standard that can be incorporated into a general monochrome monitor. A multiscanning monitor will support all of the monochrome standards. Multiscanning means that the monitor itself will switch over to the correct frequency and the correct standard as specified by the adapter.

**RGB**  The RGB is the original color display for the IBM PC and is analogous to TTL monochrome. RGB stems from the additive primary colors: red, green, and blue. These were the only colors supported by this particular standard. It was a digital standard and for a very long time the only color adapter available. If you've ever seen an RGB, you know that it's very difficult to look at.

**CGA**  The CGA (Color Graphics Adapter) was the first *real* color graphics standard. Like RGB, CGA is a very low resolution standard. CGA only supports 16 colors—13 more than RGB—and provides a very low resolution display: approximately 320 horizontal pixels × 200 vertical pixels. CGA can cause serious eyestrain in both text and graphics modes.

**EGA**  The first serious quality color standard came along with some of the later IBM PS/2 models. It was EGA (Enhanced Graphics Adapter) and represented a dramatic enhancement of RGB. The industry moved away from CGA and created a better RGB, which supported 64 colors and higher resolution: approximately 640 × 350. EGA is a digital standard that supports many of the earlier monochrome screens.

**VGA**  VGA (Video Graphics Array) is the most popular and highest resolution standard to date. It represents a dramatic improvement over EGA and supports more than just one mode. VGA can switch between high resolution/low colors and low resolution/high colors. It supports 640 × 480 resolution with 16 colors or 320 × 200 resolution with 256 colors. A recent offshoot of VGA, called Super VGA, provides much better throughput and 800 × 600 resolution or better with at least 256 colors. This is probably the best of both worlds because you're getting the high number of colors as well as the higher resolution.

*The science of today is the technology of tomorrow.*

*Edward Teller*

That completes our discussion of video display. Again, keep in mind that display quality is extremely important because it describes the interface between the user and the microcomputer. A high-quality display can increase productivity while decreasing user stress. The minor investment is well worth it.

# Input/Output

*Keep in mind that display quality is extremely important because it describes the interface between the user and the microcomputer.*

*Input/output ports define a communications path between the inside components of the microcomputer and external peripherals. There are two types of ports: parallel and serial.*

Until now, we have discussed many different hardware components that work together to define the microcomputer. We have talked about the microprocessor, the data bus, memory, disks, and video. The final components we're going to discuss are the input/output components—serial and parallel lines.

The input/output components provide an interface between the microcomputer and other external devices—modems, printers, and so on. This discussion will focus on the technology as well as the productivity of serial and parallel input/output devices. We will also explore how they work in workstations and file servers throughout the network environment. Keep in mind that the microcomputer becomes most effective when it combines its internal operations with external hardware devices.

As I mentioned above, the input/output ports define a communications path between the inside components of the microcomputer and external peripherals. There are two types of ports: parallel and serial. Parallel ports are primarily used for printers and operate as one-way communication devices. This means that when you send something out to the printer, it doesn't send anything back. Serial ports, on the other hand, operate as bidirectional devices that send and receive data at the same time. Serial ports are primarily used with data communication devices like modems.

Parallel and serial communications operate in two distinct ways. Parallel communication operates as eight different communication lines sending eight different bits simultaneously. Serial communications use one communications channel and send eight bits of data one after another. Figure 1.6 provides an illustration of the difference between parallel and serial communications.

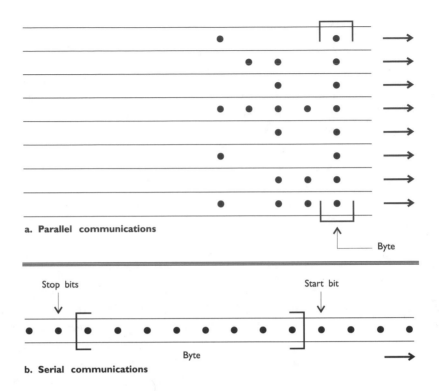

**FIGURE 1.6**
Parallel and serial
communications

a. **Parallel communications**

Byte

Stop bits          Start bit

Byte

b. **Serial communications**

## Parallel Ports

The parallel port is often called the printer port because it is almost exclusively used for printers. However, parallel ports can be used for high speed communications between internal microcomputer components and external tape drives, CD-ROMs, or add-on network interface cards. Configuration of the parallel port is extremely easy because it uses a "plug-and-play" connection—just plug it in and it works. There's no configuration, because the parallel port speaks the same language as the internal data bus. The parallel port convention, which is used on most IBM-compatible machines, was developed by the Centronix company. It describes a 25-pin female connector on the microcomputer and a 36-pin edge connector on the printer. Parallel ports are typically defined as LPT1 for the first parallel port, LPT2 for the second parallel port, and LPT3 for the third parallel port (although it's rare to have more than one parallel port per microcomputer).

The main advantage of parallel ports is their speed. Parallel communications are extremely fast because they transmit 8 bits of information simultaneously. Another advantage is cost. The technology for building parallel port communications is extremely inexpensive because it uses the same communication scheme as does the internal data bus.

Parallel communications is not without problems, however. Parallel communications, with its high speeds and parallel configurations, can only travel 10 or 25 feet. This limitation is due primarily to cross talk. Cross talk is a phenomenon that occurs when parallel communications travel long distances and two different channels interfere with one another. Another disadvantage is that since parallel communications are designed for one-way communications, parallel devices are uni-directional, and therefore less intelligent. Bi-directional communications is reserved for serial ports.

## Serial Ports

The serial port is also known as the asynchronous port or COM1. It operates according to the EIA (Electronics Industry Association) RS232C standard, and is also called the RS232 port. IBM connections call for up to four serial ports designated as COM1, COM2, COM3, and COM4. However, you can only use two serial devices at the same time because COM1 and COM3 use the same configuration and COM2 and COM4 are the same. Serial communications differ dramatically from parallel communications in that they use single channels. While this configuration is not nearly as fast as multiple channels, it is more reliable. Also, serial devices can transmit data over much longer distances.

There are two different methods for serial communications: synchronous and asynchronous. Synchronous communications describes a method in which both devices on each end of the cable are said to be synchronized. That is, they each know what bits make up a byte and how the information should be organized. Asynchronous communications, on the other hand, doesn't rely on expensive synchronizing machinery. It relies on fundamental procedures for recognizing bits and bytes. The most popular method for organizing asynchronous serial bits into bytes is the *data frame*. The data frame consists of 11 bits—8 bits of data, called a byte, 1 bit on the front end (start bit), and 2 bits on the back end (stop bits). This method is simple and reliable, but it's not very efficient.

Serial communication speeds are measured in bits per second, or bps. A device's bps rating is partially determined by its *baud* (a measurement of the device's changes of state per second). A change of state describes a movement

*A typical 2400-baud modem is really a 2400 bits per second modem that is di-bit running at 1200-baud. A typical 9600-baud modem, which is actually 9600 bits per second, is a 2400-baud modem running at quadbit.*

from one frequency state to another. In a typical monobit system, each change of state transmits one bit of data. So a 2400-baud modem would transmit 2400 bits per second. Not all devices are monobit. Many of the new faster modems are di-bit or quadbit. In a di-bit environment, each baud transmits 2 bits of data—therefore, a 2400-baud modem would have an effective throughput of 4800 bits per second. Quadbit devices follow the same principle—4 bits are transmitted for each baud. Just to give you an example, your typical 2400-baud modem is really a 2400 bits per second modem that is di-bit running at 1200-baud. Your typical 9600-baud modem, which is actually 9600 bits per second, is a 2400-baud modem running at quadbit.

Serial ports are configured using a variety of different communications parameters: transmit rate, data bits per byte, parity, and stop bits. The transmit rate is typically measured in baud, although baud is really a measure of bps. Most serial ports have a range of 110 to 19,200 bps. The next serial parameter is data bits per byte. In most serial systems there are 8 bits per byte. But some communications prefer to use 7 bits for each character. In this case, the extra bit is used for parity. Parity is an error-checking algorithm. Serial ports use even parity, odd parity, or no parity. Finally, serial ports are also configured according to stop bits. In most systems, the asynchronous serial port defines 2 stop bits, although it is possible to use just one.

The RS232 serial standard defines two different types of devices: the DTE (Data Terminal Equipment) and the DCE (Data Communication Equipment). The Data Terminal Equipment is the computer at the end of the serial line. The DCE describes the modem or the device that is actually performing the serial translation between the DTE and the phone line. Typically, the Data Terminal Equipment connects to the DCE through a serial connector. This connector can be 9-pin or 25-pin. The 25-pin port looks very similar to parallel except it uses a male connector.

*The highest transmit rates are reserved for dedicated digital lines. Most telephone lines can only support relatively low rates—from 300 to 9600 bits per second.*

In the first half of this chapter, we discussed the microcomputer and its many internal components. We have explored the CPU, data bus, memory, hard disk, video display, and the input/output ports. Now let's shift our focus from microcomputer hardware to the microcomputer operating system that controls the hardware. The operating system interfaces between the intelligent hardware devices and internal software to provide user productivity. The most popular microcomputer operating system is DOS, or the Disk Operating System. In our discussion of DOS, we'll focus on the fundamentals of DOS and the many internal and external DOS commands.

*There is one thing stronger than all the armies in the world, and that is an idea whose time has come.*

*Victor Hugo*

# Understanding DOS

DOS IS A VERY important piece of the microcomputer package because it provides an interface between the software programs that provide user productivity and the microcomputer components that provide processing and disk storage. DOS consists of a basic set of computer instructions that manage the flow of information in and out of the computer. It sits between the hard disk, memory, and the CPU. DOS controls the display of information on the screen as well as the transfer of information in and out of I/O ports. DOS can be thought of as a messenger between the computer hardware and the application programs.

There are other operating systems that perform similar messenger functions.

> *DOS can be thought of as a messenger between the computer hardware and the application programs.*

**NetWare** is a network operating system that provides file sharing and security on the file server.

**Windows NT** (New Technology) is a local operating system that runs on workstations and provides some basic file sharing functionality.

**UNIX** is similar to NT in that it provides some basic file sharing, but UNIX is more difficult to use.

**OS/2** is the second-generation operating system that provides a friendlier interface and greater functionality than DOS. Unfortunately, OS/2 never gained the support it needed.

But to this day, DOS reigns over all other local operating systems and NetWare reigns over all other network operating systems. It is a natural marriage.

DOS controls 95% of the microcomputers currently on the market because it's simple, reliable, and has been around for ten years. The two most popular types of DOS are manufactured by Microsoft (MS-DOS) and Novell (Novell DOS). Both versions currently offer much more functionality than any other local operating system, including virus protection, memory management, and file compression. In the remainder of this chapter, we will explore the basic operations of DOS and review the internal and external commands that provide the user with local resource management. Before you can begin your journey into the NetWare jungle, you must understand the fundamentals of the local operating system—DOS. Look out for crocodiles.

## Basic DOS Operations

To better understand DOS, it's important to have an appreciation for its basic parts. DOS has two main components: the operating system itself and the auxiliary utility programs that go with it. The operating system itself is made up of three files:

**IBMBIO.COM,** also known as IO.SYS, provides the basic facilities for handling the microcomputer's input and output devices—keyboard and video display. This file is hidden and stored in the root directory of the C: drive.

**IBMDOS.COM,** also known as MSDOS.SYS, is the central DOS program that controls communications between the internal microcomputer components. It is also a hidden file in the root of the C: drive.

**COMMAND.COM** is the command interpreter. It reads commands from the keyboard and decides how to carry out the request. COMMAND.COM directs user requests to appropriate internal components—CPU, memory, disk, and so on. It actually executes or interprets all commands that are entered at the keyboard.

The second part of DOS is its many utility programs, which are broken into two groups: internal and external. Internal commands are part of the operating system; that is to say, they aren't made up of separate files. Internal utilities are actually part of the COMMAND.COM file. External DOS commands are separate files with .EXE or .COM extensions. These utilities are executed from a DOS directory on the hard disk. We will discuss most of the common DOS commands later in the chapter.

DOS is activated when you turn on your computer. The three system parts of DOS—IBMBIO.COM, IBMDOS.COM, and COMMAND.COM—are executed automatically during the start-up or *boot* process.

*Booting is an important concept to learn. Besides, they want you to know each of the three bootup phases.*

*DOS is activated when you turn on your computer. The three system parts of DOS—IBMBIO.COM, IBMDOS.COM, and COMMAND.COM— are executed automatically during the start-up or boot process.*

Boot is a general computer term that comes from the *bootstrap* program (a series of basic microcomputer start-up instructions that load from the ROM BIOS (Read Only Memory Basic Input/Output System)). There are two different ways to begin the boot process. You can perform a cold boot (the power is turned off and then back on from a cold state), or a warm boot (by pressing the Control-Alt-Delete keys simultaneously to restart a running system). Either way the computer is re-initialized and the three following bootstrap steps are executed:

**Initial Power Up**—During the initial power up stage, the CPU performs two basic functions—circuitry check and ROM execution. First, the CPU checks its own circuitry to make sure that everything is functional. Second, it looks for ROM memory and performs any instructions it might find there, including the bootstrap instructions. Nothing at this point has been affected by the operating system. This is just an internal microcomputer check for component failures.

*During the initial power-up stage, the CPU performs an internal circuitry check. If any of the components fail, the system will emit "x" number of beeps. This is a BIOS error-checking feature. The number of beeps corresponds to a particular component. Six beeps, for example, point to the internal video adapter. Consult your microcomputer documentation for a list of the error beeps and corresponding hardware components.*

**DOS Search**—Once the bootstrap instructions have loaded, they say, "Let's go find the local operating system and load it into memory." The first thing the bootstrap program loads is IBMBIO.COM and IBMDOS.COM. The first place it looks is the A—or first bootable—drive. Then it looks at B, and finally C—the hard disk. This order can be changed in the CMOS.

If the bootable disk is found and the DOS components are hidden there, the system loads them into memory and goes onto the third step—DOS configuration.

**DOS Configuration**—After the two hidden files are loaded, the CPU looks for a configuration file called CONFIG.SYS. If the file is present, the system uses it to define certain operating system parameters—including device drivers, memory configuration, and so on. Next, the system looks for COMMAND.COM—the command interpreter. Once it loads COMMAND.COM, the computer is ready to perform its duties—DOS and otherwise. The very first thing the computer does once it loads COMMAND.COM is execute a file called AUTOEXEC.BAT. This file is an auto-executing batch file that contains preliminary configuration instructions. Incidentally, both CONFIG.SYS and AUTOEXEC.BAT are workstation-specific user-editable files. They can quickly become the system manager's nemesis.

*The DOS prompt is an operating system fixture on the screen that says, "I'm ready, prepared, and at your service."*

So that's how DOS does it. Besides the built-in bootstrap instructions, DOS has some basic operational components that allow it to understand the microcomputer software environment. First there's COMMAND.COM execution during the last step of the booting procedure. Then there's file maintenance (understanding how to set up files and organize them into directories). There are directory maintenance and batch files that allow you to execute large numbers of commands very easily. Finally, there's DOS configuration—CONFIG.SYS and AUTOEXEC.BAT. In the remainder of this chapter, we will explore these different DOS operations and gain an understanding of their relationship with microcomputer hardware and software. Finally, we will learn the most popular internal and external DOS commands. Let's begin with command execution.

## Command Execution

Once COMMAND.COM has been executed, the system is prepared to process any valid user request. These requests are made at the DOS command line. The command line is called the *DOS prompt.* The DOS prompt is an operating system fixture on the screen that says, "I'm ready, prepared, and at your service." The DOS prompt is typically displayed as a drive letter, A or C, and a greater than (>) sign—followed by a blinking line, called the cursor.

The blinking cursor represents the input point for user requests and looks like this:

```
C>_
```

Information is not processed until the Enter key is pressed. The PROMPT command allows you to customize the way the DOS prompt looks. You can add other information, including current directory, date and time information, text, and so on. Users can customize the DOS prompt to provide information as well as look appealing. The options are almost limitless.

DOS commands are entered at the DOS prompt using proper syntax. This means you must enter commands in uppercase or lowercase (DOS is not case sensitive), spell commands correctly, no spaces, and always press the Enter key at the end. Also, whenever specifying a drive letter, always follow it with a colon (C:). As we talked about earlier, DOS supports floppy drives A and B, and hard disks C, D, and E. These are the different drive designations you can specify when you go looking for your files. If you need to abort a command or break out of a DOS program, press Control-C or Control-Break simultaneously.

Another way of customizing command execution is to use a switch, or command parameter. The switch is a way of telling DOS that you would like to execute a particular command with a specific type of environment. Switches typically follow the command and are preceded by a forward slash.

Let's use the DIR command (which lists the files in a given directory) as an example. If the file list exceeds the length of the screen, the system will continue to scroll, and will chop off the top of the list. This is bad. Executing the DIR command with a /P switch instructs DOS to list the files one page at a time. If you would like a complete list of all the switches for a given command, type the command followed by /?. Switches can be very useful in customizing the more complex DOS commands.

## File Maintenance

Think of the hard disk as a filing cabinet. The drawers are disk drives, inside of which are folders (directories). The folders contain electronic files with file names and DOS attributes. It would be difficult to find your files without folder and file labels. Directory and file names are extremely important to the electronic filing cabinet. In the next two sections, we will explore the electronic filing cabinet through file and directory maintenance. File maintenance deals specifically with the rules and regulations of creating and maintaining DOS files, while directory maintenance deals with DOS directories.

As a file is created in DOS, the system makes note of it in the File Allocation Table (FAT). The DOS FAT keeps track of file names, extensions, and the file's physical location on the disk by track, sector, and cylinder. The DOS file-name consists of two parts: an 8-character name and a 3-character extension. The file name and extension are separated by a period. Other FAT information includes file size, creation date, modified date, and file attributes. There are a few conventions that must be followed when naming DOS files:

- Use a maximum of eight characters, followed by a period and a three-character extension.

- Use no spaces.

- Use any keyboard character except special characters.

- DOS reserves the following special characters:

    - Asterisk (*) and question mark (?), which are reserved for wildcards.

    - Period (.), which is used to separate a file name and extension.

    - Colon (:), which is used to identify drives and other types of devices like LPT1 and COM1.

    - Forward slash (/), which is used to identify switches.

    - Backward slash (\), which is used to identify directories.

    - Less than (<) and greater than (>) symbols, which are used for redirecting data.

*There are few guarantees in life, but here's one: they'll ask you questions about file names and extensions.*

Once you create a file name using the proper convention, DOS will attach an appropriate extension. Extensions are used to identify file types and functionality. Many times the application defines the extension, not the user. The following is a list of standard DOS extensions and what they mean. Understanding this list will help you identify specific files and their function in the DOS environment.

**.COM** indicates a command file. These files are typically executed at the DOS prompt and normally cannot be changed. Typically, a COM file is an external utility that is part of the DOS operating system.

**.EXE** is used for executable program files. These files contain instructions that are processed by the CPU. They are usually created by some compatible programming language.

**.BAT** identifies DOS batch files. Batch files are text files, programmed with valid DOS commands, that allow users to execute multiple commands from a single file.

**.SYS** indicates a system file. System files are used to interface between the operating system and hardware. Typically, .SYS files are drivers. MOUSE.SYS, for example, interfaces between DOS and the mouse hardware device.

**.OVL** are overlay files. Some DOS programs are so big that they cannot reside in the 640K of conventional memory. Overlay files allow programs to divide themselves into smaller pieces that can be swapped in and out of conventional RAM.

**.DAT** indicates a data file. Some programs create their own data files while they are running. These temporary files use the .DAT extension to distinguish themselves. Most permanent data files use a program-specific extension, including .XLS for Excel, .DOC for Word, and so on. Other program-specific data files, such as WordPerfect, use no extension.

**.BAK** indicates a backup file. Backup files are typically created by programs that store important data. Word processing, spreadsheet, and database applications, for example, create automatic backup copies (with a .BAK extension) of the file you're working on. These .BAK files can be lifesavers in cases of data loss, corruption, or disk crash.

**.BAS** indicates a source code file from the BASIC programming language.

**.C** indicates a source code file from the C programming language.

DOS also provides two wildcard characters: the asterisk (*) and question mark (?). These wildcards can be used for file searching, copying, and deleting. The asterisk represents any *group* of characters—in the file name, extension, or both. For example, `*.BAK` defines any file name with the .BAK extension; `DAVID.*` defines the file DAVID with any extension; and `*.*` defines any file name with any extension—i.e., all files.

The question mark represents a *single* character. For example, `?.BAK` defines any one character file name with the .BAK extension. Also, `DAVID.B?` defines the file DAVID with any 2 character extension that starts with B.

While files are the mainstay of the DOS data filing system, directories provide a higher level of organization. They are the folders in which the files are stored. And like files, directories follow a few simple DOS conventions.

---

### Directory Maintenance

*While files are the mainstay of the DOS data filing system, directories provide a higher level of organization. They are the folders in which the files are stored.*

DOS directories are organized into a tree structure that, not surprisingly, has its basis in what's called the *root* directory. The root directory is the highest level of the tree—all parent directories branch from the root. (You can think of it as the electronic drawer in which all other folders are organized.) Subdirectories provide further organization by branching from parent directories. Directories and subdirectories are denoted with the backslash (\). For example, a directory on the C: drive named 123 would have the designation—C:\123. `C:` is the volume and `\123` is the directory name. Directories use the same naming conventions as files—eight characters and a three-character extension, with a period separating the two.

The route from the root directory to a particular file is called the path. The path denotes the subdirectory structure that one travels from the root directory to any given file. For example, if the file DAVID.BAT was in the DATA subdirectory under DAVID under 123, the path would be C:\123\DAVID\DATA\DAVID.BAT. DOS uses paths to create a *search list*. The DOS search list is a table of subdirectories that are searched when users request specific files—.BAT, .COM, or .EXE. Users can use the PATH command to build a search list with a particular search order. We will discuss the PATH command later in the chapter.

Directory maintenance is extremely important because it provides a tool for organizing user data. Some programs provide graphical representations of the DOS directory format. Microsoft Windows, for example, specifies the directory tree in a format that is very easy to follow. Directory maintenance is an essential part of the system manager's job.

## Batch Files

Speaking of productivity and ease of use, DOS includes a programming feature that allows users to create simple text file with multiple DOS commands. These are called *batch files*. They make command execution extremely easy and provide a nice facility for autoloading specific programs or commands.

Batch files are text files with a .BAT file name extension. They contain a series of DOS commands that, when performed in sequence, execute a specific task. To invoke a batch file, simply type the name of the batch file without the extension and press Enter. DOS executes each of the batch commands in order. Creating batch files is as simple as creating a text file. Just make sure to follow proper batch file syntax. Batch files support any and all DOS commands and even a few non-DOS commands. The following three batch file commands are not supported at the DOS command line.

**REM** is the remark command, which enhances batch file processing by providing a way of inserting documentation into the file. Here's an example:

```
REM This line copies all files from A to B.
Copy A:*.* B:*.*
```

**ECHO,** when placed at the beginning of a batch file, will echo all commands to the screen so you can follow the batch file execution—line by line. If you do not want to confuse users and would prefer not having the commands echoed to the screen, use ECHO OFF (this command makes all execution appear transparent (invisible) to the user).

**PAUSE** is used to suspend the operation of the batch file until another key is pressed. If you put a PAUSE command anywhere in the batch file, execution will stop and the message `Press any key to continue` or `Strike a key when ready` will appear on the screen. As soon as the user strikes a key, the batch file execution will continue.

## DOS Configuration

DOS configuration is important because it provides a way of customizing each user's workstation environment. There are two specific configuration files that work in the DOS environment: CONFIG.SYS and AUTO-EXEC.BAT. Both of these configuration files are automatically loaded during the microcomputer boot process. Let's take a closer look.

**CONFIG.SYS** CONFIG.SYS is a system configuration file that automatically loads during the second stage of the boot process. CONFIG.SYS instructs DOS how to communicate with new and existing hardware. It provides some memory management functionality. There are four commands that are commonly used in the CONFIG.SYS file:

**BUFFERS** tells DOS how much memory to set aside for local disk buffers. This is an area in memory that the computer will use for temporary data storage. Data buffering speeds up the processing and movement of files from disk to memory. The BUFFER = 40 command is optimal. DOS will support any number from 3 to 99. Each buffer consists of 512 bytes of information and will make that particular area of memory directly and instantly available to the CPU.

**FILES** controls how many disk files DOS will allow to be open at the same time. Many of the popular software programs—Microsoft Windows, for example—require multiple open files, and this command can be used to accommodate them. FILES = 40 is optimal. DOS supports as many as 255 open files simultaneously.

**LASTDRIVE** is especially important for network users because it reserves the local DOS drives. As you remember, DOS reserves the drive letters A and B for floppy drives, C, D, and E for hard disks. If you have the LAST DRIVE = D command, for example, the last drive that DOS is capable of addressing is D. You can also go further and have other drives available to DOS—G and H, for example. In this case, you would use the LAST DRIVE = H command and your first available network drive would be I.

**DEVICE** is the most important CONFIG.SYS command. DEVICE tells DOS how to handle the microcomputer's internal hardware devices. Earlier we learned that device drivers are software programs that interface between microcomputer hardware and the operating system. The DEVICE command in CONFIG.SYS provides the interface for device drivers, DOS, and internal hardware. Some of the most popular device drivers are ANSI.SYS, MOUSE.SYS, and VDISK.SYS. ANSI.SYS interfaces between DOS and the input/output systems. MOUSE.SYS provides mouse support in DOS. VDISK.SYS creates a virtual disk and provides communications between the hard disk and memory.

**AUTOEXEC.BAT** The AUTOEXEC.BAT file is another DOS configuration file that helps to customize user environments. AUTOEXEC is the last file that DOS executes once the boot up process is completed. The AUTOEXEC name means that it is automatically executed when COMMAND.COM is loaded. Some common AUTOEXEC.BAT commands include PROMPT, ECHO OFF, CLS, and PATH. We will discuss these internal and external commands next.

This concludes the fundamentals of DOS operation. We talked about command execution, file maintenance, directory maintenance, batch files, and DOS configurations. In the fleeting moments of this chapter, we will explore the variety of DOS internal and external commands and learn how they work together to customize the operating system environment. These are the commands that make the computer useful.

*The mode by which the inevitable comes to pass is effort.*

*Oliver Wendell Holmes*

*When studying DOS internal and external commands, please note all the different switches. You'll thank me later when agonizing over the CNA exam ... oh, it's not that bad!*

## Common Internal Commands

Internal DOS commands, as we learned earlier, are not composed of actual .EXE or .COM files. Instead, they are part of the COMMAND.COM program. Internal DOS commands can be executed from any location, as long as you have a DOS prompt. These commands are used for file maintenance, directory movement, DOS configuration, and workstation setup. Following is a brief description of the most common internal DOS commands.

### CD

CD stands for Change Directory. This command allows you to change your current directory. DOS keeps track of where you are and the directory you're working in through the DOS prompt. You can move to another directory by typing `CD [name of directory]`. Remember the following conventions when using the CD command:

`CD\` specifies the root

`CD\123` specifies the 123 directory under the root

`CD 123` specifies the 123 directory under the current directory

*DOS includes two reserved directory names: "." and "..". The "." represents your current directory. The ".." represents the previous parent directory. For a shortcut to move to the parent directory, try typing* `CD..`

## CLS

CLS is the clear screen command. This command will clear the screen and move the prompt in the top left-hand corner. Clear screen is very effective in batch files for clearing garbage from the screen.

## COPY

The COPY command is a very useful DOS command that allows users to copy files from one location in the directory structure to another. The COPY command creates a copy of the file and moves it to another location, keeping the original file intact. The COPY command can be used to copy files within the same disk—from one level of the directory structure to another—or from one disk to another—from the C: drive to A: for example. The COPY command syntax reads `COPY [source drive and file name] [target drive and file name]`.

*An interesting variation on the COPY command is COPYCON. COPYCON is an internal DOS command that creates text files by copying the contents of the screen to a file. This is ideal for DOS configuration files such as CON-FIG.SYS and AUTOEXEC.BAT. Type in* `COPYCON` *and then the name of the file, and then press Enter. You will see a blinking cursor. Input text by typing and pressing Enter at the end of each line. To finish, type* `Control-Z` *on a line by itself. As soon as you press Enter, the system responds with* `1 file copied`. *All done.*

## DEL

The DEL (delete) command is used to delete or erase DOS files. DEL (or ERASE) can be used to delete large numbers of files when used in combination with wildcard characters. Be very careful when using the DEL command with wildcard characters; you can accidentally delete large numbers of files. DEL *.*, for example, will delete everything in the current directory.

*When a user types* DEL *.*, *DOS responds with* Are you sure? Yes or No. *This is a built-in, fail-safe feature that gives the user the option to back out of a perilous situation.*

## DIR

*A typical directory listing provides the file name, extension, size, and last update time/date.*

The DIR command provides a listing of the files and directories within the current directory or disk. A typical directory listing provides the file name, extension, size, and last update time/date. At the bottom of the file/directory listing, DOS will display the number of files in the directory and the amount of free space that is available. DIR is particularly useful in locating specific files and directories. The directory listing scrolls extremely quickly on the screen, so you can use Control-S (pressing Control and S simultaneously) to pause the scrolling at any point. Use Control-S again to continue the scrolling.

There are a few DOS switches that can be used with the DIR command:

/p causes the command to pause after a screen is filled, typically 23 lines.

/w presents the listing in five columns across the screen. This parameter only displays the file names and extensions.

## MD

MD is Make Directory. MD is identical to CD in convention and syntax, except in this case we are *making* directories, not changing them.

## MORE

The MORE command causes softcopy output to be displayed one screenful at a time. This is very similar to the /P switch for DIR, except MORE works with any command. You can type the command and send it to MORE by typing the command followed by ¦ MORE. The "¦" symbol is called a pipe, and it is one of the three DOS redirection symbols. "<" and ">" are the other two.

## PATH

The PATH command is extremely important because it builds a search list for DOS program files. The PATH command, when put in the AUTOEXEC.BAT, will specify a list of directories for DOS to search, in order, when a user requests a specific program file. For example, if you attempt to execute a particular .COM, .EXE, or .BAT program file from a directory where the file doesn't exist, the system will respond with Bad Command or Filename. The PATH command builds a search list that DOS will use to try to find your file. If DOS finds your program in any of the PATH directories, it executes the file.

   The PATH command is a variable that will be retained in memory until you either execute another PATH command or until the computer is rebooted. The DOS syntax for the PATH command is pretty simple. The PATH command alone displays the current path; PATH followed by an equal (=) sign builds a search list of DOS directories. Subdirectories are separated by semicolons (;). Keep in mind that the order that subdirectories appear (from left to right) specifies the order in which the system searches for DOS commands and program files. Here's an example:

```
PATH = C:\;C:\DOS;C:\WINDOWS
```

## PROMPT

The PROMPT command is important in that it specifies or customizes the DOS prompt. This command is useful for users who require more information than just the drive letter and a ">". DOS provides a variety of different parameters that can be used with the prompt command. Here's a brief list of some of the more common PROMPT parameters:

- $p$g—the drive letter and the full path of your current directory.

- $t—the time.

- $d—the date.

- $v—the version number of DOS.

- $n—the default dive.

- $q—an = sign.

- $$—the $ (weird?!)

- $1—a "<".

- $b—a pipe, or vertical line.

- $_—a carriage return, or line feed.

The PROMPT command also supports text. For example, you could type PROMPT Today is $d and the DOS prompt would display Today is May 3, 1994. The PROMPT command alone returns the DOS prompt back to its default state—C>.

## REN

REN is an internal DOS command that allows you to rename a file without copying it. REN creates a copy of a file, gives it a new name, and deletes the original. The rename command will rename the file and store it in the default directory. You can always rename a file to another directory but you have to copy the file there first.

## RD

RD (Remove Directory) is identical to CD and MD except it removes directories instead of changing or making them. The same conventions apply.

*You cannot remove a directory containing files or subdirectories—they must be deleted first.*

### SET

The SET command is a complex internal DOS command that provides a great deal of flexibility and DOS customization. The SET command inserts a variable string into the command processor's environment. Any program can then recall the string from DOS whenever a user asks for it.

### TYPE

The TYPE command displays the contents of a file on the screen. Users can also type a file to the printer or redirect it to a file. Text files are displayed in alphanumeric characters. Program files are not as simple—they contain all sorts of programming notations. These control characters are displayed as strange little ASCII characters (smiley faces, for example) and loud beeping noises. To redirect files to a printer, use the following notation: `TYPE > LPT1:`.

### VER

VER is a DOS internal command that displays the version number of DOS. DOS version information is important for certain programs that are sensitive to particular versions.

*Remember: Learn those switches for the test.*

## Common External DOS Commands

External commands differ from internal commands in that they exist as external files, with .COM or .EXE extensions. .COM files are command utilities while .EXE files are add-on DOS applications. External DOS commands are not part of COMMAND.COM. They are typically stored in the C:\DOS subdirectory. Most external DOS commands are specialized tools and are not part of the microcomputer's everyday operation. The following is a brief description of DOS's most popular external commands.

### ATTRIB

The attribute command, or ATTRIB, displays and changes file attributes. An attribute controls access to a file and provides a very simple level of DOS security. There are two attributes that are specifically useful in DOS: read-only and archive. The read-only attribute says, "This file can only be read, it cannot be written to." Read-only files cannot be copied or deleted. The Archive attribute says, "This particular file needs to be backed up. It's been modified since the last backup." The ATTRIB command allows you to add or subtract either of these two file attributes. To add an attribute, type ATTRIB followed by +r. To subtract an attribute, type ATTRIB followed by -r. If the read-only attribute has been disabled, the file is said to be read-write—it can be read from and written to simultaneously. Typing the ATTRIB *.* command displays the current attribute status of all files in the default directory.

### BACKUP

BACKUP is a useful DOS utility that allows users to make backup copies of files, directories, disks, and diskettes. BACKUP is the main DOS fault tolerance feature. BACKUP will make an archive of all files and all subdirectories on the disk and save the archive in a specific backup format. The DOS BACKUP format can only be restored using the RESTORE command. Also, BACKUP only works on hard disk or diskette—so imagine backing up a 40MB or 80MB hard disk to 80 high-density diskettes. Talk about boring.

*The DOS BACKUP command is misleading and unreliable. It creates a proprietary archive diskette that cannot be copied or deleted. If you want to restore one file, you have to restore the entire backup set.*

## CHKDSK

CHKDSK (CHecKDiSK) is a DOS external program that checks the integrity of data on your disk. It can also make corrections. CHKDSK, when performed alone, will check the default drive. Otherwise, you can specify a drive by typing CHKDSK [drive]. CHKDSK will tell you the size of the drive, the capacity of the drive, and how much disk space is available. It will also tell you if there are any lost clusters, lost sectors, or corrupted data. CHKDSK /F performs low-level disk maintenance and fixes any notable errors.

## COMMAND.COM

COMMAND.COM is the most important DOS command—it loads the DOS command processor. COMMAND.COM is one of the three main portions of DOS. It is also the second-to-last program that is executed during the boot-up process. If you type COMMAND at the DOS prompt, it will load a second copy of the command processor. This command is only used in specialized cases. Don't try this at home!

## DISKCOPY

The DISKCOPY command provides a method of duplicating DOS diskettes. To use DISKCOPY, the source and destination disks need to be exactly the same. For example, if the source disk is a 1.2MB high density 5¼" floppy, then the target disk must also be a 1.2MB high density 5¼" floppy. DISK-COPY makes a low-level copy of all tracks and sectors—so it will also copy any hidden protection. If the target disk is not formatted before the DISK-COPY is performed, DISKCOPY will automatically format the disk for you.

To perform DISKCOPY, you simply type DISKCOPY [source drive] [target drive]. For example, if you would like to copy two diskettes from the same drive, type DISKCOPY A: A:—in this case, the system will prompt you for the source disk and the target disk. Keep in mind that since you have limited conventional memory in DOS, DISKCOPY will require multiple swappings—often five or ten times per DISKCOPY session.

## FDISK

FDISK allows you to break a hard disk into multiple partitions or define the entire disk as one large partition. FDISK will also allow you to delete existing partitions. Once you run FDISK, the hard disk is ready to be formatted. Formatting downloads the operating system and formats the disk into sectors, tracks, and cylinders. FDISK allows you to create primary DOS partitions, secondary extended DOS partitions, or non-DOS partitions. Incidentally, when you use FDISK to create a DOS partition in NetWare 3.12, you leave a large portion of the disk unformatted. NetWare 3.12 will create a non-DOS partition for itself.

*DOS 3.30 and below allow a maximum of 32MB for each partition. DOS 4.0 and above allow unlimited partition sizes.*

## FORMAT

Once the disk has been FDISKed and partitioned, it is ready to be formatted. Formatting breaks up the disk platter into logical tracks, pie-shaped sectors, and parallel cylinders. The FORMAT command can be used to format a hard disk or floppy diskette. Keep in mind that a disk must be formatted and prepared before it can store any data. There are a variety of switches that can be used with the FORMAT command:

/s—to transfer the system files, namely IBMBIO.COM, IBMDOS.COM, and COMMAND.COM.

/v—specifies a volume label for this disk. During the format procedure, it will ask you for an 11-character volume name.

/x—required to format hard disks in DR DOS.

In addition to the above switches, FORMAT supports a variety of drive compatibility switches, to ensure that FORMAT understands the type of diskette you are using and the corresponding drive type:

FORMAT A: /F:720 formats a low-density 3½" diskette in a high-density drive. (This switch only works with DOS 5.0 and above.)

FORMAT A: /4 formats a low-density 5¼" diskette in a high-density drive.

### LABEL

The LABEL command makes it possible to create, change, or delete a volume label. This ability is important because many users like to have specific names or volume labels for their hard or floppy disks. This command gives you an electronic filing system.

### MEM

The MEM command is an external DOS (but only v5.0 and above) utility that allows you to display information about the way memory is currently being used. This command is very useful in troubleshooting and optimizing workstation RAM. After all, memory has become a central issue as more and more programs compete for limited memory resources. The MEM command, when executed alone, will display the currently available RAM as compared to the total amount installed. MEM /C provides a lot more information—it breaks up the memory into conventional, expanded, and extended. MEM /C displays the programs that are currently using RAM and how much they are using.

### PRINT

The PRINT command is a simple printing utility in DOS. It allows you to print text files to an LPT1 printer. Simply type PRINT followed by the name of the text file and the system will print the file to the default printer.

### SHARE

SHARE is a DOS command that allows multiple access to otherwise stand-alone files. File sharing is something new in a DOS environment because typically you have one user accessing one file at a time. If you have programs that are capable of multitasking, such as Microsoft Windows, and they want to access the same file simultaneously, you should have SHARE loaded. SHARE allocates DOS environment space for file sharing and locking instructions.

*File sharing is quite common in a network environment. File attributes mark files as sharable, non-sharable, and so on. But with sharable data files, the question is "Which user's changes get saved?" The answer? "Whoever saves last, wins!"*

## SYS

The SYS command allows you to transfer the system files from a hard or floppy disk to another drive. SYS copies the system files—IBMBIO.COM, IBMDOS.COM, and COMMAND.COM—from the source disk to a target drive. For example, if you format a floppy drive and forget to use the /S parameter, the SYS A: command will transfer the system files to the floppy disk A and make it bootable.

## UNDELETE

UNDELETE is an extremely useful fault tolerance feature that is only available in the newer versions of MS-DOS and DR/Novell DOS. UNDELETE allows users to recover deleted files if the files haven't been written over yet. When you run UNDELETE, the system will give you a list of files that are available for undeletion. This list is directory-specific. UNDELETE has saved many users from the proverbial firing line.

## XCOPY

XCOPY was developed primarily to aid in working with hard disks and large groups of files. The XCOPY command expands on the functionality of COPY by providing the ability to copy files and subdirectories together. XCOPY supports four main switches:

/s tells XCOPY to copy a directory including all subdirectories under it. This is found to be extremely useful moving entire branches from one part of the tree to another.

/e copies all empty subdirectories and may only be used with the /s switch.

**/v** verifies the integrity of the data copied. DOS performs a read-after-write verification while it copies the data from one area of the disk to another.

**/w** causes XCOPY to wait before it starts copying files. This is important in copying files to a floppy-based system because it gives the user more time to switch the DOS disk from the source to the target destination.

This completes our discussion of DOS. In this chapter, we have explored the fundamentals of the microcomputer through the eyes of internal hardware and DOS. As a CNA, it is important that you gain an appreciation for the complexities of microcomputer hardware. In addition, you should understand the purpose of an operating system and feel comfortable with the basic operations of DOS. As we continue throughout the book, we will refer back to these components and discuss ways of optimizing the microcomputer hardware/software in a networking environment. In the next chapter, we will use these microcomputer/DOS fundamentals as a springboard for NetWare basics. Remember, it all starts with that first step. Before you know it, you will be running the NetWare marathon.

*A journey of a thousand miles must begin with a single step.*

*Chinese Proverb*

# Exercise 1.1: Matching Microcomputer Concepts

|   |   |   |   |
|---|---|---|---|
| _____ | **1.** Extended ASCII | **A.** | Bus architecture of IBM AT class computer |
| _____ | **2.** Motorola | **B.** | Part of the computer's input system |
| _____ | **3.** ISA | **C.** | Bus architecture of IBM's PS/2 class |
| _____ | **4.** Serial | **D.** | Houses the control unit and ALU |
| _____ | **5.** CGA | **E.** | A set of 256 characters in 8 bits per byte |
| _____ | **6.** 80486 | **F.** | Chip of choice for Macintosh computers |
| _____ | **7.** VGA | **G.** | 16-bit data bus and 32-bit CPU internal bus |
| _____ | **8.** 80386SX | **H.** | Chip of choice for IBM computers |
| _____ | **9.** Extended RAM | **I.** | Brains of the Macintosh IIfx |
| _____ | **10.** CMOS | **J.** | Includes a math coprocessor and internal cache controller |
| _____ | **11.** Keyboard | **K.** | Volatile storage |
| _____ | **12.** Pixels | **L.** | Keeps track of system configurations |
| _____ | **13.** SCSI | **M.** | Optical floppies |
| _____ | **14.** Intel | **N.** | Memory used by Microsoft Windows to break the 1MB barrier |
| _____ | **15.** Floptical | **O.** | Best interface for NetWare servers |
| _____ | **16.** MCA | **P.** | 16 colors in low resolution |
| _____ | **17.** RAM | **Q.** | Picture elements |
| _____ | **18.** CPU | **R.** | Most popular disk interface for smaller disks |
| _____ | **19.** Motorola 68030 | **S.** | 16 colors in very high resolution |
| _____ | **20.** IDE | **T.** | RS232C standard |

See Appendix D for answers.

### Exercise 1.2: Using DOS Commands

In this chapter, we learned about how the DOS workstation operating system interfaces between the microcomputer hardware and NetWare user. We learned about basic DOS operations, including command execution, file and directory maintenance, batch files and DOS configuration files. The bulk of the DOS discussion focused on fourteen common internal and fourteen common external DOS commands. In this exercise, we will practice using some of the most common DOS commands and gain a comprehensive understanding of how they can be used to work productively in a DOS environment.

# Common Internal Commands

**CD** The CD command allows the user to change directories from the current directory to another one in the directory structure.

- Type CD\ and press Enter to change to the root directory. The system will return with a prompt indicating that you are currently in the root directory.

- Type CD\DOS and press Enter to move to a specified directory on the hard drive. This moves to the DOS subdirectory. Remember the backslash indicates that this directory resides directly off of the root.

**CLS** The CLS command can be used to clear the screen.

- Type CLS and press Enter.

**COPY** The DOS COPY command provides an effective strategy for copying files within a hard disk or between disk drives and floppy disks. To copy a file, you must either specify the source and target drive, or move to the source directory and specify the file from there.

- Type CD\ and press Enter to move to the source directory.

- Once at the root directory, type COPY AUTOEXEC.BAT \DOS and press Enter. This command will copy the AUTOEXEC.BAT file from the root to the DOS subdirectory.

**DEL** The delete command works similarly to the COPY command except it deletes files instead of copying them.

- Type `DEL \DOS\AUTOEXEC.BAT` and press Enter to delete the file we just copied.

**DIR** Use the DIR command to verify that the DEL, in fact, worked.

- Type `DIR \DOS\AUTOEXEC.BAT` and press Enter. The system will return with `File not found`, because we deleted the file from the DOS subdirectory.

- Now type `DIR AUTOEXEC.BAT` and press Enter. The system will respond with information about the AUTOEXEC.BAT file that resides in the root directory.

- Type `DIR/p` to gain information about more than one file. You will see all information on files and directories in the current directory, one page at a time.

**TYPE** To see the contents of the AUTOEXEC.BAT file, use the TYPE command.

- Type `AUTOEXEC.BAT` and press Enter. You will see the contents of the AUTO-EXEC.BAT text file. If the text file is larger than one screen, you can use the MORE redirection command to view one screen at a time.

- Type `AUTOEXEC.BAT | MORE`.

**PATH** The PATH command allows users to search certain directories for files.

- Type `PATH` and press Enter. You will see the current path. In order to customize the path, follow the path command with any specific set of directories separated by semicolons.

**PROMPT** The PROMPT command customizes the directory display so that users can view more information than just the directory they're in and the drive they're using.

- Type `PROMPT $d` and press Enter. The system will respond by changing the directory pointer so that it displays the date.

- Type `PROMPT $v$g` and press Enter. You will see the current version of DOS you are running followed by a greater-than (>) sign. You can also use text in your DOS prompt.

- Type `PROMPT HI, HOW ARE YOU TODAY` and press Enter. The system will respond with `HI, HOW ARE YOU TODAY` at every screen. The text can be combined with variables to provide valuable information for the user.

- Type PROMPT TODAY IS $d and press Enter. You will see TODAY IS and the date.

- Type PROMPT $p$g and press Enter to return to the prompt you're most used to. This prompt provides you with the drive and path plus a greater-than (>) sign.

**VER** The VER command allows users to gain information about the version of DOS they're using.

- Type VER and press Enter.

That completes our discussion of the use of some of the common internal DOS commands. These commands are stored in the COMMAND.COM file, which automatically loads during computer startup.

# Common External Commands

While the DOS internal commands reside in the one COMMAND.COM file, the DOS external commands all reside in the DOS subdirectory. These are utilities that exist as .EXE or .COM files and they provide additional functionality beyond the internal DOS commands. Let's explore some of the more common external DOS commands.

**CHKDSK**—The CHKDSK command allows users to keep track of the use of disk space on floppy or hard disks as well as the health of their disks. In addition, CHKDSK displays the number of hidden files found on the disk.

- Type CHKDSK and press Enter. The system will respond with a group of information. If the hard disk has some problems and there are lost clusters or sectors, the system will respond with a warning message.

- Type CHKDSK /f and press Enter to repair any existing problems on the disk. If problems do not exist, the /f switch will be ignored.

**MEM** Another valuable utility for gaining information is MEM. The MEM command provides detailed information about internal workstation RAM.

- Type MEM and press Enter. The system will respond with a few lines of information about existing and available workstation RAM. More detailed information about which programs are loaded into memory can be accessed by using the /c parameter.

- Type MEM /c and press ENTER.

**LABEL**—The LABEL command allows users to electronically label their local and floppy disks.

- Type LABEL and press Enter to label the hard disk. The system will respond with an input box asking for any label up to 11 characters.

- Type in a name for your hard disk and press Enter.

**DIR**—Now that you've labeled your hard disk you can view the label.

- Type DIR and press Enter. The system will respond with a list of files in the root directory and the label of the hard disk.

**XCOPY**—Beyond COPY, DOS provides two other utilities that can be used in DISKCOPY special copy situations: XCOPY and DISKCOPY. XCOPY allows for copying of subdirectories and files and DISKCOPY allows for the duplication of entire floppy disks.

- Try them out on your hard disk and use them to copy floppy disks of the same type.

Be aware that DOS provides the facility for not only file and directory management but disk management as well. There are two utilities, FDISK and FORMAT, that perform dangerous disk-level operations. Be very careful when toying with these two utilities.

# NetWare
# Basics

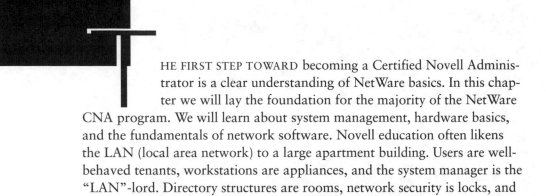

THE FIRST STEP TOWARD becoming a Certified Novell Administrator is a clear understanding of NetWare basics. In this chapter we will lay the foundation for the majority of the NetWare CNA program. We will learn about system management, hardware basics, and the fundamentals of network software. Novell education often likens the LAN (local area network) to a large apartment building. Users are well-behaved tenants, workstations are appliances, and the system manager is the "LAN"-lord. Directory structures are rooms, network security is locks, and printing is performed in the laundry room. You get the idea.

In the context of this analogy, NetWare basics is the cement foundation upon which the apartments are built. You must have a firm grasp of the LAN fundamentals before you can effectively manage the network resources. There are many challenges and responsibilities that the system manager faces each day. The difference between success and failure is a good utility belt with reliable hardware, transparent software, and technical know-how. Let's begin our discussion of NetWare basics with a look at the responsibilities and resources of the NetWare system manager.

*My precept to all who build is, that the owner should be an ornament to the house, and not the house to the owner.*

*Cicero*

# The NetWare System Manager

THE NETWARE SYSTEM MANAGER is responsible for network design, implementation, and daily network management. In addition, he/she is required to perform preventive maintenance and timely network troubleshooting. Although this is not a job for the faint-of-heart, the rewards are plentiful—fame, fortune, and continued connectivity. In this section, we will explore the detailed responsibilities of the NetWare system manager and offer some valuable network resources for your utility belt. The remainder of this chapter focuses on the hardware and software basics that comprise NetWare LANs. Pay close attention to this chapter, because you never know when you will need a special torque-head screwdriver.

## Responsibilities of a CNA

The NetWare system manager is a brave soul whose single task is to keep peace in the NetWare castle. System management is typically three full-time jobs smashed into one part-time person. In the past, the NetWare system manager was chosen by default—a dubious distinction. Nobody fully understood the time and effort it required to manage a NetWare LAN and the job was often given to the first employee who showed proficiency in using the copy machine or office microwave. Fortunately we have left the dark ages. Employers are beginning to appreciate the knowledge and skill it takes to correctly manage a LAN. The CNE and CNA certifications are gaining respect and—in many cases—are becoming a requirement.

Let's review the top ten responsibilities of a NetWare system manager:

1. **Understand NetWare**—(Covered in Chapter 2). The first order of business for a NetWare system manager is a strong foundation of NetWare basics. After all, it is hard to manage something you don't understand.

2. **Maintain trustees & security**—(Covered in Chapters 3, 4, 8 and 9). The most time-consuming responsibility a system manager has is maintaining network trustees and security. First, the users are created and organized into functional workgroups. Then their data and applications are

installed and configured into an existing file structure. This step involves network directory structures and drive mapping. Next, the users are granted specific security privileges to various LAN directories. This step involves configuring user types and NetWare trustee assignments.

3. **Monitor the file server**—(Covered in Chapters 5 and 10). The file server is at the heart of the system manager's life. It houses the NetWare operating system and provides network users with applications, data, and shared resources. NetWare provides a variety of supervisor utilities for routine monitoring and maintenance of the file server.

4. **Maintain the network**—(Covered in Chapters 5, 6, 10, and 11). Once the NetWare LAN has been created and the users are defined, it is time to turn your system management attention to maintaining the network. Network maintenance has two faces—preventive maintenance and troubleshooting. Preventive maintenance is typically proactive, while troubleshooting is reactive. The former reduces the latter and ensures job stability and a relatively high quality of life.

5. **Manage printing**—(Covered in Chapters 7 and 12). The most mysterious and misunderstood facet of system management is printing. Printing represents 50% of LAN functionality and 10% of the system manager's time. Very little is written or said about managing network printing. In Chapter 9 we will begin with a discussion of the *Essence of Printing*. A critical topic that few people pay attention to.

6. **Manage network applications**—(Covered in Chapters 6 and 11). Network applications are the functional workhorses of any NetWare LAN. They provide a purpose to the file system and give users something to do with their time. The system manager must optimize network applications by providing secure configurations and shared data directories.

7. **Establish a user environment**—(Covered in Chapters 6 and 11). Image is everything—well almost. In many cases the life or death of the network hangs in the balance of user interface. The LAN is only useful if the users are comfortable and productive with it. Involve the users in planning the network environment, but make sure they don't get in the way.

8. **Maintain a system backup**—(Covered in Chapters 6 and 11). All unemployed system managers have one thing in common: they didn't maintain a reliable system backup. System backup is the most important line

of defense against unexpected network faults. Most employed system managers spend 15% of their time maintaining a reliable network backup system.

9. **The NetWare log book**—(Covered in Chapter 11). Most system managers ignore this network documentation—and regret the decision later. A complete log of network details can save hours of guesswork during network maintenance and troubleshooting. The NetWare Log is at the heart of network documentation.

10. **Staying up to date of changing technology**—(Covered in other Network Press publications). The final system manager responsibility never ends. In addition to the previous nine responsibilities, the NetWare system manager must stay on top of changing technology. He/she must periodically reevaluate the LAN in light of new advancements. The network is dynamic; it must evolve or else it will die. As new technologies arise, the system manager must be willing to incorporate them into the existing LAN. Other Network Press publications provide an excellent library of alternative LAN technologies.

The system manager's diary is the NetWare Log. The log details valuable information about the LAN's hardware, software, and various configurations. Refer to Appendices B and C for a series of NetWare 2.2 and NetWare 3.12 worksheets, which should be included in your diary. The NetWare Log consists of:

**Identification**—company name, system manager, and date

**Version of NetWare**—serial number and number of users

**File Server Information**—physical location and hardware

**Volume Information**—locations, types, and size

**Workstation Information**—users, node address, and hardware

**Network Applications**—location and configurations

**Technical Support**—names, phone numbers, hardware, and software

**System Fault Tolerance**—UPS, mirroring, and TTS

**Recent Activity**—a daily log of LAN configuration changes.

Addiction to network documentation can be a good thing and entering information into the NetWare Log should become a habit. In addition to the NetWare Log there are many other resources that aid the NetWare system manager in accomplishing his/her responsibilities: product documentation, NetWire, NetWare Express, NetWare Buyer's Guide, Network Support Encyclopedia, on-line help, and Network Press publications. Let's take a moment to explore each of these system manager resources. Get your utility belt ready.

## System Manager Resources

The responsibilities of a NetWare system manager can be overwhelming at times. Fortunately, you have the comprehensive training of Novell's CNA program to guide you. This book and the Novell courses will prepare you for 95% of the pitfalls of system management. Unfortunately, it's the other 5% that always seem to jump up and bite you. The good news is that you don't have to do it alone. Novell provides a variety of tools that augment your impressive NetWare utility belt. Following is a brief discussion of the seven most popular Novell resources:

### Product Documentation

The NetWare 2.2 and 3.12 product documentation has been dramatically improved over the years. It contains a variety of resumes, including:

*Concepts* includes an alphabetical listing of NetWare terms. It also includes examples of critical NetWare topics, such as directory structure, login scripts, and security.

*Installing and Maintaining the Network* offers an introduction to NetWare installation and network management methodologies. It is a cookbook of system management tasks, including advanced installation, preventive maintenance, upgrade, and troubleshooting.

*Print Server* guides the system manager through the steps of designing, installing, configuring, and maintaining NetWare print services.

These are only a few of the many books available in NetWare's product documentation. There are twenty books in the NetWare 3.12 set! Keep in

*This book and the Novell courses will prepare you for 95% of the pitfalls of system management. Unfortunately, it's the other 5% that always seem to jump up and bite you.*

mind though, that while NetWare 2.2 includes all hard-copy books, NetWare 3.12 offers them only on-line.

*The books that help you the most are those which make you think the most.*

*Theodore Parker*

## NetWire

NetWire is Novell's on-line information service. It provides access to Novell product information, press releases, network services, technical support, a calendar of events, forums, and downloadable files—patches, upgrades, and shareware utilities. NetWire is available twenty-four hours a day through the CompuServe Information Service (CIS). It is structured into eighteen forums and multiple software libraries, including electronic round tables for CNEs, version-specific details, an end-user area, and thousands of downloadable files. NetWire currently services over 100,000 network end-users and professionals.

NetWire is an invaluable resource for CNEs. It requires a personal computer, a modem, communications software, and an account with CompuServe Information Service (CIS). CIS offers local access numbers with an on-line connect charge of $5—$12/hr., depending on speed. Contact CompuServe at (800) 848-8199 in the U.S. and Canada, or at (614) 457-0802 internationally.

## World Wire

World Wire is a NEW global on-line information service that provides technical support and on-line LAN experience specifically for networking professionals. It extends beyond NetWire in providing a variety of on-line NetWare LANs, "real-time" technical support, classes, technical databases, and Internet access. World Wire is a personal, virtual city with many different "Rooms," a "Library" of files, and "Doorways" to network-related services, including a shopping mall, on-line books, articles, NetWare LANs, and on-line testing.

World Wire uses the information superhighway to provide local access from anywhere in the world, twenty-four hours a day. It is an invaluable resource for CNEs and requires a PC, modem, and any communications software. World Wire connect time charges are very low, ranging from $2 to $4/hr. Contact World Wire at (510) 254-7283 or ride the superhighway to (510) 254-1193.

*Navigation through the on-line forest can be a losing proposition—the interface is very cryptic. Fortunately, there are two semi-free aids that automate much of the navigation lexicon: CIM and WIRERIP. CompuServe Information Manager (CIM) is a text-based or Windows-based (WinCIM) interface that provides menu choices for many of the cryptic CompuServe commands (it costs money). WIRERIP is a faster, graphical interface that personalizes navigation through the World Wire city (it's free). Either of these tools can triple your on-line productivity.*

### NetWare Buyer's Guide

The NetWare Buyer's Guide provides a comprehensive catalog of Novell's concepts, strategies, and products. It includes solutions for NetWare LANs, desktop computing systems, implementing wide area networks (WANs), connectivity to larger machines, and multiple workstation environments. The NetWare Buyer's Guide is a complete product catalog with four sections: Novell Corporate & Strategic Overview, Novell Product Overview, Novell Products, and Novell Support & Education. System managers can receive the guide for free by calling (800) LANKIND. The guide ships twice a year (April and October) and is currently available in paper or electronic form.

### Network Support Encyclopedia

The Network Support Encyclopedia (NSE) is an electronic information database available on CD-ROM. It contains a comprehensive list of technical support questions, bulletins, patches, application notes, and on-line documentation. NSE is available in two different volumes: the Standard Volume and Professional Volume. The Standard NSE includes Technotes, Novell Labs bulletins, product documentation, a library listing of all NetWire files, and additional product information including press releases and the NetWare Buyer's Guide. The Professional NSE contains all the information from the standard volume plus all NetWire files, troubleshooting decision trees, NetWare application notes, and additional product manuals. Both NSE volumes are available on CD-ROM and are updated four to twelve times per year. Incidentally, one of the benefits of becoming a Certified NetWare Engineer is a free introductory copy of the Professional Network Support Encyclopedia.

### On-Line Help

NetWare has an extensive HELP facility built into its products. The NetWare 2.2 help program is a hypertext infobase from a company called *Folio*. The Folio Infobase provides on-line access to NetWare utility syntax, system messages, and NetWare concepts. The NetWare 3.12 help program is a Windows-based hypertext bookshelf called *DynaText*. DynaText provides on-line access to all twenty books of product documentation. It is a dramatic improvement over Folio.

*NetWare's on-line HELP facility has dramatically improved. The latest version, called DynaText, was recently introduced with NetWare 3.12 and 4.0. DynaText is fully Windows-based, indexed, context sensitive, and fuzzy logical. The most dramatic improvement is in the search engine. It supports multiple fuzzy searches with a huge variety of criteria. The cost for this technical evolution is hard disk space. The NetWare 2.2 infobase occupies roughly 1MB of server disk space, while DynaText hogs almost 30MB of space—four times the size of the entire 2.2 product!*

### Sybex and Network Press Publications

To help you stay in touch with rapidly changing technologies in networks and other areas, Sybex has developed a library of valuable publications. At the heart of the Sybex networking library is Network Press, books on networking written and technically reviewed by experts in networking. Network Press publishes an incredibly diverse collection of networking books, ranging from *The Network Press Encyclopedia of Networking* to *The CNE Study Guide*. A few more titles designed for the NetWare system manager include *Managing an Inherited NetWare Network, Networking the Small Office,* and *The Network Press Dictionary of Networking*. To order Network Press books, call Sybex Inc. at (800) 227-2346.

*Some books are to be tasted; others swallowed; and some few to be chewed and digested.*

*Francis Bacon*

This completes our discussion of system management responsibilities and resources. Can you feel the weight of your NetWare utility belt?

To begin the transition from conceptual job responsibilities to meat and potatoes, we will spend the next few pages exploring NetWare's hardware and software basics. Then, we will dig in with Chapter 3—NetWare Directory Structure.

# Hardware Basics

THE TERM *NETWORK* HAS a variety of different meanings:

- An openwork structure of twine with periodic intersections

- An exceedingly average collection of television broadcast stations

- A system of electronic components that share a common function.

None of these definitions, however, captures the essence of NetWare. The type of network we are concerned with is:

- *A collection of distributed, intelligent machines that share data and information through interconnected lines of communication.*

Our network is a combination of hardware and software components. The hardware components control processing and communications. They include file servers, workstations, cabling components, and printing. On the other hand, the software components control productivity and intelligence. They include network operating systems, workstation shells, and network applications. In order for your NetWare LAN to operate at peak efficiency, you must balance hardware and software components with user needs and LAN

*In order for your NetWare LAN to operate at peak efficiency, you must balance hardware and software components with user needs and LAN synergy.*

synergy. In the remainder of this chapter, we will explore our definition of the network by introducing the basic concepts of LAN hardware, software, and synergy.

*Synergy is defined as: The whole is greater than the sum of its parts. When applied to NetWare LANs, synergy defines an environment in which user interface, distributed processing, and topology components work together in harmony. To achieve NetWare synergy, the system manager must spend equal time with hardware, software, and user components. LAN synergy is highly recommended for NetWare system managers who value their peace of mind.*

## Network Types

Just as a television network absorbs the minds of our young, a computer network gathers data and information. Small networks include two to five machines and one central file server. They are typically designed to share word processing documents or printers. Medium-sized systems share hundreds of machines with multiple file servers over a variety of different platforms—PCs, Macintoshes, and minicomputers. These networks are designed for large businesses with a variety of different computing needs. They share databases, electronic mail, and custom applications. Large internetworks are common in university settings, government institutions, or large corporations. These expansive internetworks include thousands of machines over large geographic areas. They incorporate a variety of different machines speaking a diverse collection of electronic languages.

*We are all fellow passengers on a dot of earth. And each of us, in the span of time, has really only a moment among our companions.*

*Lyndon Baines Johnson*

The three network scenarios discussed next provide only a snapshot of the amazing network community. Today's networks are so incredibly versatile that they touch every aspect of our lives—shopping, banking, working, and entertainment. The assumption is that networks improve our general quality of life, but the jury is still out on that one. Regardless of their philosophical value, networks make our lives easier and they are definitely here to stay.

Computer networks are categorized according to size. Here's a brief peek at the three most popular network classifications.

**LAN** (Local Area Network) is a small collection of workstations in a local geographic area. LANs typically serve small to medium-sized offices on a single floor. LANs never extend beyond one mile.

**WAN** (Wide Area Network) is a large collection of LANs—kind of a LAN of LANs. WANs extend the local network over large geographic or technical boundaries. Geographic expansion is achieved through worldwide communication lines and advanced routers. Technical expansion is achieved through the integration of dissimilar machines speaking dissimilar languages.

**MAN** (Metropolitan Area Network) is a restricted WAN confined to a specific metropolitan area. MANs share a common goal—municipal integration. MANs provide electronic communications between a variety of different municipal entities, including banking, industry, broadcast cable, home computers, shopping, utilities, and entertainment. MANs are currently being developed in a small collection of pilot cities.

All of these different network classifications share one common thread— connectivity. Connectivity is the underlying theme of all computer networks. After all, their purpose is to share electronic resources through a collection of *interconnected* lines. Network connectivity is achieved in three different ways: peer-to-peer, client/server, and interconnectivity. The following is a brief description of these three network connectivity fundamentals.

### Peer-to-Peer Networks

The first connectivity option is peer-to-peer networks. These systems are unique in that they share computer resources without the aid of one central file server or network operating system. Peer-to-peer LANs rely on the workstations to control network operations. There is no one point of control or failure. In order to achieve this distributed control, the peer-to-peer network operating system is present on all workstations. The distributed workstations can share hard disks and printers directly with other workstations. Figure 2.1 illustrates a typical peer-to-peer network with multiple workstations and

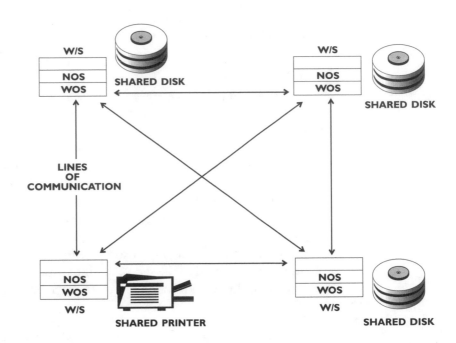

**FIGURE 2.1**
A typical peer-to-peer
network layout

direct lines of communication. The figure shows each workstation with shared resources and two operating systems: the required workstation operating system (WOS) and a peer-to-peer network operating system (NOS). Notice how the lines of communication point from each workstation directly to all the others.

| ADVANTAGES | DISADVANTAGES |
|---|---|
| low cost | slow |
| no central point of failure | difficult to maintain security |
| easy to use | limited number of workstations |

*You'll want to learn the advantages and disadvantages of peer-to-peer and client/server networks.*

Some of the most common peer-to-peer operating systems include NetWare Lite, LANtastic, Windows NT, and Windows for Workgroups. In addition, NetWare 3.12 and 4.0 will soon have some peer-to-peer functionality built into the new workstation shells.

### Client/Server Networks

The second type of network connectivity requires a central file server and dedicated network operating system. The file server houses all shared resources and provides connectivity to the workstation clients. The client/server model relies on the central PC for network control, shared resources, security, and connectivity to other systems—interconnectivity. NetWare uses the client/server model because it provides a dedicated processor for complex network operations. The clients connect to the central NetWare server through a special workstation program called the *shell*. The NetWare shell interfaces between the workstation operating system and NetWare. Figure 2.2 illustrates a typical client/server system with the central file server attending to multiple client workstations. Notice that the lines of communication point from each workstation directly to the central server. Also, the shared disk and printer are attached to the server, not the workstations. In a client/server system, the local workstation resources are not available to other network clients.

| ADVANTAGES | DISADVANTAGES |
|---|---|
| increased speed | expensive hardware |
| enhanced security | expensive NOS |
| expansion | difficult to install |
| excellent management tools | |

**FIGURE 2.2**
A typical client/server network layout

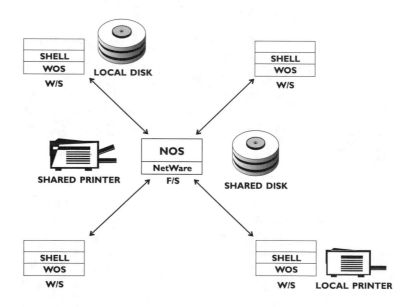

Besides NetWare, there are a few other client server operating systems that provide similar network connectivity: Banyan VINES, Microsoft LAN Manager, and AppleShare, to name a few.

### Interconnectivity

Another approach to network connectivity involves the extension of network resources beyond the local boundaries of a LAN. WANs and MANs require connectivity expansion beyond workstations and servers. This expansion is known as *interconnectivity*. Interconnectivity provides the capability of connecting multiple like or unlike LANs. Interconnectivity is achieved through one of two devices:

**Routers** allow network expandability by interconnecting multiple file servers or LAN topologies. (A topology is a geographic arrangement of network nodes and cabling components.) A NetWare router can connect up to four like or unlike topologies from within the server (internal routing) or in an external workstation (external routing). NetWare allows an external router to run in dedicated real mode, dedicated protected mode, or nondedicated protected mode. Figure 2.3 illustrates internal routing between two unlike LAN topoligies: Ethernet and ARCNet.

**Gateways** provide additional expansion and functionality by allowing connectivity between NetWare LANs and other unlike computer systems,

**FIGURE 2.3**
Internal routing for
Ethernet and ARCNet

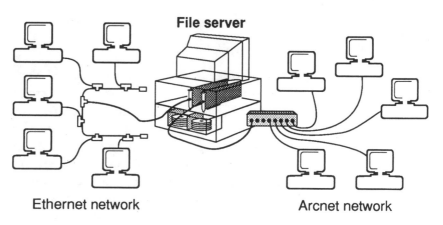

File server

Ethernet network

Arcnet network

**Internal router**

including mainframes, minicomputers, SNA, TCP/IP, or X.25. Another form of gateway allows NetWare LANs to communicate with remote workstations. These systems rely on modems and dedicated PCs as asynchronous communication gateways.

*When a NetWare workstation needs to access the services of a mainframe or minicomputer, the workstation requests a session from the gateway machine. If a session is available, the gateway grants the workstation a direct connection to the host computer and acts as a messenger between the two unlike systems. Novell provides gateway services through a variety of additional NetWare products. Refer to the NetWare Buyer's Guide for a complete list.*

Connectivity is the true purpose of a NetWare LAN. So how is it achieved? Let's take a closer look at the hardware components.

## Network Components

*File servers and workstations are the real workhorses of the LAN. They provide distributed processing, network control, and a platform for network operating systems and applications.*

Earlier we talked about synergy and wholes and parts. So what about these network parts. What are they? How do they work together? Network hardware is organized into four different categories:

- File Servers and Workstations
- Topology Components
- File Server Memory and Disk Storage
- Network Printers

File servers and workstations are the real workhorses of the LAN. They provide distributed processing, network control, and a platform for network operating systems and applications. Topology components provide network connectivity. They are the glue that binds the file servers and workstations together. Topology components include network interface cards (NICs), cabling, and hubs. Other components, namely file server memory and disk storage, increase network performance and provide the capacity for shared applications and data. Finally, network printers provide quality output for network users.

*Paying attention to the hardware differences between file servers and workstations now will help you later.*

Let's take a closer look at the four categories of network hardware:

### File Servers and Workstations

NetWare supports a variety of different workstations, but only one type of server—an Intel-based PC. NetWare 2.2 is designed for the 80286 Intel architecture and it supports 16-bit processing and 16-bit internal bus channels. The server must be at least an 80286 machine, but NetWare 2.2 will support an 80386, 80486, or Pentium processor. The two key bottlenecks for a NetWare server are the NIC channel and disk channel. NetWare 2.2 can slow down in heavy loads because it only supports 16-bit channels. NetWare 3.12, on the other hand, provides much better performance over a 32-bit 80386 architecture.

NetWare is much more accommodating from the workstation viewpoint. It inherently supports ISA, MCA, and Macintosh architectures, as well as DOS, Windows and OS/2 workstation environments. Additional support for Macintosh and Unix is provided through special NetWare products. The greatest asset of NetWare is transparent connectivity. Transparent connectivity applies to NetWare's ability to support diverse workstations while maintaining a consistent interface for all users.

### Topology Components

Topology components provide network connectivity. They create a communications path between distributed workstations and the central NetWare file server. Topology components fall into three categories:

**NICs** (network interface cards) are internal components that communicate with the file server/workstation CPU and the network topology. The topology is the organizational standard for network communications. NetWare supports a variety of different topologies, including Ethernet BUS, Ethernet 10Base-T, ARCNet, Token Ring, and LocalTalk. The NIC card plugs into the file server/workstation expansion slot and connects directly to network cabling. NetWare and the workstation shells must be specially configured to communicate with the internal NIC.

**Cabling** provides the pathway for network communications. The topology standard and NIC determine which cabling type should be used. Table 2.1 provides a simple look at the relationships between topology, NIC, and network cabling. The most popular types of LAN cabling include coaxial, unshielded twisted pair, shielded twisted pair, and fiber optics.

**Hubs** provide a control point for signal routing or packet broadcasts. All hubs perform basically the same function, although they come in many different names—Ethernet 10Base-T calls them concentrators, ARCNet has active and passive hubs, and Token Ring uses MSAUs, or MultiStation Access Units.

*What's in a name? That which we call a rose by any other name would smell as sweet.*

*William Shakespeare*

*The nemesis of network cabling is EMI, or ElectroMagnetic Interference. EMI distorts electronic signals and damages network communications. Some cabling is more susceptible to EMI than others. From worst to best, they are: unshielded twisted pair, shielded twisted pair, coaxial cabling, and fiber optics. The most common sources of EMI include elevator motors, fluorescent lighting, electrical wiring, and large generators.*

**T A B L E  2.1**
The Relationship between Topology, NIC, and Network Cabling

| TOPOLOGY | NIC | NETWORK CABLING |
|----------|-----|-----------------|
| Ethernet BUS | BNC | 0.2 inch Coaxial—50 ohm / Fiber Optics |
|  | DIX | 0.4 inch Coaxial—50 ohm / Fiber Optics |
| Ethernet 10Base-T | RJ-45 | Unshielded Twisted Pair |
| ARCNet | BNC | Coaxial—93 ohm |
|  | RJ-45 | Unshielded Twisted Pair |
| Token Ring | AUI | Shielded Twisted Pair / Fiber Optics |
| Local Talk | RJ-11 | Unshielded Twisted Pair |

### File Server Memory and Disk Storage

*The server disk houses NetWare, network applications, and shared data. It is the permanent filing cabinet for network productivity.*

NetWare LANs are heavily dependent on file server RAM (Random Access Memory). The server RAM is used to process network requests, speed up shared data requests, and buffer incoming messages. Disk storage is important for many different reasons. Although it doesn't help process requests or increase LAN performance, server disk storage is the single most important asset on the LAN. The server disk houses NetWare, network applications, and shared data. It is the permanent filing cabinet for network productivity.

NetWare RAM and disk storage work hand in hand. As requests are made for shared data, NetWare accesses the disk and moves the data into server RAM (this process occurs relatively slowly). When subsequent requests are made for the same data, NetWare can process the request from RAM (a much faster proposition). This phenomenon is known as *file caching* and it increases network performance while decreasing disk wear. File caching is described later in the chapter. Refer to Table 2.2 for a summary of NetWare features and storage capacities.

*The difference between file server RAM and disk storage is clarified by asking two simple questions: "What is your home phone number?" and "What is the Kremlin's phone number?" The first number should appear in your mind almost instantly (since you accessed it from RAM), while the second number might require a little more time and research (since you had to refer to permanent storage—a Russian phone book. If I asked the same two questions five minutes from now, file caching would be invoked.)*

### Network Printers

The second most popular NetWare resource is shared printing. And since all productive network data must eventually be represented in printed form, network printers ultimately become very important. NetWare supports the following printing configurations:

**Core Printing** refers to network printers attached directly to the file server. Core printing is established during the NetWare installation process and it provides the capacity for up to five network printers.

**Print Servers** build on core printing by expanding the number of supported printers to sixteen. A NetWare print server can be installed on the file

| MAJOR NETWARE FEATURES | NETWARE 2.2 | NETWARE 3.12 |
| --- | --- | --- |
| DOS/Windows support | Yes | Yes |
| OS/2 support | Yes | Yes |
| Macintosh support | Yes | Yes |
| NFS Unix support | No | Additional |
| AppleTalk support | Yes | Yes |
| File Server Bus | ISA, MCA | ISA, MCA, EISA |
| User Configurations | 5, 10, 50, 100 | 5, 10, 25, 50, 100, 250 |
| Maximum Disk Storage | 2 GB | 32 TB |
| Maximum Volume Size | 255 MB | 32 TB |
| Minimum RAM | 2.5 MB | 4 MB |
| Maximum RAM | 12 MB | 4 GB |
| Maximum Number of Open Files | 10,000 | 100,000 |

server or on a dedicated workstation (as PSERVER.EXE). Any print server can support users from a maximum of eight different file servers.

**Remote Printing** was invented because print servers can support up to sixteen printers throughout the LAN, but only five on one machine. Remote printing allows you to grant network access to local printers attached to distributed workstations. The workstation runs a small TSR (Terminate-and-Stay Resident) program called RPRINTER.EXE and all network users can instantly access that workstation's printer.

We will explore network printing in much more depth in Chapter 9—Printing.

# Software Basics

OUR DISCUSSION OF HARDWARE basics focused on the network components that control processing and LAN communications. We discussed network classifications and the hardware parts that contribute to LAN synergy. Now we will delve into the network components that control productivity and LAN intelligence. Software basics involve distributed processing, file server software, and workstation shells. In this section, we will explore what makes NetWare so great and try to understand its processes, specifications, and support for diverse workstation environments. In addition, we will describe the many built-in system fault tolerance features that provide stability and peace-of-mind to LANs running critical network applications. Let's start at the beginning.

## Distributed Processing

*The primary difference between a network and any other computer system is where the processing occurs. In mainframe or minicomputer systems, the central machine does all of the work. In a NetWare LAN, the clients do all the work!*

The primary difference between a network and any other computer system is where the processing occurs. In mainframe or minicomputer systems, the central machine does all of the work. The "slave"-like clients simply sit there and act dumb. Hence the name *dumb terminal*. A network is different for one very important reason—the *clients* do all of the work. In a NetWare LAN, all of the data is stored on the central file server. When a user wants to access the data, he/she attaches to the file server and downloads a copy of the data to local workstation RAM. The workstation runs the application and manipulates the network data—completely in workstation RAM. This process is known as *distributed processing*. Once the user is finished with the data, he/she uploads a copy of the new data to the file server, where it is stored for future use.

The exciting part about distributed processing is that each user has access to an entire computer system. In a centralized system, the client terminals utilize only a fraction of the central processor. Also, the overall processing power of distributed systems increase as workstations are attached. The benefits of distributed processing also include enhanced security, concurrent data sharing, and system fault tolerance.

*A harmful myth has permeated the network community—probably started by a mainframe person. It goes like this: every great network needs a really powerful file server—workstations don't matter. Even worse, people believe that all the available bells and whistles should go onto the file server, not the workstations. I have seen many installations with $10,000 file servers and $500 workstations. This thinking is absolutely wrong. The concept of distributed processing states that 95% of the LAN's work is performed by the workstations. File servers are important, but workstations are the key to NetWare nirvana.*

# File Server Software

*The file server software is at the heart of the LAN. It provides network control, security, file management, and transparent connectivity.*

The file server software is at the heart of the LAN. It provides network control, security, file management, and transparent connectivity. Novell is the leading manufacturer of file server software—nine generations of NetWare. The purpose of file server software is resource management. The network operating system must be capable of managing internal RAM, network applications, user requests, printing, and network directory structures. This is not a simple proposition. In order to achieve this level of sophistication, NetWare has evolved tremendously over the past ten years. Its ninth generation, NetWare 4.1, is over 70MB in size and offers a completely new perspective to networking—logical directory services.

In this book, we are focusing on NetWare 2.2 and 3.12. The following few pages provide some insight into NetWare's features, benefits, and specifications. Follow this section carefully because it offers some very valuable ammunition for your NetWare utility belt.

## NetWare Specifications

As with any other software package, NetWare has some built-in limitations. Although these limitations are logical in nature, they are controlled by the file server hardware architecture. The fundamental difference between NetWare 2.2 and 3.12 specifications is in the 80286 vs. 80386 hardware. The 80286 processor uses a 16-bit architecture, whereas the 80386 system includes a 32-bit processor and expansion bus. The 32-bit design provides a great deal more flexibility and exponential improvements in RAM and disk capacity.

Table 2.2 summarizes NetWare's major features and provides a comparison of the NetWare specifications for NetWare 2.2 and 3.12. For a complete list of NetWare specifications, refer to the most current NetWare Buyer's Guide.

The two most compelling improvements in NetWare 3.12 are *Maximum Volume Size* and *Maximum RAM*. With today's advanced machines and gigabyte capacities, NetWare 2.2's limitations are pretty severe. Again, this limitation is due in part to the restrictive 16-bit file server architecture.

*Learn the NetWare specifications for versions 2.2 and 3.12 as shown in Table 2.2.*

### NetWare Performance Features

NetWare utilizes myriad advanced performance algorithms that improve network processing up to 10,000%! These features are built into the NetWare operating system core and are automatically implemented each time the file server boots. The following NetWare performance features are included with NetWare 2.2, 3.12, and 4.0:

- Directory Caching
- Directory Hashing
- File Caching
- Elevator Seeking

*They will ask you about NetWare performance and SFT features. Focus on learning about file caching, hot fix, mirroring/duplexing, and UPS monitoring.*

Let's take a closer look.

**DIRECTORY CACHING**  NetWare uses two different directory tables to keep track of network data: directory entry table (DET) and file allocation table (FAT). The DET stores basic information about NetWare file names, directories, file locations, and file/directory properties. The DET's file location parameter points to entries in the corresponding FAT. The FAT lists all files on the NetWare volume and the specific disk blocks they occupy. Whenever a user requests access to a NetWare file, the system must refer to the DET and FAT tables for basic file information. Directory caching speeds up this process by storing the DET and FAT tables in file server RAM. Each reference to the DET or FAT is performed one hundred times faster from within memory, thus allowing the file server to locate the tables much more quickly and efficiently than if it had to read the information from disk.

**DIRECTORY HASHING**  Directory hashing further enhances DET access by indexing the table. This feature allows NetWare to find the correct directory entry much more quickly, and reduces the response time of disk I/O by 30 percent.

**FILE CACHING**  File caching has the largest impact on file server performance. As we learned earlier, data access from file server RAM is one hundred times faster than data access from disk. Imagine how fast the system would be if all network data was stored in file server RAM. Unfortunately, this isn't feasible. But NetWare's file caching feature does provide users with the next best thing: all the most-recently-used files are stored in file server RAM.

Here's how it works: when a file is first requested, it is brought from the disk across the network topology to workstation RAM. At the same time, the system copies a duplicate of the file into file server RAM. All subsequent requests for the file are serviced from file server RAM. Once file server RAM fills up, NetWare replaces cached files in least-used order. The system will automatically use all available RAM for file caching. This performance feature also reduces disk wear and tear.

**ELEVATOR SEEKING**  Elevator seeking is an interesting animal. It is a disk management process that borrows ideas from elevator traffic movements. Elevator seeking prioritizes file requests according to their location on the server disk. It reshuffles the order of user requests and creates the most efficient path for the disk's read/write heads. Figure 2.4 illustrates elevator seeking for four NetWare files: 1, 2, 3, and 4. Notice how the retrieval order has been reshuffled to minimize disk wear. Elevator seeking is a mind-boggling operation.

### NetWare System Fault Tolerance

NetWare has seven built-in features that protect network data from harmful system faults. These features are grouped into a data integrity benefit called System Fault Tolerance (SFT). SFT is the measure of a system's tolerance to faults.

**F I G U R E   2.4**
Prioritizing disk requests
with elevator seeking

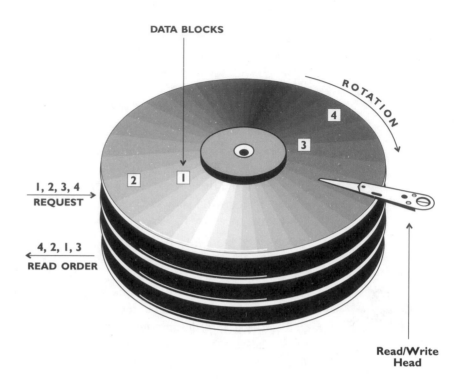

In this case, the name says it all. A high level of system fault tolerance provides data protection against a variety of possible system faults, including power outages or disk crashes. A low level of SFT means that your LAN is susceptible to many different network faults: power spikes, brownouts, data corruption, and so on. The seven features that make up NetWare SFT are included in all current versions of NetWare—NetWare 2.2, 3.12, and 4.0. Let's take a peek.

*In the past, Novell organized the seven NetWare SFT features into two categories: SFT I (Read-After-Write verification, duplicate DETs and FATs, Hot Fix) and SFT II (Disk Mirroring, Disk Duplexing, TTS, UPS Monitoring). Today, these features are all bundled into one SFT benefit. In addition, Novell has introduced another reliability feature known as SFT III. SFT III is full server duplexing and it is only available in NetWare 3.12 and 4.0.*

**READ-AFTER-WRITE VERIFICATION**   This feature assures that data written to the network disk matches the original data in file server RAM. Each time the server writes a file to the internal disk, it verifies the integrity of the data by reading it back and comparing it to the original file in memory. If the disk file matches the memory file, the server releases the data from memory and continues with the next disk operation. If the disk file doesn't match the memory file, the server retries. After a number of retries, the server gives up and marks the disk area unusable. At this point, NetWare reverts to another system fault tolerance feature called *Hot Fix*.

**HOT FIX**   Hot fix takes over when the read-after-write verification process discovers a bad disk block. Hot fix marks the bad block as unusable and redirects the data to a reserved portion of the disk called the *hot fix redirection area*. Figure 2.5 shows a typical bad block being remapped to the hot fix redirection area. Hot fix is sometimes called dynamic bad block remapping because it works on the fly. The hot fix redirection area occupies 2% of the server disk by default.

*When network data is written to the hot fix redirection area it is never returned to the main portion of the disk. As a result, the hot fix redirection area quickly fills up, thus providing a red flag to the network manager. As a general rule, the hot fix redirection area should never reach 70% occupancy. If this occurs, it is a sure sign that the server disk is near failure.*

**FIGURE 2.5**

A bad block being remapped to the hot fix redirection area

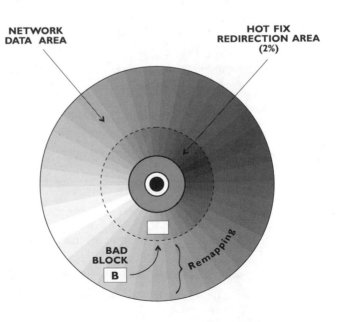

**DUPLICATE DETS AND FATS**  As we discussed earlier, DETs and FATs contain basic information for network directories and files. NetWare automatically duplicates the DETs and FATs on alternate portions of the server disk. This increases system fault tolerance by reducing the possibility of DET/FAT corruption or failure.

**DISK MIRRORING**  Disk mirroring and disk duplexing are two SFT strategies for disk crash protection. Disk mirroring duplicates the entire contents of the server disk on a second "mirrored" disk. If the first disk fails, the second disk automatically takes over. No questions asked. Disk mirroring is accomplished by attaching both drives to the same disk controller. This strategy is cheaper, but it creates a single point of SFT vulnerability—the controller.

**DISK DUPLEXING**  Disk duplexing provides an additional level of data SFT by duplicating the controller as well as the disk. In addition, duplexing mirrors the external disk power supply and the controller cable. All disk components are duplicated. This level of SFT is very expensive, but it offers the greatest protection against disk crashes and network data loss. Refer to Figure 2.6 for an illustration of disk mirroring versus disk duplexing.

*Disk duplexing also offers a performance feature that isn't possible with disk mirroring. Since disk duplexing mirrors the entire disk channel—disk, disk controller, cable, and so on—it can read and write data to both disks at the same time. While this feature doesn't help with disk writes (it has to write to both disks anyway), it dramatically improves the response time of disk reads. This performance feature is known as split seeking.*

**TRANSACTION TRACKING SYSTEM**  NetWare's transaction tracking system (TTS) provides data protection for selected network database applications. TTS tracks database transactions from beginning to end. If a system fault interrupts a transaction before it is completed, TTS will abort the transaction's updates and rollback the database to the last point of consistency. TTS protects large database files from data corruption, data loss, or transaction mismatch. In order to activate NetWare TTS, the system manager must specify it at installation and flag the network database as a TTS file. The database application must also be TTS-compatible. Ask your dealer or check with Net-Wire, NSE, or the most current NetWare Buyer's Guide.

**UPS MONITORING**  This feature protects NetWare file servers from sudden, unexpected power failures. An Uninterruptible Power Supply (UPS) is a stable energy source that provides power to network machines in the event of

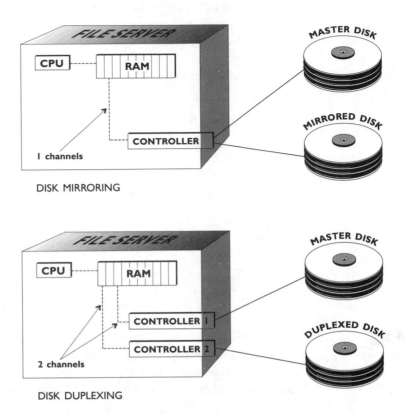

electrical brownouts or blackouts. Basically, it is a large, intelligent battery. If you don't have a server UPS, power failures can cause irreparable damage to network hard disks, data, and topology components. UPS monitoring is a combination of hardware and software that *downs* the server gracefully in the event of an electrical brownout or blackout. (It first sends a message to NetWare users encouraging them to logout, and downs the file server fifteen minutes later.) UPS monitoring is available for NetWare 2.2, 3.12, and 4.0.

This completes our discussion of file server software. But you ain't seen nothin' yet. If you think NetWare is amazing, wait until you see what the workstations can do.

# Workstation Software

If file server software is the heart of the LAN, workstation software is the brains. In a distributed processing environment, 95% of the work occurs at the network workstation. The real brains behind NetWare is in the workstation operating system (WOS). Without the WOS, NetWare would be useless. In addition, the workstation environment provides transparent connectivity to network users and a point of entrance to shared LAN resources. Novell understands these concepts very well. In fact, they have spent a great deal of time optimizing NetWare's workstation interface. NetWare's built-in interoperability allows many different users from a variety of different workstations to share the same network data. This level of interoperability is not achieved easily. It relies on a complex structure of workstation shells and network protocol stacks. After all, NetWare was originally written for DOS!

In our discussion of workstation software, we will focus on NetWare's support for DOS—namely IPX and NETx. We will, however, take a brief look at multi-protocol support (ODI) and the NEW NetWare DOS Requester (VLM). We will discuss workstation software in more depth in Chapter 11.

## IPX

IPX stands for internetwork packet exchange. It is the NetWare protocol that handles communications between NICs and workstation shells. The workstation shells handle communications between IPX and the WOS. At the server, IPX is built into NetWare. At the workstation, IPX runs from workstation memory as the file IPX.COM. IPX.COM is the union of IPX.OBJ and a NIC-specific LAN driver. IPX.COM is created with the WSGEN utility.

## NETx

When IPX receives a network message that is destined for the WOS, NETx handles the transfer. NETx is called a *shell* because it screens all workstation requests and decides whether they belong to the WOS or to IPX. It protects the WOS from the LAN just as a clam shell protects the clam. The NETx shell exists in workstation RAM as one of three different files:

- NETx.COM—the standard shell resides in conventional workstation RAM—the first 640K. NETx.COM requires about 47K or workstation RAM.

*The best way to save conventional memory is to load high NETx.COM. This feature is available in DOS 5.0 and above.*

- EMSNETx.EXE—the expanded shell resides in expanded workstation RAM—the reserved memory between 640K and 1MB. EMSNETx.COM requires the LIM 4.0 expanded memory manager and works with all versions of NetWare. It frees 34K of conventional RAM by loading primarily in expanded memory. Note: expanded memory is generally slower than conventional RAM.

- XMSNETx.EXE—the extended shell resides in extended workstation RAM—memory above the 1MB barrier. XMSNETx.COM requires the LIM 4.0 extended memory manager and also works with all versions of NetWare. It frees 34K of conventional RAM. Note: XMSNETx.COM must load in the High Memory Area (HMA)—or first 64K of extended memory. Unfortunately, this is the same area in which DOS 5.0 loads high. Therefore, the extended memory shell is not compatible with DOS 5.0 or greater if DOS is loaded high.

*NETx uses the "x" because it recently became WOS version-independent. In earlier times, NETx was NET2, NET3, NET4, or NET5. Each of the NET# shells corresponded to a specific version of DOS. Today, NETx will work with any version of DOS from v2.1 to v6.0.*

## ODI

Open Data-link Interface (ODI) is not a shell. It is a protocol interface that replaces IPX if multiple protocols are required. ODI speaks many languages and translates any ODI-compatible protocol into something the NetWare workstation can understand. It also provides support for multiple protocols within the same workstation NIC. For example, ODI allows NetWare workstations to communicate with NetWare servers using IPX and Unix servers using TCP/IP—all through the same NIC. ODI is quickly becoming the workstation wave of the future.

### NetWare DOS Requester

The NetWare DOS Requester is another new workstation technology that works in conjunction with ODI drivers to define NetWare 3.12's new workstation environment. The Requester is a set of Virtual Loadable Modules (VLMs) that provide communications between DOS and IPXODI. These VLMs are loaded automatically using the VLM Manager (VLM.EXE) and they replace the earlier NETx.COM files. The modular VLMs can be loaded and unloaded at will, thereby reducing workstation overhead while providing a development platform for third-party programmers.

*Learn as much as you can about ODI and the NetWare DOS Requester for the CNA 3.12 exam. Refer to Chapter 11.*

### Support for Non-DOS Workstations

As I mentioned earlier, NetWare supports a variety of different workstation environments. NetWare supports four additional WOSs beyond DOS—Windows, OS/2, Macintosh, and Unix. Windows support is built in but OS/2 workstations require special client drivers—the OS/2 Requester. Macintosh and Unix workstations, on the other hand, have built-in network drivers. They don't require any special client software. Support for Macintosh and Unix workstations is provided by special server software—namely, NetWare for Macintosh and NetWare for NFS, respectively.

*It takes all sorts to make a world.*

*English Proverb*

Well that does it for NetWare basics. We have discussed system manager responsibilities, available resources, and the basics of network hardware and software. In addition, we have explored the purpose of the system manager's utility belt and provided some great tools to get it started. The rest of this book is all about how to build your repertoire of NetWare knowledge so that you can be the best CNA in the world. So sit up straight and pay attention. This is going to be fun.

# Exercise 2.1: Understanding NetWare Basics

_____  **1.** A CNE responsibility     **A.** Dynamic bad block remapping

_____  **2.** Concepts     **B.** Includes tech notes and on-line documentation

_____  **3.** Interconnectivity     **C.** 32-bit operating system

_____  **4.** NetWare 3.1*x*     **D.** 32 terabytes

_____  **5.** NetWare 3.1*x* disk maximum     **E.** Decreases disk thrashing

_____  **6.** Hot fix     **F.** Two disks, one controller

_____  **7.** NSEPro     **G.** Maintain a system backup

_____  **8.** Elevator seeking     **H.** Server duplexing

_____  **9.** Disk mirroring     **I.** Uses 50 ohm coaxial

_____  **10.** NetWare 2.2     **J.** 16-bit operating system

_____  **11.** NetWare 2.2 RAM maximum     **K.** Routers and gateways

_____  **12.** Network     **L.** A collection of distributed intelligent machines

_____  **13.** WAN     **M.** Alphabetic listing of terms

_____  **14.** Coaxial     **N.** A type of LAN cabling

_____  **15.** Ethernet     **O.** A LAN of LANs

_____  **16.** File caching     **P.** 12 megabytes

_____  **17.** SFT III     **Q.** Increases disk I/O by 10,000%

See Appendix C for answers.

# Exercise 2.2: Using NetWare 3.12 DynaText

NetWare 3.12 is equipped with a powerful new Windows-based documentation tool called DynaText. DynaText is an on-line, electronic version of NetWare 3.12 documentation—all 20 books! Let's take a closer look.

**1.** Begin Microsoft Windows.

**2.** Enter DynaText by choosing File ➤ Run from Program Manager and executing ET.EXE from the SYS:PUBLIC (network) or E:\PUBLIC (CD-ROM) subdirectory.

**3.** This is the main library screen. Enter the NetWare 3.12 Manuals bookshelf.

**4.** Open the Concepts manual and find NETWIRE using the outline. Click on the "+" preceding NNN. Find "NetWire" and click on it. Find "UPS Monitoring" and "MIRRORING."

**5.** Search for information concerning the supervisor. How many times does this topic appear in the Concepts manual? How many times does it appear in the entire NetWare 3.12 library? (Hint: to search the entire library, close the Concepts manual and begin the search from the main screen.)

**6.** Experiment with the appearance of the outline screen. Open the Overview manual. Choose File ➤ Preferences. Notice the choices for positioning the outline screen. Highlight Top and Choose OK.

**7.** Explore the new features of NetWare 3.12 Review Novell DynaText. What subtopics appear under Novell DynaText? Which NetWare 3.12 manual is not available on-line?

**8.** DynaText includes hypertext references within and between books. Notice the green-colored topic, "Installing and Using Novell DynaText." This refers to a topic in Appendix B of another book—Installation and Upgrade. Jump to the hypertext reference by clicking on the green-colored sentence.

**9.** Exit the Installation and Upgrade manual. Let's explore the Printing features of DynaText. Open the System Administration book. Find the reference to Printing in the Using Novell DynaText section. Review the Procedure for printing from within DynaText. What happens when you double-click on the green camera icon?

**10.** Follow the printing procedures. First, select File ➤ Print from the title bar. Choose `Sections you choose from outline below.` Which book appears in the outline?

**11.** Let's print something. Click on the "+" preceding How to Use this Manual. Select User Comments and choose OK.

Send a note to Novell Technical Publications telling them what you think of DynaText.

Finish the exercise by exploring many of the other features of Novell DynaText. As you can see, this is a superior way of accessing critical NetWare documentation information. It's not the most natural way to read a book, but on-line documentation makes searching for details a lot easier.

*You can install Novell DynaText on the network or a local hard disk. In addition, users can access the DynaText database directly from the NetWare 3.12 system CD-ROM. For more information on installing DynaText, refer to DynaText itself.*

# Part I—Fundamentals

### ACROSS

**2.** 16-bit NetWare for workgroups

**3.** Hot fix, mirroring, etc.

**7.** Protect against power surges

**9.** The home of the Motorola CPU

**10.** A dedicated line to the CPU

**13.** Increases file access 10,000%

**15.** Initial NetWare access tool

**18.** Dynamic bad block re-mapping

**20.** Intel's new 80586 microchip

**24.** Protect against disk crashes

**25.** Internal microcomputer freeway

**26.** Create a DOS volume name

**27.** Distributed data communications

**29.** Semipermanent PC configurations

### DOWN

**1.** Novell's on-line public service

**3.** Keep the bad guys out

**4.** A binary digit

**5.** The CNA must organize his/her stuff

**6.** The goal!

**8.** The ideal file server disk interface

**11.** Workstations talking to workstations

**12.** Copy DOS files and directories

**14.** The most current NetWare shell

**16.** The chip of choice for NetWare

**17.** NetWare's built-in protocol

**19.** Keeping track of DOS files

**21.** The CNA's secret weapon

**22.** Not hardware, not software

**23.** 32-bit NetWare for large LANs

**27.** A complete technical database

**28.** The new NetWare protocol drivers

See Appendix D for answers.

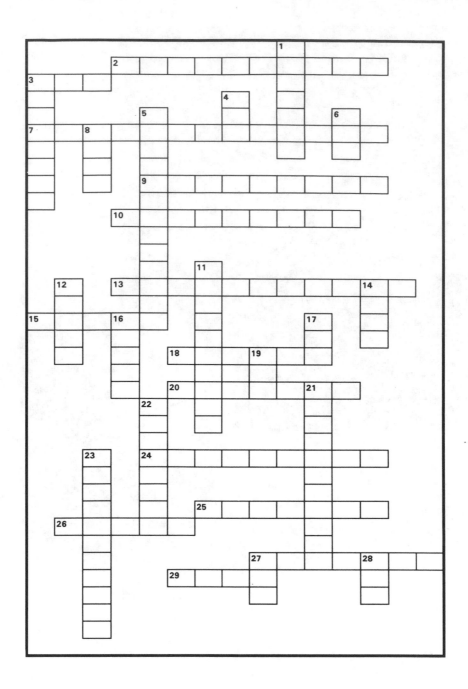

# The NetWare 2.2 CNA Program

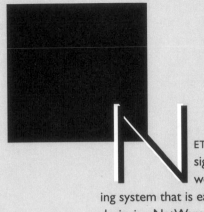

NETWARE 2.2 IS A complete, 16-bit network operating system designed to meet the needs of small businesses, professional offices, workgroups, and departments. It offers a reliable, versatile operating system that is easy to install, use, and administer. The most important goal in designing NetWare 2.2 was to build a single, versatile product that would meet the diverse needs of Novell's ever-changing client base.

NetWare 2.2 is actually more similar to NetWare 3.12 than to 2.15. NetWare 2.2 was designed as an intermediate upgrade path from existing NetWare 2.15 LANs to NetWare 3.12. The features, utilities, security, and printing components of NetWare 2.2 are dramatic improvements over its 80286-based predecessor. On the downside, 2.2 relies on a nonmodular operating system file—NET$OS.EXE—which substantially restricts the system manager's ability to customize NetWare parameters. In addition, NetWare 2.2's 16-bit architecture severely affects its ability to support multiple protocols or alternative non-DOS workstation platforms.

Overall, NetWare 2.2 is a good investment and it gives you a great deal of network functionality for a relatively low price. Enjoy the show!

# NetWare 2.2
# Directory
# Structure

CHAPTER

3

S THE NETWARE SYSTEM manager, you will inherit the LAN in the last of three construction phases—network management. The first two phases are analysis & design and installation. During the analysis & design phase, the systems analyst and network designer evaluate the existing LAN resources and determine the system's needs. They work together to develop a solid LAN design that balances user needs with network performance and cost. Once the LAN design has been completed, the installation team takes over. They purchase the LAN materials and materialize the network design. The result is an empty shell of interconnected workstations and a central NetWare file server. No applications, no users, no life. It is the system manager's responsibility to breathe life into the empty NetWare shell.

Unfortunately, the NetWare system manager is rarely included in the first two phases of building a NetWare LAN. The manager is asked to breathe life into a system he/she had nothing to do with creating. He/she inherits a minimum base system—distributed workstations, connected topology components, a functioning file server, and NetWare. The minimum NetWare setup includes four system-created directories, two users, one group, and a few system/public files. This is where your job begins. It is your responsibility to hitch up the NetWare utility belt and get busy—creating a directory structure, installing applications, developing security, and adding users and groups. The process of NetWare system management begins with the creation of an efficient, secure network directory structure.

*The process of NetWare system management begins with the creation of an efficient, secure network directory structure.*

# Directory Types

I N THE PREVIOUS CHAPTER, we likened network directories to the rooms of an apartment building. These rooms have a variety of functions. Some rooms include apartment facilities—laundry room, garage, game room—while others house apartment staff—the LANlord and his/her family. Most apartment rooms are a home for apartment families, but a few double as business offices—for lawyers, the self-employed, and so on.

NetWare directory types follow this same approach. The facility rooms are system-created directories that serve the supervisor and daily LAN operations. The homes are user directories, while the application/data directories are businesses for NetWare families. NetWare's directory structure is organized and efficient. It provides flexibility and security while maintaining user autonomy. They are based on a vertical tree structure. Figure 3.1 illustrates a typical NetWare directory structure with the volume acting as the trunk (root) of the tree.

**FIGURE 3.1**
A typical NetWare directory structure

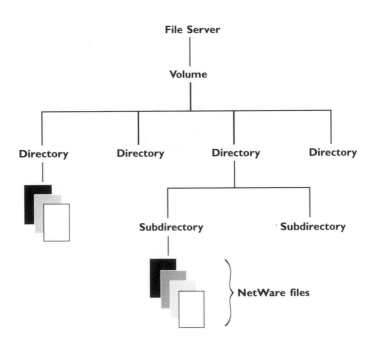

NetWare directories create functional groupings from the volume root. They house NetWare files or functionally similar subdirectories. Figure 3.2 shows this directory structure as a filing cabinet with drawers (volumes), folders (directories/subdirectories), and documents (NetWare files).

Before we begin our discussion of NetWare's four main directory types, we need to explore the rules that govern the creation of our tree. Here's a brief list of NetWare's directory rules:

File Server       Name length is limited to two to forty-five characters
First character cannot be a period
Name cannot contain special characters—* ? \ /

**FIGURE 3.2**
NetWare directories
as a filing cabinet

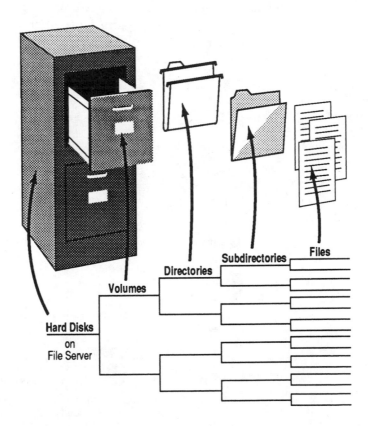

| Volume | Name length is limited to two to fifteen characters |
| --- | --- |
| | Name must end with a colon |
| | First volume on first disk must be SYS: Maximum of thirty-two volumes per server (up to 2GB) |
| | Maximum volume size is 255MB |
| Directory | Name length is limited to eleven characters (8 + 3) |
| | A period separates the first eight and last three characters |
| | Directories should be limited to functional groups |
| Subdirectory | Name length is limited to eleven characters (8 + 3) |
| | A period separates the first eight and last three characters |
| | Subdirectories share common functionality |
| | The number of subdirectories is limited by disk size |

*The rule for NetWare directory structures is KISS:* Keep It Safely Shallow. *A hierarchical tree is easiest to maintain when it is not too tall and not too wide.*

*NetWare's direc-*
*tory structure*
*includes system-*
*created directories,*
*DOS directories,*
*application/data*
*directories, and*
*user directories.*

In our discussion of NetWare's directory structure, we will focus on the four main directory types:

- System-created directories

- DOS directories

- Application/Data directories

- User directories

Let's start with the system-created directories.

## System-Created Directories

During the installation procedure, NetWare creates four system directories:

- LOGIN
- PUBLIC
- SYSTEM
- MAIL

These four directories perform vital NetWare functions and house critical system/public files. Refer to Figure 3.3 for an illustration of NetWare's four system-created directories. All of these directories contain necessary NetWare files and should *not* be deleted. The following is a description of each of NetWare's system-created directories and their functions.

*Learn the system-created directories and what they do. You never know when you might need them....*

**FIGURE 3.3**
NetWare's
system-created
directory structure

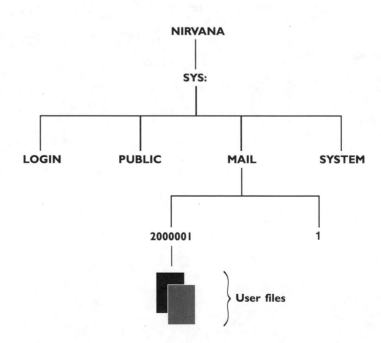

## LOGIN

The LOGIN directory is NetWare's welcome mat. It represents the first point of contact for attached NetWare users. Once a user attaches to the central file server, he/she has access to the LOGIN directory. But before the user can enter the rest of the apartment building (server), he/she must ring the door-bell (login) and provide the secret password. The process of logging-in is performed from the LOGIN directory.

The process of logging into a NetWare server consists of two main steps: workstation initialization and login procedures. Here's how it goes:

Workstation Initialization

1. Boot the workstation with a supported WOS (workstation operating system)—DOS, OS/2, etc.

2. Type IPX ↵ to load the NIC-specific NetWare protocol stack.

3. Type NETX ↵ to load the generic NetWare shell.

Login Procedures

4. Attach to the NetWare welcome mat by typing F: ↵.

5. Type LOGIN ↵.

6. Enter a valid username.

7. Enter the correct password if needed.

The NetWare welcome mat contains two system files: LOGIN.EXE and SLIST.EXE. LOGIN.EXE is the executable file that allows users to log into the NetWare server. SLIST.EXE provides a list of available file servers. Notice that the available disk space in the LOGIN directory is zero. This restriction is lifted once you properly login.

## SYSTEM

The SYSTEM directory is the second most important system-created direc-tory next to LOGIN. SYSTEM houses critical NetWare files including the operating system file (NET$OS.EXE), supervisor utilities, and value added

processes (VAPs). The SYSTEM directory is off limits to everybody except the
Supervisor.

Novell uses a curious naming scheme to designate important system files—
the "$" sign. Every critical system file in NetWare contains a $ in its name.
Here are some examples:

- NET$OS.EXE—the NetWare 2.2 operating system file

- NET$LOG.DAT—the system login script file

- NET$BIND.SYS—one of the NetWare 2.2 bindery files

It's safe to say that Novell recognizes the monetary value of these critical
system files.

## PUBLIC

The PUBLIC directory is every user's playground. It is where the public Net-
Ware programs are stored—commands, menu utilities, and other fun stuff.
The PUBLIC directory is accessible to all network users and it provides a central shared area for frequently used network programs and system-oriented
commands. Third-party utilities, for example, could be stored in the PUBLIC
directory. We will explore these public commands and utilities in Chapter 5—
NetWare 2.2 Utilities.

## MAIL

The MAIL directory is left over from earlier days when NetWare included an
electronic mail facility. Although e-mail is no longer included with NetWare,
the MAIL directory does continue to be useful. MAIL is the parent directory
for a collection of system-created user directories that correspond to each
user's randomly-assigned user ID number. The user ID is a seven- or eight-
digit, hexadecimal number that identifies each user to the NetWare operating
system. For example, the Supervisor is number 1 and Guest is number
2000001. The user ID subdirectory under MAIL is used to store two very important user-specific configuration files: the user login script (LOGIN.) and
printer configuration file (PRINTCON.DAT). The NetWare system manager
will have to delete these user-specific subdirectories when users are deleted.
This procedure is outlined in Chapter 5.

## Suggested Directories

NetWare provides the system manager with a big head start by building the four required system-created directories. The next step is to add some productive user/application directories on top of the existing directory structure. Novell suggests a variety of approaches to creating custom directories: multiple volumes, applications sorted by user, group directories, and shared data directories. No matter how you slice it, Novell's custom approach seems to boil down to four directories. Let's take a closer look.

### The DOS Directory

*User directories provide NetWare users with a home and provide them with a private subdirectory in which to begin a personal directory structure.*

The DOS directory is important because it provides support for the most common WOS—DOS. One of the most critical DOS files is COMMAND.COM—the workstation boot file. COMMAND.COM is loaded into workstation RAM whenever the workstation is turned on. During normal LAN operations, the COMMAND.COM file can be harshly removed from workstation RAM. If this happens, the workstation must be told where to find the file. The server's DOS directory and subsequent subdirectories provide the workstation with a simple path back to COMMAND.COM. In addition, the DOS subdirectories allow network users to access common DOS utilities from a centrally shared directory. For this reason, the DOS directory is typically stored under PUBLIC.

In order to provide optimal workstation support, the DOS directory structure must follow a very strict pattern. Refer to Figure 3.4 for an illustration of the strict design of NetWare's DOS directories. We will explain this pattern in more depth in Chapter 6.

*A man travels the world over in search of what he needs, and returns home to find it.*

*George Moore*

### User Directories

User directories provide NetWare users with a home and provide them with a private subdirectory in which to begin a personal directory structure. User

**FIGURE 3.4**
The suggested NetWare
directory structure

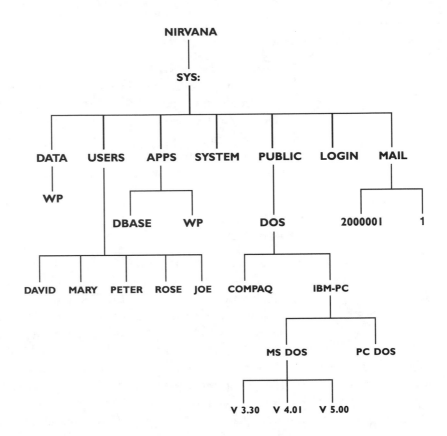

subdirectories serve two functions: security and organization. From a security viewpoint, user subdirectories provide a secure place for private user files or personal correspondence. From an organizational viewpoint, user subdirectories can become the parent directory of a complex user-specific directory structure. User subdirectories should match usernames and be stored under the USERS root directory.

*Home interprets heaven. Home is heaven for beginners.*

*Charles H. Parkhurst*

### Application/Data Directories

Proper organization of application and data directories strongly impacts user productivity. If application directories are scattered, it is difficult for users to find network applications. Furthermore, disorganized data directories can confuse users who are trying to store network files. Application subdirectories should be created for each network application and stored under the APPS root directory, so that application access is easy for network users and security management is more straightforward for the NetWare system manager. Data, on the other hand, can be stored in a variety of directories:

- **Personal data** should be stored in user directories.

- **Application-specific data** should be stored in DATA subdirectories under each network application.

- **Shared network data** should be stored directly in DATA.

Refer to Figure 3.4 for a schematic of how application and data directories should be organized.

## Directory Path Names

All of this crazy organization can seem a bit overwhelming at first. But once you have had an opportunity to work with NetWare directories for a while, you will find them very efficient and useful. The following is an example of the syntax for NetWare directory path names:

```
file server/volume:directory\subdirectory
```

The forward slash separates the file server name and volume, the colon distinguishes the root of the volume, and the backslash separates the directories and subdirectories. Keep in mind that this format is very similar to DOS, except NetWare supports both the forward slash and backslash. Here's an example of a typical NetWare directory path:

```
CNA/SYS:USERS\DAVID
```

Path names are used to define file locations, drive mapping, and utility searches. It is important to use the correct syntax when establishing NetWare directory structures.

*Sticks and stones will break my bones, but names will never hurt me.*

*English Proverb*

# Directory Structure Commands

THROUGHOUT THIS BOOK, we will be adding many new system manager command tools to our NetWare utility belt. NetWare command tools are organized into three categories:

*NetWare command tools are organized into three categories: command-line utilities, menu utilities, and file server console utilities.*

**Command-Line Utilities** (CLUs) are used to manage the LAN environment. CLUs (NetWare has over one hundred of them) reside in the SYS:PUBLIC directory and are executed at the NetWare prompt— Z:\PUBLIC>. We will explore NetWare's CLUs in appropriate sections throughout the book. In this section, we will have our first discussion of NetWare command-line utilities as they apply to directory structures.

**Menu Utilities** provide a consolidated interface for frequently used system management tools. We will explore NetWare 2.2 menu utilities in Chapter 5 and NetWare 3.12 menu utilities in Chapter 10.

**File Server Console Utilities** allow supervisors to manage NetWare file servers. We will discuss NetWare 2.2's console utilities in Chapter 5.

Let's begin our discussion of NetWare command utilities with an exploration of DOS and NetWare directory commands.

*Memorize the switches for each of these commands and utilities.*

## DOS Commands

NetWare works in conjunction with many different workstation operating systems. But it was primarily designed for DOS. Following is a description of some internal DOS commands that also work on NetWare directory structures.

### PROMPT

Sets a new DOS prompt. There are myriad prompt parameters (see Chapter 2 for a brief list). NetWare requires PROMPT $P$G to display current directory path names.

### MD

Creates a NetWare directory or subdirectory. MKDIR also works.

### CD

Changes the default DOS or NetWare directory. This command is particularly dangerous in NetWare if it is combined with search drive mappings. This is discussed later in the chapter. CHDIR also works.

### COPY CON

Captures data from the screen and creates a text file. A very useful command for creating simple NetWare configuration files. Remember to use F6 to exit the program and save your file.

### DIR

Shows a listing of files and subdirectories of a given NetWare or DOS directory. DIR also displays information about directories and files, including creation date, creation time, and size.

### TYPE

Displays the contents of a text file on the screen. The results of the TYPE command can be redirected to a printer or file by using the > sign:

- **PRINTER**—TYPE filename > PRN
- **FILE**—TYPE filename > FILE

### RD

Removes an empty DOS or NetWare subdirectory. RMDIR also works.

## NetWare Commands

NetWare directory structure commands build on the existing DOS commands by providing additional network functionality. NetWare offers network versions of most DOS utilities (but keep in mind that the NetWare utilities are designed to work on LAN drives only). Below is a discussion of the four most popular NetWare directory commands.

### NDIR

The NDIR command is a versatile NetWare utility that allows you to search through NetWare volumes for data, applications, and utilities. NDIR is the NetWare version of DIR. In addition to the basic information—creation date, creation time, and file size—NDIR displays a plethora of network statistics, including owner, directory rights, last modified date, and file attributes.

NDIR can be used to search one directory or a directory and all its subdirectories with the /SUB parameter.

Typing `NDIR *.* /SUB` displays all information about all files in this directory and all its subdirectories.

## RENDIR

The RENDIR command is a useful NetWare tool that isn't available in the DOS world. It allows you to rename an existing NetWare directory. I can't count the number of times I could have used this command in DOS.

## LISTDIR

LISTDIR displays an enhanced graphic of the NetWare directory structure in a pseudo-tree layout. LISTDIR displays more security statistics than NDIR and allows you to specify which information you would like to view. Here's a description of LISTDIR syntax and its parameters:

`LISTDIR /A` displays all information for each specified directory.

`LISTDIR /D` displays the creation date and time.

`LISTDIR /S` displays all subdirectories below this directory.

`LISTDIR /R` displays the directory rights for each specified directory.

## VOLINFO

VOLINFO is a graphic display of NetWare volume information and statistics. It lists volume sizes, total directory entries, free space, and available directory entries.

The NetWare directory structure is complex and sophisticated. It allows you to properly organize many different kinds of network information. A well-designed directory structure can increase user effectiveness and productivity. A related strategy for increasing user effectiveness is drive mapping. Drive mapping allows you to represent complex directory structures as simple alphabet letters. Let's take a look.

# Drive Mapping

I N THE DOS WORLD, we are comfortable with the idea of using letters to represent physical disk drives. The letter A represents the first floppy drive and B represents the second. C represents the first hard disk, and D and E indicate secondary disks. This scheme is simple and straightforward. It allows us to find data easily without having to bother with volume labels or physical mappings.

*D*OS drives point to physical storage devices. NetWare drives point to logical areas on the same physical disk.

In the NetWare world, we use the same approach—kind of. NetWare also uses letters as drive pointers, but the letters point to *logical* drives, not physical ones. The letter F, for example, points to a network directory (LOGIN), not a physical drive. In this case, F would represent the LOGIN directory—i.e., F:\LOGIN>. NetWare drive letters point to different directories on the same disk. This scheme is also simple and straightforward, but it takes some getting used to.

*NetWare drive mappings can be user-specific, temporary environment variables. Each user can have a different set of drive mappings in his/her own workstation RAM. They are created each time the user logs in. When users logout or turn off their machines, drive mappings are lost. Fortunately, NetWare provides an automatic login script that establishes user mappings at each login.*

NetWare uses two different types of drive pointers: regular and search. Regular drive pointers provide a convenient way of representing complex network path names with a single letter. Search drive pointers provide an additional level of functionality by building a search list for network applications. In this section, we will explore the details of these two NetWare drive pointers and learn how to implement them by using the MAP command. First, let's briefly review DOS pointers.

*In this section the terms drive pointer and drive mapping will be used interchangeably. According to Novell, they are the same thing. Technically, it can be argued that the drive pointer is the alphabet letter and drive mapping is the process of assigning it to a network directory. But let's keep it simple:* Drive Pointer = Drive Mapping.

## DOS Pointers

DOS pointers represent physical storage devices as alphabetic letters. These DOS storage devices are typically floppy drives, hard disks, or CD-ROMs. By default, DOS reserves the letters A–E for local devices. This number can be extended by using the `LASTDRIVE = <letter>` command in the workstation's CONFIG.SYS file. To move from one drive letter to another, you would simply type the drive letter followed by a colon and press Enter—i.e., `A:` ↵. Once you have moved to the correct physical drive, you can use the CD command to move between subdirectories of that drive.

*It is possible to reassign a DOS pointer as a NetWare pointer. In this case, the local drive becomes unavailable to the network user. This is an effective strategy for restricting access to local floppy drives while users are attached to NetWare servers. The DOS pointer is returned to the user when he/she disconnects from the LAN.*

## NetWare Pointers

NetWare pointers are similar to DOS pointers in a few respects, but for the most part, they are two different animals. Table 3.1 provides a comparison of DOS and NetWare drive pointers. NetWare pointers use alphabetic letters to represent logical network directories—not physical disks. NetWare pointers use the same syntax as DOS pointers, but they begin where the DOS pointers ended—the letter F. This means that NetWare pointers have twenty-one

| **TABLE 3.1** The Similarities and Differences between DOS and NetWare Drive Pointers | **FUNCTION** | **DOS POINTERS** | **NETWARE POINTERS** |
| --- | --- | --- | --- |
| | Drive Letters | alphabetic | alphabetic |
| | Syntax | <letter>: | <letter>: |
| | Alphabetic Range | A–E | F–Z |
| | Drive Type | physical drive | logical directory |
| | Destination | local workstation | network file server |

possible choices—F–Z. Figure 3.5 shows a typical NetWare directory structure with the drive letter F pointing to the SYS:USERS\DAVID directory. NetWare uses two different types of drive pointers: regular pointers and search pointers.

### Regular Drive Pointers

Regular drive mappings point to user-defined data directories. These drive pointers are typically used for convenience and directory movement. Without drive mappings, movement throughout the directory tree would consist of long path names and the CD command. This is cumbersome and time-consuming. With drive mappings, movement is consolidated into one simple step—F : ↵. Regular drive pointers represent complex directory paths as simple alphabet letters. Figure 3.5 represents the path SYS:USERS\DAVID as the letter F:. Simple.

NetWare reserves the final twenty-one letters of the alphabet for network drive mappings. Regular drive pointers are assigned by NetWare users with the MAP command. They begin with F: and move forward. Note: if the

*NetWare reserves the final twenty-one letters of the alphabet for network drive mappings.*

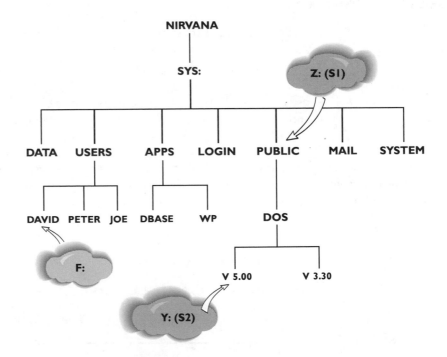

**FIGURE 3.5**
NetWare drive pointers and logical network directories

workstation CONFIG.SYS file contains the `LASTDRIVE = <letter>` command, the first available drive pointer will be the next letter. For example, `LASTDRIVE = G` will reserve A–G for DOS and the first NetWare pointer will be H.

*You can actually assign twenty-six network drive mappings (A–Z) by overwriting all existing local drives.*

### Search Drive Pointers

Search drive mappings extend one step beyond regular drive mappings by providing the user with the ability to search for network application files. When a user executes a particular network application, the system searches the current directory for the application file—.EXE, .COM, or .BAT. If the file isn't there, the system looks for a search list. If a search list doesn't exist, the system will return the message: `bad command or file name`. If a search list does exist, the system will move through the list in order until it finds the application. This method is very similar to the DOS "path" command. Search drive pointers build NetWare search lists. The maximum number of search drives in a NetWare search list is sixteen.

*The mind has its own logic but does not often let others in on it.*

*Bernard de Voto*

*N*etwork drives point to data directories, while search drives provide service to NetWare applications.

  Because search drive pointers are primarily used to build search lists, network users are more concerned with the order of the list than the letter that is assigned to the search pointer. For this reason, search drive mappings are assigned in search order by using the letter S and a number. For example, the first search drive would be assigned S1 and placed at the top of the search list. The second drive is S2 and so on. As a matter of convenience, NetWare also assigns an alphabet letter to each search pointer. This letter can be used to move around the directory structure just like a regular drive pointer.

  This strategy poses an interesting question—How do you tell the difference between a regular drive letter and a search drive letter? The answer is simple: you don't! There is no way of distinguishing one from the other by simply looking at it. So as a matter of convention, NetWare assigns search drive letters from Z and moves backwards. Therefore, S1 becomes Z:, S2 becomes Y:, and so on. Figure 3.5 shows the first two NetWare search drives as Z (S1) = SYS:PUBLIC and Y (S2) = SYS:PUBLIC\DOS\V5.00. With this in mind, you can assume that the early alphabet letters are regular pointers and the later alphabet letters are search drives. Keep in mind, this is only an assumption— and you know what they say about assumptions. Table 3.2 shows a comparison of regular and search drive pointers.

*The CD command is off-limits to NetWare users. If the CD command is used on a NetWare pointer, it reassigns the pointer to a different directory. This can be fatal for search drives that point to critical applications or utility directories. But if you must use the command, switch to the J: drive before doing so. The J: drive holds no special significance except that it is typically used as a JUNK pointer. (You can use another letter if J: is already in use.)*

*In the course of assigning search pointers, NetWare will skip any drive letter that is already defined as a regular drive pointer.*

## Using the Map Command

Now that we understand the fundamentals of NetWare drive mapping, we must learn how to implement it. The MAP command is one of the most versatile NetWare utilities. Below is a discussion of the many different MAP commands that allow system managers to implement NetWare drive mappings. Keep in mind that drive mappings are user- and/or group-specific and temporary. You'll have to do this all over again tomorrow.

**TABLE 3.2**
Comparing the Functions
of Regular and Search
Drive Pointers

| FUNCTION | REGULAR | SEARCH |
|---|---|---|
| Purpose | movement | searching |
| Assignment Method | as the letter | in search order (S1, S2, etc.) |
| Letter Assignment | by the user | by the system |
| First Letter | F: | Z: (S1) |
| Directory Types | data | applications |

### MAP

The MAP command without any parameters will display a list of the current drive mappings. It will list the alphabet pointers in order beginning with the local drives (A–E), the regular drives, and then the search drives. Here's an example of how the MAP display is organized:

```
Z:\PUBLIC>map

Drive A:  maps to a local disk.
Drive B:  maps to a local disk.
Drive C:  maps to a local disk.
Drive D:  maps to a local disk.
Drive E:  maps to a local disk.
Drive F: = NIRVANA\SYS: \LOGIN
    -----
SEARCH1: = Z:. [NIRVANA\SYS: \PUBLIC
SEARCH2: = Y:. [NIRVANA\SYS: \PUBLIC\DOS\V5.00
```

*Some of the most interesting MAP commands are MAP INSERT, MAP ROOT, and MAP NEXT.*

### MAP F:=SYS:LOGIN

MAP followed by a specific drive letter specifies a *regular* NetWare drive pointer. The above command would map the LOGIN directory to the drive letter F:.

### MAP S1:=SYS:PUBLIC

MAP followed by an S# specifies a *search* drive pointer. The # represents the pointer's place in the search list. NetWare assigns an appropriate letter beginning with Z: and moving backwards. In this example, the PUBLIC directory will be inserted at the top of the search list and receive letter Z:.

### MAP INSERT S2:=SYS:APPS\WP

The MAP INSERT command inserts a new search drive into the search list. The new pointer is inserted into the search list as the number specified. All search drives below the new pointer are bumped down one level in the list. The quirky thing about MAP INSERT is that the letter assignments are unaffected. All of the previous drives retain their original drive letter and the new pointer is assigned the next available drive. For example, if the above command was executed in Figure 3.5, the DOS drive (S2) would become S3 but still retain the drive letter Y:. The new directory, SYS:APPS\WP, would become S2 and inherit the drive letter X:.

*Search drive mappings occupy the same environment space as the DOS PATH command. For this reason, NetWare search mappings eliminate DOS PATH commands. The only way to retain the DOS path in a NetWare environment is to add the path directories to the NetWare search list. This can be accomplished by always using the MAP INSERT command. The DOS path directories are added to the end of the search list. Don't worry, the DOS path directories don't occupy any of your sixteen available search slots.*

### MAP DEL G:

MAP DEL deletes an existing NetWare drive mapping. It works with either regular or search drive pointers. MAP REM (remove) performs the same function as MAP DEL.

### MAP ROOT H:=SYS:USERS\DAVID

MAP ROOT is an intriguing command. It establishes a regular drive mapping as a false root. The user sees the drive as if it is the root directory. In the above example, the SYS:USERS\DAVID directory will be mapped to the drive letter H:. In addition, the H: drive will appear to be the root of the volume even though it is actually the SYS:USERS\DAVID subdirectory. It will appear as H:\>. False root mappings are dangerous because they limit users to specific branches of the network directory tree. In this example, no other directories would be available to the user David.

### MAP NEXT SYS:DATA

The MAP NEXT command assigns the next available drive letter as a regular drive pointer. This command doesn't work with search drive mappings. In Figure 3.5, the above MAP NEXT command would assign the letter G: to the SYS:DATA directory. MAP NEXT is useful to system managers because it keeps track of the alphabetic letters for you.

*Although MAP NEXT doesn't work with search pointers, there is a way to achieve the same effect. Simply use MAP S16. NetWare will not allow you to assign search drive mappings out of order. So if you specify S16, NetWare will automatically assign the directory to the next available spot in the search list.*

That's it for NetWare directory structure. In this chapter, we explored logical trees, system-created and suggested directories, path names, and drive mapping. I'd say we got a pretty good head start on network management and LAN configuration. The next step in building our vital NetWare LAN is security. Security configuration establishes integrity and protection for network users and shared data files. In the next chapter, we will install locks for rooms in our network apartment building, and pass out user keys.

*Security is mostly a superstition. It does not exist in nature, nor do the children of men as a whole experience it. Avoiding danger is no safer in the long run than outright exposure. Life is either a daring adventure, or nothing.*

*Helen Keller*

# Exercise 3.1: Using the Map Command

Use the directory structure illustrated in Figure 3.1E to provide the appropriate syntax for mapping logical drive letters to the directories indicated.

**F I G U R E  3.1E**

Using the MAP command

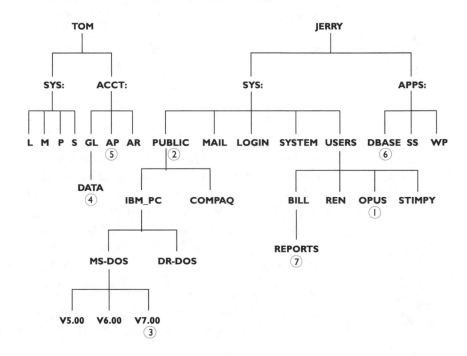

1. Give Opus a drive mapping to his home directory.

   _____

2. Map the first search drive to PUBLIC.

   _____

3. Map the next search drive to the appropriate DOS subdirectory.

   _____

4. Map the next available network drive mapping to the data subdirectory.

   _____

**5.** Map an appropriate search or network drive mapping to the accounts payable application.

_____

**6.** Insert the third search drive mapping to the database subdirectory.

_____

**7.** Map a pseudo-root to Bill's report subdirectory.

_____

See Appendix D for answers.

# Exercise 3.2: The Effects of CD on MAP

This exercise provides an illustration of the effects of the change directory command on search drive mappings. Carefully follow these steps:

**1.** Login to the network.

**2.** Type `Z:` and press Enter. Doing so should move you to the PUBLIC subdirectory.

**3.** Type `MAP` and press Enter. The system will respond with a list of all logical mappings and their appropriate directories.

**4.** Type `CD ..` at the prompt and press Enter. Doing so should move you from the PUBLIC subdirectory to the root.

**5.** Type `MAP` and press Enter. What happened and why?

_____

_____

**6.** Once you have pondered this factoid, type `CD PUBLIC` and press Enter. You will move back to the PUBLIC subdirectory.

**7.** Now that your Z: drive has been remapped to the PUBLIC subdirectory, type `MAP` and press Enter. What happens and why?

_____

_____

**8.** Now let's view the effects of CD on mapping search drives from other drive pointers. Once again, from the PUBLIC subdirectory Z: drive, type `F:` and press Enter. You should move to the F drive.

**9.** At this point, type `MAP` and press Enter. Notice the system responds with a list of current drive mappings. This response occurs because the Z: drive at PUBLIC is a search drive and the system finds the MAP command in that directory.

**10.** Move to the PUBLIC subdirectory once again by typing `Z:` and pressing Enter.

**11.** Remap the Z drive by typing CD .. and pressing Enter. The search drive Z: will be remapped to the root subdirectory.

**12.** Now move back to the F drive by typing F: and pressing Enter.

**13.** Type MAP and press Enter. What happened and why?

_____

_____

**14.** Return to the Z: drive by typing Z: and pressing Enter. Now remap the Z: drive back to PUBLIC by typing CD PUBLIC and pressing Enter.

**15.** Return to the F: drive, type F:, and press Enter.

**16.** Now type MAP and press Enter. What happened and why?

_____

_____

**17.** Now let's view the effects of creating search drive and network drive mappings of our own. Return to the Z: drive by typing Z: and pressing Enter.

**18.** Remap the Z: drive by typing CD .. and pressing Enter.

**19.** Return to the F: drive. Type F: and press Enter.

**20.** Type MAP and press Enter. Notice the MAP command does not work.

**21.** Create your own network drive mapping by typing MAP NEXT SYS:PUBLIC and pressing Enter. The system will respond with the next available drive mapping, which in most cases will be G.

**22.** Now type MAP and press Enter. What happened and why?

_____

_____

**23.** Let's attempt the same exercise but create a search drive mapping instead. Type `MAP S16:=SYS:PUBLIC` and press Enter. This will create a search drive mapping with the next available search letter to the PUBLIC subdirectory.

**24.** Now type `MAP` and press Enter. What happened and why?

_____

_____


**25.** Now to complete the exercise, be sure to return to the Z: drive and remap it to PUBLIC. Type `Z:` and press Enter.

**26.** Type `CD PUBLIC` and press Enter.


When you're through, refer to Appendix D to verify your answers.

# NetWare 2.2 Security

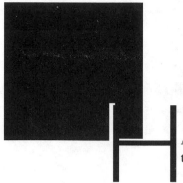

AVE YOU EVER WANTED to be a locksmith? Just imagine the things you could do:

- Build unbreakable locks

- Design reliable keys

- Protect countless valuable treasures

- Provide peace of mind and security for your clients.

But the locksmith has a difficult job. He/she is burdened with the responsibility of protecting the world's assets. The goal is to create a reliable security system that locks out the bad guys but welcomes everybody else in. While the job is not easy, locksmithing typically pays very well.

Clients generally come to locksmiths for unbreakable locks, reliable keys, and peace of mind. As the NetWare system manager, you are the locksmith of your LAN. Users come to you for application security, data organization, and general peace of mind. Your LAN locksmith duties are some of the most important responsibilities you will have and you must take them very seriously.

In this chapter, we will learn about NetWare security from the locksmith's point of view. We will discover NetWare's multilayered security model and explore each layer in depth. In addition, we will discuss some of the command line and menu utilities that NetWare provides to help manage LAN security. Keep in mind, locksmithing is a very important tool in your NetWare utility belt—LAN locksmithing is somewhat of a lost art.

*The goal is to create a reliable security system that locks out the bad guys but welcomes everybody else in.*

# The NetWare Security Model

THE MULTILAYERED NETWARE SECURITY model provides a level of protection for entrance to the LAN. Since the data on a network is typically shared, it is important to secure the data in directories to which only authorized users have access. In a stand-alone environment, security isn't as critical. The only way to access stand-alone data is to physically walk over to another user's workstation. However, in a network environment, you can let your fingers do the walking. Without security on the central LAN hard disk, it would be easy for users to access each other's data. This is bad.

The NetWare security model provides a level of data protection by forcing users through a specific series of security events on their way towards shared data. NetWare security consists of access restrictions, privileges, and file conditions. This way you can store data in certain directories on the server disk without having to worry about anybody accessing that data.

The NetWare security model consists of three layers (see Figure 4.1 for an illustration).

*The NetWare security model consists of three layers: login/password security, access rights, and file attributes.*

**FIGURE 4.1**
The NetWare security model

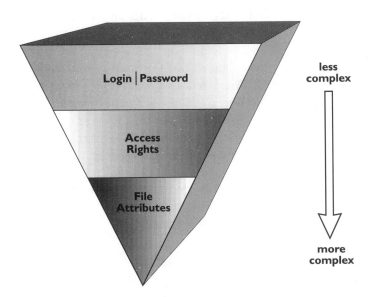

- Login/password security
- Access rights
- File attributes

Login/password security governs initial access to the file server and provides a system for user authentication. In addition, NetWare's login/password security level includes a variety of login restrictions that prevent users from accessing the system during unauthorized time periods, from unauthorized workstations, or with unauthorized configurations. Access rights define a complex set of privileges that can be assigned to directories and to users. When in combination, they create what is called *effective rights*. Effective rights define a user's actual privileges in a given directory on the disk. NetWare 2.2 provides seven different access rights. As the LAN locksmith, it is imperative that you understand each of these rights intimately and have a firm handle on how they are combined, both at the directory level and at the user level, to create effective rights. Access rights are the most common form of NetWare security and provide a very versatile system for controlling who has what privileges to which files.

The final layer of NetWare security is attribute security. File attributes are conditional privileges that control file sharing, reading, writing, executing, hiding, tracking, and archiving. Access rights define which users can have access to a file, while file attribute security controls what the users can do with the file once they are there. NetWare provides two different types of file attributes: security attributes and feature attributes. Security attributes affect how users access files and feature attributes affect how the system accesses files. File attribute security is a very complex level of NetWare security, and it is never implemented by most system managers. The first two layers of the NetWare security model provide more than enough security for 95% of the NetWare 2.2 LANs. File attributes are the infrared motion detectors of LAN security.

Let's being our discussion of the NetWare security model with an exploration of login/password security.

*The first two layers of the NetWare security model provide more than enough security for 95% of the NetWare 2.2 LANs.*

*Spoken language is merely a series of squeaks.*

*Alfred North Whitehead*

# Login/Password Security

L OGIN/PASSWORD SECURITY is the first layer of the NetWare security model. This level controls LAN access at the first point of entrance—login name and password. Login/password security is effective because it requires two pieces of information—an authorized login name and valid password. Keep in mind that the password and login name must match the system exactly. Any discrepancy is grounds for LOGOUT!

Once the login name has been entered and the password has been matched, the user is granted conditional access to the system. Permanent access is contingent on the user passing through a supplemental level of login/password security called *login restrictions*. Login restrictions further scrutinize LAN access by matching the login name with a variety of other qualifications: Is this user authorized to log in during this time period? Is this user authorized to log in from this particular machine? Is this user authorized to log in on this date? And so on. In addition, NetWare login restrictions incorporate an access tracking feature called Intruder Detection/Lockout. This security feature tracks unauthorized login attempts and automatically locks accounts that exceed a given bad login threshold count. The user account can only be unlocked by the NetWare supervisor.

*Login restrictions (which are discussed in more depth in Chapter 6) are important. Review what they are and explore their implementation in SYSCON.*

To review, here's the login process:

1. Load `IPX`.

2. Load `NETx`.

3. Move to `F:\LOGIN>`.

Once a user accesses the F:\LOGIN> directory, he/she is on the doorstep of the LAN. At this point, the user has limited access to only two NetWare files—LOGIN.EXE (to login) and SLIST.EXE (for a list of available servers). The user is ready to exercise his/her login security. The user logs into the network by specifying the file server name and a login name. Once the system verifies the login name, it will respond with Password:. If the user enters the correct password for this login name, he/she will be granted conditional access to the LAN. Next, the system will match the user's login name with a collection of login restrictions and apply another level of security. Once the user passes the scrutiny of login restrictions, he/she will be greeted with a NetWare prompt.

Upon receipt of the long-awaited NetWare prompt, the user has completed level one of the NetWare security model. The next level—access rights security—controls the user's movements throughout the directory structure and provides limited access to only authorized areas of the disk.

NetWare responds curiously to a variety of different login conditions:

- If the username is valid and there is no password, the system grants immediate access.

- If the username is valid and there is a password, the system prompts the user for a password. If the password is entered correctly, the user is granted access.

- If the username is not valid, the system prompts the user for a password anyway. This is to fool would-be hackers into thinking the username is valid.

*M*ovement
*throughout the*
*network directory*
*structure is controlled*
*by access rights.*

NetWare is designed on the principle of "What you don't know can't hurt us!"

There are numerous command line utilities that allow the supervisor to customize login password security and login restrictions. We will discuss a few of these commands at the end of the chapter. Also, login restrictions are covered in greater depth in Chapter 6—Network Management.

# Access Rights

ONCE THE USER HAS passed login/password security and login restrictions, he or she is greeted with a NetWare prompt. Users cannot freely access all files and directories in the system—this would be entirely too 1960s. Instead, users are limited to only those files and directories in which they have been given specific privileges.

Access to shared network data is controlled at two different levels: the user level—Trustee Assignments—and the directory level—directory rights, or the maximum rights mask (MRM). We will discuss each of these two levels of security and talk about how they combine to create effective rights. But before we dive into trustee assignments and directory rights, we must take a moment to understand the access privileges themselves and appreciate how they are used to limit specific user actions in NetWare directory structures.

## Understanding Access Rights

In understanding access rights, you need to ask one simple question: "What are the types of things users do in a network directory?" Ready for the answer?

- Read from files
- Write to files
- Copy files
- Change the names of files
- Access applications
- Erase files
- Create directories

Wow, users are extremely active. Fortunately, NetWare provides a simple facility for controlling their actions. Each of these user activities corresponds with a specific NetWare access right. In NetWare 2.2, there are seven different access privileges.

| | |
|---|---|
| **W—Write** | write to an existing file |
| **R—Read** | read an existing file |
| **M—Modify** | modify file names and attributes |
| **F—File Scan** | search the directory or subdirectory |
| **A—Access Control** | determine access rights |
| **C—Create** | create and write to new files or subdirectories |
| **E—Erase** | delete existing file or subdirectories |

*Notice that the NetWare 2.2 rights spell a word—WoRMFACE. (The "o" is silent.) Ironically, the "o" (open) is a NetWare 2.15 right that has been incorporated into W and R. Funny how it falls into place so nicely—almost as if we planned it that way.*

Each of these seven access rights corresponds with a particular user function. Five of them correspond with common functions—writing, reading, creating, erasing, and searching. The other two are a little more quirky—modify and access control. These rights pertain to the process of assigning and modifying NetWare security. Modify provides the ability to customize file attributes and Access Control allows users to change their access privileges—this is dangerous.

*These rights evolve as you move from one version of NetWare to another. Access rights in NetWare 2.2 are different from those in 2.15 and also change as you move forward to NetWare 3.12. Pay attention to the version of NetWare you are using and understand the differences—however subtle they may be.*

*It's not sufficient to learn the seven access rights. You need to understand how they are implemented (refer to Table 4.1).*

The key to access rights is understanding which rights it takes to perform common NetWare activities. Table 4.1 provides a list of some common NetWare activities and the rights that are required to perform those activities. As the LAN locksmith, it is your responsibility to go through the directory structure and assign specific access rights to specific directories for specific users on the basis of the types of activities they perform in those directories. Sounds simple, right?

If we return for a moment to our earlier analogy of the system manager as a locksmith, you can think of the LAN locksmith as having two major responsibilities—keys and locks. The first responsibility is to create the keys that unlock all doors in the building. The other locksmith responsibility is to install the locks in appropriate network directories. Once the keys have been created and the locks are in place, each user is given an appropriate set of keys—the NetWare key ring. This analogy is actually very close to what happens in the NetWare security model—the keys are analogous to trustee assignments and the locks are analogous to directory rights. If a lock exists and the user has the correct key, that user is said to have the effective right or privilege to

*Think of the LAN locksmith as having two major responsibilities—keys and locks.*

| | ACTION | RIGHTS REQUIREMENT |
|---|---|---|
| **TABLE 4.1**<br>Rights Requirements<br>for Common<br>NetWare Activities | Read from a closed file | R |
| | Write to a closed file | W |
| | Create and write to a file | C |
| | Make a new directory | C |
| | Delete a file | E |
| | Search a directory | F |
| | Change file attributes | F M |
| | Rename a file | M or C W |
| | Change directory rights | A |
| | Change trustee assignments | A |

unlock the directory. Remember, users can only perform the privileges that match the notches on their key.

## Trustee Assignments

When a user or group is given a trustee assignment to a given directory, he/she is said to be a trustee of that directory. In addition, trustee assignments flow from parent directories to their children. So when an access right is granted to a trustee for a given directory, the privilege is inherited by all subdirectories. Figure 4.2 shows an example of flowing trustee assignments. Access rights do not flow up, however, and so it would be impossible to grant user trustee assignments to a parent directory unless you went to that directory and assigned them specifically at that point. You can, however, assign large sweeping sets of privileges by granting trustee assignments to global parent directories—like APPS, for example.

Another interesting side effect of trustee assignments is that when access privileges are given in a subdirectory, all other keys are taken away. It's not an

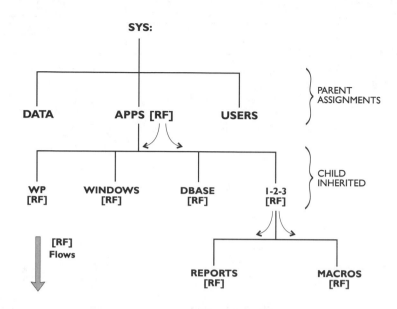

**FIGURE 4.2**
The flow of trustee assignments from parent to child

additive effect. On the other hand, trustee assignments are additive from the viewpoint of users and groups. In other words, a user's trustee assignment in a given directory is the combination of his/her user assignment and the assignment of groups to which he/she belongs. Here's an example: Bob is granted the read and write privileges in the APPS\WP directory as a user. In addition, he is a member of the ADMIN group, which is assigned file scan, access control, and modify. So Bob's actual trustee assignment in APPS\WP is read, write, file scan, access control, and modify. See Figure 4.3 for an illustration.

This strategy is particularly useful because it allows the LAN locksmith to assign keys to large groups of individuals—all in one swoop. It might seem trivial at this point but as soon as you begin assigning trustee assignment and directory rights throughout the system, you'll find that it can become quite a monumental task. An intelligent approach to trustee assignments would involve group assignments for global directories—PUBLIC, APPS, DATA, and so on—and user assignments for user-specific directories—USERS\BOB. Also, keep track of how the rights flow. Use inherited rights for multiple subdirectories of global parents—APPS\WP, APPS\DBASE, and APPS\WINDOWS for example.

**FIGURE 4.3**
Combined trustee
assignments

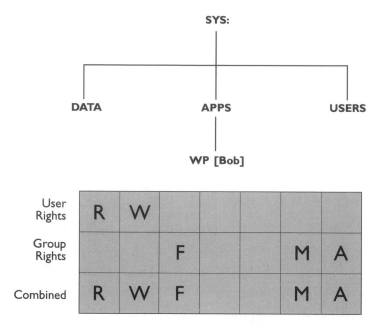

In order to create a trustee assignment for users and groups, NetWare needs three pieces of information:

**1.** The name of the trustee

**2.** The trustee rights to be assigned

**3.** The path to the directory in which the assignment begins

Trustee assignments can be granted in two ways: SYSCON or GRANT. Assignments can be made in the SYSCON utility using the User Information or Group Information screens. (We will explore this utility in great depth in Chapter 5—Menu Utilities.) Assignments can also be made using the GRANT command (which we will explore later in this chapter).

There are a few users and groups that automatically exist when you first take over the LAN. These system-generated users and groups include the GUEST user, which has basically no rights, the SUPERVISOR user, which has unlimited rights, and the group EVERYONE, which has specialized default rights. These system-generated users and groups have default trustee assignments, which are also created by the system. Here's a brief description of the default user/group trustee assignments:

- **EVERYONE** includes all users who currently exist and all users who will eventually exist. Most global assignments are granted to EVERYONE because it provides an effective strategy for assigning sweeping trustee privileges. EVERYONE is assigned the read and file scan privileges to SYS:PUBLIC and the create right to SYS:MAIL.

- **SUPERVISOR** inherits all rights to everything. Also, these rights cannot be removed and the SUPERVISOR account cannot be deleted.

- **GUEST** provides the bare minimum NetWare security. GUEST assumes the trustee privileges of EVERYONE, plus all rights except access control to his/her own SYS:MAIL\userid directory.

In addition, each user is given a default trustee assignment of create, erase, file scan, modify, read, and write to their own specific user SYS:MAIL\ userid directory. Also, users are given the same rights to their own specific SYS:USERS\username directory (assuming, of course, that the directory has been created).

Let's return for a moment to the locksmith analogy. If the trustee assignments are keys, then the keys are only effective in directories that have locks. If there are no locks, the key can't work. The absence of a lock in the NetWare analogy does not mean you have all access. In fact, it means the opposite—you have *no* access. In order for a user to have effective rights in a given directory, the user must be granted both the key and the lock to that directory. Let's see how directory rights fit into this puzzle.

*If the trustee assignments are keys, then the keys are only effective in directories that have locks. If there are no locks, the key can't work.*

*Some problems are so complex that you have to be highly intelligent and well informed just to be undecided about them.*

*Laurence J. Peter*

## Directory Rights

Directory locks, or directory rights, are directory specific, *not* user/group specific. Directory rights are assigned to directories, and do not flow down. In addition, the existence of a directory lock is independent from the existence of a user key. If the locksmith decides to put a lock on a given directory, that lock is susceptible to any user key that matches (see Figure 4.4). This level of NetWare security can get out of hand very quickly.

Fortunately, the directory rights in NetWare 2.2, by default, include all locks on all directories—so every directory in the entire system has all locks available. This is useful because it eliminates the directory rights facility and makes NetWare 2.2 security dependent only on trustee assignments. This dramatically simplifies the locksmith's job. If the LAN locksmith is specifically concerned about a given directory, the locksmith can remove the lock from that directory. Otherwise, he/she can leave it alone.

Directory locks are only necessary in sensitive directories—such as applications, users, or the SYSTEM directory. NetWare directory rights are called the Maximum Rights Mask, or MRM. The MRM is based on the following assumption—"Here are the maximum rights you can have in this directory." For example, if the SYS:APPS\WP subdirectory has sensitive application files that shouldn't be deleted, you can remove the erase lock from that directory.

**FIGURE 4.4**
The flow of
keys and locks

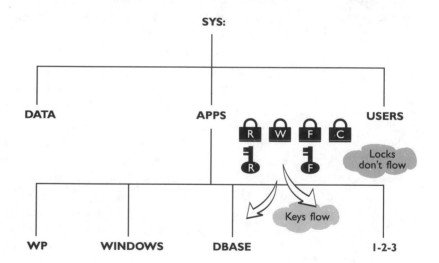

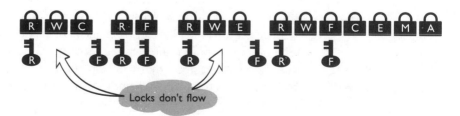

This way, no matter who has access—even if they have the erase key—users will not be able to exercise the erase right in the SYS:APPS\WP directory. Remember, the maximum rights mask is only useful in very specialized circumstances and can become quite confusing in calculating effective rights. An effective way to implement NetWare security is to leave all directory locks in their default state and rely 100% on trustee assignments—user keys.

## Calculating Effective Rights

So what does all this really mean? The bottom line is this: A user's actual privileges in a given directory are calculated as the intersection of the user's trustee assignments and the directory's MRM. These are defined as effective rights.

*Trustee assignments and the MRM are only the beginning. The real show stopper is effective rights. Pay attention to this discussion, and practice with the exercises at the end of this chapter.*

*Effective rights is defined as the combination of a privilege key and the existence of that privilege lock. If either is absent, the privilege is revoked.*

If you look at it in a global sense, a user's trustee assignments and a directory's MRM are meaningless until you put them together and calculate what the user's real effective rights are. After all, the effective rights are the only rights that a user can exercise in a given directory.

Effective rights is defined as the combination of a privilege key and the existence of that privilege lock. For example, in the APPS\WP subdirectory, all locks exist—by default. In addition, the user has been granted the read, write, and file scan keys. Therefore, the user's effective rights are read, write, and file scan (see Figure 4.5). If, for some reason, the LAN locksmith (system manager) decided that this person should not have the write privilege in the directory, the system manager has two choices: remove the user's write key or remove the write lock. The first choice would affect the one user only, while the second choice would restrict the write privilege for ALL users in the LAN.

If all of this is a little confusing and overwhelming, don't be concerned. When we get into the Network Management section in Chapter 6, we'll talk a little bit more about implementing security. Also, there are some exercises at the end of this chapter that will help you understand effective rights for certain cases. As the LAN locksmith, you must fill your NetWare utility belt

**FIGURE 4.5**
User keys, directory
locks, and effective rights

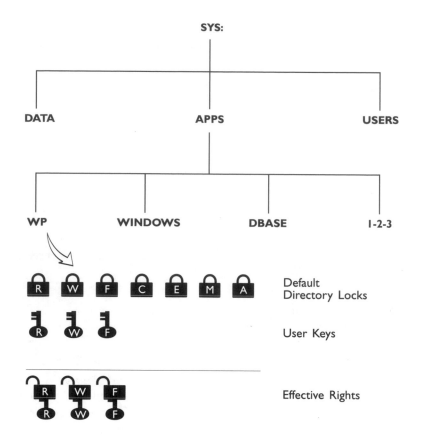

with a strong understanding of NetWare security and some efficient methods
for implementing trustee assignments (keys) and directory rights (locks).

# File Attributes

ILE ATTRIBUTES PROVIDE a very complex level of security that allows
you, as the LAN locksmith, to specifically affect what users do with
files once they have access to them. File attributes are global security
elements that affect all users regardless of their rights. Attributes can be used

to override all previous levels of security. For example, let's say your effective rights are read, file scan, and write privileges to the SYS:APPS\WP directory. The system manager can still restrict you from writing to a specific file by assigning the READ-ONLY file attribute. This level of NetWare security overrides all previous security.

The true effective rights to a given file in a given directory is determined by the combination of trustee assignments, directory rights, *and* file attributes. NetWare 2.2 supports two different types of file attributes: security and feature. Security attributes affect each user's security access. Features attributes affect how the system interacts with files—whether or not the files can be archived and whether or not transactional tracking has been activated. In this section, we will describe NetWare 2.2's different security and feature attributes and then move on to the many command line utilities that allow the LAN locksmith to implement NetWare's three-layered security model.

## Security Attributes

The first set of file attributes in NetWare 2.2 are security attributes. Security file attributes protect information at the file level within directories by controlling two kinds of file access: file sharing and file alteration. File access security controls not so much who has access to the files but what kind of access people have. Once a user has been given the proper trustee assignments to a given directory, that user has the ability to access any of the files within that system. File attributes tell that person what they can do with the files once they have access. The file alteration attributes not only tell you what you can do with them but limit file access to execute only or hidden. If a file has the hidden attribute, users cannot see, use, delete, or copy over the file.

Here's a list of the filing sharing and filing alteration attributes.

| | |
|---|---|
| NS—Non-Sharable | Access is limited to one user at a time. |
| S—Sharable | Simultaneous access by multiple users. |
| RW—Read/Write | Users may see the file and alter its content. |
| RO—Read/Only | Users may only see the file; no changes. |
| X—Execute Only | Execution only; users cannot copy or delete. |
| H—Hidden | Users cannot see, use, delete, or copy over. |

*The execute only attribute is extremely sensitive and provides the highest level of NetWare security.*

The nonsharable and sharable attributes limit access to files to either one user at a time or provide simultaneous access by multiple users. When multiple users have access to a directory and the files are flagged sharable, you run into a problem in which multiple users are accessing the same data and trying to save their version of the file. If the file is flagged sharable, the last person who saves the file will win the race. This is when the nonsharable attribute comes in handy. If you want only one person to access a file at a time, you can assign the nonsharable attribute to a file—the system will keep track of who gets to save and who doesn't.

The read/write and read/only attributes also affect file access but in a different way. These attributes affect what the user can do once he/she has the file open. The read/write attribute allows users to see the file and alter its contents whereas read/only means they can open the file but cannot make any changes. The read/only attribute is useful for application files that you want users to be able to access—but not change—in a shared environment.

The execute only attribute is extremely sensitive and provides the highest level of NetWare security. The execute only attribute can only be assigned by the supervisor to an executable file or .COM file. Execute only files cannot be copied or deleted—just executed. Also, once the execute only attribute has been set, it cannot be removed.

The hidden attribute is reserved for special files that should not be seen, used, deleted, or copied over. The hidden attribute is for archived files. In order to access a file that has been flagged hidden, the supervisor must remove the hidden attribute.

## Feature Attributes

The next set of file attributes is feature attributes. Feature attributes provide access to special NetWare functions or features including backup, indexing, and transactional tracking. The feature attributes are listed below.

| | |
|---|---|
| TTS—Activate TTS | Identifies this file for transactional tracking. |
| I—Indexed | Identifies this file for turbo FAT indexing. |
| SY—System | Identifies this file as system owned. |
| A—Not yet Archived | This file has been modified since last backup. |

The one that warrants the most attention is the system (SY) attribute, which is assigned by the system. The system attribute identifies the file as being system owned and can only be used for system functions. The NetWare 2.2 operating system file—NET$OS.EXE—is flagged as system owned so that nobody can delete, copy, or write to that file. The archive (A) attribute is interesting. It allows the system to keep track of which files have been modified since the last backup. The indexed attribute (I) allows turbo FAT indexing. This feature speeds access to very large data files (over 64 FAT entries). The TTS attribute is assigned to files that need to be transactionally tracked by NetWare's internal transactional tracking system (for a review, see Chapter 2).

*Learn how security attributes are implemented in the "real world." Here's a list just for you ... because I care!*

These file attributes, in combination, can create very effective security tools in controlling who has access to do what with very specialized NetWare files. The default attribute combination for all files on the system is non-sharable read/write (NSRW). This setup is fine for most applications and most data files. There are specialized instances, however, when you can justify customizing these attributes. Here's a brief list:

- Stand alone applications that are not to be shared should be flagged nonsharable read/only.

- Data files that are shared but should not be written to simultaneously should be nonsharable read/write.

- Data files that are part of larger multi-user applications that provide specialized record locking and other advanced features and can keep track of file sharing and data sharing on their own should be flagged sharable read/write.

- Application files that are accessed by simultaneous users should be flagged sharable read/only.

- Large database files that are important to the system should be flagged with the transactional tracking attribute.

- Very sensitive archive files—records that are rarely accessed, payroll records or general ledgers that are accessed once a month—should be hidden.

- All system files that are owned in the most part by the system are flagged system. But again, this is an attribute assigned by the system, not by the user.

- Sensitive application files that cost lots of money and are shared on the system should be flagged executable so that the supervisor is not liable should piracy occur.

*Recently, a very popular software manufacturer sued a company for piracy when it was found that many of the company's network users had taken copies of the network application home with them. The manufacturer won the case because of system manager negligence. Evidently, the system manager had not flagged the executable application file execute only. Doing so is not only a good idea, it can probably save your job.*

This completes our discussion of the NetWare security model and the concepts that combine to create the complex level of NetWare security that is necessary in this type of shared environment. We're going to have a chance to practice these concepts as we go along. You should feel much more comfortable with NetWare security once you get an opportunity to get your locksmith feet wet. In the remainder of this chapter, we will learn about many valuable LAN locksmith tools and begin to build the security portion of our NetWare utility belt. Don't let it weigh you down.

# Security Command Line Utilities

HAVE YOU EVER WATCHED a locksmith make a key? This amazing process involves a very complex set of specialized tools and fine precision. The process of building locks is also an amazing one. The intricate machinery inside combines to create not only the strength of the unbreakable locks, but also their reliability. Imagine what's required to make the lock match only one key.

This process in analogous to what the LAN locksmith must go though in implementing access right keys and directory locks. The process of building keys and locks is not easy—it's time-consuming, complex, and grand in scope. The LAN locksmith must be aware of the many ramifications of assigning NetWare security. NetWare security tools, or command line utilities, are broken into three different categories—login/password security, access rights, and file attributes. The command line utility tools with respect to access rights are further broken down into trustee assignment tools and directory rights tools.

These tools are augmented by the menu utilities that we'll discuss in the next chapter. Most of the login/password security and access rights tools can be found in the SYSCON menu utility. While the directory rights and file attribute tools can be implemented in the FILER menu utility. The menu utilities provide a great deal more functionality and a much friendlier format than command line utilities—but the Command Line Utilities (CLUs) are fast and to the point.

## Login/Password Security—CLUs

The first level of security tool is login/password security. As we mentioned above, login/password security deals with initial user access to the system. It incorporates a login name, a password, and specific login restrictions. There are five login/password security tools that can be used by the LAN locksmith to set passwords and get information about who is logged in. Also, these tools provide a list of servers and allow users to attach to other file servers. Login/password CLUs are not only used by the LAN locksmith, but can also be used by any user to gain general login information.

### SETPASS

The first login/password security tool is SETPASS. SETPASS is a command line utility that allows users to set their own password. At any NetWare prompt, type SETPASS. The system takes a look at who you're logged in as and goes out and gathers information about your authorized password. If a password already exists, the system will then ask you to enter your password followed by a new one if you pass the first test. The reason for this security is so that not just anybody could log in as a different user and change that user's password.

## ATTACH

ATTACH allows user and supervisor access to other file servers. Within Net-Ware, a user can log in to only one file server because the key component of the login is the execution of what is called a login script. The login script contains many specific variables for a file server and loads specific variables into workstation memory. While it is possible to attach to multiple servers, you can only log in to one server because if you logged into multiple servers, each server's login script would overwrite the other. The main difference between logging in and ATTACH is the execution of the login script. If you log in to a server, it does execute the system login script. Attaching to a server performs exactly the same task except it does not execute the system login script.

Keep in mind, in order to map drives or to access directories on other file servers, you must be physically attached to those file servers through the ATTACH command. The ATTACH command will ask for a user name and a password and you will be subject to the same login restrictions as if you had logged in. The only difference is, again, that ATTACH does not execute the file server's host login script. The syntax of ATTACH is the same as LOGIN: type `ATTACH [name of filer server]\[name of user]`. The system will then prompt you for a password if there is one. Keep in mind that NetWare lets you attach only up to eight file servers at one time.

## SLIST

Another login/password security tool that works in conjunction with ATTACH is SLIST. SLIST allows the user to view a list of all available servers that they are currently physically attached to so that they can decide whether they would like to logically log in or attach to those multiple servers. In large complex internetworks, the SLIST command is extremely useful because it provides a simple list of all servers that are currently available. The SLIST does not tell you whether you have a valid login account on any of those servers; it simply gives you a list of all servers that are physically recognized by your internal NIC.

## USERLIST

Another listing command login/password tool that is useful for users as well as system managers is USERLIST. USERLIST does not provide a list of servers but instead provides a list of *users*. USERLIST is useful because it will only give you a list of the users who are currently logged in to the file server you're specifying. The USERLIST command displays login information about those users and what they're currently doing on the system. There are some command switches that work with USERLIST—specifically /e, which lists network and node addresses and tells you where these users are logged in. Also, you can specify as a switch the specific user name and gain valuable information about specific users. For example, if you type `USERLIST GUEST`, the system will respond with relevant information specifically for the user GUEST. That only works again if the user is logged in.

*One possible use of USERLIST for the network supervisor is USERLIST /e for all network and node addresses. Then use that information to restrict users to logging in only from their authorized workstations. This type of login restriction is extremely useful for users who have a tendency to migrate through the LAN and log in from multiple workstations.*

## WHOAMI

The final login/password security tool is WHOAMI, which at first hearing has an existentialist tone to it. The WHOAMI utility displays information about user name, file servers you're currently attached to, your connection number, and the date and time of your last login. WHOAMI can be a useful tool for users who find it difficult to come to grips with their purpose in life, and also provides valuable information about users and their current network environment.

*WHOAMI provides a dual purpose: to display user information and to help out during an identity crisis.*

There are four WHOAMI switches that provide more focus for the WHOAMI command. They allow you to focus in on only specific types of information.

**WHOAMI /G** lists the groups you belong to.

**WHOAMI /S** lists your security equivalences. Again it's possible for you to be equivalent to another user in your security.

WHOAMI /R lists the effective rights in the network directory structure.

WHOAMI /A stands for *all* of the above switches.

Again, WHOAMI is useful only for the user who is logged in, because it takes a look at who you're logged in as and grabs information about you from the NetWare bindery.

# Trustee Assignments—CLUs

The next set of NetWare security tools refer to access rights—specifically trustee assignments and directory rights. We'll break it out according to those two different categories so that we'll first discuss the tools that apply to trustee assignments and then move on to directory rights.

Trustee assignment security tools apply almost exclusively to the LAN locksmith. These tools are very powerful and are easily abused. Keep in mind that in order to assign trustee rights or directory rights, the user in question must be granted the access control right to that particular directory. Again, the only person who has global access rights to assign all rights or privileges to the system is the supervisor or somebody who is granted what is called *supervisor equivalents*.

## TLIST

The first trustee assignment tool is TLIST. The TLIST command line utility displays the trustees and their effective rights in a specific directory. TLIST is generally for information only and can only be applied to a specific directory or drive letter in the mapping environment. TLIST is useful because it provides information about all the different trustees that are assigned access to a directory and their effective rights in that directory. It calculates the combination of trustee assignments and directory rights to display the effective rights. This information could be very useful for the LAN locksmith who is trying to figure what security should be granted to whom in a given directory. They can first type `TLIST` and get information about what already exists.

The next three trustee assignment tools apply to the actual implementation of trustee assignments.

### GRANT

The GRANT CLU is the most effective for trustee assignment. GRANT allows the supervisor to assign or grant specific privileges to specific users within specific directories. The syntax for GRANT is `GRANT [rights] for [directory or drive name] to [user or group]`. For example, if I wanted to assign the R and F rights to user DAVID in the SYS:APPS\WP directory, the syntax would be `GRANT R F for SYS:APPS\WP to DAVID`.

GRANT is a particularly useful and efficient CLU because it allows very quick access to the security system and quick implementation of trustee assignments. GRANT is hard to use, though, because it doesn't provide a list of existing trustee assignments for given users or groups and it provides a very specific syntax. If you do not follow it exactly, you can get into trouble. The SYSCON menu utility is a lot more friendly in the assignment of trustee privileges.

### REVOKE

REVOKE is exactly the opposite of GRANT. The REVOKE syntax is exactly the same as GRANT, but instead of granting rights to a user, you are revoking rights from a user. Again, REVOKE is very specific in its syntax and does not provide a simple way of viewing all trustee assignments for given users.

### REMOVE

REMOVE is dramatic in its scope—it removes all rights for a given trustee in a directory and completely removes that user as a trustee so that user has no rights whatsoever to that directory.

*Use GRANT if you want to grant any rights for a given user to a directory, REVOKE to revoke partial rights, or REMOVE to revoke all rights.*

# Directory Rights—CLUs

There are two security access right tools that work in conjunction with the trustee assignment CLUs—they are the directory rights command line utilities, namely RIGHTS and LISTDIR. These command line utilities are specifically used in directory situations and do not apply to users, groups, or trustee assignments. RIGHTS and LISTDIR are used to allow you to view not only the directory rights of a given directory but the trustees and the effective rights of a given directory. All the previous access right tools allow you to view information about trustees. These particular tools allow you to view information about directories and effective rights.

Again, RIGHTS and LISTDIR, which are the directory rights tools, are not only used by system managers but by users as well. The RIGHTS and LISTDIR utilities provide valuable information about effective rights and directory structure not only for system managers but also for users.

## RIGHTS

RIGHTS is similar to TLIST in that it displays effective rights in a specific directory. It does not, however, display all the trustees of that directory. RIGHTS displays your trustee rights and effective rights for a particular directory. The RIGHTS command takes a look as who you're logged in as and reads your trustee assignment from the bindery. It uses the directory rights to calculate effective rights.

## LISTDIR

LISTDIR is a lot more effective at providing information about directory rights than the RIGHTS command. LISTDIR displays the effective and directory rights and all information pertaining to the directory including all subdirectories of a parent directory. There are six switches that are relevant here and that work in conjunction with the LISTDIR command.

**LISTDIR /e** shows the effective rights you have in the directory and subdirectories of a parent directory.

**LISTDIR /r** shows the directory rights for this directory and all subdirectories of the directory.

**LISTDIR /a** shows the maximum rights mask, the effective rights, and all of the other date and time information.

**LISTDIR /d and /t** show the creation date and time of the directory and subdirectories.

**LISTDIR /s** shows the subdirectory information in an entire tree structure of all subdirectories of a given parent directory.

Again, LISTDIR is a useful utility that provides subdirectory information and a directory tree structure including effective rights, MRM, and creation date and time of directory structures.

# File Attributes

There are two file attribute command line utilities: FLAG and NCOPY. These two command line utilities are designed to provide the system manager with the ability to view and assign file attributes as well as copy files with their attributes attached. Let's take a closer look.

## FLAG

The FLAG command line utility allows supervisors and users with the modify access right to view or change the file attributes of a given file. The syntax with the FLAG command is `FLAG [file name]`. The flags consist of the first few letters of the attribute name. If you refer to the earlier bullet list of security/feature file attributes, the bolded letter corresponds to the flag switch that would be used with this command. One switch that is not included on that list is the N switch, which allows the supervisor to assign the normal series of attributes to files and thus return the file attributes to the default state—nonsharable read/write.

## NCOPY

The NCOPY command is extremely useful for a variety of reasons. It is included at this point because it does retain the file attributes for files that are copied using the NCOPY command. This is not the case for files that are copied using the DOS COPY command. NCOPY works exactly the same way as the COPY command. The syntax is similar. Type `NCOPY [file name] to [file name]`. Again, you can also leave out the "to" and insert a space between the two file names, in which case NCOPY would assume a "to" in between.

*Because NCOPY is a NetWare utility, it accesses the NetWare FAT and DET with a great deal more efficiency than DOS COPY does. Because NCOPY works within the memory of the file server, NCOPY provides a much safer, much faster means of copying files across the network. If files are copied from one directory on the file server to another, NCOPY does not copy the files down to workstation memory and back up (thereby creating a load on the network). Instead, it copies the files in file server RAM—a process that is much faster and does not create a load on the network. It's safer because NCOPY utilizes the read-after-write verification fault tolerance feature that is incorporated into NetWare. This read-after-write verification is not performed if you use the DOS COPY command.*

The NCOPY command supports all wildcard characters, including the ?, which is also supported with the DOS COPY command.

That completes our discussion of the NetWare security tools and our discussion of NetWare 2.2 security. Keep in mind that the responsibilities of the LAN locksmith are to make sure that all the user data is safe and that sufficient access and data integrity security has been implemented. That way unauthorized users are left out, but the system is still efficient and transparent enough so that it doesn't get in the way of normal operations for authorized users. Many times the LAN locksmith gets caught up in the whole complex security model of NetWare and creates such a secure system that it's impossible to use. Keep in mind that security and productivity must be balanced. NetWare's security functionality is extensive, and supports a great many options. But use my next KISS principles: Keep It Safe and Simple.

In the next chapter we'll talk a little bit more about directory structures, drive mapping, and security from the menu utilities standpoint. Throughout these first three chapters, we have discussed the command line utilities tools that have bolstered your NetWare utility belt. Now what I'd like to do is spend some time discussing the menu utilities, which can only enhance the power of your NetWare utility belt. In the chapters that follow, I'll go into much more depth on network management and printing. The NetWare menu utilities will provide a springboard for that discussion.

Without any further ado, let's get on with the shew!

---

## Exercise 4.1: Calculating Effective Rights

In this exercise, we will calculate the effective rights for a number of different security cases. In each case, you will be provided with the user rights and the maximum rights mask and you will be asked to calculate the effective rights using the worksheets provided. Remember that in all cases, the maximum rights mask limits the user rights that can be exercised in a given directory.

Use the accompanying forms for each of the scenarios below. Check your answers in Appendix D.

1. As a user, you are granted the R, W, C, and F privileges. The maximum rights mask is set at the default. What are your effective rights?

---

| | R | W | C | E | M | F | A |
|---|---|---|---|---|---|---|---|
| USER RIGHTS | | | | | | | |
| MRM | | | | | | | |
| **EFFECTIVE RIGHTS** | | | | | | | |

2. This directory is a subdirectory of the one from Case #1. The maximum rights mask has been set to R and F. What are your effective rights?

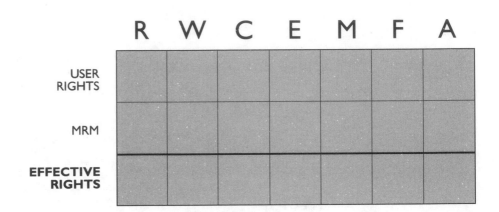

| | R | W | C | E | M | F | A |
|---|---|---|---|---|---|---|---|
| **USER RIGHTS** | | | | | | | |
| **MRM** | | | | | | | |
| **EFFECTIVE RIGHTS** | | | | | | | |

3. Your user rights in a given directory are R, C, E, and F. The maximum rights mask has been set to W, M, A. What are your effective rights?

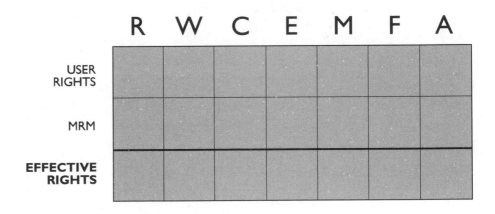

| | R | W | C | E | M | F | A |
|---|---|---|---|---|---|---|---|
| **USER RIGHTS** | | | | | | | |
| **MRM** | | | | | | | |
| **EFFECTIVE RIGHTS** | | | | | | | |

**4.** As a user, you are granted R and F rights to a given directory. As a member of the group EVERYONE, you inherit the W and C rights. What are your combined rights? In the same directory, the maximum rights mask is set to R, F, W, and E. What are your effective rights?

| | R | W | C | E | M | F | A |
|---|---|---|---|---|---|---|---|
| USER RIGHTS | | | | | | | |
| MRM | | | | | | | |
| **EFFECTIVE RIGHTS** | | | | | | | |

**5.** As a system manager, you want to restrict a particular user from having any rights in the SYS:PUBLIC subdirectory. Using their default user rights, how would you configure the maximum rights mask so that this particular user would have no rights in the SYS:PUBLIC subdirectory?

| | R | W | C | E | M | F | A |
|---|---|---|---|---|---|---|---|
| USER RIGHTS | | | | | | | |
| MRM | | | | | | | |
| **EFFECTIVE RIGHTS** | | | | | | | |

# NetWare 2.2
# Utilities

N CHAPTER 2, WE defined the NetWare system manager as "a brave soul whose single task is to keep peace in the NetWare castle." The system manager is the LANlord of his/her network apartment—managing workstation appliances, directory rooms, and user tenants. It's definitely a challenging, rewarding, and exciting life.

In order to accomplish his/her many LAN management duties, the NetWare system manager relies on a variety of CNA resources, including Product Documentation, Netwire, NetWare Express, the NetWare Buyer's Guide, Network Support Encyclopedia, On-Line Help, and valuable Network Press Publications. But the most important system manager resource of all is the magic NetWare utility belt—Batman for the LAN.

The NetWare utility belt is composed of a variety of tools—command line utilities (CLUs), menu utilities, supervisor utilities, and console commands. CLUs are productive management tools that provide NetWare customization from the workstation command line. CLUs are the mainstay of the NetWare arsenal. These utilities are primarily designed for system managers, but there are a few tools that appeal to NetWare users as well. Menu utilities provide the same functionality as CLUs, but with a friendly menu interface. In addition, some menu utilities provide extended functionality beyond what the CLUs offer. Menu utilities are more popular than CLUs and comprise 85% of most system manager utility belts. Supervisor utilities are specialized CLUs and menu tools that have been designed for supervisor use only. Most supervisor utility tools come equipped with a warning label—"WARNING : This tool contains explicit supervisor functionality. Keep out of the reach of children and NetWare users." Finally, console commands are NetWare tools that provide customization of the network operating system environment. Console commands are advanced utilities and must be executed at the file server console. These tools can be very hazardous if not handled correctly.

*The most important system manager resource of all is the magic NetWare utility belt—Batman for the LAN.*

*There is no knowledge that is not power.*

*Ralph Waldo Emerson*

In many cases, a good NetWare utility belt can be the difference between system management success and failure. In Chapters 1 and 2, we started our NetWare utility belt with a holster of microcomputer/DOS fundamentals and NetWare basics. In this chapter, we will fill the holster with valuable NetWare tools—menu utilities, supervisor utilities, and console commands. In addition, we will examine practical applications for these tools and even practice them with some lab exercises and NetWare simulations.

Let's begin with NetWare menu utilities.

*In this chapter, you may have noticed that the command line utilities are missing. Because there are so many CLUs and they represent the mainstay of your utility belt, I have opted to cover them in detail throughout the chapters as they apply to CNA objectives. This is a much more effective strategy for learning the many CLUs and gaining practical experience using them in a "real world" environment.*

# Menu Utilities

NETWARE MENU UTILITIES ARE the most productive and friendly of the NetWare system management tools. Menu utilities provide all the same functionality as command line utilities plus some additional features all wrapped up in a friendly user interface. These tools can be broken down into two basic categories—user menus and supervisor menus. Some user menus double as supervisor menus and allow supervisors to perform additional administrative tasks, including user creation, directory maintenance, and security and login password configurations.

In this section, we will discuss the three most popular NetWare menu utilities: SYSCON, FILER, and SESSION. These utilities are for users and system managers. The next section focuses on supervisor-only menu utilities. But before we begin, let's take a moment to discuss the look and feel of NetWare menu utilities.

NetWare menu utilities are a progression of screens that provide additive levels in an easy-to-use format. Each menu screen consists of a border—either single-lined or double-lined. The single-lined border denotes an information-only box (the contents of this box cannot be edited—it is for viewing only).

*In this section, we will discuss the three most popular Net-Ware menu utilities: SYSCON, FILER, and SESSION.*

On the other hand, a double-lined border denotes a box that contains information that can either be viewed or edited. All NetWare menu utilities are displayed in a blue and gold color format, which is the default color palette.

*The color palettes for NetWare's menu utilities are configurable using the COLORPAL menu utility. The default menu colors are defined as Palette 0.*

## Function Keys

Learning to use a menu is not something I think you're going to have a lot of trouble with. These menus are designed to be simple, straightforward, and provide basic system management facilities—all in an easy-to-use framework. Most of the menu functions are self explanatory, but there are a few function keys you should be aware of that will help you navigate through NetWare's menu utilities:

**RETURN** key or **ENTER** moves you to the next screen.

**ESCAPE** key returns you to the previous screen.

**INSERT** adds an entry in a particular double-bordered box.

**DELETE** removes an entry.

**F1** provides help.

**F1 F1** (two in a row) identifies the function keys that we're talking about now.

The last three function keys are NetWare-specific and provide specialized functionality within NetWare menu utilities only.

**F3** modifies the highlighted choice and allows you, for example, to rename users and directories as well as modify security rights.

**F5** is a toggle switch that marks and unmarks multiple options. Marking multiple options with F5 is particularly useful in environments in which you're configuring multiple options.

**Alt-F10** combination will quickly exit you from a NetWare menu utility without saving. Alt-F10 is useful if you want to jump out of a menu from within multiple nested screens without saving any of the work you've accomplished.

*When you come across a list screen with a double border, NetWare allows you to highlight particular options within that list and continue. If the double-bordered list is empty, it is a perfect opportunity for using the INSERT key to insert a choice into the list. Doing so is particularly useful when assigning rights and user names.*

NetWare menu utility navigation is a little quirky at first but you'll soon get the hang of it and find yourself buzzing through the screens like a pro. Now we will move onto the three most popular NetWare menu utilities in a little more detail.

*Learn the function keys—it's for your own good!*

## SYSCON

SYSCON is the mother of all utilities. SYSCON stands for SYStem CONfiguration and it is used for most of the system management tasks. It is used to configure trustees, trustee assignments, account restrictions, login restrictions, accounting, login scripts, users and group information. During our discussion of menu utilities, we will focus on both the command line utilities, which are integrated into the menu utility, and the extended functionality that the menu utility provides.

SYSCON incorporates the seven command line utilities we've introduced so far.

- GRANT
- REMOVE
- REVOKE
- RIGHTS
- SETPASS

*SYSCON is the mother of all utilities.*

- SLIST

- TLIST

The SYSCON menu and its submenus can be viewed in Figure 5.1. The standard NetWare menu utility format calls for the name of the menu utility across the top header with the date and time. In addition, it provides the next

**FIGURE 5.1**
The SYSCON
menu utility

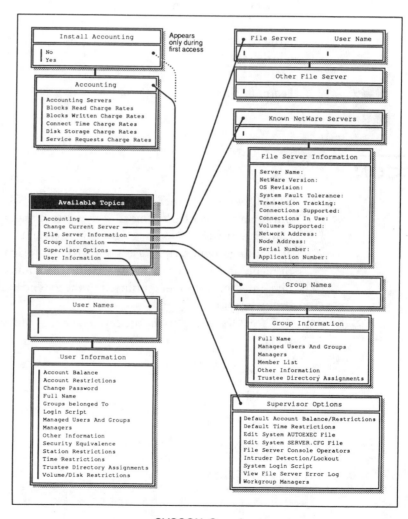

SYSCON Overview

line with user information and the filer server that you're currently attached to. The available topics menu in SYSCON contains six choices:

- Accounting
- Change Current Server
- File Server Information
- Group Information
- Supervisor Options
- User Information

*The best advice for learning SYSCON is to use it. Practice at home or on World Wire.*

Now let's take a moment to go into each of these available topic menus in a little more depth.

### Accounting

The Accounting submenu of SYSCON is where the system manager installs and manages NetWare accounting. NetWare accounting is a feature that allows system managers to monitor and charge customers for using specific file server resources. Another strategy for using NetWare accounting is to track network usage and resource utilization by charging specific prices for particular network resources such as disk blocks read, disk blocks written, file server attach time, and processor utilization. NetWare 2.2 includes an elaborate reporting system.

To install accounting, simply highlight the accounting option from the available topics menu in SYSCON and press Enter. The system will ask you whether you would like to install accounting. Highlight YES and it will install accounting on the default server. It's possible to install accounting on multiple servers from this SYSCON menu by inserting multiple file servers in the accounting servers window.

*Either I will find a way, or I will make one.*

*Phillip Sidney*

The accounting submenu provides six choices: Accounting Servers—where you would add the servers that are going to support NetWare accounting—and the five different resource accounting features: blocks read, charge rates, blocks written, connect time, disk storage, and service requests. Network accounting supports two other command line utilities that provide reporting functionality. They are ATOTAL, which provides a summary of weekly accounting charges, and PAUDIT, which provides a detailed tracking of all user logins, logouts, and accounting charges. We will discuss accounting in more detail in Chapter 6—Network Management.

### Change Current Server

The next choice in the available topics menu is Change Current Server. This choice simply allows the user or the system manager to change the server upon which he/she is using SYSCON. This changes their default server from the current server to any server that is currently attached to the internetwork. Change Current Server displays a menu with the current default file servers on the left-hand side and the user names that are used to log in on the right-hand side. To add a server to this list, attach to another server, or change current servers, you can press INSERT at the Change Current Server menu screen and the system responds with a list of available servers. Highlight a server from the Other File Server screen and the system will ask for a user name and password. Keep in mind you are attaching to another file server so it is important that you follow the same login security levels as you would if you were logging in.

*The only difference between attaching and logging in is that when you attach, you do not execute the login scripts.*

### File Server Information

The File Server Information screen is a single-bordered box that displays relevant details about the current default file server. These details include server name, NetWare version, operating system revision, level of system fault tolerance, network address, serial number, and the number of connections supported and in use.

*A connection is not a user but a physical workstation connection to the server. It is also a print server, a router, or any other device that requires communication with the NetWare file server. If, for example, you buy a 100-user version of NetWare, you are actually buying 100 connections for this server. Since you're buying a 100-connection license and the print servers and routers cut into these connections, NetWare supports 16 additional connections beyond the 100—to support print servers and routers. If you have more than 16 print servers and routers, you will start to lose user connections. The moral of the story is a 100-connection version of NetWare will support 116 connections but only 100 user connections because NetWare discerns between user connections and print server and router connections.*

### Group Information

The Group Information submenu provides information and configuration options for NetWare groups. The Group Information submenu is similar to the user information submenu in functionality but provides fewer choices. The Group Information submenu of SYSCON provides seven choices:

- Full name
- Managed users and groups
- Managers
- User list
- Other information
- Trustee directory assignments
- Trustee file assignments

Before you can enter the Group Information screen, you must identify which group you would like to view. This choice is made in an intermediate menu called the Group Names menu, which is a double-bordered box. At this point, you are allowed to either insert, delete, or choose a specific existing NetWare group. The Group Information box in SYSCON is particularly useful for assigning group specific or group-wide security options. Trustee assignments can be made for large groups of users by using the group information window to assign trustee assignments to a group and then using the member list option to assign users to this group. This is a very effective way to cure baldness in system managers who worry too much about user-specific security.

### Supervisor Options

*The Supervisor Options submenu of SYSCON is where the NetWare system manager will spend most of his/her time.*

Supervisor Options is the submenu in which the system manager spends most of his or her time and which provides the most system administrative functionality. In NetWare 2.2, the Supervisor Options menu provides eight different choices and can only be accessed by a supervisor or supervisor equivalent:

- Default account balance restrictions

- Default time restrictions

- Edit system AUTOEXEC file

- File server console operators

- Intruder detection/lockout

- System login script

- View file server error log

- Work group managers

All these choices will be explored in greater depth in Chapter 6, Network Management, when we discuss the intricacies of advanced system management. If the NetWare system manager can spend most of his or her time in the Supervisor Options screen and stay away from customizing group information and user information, he or she will be much better off with respect to file server maintenance—and general quality of life.

### User Information

The User Information option in SYSCON is the largest and most useful of the SYSCON submenus. In NetWare 2.2, the User Information submenu provides fourteen different options, including full name, password, login script, security equivalences, time restrictions, trustee directory assignments, and volume disk restrictions. See Figure 5.1 for a complete list. The User Information configuration follows the same format as Group Information in that the intermediate user names lists all known users of the system and users at this point can be deleted, inserted, or highlighted.

*NetWare provides a hidden facility for configuring small, select groups of users. The system manager can use F5 to mark multiple users in the User Names window of SYSCON. Pressing Enter provides a limited configuration window for setting specific parameters for the marked users. The window is called Set User Information and it consists of four choices—Account Balance, Account Restrictions, Station Restrictions, and Time Restrictions. This is as close as you are going to get to configuring global login restrictions.*

*The User Information option in SYSCON is the largest and most useful of the SYSCON submenus. In NetWare 2.2, the User Information submenu provides fourteen different options.*

    The User Information submenu is used to specifically configure security and environmental variables. The system manager can use the User Information submenu of SYSCON to fine tune group-wide and system-wide security down to the user level. This is done through the user login script, user-specific passwords, trustee assignments, and account restrictions. The less time system managers spend in the user information screen, the better off they are because each time a configuration is performed in the user information screen, it must be performed not only for this user but for all other users as well. This can be quite overwhelming in an environment in which five hundred or one thousand users exist on one server or on one LAN.

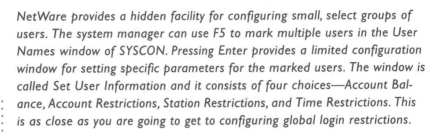

*The User Information submenu in SYSCON can also be used by users to customize their environment or to change their login scripts, passwords, or full name. The user information screen will appear with all fourteen options as long as a specific user is accessing his or her own user information options. A severely abbreviated version of this User Information menu will appear if a user tries to access the configurations of any other user. The User Information menu will appear for other users except that it will have two options: full name and groups belonged to. The idea here is to provide information about users to anyone in the LAN without allowing just anybody to come along and change other user configurations.*

    As you can see, the SYSCON menu utility is quite extensive and provides a great deal of functionality for NetWare system managers. It is very important that you become well aware of the many features of the SYSCON menu utility and become familiar with its use. The next menu utility we'll talk about involves the configuration of the NetWare directory structure.

*Great thoughts reduced to practice become great acts.*

*William Hazlitt*

# FILER

The FILER NetWare menu utility is designed to control volume, directory, file, and subdirectory information. FILER is just as extensive as SYSCON in its approach but instead of configuring users and groups, FILER specifically configures files, directories, volumes, and subdirectories. The associated command line utilities that are incorporated into the FILER menu utility are:

- FLAG
- LISTDIR
- NCOPY
- NDIR
- RENDIR
- DOS XCOPY command

The FILER menu utility is extremely refreshing for users who are used to using the DOS interface or the DOS command line for directory management. FILER provides exceptional functionality beyond DOS by allowing you to rename directories, delete entire branches of the tree, and change file security from within one menu. These functionalities are very similar to the third-party utilities such as Norton Utilities and XTree, which have been incorporated into the DOS environment.

The FILER Available Topics menu can be viewed in Figure 5.2 and includes these five choices:

- Current Directory Information
- Directory Contents
- Select Current Directory
- Set FILER options
- Volume Information

*The FILER menu utility is extremely refreshing for users who are used to using the DOS interface or the DOS command line for directory management.*

F I G U R E   5.2
The FILER menu utility

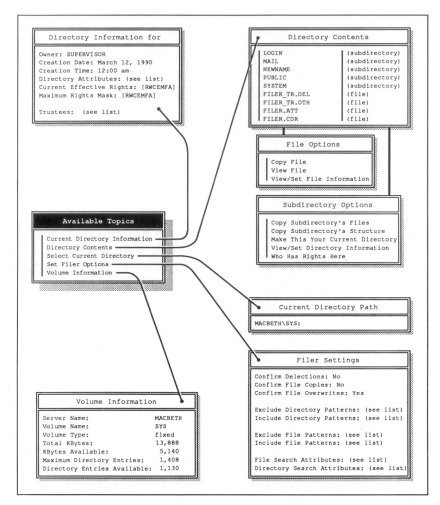

FILER Overview

FILER provides a consistent interface with SYSCON and the other menu utilities by using double-bordered and single-bordered boxes. It uses the same blue and gold format and the same header across the top. The header in FILER's case, instead of describing the user and the file server you're attached to, describes your current default directory. While FILER can be used by both users and system managers, it does limit the functionality to directories and files with which users have rights. The system manager has full functionality within the FILER utility. Let's take a moment to explore the five submenus under the FILER available topics menu.

### Current Directory Information

Current Directory Information provides detailed information about the current default directory. It provides information such as the owner, the creation date and time, the directory attributes, and other security information. Some of the most valuable information in the current directory information box is security related. It provides a detailed list of directory and file attributes, maximum rights mask, trustees and their trustee assignments, and the calculated effective rights. This is the only menu utility that provides calculated effective rights because it incorporates both trustee assignments and the maximum rights mask.

*The trustee assignments and maximum rights mask boxes within the directory information screen of FILER are double-bordered, indicating that this information can be edited by the system manager or anybody with access control rights in this directory. This FILER screen provides an effective strategy for calculating and managing NetWare security at the directory level.*

### Directory Contents

The Directory Contents menu provides a listing of all files and directories within and underneath the current default directory. The directory contents menu is where the system manager can perform file and subdirectory creation, deletions, pruning, and general maintenance. Besides subdirectories and files, the directory contents menu includes two other components: the double dot (..), which represents the parent directory, and the backslash (\), which represents the root directory.

System managers and users can highlight subdirectories/files and press Enter to receive a third submenu, which provides additional functionality—subdirectory options and file options. The subdirectory options screen includes functionality for copying subdirectories, making this your current directory, viewing directory information, or getting a list of who has rights to this subdirectory. The file options submenu provides information about copying, moving, and viewing files. You can also get information about viewing and editing file information and who has rights to this file.

The directory contents option within FILER is probably one of the most versatile menu utilities provided by NetWare. The system manager can insert or create directories at this point by pressing the INSERT key, or delete directories by using the DELETE key. Another interesting feature provided by the directory contents screen is pruning. When the system manager highlights a directory and presses DEL, the system responds with two choices—delete only a subdirectory's files or delete the entire subdirectory structure. In the latter case, you would prune the directory tree at the branch level. This is a very effective strategy for deleting entire portions of the subdirectory structure without having to delete each of the files first and then remove the directories.

### Select Current Directory

The Select Current Directory option simply allows you to move throughout the directory structure and change your default directory. This ability is useful when moving back and forth between current directory information and the Select Current Directory options box.

### Set FILER Options

The Set FILER Options choice allows you to set the parameters that are currently used by the FILER utility for accessing, editing, and viewing NetWare directories/files. Numerous parameters can be configured in the Set FILER Options, including confirm deletions, confirm file copies, preserve file attributes, include and exclude patterns, and search attributes. The last choice is particularly useful when searching for hidden and system files, which are not normally displayed in the directory contents box of FILER.

### Volume Information

Volume information is similar to SYSCON's file server information in that it is a single-bordered box that provides information only about the default volume. Volume Information includes the file server name, the volume name, the type of volume, the total size, the kilobytes available, and information about directory entries.

SYSCON and FILER comprise 95% of the system manager's utility needs. They are both extensive in functionality and easy to use. The final of the three most popular NetWare menu utilities is SESSION, not because of its system manager functionality, but because it provides a simple user interface for some common user tasks. These tasks include drive mappings, user lists, and so on. Let's take a closer look at the SESSION user tool.

# SESSION

The SESSION menu utility is extremely useful because it provides a single central point for accessing NetWare's user-specific configurations and features. The SESSION menu controls file servers, default drive mappings, search drive mappings, messages, and lists of users and groups. There are four associated command line utilities that work in conjunction with the SESSION menu utility.

- MAP
- SEND
- USERLIST
- WHOAMI

The SESSION menu (Figure 5.3) includes six different available topic options:

- Change Current Server
- Drive Mappings
- Group Lists
- Search Mappings
- Select Default Drive
- Userlist

*The SESSION menu controls file servers, default drive mappings, search drive mappings, messages, and lists of users and groups.*

SESSION uses the same NetWare menu interface with the blue and gold colors and the header across the top describing the SESSION manager utility.

The Change Current Server option works the same way as it does in SYS-CON. In addition, the Select Default Drive option in SESSION is similar to the Change Current Directory option from FILER. The remainder of the SESSION functionality is grouped into two categories—user group lists and drive mappings. Let's spend a moment discussing each of these different categories and learn how they can be used in a productive NetWare environment.

**FIGURE 5.3**
The SESSION
menu utility

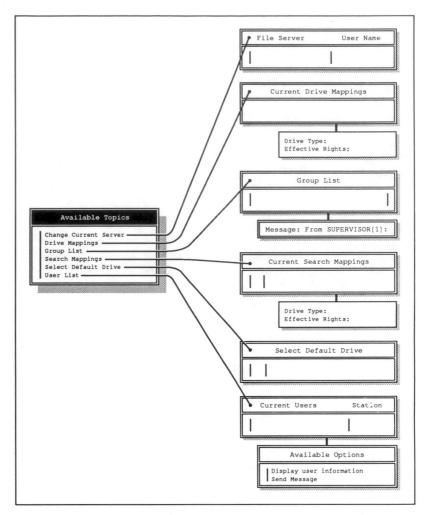

SESSION Overview

## User List/Group List

The User and Group List option in SESSION provides a quick and simple
way to access or view a list of who is logged in and which groups exist on the
system. The User List option provides only a list of users who are currently
logged in, and allows users to view connections that are currently open. A
not-logged-in user would appear in cases in which users have logged out but
not turned off their machines (doing so doesn't clear the connection). Both

the Group List and the User List allow users to send messages to other users. Simply by highlighting a user from the User List, or a group from the Group List and pressing Enter, the system displays a message input screen. The message input screen can include any message of forty characters or fewer, which will then be sent to the bottom console session of each person's screen. This functionality is identical to that of the SEND command.

*The down side of the SEND and the User List and Group List message options is that they lock up the destination computer until the combination Control-Enter is input. For example, the computer is unattended and a message is sent to that computer. The process will halt and the message will not be cleared until a user comes up to that machine and presses Control-Enter. To avoid having messages lock up, unattended machines use CASTOFF and CASTON. CASTOFF blocks the display of broadcast messages on any machine. CASTON reopens the machines.*

### Drive Mappings

The Drive Mappings options in SESSION provide users with a simple user menu interface for deleting, inserting, and changing drive mappings. The drive mappings option from the available topics within SESSION provides a double-bordered list of all network drive mappings, while the search mappings option provides a double-bordered list of all search drive mappings. Within the double-bordered list of mappings the user can press INSERT to insert a mapping and DELETE to remove a mapping. In addition, users can use the F3 key when highlighting a directory to change an existing drive mapping.

*While selecting a directory to either insert or change for a given drive mapping within SESSION, the user can press INSERT during the Select Directory prompt box and the system will respond with a list of available directories and subdirectories within that structure. This very useful feature allows users to quickly navigate the system.*

SESSION is a nice utility that provides simple message and list functionality as well as drive mapping for network users who are not savvy in the ways of NetWare management. Incidentally, Microsoft Windows provides a utility, called NetWare Tools for Windows, that is in effect the SESSION utility in a graphical user environment. This has been a very successful tool for users who are comfortable in the Windows environment and would like the same functionality that SESSION provides.

That finishes our discussion of NetWare menu utilities from the system manager and user viewpoint. The next set of NetWare tools for the system manager's utility belt is Supervisor Utilities. These utilities are designed specifically for the supervisor and are not to be used by general users.

*To be absolutely certain about something, one must know everything or nothing about it.*

*Olin Miller*

# Supervisor Utilities

S UPERVISOR UTILITIES ARE Batman tools designed especially for Net-Ware system managers. They allow system managers to customize and configure dangerous NetWare environments. Supervisor utilities come in two flavors: command line utilities and menu utilities. Some of the most hazardous supervisor utilities are tucked away in the SYS:SYSTEM directory. Less serious supervisor utilities reside in PUBLIC. By placing supervisor utilities in the SYSTEM subdirectory, NetWare is restricting access to only those users with rights to SYSTEM. By default, nobody has rights to SYS-TEM except the supervisor and supervisor equivalents. This is an effective strategy for limiting the use of supervisor utilities to system managers and users with appropriate rights.

In this section we will discuss the most popular supervisor command line utilities and the most effective NetWare menu utilities. Once we have a firm grasp on the purpose and functionality of supervisor utilities, we will move on to the console commands, which provide customization at the file server console itself.

*Supervisor Utilities are Batman tools designed especially for NetWare system managers. They allow system managers to customize and configure dangerous NetWare environments.*

# Supervisor Command-Line Utilities

NetWare provides eight supervisor command-line utilities. Their functions range from accounting to bindery restoration to workstation shell updates. As system manager, it is important to get a firm grasp on the use of these utilities, because they will provide a very specialized and powerful set of tools for your NetWare utility belt. Here's a detailed look.

### ATOTAL

The ATOTAL utility provides a daily and weekly summary of NetWare accounting services. NetWare accounting is a very useful tool, not only for charging back against shared network resources, but also for system managers to track resource utilization and user logins/logouts. ATOTAL does not provide a breakdown of user resource utilization but does provide a weekly and daily summary.

### BINDFIX

BINDFIX is an extremely important supervisor utility that allows for corruption recovery and restoration of the NetWare bindery. Earlier we spoke about the NetWare bindery as being the flat file database that keeps track of all NetWare objects, properties, and their values. The NetWare bindery is the most important system file within NetWare besides the operating system file itself (NET$OS.EXE). The NetWare bindery keeps track of users, groups, file servers, print servers, routers, and anything else with a name. It stores their rights, connections, configurations, and so on. All objects that use the network, all properties, and all values that define the NetWare LAN are tracked in the NetWare bindery. The NetWare 2.2 bindery consists of two files: NET$BIND.SYS and NET$BVAL.SYS.

*BINDFIX is a very important CNA utility. Try using it weekly as a maintenance tool.*

The system manager can run BINDFIX from the SYSTEM subdirectory when he or she suspects foul play (somehow the bindery has been corrupted or objects and values are not tracking correctly). BINDFIX has the ability to run consistency checks on the bindery and track relationships between objects, properties, and values. If an error is found, BINDFIX will restore the error and de-corrupt the bindery. Two other functionalities that are built into BINDFIX include deleting rights and trustees for users who no longer exist and deleting MAIL\userid subdirectories for users who no longer exist. BIND-FIX, while fixing the bindery, creates a backup of the original bindery in the names of NET$BIND.OLD and NET$BVAL.OLD. These .OLD files are text files that can be copied from the network and kept on a diskette.

*It's always a good idea to run a BINDFIX on a new network so the pristine bindery can be saved as the .OLD files and kept on a diskette—just in case corruption occurs and BINDFIX does not solve the problem in the future. Also, run BINDFIX twice before making backups—once for de-corruption and once for backup.*

### BINDREST

BINDREST is a related utility that restores .OLD files—files that have been created during a BINDFIX session. BINDREST can restore .OLD files from previous or new BINDFIX sessions. BINDREST can also be used to restore old copies of the bindery that were backed up onto a floppy diskette from earlier bindery sessions. Using BINDFIX and BINDREST on a daily basis or routine basis, such as once a month, is a good strategy for saving thousands of hours of work in creating users over again and reconfiguring NetWare security. Remember, when running BINDFIX and creating a backup copy of the bindery, it's a good idea to run BINDFIX twice.

### DCONFIG

DCONFIG is a very useful utility in NetWare 2.2 that changes the configuration information of routers, IPX files, and the NET$OS.EXE NetWare operating system file. DCONFIG is important in NetWare 2.2 because the LAN driver configuration options, network address, node address, disk controller type, and configuration are built into the NET$OS.EXE file. This information is defined during the NetWare 2.2 installation process and cannot be changed once the file has been installed. The only way to change this information without having to reinstall the entire operating system is to run DCONFIG. This is particularly useful in file servers that gain hardware conflicts later in their lives and the configuration options of the LAN drivers or disk drivers need to be changed. Incidentally, DCONFIG is not automatically copied to the SYSTEM subdirectory during the install procedure and should be copied from the SYSTEM-2 diskette manually.

## DOSGEN

*The SECURITY supervisor utility is excellent for identifying weaknesses in NetWare security.*

DOSGEN is an extremely useful supervisor utility that creates a remote boot image for files that can be used for logging in from *diskless workstations*. Diskless workstations—or remote booting—define an environment in which users are logging in from workstations with no floppy or hard disks. In these cases, the user will boot from a boot PROM (Programmable Read Only Memory) chip, which is located on the network interface card. The boot PROM redirects the user to the file server F:\LOGIN directory for a boot image. The boot image is downloaded to the workstation RAM and the AUTO-EXEC.BAT, CONFIG.SYS, and COMMAND.COM are executed from there. The creation of a boot image is performed using the DOSGEN utility. Remote booting in diskless workstations is effective in protecting against theft from the network or from viruses being entered into shared disks.

## PAUDIT

PAUDIT is another accounting supervisor utility that provides reporting functionality for system managers. PAUDIT provides a lot more detail in user resource utilization, specifically a full track of all user logins and logouts as well as user access of network resources. PAUDIT creates a very large and detailed file that can be imported into a database package and configured into a meaningful report. PAUDIT also provides information about security violations and intruder detection/lockout.

## SECURITY

The SECURITY supervisor utility is excellent for identifying weaknesses in file server security. The SECURITY command, when entered at the command line from the SYSTEM subdirectory, will analyze the NetWare bindery and report any instances of security weakness or violations. NetWare identifies a variety of security conditions as violations, including passwords that are fewer than five characters, and users who have security equivalents to supervisor, who have been assigned as work group managers, who are not required to enter a password, who have no full name attached, and so on.

*Too many people are thinking of security instead of opportunity. They seem more afraid of life than death.*

*James F. Byrnes*

### WSUPDATE

The WSUPDATE supervisor utility can be used to update workstation shells and configuration files from one central location. The WSUPDATE utility compares the date and time of all destination workstation configuration files with a central source file and will copy or replace existing workstation shell files with the source file if the source file is found to be newer than the workstation originals. The WSUPDATE utility is not limited to NetWare shell files. This utility can update any file including application and program files. The command syntax for WSUPDATE is

```
WSUPDATE [source file name] [destination file
    name] /[switch].
```

*WSUPDATE is important. Learn the switches and when or where it's best to use it.*

There are a variety of different switches in WSUPDATE:

**/f=[file name]** allows the system manager to set a variety of WSUPDATE files in one text file and then specify that text file for reading in source and destination information.

**/i** (the default option) forces the utility to prompt you for an action each time it finds an outdated file.

**/c** automatically copies a new file over an existing file without prompting.

**/r** copies the new file over the old file and renames the old file with a .OLD extension.

**/s** instructs the utility to search not only the destination, path, and drive name but also all subdirectories of the destination path.

**/l=[path and file name]** creates a detailed log of all activity, searches, finds, and copies.

**/o** copies over and updates Read/Only files. Since many of the NetWare shell files on the workstation are flagged Read/Only for protection, the /o parameter is required to update Read/Only files. This parameter will instruct the utility to change the attribute of the file to Read/Write, copy over it, update it, and then change the attribute back to Read/Only.

That takes care of our discussion of supervisor command line utilities. As you can see, they provide you with a variety of different system manager tasks and tools. Now let's focus on supervisor menu utilities, which will further enhance the NetWare utility belt.

## Supervisor Menu Utilities

While the supervisor command line utilities provide direct functionality from the command line, the supervisor menu utilities provide greater functionality within a friendly user interface. The supervisor menu utilities are also stored in the SYS:SYSTEM subdirectory and restricted to only supervisor, supervisor equivalents, or users with Read and File Scan rights to that directory. These ten menu utilities provide a variety of features—from printing and disk management to user setup and even downing the server. The following is a detailed description of each of the ten supervisor menu utilities and the features they provide for the NetWare system manager.

### DSPACE

DSPACE is a utility that is used to limit a user's disk space on all volumes of the file server (Figure 5.4). DSPACE provides the same functionality as the disk restriction option in SYSCON, except here you can choose users and volumes from a central location. The available options menu of DSPACE

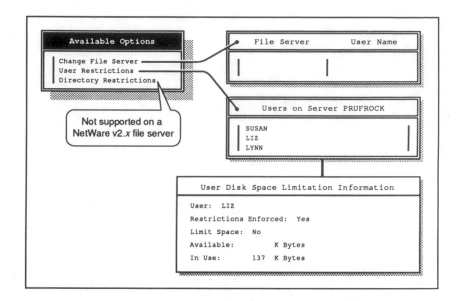

**F I G U R E 5.4**
The DSPACE
supervisor menu utility

includes three choices: change file server, user restrictions, and directory restrictions. While in 3.12 DSPACE allows system managers to limit users' disk space within directories, NetWare 2.2 does not support this feature. The user disk space limitation information screen provides the system manager with a central place to specify the user, the amount of space to restrict, and the amount of space that is available for this particular user. The DSPACE utility is one of the rare supervisor menu utilities that is placed in the PUBLIC directory during installation.

## FCONSOLE

*FCONSOLE is the mother of all supervisor menu utilities. It provides a great deal of functionality both in monitoring and configuring file server performance.*

The FCONSOLE utility is NetWare 2.2's version of the MONITOR NLM that is provided in 3.12. FCONSOLE (Figure 5.5) is the mother of all supervisor menu utilities and provides a great deal of functionality both in monitoring and configuring file server performance. In addition, experienced network programmers can use FCONSOLE to obtain information for writing, testing, and debugging their multiuser programs and advanced

**FIGURE 5.5**
The FCONSOLE
supervisor menu utility

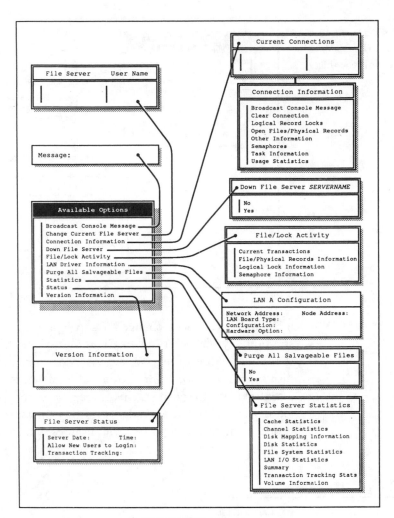

FCONSOLE Overview

system managers can use FCONSOLE to fine-tune server performance. The available options menu in FCONSOLE provides the following features:

- Broadcast Console Message

- Change Current File Server

- Connection Information

- Down File Server

- File Log Activity

- LAN Driver Information

- Purge All Salvageable Files

- Statistics

- Status

- Version Information

*In NetWare 2.2, FCONSOLE is the main supervisor server utility. CNAs should be very familiar with how it works and when to use it. Explore all the FCONSOLE options.*

The most useful feature in FCONSOLE is the File Server Statistics screen. This screen provides information on cache statistics, channel disk mapping, file system I/O statistics, and a summary statistic screen that provides invaluable information about the performance of the file server. FCONSOLE should be restricted only to supervisors because it allows remote downing of the file server.

## FILER

The FILER menu utility, which we talked about earlier, is the file structure's version of SYSCON. SYSCON is a utility used to manage users, groups, and security, while FILER is used to manage files, directories, and security. The FILER utility can also be used by the supervisor to customize the trustee assignments, the MRM, and to view effective rights. Because FILER is also used by users, it is another one of the rare supervisor menu utilities that is stored in the PUBLIC directory.

## MAKEUSER

The MAKEUSER menu utility provides the ability to design large user scripts that can be used to create or delete multiple users. The MAKEUSER functionality is based on a text script file with the .USR extension. The text file is used by the MAKEUSER program to create and delete large numbers of users, set security, define users and groups, and define home directories and login scripts.

*Learn MAKEUSER. You never know when it might pop up in your life.*

The MAKEUSER syntax is similar to login scripts in that it requires specific key commands and syntax. Below is a list of the nineteen MAKEUSER key words, which—as you can see—provide a wide range of functionality as far as creating users and groups and establishing security. Each of these key words must be preceded by a pound (#) sign:

**ACCOUNT_EXPIRATION** followed by the month, the day, and the year when the account expires.

**ACCOUNTING** followed by a balance and a low limit.

**CLEAR/RESET,** which clears the processing of the script from this point on.

**CONNECTIONS** followed by number that specifies the maximum concurrent connections.

**CREATE** followed by a user name and a variety of different options. This command creates users with specific full names, passwords, group membership, and directory rights.

**DELETE** followed by a user name.

**GROUPS** followed by a group name. This assigns users to specific groups.

**HOME_DIRECTORY** followed by a path that creates a home directory for this user.

**NO_HOME_DIRECTORY,** which overrides the creation of a default home directory.

**LOGIN_SCRIPT** followed by a path which points to a specific text file written in login script syntax.

**MAX_DISK_SPACE** and a number which establishes a maximum disk space for this user.

**PASSWORD_LENGTH** specifies a minimum password length between one and twenty characters.

**PASSWORD_PERIOD** followed by days specifies the number of days before the password will expire.

**PASSWORD_REQUIRED**

**PURGE_USER_DIRECTORY** will delete subdirectories owned by the user when the user is deleted.

**REM** (for Remark) for documentation.

**RESTRICTED_TIME** day, start and end specifies which days and hours the users cannot log in.

**STATIONS** followed by the network number and the station address for station restrictions for this user.

**UNIQUE_PASSWORD** requires new passwords that are unique.

Once a MAKEUSER script has been created, it can be used over and over again to establish new or existing user environments. This ability is particularly useful when the system is recreated every semester in school environments or when there's been a failed disk and you need to restore the bindery.

*Only the educated are free.*

*Epictetus*

## NWSETUP

NWSETUP is a NetWare 2.2 phenomenon that provides the beginning system manager with a headstart. NWSETUP is a simple menu template interface that creates users, login scripts, and home directories with default settings. If your network has a small number of users and you're just getting started, NWSETUP is for you.

## PCONSOLE

PCONSOLE (Figure 5.6) is the mother of all printing utilities. It provides a wide range of configuration options for printing, print servers, print queues, and printers. The three components that establish the printing environment in

**FIGURE 5.6**
The PCONSOLE
menu utility

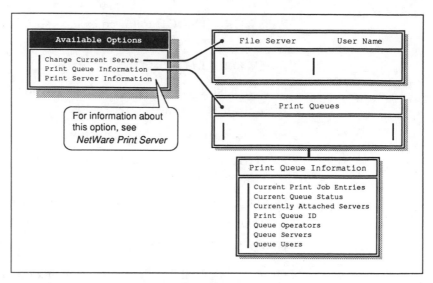

PCONSOLE Overview

NetWare are the print server, the print queue, and the printer. In order to set up NetWare printing, the print queue and print server must first be created, and finally the printers must be defined. These steps are all accomplished using the PCONSOLE utility. The available options menu in PCONSOLE includes Change Current Server, Print Queue Information, and Print Server Information. The Print Queue Information allows for the creation and management of print queues. Print server information allows for the creation and management of print servers and printers. We will discuss PCONSOLE and printing in greater depth in Chapter 7. Incidentally, the PCONSOLE utility is stored in PUBLIC because it is available to users as well as system managers.

## PRINTCON

The PRINTCON supervisor menu (Figure 5.7) utility allows for the configuration of print jobs. Once a printing system has been established using the PCONSOLE utility, the system manager has two options with respect to printing customization. He or she can either customize the print jobs that are the actual printed tasks, or customize the printers themselves. The print job configuration is accomplished through the PRINTCON utility. Printer configuration and definition are established through the PRINTDEF utility. Within

**FIGURE 5.7**
The PRINTCON
menu utility

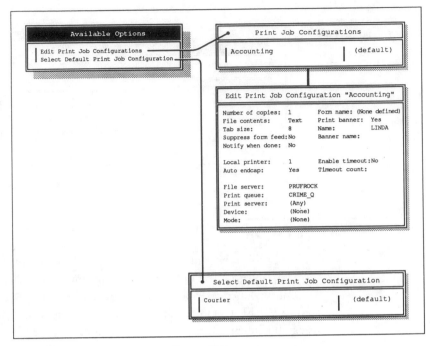

PRINTCON Overview

PRINTCON, the supervisor can configure or customize specific print job parameters such as number of copies, file contents, tab size, banner, form name, auto endcap, and default print queue. PRINTCON will also be discussed briefly in Chapter 7.

## PRINTDEF

The PRINTDEF options menu in Figure 5.8 has two choices: print devices and forms. Print devices are specific printer definitions that include escape sequences for defining customized printing orientations such as compressed print, landscape print, or specific fonts. Print devices can be imported from existing PDF or printer definition files or edited using the PRINTDEF utility. The forms option specifies the length and width of different forms that are used in the printing environment with these printers. Some example form definitions include checks, legal, greenbar, or simple 8.5 × 11. We will also discuss the PRINTDEF utility and its functionality briefly in Chapter 7.

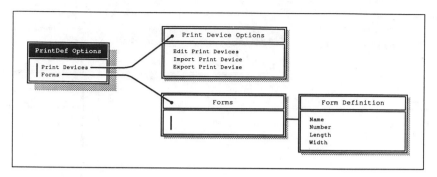

**FIGURE 5.8**
The PRINTDEF
menu utility

PRINTDEF Overview

## SYSCON

SYSCON is the mother of all utilities. SYSCON provides not only user and group information but supervisor options as well. These include default account balance restrictions, time restrictions, editing of the AUTOEXEC file or SERVER.CFG file, file server console operators, the system login script, establishment of intruder detection/lockout, the file server error log, or the creation of work group managers. Refer to the menu utilities section at the beginning of the chapter for an in-depth discussion of SYSCON and its many options.

## USERDEF

USERDEF provides the same functionality as MAKEUSER in that it allows you to create large numbers of users from one simple menu utility. The difference between USERDEF and MAKEUSER is that MAKEUSER uses a script format and allows the supervisor to create *and* delete users while USERDEF is a template that only allows the supervisor to create users. The USERDEF template (Figure 5.9) provides a more user friendly and graphic environment for the system manager to create user parameters of customization. However, it doesn't provide nearly the flexibility or versatility of options that MAKEUSER does. The USERDEF template includes user parameters such as default directory, groups belonged to, account balance, concurrent connections, require password, password changes, and unique passwords. See Figure 5.10 for an illustration of the USERDEF menus.

```
┌──────────────────────────────────────────────┐
│         Parameters for Template CLERK          │
├──────────────────────────────────────────────┤
│ Default Directory:  SYS:                       │
│ Copy PrintCon From: (see list)                 │
│ Groups Belonged To: (see list)                 │
│ Account Balance:                     1000      │
│ Limit Account Balance:               No        │
│       Low Limit:                               │
│ Limit Concurrent Connections:        No        │
│       Maximum Connections:                     │
│                                                │
│ Require Password:                    Yes       │
│       Minimum Password Length:       5         │
│ Force Periodic Password Changes:     Yes       │
│       Days Between Forced Changes:   90        │
│ Require Unique Passwords:            Yes        │
└──────────────────────────────────────────────┘
```

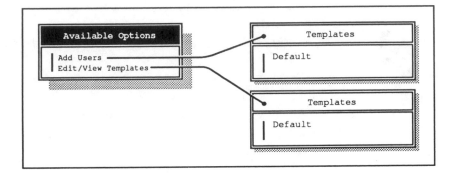

USERDEF limits the system manager to creating large groups of files using one template at a time, so the system manager can only create similar groups of users at the same time. MAKEUSER, on the other hand, provides the facility for changing configurations in mid-stream and creating all users from one script.

# Console Commands

AT THE BEGINNING OF this chapter, we defined console commands as advanced NetWare tools that provide customization of the network operating system. Console commands are advanced utilities that must be executed at the file server console. These tools can be very

*onsole com-
mands allow the
system manager to
perform a variety of
system adminis-
tration tasks.*

hazardous if not handled correctly, so please make sure to keep these console commands out of the reach of children and NetWare users.

Console commands allow the system manager to perform a variety of system administration tasks, including controlling the file servers, printers, and disk drives, sending messages, setting the server clock, and performing general control tasks. Some of the more popular console commands include MONITOR, BROADCAST, TIME, WATCHDOG, VAP, SPOOL, and, of course, DOWN. The syntax of console commands is relatively straightforward. The command itself is entered at the console prompt—a colon (:)—and various switches are displayed. Keep in mind that anybody with access to the file server console can execute a console command. This is a very good reason to limit access to the file server console and possibly to keep the file server itself under lock and key.

*Hesitancy in judgement is the only true mark of the thinker.*

*Dagobert D. Runes*

Console commands have a direct line to the operating system itself so they can perform customization of the file server code. For this reason (and the inherent lack of security), console commands are the most dangerous supervisor utilities. Let's begin with a detailed discussion of the twenty-two most popular NetWare 2.2 console commands.

*Study these advanced console commands for the CNA test: CONFIG, DISK, MONITOR, DISPLAY SERVERS, VAP, WATCHDOG, and TRACK ON/OFF.*

## BROADCAST

BROADCAST is a console command that is used to send a message of forty or fewer characters to all users who are currently logged in or attached to the file server. The BROADCAST console command syntax is BROADCAST [message in " "]. The messages users receive with the BROADCAST command are exactly the same as messages users receive with the SEND command—forty characters at the bottom of the screen with the prompt Press Control-Enter to clear. These messages will lock up the workstation until the user intervenes. Only users or workstations who are actually logged in to the system will receive the BROADCAST command. Any user who is attached to the file server's login directory will not receive that file server's BROADCAST message. Again, BROADCAST is used to send a simple message to all users in the network simultaneously.

All these console commands are internal operating system commands very similar to the DOS internal commands, and are built into the network operating system. The console commands are inherent to the operating system and therefore can only be executed at the console prompt.

## CLEAR MESSAGE

The CLEAR MESSAGE console command clears the messages from the message display area at the bottom of the file server console screen from within MONITOR. This command allows system managers to clear the message area without clearing the entire screen, and this can be useful in certain troubleshooting situations. The syntax is `CLEAR MESSAGE`.

## CLEAR STATION

The CLEAR STATION console command is a dramatic utility that allows the system manager (or anybody from the file server console) to abruptly clear a connection for a particular workstation. This command removes all file server resources from the workstation and can cause file corruption or data loss if executed while the workstation is processing transactions. This command is only useful in environments in which workstations have crashed or users have turned off their machines without logging out. In each of these particular instances, the connection would stay open even though the files are not currently being used.

The syntax for the CLEAR STATION command is `CLEAR STATION [number]`. The connection number for a specific workstation can be viewed from either the MONITOR console command or from FCONSOLE. This number is randomly allocated as workstations attach and is not the same from one session to another.

## CONFIG

The CONFIG console command is used to display the operating system's hardware configure information for all known internal components. CONFIG is useful not only for the NetWare file server but also for external dedicated routers. The type of information that is displayed using the CONFIG command includes the file server or router name, the number of service processes that have been defined, LAN network interface card configuration information and disk channel configuration information. The network interface card information includes the network address, the type of the card, the version of the shell, and the configuration settings including IRQ, I/O and memory address. The disk channel information includes the hardware type with the shell version information and the hardware settings including the I/O and the interrupt.

## DISABLE/ENABLE LOGIN

The DISABLE LOGIN and ENABLE LOGIN commands provide a feature for the NetWare system manager to use when troubleshooting or maintaining critical NetWare components. DISABLE LOGIN prevents anyone from logging in to the system from that point forward until login has been re-enabled. DISABLE LOGIN is particularly useful when system managers are working on the bindery, backing up files, loading software, or dismounting or repairing volumes. Keep in mind that DISABLE LOGIN does not affect users that are currently logged in until they log out. This command should only be used when it's absolutely necessary. The ENABLE LOGIN command enables logins for users that have been disabled. It also provides one other facility, the supervisor account, which can be reactivated if intruder detection/lockout has locked it. ENABLE LOGIN can only be used by supervisors to activate locked accounts.

The syntax for DISABLE LOGIN and ENABLE LOGIN is simply `DISABLE LOGIN` or `ENABLE LOGIN`.

## DISABLE/ENABLE TRANSACTIONS

DISABLE TRANSACTIONS and ENABLE TRANSACTIONS function similarly to DISABLE LOGIN and ENABLE LOGIN—except that instead of working on the user login, they work on NetWare's internal transactional tracking system. DISABLE TRANSACTIONS manually turns off the transactional tracking system until ENABLE TRANSACTIONS has been invoked. This command is particularly useful for application developers who are testing the performance or system fault tolerance functionality of transactional tracking when the tracking has been turned on and off.

## DISK

The DISK console command is used to monitor the status of internal file server disk drives. DISK provides a variety of different information about the status of particular drives, channels, controllers, and the hot fix redirection area. The DISK console command provides a matrix of drives and their particular interrupt values as well as the amount of hot fix redirection space that has been used. The following list shows all the information provided in the DISK table:

- The drive number assigned to NetWare

- The channel number that the disk controller is using

- The address set on the controller for the disk

- The disk address itself

- The status, which can be either OKAY (which means hot fix is running fine), NO HF (which means hot fix has been shut off), DOWN (which means the drive is not operating), M (for Mirrored), or D (for Duplexed but is not working)

- List of I/O errors (the number of input/output errors that have occurred on the drive)

- A list of the blocks free for the disk's redirection area

- A list of the number of blocks that have been used in the hot fix redirection area

The redirection information is particularly useful because as the number of used blocks increases, an indication is given that the drive is performing poorly. The DISK console command can also be followed by a volume name, which provides information about specific volumes.

## DISPLAY NETWORKS

DISPLAY NETWORKS is a particularly useful console command that provides data about all of the networks that the file server or router is currently aware of. A network consists of a unique network address cabling trunk, which is further interconnected to this particular file server or router as a network. The listing for DISPLAY NETWORKS can be seen in Figure 5.11 and provides three pieces of information. First, the network address (an eight-character hexadecimal number), followed by a number and slash (/), then another number. The first number preceding the slash is the number of hops or the number of networks that must be crossed to get from this particular file server to that network. The number following the slash is the estimated time in ticks that it would take for a packet to reach that particular network address from this server. (A tick is 1/18th of a second.)

*No brain is stronger than its weakest think.*

*Thomas L. Masson*

## DISPLAY SERVERS

DISPLAY SERVERS is similar to DISPLAY NETWORKS except that instead of displaying all of the networks a particular server or router knows of, it displays all of the *file servers*. DISPLAY SERVERS consists of two pieces of information: the file server name and the number of hops. The file server name is

**F I G U R E  5.11**
The layout of
DISPLAY NETWORKS

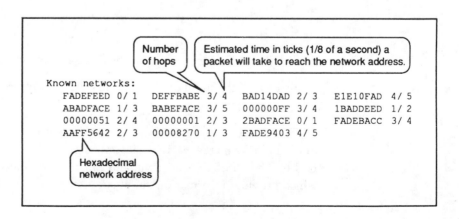

limited to the first twelve characters of the name in this particular utility. Keep in mind that a file server can have forty-five characters in its name. The output for DISPLAY SERVERS can be seen in Figure 5.12.

## DOWN

*The DOWN command is the most dramatic and harmful NetWare console command.*

The DOWN command is the most dramatic and harmful NetWare console command. It completely shuts down the file server activity and closes all open files. DOWN can be performed only from the console command, but keep in mind that the FCONSOLE supervisor utility provides its own internal downing feature. DOWN performs a variety of activities before it shuts down the operating system. First, it clears all the cache buffers and writes them to disk, and then it closes all open files. It then updates the appropriate directory and file allocation tables with the particular files that have been written to disk, dismounts all volumes, clears all connections, and finally shuts down the operating system. Once DOWN has been entered at the file server console prompt, the system responds with a command to turn off the system and turn it back on to reboot.

DOWN is particularly harmful because of its effect on maintenance background statistics. FCONSOLE relies heavily on background information and averages for providing information about statistics and file server fine tuning and performance. Once the system has been DOWNed, all these statistics are flushed and brought back to a default state. Obviously, the statistics are more meaningful the longer they're being measured.

**FIGURE 5.12**
The layout of
DISPLAY SERVERS

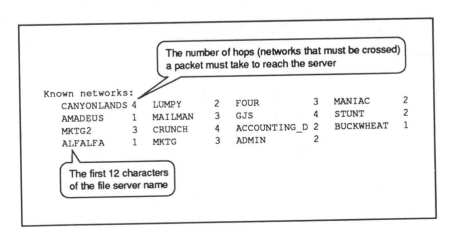

## MONITOR

MONITOR is the most popular console command because it provides a central screen for tracking file server activity, workstation connections, and who is logged in. The default monitor screen displays information on six blocks at one time, although it can support many more than that. In order to continue beyond the first six blocks, the system manager must type in `MONITOR [number]`. MONITOR also displays the operating system version, the percentage of file server utilization (updated every second), and the number of cache buffers that have been changed in memory but have not yet been written to disk. These are called *dirty cache buffers.*

Every time a workstation requests a transaction, MONITOR displays the file status message and up to five files that are being accessed. The file status message includes the following:

**PERS,** which indicates the file is logged but not locked, LOCK which indicates the file is locked

**A,** which indicates that the file server is running dedicated NetWare

**T,** which indicates that the file is flagged as transactional and is open

**H,** which indicates that the transactional file is on hold until the transaction is completed

This information is extremely useful for NetWare system managers who continually monitor file server performance for proactive maintenance strategies. Incidentally, the MONITOR console command in NetWare 3.12 is much more useful (and integrates both MONITOR and FCONSOLE) than NetWare 2.2.

## NAME

The NAME console command simply displays the name of the file server. It uses an underscore (_) to represent a space in the name. Remember, space is not a valid character. The file server name may range from two to forty-five characters.

## OFF

The OFF console command simply clears the file server console screen and conserves the file server monitor. The OFF command is not particularly useful when trying to monitor network activity, but it does provide a way of uncluttering the screen before you enter subsequent commands.

## PURGE

The PURGE utility is used to remove or completely erase all *salvageable* deleted files. In NetWare, when a user deletes a file, the system keeps track of the file and allows the user to recover it through the SALVAGE utility. These salvageable files take up space on the file server and create inefficiencies in disk access. The PURGE command, when entered at the console prompt, deletes all salvageable files from all volumes on the system and clears directory entry and file allocation tables. PURGE can be an effective strategy when file server disks become sluggish. Remember, the PURGE command is not selective—it purges everything or nothing.

## RESET ROUTER

The RESET ROUTER console command resets the file server or router table if it becomes inaccurate or corrupted. The router table is used by the filer server or router to recognize other servers and other networks and to send or receive packets between them. If any other servers, networks, or routers go down on the network, the packets will be lost and the router table will become inaccurate. In normal situations, the router table is updated every two minutes, but this time period could provide a window of errors. When the RESET ROUTER command is issued, the server (or router) sends out a service advertising packet (SAP), which advertises itself to all nearby file servers and networks. The networks then respond with information about their network address, their name, their location, and hops and ticks, which is then used to build a new router table. The syntax for RESET ROUTERS is `RESET ROUTER`.

## SET TIME

The SET TIME console command is used to set the time and the date that is kept by the file server. The syntax is SET TIME [month, day, year] [hour:minute:second]. You can enter the time in either standard or military format. If you use standard format, you may follow the time with AM or PM. The file server always displays the time in standard format. Date can be entered not only in month, day, and year, but also with numbers as well as letters in the format day, month, year. You can set the date and time separately by using two commands, or you can use them together by putting a space between them. To view the current file server date and time, simply enter the set time command without any parameters.

This console command is particularly useful for daylight saving time or when the file server clock slows down. Keep in mind, though, this can be a security risk for users who have access to the file server console, because many of the login restrictions are tied to the date. It's quite common for users whose accounts have expired to gain access to the file server console and change the filer server date, thereby granting themselves access to the system.

## SPOOL

The SPOOL command is used in NetWare 2.2 to list or change spooler assignments. A spooler assignment is necessary for the proper execution of NPRINT and CAPTURE printing utilities as well as compatibility with earlier versions of NetWare 2.x. Spooling will automatically redirect jobs from NetWare 2.0a file servers to the appropriate queue and printer. The SPOOL command by itself will list the current spooler assignments as well as the syntax for those assignments. To assign a specific printer to a specific queue, type SPOOL [printer number] to queue [queue name]. Spooler assignments are not required in NetWare 2.2. They are only recommended when the system exists with earlier versions of NetWare.

## TIME

The TIME command displays the file server's date and time. This command is the same as SET TIME, but without any parameters. TIME will not allow the system manager to alter the system date and time—it will simply allow him or her to display it.

## TRACK OFF/ON

The TRACK ON and TRACK OFF commands are used to display network service advertising packets as they are sent or received both from the file server and the router. The information is formatted according to whether the file server is receiving the information (in which it would be an IN), or broadcasting the information out to other networks. Figure 5.13 shows the format of the TRACK ON screen and provides information about the many different components that provide valuable information. These components include the sending file server's network address, node address, name, hops from that file server to this one, network addresses known by the sending file server, and the number of tics that a packet would take to get to this network from the sending file server or router. Issuing a TRACK ON command will open an auxiliary window or screen on the file server console (also known as the file server tracking screen), which will constantly display the information until the TRACK OFF command is issued. The TRACK ON command is particularly useful for system managers who are troubleshooting network connections or simply interested in what other networks or file servers exist out there.

**FIGURE 5.13**
The format of
TRACK ON

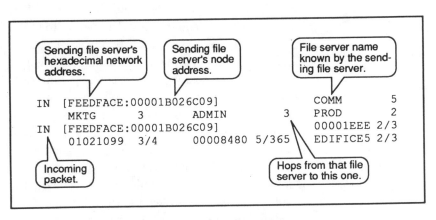

Server Information

## UPS

The UPS command is used to indicate the status of a connected uninterruptible power supply. This utility does not provide any functionality for editing the parameters of the UPS; it simply displays the status. Other uninterruptible power supply manufacturers provide software that works in conjunction with NetWare to provide what is called UPS monitoring. UPS monitoring sends a message to the file server when power falls below a particular threshold. The file server responds by sending a message to users, closing all open files, and downing the file server. This is done to avoid data corruption (which occurs when the file server's power is abruptly turned off or lost).

## VAP

System managers can use the VAP command to display a list of all value added processes that are currently loaded on the NetWare server. In addition, the VAP console command provides information about the VAP's parameters and customized commands. A value added process is a specialized network application that runs on the server (but not within the normal confines of the disk subsystem). VAP processes include printers, Macintosh connectivity, and UPS monitoring.

## WATCHDOG

*The WATCHDOG console command monitors file server connections for inactivity and lost connections.*

The WATCHDOG console command monitors file server connections for inactivity and lost connections. The syntax for WATCHDOG is `WATCHDOG START=[number] INTERVAL=[number] COUNT=[number]`. The START value defines how long the file server will wait to check a user's new connection. The default is 300 seconds (5 minutes). This value is specified in seconds with a minimum of 15 and a maximum of 1,200 or 20 minutes. The INTERVAL value is also specified in seconds with a minimum of 1 and a maximum of 600. The INTERVAL value specifies how often the system will monitor this particular connection. The default is 60 seconds. The COUNT value specifies the number of intervals after the start before it will clear an inactive connection. The minimum interval count value is 5; the maximum is 100. If all defaults are set and the WATCHDOG command is simply executed without any parameters, the system will wait 5 minutes after a new connection has arrived and then check the connection every minute for inactivity. If it finds inactivity of the connection, it will wait 10 intervals or 10 minutes before clearing the connection.

The WATCHDOG feature is important in NetWare 2.2 because it allows the system manager to automatically clear inactive connections that are reserving valuable NetWare licensing connections. Since NetWare is licensed for X number of connections, if users are turning off their machines without logging out, they are locking up valuable connections that others cannot use. In addition to users, there are other NetWare device components that use connections, including file servers, routers, and print servers.

That's it for NetWare console commands. These commands are part of the NetWare operating system and provide functionality for configuring or customizing the internal workings of NetWare. Console commands are entered at the file server console with no security and can therefore be quite dangerous. The only security against console commands is locking up the file server.

At the beginning of the chapter, we defined the NetWare system manager as a brave soul whose single task it is to keep peace in the NetWare castle. As the NetWare LANlord of his or her own apartment, the system manager's NetWare utility belt is his/her only defense against problems and user uprisings. The utility belt is composed of a variety of tools, including command line utilities, menu utilities, supervisor utilities, and console commands. In this chapter, we have explored the many different NetWare utilities and provided enough functionalities so that the system manager can fill his or her belt with the best tools available. Think of this chapter as an open tool chest providing everything you need to succeed in network management.

*My interest is in the future because I am going to spend the rest of my life there.*

*Charles F. Kettering*

*Think of this chapter as an open tool chest providing everything you need to succeed in network management.*

In the next chapter, we will explore network management in greater detail, discussing the specific tasks that the system manager must perform to fine-tune and optimize the user environment. Beyond creating users, directory structures, and drive mappings, the system manager must define login restrictions, create login scripts, install network applications, user interface, and workstation software, and perform routine NetWare backups. We will learn about all of these concepts in the next chapter. Get ready for the ultimate NetWare puzzle.

# NetWare 2.2 Network Management

*The network man-
agement phase
breathes life into an
otherwise limp and
lifeless LAN.*

N PREVIOUS CHAPTERS, I mentioned that the NetWare system manager inherits the LAN in the third of three construction phases: network management. The network management phase breathes life into an otherwise limp and lifeless LAN. The network designer and installation team leave you with wires, workstations, a file server, and some barely functional software. As the system manager, it is your responsibility to take this empty frame and fill it out with users, groups, applications, menu systems, security, login scripts, and system fault tolerance (SFT). Network management is the most challenging, exciting, and rewarding aspect of LAN construction. You can't imagine how lucky you are.

*It does not take much strength to do things, but it requires great strength
to decide on what to do.*

*Elbert Hubbard*

The world of NetWare network management is one big puzzle. At first, the NetWare components are scattered randomly throughout the LAN—users, workstations, software, and rights. None of it makes sense. But with a cool head and the right tools, the NetWare system manager can begin to arrange these puzzle pieces into a meaningful LAN picture.

- The directory structure is formed and drive mappings are created.

- Login names and passwords are assigned.

- Access rights take shape.

- Login restrictions are established.

- Numerous login scripts are written.

- Workstation software is installed.

- Application software is installed.

- The menu system is created.

- A tape backup system is established.

- The NetWare printing system is defined.

Just like any large puzzle, the organization of these many NetWare components can be overwhelming at first. But with a little patience and the right guidance, you will quickly get the hang of it. NetWare network management can really be a piece of cake. In this chapter, we will explore the network management puzzle pieces and learn how to organize them into a meaningful NetWare picture. The first three pieces from the list above were discussed in Chapter 3 and 4. The final piece, NetWare printing, will be covered in Chapter 7. *This* chapter focuses on the grunt work of NetWare network management—login restrictions, login scripts, the user interface, and NetWare backup.

 *All wish to possess knowledge, but few, comparatively speaking, are willing to pay the price.*

*Juvenal*

Clear off the table, this is going to be a BIG picture.

# NetWare Login Restrictions

N CHAPTER 4, WE discussed the three different layers of the NetWare security model. We learned that when a user logs into the system, his or her username is matched against a list of valid login names. If the username matches, the system asks for a valid password. If the password matches, the user is granted preliminary access to the LAN. He/she is not yet at the NetWare prompt. There is one more door to pass through—login restrictions. Login restrictions provide a final level of login/password security, which allows the LAN locksmith to restrict user access according to four different categories:

- account restrictions
- time restrictions
- station restrictions
- intruder detection/lockout

Account restrictions apply to user accounts and password/data restrictions. Time restrictions and station restrictions apply to login times and workstation locations. Intruder detection/lockout is a NetWare v2.2 feature which tracks invalid login attempts and locks out unauthorized users. Each of these puzzle pieces is an important component in the overall security picture. Let's begin with account restrictions.

 *This is a more detailed discussion of the second layer of NetWare's four-layered security model. Refer to Chapter 4 for an in-depth discussion of the other three layers.*

## Account Restrictions

NetWare account restrictions provide a method for controlling and restricting user access to the NetWare file server. They are established in two different ways:

- *Default Account Balance/Restrictions* in Supervisor Options of SYSCON
- *Account Balance/Restrictions* in User Information of SYSCON

Default account restrictions establish configurations for all new users and are defined in the Supervisor Options screen of SYSCON. User-specific account restrictions establish configurations for individual users and are defined in the user's specific User Information window of SYSCON. Default restrictions only take effect for users created from this point on—they do not affect current users. For this reason, you should define the default account restrictions *before* you create any users.

*Default account restrictions take effect for all users who are created after the restrictions are put in place. These restrictions will not take effect for any users who currently exist.*

*Good news. There's a little trick that can save you hours of work if you get caught in the trap described above. To configure login restrictions for large numbers of users, simply highlight those users with the F5 key in the User Information window of SYSCON. Press Enter. The Set User Information screen will appear with four choices—Account Balance, Account Restrictions, Station Restrictions, and Time Restrictions. Simply define the appropriate restrictions and they will take effect for all highlighted users. Whew, that saved a ton of time. Good thing you read this tip.*

NetWare's Account Restrictions screen (Figure 6.1) provides a variety of different options for NetWare system managers. Below is a brief discussion of each of these options.

*Study Figure 6.1. It provides a great summary of the main NetWare 2.2 login restrictions.*

**FIGURE 6.1**
Suggested default
account restrictions
in SYSCON

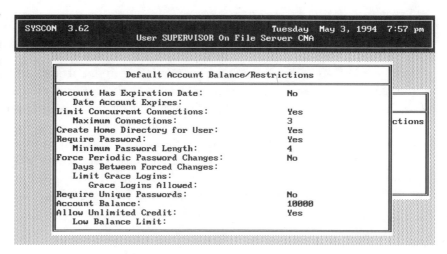

### Account Expiration Date

Account Expiration Date is a useful tool for temporary employees or students in an academic environment. It allows the system manager to lock an account after a specific date. By default, the Account Expiration Date is set to NO. If you change the value to YES, today's date will appear as the default Date the Account Expires. You can change the date at any time; keep in mind that the account locks at midnight.

### Limit Concurrent Connections

Limiting concurrent connections is useful against users who like to migrate throughout the LAN or login from multiple workstations. The system manager can limit a user's concurrent connections by changing the default from NO to YES (by default, Limit Current Connections is set to NO), then configuring Maximum Connections for 3. Three concurrent connections means that this user can login from only three workstations simultaneously. This particular account restriction works in conjunction with station restrictions. You can enhance a user's concurrent connection limitation by combining it with a specific physical workstation limitation—station restrictions (we'll discuss station restrictions a little later). A good average setting is YES, limit current connections, and set the maximum connections to 3. If you set this in the default account restrictions, it will take effect for all users created beyond this point.

### Create Home Directory for User

Create Home Directory for User is an important part of the network management puzzle because it defines a home area for each user (by default this option is set to YES). This home area is used by many other configurations, including drive mappings, login scripts, and trustee assignments. User drive mappings are created in the system login script with an identifier variable called %LOGIN_NAME. This identifier variable will create a home directory mapping for all users based on what their unique login name is. However, this only works if a home directory exists for each user.

### Require Password

Password restrictions are applied using the Require Password and other related restrictions. By default, the system does not require a password. This is a huge oversight. I recommend that you require a password for all users and that you set the minimum password length to something in excess of five characters.

*There is a password-hacking routine that can guess any five-character password in less than 20 minutes. The program connects directly to the NetWare bindery and matches random character combinations with existing password information. So if your minimum password length is four characters or less, this program can break into the system very, very quickly.*

### Force Periodic Password Changes

*I recommend that you require a password for all users and that you set the minimum password length to something in excess of five characters.*

Once a password has been required and the suggested minimum password length of seven characters has been set, you should explore using the Force Periodic Password Changes account restriction. This restriction forces users to change their password at periodic intervals. If you set Force Periodic Password Changes to YES, the system will ask you to input the days between forced changes. The default is forty-five days—this is a little short and can become a nuisance very quickly. A periodic password interval of ninety days is optimal.

Once a password interval has expired, the user must change his/her password. If the user does not change his/her password at the point of login, the system will lock the account. This is where *grace logins* come in. Grace logins allow the user to log in without changing the password. Keep in mind this is a temporary situation because even grace logins expire. Seven grace logins is ideal for most users. Once a user logs in for the seventh time and chooses not to change his/her password, the account is locked. Locked accounts can only be unlocked by the supervisor. So who unlocks the supervisor's account? Stay tuned for the answer.

*When the periodic password interval has expired, the system will respond with* Your password has expired. Would you like to change it now? *This gives users an opportunity to change their passwords right away. Otherwise, users can use SETPASS or SYSCON to change their passwords at any time.*

### Require Unique Passwords

Require Unique Passwords works in conjunction with forcing periodic password changes. When the periodic password interval expires and the user is required to change his/her password, Unique Passwords forces him/her to enter a new, *different* password. If the system manager takes the time and effort to make the users change their passwords periodically, it makes sense that those passwords should be unique each time. It does not make sense for the user to continually use the same password.

*Requiring unique passwords relies on an internal NetWare password table. The table keeps track of each user's previous ten passwords. The user can in fact reuse the eleventh previous (and older) password.*

### Account Balance

Account balance restrictions apply to NetWare's internal accounting feature. NetWare has a built-in accounting feature that tracks user logins, logouts, and access to network resources. The system manager can install accounting through the SYSCON menu utility. In addition, he/she can use SYSCON to define network resources and establish charge rates for access to those resources. Account balance is a dynamic measure of each user's accounting usage.

By default, the account balance is set to 0 and unlimited credit is set to NO. This is a problem because once the system manager installs accounting, users begin accumulating resource charges—the account balance is immediately negative. If the low balance limit is set to 0, users are instantly in violation of NetWare accounting. Once a user's account balance becomes negative, the system locks their account—they can no longer log in. So it is very important to set the account balance to at least 1,000 when you decide to install accounting. Low balance limit refers to the number that, when reached, locks the user out. Typically, an account balance of 1,000 (depending on the charge rates) and a low balance limit of 0 is optimal. It's not a good idea to set unlimited credit because that defeats the whole purpose of charging for resources.

Another interesting use of NetWare accounting in NetWare 2.2 is resource tracking. Instead of charging users for their specific resource usage, you can use accounting to track how users are accessing resources—by setting the Allow Unlimited Credit to YES and setting the account balance to 0 and the low balance limit to 0. Then you charge each user a rate of 1 unit per usage on each of the five different resources. The five different resources that can be tracked are:

- time usage
- blocks written
- disk space
- blocks read
- processor utilization

By setting each of these resource charge rates at 1, you can compare how users are using your LAN resources (you can match their time utilization with processor utilization to see if they are really working, for example). By setting the Allow Unlimited Credit to YES, you are allowing the number to go well below 0, and users will quickly accumulate a negative balance. The number that appears in their negative account balance under User Information exactly correlates with their use of NetWare resources. While NetWare does not inherently support any kind of auditing feature or resource tracking feature, clever and creative use of NetWare accounting can provide the same functionality.

## Limit Server Disk Space

*Users can be restricted to specific amounts of disk space on the shared server disk.*

Users can be restricted to specific amounts of disk space on the shared server disk. NetWare tracks disk space by who owns (created) what. Also, if you copy a file, ownership is transferred to the destination user. If Limit Server Disk Space is set to YES, the system will ask for a maximum server disk space parameter in kilobytes. Typically, this parameter works in deterring disk abuse. Also, in academic environments, it's a good idea to limit students so they don't clutter the disk with games and miscellaneous utilities. (Unless, of course, they give you a copy of the game.) A good value for limiting server disk space is 1,000 kilobytes, or 1 megabyte.

The next three login restrictions are time restrictions, station restrictions, and intruder detection lockout. They provide a certain level of login security though not near the flexibility or versatility of account balance restrictions. Let's take a quick look at them.

*The wisest man has something yet to learn.*

*George Santayana*

## Time Restrictions

Time restrictions are useful because they allow you to control how much time users have access to the system. As with account restrictions, time restrictions can be applied as a default at the user level. Remember that default time restrictions only take effect for users who are created from this point forward. Time restrictions are valuable when they are configured intelligently. But when configured carelessly, they can dramatically hinder user performance and productivity.

The default time-restriction screen (Figure 6.2) is a matrix of days and time periods. The days of the week, Sunday through Saturday, are displayed on the left-hand side of the matrix, and a 24-hour clock, in half-hour increments, is displayed across the top. Each asterisk in the system indicates a time

**F I G U R E  6.2**
Default time
restrictions in SYSCON

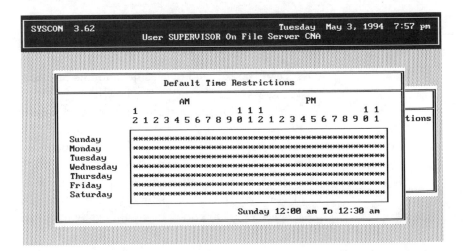

*Time restrictions are effective in protecting against mild-mannered janitors who turn into superhackers at midnight or users who spend too much time in front of the computer.*

period during which this particular user or all users can log in. By default, the Time Restriction screen has all asterisks—all users can log in at any time. To restrict users, simply move the cursor to a particular point in time and press the spacebar. This blanks the time period and makes it unavailable for user access.

Some common time restrictions include:

**Restrict entire days**—weekends, for example

**Restrict evenings**—10:00 PM to 5:00 AM

**Restrict backup time periods**—11:00 PM to midnight

These are effective strategies for protection against mild-mannered janitors who turn into superhackers at midnight or users who spend too much time in front of the computer. Keep in mind that time restrictions are dynamic—once the user enters a blank time period, the system clears your connection. Don't worry, there is a five-minute warning before the connection is cleared.

*When a time restriction is encountered and a user connection is cleared, the system does not perform a proper logout—it simply clears the workstation connection. But watch out—files are not saved. When the system prompts you with a five minute message, it's a good idea to pay attention and log out.*

The F5 key allows you to highlight blocks of time and press the asterisk key to insert an available time slot or the spacebar to restrict that time slot. Remember, intelligent time restrictions increase network security, while careless ones significantly hinder user productivity.

## Station Restrictions

Station restrictions are another effective way to control user access. But this time, you're not restricting user access with passwords, disk restrictions, or time slots. Instead, you're restricting the physical workstation users log in from.

Here's how it works: each workstation is equipped with an internal network interface card. The card has a 12-digit hexadecimal node address that is programmed at the factory. This node address is unique for all network interface cards in the world and is used by the cabling media to identify each network interface card on the LAN. The node address can also be used to identify which users can log in from which machines. In a certain sense, it can be said that the user is logically attached to a specific network interface card.

Because station restrictions are linked so closely to the user and node address, there is no such thing as default station restrictions. It wouldn't make sense to restrict all users on the network to a particular node address. If you did, all users in the network would have to log in from the same workstation. Massive gridlock!

Station restrictions are configured for specific users in the User Information screen of SYSCON. To define a station restriction for a given user, the system manager must provide two pieces of information: network address and node address. The network address defines the cabling scheme on which the workstation is attached. The node address is a 12-digit hexadecimal number that identifies the workstation network interface card. Unfortunately, this information is not readily available to NetWare system managers. The only easy way to access this information is with the USERLIST utility. USERLIST provides a list of all users currently logged in and the station addresses of the machines they are using. The best strategy is to print out a USERLIST and use the information in SYSCON to establish station restrictions.

Station restrictions are another example of how login restrictions can be used to enhance access security but—if abused or mishandled—can significantly impede user productivity. If station restrictions are set to only one workstation and that workstation is down or busy, he or she cannot log in from any other workstation. While station restrictions are a useful security tool, they can be detrimental to user relationships.

*Intruder detection/lockout tracks invalid login attempts by monitoring users who try to log in without correct passwords.*

## Intruder Detection/Lockout

Intruder detection/lockout is not so much a restriction as it is a security tracking feature. Intruder detection/lockout tracks invalid login attempts by monitoring users who try to log in without correct passwords. The Intruder detection/lockout feature keeps track of invalid password attempts and locks a user account once the threshold number of attempts has been exceeded— usually three. Intruder detection/lockout is a system-wide configuration—it is either activated for all users or none.

By default, Intruder Detection/Lockout (Figure 6.3) is set to NO. You can choose Intruder Detection/Lockout from the Supervisor Option screen of SYSCON. Intruder detection/lockout has two components: intruder detection and account lockout. Let's look at each one in detail.

### Intruder Detection

Intruder detection is activated as soon as a valid user logs in with an incorrect password. The incorrect login attempt threshold feature keeps track of the number of invalid passwords entered for the same user. As soon as the number exceeds the incorrect login attempt threshold, the system activates account lockout. The bad login count retention time is a window of opportunity, so to speak, that the system uses to count the incorrect login attempts. Here's how it works:

- Assume Incorrect Login Attempts is set to 7 and Bad Login Account Retention Time is set to 24 hours. The system will track all incorrect login activity and lock the user account if the number of incorrect login attempts exceeds 7 in a 24-hour window.

**FIGURE 6.3**
Intruder
detection/lockout

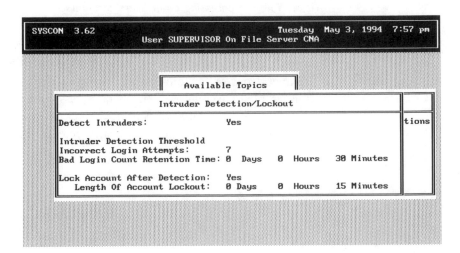

### Account Lockout

Account lockout is activated when the intruder detection threshold is exceeded and account lockout is set to YES. It doesn't make much sense to activate intruder detection/lockout without initiating a user lockout once the intruder detection threshold is exceeded. By setting the lock account after detection to YES, the system asks for a length of account lockout, the time period that the account is locked once account lockout is activated. By default, this value is set to 15 minutes, which doesn't make much sense because it invites the hacker to come back 15 minutes later and try all over again. Typically a value equal to or exceeding the bad login account retention time is adequate.

*The most common target for NetWare hackers is the supervisor. If intruder detection/lockout is activated and users try to access the supervisor account more than 7 times with an incorrect password, the system will lock the supervisor account. This is particularly disconcerting—especially because the supervisor is the only user who can unlock NetWare accounts. Fortunately, NetWare has incorporated a console command (called ENABLE LOGIN) that resets the Supervisor account.*

*When the supervisor unlocks a user account, he/she performs this function in the User Information screen of SYSCON. The Intruder/Detection Lockout screen displays the node ID of the last station that attempted an incorrect login. This is useful information if you have a problem with particular users who are accessing other users' accounts.*

That's it for login restrictions. In this section, we learned about the various account restrictions, time restrictions, station restrictions, and NetWare's intruder detection/lockout feature. These restrictions, when used in coordination with login/password security and access rights, can create a very effective security strategy for the NetWare LAN locksmith.

The next piece of our network management puzzle is login scripts.

# Login Scripts

L OGIN SCRIPTS ARE EXECUTED once a user passes through the many layers of NetWare security and becomes an active player in the LAN. Login scripts are very useful tools in customizing user environments. If you think back for a moment to our discussion of drive mappings, you'll remember that they are temporary user mappings that point to specific areas of the shared disk. Drive mappings are activated (defined) each time a user logs in. Login scripts allow the system to establish and define custom user configurations and are transparent to the user.

Login scripts are batch files for the network. As the NetWare system manager, it is your responsibility to create login scripts that are both productive and easy to maintain. NetWare provides three different types of login scripts:

**The system login script** provides user configurations and system-wide drive mappings for everybody who logs into the network.

**The user login script** is a user-specific script that provides user-customized configurations (each user executes his/her own script).

**The default login script** executes when there is no user script. The default login script contains minimum drive mappings and system configurations.

*A well-designed and well-written login script can save the system manager literally hours of individual configuration. I highly recommend that you make use of this particular NetWare tool for decreasing your maintenance load and increasing your general quality of life.*

*Ability is of little account without opportunity.*

*Napoleon Bonaparte*

## Login Script Types

All three login scripts work together to provide system-wide drive mappings and user-specific customization. In this section, we will explore the details of the three login script types. In addition, we'll bolster our NetWare holster with a comprehensive understanding of NetWare login script commands and their syntax. Let's take a closer look.

### System Login Script

The system login script provides a facility for system-wide drive mappings. The system login script is executed by all users as soon as they log in. This script can only be created and edited by the supervisor—under the Supervisor Options menu of SYSCON. The system login script is a special text file—NET$LOG.DAT. It is stored in the SYS:PUBLIC directory so all users can access it. The system login script file must consist of valid login script commands and be organized according to NetWare login script syntax and conventions.

### User Login Script

The user login script is a user-specific script. It provides customization at the user level. The supervisor can use this script to further customize user parameters beyond the system login script. The user login script typically contains user-definable drive mappings and commands that are customized for particular individuals. While the user script is a nice feature, it can quickly become a maintenance nightmare (imagine hundreds and hundreds of user login scripts to constantly maintain). The user login script is the text file LOGIN in each user's unique SYS:MAIL\userid directory. In our discussion of directory structures, we talked about a system-generated series of user directories under SYS:MAIL. This subdirectory is used to store user-specific configuration files like the user login script.

*The intelligent system manager can create an effective system login script that makes user login scripts obsolete. This is ideal because it provides the flexibility of user customization while retaining the ease of maintenance and centralization of one system script. Try as hard as you can to fit all of your login script commands into one system login script.*

### Default Login Script

*The default login script contains some basic mappings for the system and a COMSPEC command which points to the appropriate network DOS directory.*

The default login script is activated only when a user login script doesn't exist. The default login script contains some basic mappings for the system and a COMSPEC command that points to the appropriate network DOS directory. The default login script cannot be edited because it exists as part of the LOGIN.EXE system file. The default login script was created and is maintained by the NetWare system and therefore cannot be edited, modified, or deleted.

Earlier we learned that the ideal scenario is to have a system login script with no user login script. In this particular case, the default login script would execute after the system login script. The downside is that the default login script contains specific system-wide mappings that stomp all over the already-created system login script mappings. This is not good.

There are a variety of different ways to remedy this situation. One of which is to create a user login script with just one line. While this is an effective strategy, it doesn't make sense because it defeats the purpose of having one centrally located login script. The best strategy, however, is to employ the EXIT command and bypass the default login script. We will discuss this scenario later in the section.

### Login Script Execution

Login script execution plays a critical role in the effectiveness of NetWare login scripts. It's important to have a firm understanding of how the different login scripts relate to one another and how they are executed. The system login script executes first and contains system-wide configurations. If a user login script exists, the user login script will execute after the system login script. Once the user login script has been executed, the system will return to the NetWare prompt, at which point the user has control of the system. If a user login script does not exist, the system will automatically execute the default login script (which is part of the LOGIN.EXE file). The default login script will also execute when no system or user login script exists, typically the case when the system is first created.

Again, the ideal scenario is one system login script and no user or default script. We'll talk about how to do this in just a moment.

## Login Script Commands

*Identifier variables are extremely useful login script components that provide diverse customization. The idea is to establish one login script command that serves a variety of different users.*

Login scripts consist of commands and identifiers—just like any other program or batch file. A NetWare login script—whether it's a system, user, or default script—must comprise valid login script commands and recognizable identifier variables. In addition, the script must follow valid syntax and conventions. The syntax for login script programming is quite simple—each line begins with a login script command and must contain either an identifier variable or a fixed value. For example, consider the following line:

```
MAP F:=SYS:\USERS\%LOGIN_NAME
```

This follows login script syntax because it contains the login script command MAP and the login script identifier variable %LOGIN_NAME. Identifier variables are extremely useful login script components that provide diverse customization. The idea is to establish one login script command that serves a variety of different users. For example, the %LOGIN_NAME identifier variable will return the value of each user's login name, depending on who logs in. This is particularly useful for mapping user directories in a system login script. Remember, the ideal scenario is to have one login script that customizes both system-wide and user-specific environment variables. This is made possible through the use of identifier variables. Figure 6.4 shows a detailed list of all of the NetWare 2.2 identifier variables. Some of the more useful login script identifier variables include the following:

- MEMBER_OF_GROUP

- DAY

- DAY_OF_WEEK

- YEAR

- GREETING_TIME

- FULL_NAME

- LOGIN_NAME

- USER_ID

- MACHINE_OS

- OS_VERSION

FIGURE 6.4
NetWare 2.2
identifier variables

| | Identifier variable | Description |
|---|---|---|
| Conditional | ACCESS_SERVER | Returns TRUE if Access Server is Functional, otherwise FALSE |
| | ERROR_LEVEL | An Error Number, 0=No Errors |
| | MEMBER OF *"group"* | Returns TRUE if member of group, otherwise FALSE |
| Date | DAY | Day number (01-31) |
| | DAY_OF_WEEK | Day of week (Monday, Tuesday, etc.) |
| | MONTH | Month number (01-12) |
| | MONTH_NAME | Month name (January, June, etc.) |
| | NDAY_OF_WEEK | Weekday number (1-7, Sunday=1) |
| | SHORT_YEAR | Year in short format (88, 89, etc.) |
| | YEAR | Year in full format (1988, 1989) |
| DOS Environment | < > | Use any DOS environment variable as a string |
| Network | NETWORK_ADDRESS | Network number of the cabling system (8 hex digits) |
| | FILE_SERVER | Name of the file server |
| Time | AM_PM | Day or night (am or pm) |
| | GREETING_TIME | Morning, afternoon, or evening |
| | HOUR | Hour of day or night (1-12) |
| | HOUR24 | Hour (00-23, midnight = 00) |
| | MINUTE | Minute (00-59) |
| | SECOND | Second (00-59) |
| User | FULL_NAME | User's full name (from SYSCON files) |
| | LOGIN_NAME | User's unique login name |
| | USER_ID | Number assigned to each user |
| Workstation | MACHINE | The machine the shell was written for, e.g., IBMPC |
| | OS | The workstation's operating system, e.g., MSDOS |
| | OS_VERSION | The version of the workstation's DOS |
| | P_STATION | Station number or node address (12 hex digits) |
| | SMACHINE | Short machine name, e.g., IBM |
| | STATION | Connection number |

Identifier variables are preceded by a % sign and must be capitalized. In order to be an effective system manager and create productive NetWare login scripts, you must have a firm understanding of all of the login script commands and how they are used in system, user, and default login scripts. In the remainder of this section we will focus on the fourteen most recognizable NetWare 2.2 login script commands. In addition, we will discuss how they are used to optimize the system and user environment. Remember, our focus in this section is to create one system login script that can satisfy both our system-wide and user-specific needs.

*Study the following login script commands very carefully. You never know when you might need them.*

### COMSPEC

COMSPEC (COMmand SPECifier) is a very important login script command. It redirects the DOS COMMAND.COM file to the appropriate NetWare DOS directory. Redirection is required because as applications load into workstation memory, they have a tendency to knock the COMMAND .COM file out of RAM. If an application loads itself and unloads the COMMAND.COM file, the system has to know where to go to find the COMMAND.COM file. That's where COMSPEC comes in; it tells NetWare where to find COMMAND.COM. Without it, users will receive the message `Invalid COMMAND.COM` or `COMMAND.COM cannot be found` or `Insert boot disk in drive A`. This can be quite disruptive to users in a network environment.

COMSPEC is important because it tells the system where to look for the appropriate COMMAND.COM. Keep in mind that each version of DOS on each of your workstations supports a different type of COMMAND.COM. You must use the DOS directory structure we discussed earlier to store the different COMMAND.COM files. In addition, you should use a drive mapping—typically S2—to make them easier to find. There are three identifier variables that allow us to map the appropriate search drive to the appropriate DOS subdirectory based on which machine was used, a very effective strategy when used in combination with the COMSPEC command. We will talk about these identifier variables and mapping DOS directories later when we get to the MAP command. At this point, it is important to note that COMSPEC is an important login script command that provides support for COMMAND .COM redirection. The syntax for COMSPEC is `COMSPEC S2: COMMAND.COM`.

Remember, COMMAND.COM must follow the appropriate drive pointer—S2 in most cases. Refer to the MAP command later in this section for a discussion of S2, COMSPEC, and DOS.

## DISPLAY/FDISPLAY

The DISPLAY and FDISPLAY login script commands allow the system manager to display a text file as soon as users reach a certain point in the login process. The text file is displayed on the screen in its most simple format, without any control codes or formatting characters. If a text file contains control codes and formatting characters, the DISPLAY command will display those characters as ASCII bullets. This can be distracting for users who see garbage all over the screen. The FDISPLAY command will filter these types of text files and won't display control codes—the characters are filtered out and only the text is displayed. The syntax of DISPLAY and FDISPLAY are identical:

```
DISPLAY textfile
```

When the login script execution comes to this particular line, it goes out and finds the selected text file. Then it displays it on the screen. This particular command is especially useful when used in combination with the PAUSE command, which allows the system to pause execution until a key is pressed. This allows users to see the text file as it is displayed on the screen. Without the PAUSE command, the text display will go by on the screen very quickly.

## DRIVE

The DRIVE command is a useful login script command that allows the system manager to specify where NetWare should leave the user once the login script has executed. By default, the system will leave the user at the first available network drive—typically F. This can be confusing because F is usually mapped to LOGIN, and the users will think, "Wow, I've already logged in. Why am I back here?" The DRIVE command is an effective strategy for leaving users in their own home area—the system manager can accomplish this by typing `DRIVE U:`. Again, this strategy assumes you've set up a home directory for each user and it specifies the U: drive.

DRIVE can also be useful if you are going to use the EXIT command to exit to a menu program at the end of login script execution. The menu program typically will be stored either in a public place—Z:—or in each user's own subdirectory—U:. The DRIVE command can be used preceding the EXIT command. This will dump the user in the directory where the menu command is to be executed.

## EXIT

The EXIT command is a very useful login script command that provides a number of functions. EXIT terminates the login script and executes a specific network program. The network program can be any .EXE, .COM, or .BAT file and must reside in the default drive. When used in combination with the DRIVE command, EXIT can be an effective strategy for creating a transparent turnkey system whereby users log in and are left within a menu system. The syntax for the EXIT command is relatively simple: EXIT "name of program file".

It is important to note that the program inside the quotes can only be a maximum of fourteen characters long. Some system managers find this to be a harsh limitation because they might want to execute a particular program name with many switches. To remedy this situation, you can exit to a batch file, which then performs the appropriate program commands and switches.

*If the EXIT command is included in the system login script, it will skip the user and default login script. While this is an effective strategy, it is also very dangerous. Keep in mind that the EXIT statement in the system login script will bypass any user login scripts—past, present, or future.*

## FIRE PHASERS

FIRE PHASERS is a fun command that emits an ear-piercing *Star Trek*-like phaser sound from the workstation. FIRE PHASERS is a useful strategy in cases where text is displayed on screen and you want to draw users' attention to the screen. FIRE PHASERS can also be used in cases where you feel there is a breach in security. The syntax for FIRE PHASERS is simply FIRE [number].

The maximum number of phasers that can be fired in one command is 9—a 1-digit number limitation. For instance, FIRE 39 would fire 3 times because 3 is the first character found. If you would like to fire phasers more than 9 times, you can simply nest multiple fire commands—one after another. There is no limit to the number of FIRE PHASERS commands you can have in a row, although it can get quite annoying.

*Big shots are only little shots who keep shooting.*

*Christopher Morley*

## IF…THEN

The IF…THEN command is probably the most versatile login script command and provides for script programming logic. IF…THEN checks a given condition and executes your command only if the condition is met. Otherwise, the IF…THEN skips the conditional command. For example, if you would like the system to display a message and fire phasers on each person's birthday, you can use the date identifier variables and the IF…THEN command to search for a specific date. This is also useful in displaying text messages on Fridays or Tuesdays, whenever there are staff meetings, or if a report is due at the end of the week.

IF…THEN is also useful in customizing group login scripts. Because there is no facility for group login scripts, the IF…THEN command can be used with the MEMBER_OF_GROUP identifier variable to configure specific drive mappings and configurations for groups of users. The IF…THEN command in combination with all of the many different identifier variables makes it possible for the intelligent system manager to create one system login script that satisfies all user-specific customization needs.

If multiple activities are dependent on a condition, NetWare provides the BEGIN and END commands in conjunction with IF…THEN. This allows the system manager to create groups of conditional commands. For example:

```
IF DAY_OF_WEEK = "FRIDAY" THEN BEGIN
   WRITE "Welcome to Friday. Glad you could make it"
   DISPLAY Friday.txt
   MAP R:=SYS:DATA\REPORTS
END
```

This is effective in adding complexity to the login script programming. Keep in mind that NetWare 2.2 does not support any nested IF…THEN statements.

### INCLUDE

The INCLUDE login script command is provided for cases where one login script isn't enough. The INCLUDE statement branches to a DOS text file that is written using proper login script conventions. INCLUDE will execute the text file as if it were a login script. Once the INCLUDE statement is finished, the original login script continues from the point of the INCLUDE statement. This is useful, particularly when used in combination with IF...THEN to provide customization for specific users and groups.

### MAP

MAP is the most widely used user-specific configuration. Mapping is a very important part of NetWare navigation and provides a facility for representing large directory paths as drive letters. The problem with mapping is that it's both session-specific (meaning drive pointers disappear when users log out), and user-specific (meaning they're unique for each user). The temporary nature of drive mappings makes them particularly annoying—the complex map commands must be entered each time a user logs in. Fortunately, Net-Ware provides a facility for mapping automation: the system login script.

MAP commands are entered at the very top of the system login. Also, network mappings are typically activated before search drive mappings—search mappings are a lot more friendly in their acquisition of drive letters. All MAP commands work in login scripts except the MAP NEXT command, which can only be used at the NetWare prompt. The default login script includes two MAP commands:

```
MAP S1:=SYS:PUBLIC
MAP S2:=SYS:PUBLIC\%MACHINE\%OS\%OS_VERSION
```

Earlier we mentioned the importance of having different DOS versions in the network directory structure. This is to provide workstation access to the appropriate COMMAND.COM. The MAP S2 command, in conjunction with three identifier variables, allows us to intelligently MAP the appropriate DOS directory for the appropriate version of workstation DOS. The above S2 command uses three different identifier variables:

**%MACHINE** identifies the machine type. IBM_PC for example

**%OS** identifies the operating system. MS-DOS for example

**%OS_VERSION** identifies the DOS version. V5.00 for example

This one command in the system login script satisfies the COMSPEC requirement for all users on all workstations using all versions of DOS. Remember to put the correct COMMAND.COM file in each %OS_VERSION directory. Also, be very precise about the directory structure you created—it must match the parameters exactly.

## PASSWORD_EXPIRES

NetWare 2.2 introduces a new login script parameter called PASSWORD _EXPIRES, which is not really a command but more like an identifier variable (proceeded by a %). PASSWORD_EXPIRES is used in coordination with the IF...THEN command to provide a facility for letting users know when their password is on the verge of expiration. This is particularly useful when the Periodic Password restriction is set and users are forced to enter a unique password. The syntax for PASSWORD_EXPIRES is

```
IF PASSWORD_EXPIRES = VALUE "4" THEN BEGIN
   WRITE "Your password expires in 4 days"
   WRITE "You better run SETPASS sometime soon"
END
```

or

```
WRITE "Your password expires in %PASSWORD_EXPIRES
   days."
```

This provides a proactive strategy for system managers who are having problems with grace login abuse. A friendly reminder never hurts.

## PAUSE

The PAUSE command pauses execution of the login script at a certain point and asks the workstation user to `Press a key to continue`. This is useful in combination with the DISPLAY and FDISPLAY commands so large messages can be displayed one screenful at a time.

### REMARK

REMARK allows comments and documentation to be placed in the login script—without generating an error. Besides the word REMARK, NetWare 2.2 supports three other uses of the REMARK command: REM, an asterisk (*), and a semicolon (;). Any text preceded by REMARK is ignored by the system. This is an effective way to track script editing when you have multiple supervisors maintaining the system login script. This is also useful for documenting large login scripts for system managers who follow you.

*When these system login scripts get quite large and complex, it is very hard to follow exactly what is going on. Novell, for example, in their international headquarters, has a login script that supports the whole organization—it exceeds seventeen pages. This system login script must be highly documented so people can follow exactly what's going on and how it's being implemented.*

### WRITE

The WRITE command allows you to display any message on the screen. Any comment enclosed in quotes following the WRITE command is displayed during the appropriate point in login script execution. WRITE can display information not only in a text nature but can also display identifier variable type information. For example, WRITE can display:

- WRITE "Your username is %LOGIN_NAME"

- WRITE "Your workstation number is %STATION"

- WRITE "Your DOS version is %OS_VERSION"

- WRITE "Today is %DAY_OF_WEEK"

Another interesting identifier variable used with WRITE is GREETING _TIME. GREETING_TIME will return a value of "Morning," "Afternoon," or "Evening," depending on the time of day. The following WRITE command provides a nice greeting to all users:

```
WRITE "Good %GREETING_TIME, %LOGIN_NAME"
```

*Personality is to a man what perfume is to a flower.*

*Charles M. Schwab*

### # (DOS Executable)

The DOS executable (# sign) command is extremely detrimental in ANY login script. It has been included by Novell in a last-ditch effort to support commands outside the login script. But watch out—it can cause more harm than good. Any non-login script command preceded by the # can be executed from within a login script. The problem is that while the command is running, the entire login script is stored in workstation RAM. Once the # command is finished, NetWare reloads the login script from memory, but many workstations do not completely free up the workstation RAM that was occupied by the login script temporarily. In many cases, as much as 70 to 100K of workstation RAM can be lost when using the #.

A more effective way of executing non-login script commands is the EXIT command. It is a good idea to use the EXIT command and execute a batch file at the end of the login script. This will remove the login script from memory and execute any list of non-login script commands from within a batch file.

*The CAPTURE command is a critical component in NetWare printing and needs to be executed at startup.*

That completes our discussion of NetWare login scripts. Keep in mind, login scripts are very effective tools for customizing user workstation environments and providing system-wide drive mappings. A well-designed system login script can save hours of maintenance for the NetWare system manager. Once you have the login script puzzle piece in place, the picture should start to take form. At this point, you have established a NetWare directory structure, drive mappings, access rights, login/password security, login restrictions, and a login script. All that remains is the user interface.

*The DOS executable (# sign) command is extremely detrimental in ANY login script.*

# The User Interface

*One of the most important jobs for the NetWare system manager is to make users feel comfortable with the LAN.*

THE USER INTERFACE INVOLVES workstation software, application software, and menu systems. One of the most important jobs the NetWare system manager has is to make users feel comfortable with the network. There is nothing worse than users who are apprehensive, intimidated, and threatened by the idea of logging into a large network. There has been a lot of hysteria lately surrounding the Big Brother syndrome and many people are becoming LANphobic. They feel that becoming part of a larger electronic system will cause them to lose their individuality. One of the most important cures for LANphobia is to provide customization and individuality for each user. That way, even though they are part of a larger whole, they can feel unique.

Another important aspect of the user interface is productivity. It is the system manager's responsibility to set up a productive software environment for each user so he/she can perform tasks in synergy with the other LAN users while at the same time maintaining some unique job specialization. This strategy is accomplished by intelligently loading application software so it is shared by everyone on the LAN yet customized for each user's needs.

In this section, we will explore the user interface responsibilities of the NetWare system manager by focusing on the intelligent installation of application software for user productivity and the alleviation of LANphobia by installing an intelligent and friendly custom menu environment. Before we begin, let's take a look at workstation software and the many different shells that connect the user with the NetWare LAN.

## Workstation Software

As we learned in Chapter 2, the NetWare workstation software consists of IPX.COM and NETx.COM. IPX is the protocol utility that controls communications between NETx.COM and the internal network interface card. IPX is generated using the WSGEN utility and requires approximately 32K of workstation RAM. NETx.COM is the NetWare shell that handles the communications between DOS and the IPX.COM protocol. NetWare provides three versions of the NETx shell (Figure 6.5); these accommodate different workstation environments.

**NETx.COM**—the basic NETx shell that loads in conventional memory. It supports any version of DOS from v2.1 to v6.00.

**EMSNETx.EXE**—the EMS (Expanded Memory Specification) version of NETx. EMSNETx.EXE runs in expanded memory and frees approximately 34K of conventional RAM. On the downside, EMSNETx.EXE is very slow.

**XMSNETx.EXE**—the XMS (Extended Memory Specification) version of NETx. XMSNETx.EXE runs in extended memory and also frees approximately 34K of conventional RAM. On the downside, XMSNETx.EXE occupies the same 64K high memory as DOS v5.00 and v6.00. Therefore, DOS HIGH and XMSNETx can't operate together—the user must choose one or the other.

*Pay attention to the three ways NETx can be loaded in workstation RAM.*

**FIGURE 6.5**
NetWare shells and
workstation RAM

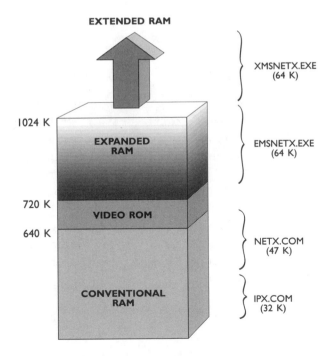

NetWare provides a variety of other solutions for non-DOS workstations, including:

**OS/2**—the OS/2 Requester, which comes with NetWare 2.2. It loads on the OS/2 workstation and controls communications between the workstation operating system and NetWare.

**Macintosh**—the NetWare for Macintosh product, which contains two components: VAP and DA. The NetWare for Macintosh VAP loads on the Net-Ware 2.2 server and provides translation tables between NetWare and AppleTalk (the Macintosh protocol). The NetWare for Macintosh DA is a group of Desk Accessories that load on the Macintosh workstation and provide elementary NetWare tools in the native Macintosh interface.

It is important to choose the correct NetWare workstation software. Keep in mind, the workstation is the user's link to the LAN. In many cases, it can make or break user productivity.

## Application Software

As mentioned earlier, one of the user interface responsibilities of the system manager is to provide synergistic LAN productivity through application software while at the same time customizing it for individual user needs. This is accomplished through a seven-step approach to installing application software. In this section, we're going to explore in detail the seven different steps and how they optimize application software in a NetWare environment. It is important to note that this is a general discussion and most application software has specific exceptions with respect to the installation process and certain configurations. For the most part, though, these seven steps will help in creating a synergy between user productivity and shared application software.

*Example is not the main thing in life—it is the only thing.*

*Albert Schweitzer*

### Step 1: NetWare Compatibility

*NetWare compatibility information can be accessed on Netwire—Novell's electronic bulletin board—or from your local Novell sales and operations center.*

The first step is determining NetWare compatibility. It is very important to determine whether or not the application software is NetWare compatible before it is purchased. There are 4,000 or more software packages that are compatible and registered with Novell. This compatibility information is important because NetWare makes demands on application software that can cause it to corrupt data or, at the very least, provide a non-productive work environment. NetWare compatibility information can be accessed on Netwire—Novell's electronic bulletin board—or from your local Novell sales and operations center. In addition, you can contact the software vendor for NetWare compatibility information.

### Step 2: Multi-user

Once you have established that the application software is NetWare compatible, it is important to establish whether or not it is a multiuser software program. For the best results and best user productivity in a NetWare environment, it is critical that the application software support multiple users simultaneously. A large number of application software programs are designed only to be used by one user at a time in a stand-alone environment. Most of your large software manufacturers with common and popular software packages are, however, creating multi-user versions of their software that provide file sharing and multi-user access. Again, to assure yourself of the most productive user environment, it is important to determine multi-user compatibility with the software before you purchase it.

Single-user software can be used in a NetWare environment. NetWare supports any DOS applications; however, they aren't as effective as those that provide not only data sharing but application sharing as well.

### Step 3: Directory Structure

Before you can install the software or configure any of its components, it's extremely important to have an intelligent organization directory structure that supports not only the application software but also the data it will generate. Each application program should have a specific subdirectory under the directory heading of APPS so as not to clutter the root directory. This also organizes application software for easy and efficient security design. Some software applications will create their own directory structure during the installation process. Unfortunately, this directory structure is typically created off of the root directory. This works fine in a local hard disk environment, but it doesn't work in a NetWare shared environment because there are many more people accessing the shared disk. You can map root the F: drive to SYS:APPS, in which case the system will be fooled into thinking that the APPS subdirectory is in fact the root and it will create its directory structure under APPS instead of the real NetWare root.

### Step 4: Installation

The fourth step in customizing network application software is installation. The installation process is typically left up to the application itself. Most applications require you to run a setup or install program so they can customize some configurations for your environment as well as unpack or decompress the files from the disk. It is not a good idea to just copy the programs off the install disks. Instead, use the INSTALL program. If you must copy the disks to the NetWare drive, don't use the DOS copy command; use NCOPY because it both retains security and is a much more efficient command line utility for file copying.

Once the network application software has been installed, there are three very important configurations that need to be taken care of before the users can access or run the application software. These three configurations comprise steps 5, 6, and 7.

### Step 5: File Attributes

It is very important that application software has the correct file attributes so it can be shared without being destroyed. Application files are normally flagged Sharable-Read Only, whereas data files are typically flagged Sharable-Read/Write. Most multi-user and NetWare-compatible application software will provide some information about specific file attributes and the flagging of files for their applications specifically.

### Step 6: User Rights

*If everyone is going to use the same applications, use the group EVERYONE to assign access rights and assign them to the APPS directory.*

It is very important to grant user access or access rights to these applications. By default, users have no rights to the new directory structure you've created. If you were to install the application software and walk away, the users would have no access to the applications and would not be able to run them.

Typically, if everyone is going to use the same applications, use the group EVERYONE to assign the access rights and assign them to the APPS directory. As you remember from our discussion in Chapter 4, access rights do flow down to all subdirectories of the parent directory. Typically, the RF (Read and File Scan rights) are sufficient for all files in an applications directory. But all rights (except modify and access control) are typically needed in data directories. Application data can be stored in a variety of different places depending on the type of data. User-specific data should be stored in the user's own home directory. Group-specific data should be stored in a group subdirectory off of the root, while data shared by all users on the system should be stored in a data directory from the root.

### Step 7: Workstation Configuration

Many programs require some DOS configuration at the workstation level for them to run properly. The most notable is the CONFIG.SYS file. In addition, there are device drivers that must be loaded for programs that use a mouse. And for large programs, environment space can be increased using the SHELL command in the CONFIG.SYS of the workstation. The actual command is SHELL = COMMAND.COM /p /e:[number] where number corresponds to the amount of environment space the application needs. Typically, a number like 1,024 provides enough environment space not only for NetWare but for all shared applications.

Once the application software has been installed and users have access to it, a friendly productive menu environment must be created to guide users from one application to another. Besides making it easy to access applications, a menu environment helps to alleviate LANphobia.

*Many a man never fails because he never tries.*

*Norman MacEwan*

# Menu Software

*NetWare's menu system uses exactly the same function keys and has the same look and feel as all other menus in the system, such as SYSCON, FILER, SESSION, and so on.*

NetWare has a built-in menu system that provides a consistent Novell-looking or NetWare-looking menu system as well as a very simple script file for system managers to create a batch file-oriented menu system. This custom menu environment allows you to have large groups of users share the same menu file or to provide each user with his or her own file. In addition, NetWare supports a customized color palette that allows each menu or each submenu of the menu to have different colors and different characteristics that distinguish it from previous menus.

The most appealing thing about NetWare's menu system is that it uses exactly the same function keys and has the same look and feel as all other menus in the system, such as SYSCON, FILER, SESSION, and so on. It is therefore very easy for users to use and for the system manager to understand and maintain.

NetWare's menu facility has specific syntax and rules for execution. Before we review those, let's spend a moment talking about a custom menu environment and creating what's called a turnkey system.

## Custom Menu Environment

A turnkey custom menu environment provides transparent use access from the point of turning on the computer to the point of bringing up applications. The idea is to perform the configuration functions and access activities in the background so the entire system is transparent to the user. The term "turnkey" comes from the notion that you can turn the key and everything takes care of itself. While this is a very nice environment and simple to use, it is somewhat complex for the system manager to set up and maintain. The turnkey system consists of four components:

1. **The workstation boot disk** should contain the hidden system files COMMAND.COM, an IPX file for accessing the NetWare protocol, and a NETx file for attaching to the server. Finally, the workstation boot disk should include an AUTOEXEC.BAT batch file, which not only loads IPX and NETx but also moves to the F: prompt and logs in the user.

2. **The system login script** and user login script should be maintained so they include an EXIT command that exits the user to a specific menu format. Whether or not that menu is user-specific or system-wide is not as important as the fact that the login script itself executes the menu.

3. **The menu** must be easily executed and customized to user needs. The menu can be executed either from a user-specific directory where a customized menu resides or from a shared directory where all users are accessing the same menu file.

4. **The menu execution options** give users access to all of the applications, functions, and utilities they need. They should all originate from within one central menu program.

*Learn this menu syntax carefully because it's very different from the syntax of NetWare 3.12. NetWare 3.11, on the other hand, shares this same menu syntax.*

### Menu Syntax

NetWare's menu facility was designed using another one of my KISS principles (Keep It Syntax Simple). The NetWare menu syntax is extremely easy to use and in many ways resembles DOS batch files. The NetWare menu file is a text file with the extension .MNU and must follow a few simple rules. The NetWare menu file consists of three different components: the title, the option, and an executable. The title defines the menu title, location, and color. The option is the choice that appears in the menu as the user sees it, and the executable is the actual program executed once the user highlights and chooses that particular option.

The title must be left justified and preceded by a "%." The location of the menu box is dictated by x and y coordinates. X is the number of rows from 0 to 23 on the screen and y is the number of columns across the top from 0 to 79. For example, a value of 12, 40 would appear in the middle of the screen. The x and y coordinates are followed by one last number indicating the color palette of the menu. (This is a number from 0 to 4, and it describes any of the five different color palettes that can be defined using the NetWare color-palette utility.) Color palette 0 is the default palette, which can be seen in all NetWare menu utilities, the blue and gold (GO CAL BEARS).

Options are also left justified but are *not* preceded by a "%." They can be any combination of characters and numbers and denote the particular option the user is choosing. The options are alphabetized automatically by the system—a feature that cannot be changed. If there is a particular order you would like your options to appear in (and it's not alphabetic), you can precede the option with a "1" or an "a" and it will alphabetize according to that format.

Finally, an executable must be indented underneath its appropriate option. Submenus are denoted by an executable with the same name as another title and preceded by a "%". For example, an executable with a submenu would say "%SUBMENU" and would branch off to the next point, which would be a left-justified title preceded by a "%" with the x and y coordinates and the palette color number.

This simple syntax produces very flexible and nice-looking menus, which use the same function keys and conventions as Novell's own menu systems.

## Menu Execution

NetWare menu execution is also straightforward. As you recall, the menu file has a .MNU extension. To execute a file, you simply type MENU [menu file name without the .MNU extension]. The menu program is stored in the PUBLIC directory so it can be accessed anywhere. Keep in mind, there are some security concerns that affect the execution of NetWare menus:

- The user must have the Read and File Scan rights to the directory that holds the .MNU file—typically their own directory or a shared directory like PUBLIC.

- The users must have all rights except Modify and Access Control in the directory they are currently logged into when they execute the menu command. This is because the menu command creates temporary batch files in the current directory. You should have users accessing or running menus from their own directory whether or not they are executing a menu file that exists there.

- If a menu file is going to be used by multiple users, it should be flagged as sharable.

That's it for menu systems and the user interface in general. Keep in mind that menus, application programs, and user configurations can be a very useful strategy in warding off LANphobia, but I think the most effective strategy is a warm touch and a kind heart.

*Consider the postage stamp, my son. It secures success through its ability to stick to one thing till it gets there.*

*Josh Billings*

# NetWare Backup

*Nowhere is the old adage more true than here: "You never miss anything until it's gone." This saying holds just as true for NetWare data as anything else.*

NOWHERE IS THE OLD adage more true than here: "You never miss anything until it's gone." This saying holds just as true for NetWare data as anything else. NetWare backup is often overlooked because it is not needed on a day-to-day basis. But as soon as the data is lost, NetWare backup is the first responsibility the NetWare manager is reminded of. In many cases, NetWare backup can be the difference between a successful and prosperous career as a NetWare system manager and the unemployment line. Make sure *never* to neglect your NetWare backup duties.

NetWare backup is not as simple as inserting a diskette and copying files. This complex process involves the bindery, NetWare compatibility, reliability of backed-up data, maintenance, and efficient restore procedures. In this section, we will briefly discuss NetWare backup considerations and talk a little bit about NetWare's own backup utility (called NBACKUP). Remember, the NetWare backup functionality or responsibility is probably one of the system manager's most volatile tasks.

# NetWare Backup Considerations

NetWare backup is different from local backup in that there are many more auxiliary components to back up. In a stand-alone environment, a backup consists primarily of the data and directories. In a network environment, the backup consists not only of data and directories but also security, file attributes, the NetWare bindery, users, and groups. This is why one of the most important considerations when choosing a NetWare backup system is NetWare compatibility. Many backup systems say they work well with NetWare or that they're NetWare comfortable. But that does not mean they're NetWare compatible. The key component in NetWare compatibility is whether or not the system can recognize the bindery. Backing up the bindery is a very serious task because it requires that the bindery be closed and re-opened (you cannot back up a file that is currently open).

Few backup systems know how to access the NetWare bindery and close and open it without bringing down the network. Most major name brands are, however, NetWare compatible and provide facilities for backing up the NetWare bindery. Keep in mind that not only is it important for the product to be NetWare compatible, but it must also be easy to use. Another consideration is who you're logged in as while you're performing the backup. To do a full NetWare backup, the user must be a supervisor or supervisor equivalent. Also, it's a good idea to perform the backup when no other users are logged into the system because the closing and opening of the bindery can cause very serious problems if any users are accessing the bindery at that moment. And if users are currently using data files or application programs, those files will not be backed up. This brings up another consideration—unattended backup. It seems contrary to want to login as a supervisor and run an unattended backup; this opens the supervisor account to anyone and leaves it vulnerable during non-working hours. The best strategy is to create a supervisor equivalent who logs in at a particular time and whose time restrictions lock the account after, let's say, 3:00 AM so the system only stays logged on for a limited period of time.

The final consideration with respect to NetWare backup is reliability. It is very important to implement an intelligent schedule that provides complete data security while avoiding having to produce 365 tapes per year. The grandfather method is a good method: It uses 24 tapes and provides at least four or five years' worth of data integrity while recycling tapes every day, week, month, and year. Reliability is maintained by performing periodic restores to nonactive disks so you can verify that the backup is truly good and that the restore functionality of the backup system works.

One of the biggest problems with backup systems these days is that you spend your days, weeks, months, and years backing up data without ever restoring any of it. It would be rather disconcerting to find out that after you have years worth of backup tapes, the system does not restore properly.

## NBACKUP

The most NetWare-compatible backup system available is NetWare's own NBACKUP. While not the most feature-rich backup utility, NBACKUP provides the facility for backing up the bindery. It is reliable, and it performs unattended backups. On the downside, though, NBACKUP only backs up to DOS devices—floppy disks, hard disks, or read/write optical. Also, you must restore exactly to the system type you backed up from, and NBACKUP only supports DOS and Macintosh file types.

NBACKUP backs up and restores 3.11 and 2.2 file servers. But you have to run NBACKUP from a workstation to back up the entire system. You also must be logged in as supervisor. If you back up a NetWare 2.2 server using NBACKUP, you must restore to a NetWare 2.2 server. The same holds true for NetWare 3.11 NBACKUP.

While the DOS device list dramatically limits the number of devices you can use for backup, Novell does allow other manufacturers to write drivers that support the NBACKUP. These drivers must be loaded in a file in the SYS:PUBLIC directory called DIBI$DRV.DAT. Unfortunately, not many manufacturers have found it necessary to write drivers for the NBACKUP utility because most manufacturers have written their own NetWare-compatible software to run with the backup system. NBACKUP exists in the PUBLIC directory, so it can be accessed by any user. For users to back up their own areas, they must have Read and File Scan rights in the directories they want to back up, and they must have Write, Create, File Scan, Erase, and Modify rights in the directories they want to restore to.

While NBACKUP is not the cream of the crop as far as NetWare backup is concerned, it provides adequate functionality and NetWare compatibility at the right price.

That's it for our discussion of NetWare backup and network management. Keep in mind network management is an extremely volatile portion of your job. It is quite a puzzle with respect to the many different activities and different responsibilities of the system manager. But once you get all of the puzzle pieces in place, the Novell picture is quite beautiful.

*I feel that the greatest reward for doing is the opportunity to do more.*

*Jonas Salk*

The final component of NetWare network management is NetWare printing. It's a dirty business, but fortunately, there's a LAN laundry room. We will learn about it next—just keep turning the pages.

# Exercise 6.1: Configuring Netware Restrictions

In this exercise, we will use each of the restriction options that have been discussed in this chapter. This exercise requires that you have access to an existing NetWare LAN and that you have supervisor equivalence. You will be asked to create three users and toy with their security restrictions. Be very careful to follow the steps precisely so you do not get lost in the maze of NetWare restrictions.

Let's begin by creating three users.

*This exercise is an excellent way to learn the ins and outs of NetWare 2.2 login restrictions. Just do it!*

1. Login as a user with supervisor equivalence and move to the NetWare prompt. Type `Z:` to move to PUBLIC. Type `SYSCON` and press Enter. Choose user information from the available topics menu in SYSCON. At the User Information menu, press Insert. Create the following three users: `FRED`, `WILMA`, `and DINO`. Don't be concerned with creating home directories or any security restrictions at this point. We will do that later in the exercise.

2. Once you've returned to the User Names window, choose DINO and press Enter. Choose the second option, Account Restrictions.

3. Disable the account. Notice that all other options have disappeared. By disabling DINO's account, DINO no longer has the ability to log in and therefore security is not required.

4. Press Escape until you reach the User's Name list and choose FRED. Press Enter.

5. Under Account Restrictions, set the Expiration Date for today's date and Limit Concurrent Connections to 1.

6. Press Escape until the Exit Confirmation window appears, then exit SYSCON. At the NetWare prompt, type LOGIN FRED. Notice that by logging in as somebody else, the system automatically logs you out from your supervisor-equivalent account. Notice that it allows you to log in FRED even though today is the expiration date. (The actual expiration date is one day after the "official" expiration date.) Go to another workstation and attempt to log in as FRED from there. Notice you will be denied because FRED has limited concurrent connections to 1. Return to your workstation.

**7.** Log in as your supervisor-equivalent account once again and change FRED's Expiration Date to yesterday's date. Exit SYSCON once again and attempt to log in as FRED. Explain what happened.

_____

_____

_____

_____

**8.** Log in as your supervisor account and enter SYSCON once again. Highlight User Information from the available topics menu and press Enter. Highlight FRED and press Enter. From the User Information window, choose Account Restrictions. Notice that FRED's account has been disabled. This is because the account expiration date had been exceeded. Enable FRED and set the password requirements as follows:

**A.** Require Password: `Yes`.

**B.** Minimum Password Length: `7`.

**C.** Force Periodic Password Changes: `Yes`.

**D.** Days Between Forced Changes: `1`.

**E.** Date Password Expires: `today's date`.

**F.** Limit Grace Logins: `Yes`.

**G.** Grace Logins Allowed: `1`.

**H.** Remaining Grace Logins: `1`.

**I.** Require Unique Passwords: `Yes`.

Exit SYSCON and log in as FRED once again. Test the above requirements to see if they have been implemented. Record the results below.

_____

_____

_____

**9.** Log in as your supervisor-equivalent account and enter FRED's account restrictions once again. Change the date the password expires to yesterday's date. Log in once again as FRED and note the changes below.

_____

_____

_____

**10.** Log in as your supervisor-equivalent account and highlight User Information from the available topics. Press Enter. Choose WILMA from the Users Name window and press Enter. In the User Information window for WILMA, highlight Volume Disk Restrictions and press Enter. Limit WILMA's server disk space to 1K.

**11.** Log in as WILMA and check her Maximum Disk Space and Disk Space in Use options from SYSCON. Note that the minimum is set to 4K. This is the lowest number Net-Ware 2.2 will accept, so it automatically updated your entry from 1K to 4K. This is because the smallest unit of measurement on a NetWare disk is 4K, called the default block size.

**12.** Let's test the disk-space restriction by creating a very small file and then expanding it. Exit SYSCON and return to the NetWare prompt. Create a very small file by typing COPY CON WILMA.TXT and press Enter. Type Yabba dabba do and press Enter. Press F6 and Enter. This will save the file.

**13.** Enlarge the file by typing COPY WILMA.TXT + Z:MAIN.MENU NEW.TXT and press Enter. Note what happens below and check the limitations in SYSCON once again for WILMA.

_____

_____

**14.** In the next portion of the exercise, we will restrict the station from which FRED can log in. Before we enter SYSCON to configure station restrictions for FRED, we must find out what the node address is for this particular workstation. Log in as your supervisor-equivalent user. At the NetWare prompt, type USERLIST /e. This will give you a list of all connections and appropriate node addresses. Pay particular attention to the user name with the asterisk next to it. This is your particular workstation. There are two pieces of information required for station restrictions. They are network number and node address. Write down the network number and the node address as they appear for your workstation.

_____

_____

**15.** Enter SYSCON and choose FRED from the User Name window. In FRED's user information box, select Station Restrictions. Restrict FRED to the network number and node address you wrote down for your workstation. Exit SYSCON and move to another workstation. Attempt to log in as FRED. Make note of what happens.

_____

_____

Now attempt to log in as FRED from your own workstation.

**16.** Log in as the supervisor equivalent and choose WILMA from the User Names window in SYSCON. Choose Time Restrictions from her User Information window and press Enter. Make note of what time it is. Restrict WILMA from logging in for the next few half hours by using F5 to highlight those time periods and pressing the spacebar. This will block out the asterisks for these times. Exit SYSCON and return to the NetWare prompt. Log in as WILMA and notice that you are allowed to log in because the restriction has not taken effect yet. Keep WILMA logged in until the half-hour period approaches. Make note below of what happens as the system approaches the half hour that is restricted.

_____

_____

**17.** Finally we will experience intruder detection/lockout firsthand. Log in as the supervisor account and highlight DINO from the Users Name list. Enter Account Restrictions from DINO's User Information window and enable his account. Next, return to the available topics menu of SYSCON. Choose Supervisor Options and press Enter. Highlight Intruder Detection/Lockout and press Enter. Set the options to the following parameters:

**A.** Detect Intruders: `Yes`.

**B.** Incorrect Login Attempts: `2`.

    **C.** Bad Login Count Retention Time: `30 minutes`.

    **D.** Lock Account After Detection: `Yes`.

    **E.** Length of Account Lockout: `15 minutes`.

    Notice that these are close to the NetWare defaults.

**18.** Enter DINO's User Information window and create a password for him. Exit SYSCON and try to log in as DINO three times, using the wrong password. Note what happens after the third attempt.

_____

_____

**19.** Log in as supervisor equivalent and highlight DINO from the Users Name window. Highlight Intruder Lockout status from DINO's User Information window. Notice that the account has been locked. In addition, the system indicates the last intruder address that was used for an incorrect login attempt. This address should match the network and node address of your workstation. Unlock DINO's account by changing Account Locked from Yes to No.

That completes our exercise for NetWare restrictions. Keep in mind that there's an incredible amount of flexibility and complexity in this level of NetWare security. This exercise has introduced you to some of the login restriction concepts. You can expand your knowledge by working with it further.

Check Appendix D for answers.

## Exercise 6.2: Writing Login Scripts

In this exercise, you will write a system login script for a fictitious NetWare LAN. This login script will contain required and optional components. In the second half of the exercise, you will have an opportunity to implement your login script for an existing NetWare LAN.

Let's begin by writing a login script.

1. Create a login script that satisfies the following drive-mapping considerations:

   **A.** MAP root to each user's home subdirectory.

   **B.** MAP drive G: to a data subdirectory from the root.

   **C.** MAP the next available network drive mapping to the login subdirectory.

   **D.** MAP the first search drive to SYS:PUBLIC.

   **E.** MAP the second search drive to the appropriate DOS subdirectory using proper syntax.

   **F.** MAP the third search drive to SYS\APPS\WP.

   **G.** MAP the next available search drive mapping to SYS:\APPS\DBASE.

   **H.** Insert the third search drive mapping to SYS:ACCT.

2. Establish a comspec for COMMAND.COM in the DOS search directory.

3. Satisfy the following WRITE conditions:

   **A.** Create a line that greets each user with their login name and the appropriate time of day.

   **B.** It's Friday, so write the following message: `Congratulations, you made it through the week! Welcome to your Friday.`

   **C.** It's May 3, the boss's birthday. To create a command that will fire phasers 27 times, write the following message: `Happy birthday to you, happy birthday to you, you live in a zoo.`

**4.** Show the following information.

    **A.** Show the date and time for each user.

    **B.** Show the DOS version each user is running on their particular workstation.

    **C.** If a user is a member of the group SALES, display the SALES.TXT file.

**5.** Switch to each user's personal user directory and exit to a batch file called START.BAT.

**6.** START.BAT should contain the following three components:

    **A.** A clear screen.

    **B.** A CAPTURE command to the laser queue with no banner, no form feed, and a timeout of 10.

    **C.** The execution of a NetWare menu file called BOB.MNU.

**7.** Finally, use the remark login script command to document each of these previous components.

In the second half of the login script exercise, you will have the opportunity to implement your system script. If you have access to a NetWare LAN, use SYSCON to alter the system login script in accordance with the script you have created here. If the LAN you have access to is a productive working LAN, avoid using the system login script and create a login script for a fictional user. Then log in as that user to view the changes that have been made.

To edit the system login script, choose Supervisor Options from the SYSCON available topics menu and press Enter. Choose System Login Script and press Enter. To edit a user's own login script, choose User Information from the available topics menu in SYSCON and press Enter. Highlight the user and press Enter. Choose Login Script from the User Information window.

NOTE: Error messages will appear if drive mappings and user configurations are defined for directories that don't exist on your LAN. Remember, this is only a learning exercise.

Check Appendix D for answers.

# Exercise 6.3: Building Menus

In this exercise, we will continue with the user interface lab from Exercise 6.2 and create a menu system for fictitious user BOB. This menu system will be executed from the system login script so BOB can simply log in and have access to all of his user configurations and the menu system as a whole.

In the first half of this exercise, you will be asked to write a menu script that satisfies a series of given conditions and uses proper menu syntax. Once the script has been written on paper, you can implement the script by inputting it into a text file and executing the NetWare menu program. The second half of this exercise requires that you have access to an existing NetWare LAN.

Using proper menu syntax, let's begin by writing a menu script for BOB that satisfies the following conditions:

**1.** **The title** will be "Bob's Personal Menu." In addition, the main menu will appear exactly in the middle of the screen and use color palette 1.

**2.** **The options** for Bob's personal menu are as follows:

    **A.** *Applications,* a submenu.

    **B.** *Utilities,* a submenu.

    **C.** *System configuration,* which will execute the Z: SYSCON utility.

    **D.** *File management,* which will execute the Z: FILER utility.

    **E.** *Logout.* The logout option will close the menu file, all open programs, and log the user out. This can be accomplished by issuing the !LOGOUT command.

**3.** **The Applications submenu** will appear on the top left corner of the screen and use color palette 2. This submenu will include the following options (all of which are under APPS):

    **A.** *Word processing,* a submenu.

    **B.** *Spreadsheet,* which will execute 1-2-3 from the LOTUS subdirectory.

    **C.** *Windows,* which will execute WIN : from the Windows subdirectory under APPS.

    **D.** *Dbase,* which will execute Paradox from APPS\PARADOX.

4. **The word processing submenu** will appear in the top right of the screen and use color palette 3. It includes the following three options:

    **A.** *WordPerfect,* executed as WP from the APPS\WP51 subdirectory.

    **B.** *Microsoft Word,* executed as WORD from the APPS\WORD subdirectory.

    **C.** *WordStar,* executed as WS from the APPS\WORDSTAR subdirectory.

5. **The utilities submenu** will appear in the bottom right-hand corner of the screen using color palette 4. It contains the following options:

    **A.** *SESSION management,* which executes SESSION from the PUBLIC subdirectory.

    **B.** *Norton Utilities,* which executes as NU from the APPS\UTILS subdirectory.

    **C.** *Print Management,* which executes as PCONSOLE from the PUBLIC subdirectory.

In the second half of this menu exercise, you will have the opportunity to implement Bob's menu. To implement Bob's menu, you must create a text file that follows exactly along with the script you have created. The text file will have the file name BOB.MNU. Bob's menu can then be executed using the menu command from the PUBLIC subdirectory of an existing NetWare LAN. Simply type MENU BOB, and it will implement your menu.

Check Appendix D for answers.

## Extracurricular Exercise

Try to add a level of complexity to Bob's menu so when users press Escape from the main menu, it doesn't exit the menu system. Instead, the Escape key brings them back to the main menu screen. Check Appendix D for an answer to this puzzling addition.

# NetWare 2.2 Printing

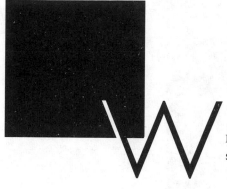

HY DO YOU USE a LAN? A recent survey of CNA students revealed some interesting answers:

- To save money

- Because they're popular

- Because I have to

- I don't know

- What's a LAN?

While there is no right or wrong answer, the most popular answer is—"to share network resources." One of the most important shared resources is the network printer. Printers produce quality hardcopy output for brochures, reports, memos, and general paperwork. Network printing is one of the most productive and useful functions of a NetWare LAN.

As the NetWare system manager, it is your responsibility to make sure that the network printing system meets or exceeds the needs of your users. Think of it as the LAN's laundry room. In this chapter, we will explore network printing from the system manager's point of view. We will discuss the two major approaches towards NetWare 2.2 printing and provide some tools for effective printing management. In addition, we will practice printing setup with some simple lab exercises. But before we begin, let's take a quick look at the fundamentals of NetWare printing.

*Why do you use a LAN? A recent survey of CNA students revealed some interesting answers.*

# The Fundamentals of NetWare Printing

ON THE SURFACE, NetWare printing may appear easy, but don't be fooled—it is probably the most troubling and mysterious management issue in the NetWare LAN. The fundamentals are relatively straightforward but it's the demands of the users that can quickly frazzle the system manager. NetWare 2.2 printing is designed around three components:

**The NetWare print queue** is a shared area on the file server that stores print jobs in the order in which they are received. The print queue lines up the print jobs and sends them to the printer in an organized and efficient manner.

**The print server** is responsible for directing the print jobs as they move from the queue to the network printer.

**The printer** is the output device in a NetWare printing system and it typically receives the jobs and prints them appropriately.

*It all starts with printing fundamentals. If you understand the relationship between NetWare print queues, print servers, and printers, the rest will be a piece of cake. Make sure you fully understand Figure 7.1 before you move on.*

Figure 7.1 illustrates the fundamental structure of the NetWare printing system. Keep in mind that the network printer is one of the most important shared resources on a NetWare LAN.

In a transparent NetWare printing environment, users print directly from their network applications and the output magically appears in the printer down the hall. This type of sophistication, while it might seem trivial to the user, is the result of great effort from the system manager.

*High aims from high characters, and great objects bring out great minds.*

*Tryon Edwards*

**FIGURE 7.1**
The NetWare
printing system

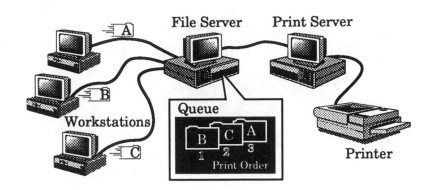

In this section we'll discuss the three printing components and make an in-depth study of how they affect the NetWare printing system. Remember, the system manager must keep on top of these components and have a firm understanding of how they relate to each other.

The word *queue* means "to stand in line." British citizens, for example, are often found queuing up—waiting for tickets to cricket matches. In a printing environment, print jobs stand in line—a queue—and wait to be sent off to the network printer. Because print jobs are simply data being translated by the printer, print queues must exist as directories on the NetWare file server. Print queues are stored as subdirectories under the SYS:SYSTEM directory and are given random eight-digit hexadecimal names. As print jobs are sent from network workstations to the print queue, they are stored in the corresponding directory as files on the hard disk. The files are ordered by the print server and are tracked on their way from the file server to the network printer. The print server never stores the print job information, it only directs and controls it.

Print jobs are sent directly to print queues in one of two ways: CAPTURE or network application printing. The CAPTURE command is a NetWare 2.2 command that literally captures the local workstation's parallel port and redirects any print jobs destined for that port to the NetWare queue. Printing from NetWare applications, on the other hand, is a little more sophisticated because those applications recognize NetWare print queues and print directly to them. In either case, the workstation NETx shell formats the print job so that the network can recognize it and place it in the correct queue on the correct file server disk. When print queues are created, the system assigns print queue operators and print queue users, which are special NetWare managers that control and use NetWare print queues. The print queue operator has the

*The NetWare print server is not so much a physical device as it is a logical process. The print server can exist as a dedicated workstation or as a process running on top of a NetWare file server or router.*

ability to add, delete, or reorder the print jobs in a given print queue. By default, the user supervisor is assigned as the print queue operator on all NetWare print queues. Print queue users have the ability to insert print jobs into NetWare queues. By default, the group EVERYONE is assigned as a queue user for all new print queues.

The NetWare print server is not so much a physical device as it is a logical process. The print server can exist as a dedicated workstation or as a process running on top of a NetWare file server or router. As a dedicated workstation, the print server process runs through a file called PSERVER.EXE, which is included with NetWare 2.2. As a non-dedicated process running on top of a NetWare file server or router, the print server exists as PSERVER.VAP or value added process.

In either case, the print server's purpose is to control and redirect print jobs as they travel from NetWare workstations to file server print queues and ultimately to network printers. The print server constantly monitors the print queues and network printers and makes logical attachments from one to the other. When a job is inserted into the print queue, it moves to the top of the line and the print server redirects it to the appropriate network printer. In addition, print servers monitor printers to make sure they're not out of paper, off line, or jammed. If any of these situations occurs with network printers, the print server will notify the print server operator or supervisor.

There are certain specifications that restrict the functionality of the NetWare print server. The print server itself can only have up to five printers attached directly to it: LPT1, LPT2, LPT3, COM1, and COM2. The print server can service print jobs from print queues on up to eight different file servers. In addition, NetWare has provided an auxiliary functionality that expands the five-printer limitation. It's called *remote printing*. Remote printing allows workstations with local printers attached to designate those printers as network devices. We will discuss remote printing in just a moment.

The real star of this show is the network printer. The network printer is the shared device that provides hard copy output to multiple NetWare users. Shared printers can be either attached to the print server, attached to the file server, or attached to local workstations using the remote printing facility. Printers attached directly to the file server use NetWare 2.2's internal printing functionality, which is called *core printing*. Core printing describes the facility for controlling network printing inside the file server itself without the use of a print server. We'll discuss core printing in just a moment.

Printers attached directly to print servers are controlled by the print server and can service users on up to eight different file servers. Printers attached directly to local workstations and shared as network devices must use the remote printing facility. Remote printing is made possible through a terminate-and-stay-resident (TSR) program called RPRINTER.EXE, which runs in workstation RAM. RPRINTER communicates directly with the print server and makes the printer available through the workstation NetWare shell.

In addition to these traditional printing configurations, the industry is providing some new, exciting, intelligent printers that are capable of communicating directly with the print server. Intelligent printers have internal network interface cards (NICs) that allow them to attach directly to the LAN trunk. These printers act as workstations with remote printers attached. Some examples of intelligent printers include the Hewlett-Packard LaserJet 4 and the LaserJet 5.

*They are able because they think they are.*

*Vergil*

In this chapter, we will explore the two different approaches to NetWare printing: print servers and core printing. We'll begin with core printing because it provides the basics of a standard printing configuration, and then we will move on to the print server approach, which provides a great deal more functionality, flexibility, and enhanced performance.

# NetWare Core Printing

DURING THE NETWARE 2.2 standard configuration and installation procedure, you'll be asked to specify whether you want to assign various parallel or serial ports on the file server to network printers. If you choose yes, you will inadvertently install NetWare core printing. Installing network printers through core printing is the simplest way to go but it does not offer much flexibility. Core printing supports up to five printers attached directly to the file server and does not rely on an external print server process.

Core printing uses print queues just as print serving does and it relies on the same intervention from the NetWare shell NETx. Once core printing has been installed, it cannot be uninstalled unless the NetWare operating system is reconfigured. Core printing and print servers can coexist in the same Net-Ware printing system but not within the same file server. If you choose to install core printing during NetWare configuration, you will be restricted from installing the print server PSERVER.VAP on this file server. In this section we will discuss when to use core printing and then evaluate the three steps that make up the installation of NetWare core printing.

## When to Use Core Printing

*Core printing should be installed in very small networks that require a maximum of five shared printers.*

Core printing is not installed as the default in NetWare 2.2 so it is a choice during NetWare installation. Core printing should be installed in very small networks that require a maximum of five shared printers. Another factor in choosing core printing is whether the users should have physical access to the NetWare file server. Remember, core printing defines which printers are attached directly to the file server. Users who have access to printers also have access to the file server itself. Core printing is a good option if the file server is readily accessible to all NetWare users.

Another limitation of core printing is that it does not allow for the distribution of printers throughout the LAN. Print servers have the functionality of remote printing, so system managers can distribute printers on local workstations. Core printing centralizes all printers at the file server so that they cannot physically be more than 15 to 25 feet (parallel) or 100 feet (serial) from the file server.

## Core Printing Installation

Installing core printing is not significantly easier than installing print servers and it severely restricts the functionality of NetWare printing. Core printing may seem simple on the surface, but there can be some hidden traps.

*The only thing to do with good advice is to pass it on. It is never of any use to oneself.*

*Oscar Wilde*

Core printing installation occurs initially at the first step of configuring the network operating system. The system will ask if you would like to install or define any ports for NetWare printing. If you choose YES to define the local parallel and serial ports on the file server, you have installed core printing. Once core printing has been installed during the configuration stage, the system managers must set up the core printing system and activate it, using three simple steps:

1. Create the print queues.

2. Define the printers.

3. Assign the queues to printers.

During the first step, the system manager creates the print queues and the system assigns a random eight-digit directory name. The print queue is stored on the same file server that is using core printing. During the second step, the system manager defines the printers and tells the system which port will be using which printers. The system managers also name the printers so that they can be easily tracked through core printing. During the third step, the system manager closes the loop by assigning the queues to the printers. Assigning queues to printers is necessary so that print jobs that are sent from workstations to print queues can ultimately find their way to the appropriate network printer.

These three setup processes are very similar to the setup processes that the print server requires. The main difference is in how they are implemented. Core printing setup is implemented entirely at the file server console while print server setup is implemented through the PCONSOLE menu utility. Here's a detailed description of the process just described.

*Core printing relies on special server console commands: QUEUE CREATE, PRINTER CREATE, and PRINTER ADD. Learn them.*

### Creating Print Queues

Creating print queues is the first step in core printing setup. Print queues are necessary because they provide a buffering holding area for print jobs while they are waiting for available network printers. Queue creation in core printing is accomplished through the QUEUE console command using the following syntax: QUEUE [queue name] CREATE and then Enter. For example: QUEUE LASERJET III CREATE would create a print queue named LASERJET III.

There are a variety of other parameters that can be used with the queue console command in creating and managing core printing queues. They are:

**QUEUE** by itself lists all print queues.

**QUEUE NAME CHANGE JOB NUMBER 2 PRIORITY X** changes the job priority in a queue.

**QUEUE NAME DELETE JOB N** deletes a given job from the print queue.

**QUEUE NAME DESTROY** deletes the entire print queue.

**QUEUE NAME JOB** lists all jobs that are currently in the print queue.

To view these options and get a full listing of the queue console parameters, simply type QUEUE HELP or QUEUE ? at the file server console. Queue name should be easily recognizable and somehow linked in name to their appropriate printer. Queue names cannot be more than forty-seven characters, but for easy management, should probably be less than ten. Remember, queues are subdirectories under the system directory. Print jobs are printed on a first in, first out basis in NetWare queues. This order, however, can be changed using PCONSOLE or the QUEUE NAME CHANGE PRIORITY console command. Queues should be assigned to their own printer, although it is possible to have a queue assigned to multiple printers or to have multiple queues assigned to one printer.

### Defining Printers

The next step in setting up core printing is defining the printers. Core printing does not allow the system manager to name his or her file server printers. The system manager is required to manage printers by number. Because there are only five printers available in core printing, the supervisor is limited to the numbers 0 through 4.

Defining the printer accomplishes three tasks:

1. Selecting a printer number

2. Specifying the port type

3. Configuring serial ports if the port type is serial

Printer definition in core printing is accomplished through the printer console command using the following syntax: PRINTER [number] CREATE PORT. For example, PRINTER 0 CREATE LPT1 will create Printer 0 and attach it to the LPT1 parallel port. If the port that is defined using the printer console command is a COM1, COM2, COM3, or COM4 port, the system manager must complete a third step: serial port configuration.

Configuring serial ports in core printing is accomplished through the PRINTER CONFIG console command. The PRINTER CONFIG console command provides a facility for viewing or changing serial printer configurations. The syntax is PRINTER [number] CONFIG, which presents a list of the different printing configuration options. To change the serial printer configuration options, type PRINTER [number] CONFIG [any of the 5 different serial configuration options]. These are:

- BAUD

- WORD SIZE

- STOP BITS

- PARITY

- XON/XOFF

An example would be PRINTER 4 CONFIG BAUD=2400 WORDSIZE=8 STOPBITS=1 PARITY=0 XOFF/ON=YES. While printer definitions in core printing are obviously extremely important, they are not very easy to grasp. One consolation is that parallel printers do not require any configuration.

## Assigning Queues to Printers

The final step in core printing installation is the assignment of the queue to the printer. Once the print queue has been defined and the printer has been installed, the system manager must assign a queue to a printer. Queue assignments tell NetWare user print jobs where to go once they leave the queue. Keep in mind, with NetWare core printing, there is no print server to help control or manage the movement from queue to printer.

The assignments of queues to printers in NetWare 2.2 core printing is accomplished through the PRINTER ADD console command. The syntax is `PRINTER [number] ADD QUEUE [queue name] AT PRIORITY [number]`. For example, to add the LaserJet III queue to printer 0 at priority 1, the following command would have to be issued at the console prompt: `PRINTER 0 ADD LASERJET III AT PRIORITY 1`. Incidentally, the default priority in core printing is 1, which means that a particular print queue will have first crack at the printer in case there are multiple queues attached to the same printer. If there are three or four queues attached to the same printer and they each have different priorities, all jobs will be printed from queue with priority 1 before any jobs are printed from other, lower-priority queues.

Once the print queue has been created, the printer has been defined, and the queue has been assigned to the appropriate printer, NetWare core printing has been accomplished. From this point on, NetWare users can send print jobs to the specific queue that was created, and those jobs will be redirected to the appropriate network printer. NetWare core printing does not provide much flexibility with respect to multiple configurations, alternative resources, or distributing printer locations.

To build on the fundamentals of core printing, the system manager has the option of installing the print server system. The print server system is much more flexible and provides a greater amount of printing functionality.

*Because core printing is installed at the file server console and because most of these configurations are not built into the operating system, all of the work that was accomplished by the system manager in setting up and installing core printing is lost once the server is down. In an effort to stay sane, the system manager should insert the previous core printing installation commands into the AUTOEXEC.SYS system configuration file. AUTOEXEC.SYS is executed whenever NetWare 2.2 file servers are booted. A sample AUTOEXEC.SYS would include a printer, a printer definition, and an assignment of the queue to the printer. Print queues are permanent directories that exist on the file server.*

*Every action of our lives touches on some chord that will vibrate in eternity.*

*Edwin Hubbel Chapin*

# NetWare Print Server

E ARLIER WE MENTIONED THAT 95% of all printing needs are satisfied using NetWare print servers. In the NetWare printing laundromat, the print server would be the washer and dryer and core printing would be the sink. Print servers are more complex than core printing but provide the PCONSOLE utility for a simple user interface and friendly printing management.

## When to Use Print Servers

Print servers are required when the number of printers exceeds the file server's limit of five, or when the physical layout of the LAN is so large that centralization of printer location is not feasible. Print servers are also required when users are utilizing specialized intelligent printers that are not attached to print servers or workstations. In NetWare 2.2, the print server functionality supports sixteen printers and queues from up to eight file servers. Print servers in NetWare 2.2 can be installed on two different devices: dedicated workstations or the file server. The creation of a dedicated print server on a workstation is made possible through the PSERVER.EXE file. In the case of a dedicated print server, the system manager should create a special configuration file called SHELL.CFG on the workstation which defines the command SPX CONNECTIONS = 60. This command is required so that communications can be maintained with multiple users, queues, and file servers.

*Print servers are required when the number of printers exceeds the file server's limit of five, or when the physical layout of the LAN is so large that centralization of printer location is not feasible.*

The non-dedicated or internal print server is defined as PSERVER.VAP, which runs on the NetWare 2.2 server or router. The VAP (value added process) runs in parallel to the operating system. While VAPs take up considerable file server resources, they are well designed and coexist peacefully with the operating system or router functions. In addition to NetWare's print server functionality, there are some third party products that provide more tasks and detailed print job accounting. One of the most popular is Bitstream's Mosaic print server software.

## Print Server Types

Regardless of which print server system you choose, the print serving setup is accomplished with four simple steps. In a nutshell, they are:

1. Create the print queues.

2. Create the print servers.

3. Define printers.

4. Assign queues to printers.

In this section we will discuss the three different print server types and when to use them. Then we will go on to evaluate the four steps in installing NetWare print servers.

To review, print servers are required for a variety of reasons:

- When the number of printers exceeds five

- When printers must be distributed throughout the LAN for location reasons

- When the system manager would like to support intelligent printing devices

- When this printing system supports other file servers from newer versions of NetWare, including 3.12 and 4.1

Available file server processes determine when print servers should be used. File server processes are internal operating system routines that are responsible for processing user requests. When the NetWare 2.2 file server is under a heavy load, file server processes can become busy and unavailable. In these instances, running core printing can severely diminish network file server performance. Running a print server offloads the file server's processes from the operating system itself—even if the print server is running on the file server. Keep in mind, the print server runs as a separate process from the file server.

While core printing limits the system manager to attaching printers directly to the file server, using a print server provides a great deal more functionality. The print server can exist as a separate process on the file server or router, or can exist as a dedicated process on a workstation. In both cases, the print server functionality is identical.

Each of these three different print server types has its own advantages and disadvantages. The advantage of a nondedicated print server is that it doesn't require additional hardware. It does, however, require you to share the print serving processes with an existing file server or router. The dedicated print server, on the other hand, operates exclusively as a print server—no sharing. Unfortunately, though, it does require additional hardware. The good news is a computer doorstop will work fine (an 8088 CPU, 1MB RAM, and a 20MB hard disk.)

## File Server

As mentioned above, running the print server process separately on a file server requires a VAP. The VAP runs in parallel to the network operating system and shares the same 286-based processor. The VAP also shares file server RAM.

*The dedicated print server file exists as PSERVER.EXE. This file runs as an application over DOS and completely takes over the processor and memory of the workstation.*

NetWare 2.2 loads all VAPs it finds in the system directory during startup. It will ask the system manager whether he or she would like to load available VAPs. At that point the system manager has one of two choices: YES to load all VAPs, and NO to load no VAPs. It's an all or nothing proposition. By default, the print server VAP is not loaded on the NetWare server, because NetWare makes no assumptions about printing configuration during installation. To activate the print SERVER.VAP, the system manager must copy the appropriate file from the appropriate NetWare diskette. The file name is PSERVER .VAP and it is stored on the PRINT 1 disk in the following subdirectory: A:\SYSTEM\VAP. Once the file has been copied from the PRINT 1 diskette to the SYSTEM directory on the file server, the file server must be downed and brought back up. Once the file server is brought back up, the system will ask the system manager whether he or she would like to install all known VAPs. If the system manager chooses YES, the print server is installed.

## Workstation

The process of installing the print server on a dedicated workstation is much simpler. The dedicated print server file exists as PSERVER.EXE. This file runs as an application over DOS and completely takes over the processor and memory of the workstation. Before PSERVER.EXE can be run, the system manager must run IPX and NETx to attach the workstation to the network cabling. The system manager does not have to log in this workstation in order for the dedicated print server facility to operate. The facility only requires an attachment so the system manager can run IPX, NETx, and PSERVER.EXE followed by a name for the print server.

PSERVER.EXE is not a large file and can be stored in the root directory of the workstation or on a diskette. Keep in mind that if you are going to run PSERVER.EXE on a dedicated workstation, you must include the SHELL.CFG file with one line: SPX CONNECTION = 60. Doing so will open up enough connections so that the print server can communicate with multiple users, print servers, and file servers.

### Router

Loading the print server functionality on a router provides two advantages over the other print server types: efficiency and connectivity. Print serving efficiency is accomplished because the router does not have nearly the overhead that the file server does. Loading a PSERVER.VAP process on a dedicated router does not hinder the network nearly as much as it does running on a file server. In addition, router functionality provides a variety of operations, including dedicated and non-dedicated routers. In order to run PSERVER .VAP, the system manager must define a dedicated protected mode router—the highest level of NetWare 2.2 routing.

The second advantage is connectivity. The purpose of a router is to connect two distinct LAN topologies. Because the print server is running on a router, the print server functionality is available not just to one but to both of the LAN topologies. This is a simple way of combining the efficiency of running the router on an existing machine with the connectivity of providing print services to more than one network at a time. A router can include up to four network interface cards, so it can connect up to four different LANs. In this scenario, the print server would support print queues on four different file servers from four different networks.

## Print Server Installation

The process of installing a print server on a router is similar to the process of installing a print server on a file server except there is no SYSTEM

*The installation process involves four steps: creating print queues, creating print servers, defining printers, and assigning queues to printers.*

subdirectory. Instead, the system manager defines a ROUTER.CFG file with the PSERVER.VAP included. Once the router is booted, the ROUTER.CFG file defines the print server function and loads the auxiliary process. From that point on, PSERVER can be used to manage and maintain the router print server.

Once you have chosen your print server type, it is time for the system manager to get down and dirty by installing the three components of a NetWare printing system: the print queues, print server, and printer.

Print server installation mirrors core printing installation in theory but that's where the similarities end. Print server installation is much more versatile and provides a workstation-based menu interface. There are no console commands included in print server installation. The installation process involves four steps:

1. Creating print queues

2. Creating print servers

3. Defining printers

4. Assigning queues to printers

During step 1, the system manager creates the print queues on the system and assigns print queue operators and users. During step 2, the system manager creates the print server and gives the print server a unique name and password. In step 3, the system manager continues with print server definition by defining the printers, assigning names to the printers, and configuring their internal parameters. These parameters include port type, interrupt, and serial configurations.

The final step in print server installation is assigning the queues to printers. This step is performed in exactly the same way as it is in core printing. This step is required so that print jobs can find their way from specific queues to appropriate printers. In the next section, we will discuss each of these four steps in some depth and provide some tips for optimizing NetWare print server installation.

*Study the four steps of NetWare 2.2 print server installation. Pay special attention to step 4, because everyone seems to skip it.*

### Creating Print Queues

Print queues are the central component in NetWare printing because they provide the link between NetWare workstations and shared printers. Print queues are created using the PCONSOLE menu utility, which is stored in the PUBLIC directory.

To create a print queue in PCONSOLE, choose Print Queue Information from the available topics menu of PCONSOLE and press Insert at the Queue Name box. Next, type in a queue name up to forty-seven characters and press Enter. At this point, the print queue name will appear in the queue names box.

Once a print queue has been created, the system will assign it an eight-digit hexadecimal number and a subdirectory under the system-generated directory. Using PCONSOLE, the system manager can define other parameters with respect to print queues, including:

- **The Current Print Job Entries** screen provides a list of all print jobs that are currently held in this queue. This screen is a central point for queue management and job reordering.

- **Current Queue Status** displays the status of the queue with respect to number of entries in the queue, number of servers being serviced by this queue, and operator flags.

- **Currently Attached Servers** is a list of print servers that can service this queue. Those print servers keep track of which network printers are also servicing this queue.

- **Print Queue ID** is the eight-digit random number that is assigned to this particular print queue. It matches the subdirectory under SYSTEM.

- **Queue Operators** is a list of users who have been assigned queue operator status. By default, the supervisor is the only queue operator.

- **Queue Servers** is a list of print servers that can service this queue. It does not mean they are currently attached. The system manager can add or delete print servers from this list.

- **Queue Users** includes a list of all users who can add jobs to this queue. By default, the group EVERYONE is assigned as a queue user for all new print queues.

Once the print queue has been created, the system manager can move on to defining and creating the print server and attaching a link between the two.

### Creating Print Servers

Print server creation consists of two steps: installation and setup. The print server installation step involves choosing a print server type and appropriate activation of print server files. For the print server on the file server, this includes the PSERVER.VAP. For a print server on a dedicated workstation, it's PSERVER.EXE and for a print server on a dedicated router, it's PSERVER .VAP and ROUTER.CFG.

Once the print server has been activated, the system manager is ready to set up the print server information. Print server setup is accomplished through the PCONSOLE utility using the printer server information menu from available options. The system manager simply presses Insert at the print server's menu screen and enters a print server name. We recommend that the system manager use the file server name followed by _PS to show the relationship between print servers and file servers they are servicing.

Once a print server has been created, the system manager can customize the print server configurations through the print server information screen, which includes the following information:

- **The Change Password** option allows the system manager to assign a password to the print server so that not just anybody can activate it.

- **The full name** provides more information about this particular print server and what queues and file servers it services.

- **Print server configuration** is used for steps 3 and 4 in print server installation.

- **Print server ID** defines the object ID of the print server. This information is not particularly useful, because it is not used by any other NetWare configuration.

- **Print server operators** displays the list of the users and groups who have been assigned as operators for the print server.

- **Print server users** is a list of users or groups who can send print jobs to printers that are defined using this print server.

By default, the supervisor is assigned as a print server operator and the group EVERYONE is defined as print server users for all newly created print servers.

Once the print server has been activated and configured, a seventh choice will appear in the print server information menu—print server status control. This option lets you view the status of the print server and provides valuable information about print servers that are currently running. This particular choice will not be available to system managers if the print server in question is not activated. Once the print server has been created, the system manager must define the printers that are going to be serviced by this particular print server.

*The wind and the waves are always on the side of the ablest navigators.*

*Edward Gibbon*

### Defining Printers

Printer definition is accomplished through the PCONSOLE utility under Print Server Information. The print server configuration menu provides four choices:

- File Servers to be Serviced
- Notify List for Printer
- Printer Configuration
- Queues Served by Printer

The printer definition choice is Printer Configuration. This option allows the system manager to define up to sixteen printers for this print server and customize their ports and configurations. By default, the sixteen print server printers are assigned numbers 0 through 15 in order. The print server also has the flexibility of assigning a name to printers so that they can be tracked for management as well as queue assignment.

To define a particular printer, choose the printer number from the top of the list (typically 0 for the first printer) and press enter. The printer 0 configuration option, which gives a variety of different options for defining, naming, and configuring NetWare printers, appears. The first option is Name, which will define it for printing management as well as for queue assignment. The Type parameter allows the system manager to define not only serial or parallel, but whether this printer is going to be attached to a local workstation. The Printer Types option appears with nineteen different choices. The first seven are parallel and are used by printers that are attached directly to the print server: LPT1, LPT2, LPT3, COM1, COM2, COM3, and COM4.

The next seven are assigned to printers that are attached to local workstations running remote printing. These include remote parallel and remote serial. The final two are Remote Other/Unknown, which is used for intelligent printers, and Defined Elsewhere. They are used for printers that are being serviced by other file servers.

Once the Printer Type parameter has been set, the system manager can choose interrupts for parallel or BAUD rate, data bit, stop bits, parity, and XON/XOFF for serial printing.

## Assigning Queues to Printers

This particular step is important because it provides a path from the NetWare file server queue to the appropriate printer. If the system manager forgets this step, users will become quite miffed. The symptom is that print jobs are sent off to the NetWare queue and they sit there forever waiting to be serviced by the print server. It is typical for up to 100 or so print jobs to gather in the print queue without any of them being serviced by the printer. If this is the case, the first place to check would be the assignment from the queue to the printer.

Queue assignments are accomplished using the print server configuration menu and the queues serviced by printer option. Choose this option and the system responds with a list of defined printers. Choose the printer that is going to be assigned a particular queue, and press Enter. The system responds with the queue list. If this is the first queue to be assigned to this printer, the queue list will be empty. The system manager will press Insert and the system will respond with a list of available queues. Choose the appropriate queue and assign a priority number, which establishes the queue assignments with the printer.

Once a print queue has been assigned to the appropriate printer and all other steps have been activated, users can now print directly to the queue and the print job will be forwarded to the appropriate printer.

*Once the print queues have been created, the printers have been defined, and the queue has been assigned to the printer, users are ready to print.*

This completes the printer installation process. Once the print queues have been created, the printers have been defined, and the queue has been assigned to the printer, users are ready to print. While print server at first glance seems more complex than core printing, it really isn't—it's just sophisticated. NetWare print servers provide much more versatility than core printing. In addition, NetWare print server functionality is compatible with NetWare 3.12 and 4.1. Core printing was abandoned in later versions of NetWare.

*Let us not be content to wait and see what will happen, but give us the determination to make the right things happen.*

*Peter Marshall*

# Printing Utilities

TO BETTER UNDERSTAND THE process of installation and management of NetWare printing, it is important to have a firm grasp on the variety of tools that are available to the system manager. NetWare 2.2 provides eight different utilities that enhance the printing system. These utilities help you perform a variety of tasks, including capturing workstation data, configuring the print jobs, managing them once they're in the queue, assigning them to appropriate printers, defining the printer escape sequences, and controlling what time of day the print jobs are printed.

In the remainder of this chapter, we will discuss these eight printing utilities and see how they are analogous to the soap in our NetWare laundry room.

## CAPTURE

The CAPTURE command is a printing utility that provides flexibility for the workstation so that printing can be done from non-NetWare applications. CAPTURE literally hijacks the local printer port and redirects all print jobs destined for that port to a NetWare queue. The syntax of the CAPTURE command is `CAPTURE QUEUE=[name of queue] /[switch].`

*Learn the CAPTURE switches. It's important to the quality of your CNA life.*

There is a huge variety of additional parameters that can be used with the CAPTURE command to customize the way print jobs are printed. Some of the more interesting CAPTURE parameters include:

**/b** for banner name

**/c** for copies

**/ff** for form feed

**/j** for job (which is a PRINTCON utility)

**/l=[number]** for the local port that needs to be CAPTUREd by default. Without the /l=[number], CAPTURE will capture the LPT1 parallel port.

**/nff** for no form feed

**/nt** for no tabs

**/sh** for show, which will display the current status of the CAPTURE command

**/t** for tabs=[number] to replace all tab characters with spaces if you specify

**/ti** for timeout, which is a timeout feature that is important for certain misbehaving non-network applications.

*Here's an example CAPTURE command that is useful in most environments:* `CAPTURE QUEUE=[queuename] /nb /nt /ti=10 /nff.`

# ENDCAP

ENDCAP is a command line utility that ends the CAPTURE session. Once CAPTURE has been loaded into memory, it cannot be unloaded or stopped unless you issue an ENDCAP command. ENDCAP allows you the flexibility to capture to specific queues for specific applications and end that capture session, then recapture the local port for another queue in another application. Incidentally, all of this can be accomplished using batch files.

## NPRINT

NPRINT is a workstation command line utility that sends a text file directly to a NetWare queue. The syntax of NPRINT is `NPRINT [queue name]` and it uses the same parameters as CAPTURE. But in this case, instead of capturing from a local port, NPRINT prints a text file from the command line directly to a NetWare queue. There's no port involved.

## PCONSOLE

PCONSOLE is the printing management installation utility that we discussed earlier. PCONSOLE is responsible for all steps in print server installation and also for the management and maintenance of print servers, print queues, and printers once NetWare printing has been installed.

## PRINTCON

PRINTCON is an advanced NetWare system management printing utility that is used to customize print job configurations. Using PRINTCON, the system manager can define a specific set of configurations for a user and then attach those configurations to a print job using the CAPTURE /j parameter. The print job parameters are identical to the switches from CAPTURE except PRINTCON provides a facility for permanently storing these parameters in a menu format.

# PRINTDEF

PRINTDEF is another advanced printing definition utility used in NetWare that provides the system manager with the ability to define or customize NetWare printers. PRINTDEF provides two facilities: form management and modes. Form management allows the system manager to define specific types of forms that are used by specific printers. These forms can include 8.5 × 11, 11 × 8.5, legal size paper, checks, etc. Forms are defined in PRINTDEF using the width and length parameters. Modes define specialized printing functions such as compressed, landscaped, bold, italic, etc. Modes can be defined using PRINTDEF for specific printers so that when print jobs are sent to NetWare queues, they can be configured using a special set of printer definition functions.

# PSC

The PSC command is a very useful printer and print server control utility that system managers use to manage and maintain NetWare print servers. PSC provides similar functionality to PCONSOLE except it performs its operations from the command line. PSC issues commands directly to the printer or print server. With PSC, you can perform the following PCONSOLE tasks:

- view the status of printers
- pause the printer temporarily
- stop printing the current job
- start the printer
- mark the top of form
- advance printer to top of next page
- mount a new form

*You can use the DOS SET command to set a default print server and printer number for PSC so you don't have to specify this information at the command line every time.*

The syntax for PSC is `PSC=printserver P=printer`.

# RPRINTER

The RPRINTER command is the workstation utility that provides the remote printing facility. RPRINTER is a terminate-and-stay-resident (TSR) program that runs in workstation RAM and controls the movement of print jobs from queues to the local workstation. The RPRINTER syntax includes RPRINTER and Enter, which will bring up the RPRINTER menu utility. Otherwise, RPRINTER parameters can be issued at the command line by typing `RPRINTER PS=PRINTERSERVER` and `P=PRINTER`. This particular command in an AUTOEXEC.BAT file will activate the RPRINTER facility. Keep in mind that RPRINTER takes up some workstation RAM and communicates directly with local printer ports. RPRINTER can be removed from memory by using the -r switch.

*RPRINTER does not require that the user be logged into the network—simply attached. An RPRINTER attachment can be accomplished by executing IPX.COM only. Once the workstation has been attached to the network, RPRINTER can be issued.*

*Congratulations! You have successfully completed the NetWare 2.2 CNA program. Don't forget your utility belt!*

Congratulations! You have successfully completed the NetWare 2.2 CNA program. We learned about NetWare directory structures, drive mapping, security, menu utilities, supervisor utilities, console commands, login scripts, user interface, backup, and printing. This has been quite a journey.

In addition, we explored the NetWare apartment building, laundry room, locksmith duties, and LANlord status. Now you should feel amply prepared for the challenges that await you. But the NetWare 2.2 world can be a jungle, so don't forget your NetWare utility belt!

# Exercise 7.1: Using the Capture Command

As we learned in this chapter, the CAPTURE command provides a facility for redirecting print jobs from local workstation ports to NetWare queues. This facility is required for applications that are not aware of the NetWare printing system. In this written exercise, we will explore some common scenarios and generate appropriate CAPTURE statements. Refer to the discussion of CAPTURE flags to choose the appropriate switches.

For each question, write the appropriate CAPTURE command.

1. Print jobs need to go to a queue named REPORTS with a timeout of 7 and four copies with no form feed. Your name and the file name should be on the banner.

2. Print jobs need to go to the SALES file server to use their graphics queue. The jobs should be a Bytestream file and have no banner. All jobs sent to the graphics should be captured from LPT2 and have a form feed following the job.

3. Print jobs captured from LPT3 should create a print file in the SYS:PLOTTER directory and should not print a hard copy.

4. Someone's print jobs aren't getting to the queue. How can I see if the file server knows to pick up their jobs and redirect them?

5. The accountant has a month-end report that will take two hours to print and would like to print it during off hours. The system manager has designed a print job configuration for this user under the name ACCOUNT. The ACCOUNT configuration defines a deferred print job to 10:00 p.m. that evening. What CAPTURE command does the accountant use to send this particular print job to the network printer and have it deferred until 10:00 p.m. that evening?

6. The sales department is using a non-network aware application that is acting quite finicky. You would like it to print with no banner, no form feed, a timeout of 10 and with no tabs.

7. The system manager's machine has a local printer attached to LPT2 but typically uses a system login script that captures both LPT1 and LPT2. He or she would like to override the redirection of print jobs from LPT2 so he or she can use the local printer. What command would he or she use?

Check your answers in Appendix D.

# Part II—NetWare 2.2

**ACROSS**

1. Displays routing info at console

4. Remote printing

8. Doorstep of the LAN

9. Next available drive mapping

10. Trustee assignment minus MRM

13. Primary drive mapping tool

16. Printing setup utility

17. Shared user tools directory

21. Folders of the NetWare filing cabinet

23. Redirects local ports to queues

25. Unwanted user

27. NetWare's built-in backup utility

**DOWN**

2. Built-in NetWare 2.2 printing

3. Search the directory structure

5. Transparent user interface

6. To rename a file

7. To view effective rights in a menu

11. Assigning file attributes

12. Load the correct COMMAND.COM

14. A NetWare 2.2 menu file

15. The directory rights analogy

18. Fix a corrupt NetWare OS

19. The user rights analogy

20. A user with privileges

21. The mother of all NetWare utilities

22. The waiting room for print jobs

24. Assigning user rights

26. To find an application with MAP

See Appendix D for answers.

# The
# NetWare 3.12
# CNA Program

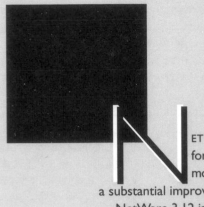

ETWARE 3.12 IS A complete network operating system designed for medium-to-large-sized LANs. It provides high performance, modularity, and flexible workstation connectivity. NetWare 3.12 is a substantial improvement over all previous versions of NetWare.

NetWare 3.12 is the first truly modular network operating system. The core operating system consists of three components: the NetWare file system, the system executive, and NLM software bus. These components are integrated into one operating system file, SERVER.EXE. All other network services are attached to the NLM bus as modular components. These components are called NetWare Loadable Modules (NLMs). They can be loaded and unloaded without disrupting the LAN. Some server applications have been written as both NLMs and operating system components. The operating system NLMs include disk drivers, LAN drivers, and name space modules. In addition, application NLMs consist of system fault tolerance, mail services, gateways, printing, multiprotocol support, and so on. Because of this modularity, NetWare 3.12 can provide a true open architecture solution. It is designed to provide file sharing, security, printing, system fault tolerance, and network management to many diverse platforms. NetWare 3.12 supports IPX/SPX, TCP/IP, AppleTalk, and OSI protocols from simultaneous workstations. These workstations can be running DOS, Windows, OS/2, System 7, or Unix operating systems.

NetWare 3.12 takes full advantage of the 32-bit file server architecture by providing almost unlimited support for disk storage, memory, and concurrently open files. NetWare's built-in high capacity file system and universal file system allow 100,000 concurrently opened files and a maximum of 2,097,152 directory entries per volume.

In addition, NetWare 3.12 supports 64 volumes and 32 disks per volume for a total of 2,048 server disks. The maximum storage capacity is well beyond current technology—4GB file size, 32TB addressable storage—that's 32 trillion (32,000,000,000,000) bytes. Fortunately, NetWare 3.12 provides a host of system fault tolerance features to protect all of this connectivity and data storage. NetWare 3.12 supports fault tolerance levels I, II, and III. SFT Level III, server duplexing, is an additional product that requires two identical servers that are connected with a 100 Mb/s (Megabits-per-second) fiber-optic line. SFT Levels I and II support read-after-write verification, hot fix, elevator seeking, disk duplexing, disk mirroring, and UPS monitoring.

NetWare 3.12's security is based on the same multilayered security model as NetWare 2.2. However, 3.12 provides some additional security enhancements—the supervisory trustee assignment, more directory and file attributes, and the concept of an inherited rights mask.

NetWare 3.12's most notable improvement is the 32-bit architecture, which provides greater memory management, performance, modularity, storage capacity, and connectivity. The 32-bit architecture has led to considerable improvements in file server throughput and response time. In addition, file service processes have been refined and the earlier dynamic memory pools have been expanded. Net-Ware 3.12's performance enhancements are optimized using two performance management utilities: SET and MONITOR. SET is a console command that offers immediate network operating system configuration. MONITOR, as an NLM, provides performance management and monitoring capabilities.

All of these features and enhancements have combined to make NetWare 3.12 the best selling network operating system in history. It's Novell's eighth generation of NetWare and is an ideal product for almost any networking environment.

# NetWare 3.12 Directory Structure

NAs HAVE THREE PRIMARY responsibilities: system administration, troubleshooting/installation, and networking technologies. This part focuses on your role as NetWare system manager.

As the NetWare system manager, it is your responsibility to understand the many flexible functions and features of NetWare. In addition, you wear the many hats required for building, managing, and maintaining such a complex system. Fortunately, NetWare provides you with all the tools you will need—including a NetWare utility belt. And this book provides you with a handy hat rack on which to hang your system manager hats.

NetWare can be thought of as a big luxurious hotel—Park Place, for example. As the NetWare system manager, it is your responsibility to make sure that all of the users pass GO and collect $200. Your system manager roles are analogous to the many people who are required to manage and maintain a luxury hotel. The following is a brief example:

- **NetWare directory structure**—In working with the NetWare directory structure, you are the architect of the LAN. The architect of a hotel designs the rooms, the lobby, and the restaurants; builds the structure; and fills the hotel with furniture and amenities. It is the architect's responsibility to create a comfortable, functional environment that is both practical and pleasing to the eye.

- **NetWare security**—In managing security, you are the detective of the LAN. The house detective builds the locks and keys for all of the rooms. In addition, he/she installs the infrared motion detection system and hires the lobby guards. The house detective ensures that the hotel guests stay where they belong and are safe and secure.

- **NetWare utilities**—In working with your NetWare utility belt, you are the handyman of the LAN. You wear your belt that contains all of the tools that are required to perform hotel maintenance. These tasks include fixer-upper projects, plumbing, electrical, heating,

*NetWare can be thought of as a big luxurious hotel— Park Place, for example. As the NetWare system manager, it is your responsibility to make sure that all the users pass GO and collect $200.*

air-conditioning, and minor equipment repairs. Whenever anything goes wrong in the NetWare hotel, it is your responsibility to fix it—using your NetWare utility belt.

- **Network management**—The NetWare system manager makes sure everything runs smoothly on a day-to-day basis. Park Place is under the guidance of the hotel manager who oversees the maids, the custodians, bellhops, reception desk staff, and all the other hotel employees. The hotel manager hat is one of the most challenging and rewarding of the system manager's responsibilities.

- **Printing**—In managing and maintaining NetWare printing, you are the chef of the LAN, in charge of preparing fine cuisine for the hotel, including the restaurants and room service. Restaurant dining is analogous to centralized printing—the printers are attached directly to the print server just as diners come to the restaurant. Room service is analogous to remote printing—the printers are distributed throughout the LAN just as the room service orders come to the guests.

- **Performance management**—The final and most exciting of your NetWare hotel roles is that of interior decorator. The interior decorator is responsible for upgrading the quality of the rooms and the lobby. Daily operations include painting, purchasing fine furniture, hanging artwork, and installing various amenities. A good interior decorator can make the difference between a mediocre hotel and a five-star resort.

In our Park Place analogy, the rooms are workstations, the lobby and the restaurants are the file server, and guests are users. The hallways and elevators are cabling that connects the rooms and the hotel lobby.

*A wonderful discovery—psychoanalysis. It makes quite simple people feel they're complex.*

*Samuel N. Behrman*

Novell's NetWare CNA program is designed to provide you with the expertise and guidance you need to wear the many hats of the NetWare system manager. In the next six chapters, we will discuss the roles and responsibilities of the NetWare architect, house detective, handyman, hotel manager, chef, and interior decorator. The discussion will focus on the responsibilities of each of these individuals and provide the system manager with a variety

*Novell's NetWare CNA program is designed to provide you with the expertise and guidance you need to wear the many hats of the NetWare system manager.*

of tools for performing his or her duties. Keep in mind that "all work and no play makes Johnny/Jane a dull child." So, while we move through these chapters, let's take time here and there to discuss the positive aspects of this job and maybe rest and relax a little. After all, life as a NetWare manager is no vacation.

*The only way the magic works is by hard work. But hard work can be fun!*

*Jim Henson*

The NetWare architect is responsible for building the directory structure, installing the applications and files, and establishing NetWare drive mappings. Once the architect has completed his/her job, the system is ready for security and user logins.

At this point, Park Place is only a dream. It consists of an empty lot with concrete foundations and lots of empty frames. The network architect will design the rooms, the lobby, and the structure of the hotel so that it will be both luxurious and practical. The architect will follow up his or her design with intense construction that will include the building of rooms, a large foyer, garage, driveways, furniture, restaurants, and so on. Once the structure has been built and the interior has been decorated, the Park Place resort will be open for guests and business conventions.

In the same manner, the NetWare system manager is responsible for building the NetWare directory structure and drive mappings so that they are both easy to use and practical. NetWare directories create functional groupings from the volume root. They house NetWare files or functionally similar subdirectories. Figure 8.1 shows this directory structure as a filing cabinet with drawers, folders, and documents. In this analogy, the drawers are volumes, the folders are directories and subdirectories, and the documents are NetWare files. The NetWare file system provides the following benefits:

- Central management and backup
- Improved data security
- Shared storage to reduce disk space requirements
- Private (unshared) storage
- Improved access to file resources

*The NetWare architect is responsible for building the directory structure, installing the applications and files, and establishing NetWare drive mappings.*

**FIGURE 8.1**
NetWare directory
structure as
a filing cabinet

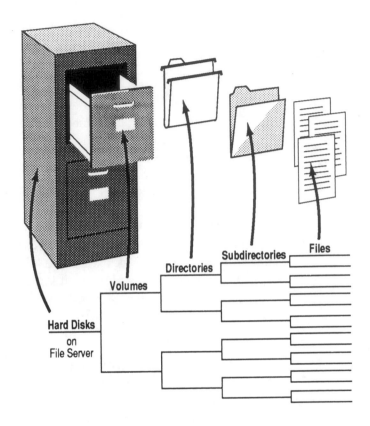

In our exploration of NetWare directory structures, we will focus on the four directory types and their contents. Tools for managing the directory structure will be provided. In addition, we will explore drive mappings to understand how network and search drive mappings provide a tool for navigating the directory tree. But before we begin, let's take a moment to explore the highest level of the NetWare directory structure—volumes.

# NetWare Volumes

THE VOLUME IS THE major division of NetWare file storage. In our earlier analogy, it represents the file cabinet drawers. Volumes are active segments of a physical server hard disk. They are further divided into directories, subdirectories, and files. A volume may be fully contained on a single hard disk or spread across multiple disks. Similarly, one disk may contain one or more volumes. By default NetWare opts for the simplest configuration—one disk = one volume.

A NetWare 3.1*x* server can support up to sixty-four volumes with 32TB of total disk space on 2,048 hard disks. NetWare 2.2 supports thirty-two volumes and 2GB of total disk space on 32 hard disks. In both cases, the default volume occupies all internal server disk space and calls itself SYS. In this chapter, we will explore proven strategies for slicing up NetWare volumes into system-created and suggested network directories. First, let's begin with a look at the types of NetWare directories.

*NetWare 3.12 includes a facility for representing server-attached CD-ROMs as NetWare volumes. System managers and their users can use this built-in CD-ROM feature to share vital informational databases such as the Network Support Encyclopedia, DynaText, and Microsoft's Bookshelf. For details, consult the DynaText CD-ROM.*

# Directory Types

THE NETWARE SYSTEM MANAGER inherits a minimum base system; that is, distributed workstations, connected topology components, a functional file server, and NetWare. The minimum NetWare setup includes four system-created directories, two users, one group, and a few SYSTEM and PUBLIC files. This is where your job begins as the NetWare architect. You will hitch up your NetWare utility belt and get busy creating a

*The process of NetWare system management begins with the creation of an efficient, secure network directory structure.*

directory structure, installing applications, developing security, and adding users and groups.

The process of NetWare system management begins with the creation of an efficient, secure network directory structure. Earlier we likened the network directory structure to a filing cabinet with drawers, folders, and documents. The NetWare directory structure in this analogy relies on the file server, volume, directory, and file components. These components are organized into a tree structure. The tree design of NetWare's directory structure is governed by a few rules. Here's a brief list of NetWare's directory rules:

| | |
|---|---|
| File Server | • Name length is limited to two to forty-seven characters. |
| | • First character cannot be a period. |
| | • Name cannot contain special characters—* + , \ / ¦ ; : = < > ? [ ]. |
| Volume | • Name length is limited to two to fifteen characters. |
| | • Name must end with a colon (:). |
| | • First volume on first disk must be SYS:. |
| | • Maximum of sixty-four volumes per server ($3.1x$) or thirty-two volumes per server (2.2). |
| | • Maximum volume size is 32TB ($3.1x$) or 255MB (2.2). |
| | • Two physical volumes on the same server cannot share the same name. |
| | • No special characters—* + , \ / ¦ ; : = < > ? [ ]. |
| Directory | • Name length is limited to eleven characters (8.3). |
| | • A period separates the first eight from the last three characters. |
| | • Directories should be limited to functional groups. |
| | • No special characters—* + , \ / ¦ ; : = < > ? [ ]. |
| Subdirectory | • Name length is limited to eleven characters (8.3). |
| | • A period separates the first eight from the last three characters. |
| | • Subdirectories share common functionality. |
| | • The number of subdirectories is limited by disk size (twenty-five deep by default). |

*The first of my KISS principles for NetWare directory structure is* Keep It
Safely Shallow. *A hierarchical tree is easiest to maintain when it is not too
tall and not too wide.*

In our discussion of NetWare's directory structure, we will focus on the
four main directory types:

- System-created directories

- DOS directories

- Application/data directories

- User directories

The system-created directories store valuable SYSTEM and PUBLIC files
that are responsible for daily LAN operations. System-created directories are
broken into two major categories: supervisor directories and user directories.
Supervisor directories contain utilities and system files that are designed for
supervisor access only. User directories contain global user management utilities that can be accessed by anybody on the network, including guests.

DOS directories provide support for common WOSs. Each version of
workstation DOS should be supported by a corresponding DOS directory. Ap-
plication/data directories are the workhorses of the LAN directory structure.
The application/data directories include both user applications and user- or
group-specific data. Finally, user directories are designed to provide a home
workspace for each user on the LAN. After all, each Park Place guest deserves
his/her own room. Let's start with system-created directories.

## System-Created Directories and Their Contents

During the installation procedure, NetWare creates four system directories:

- LOGIN

- SYSTEM

- PUBLIC

- MAIL

These four system-created directories perform vital NetWare functions and house critical system/public files. Figure 8.2 illustrates NetWare's four system-created directories. All of these directories contain necessary NetWare files and should *not* be deleted. Following is a description of each of NetWare's system-created directories and its contents.

## LOGIN

The LOGIN directory is NetWare's welcome mat. It represents the first point of contact for attached NetWare users. Once a user attaches to the central file server, he/she has access to the LOGIN directory. Before the user can enter Park Place hotel, he/she must check in at the desk (as in the login) and provide proof of reservation (password). The process of logging in is performed from the LOGIN directory.

**FIGURE 8.2**
NetWare's
system-created
directories

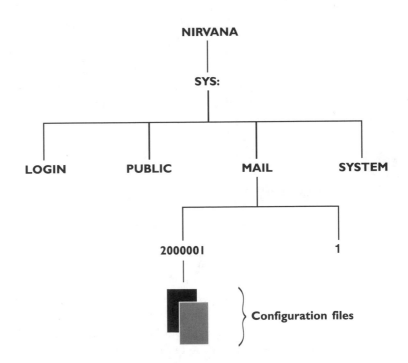

The process of logging into a NetWare server consists of two main steps: workstation initialization and login procedures.

- Workstation Initialization

  1. Boot the workstation with a supported WOS—DOS, OS/2, etc.

  2. Type IPX for NetWare 2.2 or type LSL, NE2000 (or other), and IPXODI to load the NetWare 3.1*x* protocol stacks.

  3. Next, type NETx for NetWare 2.2 or type VLM and press Enter to load the NetWare Shell or DOS Requester.

- Login Procedures

  4. Attach to the NetWare welcome mat by typing F: and pressing Enter.

  5. Type LOGIN and press Enter.

  6. Enter a valid username.

  7. Enter the correct password—if needed.

The NetWare welcome mat contains two system files: LOGIN.EXE and SLIST.EXE. LOGIN.EXE is the executable file that enables users to log in to the NetWare server. SLIST.EXE lists available file servers. Notice that the available disk space in the LOGIN directory is zero. This restriction is lifted once users properly log in.

*Only the educated are free.*

*Epictetus*

The LOGIN directory is the only network directory available to a user before he/she logs in—besides local DOS. The LOGIN directory is automatically mapped to the first available NetWare drive once the user attaches, using NETx or VLM. The first available NetWare drive by default is F. If the system manager needs to make a file available to users before they log in, that file should be placed in the LOGIN directory. For example, remote booting requires access to a boot image file that is used to load the WOS—this boot image file is stored in the SYS:LOGIN directory.

## SYSTEM

The SYSTEM directory is the second most important system-created directory next to LOGIN. SYSTEM houses critical NetWare files, including the operating system (NET$OS.EXE for NetWare 2.2), specialized bindery files, Supervisor utilities, value added processes (VAPs, in 2.2), and NetWare loadable modules (NLMs, in 3.1x). By default, all server VAPs and NLMs are loaded from the SYSTEM directory. SYSTEM is off limits to everyone except the supervisor.

Novell uses a curious naming scheme to designate important system files—the $ symbol. Every critical system file in NetWare contains a $ in its name. Here are some examples:

- NET$OS.EXE—the NetWare 2.2 operating system file

- NET$LOG.DAT—the system login script file

- NET$OBJ.SYS—one of the NetWare 3.1x bindery files

It is safe to say that Novell recognizes the monetary value of these critical system files!

*The PUBLIC directory is every user's playground. This is where the public NetWare programs, commands, menu utilities, and other fun stuff are stored. The PUBLIC directory is accessible to all network users.*

## PUBLIC

The PUBLIC directory is every user's playground. This is where the public NetWare programs, commands, menu utilities, and other fun stuff are stored. The PUBLIC directory is accessible to all network users. It provides a central shared area for frequently used network programs and system-oriented commands. Third-party utilities, for example, usually are stored in the PUBLIC directory. We will explore these public commands and utilities in Chapter 10's coverage of NetWare utilities.

In addition, the PUBLIC directory is a good central storage area for global applications and utility files—the Park Place lobby. The DOS directories, for example, are typically stored under the PUBLIC directory.

## MAIL

The final system-created directory is MAIL. The MAIL directory is left over from the old days, when NetWare included an electronic mail facility.

NetWare 3.12 reintroduced the Novell e-mail facility, greatly improved. Ironically, it doesn't use the MAIL directory. MAIL is still useful, though, because it is the parent directory for a collection of system-created user directories that correspond to each user's randomly assigned user ID number. The user ID is an eight-digit hexadecimal number that identifies each user to the NetWare operating system. For example, the supervisor is number 1 and the guest is number 2000001. Each user gets his/her own SYS:MAIL subdirectory identified by the user ID number—leading zeros removed. The user ID subdirectory under MAIL is used to store two important user-specific configuration files: the user login script (LOGIN.) and printer configuration file (PRINTCON.DAT). The NetWare system manager should never have to bother with these user-specific subdirectories under MAIL.

*NetWare 3.12 includes three other auxiliary system-created directories: ETC, DELETED.SAV, and DOC. The ETC directory supports TCP/IP interconnectivity, DELETED.SAV contains salvageable files from deleted directories, and DOC includes DynaText files.*

That completes our discussion of the system-created directories. Keep in mind that these directories are created by NetWare during installation, and they include all necessary NetWare system files and utilities. All other directories created and stored beyond this point are the responsibility of the NetWare architect. The three remaining directory types are suggested directories.

*Although the following three directory types are "suggested," NetWare doesn't operate properly without them. Also, directory design is a personal issue. There are no right or wrong answers—only shades of efficiency.*

## Suggested Directories

NetWare provides the system manager with a big head start by building the four required system-created directories. The next step is to add some productive user/application directories on top of the existing directory structure. After all, what good is Park Place without room service, laundry, and a snack bar? Novell suggests a variety of approaches to creating custom directories: multiple volumes, applications sorted by user, group directories, and shared data directories. Novell's custom approach to suggested directories boils down to the following four directories: DOS, USERS, APPS, and DATA. Let's take a closer look.

### The DOS Directory

*Novell's custom approach to suggested directories boils down to the following four directories: DOS, USERS, APPS, and DATA.*

The DOS directory is vital because it provides support for the most common WOS: DOS. One of the most critical DOS files is COMMAND.COM, the workstation boot file. COMMAND.COM is loaded into workstation RAM when the workstation computer is turned on. During normal LAN operations, the COMMAND.COM file can be harshly removed from workstation RAM. If this happens, the workstation must be told where to find the file. The server's DOS directory and subsequent subdirectories provide the workstation with a simple path back to COMMAND.COM. In addition, the DOS subdirectories enable network users to access common DOS utilities from a centrally shared directory. For this reason, the DOS directory is typically stored under PUBLIC.

In order to provide optimal workstation support, the DOS directory structure must follow a strict pattern. Figure 8.3 illustrates the strict design of NetWare's DOS directories. We will explain this pattern in more depth in Chapter 6.

*A man travels the world over in search of what he needs, and returns home to find it.*

*George Moore*

### User Directories

User directories provide NetWare users with their own little home, giving them a private and secure subdirectory to begin their own personal directory structure. User subdirectories serve two functions: security and organization. From a security viewpoint, user subdirectories provide a secure place for private user files or personal correspondence. From an organizational viewpoint, user subdirectories can become the parent directory of a complex user-specific directory structure.

*NetWare 3.1x provides a utility for specifying a parent directory for all users: SYSCON. This utility enables the system manager to specify USERS as the parent directory. NetWare does the rest—it creates a home directory for all users individually at the point of their creation, under USERS with their unique username!*

User subdirectories should match usernames and be stored under the USERS root directory, as Figure 8.3 indicates.

*Another effective user directory strategy involves functional departments. In the next chapter, you will learn about distributed security management. Distributed security is made much easier if users and their files are organized according to departments. Consider this as an alternative to the standard structure shown in Figure 8.3.*

**FIGURE 8.3**
The suggested NetWare directory structure

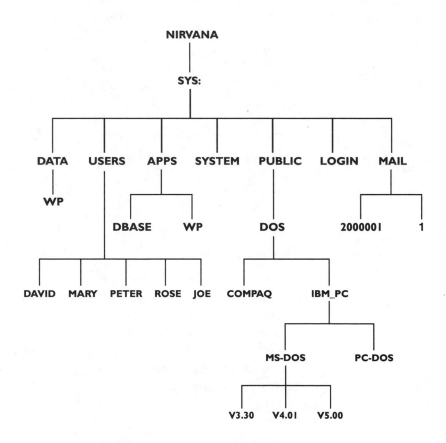

### Application/Data Directories

Proper organization of application and data directories strongly impacts user productivity. If application directories are scattered, it is difficult for users to find network applications. Furthermore, disorganized data directories can be confusing for users who are trying to store network files. Application subdirectories should be created for each network application and stored under the APPS root directory. This makes application access easy for network users and security management more straightforward for the NetWare system manager. Data, on the other hand, can be stored in a variety of directories:

■ **Personal data** should be stored in user directories.

■ **Application-specific data** should be stored in application subdirectories under the DATA root directory.

■ **Shared network data** should be stored directly in DATA.

Figure 8.3 provides a schematic of how application and data directories should be organized.

*Again, a department-oriented directory structure can prove useful as you distribute the security workload to workgroup managers. In some cases, it makes sense to organize the data and applications within the departments that use them.*

That's it for the NetWare system-created and suggested directory types. Although creating directories depends on personal preferences, there are a few rules to follow for optimal functionality:

■ Limit the number of subdirectories off of the root volume.

■ Organize directories and subdirectories according to their common functionality.

■ Stay within the confines of the one SYS volume, to avoid the problem of running out of disk space on a volume even though the disk has plenty of space.

■ Only use multiple volumes if you have more than one disk or non-DOS name space loaded.

■ Break data into three areas so that it can be easily found by users, groups, and everyone on the network.

*P*roper organization of application and data directories strongly impacts user productivity. If application directories are scattered, it is difficult for users to find network applications.

*Perhaps the reward of the spirit who tries is not the goal but the exercise.*

*E. V. Cooke*

Try this: The next three figures (8.4, 8.5, and 8.6) depict some *wrong* ways of approaching NetWare directory creation. They show similarities to building a hotel on the edge of a cliff. Try to determine what is wrong with these three sample structures before you read on.

Figure 8.4 illustrates an unorganized directory structure with all directory types defined at the root. This design has serious logic flaws. Figure 8.5 structures network data according to functional groups. Although the design seems to make sense at first, it doesn't work well in real-world situations. This design makes it difficult to find users and track network information. Figure 8.6 organizes network directories within functionally separate

**FIGURE 8.4**
The root of all bad
directory designs

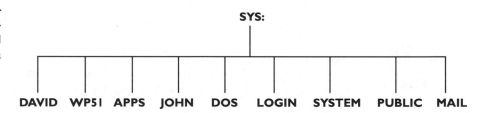

**FIGURE 8.5**
Where's the plan?

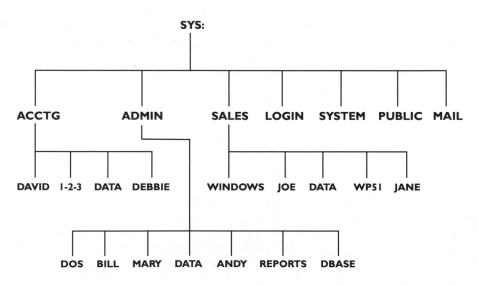

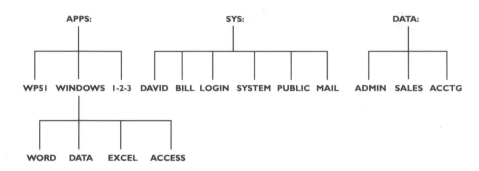

volumes. This approach is inefficient because NetWare volume restrictions are written in stone. Once the volume size is defined, it cannot be changed without destroying the volume. With multiple volumes, DATA: can run out of disk space even though there is plenty of room left in APPS:.

## Directory Path Names

All of this crazy organization can seem a bit overwhelming at first. But once you have had an opportunity to work with NetWare directories for a while, you will find them efficient and useful. Following is the proper syntax for NetWare directory path names:

```
file server/volume:directory\subdirectory
```

The forward slash separates the file server name and volume. The colon distinguishes the root of the volume, and the backslash separates the directory from the subdirectory. This format is very similar to DOS, except NetWare supports both the forward slash and backslash. A typical NetWare directory path looks like this:

```
NIRVANA/SYS:USERS\DAVID
```

Path names are used to define file locations, drive mapping, and utility searches. It's necessary to use the correct syntax when you establish NetWare directory structures.

*Sticks and stones will break my bones, but names will never hurt me.*

*English Proverb*

# Directory Structure Command-Line Utilities

THROUGHOUT THIS BOOK, WE have been bolstering your NetWare utility belt with a variety of commands. NetWare command tools are organized into three categories:

**Command-line utilities** (CLUs) reside in the SYS:PUBLIC directory and are executed at the NetWare prompt—Z:\PUBLIC>. We will explore NetWare's CLUs (NetWare has more than 100 of them) in appropriate spots throughout the book. Here, though, we will discuss NetWare directory structure command-line utilities.

**Menu utilities** provide a consolidated interface for frequently used system management tools. You will learn about NetWare menu utilities in Chapter 10.

**File server console utilities** enable system managers to directly manage NetWare file servers. We will discuss NetWare's console commands in Chapter 10.

*NetWare command tools are organized into three categories: command-line utilities, menu utilities, and file server console utilities.*

Let's begin our discussion of NetWare command-line utilities by exploring DOS and NetWare directory commands. These commands are the paper, pens, and drafting table of the NetWare architect. She wields them to design and create the organizational structure of Park Place's directories. Let's take a look.

## DOS Commands

NetWare works in conjunction with many workstation operating systems—
DOS, OS/2, System 7, Windows NT, and Unix—but was primarily designed
for DOS. In Chapter 1, we explored a variety of DOS commands and utilities. The following is a description of some internal DOS commands that
have limited use in NetWare directory structures.

| | |
|---|---|
| PROMPT | Sets a new DOS prompt. There are myriad prompt parameters—too many to mention here. NetWare requires `PROMPT $P$G` to display current directory path names. |
| MD | Creates a NetWare directory or subdirectory. MKDIR also works. |
| CD | Changes the default DOS or NetWare directory. This command is particularly dangerous in NetWare if it is combined with search drive mappings. This circumstance is discussed later in the chapter. CHDIR also works. |
| COPY CON | Captures data from the screen and creates a text file. A useful command for creating simple NetWare configuration files. Use F6 or Ctrl-Z to exit the program and save your file. |
| DIR | Shows a listing of files and subdirectories of a given NetWare or DOS directory. DIR also displays information about directories and files, including creation date, creation time, and size. |
| TYPE | Displays the contents of a text file on the screen. The results of the TYPE command can be redirected to a printer or file by using the > sign:<br><br>PRINTER—`TYPE filename > PRN`<br>FILE—`TYPE filename > TEMP.TXT` |
| RD | Removes an empty DOS or NetWare subdirectory. RMDIR also works. |

# NetWare Commands

NetWare directory structure commands build on the existing DOS commands by providing specific network functionality. NetWare offers network versions of most DOS utilities (but keep in mind that NetWare utilities have been designed to work on LAN drives only). The following is a discussion of the seven most popular NetWare directory structure commands.

### CHKDIR

The CHKDIR command is used in NetWare to view information about a directory and a volume. The CHKDIR command displays the directory space limitation for the file server and volume. It also displays maximum volume capacity in kilobytes and directory restriction information. CHKDIR displays the number of kilobytes currently in use on the volume or in the specified directory. The system manager can use CHKDIR to check the volume by simply typing CHKDIR and pressing Enter or use CHKDIR to specify information about a given directory. Following is the correct syntax for CHKDIR:

```
CHKDIR directory
```

### CHKVOL

The CHKVOL command is used to view more information about a specific volume. CHKVOL provides the same information as CHKDIR. However, it expands to include the name of the file server, the volume name, the total volume space, the space used by files, the space in use by deleted files, space available from deleted files, the space remaining in the volume, and the space available to the user. CHKVOL also supports wildcard characters. Incidentally, users can only view disk space on volumes for which they have sufficient rights.

### LISTDIR

LISTDIR displays an enhanced graphic of the NetWare directory structure in a pseudo-tree layout. LISTDIR displays more security statistics than NDIR and enables you to specify which information you would like to view. Here's a description of LISTDIR syntax and its parameters (it spells a word):

**LISTDIR /T** displays the creation time.

**LISTDIR /R** displays the directory rights for each specified directory.

**LISTDIR /E** displays only the effective rights for a directory.

**LISTDIR /A** displays all information for each specified directory.

**LISTDIR /D** displays the creation date.

**LISTDIR /S** displays all subdirectories below this directory.

### NCOPY

*NCOPY is particularly useful because it operates entirely from within file server RAM. This command is useful in a NetWare environment because it does not create any additional network traffic.*

NCOPY is a NetWare version of the DOS XCOPY command and provides much more reliability and greater functionality than XCOPY. The SYNTAX for NCOPY is as follows:

```
NCOPY source destination /switch
```

A variety of switches are available with NCOPY that are unavailable for DOS COPY (they also spell a word):

**/C** to copy files without preserving file attributes and name space

**/A** for all files that have the Archive bit set

**/V** for a verify—a read-after-write verification on the original file

**/E** for empty subdirectories

**/S** for subdirectories

*NCOPY is particularly useful because it operates entirely from within file server RAM. This command is handy in a NetWare environment because it does not create any additional network traffic. The DOS COPY command, on the other hand, copies the file into workstation RAM using LAN cabling and back up to the file server.*

*The mind is like the stomach. It is not how much you put into it that counts, but how much it digests.*

*Albert Jay Nock*

## NDIR

The NDIR command is a versatile NetWare utility that enables you to search through NetWare volumes for data, applications, and utilities. NDIR is the NetWare version of DIR. In addition to the basic information—creation date, creation time, and file size—NDIR displays a plethora of network statistics. These include owner, directory rights, subdirectory type, last modified date, security information, disk usage, and file attributes. As seen in the following example, NDIR can list all files in a single directory alone or all files in a single directory and its subdirectories.

```
NDIR *.* /SUB
```

Following is a detailed list of NDIR's many options:

**DO** shows directories only.

**FO** shows files only.

**C** is for a continuous display.

**SORT** sorts the display (UP or DOWN).

**REV SORT SI** conducts a reverse sort by size.

**OW EQ DAVID** searches for files that David owns.

**?** displays help (displays all options).

You get the idea.

## RENDIR

The RENDIR command is a useful NetWare tool that isn't available in the DOS world. It enables you to rename an existing NetWare directory. I can't count the number of times I could have used this command in DOS.

### VOLINFO

VOLINFO is a graphic display of volume information and statistics. It lists volume name, server name, volume sizes, total directory entries, free space, and available directory entries.

*NetWare 3.1x includes a graphical menu utility that automates many of these directory structure commands. It is called NetWare Tools for Windows. With this MS Windows-based utility system managers and users can manage server connections, view active users, send messages, manage directory structures and drive mappings, change directory and file properties, and manage NetWare printing. MS Windows users can quickly access NetWare Tools by pressing <F6>.*

The NetWare directory structure is complex and sophisticated. It enables you to properly organize many kinds of network information. A well-designed directory structure can increase user effectiveness and productivity. A related strategy for increasing user effectiveness is drive mapping. Drive mapping enables you to represent complex directory structures as simple alphabet letters. Let's take a look.

# Drive Mapping

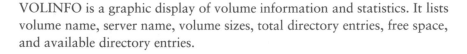

*In the DOS world, we use letters to represent physical disk drives. NetWare also uses letters as drive pointers, but they point to logical drives rather than physical ones.*

IN THE DOS WORLD, we are comfortable with the idea of using letters to represent physical disk drives. In this world, the letter A represents the first floppy drive and B represents the second. C represents the first hard disk and D and E indicate secondary disks. This scheme is simple and straightforward. It helps us to find data easily without having to bother with volume labels or physical mappings.

In the NetWare world, we use the same approach—kind of. NetWare also uses letters as drive pointers, but they point to *logical* drives rather than physical ones. The letter F, for example, points to a network directory (LOGIN), not a physical drive. In this case, F would represent the LOGIN directory—i.e., F:\LOGIN>. NetWare drive letters point to different directories on the same disk. This scheme is also simple and straightforward, but it takes some getting used to.

*NetWare drive mappings are user-specific, temporary environment variables. Each user has a different set of drive mappings in his or her own workstation RAM. They are created each time the user logs in. When the user logs out or turns off the machine, drive mappings are lost. Fortunately, NetWare provides an automatic login script that establishes user mappings at each login.*

NetWare uses two types of drive pointers: network and search. Network drive pointers provide a convenient way of representing complex network path names with a single letter. Search drive pointers provide an additional level of functionality by building a search list for network applications. Now we will explore the details of these two NetWare drive pointers, and you will learn how to implement them by using the MAP command. But first, let's briefly review DOS pointers.

*In this discussion the terms drive pointer and drive mapping will be used interchangeably. Technically, it can be argued that the drive pointer is the alphabet letter and drive mapping is the process of assigning it to a network directory. But let's keep it simple:* Drive pointer = drive mapping.

## DOS Pointers

DOS pointers represent physical storage devices as alphabetized letters. These DOS storage devices typically are floppy drives, hard disks, or CD-ROMs. By default, DOS reserves the letters A–E for local devices. The number of drives can be extended by using the LASTDRIVE = *letter* command in the workstation's CONFIG.SYS file. To move from one drive letter to another, you would simply type the drive letter followed by a colon—i.e., A:—and press Enter. Once you have moved to the correct physical drive, you can use the CD command to move between subdirectories of that drive.

*You can reassign a DOS pointer as a NetWare pointer. In this case, the local drive becomes unavailable to the network user. This is an effective strategy for restricting access to local floppy drives while users are attached to NetWare servers. The DOS pointer is returned to the user when he/she disconnects from the LAN or removes the NetWare pointer.*

# NetWare Pointers

NetWare pointers come in two varieties: network drive mappings and search drive mappings. Network drive mappings are used for directory navigation and accessing data files. Search drive mappings, on the other hand, provide an additional functionality—the NetWare search list. The search list provides easy access to distributed network applications. Here you will learn how to implement network and search drive mappings.

*If I were you, I would expend a little extra effort learning drive mapping. This concept is critical to daily LAN operations. Also, you're likely to see the following topics again: network drive letters and CD, search drive mappings and the PATH statement, drive letter conventions, and MAP ROOT.*

### Network Drive Mappings

Network drive mappings are similar to DOS pointers in a few respects, but for the most part, they are different animals. Table 8.1 compares DOS pointers and Network drive mappings. NetWare pointers use alphabetized letters to represent logical network directories—not physical disks. Network drive mappings use the same syntax as DOS pointers, but they begin where the DOS pointers end—the letter F. This means that network drives have twenty-one possible choices—F–Z. Figure 8.7 shows a typical NetWare directory structure with the drive letter F pointing to the SYS:USERS\DAVID directory.

*Network drive mappings are used for directory navigation and accessing data files. Search drive mappings, on the other hand, provide an additional functionality—the NetWare search list.*

**PURPOSE** Network drive mappings point to user-defined data directories. These drive pointers are typically used for convenience and directory movement. Without drive mappings, movement throughout the directory tree would consist of long path names and the CD command. This is cumbersome and time-consuming. With drive mappings, movement is consolidated into one simple step: type F: and press Enter. Network drive pointers represent complex directory paths as simple alphabetized letters. Figure 8.7 represents the path SYS:USERS\DAVID as the letter F. Simple.

**MAP ASSIGNMENTS** NetWare reserves the final twenty-one letters of the alphabet for network drive mappings. These drive pointers are assigned by NetWare users with the MAP command. They begin with F and move forward. Note: If the workstation CONFIG.SYS file contains the LAST-DRIVE = *letter* command, the first available drive pointer will be the next letter. For example, LASTDRIVE = G will reserve A–G for DOS and the first NetWare pointer will be H.

| | | |
|---|---|---|
| **TABLE 8.1**<br>The Similarities and Differences between DOS and NetWare Drive Pointers | | |

| FUNCTION | DOS POINTERS | NETWORK DRIVE MAPPINGS |
|---|---|---|
| Drive Letters | alphabetic | alphabetic |
| Syntax | *letter:* | *letter:* |
| Alphabetic Range | A–E | F–Z |
| Drive Type | physical drive | logical directory |
| Destination | local workstation | network file server |

**FIGURE 8.7**
NetWare drive pointers and logical network directories

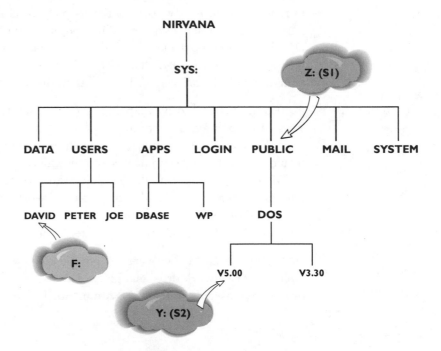

*The NetWare DOS Requester requires the LASTDRIVE = Z statement in CONFIG.SYS. Also, you can actually assign twenty-six network drive mappings (A–Z) by overwriting all existing local drives.*

### Search Drive Mappings

Search drive mappings extend one step beyond network drive mappings by enabling the user to search for network application files. When a user executes a particular network application, the system searches the current directory for the application file—.EXE, .COM, or .BAT. If the file isn't there, the system looks for a search list. If a search list doesn't exist, the system will return with the message Bad command or file name. If a search list does exist, the system will move through the list in order until it finds the application. This method is similar to the DOS PATH command. Search drive pointers build NetWare search lists. The maximum number of search drives in a NetWare search list is sixteen. It is possible, however, to have more if you incorporate the DOS PATH into the search list.

**MAP ASSIGNMENTS** Because search drive pointers are primarily used to build search lists, network users are more concerned with the order of the list than the letter that is assigned. For this reason, search drive mappings are assigned in search order by using the letter S and a number. For example, the first search drive would be assigned S1 and placed at the top of the search list. The second drive is S2, and so on. As a matter of convenience, NetWare also assigns a letter to each search pointer. This letter can be used to move around the directory structure just like a network drive mapping.

**AVAILABLE DRIVE LETTERS** This strategy poses an interesting question: How do you tell the difference between a network drive letter and a search drive letter? The answer is simple: You don't! There is no way of distinguishing one from the other by simply looking at it. So as a matter of convention, NetWare assigns search drive letters from Z and moves backward. Therefore, S1 becomes Z, S2 becomes Y, and so on. Figure 8.7 shows the first two NetWare search drives as Z: (S1) = SYS:PUBLIC and Y: (S2) = SYS:PUBLIC\ DOS\V5.00. With this in mind, you can assume that the early letters are network pointers and the later letters are search drives. Of course, this is only an assumption—and you know what they say about assumptions. Table 8.2 compares network and search drive mappings.

| | FUNCTION | NETWORK | SEARCH |
|---|---|---|---|
| **TABLE 8.2** Comparing the Functions of Network and Search Drive Mappings | Purpose | movement | searching |
| | Assignment Method | as the letter | in search order (S1, S2, etc.) |
| | Letter Assignment | by the user | by the system |
| | First Letter | F | Z(S1) |
| | Directory Types | data | applications |

*In the course of assigning search pointers, NetWare will skip any drive letter that is already defined as a network drive. The CD command is off limits to NetWare users. If the CD command is used on a NetWare pointer, it reassigns the pointer to a different directory. This reassignment can be fatal for search drives that point to critical applications or utility directories. If you must use the CD command, switch to drive J before doing so (assuming, of course, that the system manager has created one). The J drive holds no special significance except that it is typically used as a JUNK pointer. Using the CD command on the J drive doesn't hurt anybody.*

# Using the MAP Command

Now that you understand the fundamentals of NetWare drive mappings, you must learn how to implement them. The MAP command is one of the most versatile NetWare utilities. Think of it as an architect's drafting board. The following is a discussion of the many MAP commands with which system managers implement NetWare drive mappings. Keep in mind that drive mappings are user-specific and temporary. You will have to do this all over again tomorrow.

### MAP

The MAP command without any parameters displays a list of the current drive mappings. It lists the alphabet pointers in order, beginning with the local drives (A–E), the network drives, and then the search drives. Here's an example of how the MAP display is organized:

```
Z:\PUBLIC>map
Drive A: maps to a local disk.
Drive B: maps to a local disk.
Drive C: maps to a local disk.
Drive D: maps to a local disk.
Drive E: maps to a local disk.
Drive F: = NIRVANA\SYS: \LOGIN
 -----
SEARCH1: = Z:. [NIRVANA\SYS: \PUBLIC
SEARCH2: = Y:. [NIRVANA\SYS: \PUBLIC\DOS\V5.00
```

### MAP F:=SYS:LOGIN

MAP followed by a specific drive letter specifies a *network* drive pointer. The above command would map the LOGIN directory to the drive letter F.

### MAP S1:=SYS:PUBLIC

MAP followed by an S# specifies a *search* drive pointer. The # represents the pointer's place in the search list. NetWare assigns an appropriate alphabet letter beginning with Z and moving backward. In this example, the PUBLIC directory will be inserted at the top of the search list and receive the alphabet letter Z.

### MAP INSERT S2:=SYS:APPS\WP

The MAP INSERT command inserts a new search drive into the search list. The new pointer is inserted into the search list as the number specified. All search drives below the new pointer are bumped down one level in the list. The quirky thing about MAP INSERT is that the letter assignments are unaffected. All the previous drives retain their original drive letter, and the new pointer is assigned the next available drive. For example, if the previous command was executed in Figure 8.7, the DOS drive (S2) would become S3 but retain the drive letter Y. The new directory, SYS:APPS\WP, would become S2 and inherit the drive letter X.

*Search drive mappings occupy the same environment space as the DOS PATH command. For this reason, NetWare search mappings eliminate DOS PATH commands. The only way to retain the DOS path in a NetWare environment is to add the path directories to the NetWare search list. You can accomplish this by always using the MAP INSERT command. The DOS path directories are added to the end of the search list. Don't worry; the DOS path directories don't occupy any of your sixteen available search slots.*

### MAP DEL G:

MAP DEL deletes an existing NetWare drive mapping. This command works with either network or search drive pointers. MAP REM performs the same function as MAP DEL.

### MAP ROOT H:=SYS:USERS\DAVID

MAP ROOT is an intriguing command. It establishes a network drive mapping as a false root. The user sees the drive as if it were the root directory. In the preceding example, the SYS:USERS\DAVID directory would be mapped to the drive letter H. In addition, the H drive would appear to be the root of the volume even though it is actually the SYS:USERS\DAVID subdirectory. It would appear as H:\>. False root mappings are dangerous, because they limit users to specific branches of the directory tree. In this example, no other directories behind SYS:USERS\DAVID would be available to David. Booo.

*Although false root mappings can be dangerous, many CNAs embrace them enthusiastically. These root drives can contain mischievous users by limiting their knowledge of the directory structure. Some CNAs even go as far as MAP ROOTing search drives. Brave souls!*

### MAP NEXT SYS:DATA

The MAP NEXT command assigns the next available drive letter as a network drive pointer. This command doesn't work with search drive mappings. In Figure 8.7, this MAP NEXT command would assign the letter G to the SYS:DATA directory. MAP NEXT is useful to system managers because it keeps track of the alphabet letters for you.

*Although MAP NEXT doesn't work with search pointers, there is a way to achieve the same effect. Simply use MAP S16. NetWare will not allow you to assign search drive mappings out of order. So, if you specify S16, NetWare will automatically assign the directory to the next available spot in the search list.*

That completes our discussion of the NetWare directory structure. In this chapter, we explored logical trees, system-created and suggested directories, path names, and drive mapping. I'd say we got a pretty good head start on system administration and LAN configuration. The next step in hotel management is security. Security configuration establishes integrity and protection for network users and shared data files. In the next chapter, we will put on our house detective trenchcoat and install locks for hotel rooms, pass out guest keys, install an infrared motion-detection system, and hire some guard dogs. I can barely wait!

*Security is mostly a superstition. It does not exist in nature, nor do the children of men as a whole experience it. Avoiding danger is no safer in the long run than outright exposure. Life is either an adventure, or nothing.*

*Helen Keller*

# Exercise 8.1: Understanding Directory Structure

In this exercise, we will explore a fictitious directory structure for two servers: Tom and Jerry. Use Figure 8.1E to help you answer the following questions:

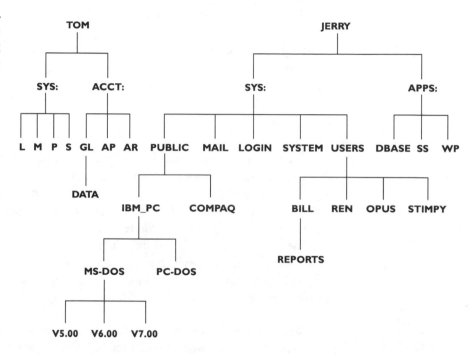

1.  How many volumes have been defined in this directory structure?

2.  Assuming that this is a NetWare 3.12 directory structure, which default system directories are missing?

3.  How is the volume structure organized in the accompanying graphic? What are the benefits of this structure? What are the possible pitfalls of this structure?

4.  Draw the path to each of the following directories:

    **A.** The REPORTS directory under BILL.

    **B.** MS-DOS v7.00.

**C.** The user directory for OPUS.

**D.** The data directory for GL.

**5.** How would you communicate or copy files from one subdirectory to another? Indicate the NetWare command you would use to copy a file from STIMPY's user directory to the data directory under GL.

**6.** What NetWare command would you use to view a graphical tree of the JERRY/SYS: directory structure?

**7.** What NetWare directory command would you use to view the space available on the TOM/ACCT: volume?

# Snouzer, Inc.— A Case Study

Welcome to Snouzer, Inc., world-renowned designer of doggie fashions. This year, Snouzer, Inc. is celebrating its silver anniversary. (Snouzer was formed twenty-five years ago in San Francisco, California, to satisfy the need for canine fashions.) At that time, nobody was giving the dog its due, so to speak, but today doggie fashions are a multibillion-dollar industry with thirty-two companies operating world wide. Snouzer, Inc., the founder of the doggie fashion industry, is the leader of the pack.

Snouzer, Inc., is best known for its top-of-the-line doggie accessories, including:

- **Classy collars**—a line of top notch dog necklaces including diamonds or cubic zirconia

- **Bowser booties**—a collection of all-leather high tops for canines

- **Eel skin leashes**—for the discerning owner

- **Doggie doos**—a collection of fine hair pieces for dogs (their best-selling product)

Snouzer, Inc., is a family-owned business. It operates out of a large factory facility in San Francisco. Management consists of seven brothers and sisters. They operate all administration, design, and production departments. Figure 8.2E shows Snouzer, Inc.'s, organizational chart. After many years operating with pen and pencil, Sophy Snouzer has decided that Snouzer, Inc., will move into the 21st century. She hired the LAN*imation* group in San Francisco to purchase her networking equipment and install the NetWare LAN. They did a tremendous job, installing seven workstations and one 486 file server. In addition, the LAN*imation* group installed NetWare 3.12 and all the workstation shells. Sophy is now coming to you to complete her dream. Your responsibility is to design, install, and manage the directory structure, users, groups, and applications. In addition, you will develop a security model and implement performance management facilities.

In the case studies that follow, we will walk through the requirements of Snouzer, Inc., discussing some possible solutions in the areas of:

- Directory structure

- Drive mappings

- Security

- Configurations

- Login scripts

- User interface

- Performance management

You will be asked to follow through from beginning to end the development of a productive and friendly NetWare LAN. Make sure to refer to the accompanying organization chart throughout these case study exercises. It will provide you with the background information to make the right decisions concerning user-specific and group-specific configurations. Remember, Sophy and all of her brothers and sisters at Snouzer, Inc., are counting on *you* to make their dream come true and bring them into the 21st century. Let's start with the development of a NetWare directory structure.

**FIGURE 8.2E**
Snouzer, Inc.'s
organization chart

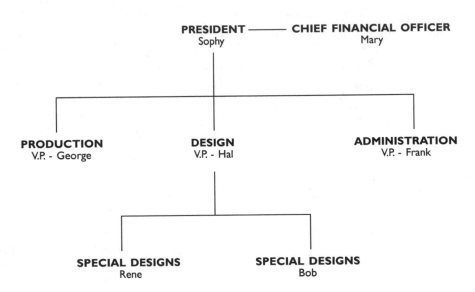

# CASE STUDY 1

## Creating a Directory Structure for Snouzer, Inc.

IN EACH OF THESE case exercises, you will be given a description of Snouzer, Inc.'s, environment and NetWare requirements. In the first half of the exercise, you will use pen and paper to draw a design of directory structures, drive mappings, security, login scripts, and so on. In the second half, you will get experience using the appropriate NetWare menu utility to implement your written design. These exercises have been written to maximize reality and fun. Have a good time!

As you can see from the organizational chart, Snouzer, Inc., is composed of three main departments:

▪ Administration

▪ Production

▪ Design

These three departments are managed by seven different employees:

▪ Sophy, President

▪ Frank, Vice President of Administration

▪ Hal, Vice President of Design

▪ George, Vice President of Production

▪ Rene and Bob, Special Designers

▪ Mary, Chief Financial Officer

When you first begin your journey at Snouzer, Inc., the LAN*imation* group has left you with functioning workstations, an active NetWare 3.12 file server and some system-created users, groups, and directories. Figure 8.3E illustrates a skeleton directory structure for Snouzer, Inc., with the following four system-created directories.

▪ SYSTEM

▪ MAIL

▪ PUBLIC

▪ LOGIN

As the Snouzer system manager, it is your responsibility to build a productive and efficient network directory structure that satisfies their application and data needs.

**FIGURE 8.3E**
A skeleton directory structure for Snouzer, Inc.

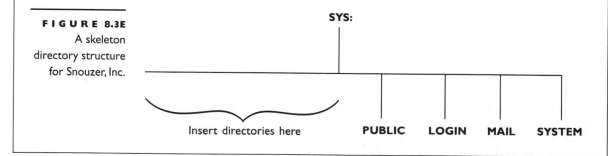

Insert directories here    PUBLIC    LOGIN    MAIL    SYSTEM

Let's review those needs for just a moment. Beyond the four system-created directories, Snouzer has requirements for three more suggested directory structures:

- DOS directories
- Users directories
- Application/data directories

Let's explore each of these in a little more detail.

## DOS Directory

LAN*imation* felt that Snouzer, Inc.'s, production and application requirements could best be satisfied by a variety of WOSs. LAN*imation* installed four types and versions of DOS:

- Compaq DOS v5.00
- Compaq DOS v3.30
- MS-DOS v5.00
- MS-DOS v6.00

In addition, the engineers installed two different types of workstations: Compaq and IBM-clone workstations. As the system manager, it is your responsibility to develop a DOS directory structure that satisfies the need for these four different types of DOS COMMAND.COM files. Incidentally, this structure should be designed within the PUBLIC directory.

Each of the seven Snouzer management employees should have his/her own user subdirectory within USERS. In addition, there are three groups: ADMIN, PROD, and DESIGN. Each of these groups should also have its own subdirectories under a GROUPS directory for storing group-specific data.

## Application/Data Directories

Snouzer, Inc. uses five main applications:

- DESIGN
- WP
- ACCT
- DBASE
- 123

The WP, dBASE, and 123 applications are generic off-the-shelf network applications. The DESIGN application is a special doggy fashion design program that is actively used by Snouzer's design group. In addition, the design program writes special macros and data files within the same directory. The ACCT program relies on three subcomponents:

- GL
- A/R
- A/P

These three components are integrated into the application but require separate subdirectories under ACCT for the storage of specific data and macros. User-specific data will be stored in each user subdirectory. Group-specific data will be stored in group-specific subdirectories. Application data is stored within the directory of the specific application. Finally, a global data subdirectory should provide all users on the LAN a place to store public files.

That completes the requirements for the Snouzer, Inc., network directory structure. After you have completed your design in Figure 8.3E, use the common NetWare tools discussed in this chapter to implement and build the network directory structure on Snouzer's shared 3.12 disk. The tools include the following:

▪ FILER Menu utility

▪ CD to change directories

▪ MD to make directories

▪ RD to remove directories

Once you have finished designing and implementing the Snouzer, Inc., directory structure, you can move onto Case Study II—Drive Mappings for Snouzer, Inc.

# Exercise 8.2: Using the MAP Command

In this exercise, you get an opportunity to work with drive mappings on an existing NetWare LAN. Using the MD command, create a directory structure that matches the one shown in Figure 8.4E. Follow these steps:

1. MAP drive G as a root to the DATA subdirectory.

2. MAP drive U to JACK's user directory.

3. MAP the next three search drives to APPS, WP, and DBASE, in that order.

4. Verify that the maps were created by typing MAP and pressing Enter. How does the system indicate a map root drive?

5. Remove the U drive, which was mapped to JACK, and remap it to JILL.

6. Insert a search drive mapping at search drive 3 for APPS\WINDOWS.

7. Move to the G drive. Now type CD \ to return to the SYS: root. What happens?

8. Return to the U drive. Map the next available network drive mapping to SYS:DATA.

**9.** Type MAP and press Enter to verify that your changes have taken effect.

**10.** How does the system execute the MAP command from the U drive?

**11.** To view the effects of the CD command on search drive mappings, type Z: and press Enter to move to the PUBLIC subdirectory. The PUBLIC subdirectory is mapped as the first search drive because it contains all the NetWare utilities including MAP.

**12.** Type CD .. at the prompt and press Enter to remap the Z drive (the first search drive) to the root.

**13.** Go to the U drive and press Enter.

**14.** Type MAP once again to verify your drive mappings. What happened and why?

**15.** Go back to the Z drive by typing Z: and pressing Enter. Type CD PUBLIC to remap the first search drive back to PUBLIC.

**16.** Go back to the U drive by typing U: and pressing Enter. Now type MAP and notice what happens.

Keep in mind that it is extremely dangerous to use the CD command on search drives, especially search drives as important as S1. That's the end of the show. Good work!

**FIGURE 8.4E**
Using the MAP command

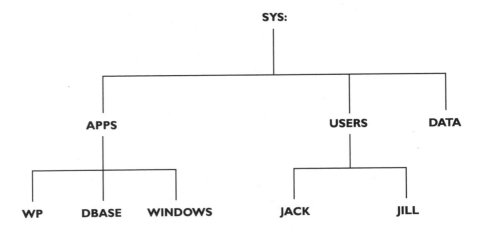

**CASE STUDY 11**

## Drive Mappings for Snouzer, Inc.

Network and search drive mappings provide a navigation tool for moving around the Snouzer, Inc., directory structure. These tools are particularly important for running network applications and storing user-specific and group-specific data. Snouzer has pretty standard drive mapping requirements. The company requires a network drive mapping to each user subdirectory, a group-specific drive mapping (Q) for each group and a global network drive mapping (T) to a shared DATA subdirectory.

The search drive mapping requirements are a little more complex. The first search drive mapping should point to PUBLIC and the second search drive mapping to DOS. These two search drive mappings are standard for all NetWare LANs. The next five search drive mappings should be mapped to each of the five different applications. It is important to assign search drive mappings in priority order. The Snouzer, Inc., managers have a tendency to use the WP application more than any other, then the DESIGN team and ACCT applications in that order. Finally, DBASE and 123 are used the least often.

Once you have completed your design, it is time to implement Snouzer, Inc.'s, drive mapping structure. The following NetWare tools can be very useful in assigning NetWare drive mappings:

MAP, the command-line utility with all of its variations that provide drive mapping creation from the command line

SESSION, a menu utility that can be used to assign network and search drive mappings

Remember that the drive mappings you create here are only temporary. They will disappear once the user exits the system. The design you created will be used during the login case study as a template for creating drive mappings in the system login script.

# NetWare 3.12
# Security

CHAPTER

9

ARK PLACE IS A beautiful hotel. It has water fountains, ice sculptures, atriums, and an indoor golf course. And as with any popular resort, Park Place needs security:

- To protect the guests
- To protect the staff
- To guard the ice sculptures
- To lock away valuable treasures

The king of Park Place security is the hotel's house detective. He/she oversees registration, guards the lobby, builds room keys, installs door locks, and locks away valuable treasures. He/she bears the responsibility of protecting the hotel's assets. The goal is to create a reliable security system that locks out the bad guy and welcomes everybody else in. To perform these duties, the house detective has four main responsibilities:

- Overseeing registration
- Guarding the lobby
- Locksmithing
- Locking away valuable treasures

In overseeing hotel registration, the house detective ensures that all guests are registered and have an appropriate form of payment: credit card, cash, check, and so on. If guests are not registered, they cannot go beyond the confines of the hotel lobby. The passageway from the lobby to the rest of Park Place is guarded by two large gold-plated gates that separate the small lobby from the rest of the hotel's rooms and amenities. The house detective guards these gates and makes sure that only appropriate registered guests (who have made payment arrangements) can pass through at appropriate times. Once guests have passed through the gates, they can roam freely through most of the resort, sampling the restaurants, enjoying the pools, ogling the ice sculptures, and resting in their rooms.

The house detective ensures that each guest is granted a user key that gives him/her access to appropriate rooms in the hotel. The house detective not only builds the user keys but installs each room's door locks as well. These functions are grouped on the detective's job description as hotel locksmithing.

Finally, the house detective locks away guests' valuable treasures in the hotel safe. These treasures can only be accessed—at appropriate times—by special guests with special privileges. Once guests leave the hotel, they must take their valuables with them.

As the NetWare system manager, you are the house detective of your LAN. Users come to you for application security, data organization, and general peace of mind. The following LAN security duties are some of the most important responsibilities you will have, and you must take them seriously:

- Overseeing user registration
- Guarding access to the LAN
- LAN locksmithing
- Locking away valuable directories and files with attribute security

*The weakest link in a chain is the strongest because it can break it.*

*Stanislaw J. Lec*

The goal is to create a reliable security system that locks out the bad guys and welcomes everybody else in. Sound familiar? With NetWare security, organization is the key. You must fully understand the ramifications of each of these responsibilities so that you can navigate through the complex layers of the NetWare security model.

In this chapter, you will learn about NetWare security from the NetWare house detective's point of view. We will explore each layer of NetWare's multilayered security model in depth. We'll also meet the NetWare house detective's deputies: distributed security managers. In addition, we will investigate some of the command-line and menu utilities that NetWare provides to help manage LAN security. Keep in mind that good security is an important tool in your NetWare utility belt. Good LAN security is becoming a lost art.

*Happiness has many roots, but none more important than security.*

*E. R. Stettinius, Jr.*

# The NetWare Security Model

THE MULTILAYERED NETWARE SECURITY model provides a level of protection for entrance to the LAN. Because the data on a network is typically shared, it is important to secure it in directories to which only authorized users have access. In a stand-alone environment, security isn't as critical. The only way to access stand-alone data is to physically walk over to another user's workstation. However, in a network environment, intruders can let their fingers do the walking. Without security on the central LAN hard disk, it would be too easy for users to access each other's data.

The NetWare security model provides a level of data protection by forcing users through a specific series of security events on their way toward shared data. NetWare security consists of access restrictions, privileges, and file conditions. Thus, users can store data in certain directories on the server disk without having to worry about anybody accessing that data.

The NetWare security model consists of four layers:

1. Login/password security

2. Login restrictions

3. Access rights

4. Attributes

As the NetWare house detective you oversee registration (login/password), guard the lobby (login restrictions), build keys and locks (access rights), and finally, hide the guest's special treasures (attributes). Following is an overview of these four security levels and a discussion of how they incrementally increase file and directory protection (Figure 9.1). Let's begin with login/password security.

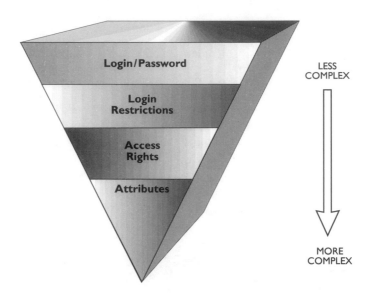

FIGURE 9.1
The multilayered
NetWare security model

## Login/Password Security

As mentioned earlier, login/password security governs initial access to the file server and provides a system for user authentication. Login/password security is analogous to duties of the Park Place registration desk. When guests register at the hotel, they provide valid identification. In NetWare 3.1$x$, the user is authenticated once he/she issues the LOGIN command. Furthermore, if the username is valid, the system must match it against an appropriate password—the Park Place guests' form of payment.

## Login Restrictions

Login restrictions form an additional level of login security that monitors a variety of security conditions. Login restrictions make up the second layer of the NetWare security model. They provide the system manager with a means of further filtering out users according to a variety of security conditions. These security conditions include:

- Account restrictions
- Time restrictions

- Station restrictions

- Intruder/detection lockout

- NCP packet signature

Login restrictions are analogous to having the house detective guard the hotel gates. Beyond payment, the house detective can make decisions about guests as they travel from the lobby into the hotel proper by asking questions or searching their belongings. This level of security can be as simple as saying "hello" or as complex as an x-ray search for weapons. In much the same way, login restrictions interrogate users about their login time, workstation ID, and so on.

# Access Rights

*Access rights define a complex set of privileges that can be assigned to users or to directories. A user's rights are analogous to room keys. Directory rights are analogous to door locks.*

Once guests have passed through the gates into the hotel proper, their movements throughout the hotel and its many facilities are restricted by their collection of room keys. This level of hotel security is known as *locksmithing*.

The third layer of network security is governed by access rights. *Access rights* define a complex set of privileges assigned to users or to directories. A user's rights are analogous to room keys. Directory rights are analogous to door locks. If a guest has a valid key and access to the appropriate lock, he/she is granted access to the room. In the same manner, if a NetWare user has a user key and the appropriate directory lock, he/she is granted access to the directory. This combination of user and directory security is known as *effective rights* and defines a user's actual privileges in a given directory on the disk. NetWare 3.1x provides eight different access rights; NetWare 2.2 uses only seven. As part of your LAN locksmith duties, you must understand each of these rights intimately and have a firm handle on how they are combined at both the user and directory levels to create effective rights. Access rights are the most common form of NetWare security and provide a versatile system for controlling who has what privileges to which files.

## Attributes

The final level of NetWare security is attribute security. *Attributes* are conditional privileges that control file sharing, reading, writing, executing, hiding, tracking, and archiving. Access rights define which users can access a file or directory; file attributes control what the users can do with the files once users open them. Attribute security is analogous to locking away a guest's treasures. Some guests do not wish to rely on the keys and locks, so they ask the hotel house detective to secure their valuable treasures in the hotel safe. In the same way, NetWare attributes provide a higher level of security for special files and directories.

NetWare provides two types of attributes: security and feature. *Security attributes* affect how *users* access files; *feature attributes* affect how the *system* accesses files. Attribute security in general is a complex level of NetWare security and is rarely implemented by most security managers. The first three layers of the NetWare security model provide more than enough security for 95% of NetWare LANs.

*The only fence against the world is a thorough knowledge of it.*

*John Locke*

## The NetWare Bindery

The multilayered NetWare security model is implemented through a flat-file database called the *NetWare bindery*. The bindery is an object-oriented database that contains definitions for users, groups, and other objects on the network. The system manager uses the bindery to organize the user structure and define NetWare security. Before we begin our in-depth discussion of the four layers of NetWare security, let's explore the three components of the NetWare bindery:

- Objects
- Properties
- Values

A NetWare bindery *object* defines any LAN component with a name—such as file servers, users, groups, print servers, and so on. The NetWare bindery tracks LAN objects and defines a variety of their *properties*. Properties are object characteristics, which differ for each type of object. For example, user objects have characteristics or properties such as passwords, account restrictions, account balances, security, and login restrictions. File server objects, on the other hand, have a different set of properties, such as file server name, NetWare version number, network address, and node address. The NetWare bindery tracks objects and their properties, and includes a database of values for those characteristics.

Bindery *values* are the actual data sets that correspond to object properties. For example, a bindery object USER would have a property of NAME and a value of DAVID. NetWare 3.1*x* bindery objects, properties, and data sets are tracked through three hidden system files: NET$OBJ.SYS for objects, NET$PROP.SYS for properties, and NET$VAL.SYS for values. The NetWare 2.2 bindery, on the other hand, exists as two system hidden files: NET$BIND.SYS and NET$BVAL.SYS. All of these files are hidden and system owned in the SYS:SYSTEM subdirectory.

*The NetWare bindery is an extremely sensitive database and must be guarded closely. If the file server crashes or power goes out in the middle of a user upgrade or configuration, the bindery can become corrupted quite easily. In this case, the system manager must use the BINDFIX or BINDREST utility to decorrupt these files.*

That's it for our overview of the NetWare security model. You will spend the majority of this chapter learning how it works and what steps can be taken to ensure the highest level of NetWare security. Before we begin, let's take a quick look at how the system manager can distribute the security load through distributed security managers.

# Special User Accounts

UNFORTUNATELY, THE PARK PLACE house detective cannot be everywhere at once. Every day, he/she has various responsibilities in various locations. To help the hotel house detective manage these security details, the hotel manager has agreed to provide a security staff. The security staff includes registration clerks, lobby guards, locksmiths, and safe monitors.

In NetWare, the NetWare house detective's assistants include:

**NetWare supervisor equivalents**—distributed users who have all the same rights as the supervisor.

**Managers**—users authorized to create, manage, and delete user accounts and groups. Managers are designed to help with organizing user activities and login restrictions.

**Operators**—users who provide specialized assistance. NetWare supports three types of operators: console operators, print queue operators, and print server operators.

Supervisor equivalents, managers, and operators compose an effective team to lighten the NetWare house detective's load. Let's take a closer look at NetWare special user accounts.

*If I were you, I would learn all I could about special user accounts. Special users, especially workgroup and user account managers, can alleviate your daily administration grind.*

## The Supervisor

The supervisor is the all-knowing, all-wise guru of the LAN—NetWare Yoda. He/she has all rights everywhere but is still subject to the password and attribute levels of security. When NetWare is first installed, two users are created by default:

- SUPERVISOR

- GUEST

Both accounts are created during NetWare installation. During initial login, the SUPERVISOR account has no password but still has all rights and access to all server configurations. Clearly, then, it is extremely important to give the SUPERVISOR a password immediately. The GUEST account, on the other hand, has severely limited security. The GUEST account is initially created so guest users can log in to the NetWare server and access the following fundamental shared resources:

- Printing

- Public utilities

- Simple network applications

In addition to SUPERVISOR and GUEST, the NetWare installation creates one other bindery object: the group EVERYONE. EVERYONE is created to provide global configuration and security access for the system manager. The EVERYONE group contains all users on the system, present and future. By default, the EVERYONE group has limited access rights and login restrictions.

Beyond these default bindery objects, the system manager can create a staff of distributed security managers. The most skilled of the staff members includes the supervisor equivalent.

*Some people blow their own horn, while others play a symphony.*

*Anonymous*

## Supervisor Equivalent

The supervisor can create a supervisor equivalent by entering the User Information window of SYSCON and assigning the supervisor security equivalence to a specific user. You will learn more about them in the next chapter. With the following three exceptions, the supervisor equivalent user is identical to the supervisor:

- The supervisor equivalent account can be deleted, whereas the supervisor account cannot.

- The supervisor is automatically assigned operator status.

- The supervisor account has a special User ID—1.

The supervisor equivalent special user provides an effective way to maintain the LAN. It is not a good idea to consistently log in as the supervisor, because some known network viruses search and piggyback this particular username. It is more secure to log in as a regular network user who has been given supervisor equivalence.

*You can use supervisor equivalence to create a back door. The system manager can create an account for a fictitious user with an unpredictable username and make that user equivalent to the supervisor. If the supervisor account has been locked or destroyed, the system manager can access the LAN and re-create the supervisor password from the supervisor equivalent's account. One of the most secure back-door accounts is the "null" character created by pressing Alt-255.*

## Managers

The NetWare house detective staff also consists of distributed managers who have limited additional capabilities in working with workgroups or guest members. NetWare provides two levels of manager staff:

- Workgroup manager
- User account manager

*Workgroup managers* are assistant supervisors who have been given special rights to create, manage, and delete names and login restrictions for users and groups. The supervisor or supervisor equivalent creates workgroup managers and assigns them specific users and groups to manage. The workgroup manager can create further users under his/her group or delete existing users from the group. The workgroup manager is restricted to deleting only accounts for users he/she created or users who are under his/her workgroup.

The *user account manager* provides the facility for managing and deleting accounts for users but not creating them. The main difference is that user account managers can only manage users. They cannot create bindery objects. Workgroup managers can create user account managers for overseeing specific subsets of their workgroup. Workgroup manager and user account manager accounts are both created using the SYSCON utility. You will learn the steps for creating accounts for distributed managers in the next chapter.

*As knowledge increases, wonder deepens.*

*Charles Morgan*

## Operators

*Operators* are distributed staff who oversee specific network functions. The supervisor or supervisor equivalent can assign users to be operators of the file server console, print server, or print queue functions. File server console operators have full access to the FCONSOLE utility except for the function of downing the server or disconnecting other users.

*FCONSOLE facilities have been dramatically limited in NetWare 3.1x. Most of the useful functions from NetWare 2.2 have been incorporated into a more wondrous 3.1x utility called MONITOR.NLM.*

Print server operators are special user accounts that are given rights to manage the print server. Print server operators can specify notify lists for printers, issue commands to the printers, change forms, change the queue serviced by a print server, change queue priority, or down the print server. Print server operators cannot create new print servers or assign other users as print server operators. Only the supervisor or supervisor equivalent can assign print server operator status.

Print queue operators are special user accounts with rights to manage, disable, and enable print queues. A print queue operator can also authorize a print server to service a queue. By default, the supervisor is the print queue operator over all print queues. Only the supervisor or supervisor equivalent can assign print queue operator status. To establish the proper connection between a print queue and print server, the user must be both a print server operator and print queue operator. Otherwise, the print server operator and print queue operator would have to work together in performing this valuable printing function.

That completes our discussion of special user accounts. Table 9.1 summarizes the "cans" and "can'ts" of NetWare supervisors, managers, and operators.

*The workgroup manager or user account manager is not given any rights to the directory structure. To adequately manage their own users and groups, the distributed managers should be given supervisor rights to particular branches of the directory tree.*

Distributed security staff is a valuable tool for the system manager. It makes his/her life a lot easier and provides a more secure system for the hotel guests. It is important to assess a possible distributed manager's ability on the network and his/her comprehension of NetWare security before assigning the person to handle those responsibilities. There is nothing more dangerous than a workgroup manager run amuck.

In the remainder of this chapter, we will discuss the system manager's approach to NetWare security and discuss the four layers of the NetWare security model in detail. Let's begin with the first layer: login/password security.

| TABLE 9.1 | CANS | CAN'TS |
|---|---|---|
| Cans and Can'ts for Special User Accounts | *Supervisor/Supervisor Equivalents* | |
| | Can assign all other special user accounts, automatically acquire all rights to each volume, and change the supervisor password | |
| | *Workgroup Managers* | |
| | Create and manage user and group accounts, delete user accounts they've created, delete user accounts they have been assigned, create user account manager | Use special file rights, create a workgroup manager account, delete other than the group's own users, assign rights they have not been granted |
| | *User Account Managers* | |
| | Manage users, delete user accounts they have been assigned, create other user account managers | Create user or group accounts, manage groups, create workgroup manager accounts, assign rights they have not been granted |
| | *Print Server Operators* | |
| | Create notify list for printers, change forms, change queue priority, down the print server | Create print servers, assign print server operators, assign queues to printers |
| | *Print Queue Operators* | |
| | Manage print queues, assign queues to printers | Create/delete print queues, assign print queue operators |
| | *Console Operators* | |
| | Perform Supervisor options within FCONSOLE | Down the file server from FCONSOLE |

# Login/Password Security

*Login/password
security controls LAN
access at the point
of entrance—login
name and password.
The password and
login name must
match those stored
in the system exactly.*

LOGIN/PASSWORD SECURITY CONTROLS LAN access at the point of entrance—login name and password. Login/password security is effective because it requires two pieces of information—an authorized login name and valid password. The password and login name must match those stored in the system exactly.

Login/password security is analogous to the registration desk responsibilities of the house detective. When guests first enter the outer hotel lobby, they are required to go to the registration desk and provide a valid form of identification for their reservation and a form of payment. The username is the ID that the NetWare user enters to validate access to the LAN. The password is the form of payment. Without an appropriate password, users are not allowed to continue to the second layer of LAN access.

*In NetWare, usernames are required, whereas passwords are optional.*

Let's discuss NetWare usernames and passwords, and explore the process of logging in.

*If I were you, I would focus on learning password restrictions, especially Require Password, Minimum Password Length, and specifications for periodically changing user passwords.*

## Usernames

Usernames provide the first point of access to the LAN. Only network supervisors, supervisor equivalents, and workgroup managers can create usernames. To access the NetWare LAN, the user must log in to the network by specifying the file server name and an appropriate username. Usernames can be anywhere from two to forty-seven characters in length. Usernames are objects in the file server bindery and are assigned specific properties. As you assign values to these properties, you are in effect granting the user sufficient security clearance to do his/her job. By default, all users are automatically assigned a password property and membership to the group EVERYONE. Usernames can be assigned using the SYSCON menu utility or one of the two user creation utilities: MAKEUSER or USERDEF.

# Passwords

Once the user has provided a form of ID at the registration desk, he/she is required to make arrangements for payment. In NetWare, payment is in the form of optional (although highly recommended) passwords. Passwords provide an effective strategy for filtering out unwanted users. Password protection can be enhanced by making passwords mandatory, defining minimum password lengths, or causing passwords to expire after a limited length of time. These password restrictions are discussed later in this chapter.

Passwords can be changed by NetWare supervisors, supervisor equivalents, workgroup managers, user account managers, or the users themselves. It is a good idea to immediately assign a password when you initially create the account for each user. Users can then be allowed to choose and change their own passwords. As the system manager, you do have the choice of not allowing users to change their own passwords.

*A password's confidentiality has been a point of concern for many system managers. In NetWare 2.2 and below, the password is broadcast across the LAN cabling in text form, so any user with the appropriate equipment can siphon the password and read it easily. NetWare 3.1x protects passwords with a feature called* password encryption—*user passwords are encrypted at the workstation and sent along the cabling in a format only the file server can understand.*

# Logging In

Let's review the process of logging in:

1. Load IPX or ODI.

2. Load NETx or VLM.

3. Move to F:\LOGIN>.

*Spoken language is merely a series of squeaks.*

*Alfred North Whitehead*

Once a user accesses the F:\LOGIN> directory, he/she is on the doorstep of the LAN. At this point, the user has limited access to only two NetWare files: LOGIN.EXE (to log in) and SLIST.EXE (for a list of available servers). The user is ready to exercise his/her login security. As seen in Figure 9.2, login security consists of the following four steps:

1. The user logs into the network by specifying the file server name and a username. The system verifies the username by matching it against an object in the NET$OBJ.SYS (or NET$BIND.SYS) bindery file. Whether or not the username exists, NetWare prompts for a password, to fool would-be hackers into thinking the username is valid. NetWare is built on the premise of "What you don't know can't hurt us!"

2. If the system verifies the username, it searches the NET$PROP.SYS (or NET$BIND.SYS) file for a password property. If one exists, the system responds with Password:. If a password doesn't exist, the system jumps to step 4.

3. The user enters a password. If the username is valid, NetWare compares this input to the value in NET$VAL.SYS (or NET$BVAL.SYS). If the username is not valid, the system bypasses the search and responds with Access Denied.

4. If the user enters the correct password for this username, he/she will be granted conditional access to the LAN. If not, the system responds with Access Denied. The user is left at the NetWare doorstep. Next, the system matches the username with a variety of additional bindery values—login restrictions.

**FIGURE 9.2**

The process of logging in

```
C:\NET>lsl
NetWare Link Support Layer   v1.20 (911120)
(C) Copyright 1990, 1991 Novell, Inc.  All Rights Reserved.

Max Boards 4, Max Stacks 4

C:\NET>eplaodi
Ethernet Pocket LAN Adapter MLID v2.53 (930504)
Copyright 1993., All rights reserved.

Speed:0
Int 7, Port 378, Node Address 80C8716AD2 L
Max Frame 1514 bytes, Line Speed 10 Mbps
Board 1, Frame ETHERNET_802.3, LSB Mode

C:\NET>ipxodi
NetWare IPX/SPX Protocol   v1.20 (911120)
(C) Copyright 1990, 1991 Novell, Inc.  All Rights Reserved.

IPX protocol bound to EPLAODI MLID Board #1.

C:\NET>netx /ps=wannabeacne

NetWare Workstation Shell  v3.31 (921112)
(C) Copyright 1991, 1992 Novell, Inc.  All Rights Reserved.
Patent Pending.

Running on DOS V5.00

Established Preferred Server connection.

Attached to server WANNABEACNE
05-17-95    8:45:44 am
C:\NET>f:

F:\LOGIN>login davidiv
Enter your password:
Good morning, DAVIDIV.

Drive  A:   maps to a local disk.
Drive  B:   maps to a local disk.
Drive  C:   maps to a local disk.
Drive  D:   maps to a local disk.
Drive  E:   maps to a local disk.
Drive  F: = WANNABEACNE\SYS:  \
           ------
SEARCH1:  = Z:. [WANNABEACNE\SYS:  \PUBLIC]
SEARCH2:  = Y:. [WANNABEACNE\SYS:  \]
SEARCH3:  = C:\WTOOLS
SEARCH4:  = C:\EXCEL
SEARCH5:  = C:\
SEARCH6:  = C:\WINWORD
SEARCH7:  = C:\WINDOWS
SEARCH8:  = C:\DOS
SEARCH9:  = C:\APPS\WP70
SEARCH10: = C:\APPS\LL5\

F:\>
```

*Experienced hackers will eventually notice that invalid usernames cause the* `Access Denied` *message to appear much more quickly. This fast response is because NetWare doesn't search the bindery for invalid username passwords. For valid usernames, such as GUEST, NetWare takes noticeably longer while it searches the NET$VAL.SYS (or NET$BVAL.SYS) bindery database.*

*Upon receipt of the long-awaited NetWare prompt, the user has completed levels one and two of the NetWare security model. The third level, access rights security, controls the user's movements throughout the directory structure and provides limited access to authorized areas of the disk.*

Numerous command-line utilities (CLUs) enable the supervisor to customize login/password security. We will investigate all of these commands at the end of this chapter.

# Login Restrictions

*The golden gates offer a final level of access security, where the lobby guards can inspect the guests for firearms, contraband, and other security violations. NetWare provides a similar form of access security through login restrictions.*

ONCE THE GUESTS CHECK in at the registration desk and provide proper payment, they must complete their access to Park Place by passing through the golden gates. The golden gates offer a final level of access security, where the lobby guards can inspect the guests for firearms, contraband, and other security violations. In much the same way, *login restrictions* provide a final level of access security that enables the NetWare house detective to restrict user access according to a variety of login conditions, including time, workstation location, date, and so on. Let's take a quick look at how login restrictions work.

Once the username has been entered and the password has been matched, the user is granted conditional access to the system. Permanent access is contingent on a supplemental level of login/password security called *login restrictions*. Login restrictions further scrutinize LAN access by matching the login name with a variety of other qualifications: Is this user authorized to log in during this time period? Is this user authorized to log in from this particular machine? Is this user authorized to log in on this date? Is this user really who he/she claims to be? In addition, NetWare login restrictions incorporate an access-tracking feature called intruder detection/lockout. This security feature tracks unauthorized login attempts and automatically locks accounts when the attempts exceed a given bad login threshold count. The user account can only be unlocked by the NetWare supervisor or supervisor equivalent.

NetWare login restrictions fall into five categories:

- Account restrictions

- Time restrictions

- Station restrictions

- Intruder detection/lockout

- NCP packet signature

Account restrictions apply to user accounts and password/data restrictions. Time restrictions and station restrictions apply to login times and workstation locations. Intruder detection/lockout is a NetWare 3.1$x$ feature that tracks invalid login attempts and locks out unauthorized users. NetWare 3.1$x$ NCP packet signatures validate client/server communications. Each of these puzzle pieces is an important component in the overall security picture. It is important to take time and care in designing NetWare login restrictions. Let's discuss each one in detail.

*If I were you, I would definitely apply Account Restrictions and Intruder Detection/Lockout. The other three login restrictions are optional.*

## Account Restrictions

NetWare account restrictions provide a method for controlling and restricting user access to the NetWare file server. Account restrictions are established in two ways:

**Default account balance/restrictions** in the Supervisor Options of SYSCON

**Account balance/restrictions** in the User Information of SYSCON

Default account restrictions establish configurations for all NEW users and are defined in the Supervisor Options screen of SYSCON. User-specific account restrictions establish configurations for existing users and are defined in the user's specific User Information window of SYSCON.

*Default account restrictions take effect for all user accounts that are created from this point on, so these restrictions will not take effect for any users whose accounts currently exist. Let's say you have one hundred users and you decide you want to restrict everybody from logging in on the weekend. You waltz over the default time restrictions and restrict the weekend time periods. What's wrong with this picture? The default time restrictions only affect user accounts created from this point on. These changes will not affect your current one hundred users. The only option is to change each user's time restriction individually—all one hundred of them! The moral of the story is "set your default restrictions before you create your users."*

*Good news. A little trick can save you hours of work if you get caught in the restrictions trap just described. To configure login restrictions for large numbers of users, simply highlight those users by pressing F5 in the User Information window of SYSCON and pressing Enter. The Set User Information screen will appear with four choices: Account Balance, Account Restrictions, Station Restrictions, and Time Restrictions. Simply define the appropriate restrictions and they will take effect for all highlighted users. Whew, that saved a ton of time. Good thing you read this tip.*

NetWare's account restrictions screen provides various options for NetWare system managers. Figure 9.3 illustrates NetWare 3.1x's default account restrictions screen. Here's a brief discussion of each of its options.

### Account Expiration Date

The Account Expiration Date is a useful tool for temporary employees or students in an academic environment. It enables the system manager to lock an account after a specific date. By default, the Account Expiration Date is set to NO. If you change the value to YES, the 1st of next month will appear as the default Date the Account Expires. You can change the date at any time—the account locks at midnight.

**FIGURE 9.3**
Default account
restrictions in SYSCON

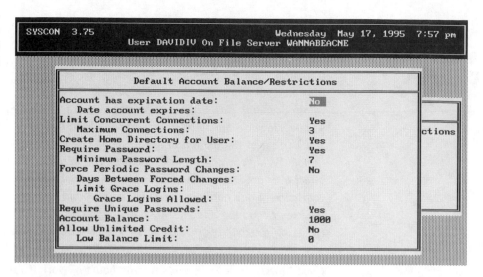

```
SYSCON  3.75                          Wednesday  May 17, 1995  7:57 pm
                    User DAVIDIV On File Server WANNABEACNE

        ┌──────────────────────────────────────────────────┐
        │          Default Account Balance/Restrictions      │
        │ Account has expiration date:              No        │
        │    Date account expires:                            │
        │ Limit Concurrent Connections:            Yes        │
        │    Maximum Connections:                    3        │
        │ Create Home Directory for User:          Yes        │
        │ Require Password:                        Yes        │
        │    Minimum Password Length:                7        │
        │ Force Periodic Password Changes:          No        │
        │    Days Between Forced Changes:                     │
        │    Limit Grace Logins:                              │
        │       Grace Logins Allowed:                         │
        │ Require Unique Passwords:                Yes        │
        │ Account Balance:                        1000        │
        │ Allow Unlimited Credit:                   No        │
        │    Low Balance Limit:                      0        │
        └──────────────────────────────────────────────────┘
```

## Limit Concurrent Connections

Limiting concurrent connections is useful against users who like to migrate throughout the LAN or log in from multiple workstations. The system manager can limit a user's concurrent connections by changing the default from NO to YES. An ideal setting is three concurrent connections, which allow the user to log in from only three workstations simultaneously. This account restriction works in conjunction with station restrictions. You can enhance a user's concurrent connection limitation by combining it with a specific physical workstation address—station restrictions. By default, Limit Concurrent Connections is set to NO. A good average setting is YES—limit concurrent connections—with Maximum Connections set to 3. If you set this in the default account restrictions, it will take effect for all users whose accounts are created subsequently.

## Create Home Directory for User

Create Home Directory for User is an account configuration that instructs the system to create a home directory for each user under the USERS subdirectory. By default, this option is set to YES. Create Home Directory for User is an important part of the overall security picture, because it defines a home area for each user. This home area is used by many other configurations, including drive mappings, login scripts, and trustee assignments. User drive mappings are created in the system login script with an identifier variable called %LOGIN_NAME. This identifier variable will create a home directory mapping for all users on the basis of what their unique login name is. But this system only works if a home directory exists for each user.

### Require Password

Password restrictions are applied using the Require Password option and other related restrictions. By default, the system does not require a password. This is a huge oversight. I recommend that you require a password of more than five characters for all users.

*One password-hacking routine can guess any five-character password in less than 20 minutes. The program connects directly to the NetWare bindery and matches random character combinations with existing password information. So if your minimum password length is four or fewer characters, this program can break into the system very quickly.*

*You can't depend on your judgement when your imagination is out of focus.*

*John F. Kennedy*

### Force Periodic Password Changes

Once a password has been required and a minimum password length of seven characters has been set, you should explore using the Force Periodic Password Changes account restriction. This restriction forces users to change their passwords at periodic intervals. If you set Force Periodic Password Changes to YES, the system will ask you to input the days between forced changes. The default is 45 days. This time period is a little short and can become a nuisance very quickly. A periodic password interval of 90 days seems to be optimal.

Once a password interval has expired, the user is required to change his/her password. If the user does not change his/her password at the point of login, the system will lock the account. This is where grace logins come in. *Grace logins* allow the user to log in without changing the password. But even grace logins expire. Seven grace logins are ideal for most users. Once a user logs in for the seventh time and chooses not to change his/her password, the account is locked and can only be unlocked by the supervisor. So who unlocks the supervisor's account? Stay tuned.

*When the periodic password interval has expired, the system will respond once the user logs in with* `Your password has expired. Would you like to change it now?` *This prompt provides an opportunity to change a password right away. Otherwise, users can use SETPASS or SYSCON to change their passwords at any time.*

### Require Unique Passwords

The Require Unique Passwords restriction works in conjunction with forcing periodic password changes. When the periodic password interval expires and the user must change his/her password, Unique Passwords forces him/her to enter a new, *different* password. This strategy is effective when combined with forcing periodic password changes and requiring passwords. If the system manager takes the time and effort to make the users change their passwords periodically, he/she should make sure those passwords are new and unique each time. It does not make sense for the user to continually use the same password.

*Requiring unique passwords relies on an internal NetWare table that keeps track of the last ten passwords any user has set. After the tenth different password has been used, the user can reuse the first password.*

### Account Balance

NetWare has a built-in accounting feature that tracks user logins, logouts, and access to network resources. The system manager can install accounting through the SYSCON menu utility. In addition, he/she can use SYSCON to define network resources and establish charge rates for access to those resources. The account balance is a dynamic measure of each user's accounting usage.

*NetWare has a built-in accounting feature that tracks user logins, logouts, and access to network resources.*

By default, the Account Balance is set to 0 and Unlimited Credit is set to NO. Once the system manager installs accounting, users begin accumulating resource charges, so the Account Balance is immediately negative. If the Low-Balance Limit is set to 0, users are instantly in violation of NetWare accounting. Once a user's Account Balance becomes negative, the system locks the account—he/she can no longer log in. So it is important to set the Account Balance to at least 1,000 when you decide to install accounting. The Low-Balance Limit refers to the number at which the user is locked out. Typically, an Account Balance of 1,000—depending on the charge rates—and a Low-Balance Limit of 0 are optimal. Setting Unlimited Credit defeats the whole purpose of charging for resources.

Another interesting use of NetWare accounting is resource tracking. Instead of charging users for their specific resource usage, you can use accounting to track how users are accessing resources, by setting Allow Unlimited Credit to YES, the Account Balance to 0, and the Low-Balance Limit to 0. Then, you charge each user a rate of 1 unit per usage on each of the following five resources:

- Time usage
- Blocks written
- Disk space used
- Blocks read
- Processor usage

By setting each of these resource charge rates at 1, you can receive a comparative view of how users are using your LAN resources. For example, match their time usage with processor usage to see whether they are really working. By setting the Allow Unlimited Credit option to YES, you are allowing the number to go well below 0 and users will quickly accumulate a negative balance. The number that appears in their negative Account Balance under User Information exactly correlates with their use of NetWare resources. Although NetWare does not inherently support any kind of auditing or resource-tracking feature, clever and creative use of NetWare accounting can provide the same functionality. We will explore NetWare accounting in greater depth in the next chapter.

*NetWare 4.1 finally includes a sophisticated auditing feature that allows system managers to track over one hundred different types of NetWare resources. Cool.*

### Limit Server Disk Space

Users can be restricted to specific amounts of disk space on the shared server disk. NetWare tracks disk space by who owns (created) what file. Also, if you copy a file, ownership is transferred to the destination user. If Limit Server Disk Space is set to YES, the system will ask for a Maximum Server Disk Space parameter (in kilobytes). Typically, this parameter deters disk abuse. Also, in academic environments, it is a good idea to limit students so that they don't clutter the disk with games and miscellaneous utilities—unless, of course, they give you a copy of the game (just kidding!). A good value for limiting server disk space is 10,000KB or 10MB.

The next three login restrictions support account restrictions supplementally. They provide a certain level of login security but not nearly the flexibility or versatility of account balance/restrictions. Let's take a quick look at them.

*Adventure is the champagne of life.*

G. K. Chesterton

## Time Restrictions

Time restrictions enable you to control how much time users have access to the system. Time restrictions can be applied as a default at the user level just as account restrictions are. Keep in mind that default time restrictions only take effect for user accounts that are created subsequently. When they are configured intelligently, time restrictions help increase the security of the system. But when configured carelessly, time restrictions can dramatically hinder user performance and productivity.

The default time restrictions screen, shown in Figure 9.4, is a matrix of days and time periods. The days of the week, Sunday through Saturday, are displayed on the left-hand side of the matrix and a 24-hour clock (in

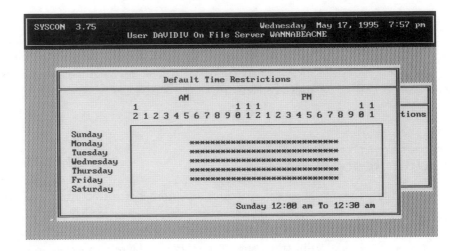

```
SYSCON  3.75                    Wednesday  May 17, 1995  7:57 pm
                   User DAVIDIV On File Server WANNABEACNE
```

```
                         Default Time Restrictions
                     AM                      PM
            1                   1 1 1                    1 1
            2 1 2 3 4 5 6 7 8 9 0 1 2 1 2 3 4 5 6 7 8 9 0 1      tions
    Sunday
    Monday          *********************************
    Tuesday         *********************************
    Wednesday       *********************************
    Thursday        *********************************
    Friday          *********************************
    Saturday
                              Sunday 12:00 am To 12:30 am
```

half-hour increments) is listed across the top. Each asterisk in the system indicates a time period when a specific user or all users can log in. By default, the time restriction screen contains all asterisks—meaning all users can log in at any time. To restrict users, simply move the cursor to a particular point in time and press the spacebar. Doing so blanks the time period and makes it unavailable for user access.

Some common time restrictions include:

**Restrict entire days**—weekends, for example

**Restrict evenings**—10:00 PM to 5:00 AM

**Restrict backup time periods**—11:00 PM to midnight

These are effective strategies for protection against mild-mannered janitors who turn into superhackers at midnight or users who spend too much time in front of the computer. Time restrictions are dynamic—once you come across a blank time period, the system clears your connection. But don't worry, there is a five-minute warning before the connection is cleared.

*When a time restriction is encountered and a user connection is cleared, the system does not perform a proper logout; the system simply clears the workstation—without saving the file. When you see a five-minute warning message, it's a good idea to pay attention and log out.*

You can use the F5 key with time restrictions to highlight blocks of time. Then simply press the asterisk key to insert an available time slot or press the spacebar to restrict that time slot. Remember, intelligent time restrictions increase network security, but careless time restrictions significantly hinder user productivity.

## Station Restrictions

Station restrictions are another way to control user access. But instead of restricting user access with passwords, disk restrictions, or time slots, you're restricting the physical workstation from which users can log in. Figure 9.5 illustrates station restrictions. Here's how they work. Each workstation is equipped with an internal network interface card. The card has a twelve-digit hexadecimal node address that is programmed at the factory. This node address is unique for all network interface cards in the world and is used by the cabling media to distinguish this network interface card from all others on the LAN. The node address can also be used to identify which users can log in from which machines. In a certain sense, the user is logically tied to a specific network interface card.

**FIGURE 9.5**
Station restrictions
in SYSCON

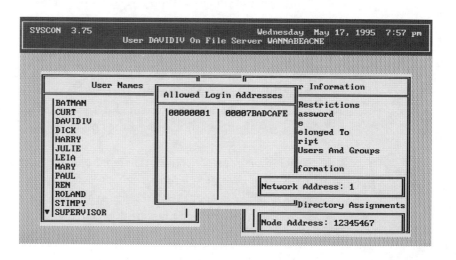

*Because station restrictions are linked so closely to the user and node address, there is no such thing as default station restrictions. It wouldn't make sense to restrict all users on the network to a particular node address. If you did, all users in the network would have to log in from the same workstation. Massive gridlock!*

Station restrictions are configured for specific users in the User Information screen of SYSCON. To define a station restriction for a given user, the system manager must provide two pieces of information: network address and node address. The *network address* defines the cabling scheme on which the workstation is attached. The *node address* is a twelve-digit hexadecimal number that identifies the workstation network interface card. Unfortunately, this information is not readily available to NetWare system managers. The only easy way to access network/node information is the USERLIST utility. USERLIST provides a list of all users who are currently logged in and the station addresses of the machines they are using. The best strategy is to print out a list of each user's USERLIST and use the information in SYSCON to establish station restrictions.

Station restrictions, like other login restrictions, can be used to enhance access security. If they are abused or mishandled, they can significantly impede user productivity. If station restrictions are set to only one workstation and a user's workstation is down or busy, he/she cannot log in from any other machine. Although this can be a useful security tool, it can be detrimental to user relationships.

## Intruder Detection/Lockout

*Intruder detection/ lockout tracks invalid login attempts by monitoring users who try to log in without correct passwords.*

The fourth login restriction strategy is intruder detection/lockout. This is not so much a restriction as it is a security-tracking feature. Intruder detection/lockout tracks invalid login attempts by monitoring users who try to log in without correct passwords. This feature keeps track of invalid password attempts and locks a user account once the threshold number of attempts has been exceeded—usually three. Intruder detection/lockout is a system-wide configuration—it is either activated for all users or none.

By default, intruder detection/lockout is set to NO. You can choose intruder detection/lockout from the Supervisor Option screen of SYSCON

(Figure 9.6). Intruder detection/lockout consists of two components: intruder detection and account lockout. The following is a brief discussion of each.

### Intruder Detection

Intruder detection is activated as soon as a valid user logs in with an incorrect password. The Incorrect Login Attempt Threshold setting is a number that continues to increment as invalid passwords are entered for the same user. As soon as the incrementing number exceeds the Incorrect Login Attempt Threshold, the system activates account lockout. The Bad Login Count Retention Time is a window of opportunity, so to speak, that the system uses to increment the incorrect login attempts.

Here's how it works: Assume the Incorrect Login Attempts is set to 7 and Bad Login Account Retention Time is set to 23 Hours 59 Minutes. The system will track all incorrect login activity and lock the user account if the number of incorrect login attempts exceeds 7 in this 24-hour window.

*The most common target for NetWare hackers is the supervisor. If intruder detection/lockout is activated and users try to access the supervisor account more than seven times with an incorrect password, the system will lock the supervisor account. This situation is particularly disconcerting because the supervisor is the only user who can unlock NetWare accounts. Fortunately, NetWare has incorporated a console command called ENABLE LOGIN that resets the supervisor account.*

**FIGURE 9.6**
Intruder
detection/lockout

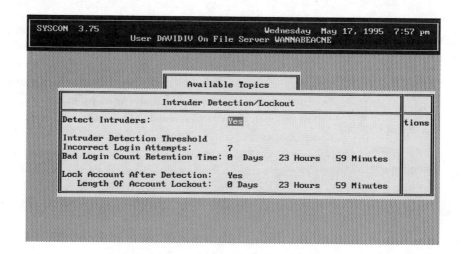

### Account Lockout

Account lockout is activated when the Intruder Detection Threshold setting is exceeded and Account Lockout is set to YES. It doesn't make much sense to activate intruder detection/lockout without initiating a user lockout once the Intruder Detection Threshold is exceeded. By setting the Lock Account After Detection to YES, the system asks for a Length of Account Lockout. It is the time period that the account is locked once Account Lockout is activated. By default, this value is set to 15 minutes (doesn't make much sense, does it?). This value invites the hacker to come back 15 minutes later and try all over again. Typically, a value equal to or exceeding the Bad Login Count Retention Time is adequate.

*The supervisor unlocks a user account on the User Information screen of SYSCON. The Intruder/Detection Lockout screen displays the node ID of the last station that attempted an incorrect login. This is useful information if you have a problem with particular users accessing other users' accounts. This information becomes especially valuable when it is combined with station restrictions—an open-and-shut case.*

# NCP Packet Signature

The new NetWare 3.12 NCP packet signature feature is designed to protect the LAN from experienced hackers who forge data packets or pose as unauthenticated clients—NetWare incognito. The best way to understand the NCP packet signature feature is to review the steps that occur between a workstation and a server during normal LAN operations:

1. When a workstation client logs into a NetWare 3.12 server, the server and the client establish a shared key referred to as the *session key*. This key is unique for each client logged into the server and for each unique session.

2. When the client requests services from the server, the client appends a unique signature to the data packet.

3. The server validates the signature as soon as the server receives the packet. If the signature is correct, the NetWare 3.12 server processes the

request and attaches a new signature to the reply. If the client's signature is incorrect, the packet is discarded and an alert message is sent to the server console and error log.

*The NCP packet signature feature causes a slight decrease in server performance. To alleviate this problem, consider enabling packet bursting or large Internet packets (LIPs).*

NCP packet signing occurs at both the workstation and the server. NetWare 3.12 contains a default level of packet signing. By default, the client signs only if the server requests it and the server signs if the client is capable. Therefore, signing always occurs. The system manager can customize NCP packet signing by using the SET server command and NET.CFG workstation file:

*At the Server (SET):*

```
SET NCP PACKET SIGNATURE OPTION =
```

*At the WORKSTATION in NET.CFG (NetWare DOS Requester):*

```
SIGNATURE LEVEL =
```

NCP packet signature settings can vary for clients and servers depending on the security needs of the network. Table 9.2 illustrates the available options for NCP packet signing.

*NCP packet signatures recently became necessary because of the overzealous activities of a group of students at Leiden University in the Netherlands. These mischievous students discovered a simple piggyback intrusion mechanism for NetWare 2.2 and 3.11 servers. The NCP packet signature feature slams the door on such would-be hackers.*

That's it for login restrictions. In this section, we covered the various account restrictions, time restrictions, station restrictions, NetWare's intruder detection/lockout feature, and NCP packet signature. These restrictions, used in coordination with login/password security, can create an effective security strategy for the NetWare LAN house detective.

**TABLE 9.2**
NCP Packet
Signature Levels

| Server Level | 0 | 1 | 2 (DEFAULT) | 3 |
|---|---|---|---|---|
| | Server does not sign packets | Server signs only if client requests it | Server signs if client is capable of signing | Server always signs and requires *all* clients to sign (or login will fail) |
| **Client Level** | | | | |
| **0** Client does not sign packets | No packet signature | No packet signature | No packet signature | No logging in |
| **1 (DEFAULT)** Client signs only if server requests it | No packet signature | No packet signature | PACKET SIGNATURE | PACKET SIGNATURE |
| **2** Client signs if server is capable of signing | No packet signature | PACKET SIGNATURE | PACKET SIGNATURE | PACKET SIGNATURE |
| **3** Client always signs and requires server to sign (or login will fail) | No logging in | PACKET SIGNATURE | PACKET SIGNATURE | PACKET SIGNATURE (maximum protection) |

# Access Rights

WELCOME TO PARK PLACE. Once you have checked in at the registration desk and provided a valid form of payment, the lobby guards inspect your belongings. If you pass the lobby guards' inspection, you are allowed through the Park Place gates. Once inside the hotel proper, you will find that Park Place fountains, atriums, and golf courses are quite overwhelming. The grandness of the hotel can cause your mind to spin. Fortunately, tour guides and maps provide an effective strategy for finding your way around. Movement throughout the hotel grounds is generally unrestricted. Access to certain areas of the grounds, however, is restricted to guests with specific user keys and door locks. In this section, we will delve into the house detective's responsibilities in using locksmith tools for enhanced hotel security.

Access rights define the third level of the NetWare security model. Once the user has passed login/password security and login restrictions, he/she is greeted with a NetWare prompt. Movement throughout the network directory structure is controlled by access rights. Users cannot freely access all files and directories in the system—this would be entirely too 1960s. Instead, users are limited to those files and directories for which they have been given specific privileges.

Access to shared network data is controlled at two levels: the user level (using trustee assignments) and the directory level (using directory rights). We will discuss each of these levels of security and talk about how they combine to create *effective rights*. But before we dive into the deep end with trustee assignments and directory rights, take a moment to understand the access privileges themselves and appreciate how they limit specific user actions in NetWare directory structures.

*Once the user has passed login/password security and login restrictions, he/she is greeted with a NetWare prompt. Movement throughout the network directory structure is controlled by access rights.*

*This is no time for ease and comfort. It is the time to dare and endure.*

*Winston Churchill*

# Understanding Access Rights

To understand access rights, you need to ask one simple question: "What are the types of things users do in a network directory?" Ready for the answers?

- Read from files
- Write to files
- Copy files
- Change the names of files
- Access applications
- Erase files
- Create directories

Wow, users are extremely active! Fortunately, NetWare provides a simple facility for controlling user actions. Each of these user activities corresponds with a specific NetWare access right. In NetWare 3.1*x*, there are eight access privileges:

**W—Write** to write to an existing file

**R—Read** to read an existing file

**M—Modify** to modify file names and attributes

**F—File Scan** to search the directory or subdirectory

**A—Access Control** to determine access rights

**C—Create** to create and write to new files or subdirectories

**E—Erase** to delete existing file or subdirectories

**S—Supervisory** for all rights in the directory and all subdirectories

*Notice that the NetWare 3.1x rights spell a word—WoRMFACES. The o is silent. Ironically, the o (open) is a NetWare 2.15 right that has been incorporated into W and R. Funny how the o falls into place so nicely. It's almost as if Novell planned it that way.*

*T*he key to using access rights is under-standing which rights are necessary to perform common NetWare activities.

Each access right corresponds with a particular user function. Five of them correspond with common functions—writing, reading, creating, erasing, and searching. The other three rights are a little more quirky—Modify, Access Control, and Supervisory. These rights pertain to the process of assigning and modifying NetWare security. *Modify* provides the ability to customize file attributes, *Access Control* allows users to change their access privileges, and Supervisory grants all rights—these are dangerous.

The key to using access rights is understanding which rights are necessary to perform common NetWare activities. Table 9.3 lists some common Net-Ware activities and the rights required to perform those activities. As the system manager, you are responsible for assigning specific access rights to specific directories for specific users based on the types of activities they perform in those directories. Sounds simple, right?

One of the system manager's security responsibilities is locksmithing. Have you ever seen a locksmith in action? It's awesome. The LAN locksmith has two major responsibilities: keys and locks. The first responsibility is to create the keys that unlock specific doors in the hotel. The other locksmith responsibility is to install the locks in appropriate network directories. Once the keys have been created and the locks are in place, each user is given an appropriate set of keys—the NetWare key ring.

*If I were you, I would spend time learning what rights are needed for certain tasks rather than simply memorizing the eight rights themselves. After all, you will need this knowledge to use access rights in the "real world." Also, focus on SAM (Supervisory, Access Control, and Modify).*

This analogy is actually close to what happens in the NetWare security model—the keys are analogous to trustee assignments, and the locks are analogous to directory rights. If a lock exists and the user has the correct key, that user is said to have *effective right* to unlock the directory. Remember, users can only perform the privileges that match the notches on their key.

*NetWare 3.1x access rights apply to both files and directories, whereas Net-Ware 2.2 rights are limited to directories only. Most system managers apply access rights at the directory level, because most files in a directory share a common purpose. Keep in mind, though, that you can apply access rights security to a single file within a directory.*

| | ACTION | RIGHTS REQUIREMENT |
|---|---|---|
| **TABLE 9.3**<br>Rights Requirements<br>for Common<br>NetWare Activities | Read from a closed file | R |
| | See a filename or directory | F |
| | Write to a closed file | W, C, E, M (in special cases) |
| | Execute an .EXE file | RF |
| | See the root directory | Any of the eight rights |
| | Create and write to a file | C |
| | Make a new directory | C |
| | Delete a file | E |
| | Change attributes | M |
| | Rename a file | M |
| | Copy files into a directory | W, C, F |
| | Copy files from a directory | R, F |
| | Modify disk space restrictions | A |
| | Change directory rights | A |
| | Change trustee assignments | A |
| | Salvage deleted files | R, F, C |

*W*hen a user or group is given a rights assignment to a particular directory, he/she/it is said to be a trustee of that directory.

# Trustee Assignments

Trustee assignments—access right keys—are assigned to users and groups. When a user or group is given a rights assignment to a particular directory, he/she/it is said to be a *trustee* of that directory. In addition, trustee assignments flow from parent directories to their child subdirectories. So when an access right is granted to a trustee for a given directory, the privilege is inherited by all subdirectories. See Figure 9.7 for an example of flowing trustee

**FIGURE 9.7**
The flow of trustee keys

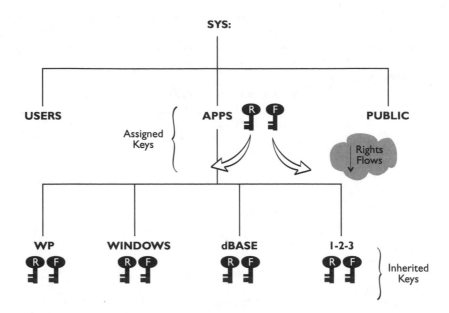

keys. Access rights do not flow upward, however, so it would be impossible to grant user trustee assignments to a parent directory unless you went to that directory and assigned them specifically at that point. You can, however, assign large, sweeping sets of privileges by granting trustee assignments to global parent directories such as APPS.

This strategy for assigning user keys defines two types of trustee assignments: explicit and inherited. *Explicit trustee assignments* are the rights explicitly granted to a user in a specific NetWare directory. *Inherited trustee assignments* are the rights that flow down from parent directories. Figure 9.8 illustrates how explicit assignments in a parent directory become inherited rights for the children subdirectories. This is important for NetWare 3.1*x*,

**FIGURE 9.8**
The flow of trustee
assignments from
parent to child

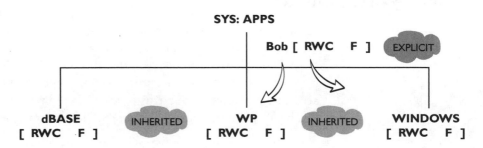

because it responds differently to explicit and inherited rights. NetWare 2.2, on the other hand, treats them the same. You will learn how in a moment.

Another interesting side-effect of trustee assignments is that they can be both additive and nonadditive. Let me explain.

**Additive** means that a user's trustee assignment in a given directory is the combination of his/her user assignment and the assignment of groups to which he/she belongs. Figure 9.9 provides an example: Bob is granted the Read and Write privileges in the APPS\WP directory as a user. In addition, he is a member of the ADMIN group that is assigned File Scan, Modify, and Access Control. So Bob's actual trustee assignment in APPS\WP is Read, Write, File Scan, Modify, and Access Control.

**Nonadditive** means that when a user is granted explicit assignments in a given directory, all other keys are taken away. That is, explicit assignments override inherited rights.

This strategy is a real time-saver, because it enables the system manager to assign keys not just to individuals but to large groups of individuals—all in one swoop. It might seem trivial, but as soon as you begin assigning trustee assignments and directory rights throughout the system, you'll find that it can become quite a monumental task. An intelligent approach to trustee

**FIGURE 9.9**
Combined trustee
assignments

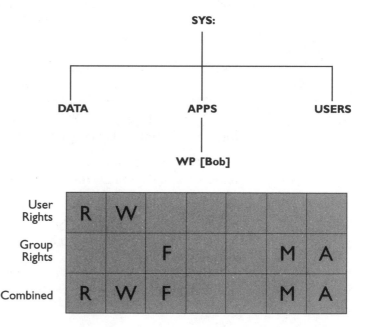

assignments would involve group assignments for global directories—PUBLIC, APPS, DATA, and so on—and user assignments for user-specific directories—USERS\BOB. Also, keep track of how the rights flow. Use inherited rights for multiple subdirectories of global parents—APPS\WP, APPS\DBASE, and APPS\WINDOWS, for example.

To create a trustee assignment for a user or group, NetWare needs three pieces of information:

- The name of the trustee

- The trustee rights to be assigned

- The path to the directory where the assignment begins—the parent directory name

Trustee assignments can be granted in two ways: SYSCON or GRANT. Assignments made using the SYSCON utility are set in the User Information or Group Information screen. We will explore SYSCON in great depth in Chapter 10, "NetWare 3.12 Utilities." Assignments can also be made using the GRANT command. We will explore the GRANT utility later in this chapter.

A few users and groups automatically exist when you first take over the LAN. These system-generated users and groups include GUEST (which has severely limited rights), SUPERVISOR (NetWare Yoda with unlimited rights), and the group EVERYONE (which has specialized default rights). The following is a brief description of the default assignments for these three user/groups:

*Directory locks, or directory rights, are directory specific— not user/group specific. Directory rights are assigned to directories. In addition, the existence of a directory lock is independent from the existence of a user key.*

**EVERYONE** includes all users whose accounts currently exist and all users whose accounts will eventually exist. Most global assignments are granted to EVERYONE because it provides an effective strategy for assigning sweeping trustee privileges. EVERYONE is assigned the Read and File Scan privileges to SYS:PUBLIC and the Create right to SYS:MAIL.

**SUPERVISOR** is granted all rights to everything. These rights cannot be removed, and the SUPERVISOR account cannot be deleted.

**GUEST** provides the minimum NetWare security. GUEST assumes the trustee privileges of EVERYONE, plus all rights except Access Control and Supervisory to his/her own SYS:MAIL\\*userid* directory.

Each user is given a default trustee assignment of Create, Erase, File Scan, Modify, Read, and Write to his/her own specific SYS:MAIL\\*userid* directory.

Also, users are given the same rights to their own specific SYS:USERS\username directory, including Access Control.

*Too many people are thinking of security instead of opportunity. They seem more afraid of life than death.*

*James F. Byrnes*

Returning for a moment to the locksmith analogy: If the trustee assignments are keys, the keys are only effective in directories that have locks. If there are no locks, the keys can't work. The absence of a lock in the NetWare analogy does not mean you have total access. In fact, it means the opposite: You have *no* access. In order for a user to have effective rights in a given directory, the user must be granted both the key and the lock to that directory. Let's see how directory rights fit into this security puzzle.

# Directory Rights

Directory locks, or directory rights, are *directory specific*—not *user/group specific*. Directory rights are assigned to directories. And they do not flow down. In addition, the existence of a directory lock is independent from the existence of a user key. If the locksmith decides to put a lock on a given directory, that lock is susceptible to any user key that matches. This level of NetWare security can quickly get out of hand. Figure 9.10 depicts the non-flow of directory locks.

Fortunately, the directory rights in NetWare 2.2 and 3.1*x*, by default, include all locks on all directories. This means that every directory in the entire system has all locks available. This strategy eliminates the need for directory rights and makes NetWare security dependent only on trustee assignments, therefore dramatically simplifying the system manager's job. If the system manager is specifically concerned about a given directory, he/she can remove the lock from that directory. Otherwise, leave it alone.

NetWare 3.1*x* directory rights are called the inherited rights mask (IRM). The IRM is based on the following assumption: "Here are the maximum rights you can inherit in this directory."

For example, if the SYS:APPS\WP subdirectory has sensitive application files that shouldn't be deleted, you can remove the Erase lock from that

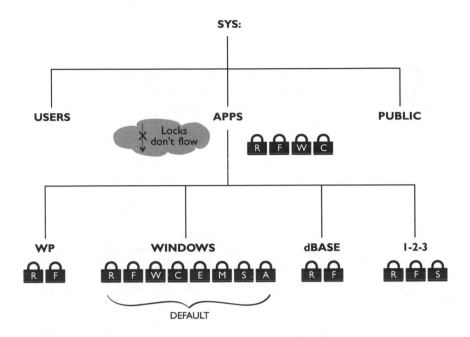

**FIGURE 9.10**
The non-flow of
NetWare directory locks

directory (Figure 9.11). Without the Erase lock, it doesn't matter who has access to or possession of the Erase key. Key holders will not be able to exercise the Erase right in the SYS:APPS\WP directory. The user must be granted explicit rights in the SYS:APPS\WP subdirectory. Remember, the I in IRM stands for *Inherited*, and the IRM only applies to *inherited* rights. Explicit rights override it.

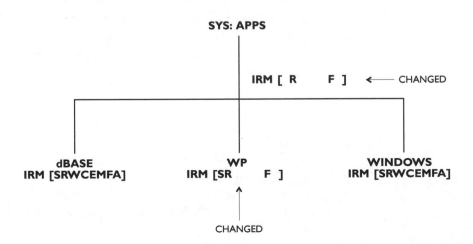

**FIGURE 9.11**
Blocking rights with the
inherited rights mask

The IRM is only useful in specialized circumstances and can become quite confusing in calculating effective rights. A useful way to implement NetWare security is to leave all directory locks in their default state and rely 100% on trustee assignments—user keys.

*If I were you, I would concentrate all my brain energy on learning about calculating effective rights. The exercises at the end of this chapter provide an excellent example of what to expect on the test.*

## Calculating NetWare 3.1x Effective Rights

So what does all this really mean? The bottom line is this: A user's *actual* privileges in a given directory are calculated as the intersection of the user's trustee assignments and the directory's IRM. These are defined as *effective rights.*

If you look at it in a global sense, a user's trustee assignments and a directory's IRM are meaningless until you put them together and calculate what the user's effective rights are. After all, the effective rights are the only rights that a user can exercise in a given directory.

Effective rights combine a privilege key with the existence of that privilege lock. Refer to Figure 9.12. Assume that only certain locks exist in the APPS\WP subdirectory [SRWCF]. In addition, Bob has inherited the Read, Write, Create, and File Scan keys from SYS:APPS. Therefore, Bob's effective rights are Read, Write, Create, and File Scan. If the system manager decided that Bob shouldn't have the Write or Create privileges in APPS\WP, he/she

**FIGURE 9.12**
Calculating NetWare
3.1x effective rights

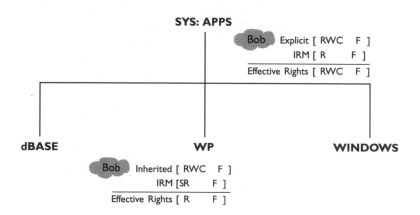

could use one of two strategies: remove Bob's W and C keys, or remove the W and C locks. The first choice would affect Bob only, whereas the second choice would restrict the Write and Create privileges for *all* users in the LAN (unless they are explicitly granted there).

In Figure 9.12, the system manager opted for a more global strategy and restricted the W and C locks with the IRM. Bob's effective rights become Read and File Scan in SYS:APPS\WP.

The process of calculating effective rights is not always this straightforward (if you can call it that). In many cases, effective rights are subject to NetWare 3.1*x* exceptions:

- The Supervisory right is immune to any effect from the IRM. In addition, inheritance of the S privilege cannot be revoked from subdirectories below the parent directory in which it is explicitly granted.

- Explicit trustee assignments override the effects of the IRM. The IRM is only effective against inherited rights.

- Trustee assignments granted to users operate separately from trustee assignments assigned to groups. For example, in a given directory, Bob's trustee assignments are the combination of his user rights and group rights. If his user rights are inherited and his group rights are explicit, his user rights will be affected by the IRM, whereas his group rights will not.

- Inherited trustee assignments are actually the effective rights from the parent directory.

To illustrate the complexity of calculating effective rights, let's review the figures from this section. First, Figure 9.8 shows Bob's explicit assignments of Read, Write, Create, and File Scan assigned to the APPS parent directory. These assignments become inherited rights in the three subdirectories of DBASE, WP, and WINDOWS.

In Figure 9.11, the directory locks or IRM in APPS allows R and F (which is different from the default). As the graphic shows, the IRM is not inherited by subdirectories of APPS. The DBASE and WINDOWS subdirectories maintain the default IRM, whereas the WP subdirectory has an IRM of S, R, and F.

Figure 9.12 shows a simple calculation of Bob's effective rights. Bob's explicit assignments of R, W, C, and F in the APPS directory combined with the IRM of R and F give him effective rights of R, W, C, and F, because explicit rights override the IRM.

In contrast, the WP subdirectory, which has an IRM of S, R, and F, does, in fact, block rights from Bob's inherited trustee assignments. His inherited trustee assignments in WP are R, W, C, and F, and you can see that his effective rights are calculated as R and F in the WP subdirectory.

To further complicate the issue, Bob is a member of the WP group that is assigned a group explicit assignment of E and M in the WP subdirectory of APPS. Figure 9.13 shows that the IRM blocks W, C, E, and M from Bob's inherited user assignment but does not block the explicit group assignment of E and M. Therefore, Bob's combined effective rights become R, E, M, and F.

Finally, in Figure 9.14 you learn the effect of the Supervisory privilege. Bob is also a member of the ADMIN group, which is assigned the explicit trustee assignment of Supervisory at the APPS parent directory. This Supervisory assignment overrides the IRM and gives Bob effective rights of S, R, W, C, E, M, F, and A in the parent directory of APPS and all subdirectories below.

*The Supervisory right cannot be blocked by the IRM.*

If all of this information is confusing and a little overwhelming, don't be concerned. LAN security at this extreme is rarely justified. Most NetWare LANs can easily afford a less complex security system—group trustee assignments and no IRMs. See Table 9.4 for a simple summary of calculating effective rights. In addition, some of the exercises at the end of the chapter will help you to understand effective rights for certain cases. It is important, however, that you understand the full scope of effective rights ramifications. After all, LAN locksmithing is one of your most important detective responsibilities. You should fill your NetWare utility belt with a strong understanding of how to implement trustee assignments (keys) and directory rights (locks).

**FIGURE 9.13**
Combination trustee assignments and effective rights

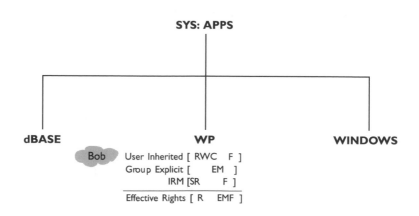

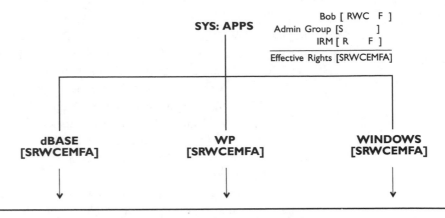

**FIGURE 9.14**
Understanding the effects
of the Supervisory right

| | |
|---|---|
| **TABLE 9.4**<br>A Summary of Calculating<br>Effective Rights | "Is the Supervisory (S) right granted in this or the parent directory?" |

**TABLE 9.4**
A Summary of Calculating
Effective Rights

| | |
|---|---|
| "Is the Supervisory (S) right granted in this or the parent directory?" | YES ● Effective Rights = All Rights<br>NO ● Move to next question |
| "Has the user been granted explicit rights in this directory?" | YES ● Effective Rights = Explicit Rights<br>NO ● Move to next question |
| "Is the IRM set to default (allowing all rights)?" | YES ● Effective Rights = Inherited Rights or Effective Rights of Parent Directory<br>NO ● Effective Rights = Inherited Rights − IRM |

*A man, to carry on a successful business, must have imagination. He must see things as in a vision, a dream of the whole thing.*

*Charles M. Schwab*

# Attributes

THE FINAL LAYER OF the NetWare security model is attribute security. *Attributes* are special assignments or properties that are assigned to individual directories or files. Attribute security overrides all previous trustee assignments and effective rights. Attribute security can be used to prevent a user from deleting a file, copying a file, viewing a file, or

*T*he final layer of
the NetWare secu-
rity model is attribute
security. Attributes
are special assign-
ments or properties
that are assigned to
individual directories
or files. Attribute
security overrides all
previous trustee
assignments and
effective rights.

writing to a specific file. Attributes also control whether files can be shared, mark files as modified since the last backup, or protect files from data corruption by ensuring that they are transactionally tracked.

Attribute security is analogous to the Park Place vault. When guests are concerned about particular belongings, they can go beyond existing door lock security and have them locked into a safety deposit box that can never be opened—except by the user or the house detective.

Attributes provide a complex level of security that enables you, as the system manager, to manage what users can do with files once they access them. Attributes are global security elements that affect all users regardless of their rights. Attributes can be used to override all previous levels of security. For example, let's say a user has the Read, File Scan, and Write privileges to the SYS:APPS\WP directory. The system manager can still restrict the user from writing to a specific file by assigning the read-only file attribute (RO). This level of NetWare security overrides all previous security.

The true effective rights to a given file in a given directory are determined by the combination of trustee assignments, directory rights, *and* file attributes. NetWare supports two types of attributes: security and feature. Security attributes affect users' security access (what they can do with specific files). Feature attributes affect how the system interacts with files (whether the files can be archived or whether transactional tracking has been activated). In the next section, we will describe NetWare's security and feature attributes and then move on to the many command-line utilities that allow the system manager to implement NetWare's multilayered security model.

## Security Attributes

*S*ecurity attributes
protect information
at the file and
directory level by
controlling two kinds
of file access: file
sharing and
file alteration.

Security attributes protect information at the file and directory level by controlling two kinds of file access: file sharing and file alteration. File access security controls not so much *who* has access to the files, but *what kind of access* they have. Once a user has been given the proper trustee assignments to a given directory, that user then has the ability to access any of the files within that system. Security attributes tell that person what he/she can do with the accessed files. The file alteration attributes not only tell you what you can do with them but also *limit* your file access.

Here's a list of the file sharing and file alteration attributes. An asterisk (*) indicates any attribute that affects both directories and files.

**NS—Nonsharable:** Access is limited to one user at a time.

**S—Sharable:** Files are available for simultaneous access by multiple users.

**RW—Read/Write:** Users may see the file and alter its content.

**RO—Read-Only:** Users may only see the file; they can make no changes to it.

**X—Execute Only:** File is for execution only; users cannot copy the file or delete the attribute.

**H (\*)—Hidden:** Users cannot see, use, delete, or copy over the file.

**D or DI (\*)—Delete-Inhibit:** Users cannot delete the file or directory.

**R or RI (\*)—Rename-Inhibit:** Users cannot rename the file or directory.

**C or CI—Copy-Inhibit:** Macintosh users cannot copy the file.

The nonsharable and sharable attributes limit file access to a single user at a time or provide simultaneous access by multiple users. When multiple users have access to a directory and the files are flagged sharable, you run into a problem. When these users access the same data and try to save their version of the file, the last person who saves the file will win the race. This is where the nonsharable attribute comes in handy. If you want only one person to access a file at a time, you can assign the nonsharable attribute to the file—the system will keep track of who gets to save and who doesn't.

The read/write and read-only attributes also affect file access but in a different way. These attributes affect what the user can do once he/she has the file open. The read/write attribute enables users to see the file and alter its contents. Read-only means they can open the file but cannot make any changes. The read-only attribute is useful for application files that you want users to be able to access (but not change the contents of) in a shared environment.

The execute only attribute is extremely sensitive and provides the highest level of NetWare security. The execute only attribute can only be assigned by the supervisor to .EXE and .COM files. Execute only files cannot be copied or backed up—just executed or deleted. Also, once the execute only attribute has been set, it cannot be removed. Hidden is reserved for special files or directories that cannot be seen, used, deleted, or copied over. The hidden attribute is used for archived files or directories. To access a file that has this flag, the supervisor must remove the hidden attribute.

*Some applications don't work properly with the execute only attribute.*

Inhibit attributes are new to NetWare 3.1*x*, and they restrict users' access to delete, copy, and rename files and directories. The delete-inhibit attribute prevents users from erasing directories or files even if they have been granted the Erase access right. If users have been granted the Modify right, they can remove the delete-inhibit attribute. Rename-inhibit restricts users from renaming directories and files even if the users have the Modify right. If they have the Modify right, they must remove the rename-inhibit attribute before they can rename the file or directory. The Modify right thus eradicates the function of rename-inhibit, which then becomes useless.

The copy-inhibit attribute restricts only the copy rights of users logged in from Macintosh workstations. If these users have been granted Read and File Scan rights, they still cannot copy the specific file. Macintosh users can, however, remove the copy-inhibit attribute if they have been granted the Modify access right.

That completes our discussion of security attributes. Now let's take a closer look at NetWare feature attributes.

## Feature Attributes

*Feature attributes provide access to special NetWare functions or features, including backup, indexing, and transactional tracking.*

Feature attributes provide access to special NetWare functions or features, including backup, indexing, and transactional tracking. The feature attributes are:

**T—Activate TTS**: Identifies this file for transactional tracking.

**I—Indexed**: Identifies this file for turbo FAT indexing.

**SY (\*)—System**: Identifies this file or directory as system-owned.

**A—Not Yet Archived**: Flags a file as modified since last backup.

**P (\*)—Purge**: Flags a file or directory to be purged when it is deleted.

**P—Private**: (NetWare 2.2 only) Allows users to view a directory but not its contents; used mostly by Macintosh clients.

**Ra—Read Audit**: Performs no function.

**Wa—Write Audit**: Performs no function.

The feature attribute that warrants the most attention is system (SY), which is assigned by the system. The system attribute identifies the file or directory as being system-owned and as usable only for system functions. For example, NetWare bindery files are flagged as system so that nobody can delete, copy, or write to them. The archive (A) attribute allows the system to track which files have been modified since the last backup. The indexed (I) attribute allows turbo FAT indexing. The T attribute is assigned to files that need to be transactionally tracked by NetWare's internal transactional tracking system. Finally, the purge (P) attribute is assigned to files and directories that should be completely deleted and not available to be salvaged. Use of this attribute is an effective strategy for wiping away any trace of sensitive files.

*SALVAGE is a useful NetWare tool that enables users to recover files after they have been deleted. It is also a hacker's tool for covertly stealing valuable information. Keep in mind that even after a file has been deleted it is still available to any user with appropriate access rights (R, W, C, and F). The purge attribute wipes away any trace of the file.*

These files attributes, in combination, can create effective security tools to control who has access to do what with specialized NetWare files. The default attribute combination for all files on the system is nonsharable read/write (NSRW)—this combination is fine for most applications and most data files. There are specialized instances, however, when you can justify customizing these attributes. Here's a brief list:

- Stand-alone applications that are not to be shared should be flagged nonsharable read-only.

- Data files that are shared but not written to simultaneously should be nonsharable read/write.

- Data files that are part of larger multiuser applications that provide specialized record locking and other advanced features and can track file sharing or data sharing on their own should be flagged sharable read/write.

- Application files that are accessed by simultaneous users should be flagged sharable read-only.

- Large, important database files should be flagged with the transactional tracking attribute.

- Sensitive archive files—records that are only accessed once a month, such as payroll records or general ledger—should be hidden.

- All system files owned by the system should be flagged system. This attribute is assigned by the system, not by the user.

- Sensitive application files that cost lots of money and are shared on the system should be flagged execute only so that the supervisor is not liable should piracy occur.

*Recently, a popular software manufacturer sued a company for piracy when it was found that many of the users had taken copies of the application home with them. The software manufacturer won the case on the basis of system manager negligence. Evidently, the system manager had not flagged the executable application file execute only. Doing so is not only a good idea, it can probably save your job.*

That's it for our discussion of the NetWare security model and the concepts that combine to create the complex level of NetWare security that is necessary in a shared environment. You're going to have a chance to practice these concepts as we go along. You should feel much more comfortable with NetWare security once you get your locksmith feet wet. In the remainder of this chapter, you will learn about many valuable system manger tools and begin to build the security portion of your NetWare utility belt. Don't let it weigh you down!

*Few enterprises of great labor or hazard would be undertaken if we had not the power of magnifying the advantages we expect from them.*

*Samuel Johnson*

# Security Command-Line Utilities

*The process of building keys and building locks is not easy—it's time-consuming, complex, and grand in scope.*

HAVE YOU EVER WATCHED a locksmith make a key? It's quite an amazing process involving a complex set of specialized tools and fine precision. The process of building locks is also amazing to watch. The intricate machinery inside combines to create not only the strength of the unbreakable locks but their reliability as well. Imagine what's required to make the lock match only one key.

This process is analogous to what the system manager must endure to implement access right keys and directory locks. The process of building keys and building locks is not easy—it's time-consuming, complex, and grand in scope. The system manager is like a LAN locksmith, who must be aware of the many ramifications of assigning NetWare security. NetWare security tools, or CLUs, are broken into three categories: login/password security, access rights, and file attributes. The CLU tools for managing access rights are further broken down into trustee assignment tools and directory rights tools.

These tools are augmented by the menu utilities that we'll explore in the next chapter. Most of the login/password security and access rights tools can be found in the SYSCON menu utility; directory rights and file attribute tools are implemented in FILER. The menu utilities provide a great deal more functionality and a much friendlier format than CLUs—but the CLUs are fast and to the point.

*If I were you, I would learn what these security CLUs can do. But more importantly, I would learn their relationship to SYSCON and FILER—that's where you'll be spending most of your time. Here are the top few security CLUs: USERLIST, WHOAMI, GRANT, RIGHTS, FLAG, and ALLOW.*

## Login/Password Security—CLUs

The first security tools deal with login/password security. As mentioned earlier, login/password security deals with initial user access to the system. It incorporates a login name, a password, and specific login restrictions. There are five login/password security tools in the LAN locksmith's belt to help you set passwords and get information about who is logged in. Also, these tools provide a list of servers and allow users to attach to other file servers. Login/ password CLUs are available not only to the LAN locksmith but also to any user for gaining general login information.

## SETPASS

The first login/password security tool is SETPASS. The SETPASS command-line utility enables users to set their own password. At any NetWare prompt, type SETPASS. The system takes a look at your user identification and gathers information about your authorized password. If a password already exists, the system prompts you to enter your password and then enter a new one if you pass the first test. The reason for this level of security is so that not just anybody can log in as a different user and change passwords.

## ATTACH

ATTACH permits user and supervisor access to other file servers. Within Net-Ware, a user can log in to only one file server, because the key component of the login is the execution of a *login script*. The login script contains many specific variables for that file server and loads these variables into workstation memory. Although it is possible to attach to multiple servers, you can only log in to one server; if you logged into multiple servers, each server's login script would overwrite the other. The main difference between logging in and using ATTACH is the execution of the login script. If you log in to a server, it executes the login script. ATTACHing to a server performs exactly the same function, except the server does not execute the login script.

Keep in mind that in order to map drives or to access directories on other file servers, you must be logically attached to each file server through the ATTACH command. The ATTACH command will ask for a username and a password, and you will be subject to the same login restrictions as if you had logged in. The only difference is, again, that ATTACH does not execute the file server's host login script. The syntax of ATTACH is the same as LOGIN:

```
ATTACH server/username
```

The system then prompts you for a password if there is one. Keep in mind that NetWare enables you to attach to only eight file servers at one time with NETx, but up to fifty with VLMs.

## SLIST

Another login/password security tool that works in conjunction with ATTACH is SLIST. SLIST enables the user to view a list of all available servers to which the user is currently attached. The user can then decide whether to logically log in or attach to those multiple servers. In large, complex inter-networks, the SLIST command is extremely useful because it provides a simple list of all servers that are currently available. SLIST does not tell you whether you have a valid login account on any of those servers; it simply gives you a list of all servers that are physically recognized by your configuration's internal network interface card.

## USERLIST

USERLIST does not provide a list of servers but instead lists users who are currently logged in to your file server. USERLIST displays login information about those users and what they're currently doing on the system. USERLIST includes some command switches, specifically /A, which lists network and node addresses and tells you where their users are logged in. Also, you can specify as a switch the specific username and gain valuable information about specific users. For example, if you type `USERLIST GUEST`, the system will respond with relevant information specifically for the user GUEST. Again, this only works if the user is logged in.

*One possible trick with USERLIST is to type* `USERLIST /A` *for all network and node addresses and then use that information to restrict users to logging in from only their authorized workstations. This type of login restriction helps to manage users who tend to migrate through the LAN, logging in from multiple workstations.*

### WHOAMI

The final login/password security tool is WHOAMI, which at first sight has an existentialist tone to it. The WHOAMI utility displays information about your username, file servers you're currently attached to, your connection number, and the date and time of your last login. WHOAMI can assist users who find it difficult to come to grips with their purpose in life. It also provides valuable information about users and their current network environment.

There are four WHOAMI switches that enable you to focus on specific types of information.

**WHOAMI /G** lists the groups you belong to.

**WHOAMI /S** lists your security equivalences.

**WHOAMI /R** lists the effective rights in the network directory structure.

**WHOAMI /A** lists all of the above switches.

WHOAMI is useful only for the user who is logged in, because it looks at the username under which you're logged in and grabs information about you from the NetWare bindery.

# Trustee Assignments—CLUs

The next set of NetWare security tools refers to access rights—specifically, trustee assignments and directory rights. We'll break the set out according to those two categories, first discussing the tools that apply to trustee assignments and then moving on to directory rights.

Trustee assignment security tools apply almost exclusively to the LAN locksmith. These tools are powerful and can be abused quite easily. Keep in mind that in order to assign trustee rights or directory rights, a user must be granted the Access Control right to that particular directory. Again, the only person who has global access rights to assign all rights or privileges to the system is the supervisor or somebody who is granted supervisor equivalence.

### TLIST

The first trustee assignment tool is TLIST. The TLIST CLU displays a directory's trustees and their effective rights. TLIST is generally for information only and can be applied just to a specific directory in the mapping environment. TLIST provides information about all the trustees that are assigned access to a directory and their effective rights in that directory. It calculates the combination of trustee assignments and directory rights to display the effective rights. Be careful, though, because it doesn't always calculate rights correctly, especially if groups are involved. This tool could be useful for the LAN locksmith who is trying to figure what security should be granted to whom in a given directory. He/she can first type TLIST and get information about what already exists, and then build from there.

The next three trustee assignment tools apply to the actual implementation of trustee assignments.

### GRANT

The GRANT CLU is the most effective for trustee assignment. GRANT enables the supervisor to assign or grant specific privileges to specific users within specific directories. The syntax for GRANT is:

```
GRANT rights FOR directory/drive TO user/group
```

For example, to assign the R and F rights to user DAVID in the SYS:APPS\WP directory, the syntax would be:

```
GRANT R F FOR SYS:APPS\WP TO DAVID
```

This CLU is particularly efficient, because it allows quick access to the security system and quick implementation of trustee assignments. GRANT is hard to use, though, because it doesn't provide a list of existing trustee assignments for given users or groups, and it requires a specific syntax that—if you do not follow it exactly—can get you into trouble. The SYSCON menu utility is a much more friendly way to assign trustee privileges.

### REVOKE

REVOKE is exactly the opposite of GRANT. The syntax of REVOKE is exactly the same as for GRANT, but instead of granting rights *to* a user, you are revoking rights *from* him/her. Again, REVOKE requires you to adhere to specific syntax and does not provide a simple way of viewing all trustee assignments for given users.

### REMOVE

REMOVE is used not to revoke specific rights but to remove a trustee and all of his/her rights from a directory. REMOVE is dramatic in its scope in that it removes all rights for a given trustee in a directory and completely removes that user as a trustee. Thus, a removed user has no rights to a given directory.

*Use GRANT if you want to grant any rights for a given user to a directory, REVOKE to revoke partial rights, and REMOVE to revoke all rights.*

## Inherited Rights Mask—CLUs

Three security access right tools work in conjunction with the trustee assignment CLUs: the directory rights command-line utilities ALLOW, RIGHTS, and LISTDIR. These CLUs are specifically used in directory situations and do not apply to users, groups, or trustee assignments. ALLOW is used to create an IRM, and RIGHTS and LISTDIR enable you to view not only the directory rights of a given directory but also the trustees and effective rights. All the previous access rights tools enable you to view information about trustees. These particular tools permit you to view information about directories and effective rights.

*Computers are useless. They can only give you answers.*

*Pablo Picasso*

## ALLOW

ALLOW is identical to GRANT, except it creates an IRM at the directory level instead of assigning access rights at the user level. The syntax for ALLOW is:

```
ALLOW rights FOR directory/drive
```

For example, to allow only the Read and File Scan privileges in the SYS:APPS\WP directory, you would type:

```
ALLOW S R F FOR SYS:APPS/WP
```

Remember, you can't block the S right with an IRM. ALLOW is useful, but FILER (menu utility) is much easier to use.

> *The RIGHTS command looks at the directory rights for a given directory and then calculates your effective rights.*

## RIGHTS

RIGHTS is similar to TLIST in that it displays effective rights in a specific directory, but RIGHTS does not display all the trustees of that directory. It only displays your trustee rights and effective rights for a particular directory. The RIGHTS command takes a look at the username under which you're logged in and reads the information from the bindery as to what your trustee assignments are. It looks at the directory rights for that given directory and then calculates your effective rights.

## LISTDIR

LISTDIR is a lot more effective at providing information about directory rights than is the RIGHTS command. LISTDIR displays the effective and directory rights and all information pertaining to the directory, including all subdirectories of a parent directory. Six switches work in conjunction with the LISTDIR command that are relevant here:

**LISTDIR /T** shows the time of creation of the directory and subdirectories.

**LISTDIR /R** shows the directory rights for this directory and all subdirectories of the directory.

**LISTDIR /E** shows the effective rights you have in the directory and sub-directories of a parent directory.

**LISTDIR /A** shows the IRM, the effective rights, and all of the other date and time information.

**LISTDIR /D** shows the date of creation of the directory and subdirectories.

**LISTDIR /S** shows the subdirectory information in a tree structure.

Again, LISTDIR is a handy utility that provides subdirectory information and a directory tree structure including effective rights, IRM, and creation date and time of directory structures.

# Attributes—CLUs

NetWare provides two file attribute CLUs: FLAG and NCOPY. These two CLUs empower the LAN locksmith to view and assign file attributes as well as copy files with their attributes attached. Let's take a closer look.

### FLAG

The FLAG CLU enables supervisors and users with the Modify access right to view or change the file attributes of a given file. The syntax for the FLAG command is:

```
FLAG filename flags
```

The flag consists of the first few letters of the attribute name. If you refer to the earlier list of file attributes, the bolded letter corresponds to the flag switch you would use with this command. One prominent flag is the N switch, which enables the supervisor to assign the normal series of attributes to files. Doing so returns the file attributes of that file to the default state—nonsharable read/write. Incidentally, FLAGDIR is used to change directory attributes.

### NCOPY

The NCOPY command is extremely important because it retains the file attributes for files that are copied using the NCOPY command. This is not the case for files that are copied using the DOS XCOPY command. NCOPY otherwise works in the same way as the XCOPY command. The syntax is similar:

```
NCOPY filename TO location
```

You can also leave out the `to` and insert a space between the two file names, in which case NCOPY would assume a "to" in between.

*Because NCOPY is a NetWare utility, it accesses the NetWare file allocation table and directory entry table with a great deal more efficiency than DOS COPY does. This increased efficiency makes NCOPY a much safer means of copying files across the network. It's faster, too, because NCOPY works within the memory of the file server. If files are copied from one directory on the file server to another, NCOPY does not copy them down to workstation memory and back up, thereby creating a load on the network. Instead, NCOPY copies the files in file server RAM, which is much faster and does not create a load on the network. It's safer because NCOPY uses the read-after-write verification fault tolerance feature that is incorporated into NetWare. This read-after-write verification is not performed if you use the DOS COPY command.*

Also note that the NCOPY command supports all wildcard characters that the DOS COPY command supports.

That's it for NetWare security tools and for our discussion of NetWare security. Keep in mind that the LAN locksmith's responsibilities are to ensure that all the user data is safe and that sufficient access and data integrity security has been implemented. The reasons for security are not only to exclude unauthorized users but also to be efficient and transparent enough not to get in the way of normal operations. Many times the LAN locksmith gets caught up in the whole complex security model of NetWare and creates such a secure system that it's impossible to use. For this reason, NetWare security and user productivity must be balanced. NetWare's security functionality is extensive and supports a great many options. But keep in mind one of my KISS principles: Keep It Safe and Simple.

In the next chapter we'll delve a little bit deeper into directory structures, drive mapping, and security from the standpoint of menu utilities. Throughout these first chapters, we have discussed the CLU tools that have helped bolster your NetWare utility belt. Now let's spend some time discussing the menu utilities that will augment your NetWare utility belt. Also, in the following chapters, we'll go into much more depth on network management and printing. The NetWare menu utilities will provide a springboard for that discussion.

Without any further ado, let's get on with the shew!

*K*eep in mind that security and user productivity must be balanced. NetWare's security functionality is extensive and supports a great many options.

# Exercise 9.1: Understanding Special User Accounts

| TABLE 9.1E Understanding Special User Accounts | S | SE | WGM | UAM | CO | PQO | PSO |
|---|---|---|---|---|---|---|---|
| Grant supervisor equivalence | | | | | | | |
| Automatically acquire all rights to directory/file | | | | | | | |
| Create other users/ group accounts | | | | | | | |
| Manage all user accounts | | | | | | | |
| Manage special users accounts | | | | | | | |
| Manager/operator type can be user or group | | | | | | | |
| Create WGM | | | | | | | |
| Assign managed users as UAMs | | | | | | | |
| Delete any user account | | | | | | | |
| Delete special user accounts | | | | | | | |
| Use Supervisor functions of FCONSOLE | | | | | | | |

| | S | SE | WGM | UAM | CO | PQO | PSO |
|---|---|---|---|---|---|---|---|
| | | | | | | | |
| Create print queues | | | | | | | |
| Manipulate print queues | | | | | | | |
| Delete print queue entries | | | | | | | |
| Create print servers | | | | | | | |
| Manage print server | | | | | | | |

# Exercise 9.2: Calculating NetWare 3.12 Effective Rights

In this exercise, you will get some experience calculating effective rights for a variety of scenarios. In each scenario, you will be given enough information to calculate the appropriate effective rights. The information is provided according to the following components: explicit user rights, inherited user rights, explicit group rights, and IRM. Use the accompanying worksheets to follow the flow of rights and the effect of the IRM.

As the scenario study provides you with the appropriate information, put the right letter in the appropriate box (from the matrices below) and use the effective rights rules you learned in this chapter to calculate the appropriate privileges. Put on your thinking cap for this one!

1. As a user, you are granted the R, W, C, and F privileges to a given directory. The IRM for the same directory is S, R, and F. Calculate the effective rights.

| | S | R | W | C | E | M | F | A |
|---|---|---|---|---|---|---|---|---|
| EXPLICIT TRUSTEE RIGHTS | | | | | | | | |
| IRM | | | | | | | | |
| **EFFECTIVE RIGHTS** | | | | | | | | |

2. In a different subdirectory, you are granted explicit user rights in reverse order; that is, the trustee assignments are S, R, and F and the IRM is R, W, C, and F. What would your effective rights be in this subdirectory?

| | S | R | W | C | E | M | F | A |
|---|---|---|---|---|---|---|---|---|
| EXPLICIT TRUSTEE RIGHTS | | | | | | | | |
| IRM | | | | | | | | |
| **EFFECTIVE RIGHTS** | | | | | | | | |

**3.** This directory is a subdirectory of the one from scenario 2. The effective rights from scenario 2 then become the inherited rights for this scenario. In addition, the IRM is set to R, W, and M. What are your effective rights?

| | S | R | W | C | E | M | F | A |
|---|---|---|---|---|---|---|---|---|
| EXPLICIT TRUSTEE RIGHTS | | | | | | | | |
| INHERITED TRUSTEE RIGHTS | | | | | | | | |
| IRM | | | | | | | | |
| **EFFECTIVE RIGHTS** | | | | | | | | |

**4.** As a user, you inherit the R, W, E, and M privileges from the parent directory. In addition, the IRM has been set to W, C, M, and A. What are your effective rights?

| | S | R | W | C | E | M | F | A |
|---|---|---|---|---|---|---|---|---|
| EXPLICIT TRUSTEE RIGHTS | | | | | | | | |
| INHERITED TRUSTEE RIGHTS | | | | | | | | |
| IRM | | | | | | | | |
| **EFFECTIVE RIGHTS** | | | | | | | | |

**5.** As a member of the group ADMIN, you inherit the R, W, C, M, and F rights from the directory above. The IRM, though, blocks these rights and only allows the S, E, and A. What are your effective rights?

| | S | R | W | C | E | M | F | A |
|---|---|---|---|---|---|---|---|---|
| EXPLICIT TRUSTEE RIGHTS | | | | | | | | |
| INHERITED TRUSTEE RIGHTS | | | | | | | | |
| IRM | | | | | | | | |
| **EFFECTIVE RIGHTS** | | | | | | | | |

**6.** As a member of the group EVERYONE, you are explicitly granted the R and F rights to the PUBLIC subdirectory. In addition, as a user, you are explicitly granted the additional rights of W, C, and E. What are your combined explicit assignments? The system manager has decided that she would like to restrict the W, E, and M rights in the PUBLIC/DOS subdirectory with an IRM of S, C, F, and A. What are your effective rights in the PUBLIC/DOS subdirectory?

| | S | R | W | C | E | M | F | A |
|---|---|---|---|---|---|---|---|---|
| EXPLICIT GROUP RIGHTS | | | | | | | | |
| EXPLICIT USER RIGHTS | | | | | | | | |
| COMBINED | | | | | | | | |
| IRM | | | | | | | | |
| **EFFECTIVE RIGHTS** (Public\DOS) | | | | | | | | |

**7.** As a member of the group ACCT, you are granted the explicit rights of R and F to the APPS/ACCT subdirectory. In addition, as a user, you inherit the rights W, C, M, and A from the APPS parent directory. What are your combined rights in APPS\ACCT? In addition, the system manager has set the IRM for APPS\ACCT to S, C, E, and A. What are your effective rights in APPS\ACCT?

|  | S | R | W | C | E | M | F | A |
|---|---|---|---|---|---|---|---|---|
| EXPLICIT GROUP RIGHTS |  |  |  |  |  |  |  |  |
| INHERITED USER RIGHTS |  |  |  |  |  |  |  |  |
| COMBINED |  |  |  |  |  |  |  |  |
| IRM |  |  |  |  |  |  |  |  |
| **EFFECTIVE RIGHTS** |  |  |  |  |  |  |  |  |

# CASE STUDY III

## Assigning Security to Snouzer, Inc.

ASSIGNING NETWARE SECURITY to a complex LAN design can be your most challenging task as the Snouzer, Inc. system manager. As you learned from this chapter, NetWare security relies on a multilayered model. This multilayered model calls for login password security, login restrictions, access rights, and attribute security. In addition, NetWare provides a facility for creating special user accounts and distributed system managers. In this case study, we will build on the existing Snouzer, Inc. directory structure and design appropriate security at each layer of the NetWare security model. In addition, we will explore the use of workgroup managers, user account managers, and supervisor equivalents as distributed system managers.

Let's take a look at Snouzer, Inc.'s security needs. Being in the doggy fashion business, Snouzer, Inc.'s most valuable assets are ideas. These ideas are stored in designs on the NetWare shared disk. Snouzer, Inc. is extremely sensitive to security—both inside and outside the company. Sophy has asked you to create a distributed security management force that follows the responsibilities of the organization chart. Frank should be a workgroup manager over all the users in design and production. In addition, Hal should be a user account manager over his two special designers, Rene and Bob. The Snouzer, Inc. managers are organized into three NetWare groups: Admin, Design, and Production.

Here is a list of the groups and their corresponding users:

**ADMIN:** Sophy, Frank, Mary

**DESIGN:** Hal, Rene, Bob

**PRODUCTION:** George, Mary, Frank

These three functional groups enable you to effectively manage Snouzer, Inc.'s security without having to maintain the setup individually. The Snouzer, Inc. managers are particularly concerned about outside competition gaining access to their valuable designs. They have heard of a new hacker program that can access a five-character password in less than five minutes. For this reason, they would like you to require passwords that are more than five characters for all users. In addition, the managers would like you to have all users change their password to something new and unique every three months. Frank is particularly concerned about the people within his workgroup and would like a facility to be able to track their logins and logouts. Hal is concerned about his special designers and their use of shared disk space. Rene and Bob have been liberal and somewhat lazy about consuming directory space for the designs—they haven't been purging their old ones. For that reason, Hal would like you to limit their disk space to 50MB each.

Sophy's a little concerned about Mary because she thinks that Mary works entirely too hard. Mary has a tendency to stay around until 9:00 or 10:00 at night; Sophy is concerned about burnout. For this reason, she would like you to restrict Mary—log her out at 7:00 each evening and not allow her to log in until 8:00 AM the next morning. Sophy would also like you to ensure that nobody can log into the network on the weekends because Snouzer's seven managers—who like to work hard and play hard—never work on the weekends.

That completes the requirements for general Snouzer, Inc. restrictions. Now let's take a look at access rights security. Snouzer, Inc. believes in empowering employees. For that reason, they don't feel that it's necessary to restrict rights in the PUBLIC subdirectory. They would, however, like you to refrain from using the SAM access rights in any directories unless it is absolutely necessary. Incidentally, the SAM access rights are the following user rights that are rarely assigned:

- **S** for Supervisory

- **A** for Access Control

- **M** for Modify

All users should have all rights except SAM to the shared data subdirectory as well. In keeping with their trend to empower the people, Snouzer, Inc. believes in granting all user rights to each user in his/her own subdirectory. The same goes for groups and group directories.

In addition, a few special circumstances exist within the user and group subdirectories. Hal and George, who are the non-Admin vice presidents, need a drop box to the ADMIN subdirectory where they can drop reports and employee evaluations. A *drop box* is a subdirectory in which users can store files

but not read, retrieve, or delete them. Production also needs a drop box to DESIGN so they can inform the designers of deadlines and production schedules. Bob and Rene need to see each other's stuff but should not have access to delete, erase, or write any files within the other user's subdirectory. Mary and Sophy have the same directory relationship.

The application security is extremely important to Snouzer, Inc. The managers feel strongly about the type of data that is stored here and they're worried about nonauthorized users having access to applications. For this reason, all users on the LAN are given Read and File Scan rights to the APPS subdirectory and all applications within it. The DESIGN group has all rights except Supervisory and Access Control to the design application. All other users have only Read and File Scan. The production group has all rights to the accounting program, except group members cannot rename files, change their rights, or do anything supervisory there. In addition, the production group has rights to the 123 subdirectory except that group members cannot erase any files, rename files, change their access rights, or have supervisory access there.

Finally, nobody should be allowed to erase any files from the GL data subdirectory under ACCT and the A/P subdirectory under ACCT except Admin. Admin should have all rights to all applications and data subdirectories within applications. Once you have established the access right security, you should augment it with attribute security, making all application data files sharable and WP and DBASE applications sharable/read-only.

That completes the NetWare security requirements of Snouzer, Inc. Once you have completed this design, you can move on to implementing it through NetWare's built-in security management tools:

> SYSCON—which allows system managers to assign login password security, login restrictions, and user access rights

> FILER—which provides the facility for implementing IRM and attribute level security

In combination, SYSCON and FILER should provide you with all the functionality you need to implement Snouzer, Inc.'s NetWare security model. Let's take a closer look at these two utilities and the screens with which system managers implement the layers of NetWare security.

## SYSCON

The SYSCON menu utility enables system managers to implement login/password security, login restrictions, and the first half of access rights. In addition, SYSCON provides menus for assigning special user accounts. Before we begin using SYSCON to implement security for Snouzer, Inc., we need to create the Snouzer, Inc. user and group accounts.

1. To create users, enter the SYSCON utility.

   A. Type SYSCON and press Enter.

   B. From the Available Topics menu, choose User Information and press Enter. The user names window will appear.

   C. At the user name window, press Ins and the user name input box appears.

   D. Type in SOPHY and press Enter. The system will ask for a Path to Create User's Home Directory.

   E. Backspace to the SYS: and type USERS\SOPHY and press Enter. The system will ask you to Verify Creation of a New Directory.

   F. Highlight YES and press Enter.

Sophy's account has now been created. In order to customize the account, you can press Enter at the User's Name window to display the User Information window. This screen provides fourteen to fifteen options for customizing NetWare user accounts. We will use this screen later to implement certain aspects of the Snouzer, Inc. security model. For now, press Esc and return to the User Name window. Now create the other Snouzer, Inc. manager accounts.

2. To create Snouzer, Inc.'s three groups, press Esc to return to the Available Topics menu.

   A. Choose Group Information and press Enter. The Group Names box appears. This is exactly the same type of format as the user name box.

   B. Press Ins to display the New Group Name input box.

   C. Type ADMIN and press Enter. The group name ADMIN has now been created.

Using the same procedure, create the other two groups: PROD and DESIGN. Once the

Snouzer, Inc. users have been created, we can use these new user accounts to implement the four different aspects of Snouzer, Inc. security. Let's begin with assigning special user accounts.

SPECIAL USER ACCOUNTS

**1.** Sophy has decided that she does not want to use the SUPERVISOR account and wants to be supervisor equivalent. To assign supervisor equivalence to Sophy, highlight User Information from the Available Topics menu and press Enter.

**A.** Highlight Sophy from the User Name window and press Enter. You'll get Sophy's user information box.

**B.** Move down to Security Equivalences and press Enter. The Security Equivalences list will appear with the group EVERYONE. These are all the users and groups to which Sophy is equivalent. By default, every user has the security equivalence to the group EVERYONE.

**C.** Press Ins for a list of other users and groups.

**D.** Highlight Supervisor and press Enter. At this point, Sophy has been made security equivalent to the supervisor. She can now perform all operations and have access to all security rights that the supervisor has.

**E.** Press Esc to return to Sophy's user information screen.

**2.** Frank is assigned to be a workgroup manager. In order to create a workgroup

manager, you must be the supervisor or a supervisor equivalent. Press Esc to move to the Available Topics window.

**A.** Once there, highlight Supervisor Options and press Enter. The final choice under Supervisor Options is Workgroup Managers.

**B.** Highlight Work Group Managers and press Enter. A list of workgroup managers will appear. If the managers list is blank, don't be concerned—it means no workgroup manager accounts have been created yet.

**C.** Press Ins to list other users and groups.

**D.** To make Frank a workgroup manager, highlight the FRANK user and press Enter. Frank's name will now appear on the workgroup manager's list. To assign users and groups to Frank as workgroup managers, you must go to Frank's User Information menu.

**E.** Press Esc twice to move to Available Topics.

**F.** Highlight User Information and press Enter.

**G.** Highlight FRANK and press Enter. Frank's User Information window will appear.

**H.** Highlight Managed Users and Groups and press Enter to see a list of all the users and groups over which Frank has been made a workgroup manager. Currently the list for Frank shows only the group EVERYONE.

**I.** Press Ins and other users and groups will appear.

**J.** Use F5 to highlight both the DESIGN group and the PROD group.

**K.** Once they are highlighted, press Enter. The DESIGN and PROD groups now appear under Managed Users and Groups. Frank has been made a workgroup manager over these two groups.

**3.** In order to make Hal a user account manager over Rene and Bob, we must move to Hal's User Information window.

**A.** Press Esc a few times to exit to the User Names window and highlight HAL and press Enter.

**B.** At Hal's User Information window, perform the same operation as you did with Frank, except this time adding Rene and Bob to Managed Users and Groups for Hal. Because we did not insert Hal as a workgroup manager under Supervisor Options, Hal by default becomes a user account manager over these users.

This chapter's text details the difference between workgroup managers and user account managers.

## Login/Password

The next layer of the Snouzer, Inc. security model is login/password security. At this level, Snouzer, Inc. is concerned about users' password length, password uniqueness, and the frequency with which passwords are changed.

**I.** To change the login/password restrictions for all users in the system, you must have set these login restrictions before you created the users. Remember, the default account balance/restriction option in Supervisor Options only applies to user accounts created beyond this point. We have already created the users, so we are stuck—or so it seems. Remember the little trick—pressing F5 lets you highlight specific users and change only their configurations.

**A.** Use F5 now to highlight all users from the user name window and press Enter. A Set User Information box appears with the following four choices:

- Account Balance
- Account Restrictions
- Station Restrictions
- Time Restrictions

**B.** To change the login/password security for these users, highlight Account Restrictions and press Enter. The Set Marked Users Account Restrictions screen appears.

**C.** Change the appropriate settings and press Esc. The system now asks whether you want to change all marked users restrictions to these settings.

**D.** Highlight YES and press Enter.

Don't you just love it when a plan comes together?

### LOGIN RESTRICTIONS

Login restrictions are the gates that separate the Snouzer lobby and its main office. These restrictions enable you to apply a final layer of security, blocking users from accessing the system at specific times or limiting staff to certain amounts of disk space. Within this area of security, Snouzer, Inc., has the requirements of limiting disk space for Rene and Bob, creating time restrictions for Mary, preventing use on weekends for everybody, and tracking Frank's people. Limiting disk space can be performed under the User Information options for Rene and Bob. The same options handle Mary's time restrictions. In order for Frank to track his people's logins and logouts, he must activate NetWare accounting by highlighting Accounting from the Available Topics menu and pressing Enter. Finally, in order to restrict all users from not logging in on the weekend, you must highlight Time Restrictions from the Set User Information option discussed earlier.

### ACCESS RIGHTS

Access rights comprise two parts:

- User trustee assignments

- Directory IRM

User trustee assignments are granted within the User Information and Group Information menus of SYSCON. The IRM is assigned within the subdirectory information option of FILER. This phase of the case study describes the steps for assigning one set

of rights; then you can use this model to continue the application of Snouzer, Inc. access requirements. Let's begin by assigning the group EVERYONE all rights to the shared data subdirectory.

**I.** In order to assign the group EVERYONE as a trustee of the shared data subdirectory, you must highlight Group Information from the Available Topics menu. Press Enter.

  **A.** At the Group Names menu, choose EVERYONE and press Enter. The Group Information Box appears.

  **B.** One of the choices in the Group Information Box is Trustee Directory Assignments. Press Enter. The Trustee Directory Assignment list appears. This list shows all directories to which the EVERYONE group is a trustee. It also shows all the rights. On the left side is a list of all directories to whom the group EVERYONE is a trustee, and on the right side all the rights.

  **C.** To add a directory, press Ins. The system responds with `Directory In Which Trustee Should Be Added`.

  **D.** Type `SYS:DATA` and press Enter. The system will automatically add the DATA directory to the trustee directory assignments list. By default, all new directories are assigned read and file scan rights.

  **E.** To add more rights, highlight DATA and press Enter. The trustee rights granted list appears, containing File Scan and Read.

**F.** Press Ins. The system responds with `Trustee Rights Not Granted.`

**G.** To grant all rights, use F5 to mark Access control, Create, Erase, Modify, Supervisory, and Write. Press Enter. All the rights are now moved over to the Trustee Rights Granted window.

**H.** Press Esc and notice that all rights are added to the rights list for the DATA subdirectory.

**I.** Press Esc three more times to return to the Available Topics window.

Use this same procedure to assign your user- and group-specific trustee assignments from the appropriate worksheets in Appendix C.

**2.** To assign the IRM for the GL subdirectory, we will use the FILER utility. Escape SYSCON and return to the PUBLIC subdirectory, type `FILER`, and press Enter.

**FILER**

Filer provides a facility for managing NetWare directories, files, and volumes. In this phase of the case study, we will use FILER to manage the inherited rights mask and attribute levels of the Snouzer, Inc., security model.

**1.** At the Available Topics menu of FILER, highlight Select Current Directory and press Enter. The system will respond by displaying the Current Directory Path menu. At this point you will input the directory you are customizing.

**A.** Backspace over PUBLIC and type `APPS\ACCT\GL`. NetWare will move you back to the Available Topics menu. Notice that in the header of the FILER utility, the default directory has now been moved to APPS\ACCT\GL.

**B.** To view current information about this directory, highlight Current Directory Information and press Enter. Among many other choices, the system lists the IRM. By default, the IRM for all new subdirectories is *all rights*.

**C.** Highlight Inherited Rights Mask and press Enter. The system responds with a list of available inherited rights.

**D.** Highlight the Erase Directory File right and press Delete. The system will respond with a question: `Revoke Right?`

**E.** Highlight YES and press Enter. Now the Erase right has been removed as an option in this subdirectory.

**F.** Press Esc and notice that the IRM now includes all rights except Erase.

**G.** Perform the same procedure to restrict the Erase right from the IRM of the AP subdirectory of Accounting.

**2.** The next level of FILER functionality is attribute security. In attribute security, we will modify the attributes of the WP and DBASE subdirectories of APPS.

**A.** To move to the WP subdirectory of the current directory, choose Select

Current Directory from the Available Topics menu and press Enter.

**B.** Backspace over ACCT\GL and input `APPS\WP`. Notice that the current subdirectory changes in the FILER Available Topics menu. Now that we have moved to the APPS\WP subdirectory, we can alter its attribute security. At this point, we are not altering the directory information; we are altering the information of the files underneath.

**C.** To access information about files in a particular directory, highlight Directory Contents from Available Topics and press Enter. The system will respond with a directory contents window including all files in the subdirectory. In addition, it displays a double dot (..), which is the parent directory, and a backslash (\), which is the root directory.

**D.** Use F5 to mark all the files. Press Enter. The Multiple Operations window appears. One of the choices in this window is Set Attributes.

**E.** Highlight Set Attributes and press Enter. The File Attributes window appears; it should be empty, which means all these files have been set to the default nonsharable-read/write attribute. Press Ins to get a list of available attributes.

**F.** From the other File Attributes option, highlight Sharable and Read Only. Press Enter. The system adds Sharable, Read Only, Delete Inhibit, and Rename Inhibit to the File Attributes screen. Rename Inhibit and Delete Inhibit are automatically given with the read-only attribute, because read-only files are not normally renamed or deleted.

**G.** Press Esc. The system asks whether you would like to set marked files to the specified attribute. Highlight YES and press Enter.

Now you have completed the attribute level of security for the Snouzer, Inc. security model. Use the same procedure to apply sharable/read-only attributes to the DBASE subdirectory.

That's it for the implementation of Snouzer, Inc.'s security model. This case study explored the multiple layers of NetWare security and used SYSCON and FILER to implement special user accounts, login password security, login restrictions, access rights, and attribute security. Once the security model has been created and put into place, the system manager must focus on general network management. As far as Snouzer, Inc. is concerned, the general management entails creating and implementing login scripts and user interface. Let's begin with login scripts.

# NetWare 3.12 Utilities

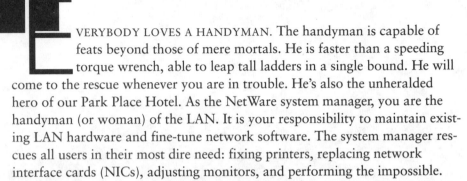

EVERYBODY LOVES A HANDYMAN. The handyman is capable of feats beyond those of mere mortals. He is faster than a speeding torque wrench, able to leap tall ladders in a single bound. He will come to the rescue whenever you are in trouble. He's also the unheralded hero of our Park Place Hotel. As the NetWare system manager, you are the handyman (or woman) of the LAN. It is your responsibility to maintain existing LAN hardware and fine-tune network software. The system manager rescues all users in their most dire need: fixing printers, replacing network interface cards (NICs), adjusting monitors, and performing the impossible.

The system manager relies on a variety of CNA resources, including product documentation, NetWire, World Wire, the *NetWare Buyer's Guide, Network Support Encyclopedia,* on-line help, and valuable Network Press publications. But by far the most important handyman tool is the NetWare utility belt—Batman for the LAN.

*What the world calls originality is only an unaccustomed method of tickling it.*

*George Bernard Shaw*

The NetWare utility belt comprises a variety of tools—command-line utilities (CLUs), menu utilities, supervisor utilities, console commands, and NetWare 3.1*x* loadable modules (NLMs). CLUs are productive management tools that enable system managers to customize the network from the workstation command line. CLUs are the mainstay of the NetWare arsenal. These utilities are primarily designed for system managers, but a few tools appeal to NetWare users as well.

Menu utilities provide the same functionality as CLUs, but with a friendly menu interface. In addition, some menu utilities provide extended functionality beyond what the CLUs offer. Menu utilities are more popular than CLUs and make up 85% of most Batman utility belts.

*A handyman is capable of feats beyond those of mere mortals. As the NetWare system manager, you are the handyman of the LAN.*

Supervisor utilities are specialized CLUs and menu tools designed for supervisor use only. Most supervisor utility tools come equipped with a warning label—"WARNING: This tool contains explicit supervisor functionality. Keep out of the reach of children and NetWare users."

Console commands are NetWare tools that provide NetWare customization at the file server. Console commands are advanced utilities and must be executed at the file server console. These tools can be very hazardous if not handled correctly.

Finally, NLMs are specialized NetWare 3.1$x$ server tools that provide powerful configuration and management features. The NetWare handyman can use NLMs to install, activate, manage, and maintain NetWare 3.1$x$ servers.

In the Park Place Hotel, many guests and staff don't recognize the contributions of the handyman. The handyman is always there when you need him but never around to be thanked. Without the hotel handyman, all of the luxurious furniture and equipment would break down and melt into a useless heap. The handyman performs emergency repairs when the ice machine goes down. Besides fixing elevators when they get stuck, adjusting air-conditioning in the guests' rooms, and fixing the shower nozzle when the water doesn't come out just right, the handyman also fine-tunes hotel electrical, phone, and plumbing systems. In many cases, a skilled handyman can spell the difference between a hotel's success and failure. So never underestimate the value of the hotel handyman.

In the same way, a good NetWare handyman can mean the difference between success and failure of the LAN. In Chapters 1 and 2, we started our NetWare utility belt with a holster of microcomputer/DOS fundamentals and NetWare basics. In this chapter, we will fill the holster with valuable NetWare tools: menu utilities, supervisor utilities, and console commands. In addition, we will examine practical applications for these tools and practice using them with lab exercises and NetWare simulations. Let's begin with NetWare menu utilities.

*You may have noticed that the CLUs are missing in this chapter. Because there are so many CLUs and they represent the mainstay of your utility belt, we have opted to cover them in detail throughout the chapters as they apply to CNE objectives. With the information spread out in this way, you will have a much easier time learning the many CLUs and gaining practical experience using them in a "real-world" environment.*

# *M*enu *Utilities*

*M*enu utilities
are the most produc-
tive and friendly of
the NetWare system
management tools.

ENU UTILITIES ARE THE most productive and friendly of the Net-Ware system management tools. NetWare menu utilities provide all of the same functionality as CLUs plus some additional features all wrapped up in a friendly user interface. NetWare provides various menu utilities that perform various tasks. These tools can be broken down into two basic categories: user menus and supervisor menus. Some user menus double as supervisor menus. This duality enables supervisors to perform additional administrative tasks—including user account creation, directory maintenance, security, and login/password configurations.

In this section, we will discuss the three most popular NetWare menu utilities: SYSCON, FILER, and SESSION. These utilities are for users and system managers. The next section focuses on supervisor-only menu utilities. But before we begin our discussion of NetWare's three most popular menus, let's take a moment to discuss the look and feel of NetWare menu utilities.

*There is no knowledge that is not power.*

*Ralph Waldo Emerson*

## Look and Feel

NetWare menu utilities are a progression of screens that provide additive levels of functionality in an easy-to-use format. Each menu screen consists of a border—either single-lined or double-lined. The single-lined border denotes an information-only box, which means that the contents of this box cannot be edited—it is for viewing only. A double-lined border denotes an editable box that contains information that can either be viewed or edited. All NetWare menu utilities are displayed in the default color palette: blue and gold colors.

*The color palette for NetWare's menu utilities are configurable using the COLORPAL menu utility. The default menu colors are defined as Palette 0.*

Learning to use the NetWare menu system is not something you'll have a lot of trouble with. These menus are designed to be simple, offer straightforward choices, and provide basic system management facilities—all within an easy-to-use framework. Most of the menu functions are self-explanatory, but there are a few keys that you should be aware of to help you navigate through NetWare's menu utilities:

**Return** or **Enter** key moves you to the next level.

**Esc** key returns you to the previous level.

**Ins** adds an entry in a particular double-bordered box.

**Delete** removes an entry.

**F1** provides help.

**F1 F1** (pressing F1 two times) identifies the function keys that we are talking about now.

The last three function keys are NetWare-specific keys that provide specialized functionality solely within NetWare menu utilities.

**F3** modifies the highlighted choice and enables you, for example, to rename users and directories as well as modify security rights.

**F5** marks multiple options. It is a toggle switch. If you press F5 again, it is unhighlighted. Marking multiple options with F5 is particularly useful in environments in which you are configuring multiple options.

**Alt-F10** quickly exits a NetWare menu utility without saving. We call it the menu "ejection seat." Press Alt-F10 if you want to jump out of a menu from within multiple nested screens without saving any of your work.

*When you come across a list screen with a double border, NetWare enables you to highlight particular options within that list and continue. If the double-bordered list is empty, it is a perfect opportunity for using the Ins key—to insert a choice into the list. This is particularly evident when you are assigning rights and usernames.*

In addition to the main menu utility interface, NetWare 3.12 includes two graphical-interface utilities: NetWare User Tools for Windows and DynaText. These two utilities provide basic user and documentation functionality in an easy-to-use MS Windows interface. See Figure 10.1.

**FIGURE 10.1**
The DynaText
graphical interface

And the manuals are still here.

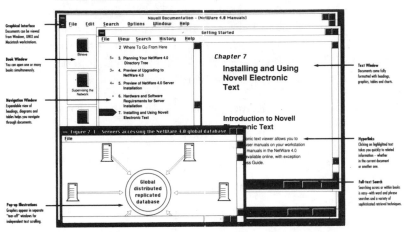

NetWare menu utility navigation is a little quirky at first, but you'll soon get the hang of it and find yourself buzzing through windows like a pro. Now we will move on to the three most popular NetWare menu utilities in a little more detail: SYSCON, FILER, and SESSION. Let's start with SYSCON, which is the most popular administrative utility within NetWare.

*If I were you, I would get intimate with SYSCON and FILER. You should spend hours practicing with them—it will pay off in both the short run and the long run.*

# SYSCON

*SYSCON (for SYStem CONfiguration) is the mother of all utilities. It is used for most of the system management tasks.*

SYSCON (for SYStem CONfiguration) is the mother of all utilities. It is used for most of the system management tasks: to configure trustees, trustee assignments, account restrictions, login restrictions, accounting, login scripts, users, and group information. During our discussion of menu utilities, we will focus on both the CLUs that are integrated into the menu utility and the extended functionality that the menu utility provides.

The SYSCON menu and its submenus can be viewed in Figure 10.2. The standard NetWare menu utility format displays the name of the menu utility across the top header with the date and time. The next line provides user

FIGURE 10.2
The SYSCON
menu utility

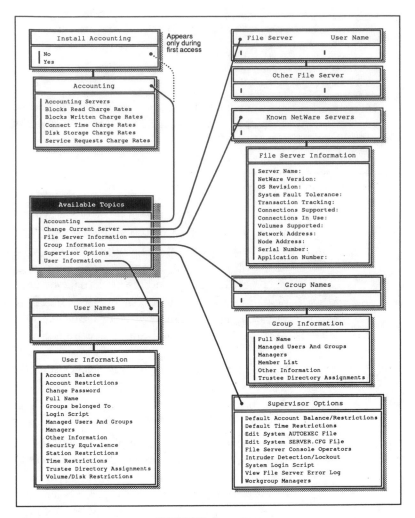

SYSCON Overview

information and the file server to which you are currently attached. The Available Topics menu in SYSCON contains six choices:

- Accounting

- Change Current Server

- File Server Information

- Group Information

- Supervisor Options

- User Information

Following is a detailed description of these six SYSCON options. Study them carefully, because SYSCON will be your friend.

### Accounting

The Accounting submenu of SYSCON is where the system manager installs and manages NetWare accounting. *NetWare accounting* is a feature that system managers employ to monitor and charge customers for access to specific file server resources. Another strategy for using NetWare accounting is to track network usage and resource usage by charging specific prices for particular network resources, such as disk blocks read, disk blocks written, file server attach time, and processor usage. Accounting, including an elaborate reporting system, is built into NetWare.

*Nine-tenths of wisdom consists in being wise in time.*

*Theodore Roosevelt*

To install accounting, simply highlight the Accounting option from the Available Topics menu in SYSCON and press Enter. The system will respond with Would you like to install accounting? Highlight Yes and NetWare will install accounting on the default server. You can install accounting on multiple servers from this SYSCON menu by inserting each name of multiple file servers in the Accounting Servers window.

The Accounting submenu provides six choices: Accounting Servers and the five resource accounting features (Blocks Read, Blocks Written, Connect Time, Disk Storage, and Service Requests). NetWare accounting supports two other CLUs that provide reporting functionality: ATOTAL (which summarizes weekly accounting charges) and PAUDIT (which provides a detailed tracking of all user logins, logouts, and accounting charges). These utilities rely on two NetWare system files for accounting data: NET$ACCT.DAT and NET$REC.DAT. NET$ACCT.DAT is a binary file in the SYS:SYSTEM directory that records all user login and logout activity. NET$REC.DAT provides a translation table for the PAUDIT reporting utility.

Figure 10.3 shows a sample accounting screen with many 30-minute time intervals. Each tracked resource supports twenty charge rates at any time interval during the day or week. Charge rates are calculated by dividing the cost of the resource by its estimated life. This is an effective strategy for fairly allocating resource costs throughout the life of a server disk or internal processor. Users are charged the entire charge rate only if they access the resource during the 30-minute time interval. Keep in mind that some charge rates (like disk usage) are charged per day.

**FIGURE 10.3**
NetWare accounting
charge rates

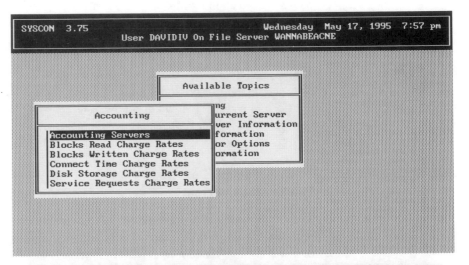

### Change Current Server

Change Current Server simply allows the user or the system manager to change the server on which he/she is using SYSCON. This changes the default server from the current server to any one that is currently attached to the network. Change Current Server displays a menu with the current default file servers on the left-hand side and the usernames that are used to log in on the right-hand side. To add a server to this list, attach to another server or change current servers, and then press the Ins key at the Change Current Server menu screen. The system responds with a list of available servers. Highlight a server from the Other File Server screen; the system will ask for a username and password. Keep in mind that you are attaching to another file server, so it is important to follow the same login security levels as you would if you were logging in.

*The only difference between attaching and logging in is that when you attach, you do not execute the login scripts. NetWare 3.11 NETx enables you to attach to eight file servers at a time, whereas NetWare 3.12 VLMs support up to fifty server connections simultaneously.*

### File Server Information

The File Server Information screen is a single-bordered box that displays relevant details about the current default server. These details include server name, NetWare version, operating system revision, level of SFT (system fault tolerance), network address, serial number, and the number of connections supported and in use.

*A connection is not a user but a physical workstation connection to the server. A connection is also a print server, router, or any other device that requires communication with the NetWare file server. If, for example, you buy a 100-user version of NetWare, you are actually buying 100 connections for this server. Because you are buying a 100-connection license and the print servers and routers cut into these connections, NetWare supports 16 additional connections beyond the 100 to support print servers and routers. If you have more than 16 print servers and routers, you will start to lose user connections. The moral of the story is that a 100-connection version of NetWare will support 116 connections but only 100 user connections,*

*because NetWare discerns between user connections and print server and router connections.*

## Supervisor Options

The next option in the Available Topics menu of SYSCON is Supervisor Options. The Supervisor Options submenu is where the system manager spends most of his/her menu time, because that submenu offers the most system administrative functionality—eight choices that can only be accessed by a supervisor or supervisor equivalent:

**Default Account Balance/Restrictions** enables the system manager to set global default accounting balances and login restrictions for user accounts that are subsequently created.

**Default Time Restrictions** allows the same functionality for time restrictions.

**Edit the System AUTOEXEC File** enables the system manager to edit the AUTOEXEC file server boot file from within SYSCON. This ability comes in handy because the only other option would be to access the file server console itself.

**File Server Console Operators** creates console operators who can access the FCONSOLE utility.

**Intruder Detection/Lockout** activates this login tracking feature and enables the system manager to set global parameters.

**System Login Script** is the most valuable login script. It executes for all users. By the way, the supervisor is the only person who can edit the system login script.

**View File Server Error Log** gives the supervisor the ability to access all system errors that have occurred since the error log was last cleared.

**Workgroup Managers** assigns workgroup manager status to distributed supervisors.

*The Supervisor Options submenu in SYSCON is the most productive system administration facility. The supervisor will spend most of his/her time here.*

We'll explore these choices in greater depth in Chapter 11, "NetWare 3.12 Network Management." The NetWare system manager will be much better off if he/she can spend most of his/her time in the Supervisor Options screen—and stay away from customizing user and group information.

### User/Group Information

The User Information option in SYSCON is the largest and most useful of the SYSCON submenus. The User Information submenu includes fourteen options, including Full Name, Password, Login Script, Security Equivalences, Time Restrictions, Trustee Directory Assignments, and Volume/Disk Restrictions. Refer to Figure 10.2 for a complete list. The User Information window is preceded by a list of users in the Users List screen. At this point, user accounts can be deleted, inserted, or highlighted.

*NetWare provides a hidden facility for configuring small, select groups of users. The system manager can press F5 to mark multiple users in the User-names window of SYSCON. Pressing Enter provides a limited configuration window, Set User Information, for setting specific parameters for the marked users. It consists of four choices: Account Balance, Account Restrictions, Station Restrictions, and Time Restrictions. This is as close as you are going to get to configuring global login restrictions for existing users.*

The User Information submenu is used to specifically configure security and environmental variables, to focus group-wide and system-wide security down to the user level. This is done through the user login script, user-specific passwords, trustee assignments, and account restrictions. The less time system managers spend using the User Information screen, the better. The assumption is that each time a change is made in the User Information screen, it must be performed for all other users as well. This can be quite overwhelming when 500 or more user accounts exist on one server.

*Network users can also customize their own environment using the User Information submenu in SYSCON. Users' changes include their login scripts, passwords, or full name. The User Information screen displays all fourteen options for a specific user as long as he/she is accessing personal user information options. An abbreviated version of this User Information menu will appear if a user tries to access the configurations of any other user. The User Information menu displays two options for other users: Full Name and Groups Belonged To. The idea here is to provide information about users to anyone in the LAN without allowing just anybody to come along and change other users' configurations. The supervisor can gain full access to the user information for all users.*

The Group Information submenu coordinates information and configuration options for NetWare groups. The Group Information submenu is similar to the User Information submenu in functionality but provides only the following options:

- Full name

- Managed users and groups

- Managers

- User list

- Other information

- Trustee directory assignments

- Trustee file assignments

But before you can enter the Group Information screen, you must identify the group you would like to view using an intermediate menu, Group Names, which is a double-bordered box. At this point, you can insert, delete, or choose a specific NetWare group. The Group Information box in SYSCON is particularly useful for assigning group-specific or group-wide security options. Trustee assignments can be made for large groups of users by using the group information window. This is an effective strategy for curing gray hair in system managers who obsess about user-specific security.

*Worry gives a small thing a big shadow.*

*Swedish Proverb*

### Assigning Managers

The system manager's job can become overwhelming as more and more users are added to the LAN. User demands and daily management tasks can take their toll on even the most robust system manager, so NetWare provides the facility for distributed network management. NetWare enables the system manager to create special accounts for a variety of distributed managers and operators. As you remember from Chapter 9, these managers and operators have unique privileges for overseeing small groups of users. SYSCON provides the facility for assigning four of the six distributed network managers: supervisor equivalent, workgroup manager, user account manager, and console operator.

The supervisor equivalent is assigned under the User Information option from SYSCON. Supervisor equivalents are assigned by accessing a specific User's Information window and choosing Security Equivalences. At the Security Equivalences window, you should press Ins and highlight the supervisor as a security equivalent for this user.

*Be careful; the supervisor equivalent can perform all functions of the supervisor, including downing the server and changing the supervisor password.*

The workgroup manager is the next level below supervisor equivalent. The workgroup manager can create, delete, and manage workgroups of NetWare users. Workgroup managers can be assigned by only the supervisor and must be assigned in the Supervisor Options window of SYSCON. To create a workgroup manager account, simply choose the Workgroup Managers choice from Supervisor Options and press the Ins key to add the user's name. Once the workgroup manager has been created, the system manager must go to that user's User Information window and assign a group of users to be managed.

User account managers are distributed managers who have less functionality than workgroup managers but can also help out. User account managers can be created by other user account managers, workgroup managers, or supervisor equivalents. The user account managers cannot create user accounts and have limited functionality over their particular workgroups. User account managers are created in the User Information window of SYSCON by going into Managed Users or Groups and inserting a group of users. Once these users have been inserted, they will become a workgroup for this user account manager.

Finally, console operators are created through the Supervisor Options window in SYSCON. Console operators can access all the facilities of FCON-SOLE except downing the server or clearing connections. Keep in mind that assigning distributed managers in a NetWare environment is a good idea, because it provides stress relief for the system manager and keeps the workload manageable.

### Related Commands

SYSCON incorporates eight CLUs that we've introduced so far:

- ATTACH

- GRANT

- REMOVE

- REVOKE

- RIGHTS

- SETPASS

- SLIST

- TLIST

As you can see, the SYSCON menu utility is quite extensive and provides a great deal of functionality for NetWare system managers. It is vital for you to become familiar with the many features of the SYSCON menu utility. FILER, the next menu utility, is as broad in scope, but it doesn't affect users and groups—it helps manage the NetWare directory structure.

# FILER

*FILER is just as extensive as SYSCON, but instead of configuring users and groups, FILER configures files, directories, volumes, and subdirectories.*

The FILER NetWare menu utility is designed to control volume, directory, file, and subdirectory information. FILER is just as extensive as SYSCON, but instead of configuring users and groups, FILER configures files, directories, volumes, and subdirectories. The FILER menu utility is extremely refreshing for users who are restricted by the DOS interface. FILER provides exceptional functionality beyond what DOS does by allowing you to rename directories, delete entire branches of the tree, and change file security. These features are similar to some of the third-party DOS utilities, such as Norton Utilities and XTree.

The FILER Available Topics menu (Figure 10.4) includes five choices:

- Current Directory Information

- Directory Contents

- Select Current Directory

- Set FILER options

- Volume Information

FILER provides a consistent interface with SYSCON and the other menu utilities in that it uses double-bordered and single-bordered boxes. It uses the same blue and gold format and the same header across the top. The header in

**FIGURE 10.4**

The FILER menu utility

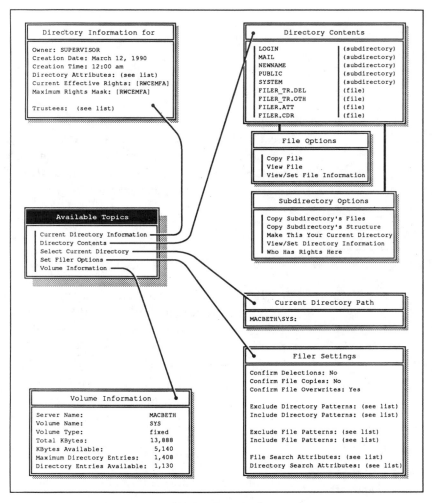

FILER Overview

FILER's case, instead of describing your user ID and file server, describes your current default directory. Although FILER can be used by both users and system managers, it does limit the functionality to directories and files for which users have rights. The system manager has full functionality within the FILER utility. Let's take a moment to explore the five submenus under the FILER Available Topics menu.

### Volume Tasks

Volume Information is similar to SYSCON's File Server Information in that it is a single-bordered box that provides information only about the default volume. Volume Information includes the file server name, the volume name, the type of volume, the total size, the kilobytes available, and information about directory entries.

### Directory/File Tasks

The second Available Topics menu choice is Directory Contents. The Directory Contents menu lists all files and directories within and underneath the current default directory. The Directory Contents menu is where the system manager can perform file and subdirectory creation, deletions, pruning, and general maintenance. Besides subdirectories and files, the Directory Contents menu includes two other components: the double dot (..)—which represents the parent directory—and the backslash (\)—which represents the root directory.

System managers and users can highlight subdirectories/files and press Enter to receive a third submenu that provides additional functionality—subdirectory options and file options. The Subdirectory Options screen includes functionality for copying subdirectories, making this your current directory, viewing directory information, or getting a list of who has rights to this subdirectory. The File Options submenu provides information about copying, moving, and viewing files. You can also get information about viewing and editing file information and again, who has rights to a file.

The Directory Contents option within FILER is probably one of the most versatile menu utilities NetWare offers. The system manager can create or delete directories at this point by pressing Ins or Delete, respectively. Another time-saver provided by the directory contents screen is pruning. When the system manager highlights a directory and presses Delete, the system offers two choices: deleting only a subdirectory's files or deleting the entire subdirectory structure. In the latter case, you could prune the directory tree at the branch level—effectively deleting entire portions of the directory structure without deleting each of the files and subdirectories separately.

*One of the best options in Directory Contents is Who Has Rights Here. This options displays all of the users who have effective rights in a given directory. This utility is the only one that provides this valuable information.*

The Select Current Directory option simply enables you to move through the directory structure and change your default directory. This option is useful when you need to move back and forth between current directory information and the Select Current Directory options box. With the Set FILER Options choice you can set the parameters currently used by the FILER utility for accessing, editing, and viewing NetWare directories/files. Numerous parameters can be configured in the Set FILER Options, including confirm deletions, confirm file copies, preserve file attributes, include and exclude patterns, and search attributes. The last choice is specifically helpful as you search for hidden files and ones not normally displayed in the directory contents box of FILER.

### Security Tasks

Current Directory Information provides detailed information about the current default directory: the owner, the creation date and time, the directory attributes, and other security information. Some of the most valuable information in the Current Directory Information box is security related: a detailed list of directory and file attributes, the IRM, trustees and their trustee assignments (including effective rights). This is the only menu utility that provides calculated effective rights, because it incorporates both trustee assignments and the IRM.

*The trustee assignments and IRM boxes within the Current Directory Information box of FILER are double-bordered, indicating that this information can be edited by the system manager—or anyone with Access Control rights in this directory. This FILER screen provides an effective strategy for calculating and managing NetWare security at the directory level.*

### Related Commands

The associated CLUs that are incorporated into the FILER menu utility are:

- DOS XCOPY command
- FLAG
- FLAGDIR
- LISTDIR
- NCOPY
- NDIR
- RENDIR

*SYSCON and FILER make up 95% of the system manager's utility needs. They are both extensive in functionality and easy to use.*

SYSCON and FILER make up 95% of the system manager's utility needs. They are both extensive in functionality and easy to use. An additional utility—SESSION—provides an abbreviated list of user functions—including drive mappings, user lists, and so on. Let's take a look.

## SESSION

The SESSION menu utility provides a central point for accessing NetWare's user-specific configurations and features. The SESSION menu controls file servers, default drive mappings, search drive mappings, messages, and lists of users and groups. Four associated CLUs work in conjunction with SESSION.

- MAP
- SEND
- USERLIST
- WHOAMI

The SESSION menu, shown in Figure 10.5, includes six choices in its Available Topics menu:

- Change Current Server
- Drive Mappings

- Group Lists

- Search Mappings

- Select Default Drive

- User List

SESSION uses the same NetWare menu interface with the blue and gold colors and the header across the top describing the SESSION manager utility.

**FIGURE 10.5**
The SESSION menu utility

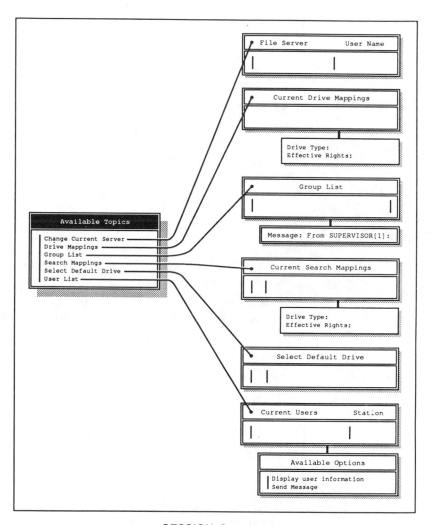

SESSION Overview

The Change Current Server option works the same way as it does in SYS-CON. In addition, the Select Default Drive option in SESSION is similar to the Change Current Directory option from FILER. The remainder of the SESSION functionality is grouped into two categories—user group lists and drive mappings. Let's spend a moment discussing each of these categories and learn how they can be used by productive NetWare users.

### User List/Group List

The User and Group List options in SESSION provides a quick, simple way to access or view a list of who is logged in and which groups exist on the system. The User List option only lists users who are currently logged in and enables users to view connections that are currently open. A not-logged-in user would appear if users have logged out but not turned off their machines (because logging out doesn't clear the connection). Both the Group List and the User List enable users to send messages to other users. Simply by highlighting a user from the User List (or a group from the Group List) and pressing Enter, you display a message input screen. The message input screen can include any message of forty or fewer characters that is broadcast to the bottom console session of each person's screen. This functionality is identical to the SEND command.

*The downside of the SEND, User List, and Group List message options is that they lock up the destination computer until the key combination of Ctrl-Enter is pressed. For example, assume a computer is unattended when a message is sent to it. The process will halt and the message will not be cleared until a user comes up to the machine and presses Ctrl-Enter. To avoid having messages lock up unattended machines, use CASTOFF and CASTON. CASTOFF blocks the display of broadcast messages on any machine, and CASTON reopens the machine.*

### Drive Mappings

The Drive Mappings options in SESSION offer users a simple user menu interface for deleting, inserting, and changing drive mappings. The Drive Mappings option from the Available Topics submenu within SESSION provides a double-bordered list of all network drive mappings, whereas the

Search Mappings option provides a double-bordered list of all search drive mappings. Within the double-bordered list of mappings, the user can press Ins to insert a mapping and Delete to remove one. In addition, users can use the F3 key to highlight a directory to change an existing drive mapping.

*When a user selects a directory within FILER or SESSION, he/she can press Ins at the Select Directory prompt box to display a list of available directories. Using this handy feature, users navigate the system more quickly.*

SESSION is a helpful utility that provides simple message and list functionality as well as drive mapping for network users who are not savvy in the ways of NetWare management. Incidentally, MS Windows provides a utility called NetWare Tools for Windows that is in effect the SESSION utility in a graphical user environment. This has been a successful tool for users who are comfortable in the Windows environment and would like the same functionality that SESSION provides.

*NetWare 3.1x includes a MS Windows-based version of SESSION called NetWare User Tools for Windows. The User Tools interface can be activated by pressing F6 from within Windows (provided you are logged in to a NetWare 3.1x server using the NetWare DOS Requester). User Tools is set up as the Requester client is installed.*

That completes our discussion of NetWare menu utilities from the user's and system manager's points of view. The next set of NetWare tools is supervisor utilities. These utilities are designed specifically for the supervisor and should not be shared with NetWare users.

*To be absolutely certain about something, one must know everything or nothing about it.*

*Olin Miller*

# Supervisor Utilities

*Supervisor utilities are Batman tools designed especially for NetWare system managers. They customize and configure dangerous NetWare environments.*

SUPERVISOR UTILITIES ARE BATMAN tools designed especially for NetWare system managers. They customize and configure dangerous NetWare environments. Supervisor utilities come in two flavors—CLUs and menu utilities. Some of the most hazardous supervisor utilities are tucked away in the SYS:SYSTEM directory, whereas the harmless user utilities reside in PUBLIC. By placing supervisor utilities in the SYSTEM subdirectory, NetWare restricts access to only those users with rights to SYSTEM. By default, nobody has rights to SYSTEM except the supervisor and supervisor equivalents. This restriction effectively limits the use of supervisor utilities to only system managers and users with appropriate rights.

In this section we will discuss the most popular supervisor CLUs and the most effective supervisor menu utilities. Once you have a firm grasp on the purpose and functionality of supervisor utilities, we will move on to the console commands that enable customization at the file server console.

## Supervisor Command-Line Utilities

As the system manager, it is important for you to get a firm grip on the benefits and operations of these utilities. They are a specialized and powerful set of tools for your NetWare utility belt. Here's a detailed look.

### ATOTAL

The ATOTAL utility generates a daily and weekly summary of NetWare accounting services. NetWare accounting, as noted earlier, helps the budget-minded people to charge back against shared network resources and also helps system managers who wish to track resource usage and user logins/logouts. ATOTAL does not break down user resource usage but does provide a weekly and daily summary.

## BINDFIX

*All objects that use the network, all properties, and all values that define the NetWare LAN are tracked in the Net-Ware bindery.*

BINDFIX is an extremely dangerous supervisor utility that permits corruption recovery and restoration of the NetWare bindery. The NetWare bindery is the most important system file within NetWare besides the operating system file itself—SERVER.EXE (3.1*x*) or NET$OS.EXE (2.2). The NetWare bindery keeps track of users, groups, file servers, print servers, routers, and anything else with a name. It stores rights, connections, configurations, and so on. All objects that use the network, all properties, and all values that define the NetWare LAN are tracked in the NetWare bindery. The NetWare 2.2 bindery consists of two files: NET$BIND.SYS and NET$BVAL.SYS. The Net-Ware 3.1*x* bindery consists of three files: NET$OBJ.SYS, NET$PROP.SYS, and NET$VAL.SYS.

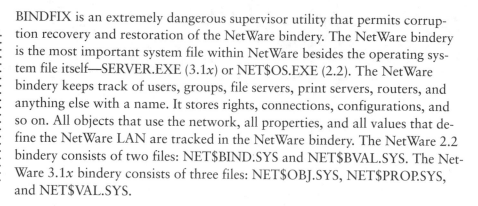

*If I were you, I would get to know BINDFIX. It will increase your quality of life and your chances of passing a certain exam.*

The system manager can run BINDFIX from the SYS:SYSTEM subdirectory if he/she suspects foul play—say that somehow the bindery has been corrupted or objects and values are not tracking correctly. BINDFIX should be used in any of the following situations:

- A username cannot be deleted or modified.

- A user's rights or password cannot be changed.

- The error `unknown server` occurs when a file is printing.

- Bindery error messages occur at the server console.

- The TTS$LOG.ERR text file shows evidence of TTS shutdown.

BINDFIX runs consistency checks on the bindery and tracks relationships among objects, properties, and values. If an error is found, BINDFIX will correct it and decorrupt the bindery. Two other built-in BINDFIX capabilities include deleting rights and trustees for users whose accounts no longer exist, and deleting MAIL\\*userid* subdirectories for user accounts that no longer exist. BINDFIX, as it fixes the bindery, creates a backup of the original bindery using the names of NET$OBJ.OLD, NET$PROP.OLD, and NET$VAL.OLD. These .OLD files are simple binary files that can be copied from the network and kept on a diskette.

*It is always a good idea to run a BINDFIX on a new network so that the pristine bindery can be saved as .OLD files on a diskette—just in case corruption later occurs and BINDFIX does not solve the problem. Also, you should run BINDFIX twice before you make backups—once for decorruption and once to back up the repaired bindery.*

### BINDREST

BINDREST is a related utility that restores .OLD files from a BINDFIX session. BINDREST can also restore old copies of the bindery that were backed up onto a floppy diskette from earlier bindery sessions. Using BINDFIX and BINDREST routinely, such as once a month, can help you save thousands of hours of work in re-creating user accounts and reconfiguring NetWare security. Remember, when you are running BINDFIX and creating a backup copy of the bindery, it's a good idea to run BINDFIX twice, because the first run fixes any problems and the second run creates a valid set of .OLD files.

### DOSGEN

The handy DOSGEN supervisor utility creates a remote boot image for files that can be used for logging in from diskless workstations. *Diskless workstations*—or remote booting—define an environment in which users are logging in from workstations with no floppy or hard disks. The user boots from a boot programmable read-only memory (PROM) chip that is located on the network interface card. The boot PROM redirects the user to the file server F:\LOGIN directory for a boot image. The boot image is downloaded to the workstation RAM and the AUTOEXEC.BAT, CONFIG.SYS, and COMMAND.COM files are executed from there. The creation of a boot image is performed using the DOSGEN utility. Remote booting in diskless workstations helps protect against theft from the network and keep viruses off of shared disks.

### PAUDIT

PAUDIT is another accounting supervisor utility that provides reporting functionality for system managers. PAUDIT provides a lot more detail in user resource usage, specifically a full track of all user logins and logouts as well as user access of network resources. PAUDIT creates a large and detailed file that can be imported into a database package and configured into a meaningful report. PAUDIT also provides information with respect to security violations and intruder detection/lockout.

## SECURITY

*The SECURITY supervisor utility is excellent for identifying weaknesses in file server security.*

The SECURITY supervisor utility is excellent for identifying weaknesses in file server security. The SECURITY command, when entered at the command line from the SYS:SYSTEM subdirectory, will analyze the NetWare bindery and report any instances of security weakness or violation. NetWare identifies a variety of security conditions as violations, including:

- Passwords that are fewer than five characters

- Users who have security equivalence to supervisor

- Users who have been assigned as workgroup managers

- Users or Print Servers who are not required to enter a password

- Users or Print Servers who have no full name assigned

The security report is long, so consider redirecting it to a file or printer.

*Too many people are thinking of security instead of opportunity. They seem more afraid of life than death.*

*Anonymous*

## WSUPDATE

The WSUPDATE supervisor utility can update workstation shells and configuration files from one central location. WSUPDATE compares the date and time of all destination workstation configuration files with a central source file and copies or replaces existing workstation shell files with the source file if the source file is found to be newer than the workstation originals. The WSUPDATE utility is not limited to NetWare shell files. This utility can update any file, including application and program files. The command syntax for WSUPDATE is:

```
WSUPDATE source:filename destination:filename
/switch
```

There are numerous switches in WSUPDATE, most notably:

**/F=***filename*, which enables the system manager to set a variety of WSUPDATE files in one text file and then specify that text file for reading in multiple source and destination information.

**/I** forces the utility to prompt you for an action each times it finds an outdated file. This is the default option.

**/C** automatically copies a new file over an existing file without prompting.

**/R** copies the new file over the old file and renames the old file with the .OLD extension.

**/S** instructs the utility to search beyond the destination path and include all subdirectories.

**/L=***path and file name* creates a detailed log of all activity, all searches, all finds, and all copies.

**/O** copies over and updates Read/Only files. Because many of the NetWare shell files on the workstation are flagged read-only for protection, the /O parameter is required to update read-only files. This parameter instructs the utility to change the attribute of the file to read/write, copy over it, update it, and then change the attribute back to read-only.

**ALL_LOCAL** specifies to search all local drives for the workstation version. This option appears as part of the destination file name.

**ALL** searches all mapped drives. This option appears as part of the destination file name.

**/V=***drive letter* places LASTDRIVE=Z in local CONFIG.SYS file. It is only used with the NetWare DOS Requester.

*If I were you, I would learn the WSUPDATE switches. Who knows when they might pop up?*

One of the best places to use WSUPDATE is the system or user login script. The login script automatically executes specific configuration commands each time users log in. Placing the WSUPDATE command in the login script automates workstation shell update procedures. The following command in the system login script searches all local drives and updates workstation VLM files only if they are an older version than 1.2:

```
IF DOS_REQUESTER <> "v1.2" THEN BEGIN
    #WSUPDATE Z:\PUBLIC\VLM.EXE ALL_LOCAL:VLM.EXE
        /S /O /C
END
```

That completes our discussion of supervisor CLUs. As you can see, they provide a wealth of system manager tasks and tools. Now we will focus on supervisor menu utilities that will further enhance the NetWare Batman utility belt.

# Supervisor Menu Utilities

Although the supervisor CLUs provide direct functionality from the command line, the supervisor menu utilities provide greater functionality within a friendly user interface. Some of the supervisor menu utilities are also stored in the SYS:SYSTEM subdirectory, and their use is restricted to the supervisor, supervisor equivalents, or users with Read and File Scan privileges to SYSTEM. These nine menu utilities provide varied features—from printing and disk management to user setup and even downing the server. The following is a detailed description of each of the nine main supervisor menu utilities and the features they provide for you.

## DSPACE

DSPACE provides the same functionality as the Disk Restriction option in SYSCON, except here you can choose users and volumes from a central location. The Available Options menu of DSPACE includes three choices: Change File Server, User Restrictions, and Directory Restrictions (see Figure 10.6). In NetWare 3.1*x*, DSPACE enables system managers to limit users' disk space within directories; NetWare 2.2 does not support this feature. The

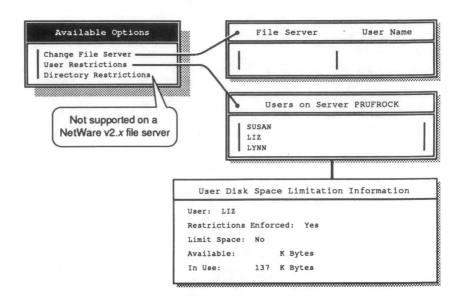

FIGURE 10.6
The DSPACE supervisor
menu utility

User Disk Space Limitation Information screen provides the system manager with a central place to specify the user, the amount of space to restrict, and the amount of space that is available for each user. The DSPACE utility is one of the rare supervisor menu utilities that is placed in the SYS:PUBLIC directory during installation.

### FCONSOLE

The FCONSOLE utility is NetWare 2.2's version of MONITOR.NLM—the main NetWare 3.1*x* maintenance utility. FCONSOLE is also available in Net-Ware 3.1*x*, but most of its features have been moved into MONITOR.NLM. FCONSOLE (Figure 10.7) is the mother of all NetWare 2.2 supervisor menu utilities and provides a great deal of functionality, both in monitoring and configuring file server performance (see Chapter 13, "NetWare 3.12 Performance Management").

In addition, experienced network programmers can use FCONSOLE to obtain information for writing, testing, and debugging their multiuser programs. Advanced system managers can use FCONSOLE to fine-tune server

**FIGURE 10.7**
The NetWare 2.2
FCONSOLE supervisor
menu utility

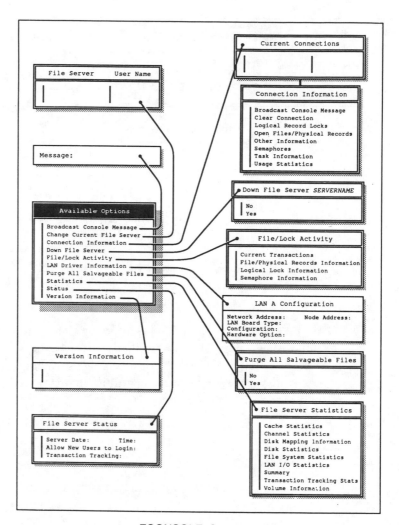

FCONSOLE Overview

performance. The Available Options menu in FCONSOLE provides the following features:

- Broadcast Console Message

- Change Current File Server

- Connection Information

- Down File Server

- File Log Activity

- LAN Driver Information

- Purge All Salvageable Files

- Statistics

- Status

- Version Information

The most useful feature in FCONSOLE is the File Server Statistics screen. This screen provides information about cache statistics, channel disk mapping, file system I/O statistics, and a summary statistics screen that displays invaluable information about the file server's performance. FCONSOLE use should be restricted to supervisors, because it allows remote downing of the file server. We will explore FCONSOLE in greater depth in Chapter 13.

## FILER

The FILER menu utility, which we talked about earlier, is the file structure's version of SYSCON. SYSCON is a utility used to manage users, groups, and security, whereas FILER is used to manage files, directories, and security. The supervisor can also use FILER to customize the trustee assignments, customize the Inherited Rights Mask (IRM), and view effective rights. Because FILER can also be run by users, it is another one of the rare supervisor menu utilities that is stored in the SYS:PUBLIC directory.

## MAKEUSER

The MAKEUSER menu utility enables system managers to design large user scripts that create or delete multiple user accounts. The MAKEUSER functionality is based on a text script file with the extension .USR. This file is used by the MAKEUSER program to create and delete large numbers of user accounts, set security, establish groups, and define home directories and login scripts.

The MAKEUSER syntax is similar to login scripts in that it requires specific key commands and syntax. Following is a list of the nineteen MAKEUSER key words. Each command must be preceded by a pound (#) sign:

**ACCOUNT_EXPIRATION** is followed by the month, the day, and the year when the account expires.

**ACCOUNTING** is followed by a balance and a low limit.

**CLEAR or RESET** clears the processing of the script from this point on.

**CONNECTIONS** specifies the maximum number of concurrent connections.

**CREATE** is followed by a username and a variety of options. This command creates users with specific full names, passwords, group membership, and rights.

**DELETE** is followed by a username.

**GROUPS** is followed by a group name. This assigns users to specific groups.

**HOME_DIRECTORY** is followed by a path that creates a home directory for this user.

**NO_HOME_DIRECTORY** overrides the creation of a default home directory.

**LOGIN_SCRIPT** is followed by a path that points to a specific text file written in login script syntax.

**MAX_DISK_SPACE** and a number establishes a maximum disk space for this user.

**PASSWORD_LENGTH** specifies a minimum password length between 1 and 20.

**PASSWORD_PERIOD** specifies the number of days before the password will expire.

**PASSWORD_REQUIRED** forces users to enter passwords.

**PURGE_USER_DIRECTORY** deletes subdirectories owned by the user when the user account is deleted.

**REM** (for Remark) is used for documentation.

**RESTRICTED_TIME** day, start, and end specifies which days and hours the users cannot log in.

**STATIONS** is followed by the network number and the station address for a user's station restrictions.

**UNIQUE_PASSWORD** requires new and unique passwords.

That rounds out the coverage of MAKEUSER key words. Keep in mind that once a MAKEUSER script has been created, it can be reused to establish new or existing user environments. A likely application of such scripts is in academia, where a similarly structured environment is re-created every semester. Another example is restoring the user bindery after a hard disk fails.

*If I were you, I would learn the MAKEUSER switches. Not only will they help you in your daily NetWare management duties, but they'll make you the smartest person on your block!*

*Only the Educated are Free.*

*Epictetus*

### PCONSOLE

PCONSOLE, illustrated in Figure 10.8, is the mother of all printing utilities. It offers a wide range of configuration options for printing, print servers, print queues, and printers. The three components that establish the printing environment in NetWare are the print server, the print queue, and the printer. To set up NetWare printing, the print queue must first be created, then the print server is created, and finally the printers are defined. These steps are accomplished using the PCONSOLE utility.

The Available Options menu in PCONSOLE includes the options Change Current Server, Print Queue Information, and Print Server Information. The Print Queue Information option coordinates the creation and management of print queues. Print server information allows for the creation and management of print servers and printers.

We will discuss PCONSOLE and printing in greater depth in Chapter 12. Incidentally, the PCONSOLE utility is stored in SYS:PUBLIC, because it is available to users as well as system managers.

**FIGURE 10.8**
The PCONSOLE
menu utility

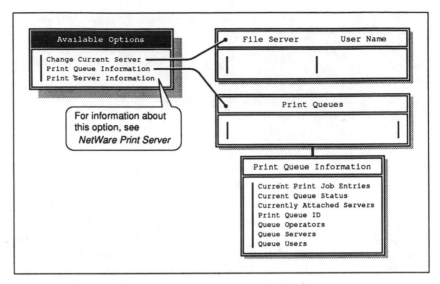

PCONSOLE Overview

## PRINTCON

The system manager uses the PRINTCON supervisor menu utility shown in Figure 10.9 to configure print jobs. Once a printing system has been established using the PCONSOLE utility, the system manager has two options for customizing printing. He/she can customize either the print jobs or the printers themselves. The print job configuration is handled through the PRINTCON utility. Printer configuration and definition are established through the PRINTDEF utility. Within PRINTCON, the supervisor can configure or customize print job parameters such as number of copies, file contents, tab size, banner, form name, auto endcap, and default print queue. PRINTCON will also be discussed in more detail in Chapter 12.

## PRINTDEF

The PRINTDEF options menu in Figure 10.10 has two choices: print devices and forms. Print devices are specific printer definitions that include escape sequences for defining customized printing orientations such as compressed print, landscape print, or specific fonts. Print devices can be imported from existing .PDF (printer definition) files or edited using the PRINTDEF utility.

F I G U R E   10.9
The PRINTCON
menu utility

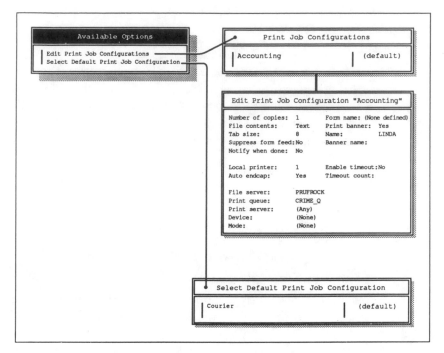

**PRINTCON Overview**

The forms option specifies the length and width of forms that are used in the printing environment with these printers. Some sample form definitions include checks, legal, envelopes, or a simple 8.5 × 11 type. We will also discuss the PRINTDEF utility and its functionality in Chapter 12.

F I G U R E   10.10
The PRINTDEF
menu utility

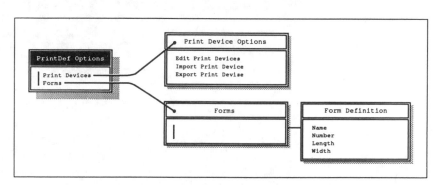

**PRINTDEF Overview**

### SALVAGE

The SALVAGE utility is used to recover or purge files that have been erased from the network. SALVAGE recovers data from its original directory. If the directory was also deleted, SALVAGE stores these files in a special directory called DELETED.SAV—which is a hidden system directory off the root of each volume. The SALVAGE main menu (Figure 10.11) consists of four options available to the system manager and to users:

**Salvage from Deleted Directories** salvages files that have been deleted from directories that have been deleted. This facility works from the DELETED.SAV directory.

**Select Current Directory** changes the default directory.

**View/Recover Deleted Files** lists all deleted files in the current directory. At this point you can choose whether to restore them.

**Set Salvage Options** sets the default parameters, such as sort list by deletion date, file size, file name, or owner.

*Deleted files are only salvageable when the system has enough space not to overwrite them. If the system runs out of space, it begins to write over salvageable files. In NetWare 2.2, if the file server is downed, all salvageable files are lost.*

**FIGURE 10.11**
The SALVAGE
supervisor utility

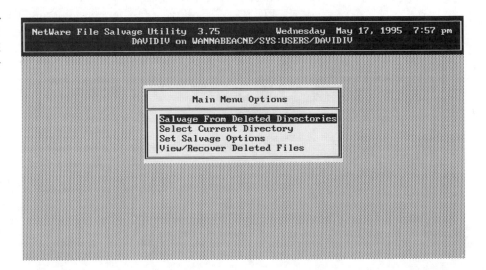

## USERDEF

USERDEF provides the same functionality as MAKEUSER, in that you can use one menu utility to create large numbers of user accounts. The difference between USERDEF and MAKEUSER is that MAKEUSER uses a script format and permits the supervisor to create *and* delete user accounts, whereas USERDEF is a template format that only allows the supervisor to create users. The USERDEF template that appears in Figure 10.12 provides a more user-friendly, graphic environment with which the system manager can customize user parameters. However, USERDEF doesn't provide nearly the flexibility or versatility that MAKEUSER does. The USERDEF template includes user parameters such as default directory, groups belonged to, account balance, concurrent connections, required password, password changes, and unique passwords. Figure 10.13 shows the USERDEF menus.

USERDEF limits the system manager to creating large groups of files using one template at a time, so the system manager can only create similar groups of users simultaneously. MAKEUSER, on the other hand, provides the facility

**FIGURE 10.12**
The USERDEF template

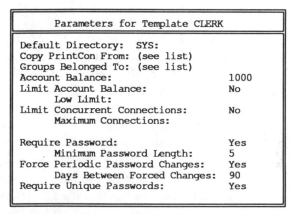

```
┌─────────────────────────────────────────────┐
│        Parameters for Template CLERK          │
├─────────────────────────────────────────────┤
│ Default Directory:  SYS:                      │
│ Copy PrintCon From: (see list)                │
│ Groups Belonged To: (see list)                │
│ Account Balance:                      1000     │
│ Limit Account Balance:                No       │
│     Low Limit:                                 │
│ Limit Concurrent Connections:         No       │
│     Maximum Connections:                       │
│                                                │
│ Require Password:                     Yes      │
│     Minimum Password Length:          5        │
│ Force Periodic Password Changes:      Yes      │
│     Days Between Forced Changes:      90       │
│ Require Unique Passwords:             Yes      │
└─────────────────────────────────────────────┘
```

**FIGURE 10.13**
The USERDEF
supervisor menu utility

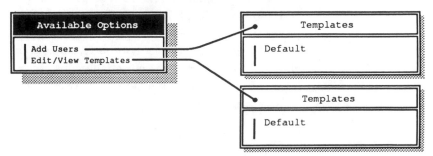

for changing configurations in midstream and creating all users from one script.

# Console Commands

A T THE BEGINNING OF the chapter, we defined console commands as advanced NetWare tools that provide customization of the NetWare operating system. Console commands are advanced utilities that must be executed at the file server console.

*The most thoroughly wasted of all days is that on which one has not laughed.*

*Chamfort*

Console commands enable the system administrator to perform various administrative tasks: controlling file servers, printers, and disk drives; sending messages; setting the server clock; and performing general LAN maintenance. Some of the more popular console commands are LOAD, BROADCAST, CLS, EXIT, MOUNT, BIND, and, of course, DOWN. These console commands are dangerous if not used properly. The syntax of console commands is relatively straightforward. The command itself is entered at the console prompt— which is a colon (:)—and various switches are displayed. Keep in mind that anybody can execute a console command as long as he/she has access to the file server console, so it's a good idea to severely limit access to the file server and possibly keep the machine itself under lock and key.

Console commands have a direct line to the operating system so they can customize the SERVER.EXE or NET$OS.EXE code. In addition, NetWare 3.1*x* provides remote access to the server console through the Remote Management Facility (Chapter 11). For this reason and the inherent lack of security, console commands are the most dangerous of the supervisor utilities. Let's begin with a detailed discussion of the twenty-five most popular NetWare console commands.

*Console commands enable the system manager to perform various administrative tasks, including controlling file servers, printers, and disk drives; sending messages; setting the server clock; and performing general LAN maintenance.*

# Screen

NetWare provides a wealth of screen console commands. With these supervisor tools the system manager can broadcast or send messages, clear the screen, or exit from the file server console. In addition, he/she can track attached workstations and open files. Keep in mind that the screen console commands only affect what is on the screen.

### BROADCAST

BROADCAST is a console command that is used to send a message of forty or fewer characters to all users who are currently logged in or attached to the file server. The BROADCAST console command syntax is:

    BROADCAST *message*

The messages users receive with BROADCAST are exactly the same as messages users receive with the SEND command. That message is up to forty characters at the bottom of the screen with the prompt Press <Control-Enter> to Clear. These messages will lock up the workstation until the user intervenes, unless of course he/she issues the CASTOFF /ALL command. Only users who are actually logged in to the system will receive the BROADCAST command. Any user who is simply attached to the file server's SYS:LOGIN directory will not receive that server's BROADCAST message. Again, BROADCAST is used to send a simple message to all users in the network simultaneously.

*All these console commands are internal operating system commands that are similar to DOS's internal commands. They are built into the network operating system—SERVER.EXE or NET$OS.EXE. Earlier we talked about the menu utilities, CLUs, and supervisor utilities that were stored in either SYS:SYSTEM or SYS:PUBLIC. The console commands are not stored in either of these directories; console commands are inherent to the operating system and therefore can only be executed at the console prompt.*

### SEND

The SEND console commands focuses on the broadcast command by providing the facility to send a file server console message to either all users who are logged in or to a list of specific users—or connection numbers. The SEND message can be up to fifty-five characters long, and you can send a list to either a username or a connection number. SEND also supports the AND delimiter, which provides the facility for sending a message to a group of users or connection numbers. The syntax for SEND is:

```
SEND "message" TO usernames or connection numbers
```

*The downside of BROADCAST and SEND is that they lock up the destination computer until the key combination Ctrl-Enter is pressed. This lockup creates harmful effects when a particular process is running on a computer—for example, when the computer is used for unattended backups. The process will halt and the message will not be cleared until a user comes up to that machine and presses Ctrl-Enter. To avoid having messages lock up unattended machines or having messages broadcast on your machine, NetWare offers two CLUs: CASTOFF (which will block these messages) and CASTON (which will reopen the channel) messages.*

### EXIT

The EXIT command enables the NetWare 3.1*x* system manager to return to DOS at the file server console once the file server has been brought down. The EXIT command enables NetWare 3.1*x* system managers to access the DOS partition and rerun SERVER.EXE with new parameters.

*The EXIT command can be used in conjunction with the REMOVE DOS console command to reboot the file server.*

### CLS

The CLS (Clear Screen) console command is a NetWare 3.1*x* command with which the system manager clears the file server console. CLS disposes of the clutter on the file server console when it displays binding LAN drivers, disk drivers, and other console commands. In addition, CLS can be useful for troubleshooting if the system manager suspects other people are accessing the file server console. The system manager simply issues a CLS and later checks whether the screen has been accessed.

## OFF

OFF performs the same function as CLS, but it works on NetWare 2.2 as well as 3.1$x$ servers.

# Installation

The installation console commands are new to NetWare 3.1$x$ and provide the system manager with the necessary tools for installing a NetWare 3.1$x$ server. Bear in mind that the NetWare 3.1$x$ installation is not menu driven as in 2.2. NetWare 3.1$x$ installation consists of a simple group of tasks that must be executed in order from the file server console. These tasks include LOAD, BIND, and MOUNT.

*If I were you, I would concentrate on learning the INSTALLATION and MAINTENANCE console commands. They are the most useful and important commands for the tests.*

## LOAD

The LOAD console command is used to load and unload NetWare loadable modules (NLMs)—Lego pieces. Later in this chapter we will discuss the four types of NLMs and their functionality. For now, simply note that NLMs are the Lego pieces that bind together to add functionality to the file server's operating system core. As you recall, NetWare 3.1$x$ architecture consists of an NLM software bus and loadable modules. The NLMs add incremental functionality to SERVER.EXE. The LOAD console command is used to load these file server modules into memory and bind them to the software NLM bus. Some of the most common NLMs are LAN drivers and disk drivers. The LAN driver is loaded during NetWare 3.1$x$ installation to initialize the file server network interface card. The disk driver is loaded during installation to initialize and open communications between the operating system and internal shared hard disk. The syntax for the LOAD command is:

```
LOAD module
```

### BIND

The BIND console command links LAN drivers to a specific communication protocol for the current server. Once a LAN driver has been loaded, the communications protocol must be bound to the LAN board so that the network interface card can start to receive packets. If the LOAD command is issued but the BIND command is not, the file server NIC will not be able to receive network packets. The default server communication protocol is IPX. The syntax for BIND is:

```
BIND IPX TO LAN driver
```

### MOUNT

The MOUNT console command activates internal file server volumes. The MOUNT command makes volumes available to users and can be used either to mount or dismount several volumes while the file server is running. The MOUNT command must be issued for a volume to be active. If MOUNT is not issued, the file server volume is not available to users, and they cannot access or distribute NetWare files.

*Mounting and dismounting volumes can be used as a security feature for volumes that are rarely accessed. Mount them during access hours and dismount them when they are not in use. No matter what security a user has, he/she cannot access a dismounted volume.*

*The term mount comes from the mainframe world, where it was typical for computer operators to have to mount a reel of tape in order for users to access data. Although the NetWare mounting process is not nearly as complex, it does follow the same general rule.*

# Maintenance

Maintenance console commands are used by the system manager for general file server maintenance. These console commands can proactively address problems. The maintenance console commands can also be used for less-than-daily operations, such as clearing workstation connections, removing DOS from the background of server memory, downing the server, and enabling or disabling logins. Let's take a closer look.

## CLEAR STATION

The CLEAR STATION console command is a dramatic utility that enables the system manager or anyone from the file server console to abruptly clear a workstation's connection. This command removes all file server resources from the workstation and can cause file corruption or data loss if it is executed while the workstation is processing transactions. This command is only useful if workstations have crashed or users have turned off their machines without logging out. In each of these particular instances, the connection would stay open even though the file server was not currently being used. The syntax for the CLEAR STATION command is:

```
CLEAR STATION number
```

The connection number for a specific workstation can be viewed from MONITOR.NLM, FCONSOLE, or USERLIST /A. This number is incrementally allocated as workstations attach and is not the same from one session to another.

## DISABLE/ENABLE LOGIN

The DISABLE LOGIN command provides a feature for the NetWare system manager to use in troubleshooting or maintaining critical NetWare components such as the bindery or volumes. DISABLE LOGIN prevents anyone from logging in to the system until login is reenabled. DISABLE LOGIN is particularly useful when system managers are working on the bindery, backing up files, loading software, or dismounting or repairing volumes. Keep in mind that DISABLE LOGIN does not affect users who are currently logged in. This command should only be used when it's absolutely necessary.

The ENABLE LOGIN command enables file server logins. It also provides one other facility: The supervisor account can be reactivated when intruder detection/lockout has locked it. ENABLE LOGIN only works on the supervisor account in this instance.

*Hesitancy in judgment is the only true mark of the thinker.*

*Dagobert D. Runes*

## DISABLE/ENABLE TRANSACTIONS (TTS)

DISABLE TRANSACTIONS (TTS) and ENABLE TRANSACTIONS (TTS) function similarly to DISABLE LOGIN and ENABLE LOGIN—except that instead of working on the user login, they work on NetWare's internal transactional tracking system (TTS). DISABLE TRANSACTIONS (TTS) manually turns off the TTS until ENABLE TRANSACTIONS (TTS) has been invoked. The enabling command is particularly useful for application developers who are testing the performance or SFT functionality of their own TTS-compatible programs.

## DOWN

The DOWN command is the most dramatic and potentially harmful NetWare console command. It completely shuts down the file server activity and closes all open files. Although the FCONSOLE supervisor utility provides its own internal downing feature, DOWN performs a variety of activities before it shuts down the operating system. First it clears all the cache buffers and writes them to disk, and then it closes all open files. It proceeds to update the appropriate directory and file allocation tables with the particular files that have been written to disk. It dismounts all volumes, clears all connections, and finally shuts down the operating system. Once DOWN has been entered at the file server console prompt, the system responds with a message to type EXIT to return to DOS.

*DOWN is potentially harmful because of its effect on maintenance background statistics. MONITOR NLM relies heavily on background information and averages for providing information about statistics and fine-tuning performance. Once the system is down, all of these statistics are flushed and brought back to a default state. Obviously, the statistics are more meaningful the longer they are being measured.*

*Do not take life too seriously; you will never get out of it alive.*

*Elbert Hubbard*

## RESET ROUTER

The RESET ROUTER console command resets the file server or router table if it becomes inaccurate or corrupted. The router table is used by the file server or router to recognize other servers and other networks and to send or receive packets among them. If any other servers, networks, or routers go down on the network, the packets will be lost and the router table will become inaccurate.

Normally, the router table is updated every 30 seconds, but this time period could provide a window for errors. When the RESET ROUTER command is issued, the server (or router) sends out a service advertising packet (SAP) that advertises itself to all nearby file servers and networks. The networks then respond with information about their network address, their name, their location, hops, and ticks. This information is then used to build a new router table. The syntax for RESET ROUTERS is:

```
RESET ROUTER
```

> *The DOWN command is the most dramatic and potentially harmful NetWare console command. It completely shuts down the file server activity and closes all open files.*

## REMOVE DOS

The REMOVE DOS command is a NetWare 3.1*x* console command that removes the DOS command processor, COMMAND.COM, from file server memory. Then the memory that was used for DOS is returned to the operating system for file caching. This extra memory is particularly important when file server memory is low and users need the additional memory. REMOVE DOS can also be used to increase file server security.

When DOS is removed, loadable modules cannot be loaded from the file server's DOS drives, because they do not exist. Also, users cannot issue DOWN and EXIT commands at the console and return to the DOS partition. If this particular instance occurs while DOS is removed, the file server will issue an automatic reboot—weird, huh?! Once this NetWare 3.1*x* command is issued, the file server cannot access DOS afterward without downing the server, exiting, and rebooting.

## SET TIME

The SET TIME console command sets the time and the date kept by the file server. The syntax is:

```
SET TIME month,day,year hour:minute:second
```

You can enter the time in either standard or military (24-hour) format. If you use standard format, you may follow the time with AM or PM. The file server always displays the time in standard format. The date can be entered not only in month, day, year format but also with numbers as well as letters in the format day, month, year. You can set the date and time separately using two commands, or you can use them together by inserting a space between them. To view the current file server date and time, simply enter the SET TIME command without any parameters.

This console command is particularly helpful when it's time to switch in or out of daylight saving time or when the file server clock slows down. Keep in mind, though, that this command can be a security risk for users who have access to the file server console, because many of the login restrictions are tied to the date. It's quite common for users whose accounts have expired to gain access to the file server console and change the file server date, thereby granting themselves access to the system.

## SET TIMEZONE

This NetWare 3.1*x* console command configures time zone information in the C-Library—CLIB. NLMs use this command to make calls to CLIB. Incidentally, this command does not automatically change the server's time status from standard to daylight saving time.

## TIME

The TIME command simply displays the file server's date and time. This command is the same as SET TIME but has no parameters. TIME will not allow the system manager to alter the system date and time—it will simply enable him/her to display it.

## TRACK OFF/ON

The TRACK ON and TRACK OFF commands display network service advertising packets as they are sent or received both from the file server and the router. The information is formatted according to whether the file server is receiving the information (in which case it would be an IN), or broadcasting the information out to other networks. Figure 10.14 shows the format of the TRACK ON screen and provides information about the many components that provide valuable information. These components include the sending file server's network address, node address, name, hops from that file server to this one, network addresses known by the sending file server, and the number of ticks it takes to traverse the network.

Issuing a TRACK ON command will open an auxiliary window on the NetWare 3.1*x* file server console that is known as the *file server tracking screen*. It will constantly display the information until the TRACK OFF command is issued. The TRACK ON command helps system managers to

**FIGURE 10.14**
The format of TRACK ON

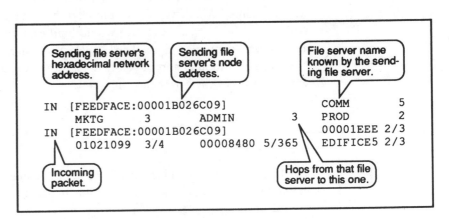

Server Information

troubleshoot network connections or to learn what other networks or file servers exist out there.

## UNBIND

The system manager uses UNBIND to remove communication protocols from a LAN driver after it has been bound (using the BIND command). UN-BIND disables communications for each internal NIC. Once the UNBIND command has been used, the NIC cannot receive communications or packets from the network. UNBIND is an effective tool for disconnecting a particular LAN network from the file server. The syntax for UNBIND is:

```
UNBIND protocol FROM LAN driver
```

You can replace *protocol* with IPX, for example, which is NetWare's native default protocol. The UNBIND command offers a strategy for removing communications from network interface cards that are disrupting the LAN— or sending incomplete packets that are conflicting with other external or internal routers.

Incidentally, the BIND and UNBIND commands include various parameters that customize the NIC environment. The most notable of these parameters is the network address parameter that tells the network what the unique address will be for a particular NIC. If the network address parameter is not used with BIND or UNBIND, the system will prompt you for it. These parameters are also useful because multiple cards can exist in the file server with the same LAN driver. For example, if there were two or three NE2000 NICs in the file server, the system would bind each of these with an interrupt and different network address. The UNBIND command must specify which NIC is to be unbound and therefore must indicate the interrupt and the network address of the card being unbound.

## UNLOAD

The UNLOAD command is a NetWare 3.1*x* console tool that unloads a loadable module that was loaded previously using the LOAD command. All resources are then returned to the operating system memory for file caching. The syntax for UNLOAD is:

    UNLOAD `module`

The UNLOAD command is particularly handy when the file server is running out of RAM or internal loadable modules are causing intermittent problems. When the system manager unloads the LAN driver, the driver is automatically unbound from all communication protocols and removed from all network boards. Once the LAN driver is unloaded, logged-in users will receive the message `Error receiving from network; abort, retry?`. This message indicates that the file server communications have been terminated. Also, before unloading name space modules, the system manager must dismount all volumes that are using the module. Finally, when a disk driver is unloaded, all volumes on the system are dismounted and data is no longer available to be shared.

*When you load and unload NLMs that rely on other NLMs, the order in which they're unloaded must be the reverse of the order in which they were loaded. For example, to use remote management, the system depends on two NLMs: RSPX and REMOTE. The REMOTE NLM is loaded first; RSPX is loaded second. So, if the system manager tried to unload REMOTE without unloading RSPX, the system would respond* `Unable to unload module remote—Error 2`, *which indicates that REMOTE was relying on other NLMs that had not yet been unloaded.*

## Configuration

The configuration console commands are tools with which the system manager configures, maintains, and monitors the file server operating system. Although most of the configuration console commands are informational only, some of them help to optimize the NetWare environment. Let's check them out.

## CDROM

NetWare 3.12 includes an NLM for accessing server CD-ROMs as NetWare volumes. Several server console commands configure and manage the CD-ROM once it has been activated. The most notable is CDROM. This command and others enable system managers to:

- Change media

- List devices

- List volumes

- Mount and dismount volumes

- View the root directory of the volume

## CONFIG

The CONFIG console command displays the operating system's hardware information for all known internal components. CONFIG lists hardware not only for the NetWare file server but also for external dedicated routers. The type of information displayed using CONFIG includes the file server or router name, the number of service processes that have been defined, LAN NIC configuration information, and the disk channel configuration. The NIC information includes the network address, the card's hardware type, the version of the shell, and the configuration settings (IRQ, I/O, and memory address). The disk channel information includes the hardware type with the shell version information and the hardware settings including the I/O and the interrupt.

## DISPLAY NETWORKS

DISPLAY NETWORKS, a particularly helpful console command, reports data about all the networks that the file server or router is currently aware of. A *network* is represented by a unique network address cabling trunk. The listing for DISPLAY NETWORKS can be seen in Figure 10.15. It provides three pieces of information: the network address (an eight-character hexadecimal number), followed by a number and slash (/), then another number. The first

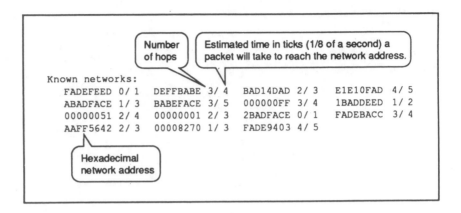

**FIGURE 10.15**
The layout of
DISPLAY NETWORKS

number preceding the slash is the number of hops or the number of networks that must be crossed to get from this file server to that network. The number following the slash is the estimated time in ticks that it would take for a packet to reach that network address from this server. (A *tick* is 1/18th of a second.)

*No brain is stronger than its weakest think.*

*Thomas L. Masson*

## DISPLAY SERVERS

DISPLAY SERVERS is a command similar to DISPLAY NETWORKS, except that instead of displaying all of the networks a particular server or router knows of, it displays all the *file servers*. DISPLAY SERVERS data consists of two components: the file server name and the number of hops. The file server name is limited to the first twelve characters of the name in this utility. Keep in mind that a file server name can contain forty-seven characters. Sample output for DISPLAY SERVERS appears in Figure 10.16.

## NAME

The NAME console command simply displays the name of the file server. It uses an underscore (_) to represent a space in the name. Remember, a space is

**FIGURE 10.16**
The layout of
DISPLAY SERVERS

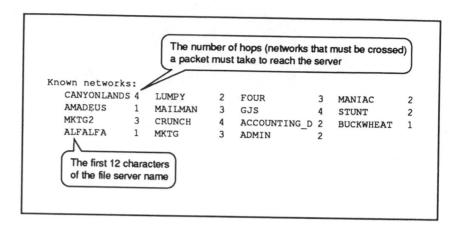

not a valid character. The file server name may range from two to forty-seven characters.

## SPOOL

The SPOOL command lists or changes spooler assignments. A spooler assignment is necessary for the proper execution of NPRINT and CAPTURE printing utilities as well as compatibility with earlier versions of NetWare 2.*x*. Spooling will automatically redirect jobs from NetWare 2.0a file servers to the appropriate queue and printer. The SPOOL command entered without parameters lists the current spooler assignments as well as the syntax for those assignments. To assign a specific printer to a specific queue, type

```
SPOOL printer number TO QUEUE queue name
```

Spooler assignments are not required in NetWare 2.2 or 3.1*x*. They are only recommended if the system coexists with earlier versions of the NetWare operating system.

## UPS STATUS

The UPS STATUS command (or simply UPS in NetWare 2.2 LANs) indicates the status of a connected uninterruptible power supply (UPS). This utility does not provide any functionality for editing the parameters of the UPS; it simply displays the status. Other UPS manufacturers provide software that works in conjunction with NetWare to provide *UPS monitoring*. UPS monitoring sends a message to the file server when power falls below a particular threshold. The file server responds by sending a message to users, closing all open files, and downing the file server. This process avoids data corruption that occurs when the file server's power is abruptly turned off or lost.

## VOLUMES

The VOLUMES console command lists all volumes currently mounted on the file server. The VOLUMES command can help the system manager determine which volumes are mounted and which are dismounted. As you remember from our earlier discussion, the MOUNT console command can be a security feature that enables the system manager to restrict volumes at times when they are not needed.

*My interest is in the future because I am going to spend the rest of my life there.*

*Charles F. Kettering*

That's it for NetWare console commands. They are vital to the NetWare operating system, because they provide functionality for configuring or customizing the internal workings of NetWare—SERVER.EXE or NET$OS.EXE. Because console commands are entered at the file server console with no security, they can be quite dangerous. The only security against console commands is locking up the file server.

# NetWare Loadable Modules

*NetWare load-able modules are the Lego pieces of our LAN. The NetWare 3.1x operating system core consists of SERVER.EXE. All other functionality is made possible through the attachment of modular Legos.*

NLMs, YOU WILL RECALL, are the Lego pieces of our LAN. Our discussion of NetWare 3.1x architecture noted that the operating system core consists of SERVER.EXE. All other functionality is made possible through the attachment of modular Legos. The modular functionality available from these NLMs provides the operating system with communications, file sharing, security, monitoring, and configuration.

NLMs are made possible because of NetWare 3.1x's 32-bit architecture. The 32-bit modularity provides a great deal of flexibility for NetWare system managers in loading and unloading certain modules. NLMs are valuable for various reasons:

- They are versatile.

- They unload and load without disrupting the LAN—this feature helps to optimize file server memory.

- They can configure the system and customize it for whatever needs the users have at the time.

- They provide a facility with which independent programmers can develop applications that can run on the NetWare server without disrupting the operating system core.

NLMs are broken into four categories: disk drivers, LAN drivers, name space, and management NLMs. Disk drivers are primarily responsible for the interface between the NetWare operating system and internal hard disks. LAN drivers initiate communications with the internal server network interface card. Name space modules provide support for non-DOS naming schemes. Management NLMs are used for monitoring, maintenance, and configuration of the NetWare environment. By default, all NLMs are located in the SYS:SYSTEM subdirectory and are accessible solely by the NetWare supervisor. Let's take a closer look at these four types of loadable modules.

## Disk Drivers

As mentioned earlier, disk drivers control communications between the Net-Ware operating system and the internal shared disk. You can load and unload disk drivers as needed. The NLM must be loaded in order for the disk to be shared or accessed by users. Disk drivers have a .DSK extension and are stored on the server DOS partition in the C:\SERVER.312> subdirectory. During the installation procedure, the first task for the NetWare system manager is to load the .DSK driver. Some common .DSK drivers include ISA-DISK.DSK, IDE.DSK, SCSI.DSK, and DCB.DSK for disk coprocessor boards.

## LAN Drivers

LAN drivers control communication between the NetWare operating system and the internal network interface cards. You can load and unload these drivers as needed to make communications available to all LAN users. Bear in mind that when a LAN driver is loaded, the system manager must specify the configuration options that are being used by this card. Options include interrupt, memory address, I/O port, and DMA. LAN drivers have the .LAN extension and are also stored in the SYS:SYSTEM subdirectory. Some popular LAN drivers that are available from Novell are TRXNET for ARCNet, NE2000, NE3200 for Ethernet, and TOKEN.LAN for Token Ring NICs.

## Name Space

Name space modules allow non-DOS naming conventions to be stored on the server directory and file system. Name space is important so that Macintosh, Unix, and OS/2 names can be supported in cooperation with the DOS environment. Name space modules have the .NAM extension and are stored in the SYSTEM subdirectory. Some common name space modules include MAC.NAM for Macintosh and OS2.NAM for OS/2.

Once a name space module has been loaded, the system manager must execute the ADD NAME SPACE console command to activate the name space on each particular volume. Name spaces support access from simultaneously different workstation platforms. There are only a few special backup systems that recognize NetWare's additional name space. NBACKUP recognizes only DOS and Macintosh name spaces, whereas SBACKUP—a NetWare server backup utility—recognizes DOS, Macintosh, OS/2, and Unix name spaces.

## Management NLMs

Management NLMs provide the functionality for configuration, maintenance, and monitoring of the NetWare 3.1$x$ file server environment. These NLMs do not manage the customization or optimization of the file server core, because they are only additional Lego pieces that are attached to the core. In order to optimize SERVER.EXE, the system manager must use the SET console parameters. We will discuss them in depth in Chapter 13.

Management NLMs all have the .NLM extension and are typically stored in the SYS:SYSTEM subdirectory. These NLMs range in function from installation to monitoring to repair. Four of the most common NLM management utilities are INSTALL, MONITOR, VREPAIR, and UPS. Let's take a closer look.

### INSTALL.NLM

The INSTALL.NLM (Figure 10.17) is a menu-driven program that provides the last 25% of the install procedure. INSTALL enables system managers to:

- Mirror hard disks
- Create NetWare partitions
- Create volumes
- Create or modify NetWare boot files
- Copy the SYSTEM and PUBLIC files onto the file server
- Load the 3.12 diskettes
- Install and configure additional products on the file server, including DynaText, Basic MHS, Macintosh, or Unix support

**FIGURE 10.17**
INSTALL.NLM

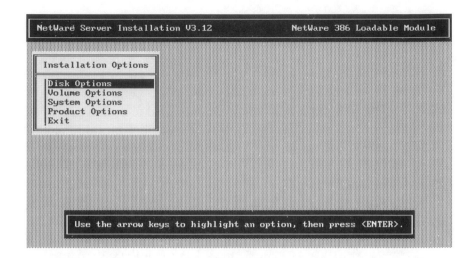

*If I were you, I would really learn MONITOR.NLM. Practice with it, play with it, even do aerobics with it. Just learn all of MONITOR.NLM's ins and outs, because you'll see it many more times before we're through.*

## MONITOR.NLM

The MONITOR.NLM utility (Figure 10.18) is the most useful file server management tool, because it provides a plethora of information about key

**FIGURE 10.18**
The MONITOR
main screen

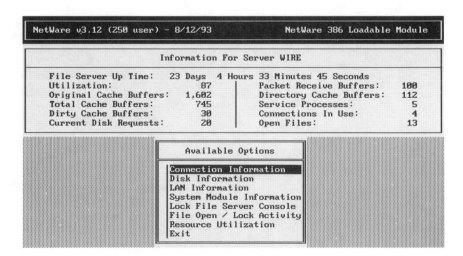

memory and communication processes. The types of resources that can be tracked using MONITOR include file connections, memory, disk information, users, file lock activity, and processor usage.

One of the most important MONITOR.NLM tasks is routine disk maintenance. The Disk Information option (Figure 10.19) displays myriad server disk statistics that can be used to track redirection errors, disk usage, and rising bad blocks. If your system's number of "redirected blocks" plus the number of "reserved blocks" reaches half the number of "redirection blocks," hot fix may be close to failing on the hard disk. In this instance, you should:

1. Back up the entire server disk.

2. Use INSTALL.NLM to run a destructive or nondestructive surface test.

3. Replace the disk if it fails the surface test.

Also, when blocks are redirected or mirroring/duplexing fails, messages are sent to the file server console and internal error log. The moral of the story: Pay attention to your server disk. In Chapter 13, you will learn more about how to use the MONITOR.NLM tool to answer all of your tough questions.

**FIGURE 10.19**
The Disk Information screen in MONITOR.NLM

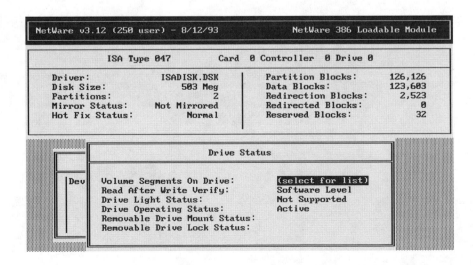

### VREPAIR.NLM

Another important management NLM is VREPAIR.NLM. VREPAIR corrects problems with NetWare volumes. It should be used in any of the following situations:

- A hardware failure causes a disk read error.

- A hardware error prevents the volume from mounting.

- A power failure corrupts a volume.

- The server console displays mirror mismatch errors when booting.

- The server console displays memory errors when loading a name space.

To activate VREPAIR, you must first DISMOUNT the volume. Then, LOAD VREPAIR from the SYS:SYSTEM subdirectory or C:\SERVER.312> on the DOS partition. Make sure to use the most recent version of VREPAIR.NLM.

*In addition to repairing volumes, VREPAIR can be used to remove a non-DOS name space.*

In addition to VREPAIR, NetWare includes a few other command-line tools for maintaining server volumes, including CHKVOL for space in use by deleted files, VOLINFO to monitor directory growth, LISTDIR /S for subdirectory depth, and the VOL$LOG.ERR error log for monitoring system alerts and volume corruption.

### UPS.NLM

SFT support is available through UPS.NLM. This NLM utility enables the system manager to install the UPS monitoring functionality. UPS monitoring provides a connection between the file server through a serial port and the UPS. The monitoring will determine when the UPS is low on battery power and will instigate automatic UPS shutdown. UPS shutdown procedures on the file server include sending a message to all users and downing and exiting the server console.

Finally, other management NLMs provide the capability for multiple protocols, source routing in a Token Ring environment, and remote booting for diskless workstations.

*Man will not live without answers to his questions.*

*Hans J. Morgenthau*

That completes our discussion of the roles and responsibilities of the NetWare handyman. The beginning of this chapter described the NetWare handyman as a true hero in proactively maintaining the health of the NetWare LAN. In this chapter, we explored the role of the NetWare handyman and elaborated on the large variety of tools for your NetWare utility belt. These tools have included many utilities, including supervisor utilities and console commands as well as NLMs. NetWare provides a large, diverse collection of tools. As the system manager, you should master these tools, so that in times of need you can put on your red cape and save the day.

In the next chapter, we will explore NetWare management in greater detail, discussing the specific tasks that the system manager performs in fine-tuning and optimizing the user environment. We will shift roles from the hotel handyman to the hotel manager, who is responsible for overseeing the smooth operations of the hotel. Park Place, being a luxury hotel, relies heavily on the hotel manager to optimize the hotel's image and motivate the staff. The goal is for all guests to be treated as kings and queens.

Like the hotel manager, the system manager is responsible for understanding servers, workstations, login scripts, user interfaces, application software, menus, multiprotocol support, system backup, and the remote management facility. In order to wrap all these functions up into a nice package, we will begin our discussion of NetWare management with a detailed exploration of the NetWare server and workstation. This should be fun.

*NetWare provides a large, diverse collection of tools. As the system manager, you should master these tools, so that in times of need you can put on your red cape and save the day.*

# NetWare 3.12
# Network
# Management

HE KEY TO PARK PLACE'S success is the hotel manager. She oversees the resort's daily hustle and bustle and projects long-term strategies for growth and success. The hotel manager has various responsibilities:

- Managing the lobby and its supporting components

- Selecting the room decor

- Managing the cleaning staff

- Making sure the guests have a mint on their pillow

- Overseeing registration

- Managing marketing and public relations

- Managing the staff

- Coordinating conventions

- Coddling VIPs

- Creating contingency plans

- Marking emergency exits

It all begins with the hotel lobby. The lobby and its many supporting components—lounge, restaurants, and gift shop—are the pulse of the Park Place Hotel. The hotel manager must make sure that the lobby creates a warm, welcoming feeling. She also must ensure that the same warm feeling extends into each guest's room. She must oversee the room's decor, monitor the number of towels used, and provide plenty of robes to take home. These fine touches keep guests coming back, and ensure that Park Place stays in business.

Registration is extremely important to the success of a hotel because this is where the clients check in and check out. In addition, the registration desk establishes the initial client environment by making the guests feel

*The key to Park Place's success is the hotel manager. She oversees the resort's daily hustle and bustle and projects long-term strategies for growth and success.*

comfortable and at home. A nice touch is providing the guests with a welcome pack including complimentary drinks and a mint on their pillow.

Marketing is another extremely important responsibility of the hotel manager. This facet of the job provides an avenue for displaying the resort's many benefits through the local and national media. Public relations helps to develop an image of the hotel that is both appealing and nonthreatening. In addition to marketing and public relations, the hotel manager must oversee the hotel staff and work closely with the interior decorator to create an ideal resort environment.

The hotel manager also must be involved in the organization of conventions and the creation of competitive convention packages. In addition, when VIPs visit Park Place, the hotel manager must make them feel special and ensure that their every need is satisfied. VIPs must also be able to find their Park Place suites.

Finally, the hotel manager ensures that all staff and guests are aware of emergency plans. She must develop and implement emergency strategies in the case of natural or unnatural disasters. Unfortunately, this facet of the hotel manager's position is often overlooked—until, of course, there's a major emergency.

In a nutshell, the hotel manager should be fair, congenial, firm, and well-organized—all at the same time. Most successful hotel managers employ a strategy for approaching these responsibilities: a hotel management plan.

As the manager of your NetWare hotel, you will have many of the same responsibilities as our friend at Park Place.

- Your lobby management duties focus on the file server. Server management is at the heart of the CNA's job. After all, the file server is the heart of the NetWare LAN. Here, you will prepare automated startup procedures and perform routine maintenance tasks.

- Your guest room duties are performed at the workstation. Here, you will create a warm, comfortable environment for your users with shell management, configuration files, and advanced workstation management strategies. Be careful though: Users can be as fickle as cheese!

- The conventions and VIPs of your LAN are the non-DOS workstations. NetWare employs a multiprotocol management model—Open Datalink Interface (ODI)—that allows for the integration of DOS, Macintosh, OS/2, and Unix workstations. It is your responsibility to implement ODI for the nonroutine guests.

- Your registration duties will consist of the development and maintenance of login scripts. Login scripts create an environment for users when they first log in to the system.

- Your marketing and public relations duties will involve the creation of a productive and friendly user interface. In addition, as you oversee your user staff, components such as menu software, application systems, and e-mail will help keep them organized.

- Your final NetWare system manager responsibility is file backup. To back up NetWare, you'll use a new powerful system called storage management services (SMS). You will never fully appreciate the importance of a backup until all of your data is lost.

In general, as the NetWare system manager, you will breathe life into an otherwise limp and lifeless LAN. The network designer and installation team have left you with wires, workstations, a file server, and some barely functional software. You will connect the staff and hotel amenities as you create a productive, integrated NetWare environment.

During your stint as the NetWare system manager, you will take an empty frame and fill it with users, groups, applications, menu systems, security, login scripts, and system fault tolerance (SFT). Network management is the most challenging, exciting, and rewarding aspect of the NetWare hotel. In this chapter, we will explore these management responsibilities by discovering the server, workstations, login scripts, user interface, and NetWare backup. In addition, we will learn about remote management facilities—NetWare's support for management from a remote site. But before we begin our trek into the challenging world of network management, we need to take a moment to explore some general management strategies and develop an approach to your daily network management duties. Roll up your sleeves; this is going to be a fun chapter!

*Experience shows that success is due less to ability than to zeal. The winner is he who gives himself to his work, body and soul.*

*Charles Buxton*

# Management Strategies

J UST AS THE PARK PLACE manager devises a hotel management strategy, you must have an approach to NetWare system management. A management plan will help you integrate the diverse facets of your job. The plan can act as a reminder for daily maintenance duties or user setup procedures. In addition, the management plan can act as a guideline for backup managers who need to follow your previous configurations. Novell provides a wealth of tools to aid the NetWare system manager in creating a management plan:

- NetWare worksheets

- Documentation

- The foundation of a NetWare log book

These tools in combination can create an effective strategy for effective NetWare system management. In this section, we will take a brief look at these system management tools as you learn how to use them for your NetWare management plan. Use this plan to help you attack the five areas of NetWare network management:

*N ovell provides various worksheets that you can use to detail hardware and software LAN configurations.*

- The server

- The workstations

- Login scripts

- User interface

- NetWare backup

Let's start with the NetWare 3.1*x* worksheets.

## NetWare Worksheets

Novell provides various worksheets that you can use to detail hardware and software LAN configurations. These system management worksheets form the beginning of the NetWare log book. Refer to NetWare Installation or System Administration documentation for copies of the NetWare worksheets. They detail, among other things:

- File server hardware information

- Workstation hardware information

- Configuration of boot files

- NetWare directories

- Users and group information

- Default login restrictions

- Trustee assignments

- Login scripts

Keep these worksheets by your side at all times. They can provide the means for documenting updates and initial configurations. Don't ignore this valuable resource. Let's take a look at the eight most important NetWare worksheets.

### File Server Worksheet

The file server worksheet provides information about the file server name, the make and model of the machine, and the system manager who installed it. The file server worksheet is hardware-oriented. It prompts you to record detailed information about the network board, internal network number, floppy disk drives, and internal hard disks. In addition, the file server worksheet encourages you to document all of the LAN driver and network interface card (NIC) configurations. Additional information you can add to the file server worksheet could include details about the make and model of the NetWare operating system.

### Workstation Configuration Worksheet

The workstation configuration worksheet details hardware and software information about each workstation. The worksheet lists details about the user who uses this workstation, the serial number of the machine, who installed it, the type of workstation it is, and node address information about the internal NICs. In addition, the workstation configuration worksheet details memory, internal hard disk types, and configurations for NICs—addresses for I/O, interrupt, and memory.

The workstation configuration worksheet also includes software information: details about how the machine is booted, whether it boots from a remote boot PROM, the DOS version installed, and the files that are needed to attach to the network. Each workstation should have its own detailed configuration worksheet.

### Directories Worksheet

The directories worksheet is a matrix of directory structure and internal security. On the left side the worksheet lists volumes, directories, and subdirectories including names and a description of host files. In addition to directory organization information, the directories worksheet includes a list of detailed file attributes, directory attributes, and each directory's inherited rights mask (IRM). This information can prove valuable when you develop access rights security.

### Users Worksheet

The users worksheet details all usernames, full names, and the groups they belong to. In addition, the users worksheet documents the applications that users use, what their access rights are, and any restrictions. Finally, the user worksheet can be used as a central source for tracking special user accounts.

### Group Worksheet

The group worksheet is similar to the users worksheet in that it includes a detailed list of group names and access rights to directories. In addition, the group worksheet provides a list of all users who are currently members of this group—in alphabetical order. Finally, the group worksheet details trustee directory assignments, access to files, and trustee file assignments. You can use group worksheets in conjunction with user worksheets to house all information about NetWare user/group configurations centrally.

## User Defaults

The user defaults worksheet documents the global login restrictions. These defaults are set in the Supervisor option screen of SYSCON and control login restriction configurations for all user accounts that are created subsequently. The user defaults worksheet is extremely important because you can use it to track which users were created using which login restriction defaults. The user defaults worksheet lists information about account restrictions, intruder detection/lockout, password restrictions, accounting, and time restrictions. The user defaults worksheet should be kept with the file server worksheet.

## Trustee Directory Security Worksheet

*The trustee directory security worksheet provides a central document outlining all trustees of all directories and what their corresponding rights are.*

The trustee directory security worksheet provides a central document outlining all trustees of all directories and what their corresponding rights are. This worksheet can become quite large, but it is important for you to use it as you create access rights security. The trustee directory security worksheet can be included in the NetWare log so that current and future system managers have a place to reference NetWare security. The structure of the trustee directory security worksheet is a matrix. On the left-hand side, it provides a list of all directories in the system. Across the top is a list of the trustees of that directory and in the corresponding box an inventory of their rights. The trustee directory security worksheet should be cataloged with the users and group worksheets in the NetWare log.

## Login Scripts Worksheet

The login script worksheet comes into play as you create system and user login scripts. The worksheet groups corresponding dialog boxes along with suggested login script topics. These topics include:

- Preliminary commands
- Greetings

- Displayed login messages

- Attaching to other file servers

- Utility mappings

- DOS directory mappings

- Application directory mappings

- Miscellaneous search drives

- Preliminary commands

- Username mappings

- Work directory mappings

- Default printer mappings

- Exiting to a program

The login script worksheet provides a tool for the system manager to create effective, efficient, and comprehensive system and user login scripts. The login script worksheet also documents updates and future modifications. The system manager should keep the login script worksheets with the file server and user default worksheets in the NetWare log.

The management worksheets just described can be effective tools as you track network management activities.

*Business is like riding a bicycle—either you keep moving or you fall down.*

*Anonymous*

## Documentation

Novell provides a full set of documentation with NetWare products. The NetWare 2.2 documentation includes eight books, and the 3.12 reference set consists of twenty electronic, on-line books in DynaText. Both sets include:

- Installation

- System Messages

- Utilities Reference

- System Administration

- Concepts

- Print Server

The NetWare *Installation* documentation includes site preparation, upgrade procedures, file server and workstation installation, and a detailed cookbook method for network setup. *System Messages* is a fully indexed catalog of command-line, operating system, NLM, printing, and shell messages. The *Utilities Reference* is an encyclopedia-oriented alphabetic reference of all utilities and complete instructions on syntax and execution. The *System Administration* book includes a more detailed reference of file server utilities, remote console, and some troubleshooting items. *Concepts* is an extended glossary of NetWare terms in alphabetic order. Finally, the *print server* documentation runs the system manager through the process of designing, installing, and configuring NetWare printing services.

# The NetWare Log Book

The final NetWare system management strategy is the pièce de résistance. The NetWare log book is the most important tool a system manager can have. It is a detailed step-by-step log of all activity from the point of LAN conception to the present. The NetWare log book includes worksheets, floor plans, receipts, restrictions, a list of all NetWare files on the shared disk, pictures of the hardware, pictures of the system manager's mother, cabling layouts, application installation information, and various random notes.

It's vital for the system manager to take the log book seriously. He/she must start the log book before the network is installed and diligently maintain it as long as management duties continue. The log book should be tab-indexed with an easy-to-follow table of contents and written on acid-free paper. If nothing else, the NetWare log book can be used by the system manager to justify his/her existence.

That's it for NetWare management strategies. NetWare management is an extremely important facet of the system manager's role and should be approached with caution and excitement. In this chapter, we will explore the five areas of NetWare network management. This is where the fun begins!

# Managing the NetWare Server

*NetWare 2.2 and 3.1x differ dramatically in the way they approach the server architecture. NetWare 2.2, being a 16-bit operating system, relies too heavily on its initial configuration. NetWare 3.1x, on the other hand, is a flexible modular 32-bit operating system.*

NETWARE 2.2 AND 3.1*x* differ dramatically in the way they approach the server architecture. NetWare 2.2, being a 16-bit operating system, relies too heavily on its initial configuration. Once 2.2 has been configured and installed, it cannot be changed. One could say that the NetWare 2.2 server is set in stone.

NetWare 3.1*x*, on the other hand, is a flexible, modular 32-bit operating system. It can be configured and reconfigured at will. As we consider the difference between the NetWare 2.2 and 3.1*x* architecture, a simple playroom analogy comes to mind—Play-Doh and Legos. Play-Doh is flexible and willing at first, molding itself into various shapes. But once Play-Doh dries overnight, it becomes a stone statue. As I'm sure you've experienced in your own childhood, it's impossible to reshape a Play-Doh toy truck into a monster once it has dried. At this point, the only thing that Play-Doh is good for is eating!

Legos, on the other hand, are much more flexible and modular. They can be snapped in and out of place easily without disrupting the overall structure or any of the pieces themselves. If left overnight, the Legos truck can be easily disassembled and reassembled into Godzilla. Legos, however, are not good for eating.

In our analogy, the NetWare 3.1*x* Lego pieces are NetWare loadable modules (NLMs). These NLMs can be loaded and unloaded without disrupting the server architecture or overall productivity of the LAN. Certain Legos pieces, of course, are more important than others. To return to our toy truck analogy, the base drive train with the wheels attached provides a foundation for the Legos door, engine, and so on. This is analogous to the SERVER.EXE NLM software bus. If the wheel base were removed, the toy truck would cease to exist. Such is the case with critical NetWare 3.1*x* NLMs such as disk drivers and LAN drivers.

*The first rule of intelligent tinkering is to save all the parts.*

*Paul Erlich*

NetWare 2.2 installation consists of a great deal of configuration up front and the development of a compiled server file: NET$OS.EXE. Once loaded, the NET$OS.EXE file cannot be modified. This is analogous to dried-up Play-Doh. NetWare 3.1$x$ installation, on the other hand, consists of loading the SERVER.EXE NLM bus and auxiliary NLM Legos pieces. NLMs can be loaded and unloaded at will to create various configurations.

In addition to server startup management, NLMs provide a communications path for various protocols and workstation languages. After all, variety is the spice of life. In this section, we will focus on NetWare 3.1$x$'s strategy toward startup and multiprotocol management. NetWare 2.2 really doesn't offer much in the way of server flexibility and management. Once configured, it simply sits there looking pretty.

Let's begin our discussion of managing the NetWare 3.1$x$ server with a look at startup management.

## Server Startup Management

As we discussed earlier, NetWare 3.1$x$ consists of an operating system base and auxiliary NLMs. The base is created by SERVER.EXE. Once SERVER.EXE is loaded, the system manager is greeted with a colon ( : ) prompt, which indicates that all is well and the server is ready for further initialization. The complete process of server initialization consists of five steps, starting with loading DOS. Let's take a look at these steps and then explore how they can be automated and customized.

*If I were you, I would spend most of my time learning the order of events for NetWare server startup. Also, pay attention to the location and types of files that are executed in specific order.*

### Step 1: Loading DOS

The NetWare 3.1$x$ server is unusual in that it actually uses DOS and NetWare. SERVER.EXE is a DOS file that must be executed from a DOS partition. As you can see in Figure 11.1, the NetWare server disk consists of two partitions: a small DOS partition and a large NetWare partition. On the small DOS partition, the system manager stores SERVER.EXE and various required NLMs, including the disk driver NLM. In step 1, the server is booted under DOS. COMMAND.COM is loaded into memory and the system responds

**FIGURE 11.1**
NetWare 3.1x
partition management

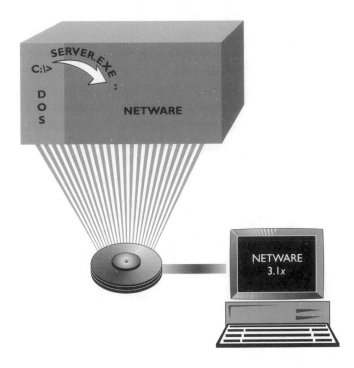

with a C:\> prompt. The NetWare startup files are located in a subdirectory on the C drive called SERVER.312.

*In this section, we are focusing on the daily processes of NetWare 3.1x startup management. At first, the small DOS partition is created using FDISK. The much larger NetWare partition is created at a later stage using INSTALL.NLM. Stay tuned.*

### Step 2: SERVER.EXE

In step 2, the system manager moves over to the C:\SERVER.312 directory and executes SERVER.EXE. Once SERVER.EXE has been executed, control shifts from the DOS partition to the NetWare partition, and the system responds with a colon prompt. At this point, the NetWare 3.1x server is alive but nobody can really accomplish anything. Files cannot be accessed and communications cannot be initiated.

In order for SERVER.EXE to establish a unique foundation for this server, it needs two important pieces of information: a server name and internal IPX address. The server name uniquely identifies this server for communications with all other servers on the LAN or WAN. The internal IPX network number performs a similar function in providing a unique internal network for communication between NLMs and the SERVER.EXE base. The file server name is alphanumeric and consists of between two and forty-seven characters. The internal IPX network number is any 8-digit hexadecimal address using numbers 0 through 9 and letters A through F. We will discuss addressing strategies in a little while.

*Once SERVER.EXE is executed and command shifts to the NetWare partition, COMMAND.COM is still loaded in memory. At this point, the system manager or any would-be hacker can exit the NetWare partition and return to the DOS partition. This is not good, because many valuable NetWare files reside on the DOS partition. In order to eliminate this security loophole, the system manager can issue the REMOVE DOS or SECURE CONSOLE console commands to remove COMMAND.COM from the server console prompt.*

### Step 3: Load Server Disk Driver

With SERVER.EXE in position and the colon prompt activated, the server startup procedures proceed to step 3. Now the system manager begins activating internal components by loading the disk driver. The disk driver, discernible by its .DSK extension, must reside on the DOS partition, because the file structure on the NetWare partition has not yet been activated. NetWare supports various architectures, including SCSI, IDE, ISA, EISA, and Micro Channel. The disk driver is loaded into server memory and attached to SERVER.EXE using the following LOAD command:

```
LOAD C:\SERVER.312\ISADISK.DSK
```

As you can see from this example, the ISADISK.DSK driver is loaded from the DOS partition. Once the disk driver has been loaded, the system automatically mounts the default system volume—SYS. Any other volumes must be mounted manually using the MOUNT console command:

```
MOUNT ACCT
```

or

```
MOUNT ALL
```

*The next "one-time" installation step involves the creation of the NetWare volumes. It all starts with the required default volume—SYS. Volumes are created from the Volume Options menu of INSTALL.NLM. Once the volumes have been installed, they can be mounted and dismounted at will.*

### Step 4: Load Server LAN Driver

With the disk driver in place and all volumes mounted, the system can now access server files from the SYS:SYSTEM subdirectory. One such important server file is the LAN driver. LAN drivers control communications between the NetWare operating system and internal server NICs. NetWare 3.1$x$ supports myriad LAN drivers, including NE2000, Intel, 3C509, NE3200, SMC, TOKEN, and RXNET for ARCNet. LAN drivers are activated and attached to the SERVER.EXE backbone in much the same way as disk drivers:

```
LOAD NE2000.LAN
```

Notice that a location was not given; this is because the system automatically searches the SYS:SYSTEM subdirectory once the SYS volume has been mounted. In many cases, the system will need additional information about the LAN driver settings in order to communicate with the NIC. The previous command would load the LAN driver NLM with its default settings. In order to specify other settings, use the following command:

```
LOAD NE2000 INT=3 PORT=300
```

This command would specify an interrupt of 3 and I/O port address of 300.

*The SYS:SYSTEM subdirectory and default LAN drivers are copied to the SYS volume during the next "one-time" installation step—copying system and public files. This option is accessed from the System Options menu of INSTALL.NLM. Once all of the system and public files have been copied to the default SYS directory structure, system managers and users can access them at any time.*

### Step 5: Bind IPX to Server LAN Driver

Once the LAN driver is loaded, the system manager activates the internal NIC and initializes communications by binding a specific protocol to the LAN driver NLM. During the binding process, the system manager specifies two important pieces of information: the protocol to be bound and the logical network address for the NIC. The default protocol for NetWare LANs is IPX. NetWare 3.1$x$ supports various other protocols including TCP/IP and AppleTalk. To initialize IPX communications for a given NIC such as the NE2000, system managers would type in the following command:

```
BIND IPX TO NE2000
```

In addition to specifying the protocol, the system manager must also specify a logical network address for this NIC. The network address uniquely identifies this cabling segment from any other on this or other LANs. The network address is an 8-digit hexadecimal number that is established by the system manager. Do not confuse the network address with the internal IPX address, which distinguishes this server from any other server on the LAN. Most people use the NetWare serial number as the internal IPX address. This number is always unique.

*In order to clearly separate internal IPX addresses from network addresses, follow this simple convention: Because both are 8-digit hexadecimal numbers, the internal IPX network number should contain only letters, whereas the external network address should contain only numbers. You can get creative with the internal IPX address. Some sample addresses include BAD and CAFE. You can also combine them to create fun words like BADCAFE. Sorry, external network addresses aren't nearly as creative—try 007.*

The external network address is established with the BIND command by using the NET parameter, such as in:

```
BIND IPX TO NE2000 NET=007
```

That completes our discussion of NetWare 3.1x startup management. Table 11.1 summarizes each of these five steps and the activities performed during each one.

*Computers can figure out all kinds of problems, except the things in the world that just don't add up.*

*James Magary*

## Automating Server Startup

As you can see, the NetWare server startup procedure, although flexible, is tricky. It would be a drag if the system manager had to implement all of these steps every time the server was brought down and back up. Fortunately, NetWare provides the facility for automating the server startup. Automation is achieved with the help of server configuration files. The two most important server configuration files are analogous to the DOS boot files, CONFIG.SYS

| **TABLE 11.1**<br>NetWare 3.1x Startup<br>Management Summary | **STEP** | **ACTION** |
|---|---|---|
| | Boot server with DOS. | DOS partition is made active. COMMAND.COM is loaded into memory. |
| | Execute SERVER.EXE from C:\SERVER.312. | NetWare operating system base is loaded into server RAM. Control shifts from DOS to NetWare partition. |
| | Load disk driver from DOS partition. | Server file system is activated. Default SYS volume is mounted. |
| | Load LAN driver from SYS:SYSTEM. | Internal server NIC is activated and configuration settings are defined. |
| | Bind protocol to LAN driver. | Initializes communications for server NIC and establishes external network address for LAN cabling. |

and AUTOEXEC.BAT. The corresponding NetWare files are STARTUP.NCF and AUTOEXEC.NCF. The NetWare 3.1*x* server executes these configuration files in respective order. Let's take a look at how they work.

**STARTUP.NCF** Once SERVER.EXE has been executed, it searches for the configuration file STARTUP.NCF in the same DOS directory where SERVER.EXE resides. STARTUP.NCF's main purpose is to load the server disk drivers. In addition to disk drivers, STARTUP.NCF can load file system-specific SET parameters. We'll talk more about these in Chapter 13.

A sample NetWare 3.12 STARTUP.NCF file would contain one line:

```
LOAD C:\SERVER.312\ISADISK.DSK PORT=1F0 INT=E
```

This command will automatically load the ISADISK disk driver with the correct parameters once SERVER.EXE has been activated.

*To fully automate server startup procedures, consider programming the AUTOEXEC.BAT file to automatically change directories to C:\SERVER.312 and execute SERVER.EXE once the server is booted.*

STARTUP.NCF is generated automatically by the INSTALL.NLM utility during the installation procedure. System managers can use the same NLM utility to edit the STARTUP.NCF file.

*To boot with an alternate STARTUP.NCF, use the following syntax:*
```
SERVER -S C:\SERVER.312\filename
```

*To boot without a STARTUP.NCF file, use the following syntax:*
```
SERVER -NS
```

**AUTOEXEC.NCF** The AUTOEXEC.NCF file executes after STARTUP.NCF. AUTOEXEC.NCF is located in the SYS:SYSTEM directory, and it guides the file server through the remainder of the booting process. A typical AUTOEXEC.NCF file contains the following information:

- File server name
- Internal IPX network number
- LOAD LAN driver
- BIND

- Other LOAD commands

- Other console commands

A sample AUTOEXEC.NCF file contains many more commands than does the STARTUP.NCF file:

```
FILE SERVER NAME CNE
IPX INTERNAL NETWORK DAD
LOAD NE2000 INT=3 PORT=300
BIND IPX TO NE2000 NET=007
LOAD MONITOR
SECURE CONSOLE
```

The AUTOEXEC.NCF file is also automatically created by the INSTALL.NLM utility during the installation procedure. System managers can use the same NLM utility to edit the AUTOEXEC.NCF file at any time.

*To boot the NetWare 3.1x server without an AUTOEXEC.NCF file, use the following syntax:* SERVER -NA .

## Customizing Server Startup

In addition to using the standard STARTUP.NCF and AUTOEXEC.NCF commands, the system manager can use other server tools to customize the startup procedure: NLMs, console commands, and supplemental server batch files. Let's take a closer look.

**NLMs**  In addition to using the standard disk drivers and LAN drivers, the system manager can use auxiliary NLMs such as the following to customize server startup:

- LOAD REMOTE and LOAD RSPX—defines the remote management facility (we will discuss the remote management facility in greater depth later in this chapter)

- LOAD INSTALL—edits standard configuration files

- LOAD EDIT —edits supplemental server batch files

- LOAD MONITOR—files used for server performance management and optimization

**CONSOLE COMMANDS** NetWare provides various server console commands that you can also use to customize the startup procedures:

- VOLUMES—display mounted volume information

- CONFIG—display server configuration information

- MODULES—display all loaded NLMs

- SEARCH—create a search path other than SYS:SYSTEM for loading NLMs

- REMOVE DOS—remove COMMAND.COM from background server memory

- SECURE CONSOLE—increase server access security

- SET MAXIMUM DIRECTORY TREE DEPTH=25—restrict the depth of directories in the NetWare server file system

- SET REPLY TO GET NEAREST SERVER=ON—allow this server to respond to workstation connection requests

- SET DISPLAY LOST INTERRUPT ALERTS=OFF—remove annoying interrupt alerts from the server console

- SET ALLOW UNENCRYPTED PASSWORDS=OFF—enhance workstation server security

*Man will occasionally stumble over the truth, but most times he will pick himself up and carry on...*

*Winston Churchill*

**SUPPLEMENTAL SERVER BATCH FILES** In addition to STARTUP.NCF and AUTOEXEC.NCF, system managers can create any supplemental server batch file by using the LOAD EDIT command. These batch files can be created to perform various startup customization procedures, including:

- REBOOT.NCF for rebooting the server

- RMF.NCF for activating the remote management facility

- OPTIMIZE.NCF to activate a preselected group of SET parameters

A REBOOT.NCF file might look something like this:

```
REMOVE DOS
DOWN
EXIT
```

When this command is executed, it removes DOS, downs the server, and exits the server. This combination causes the server to exit to an empty shell and perform a warm boot.

As you can see from this discussion, the NetWare 3.1*x* startup procedures are much more complex than their NetWare 2.2 predecessors. However, with this complexity comes sophistication and flexibility. Instead of simply having one NET$OS.EXE file to execute all server functions, system managers have various NLMs and configuration options. Some people see advancement as an obstacle, but visionary system managers will view this as the movement of power from the operating system to the system manager's hands. Speaking of power and sophistication, now it's time to shift our attention away from starting up the server and toward multiprotocol management. With multiprotocol management, the system manager can customize the server environment so it will simultaneously support various systems. Let's take a closer look.

> *L*ife would be so easy if NetWare only supported one type of user and one type of workstation. In our "make-believe" kingdom, the NetWare knight could focus all of his energy on DOS workstations, DOS shells, and saving the princess.

## Multiprotocol Management

Life would be so easy if NetWare only supported *one* type of user and *one* type of workstation. In our "make-believe" kingdom, the NetWare knight could focus all of his energy on DOS workstations, DOS shells, and saving the princess. This would be analogous to having only one type of guest at the Park Place Hotel: regular, well-behaved, and high-tipping. The hotel manager wouldn't have to deal with the huge variety of personalities, the conventions, the VIPs, and the complaints. Unfortunately, though, this is not a perfect world—and besides, where would the fun be? Remember, variety is the spice of life! Well, NetWare has embraced multiprotocol variety with three different arms—OS/2, Unix, and Macintosh. In addition, NetWare 3.1*x* supports various protocols: FTAM for OSI, AppleTalk for Macintosh, and TCP/IP for Unix-type machines.

One of the hotel manager's most challenging responsibilities is planning and organizing unique events such as VIP visits, press conferences, and weekly or monthly conventions. Although unique visits create stress in the hotel manager's life, they also provide an entertaining variety. In the same way, the system manager is responsible for supporting unique workstations (DOS, OS/2, Macintosh, Unix, and Windows NT); different types of protocols; other network operating systems (NetWare, LAN Manager, and NT Advanced Server); and connections to larger host machines (such as mini- and mainframe hosts).

In this context, *protocol* refers to the rules used by these different machines to communicate with one another. Protocols perform three tasks: accessing the media, transporting information across the network, and allowing for sharing of resources. Accessing the media enables communications across the physical network media. The internal server NIC uses media access (MAC) protocols to communicate with other boards over the media. These boards use packets for formatting data into network units. Each MAC packet uses a specific frame type that defines the shape and organization of the packet architecture.

Other protocols at a higher, more intelligent level determine how data is transferred and routed across the network. NetWare IPX and TCP/IP, for example, are two popular higher-level protocols. And finally, protocols allow for sharing dissimilar resources through routing information protocol (RIP), the NetWare core protocol (NCP), and name space support.

Multiprotocol management is supported through the ODI architecture model. Open Datalink Interface is an industry standard for supporting and sharing multiprotocols over one LAN medium. In addition, ODI-compliant NICs can simultaneously support IPX, TCP/IP, and AppleTalk protocols. This level of transparent access does not come without a price. ODI architecture is complex and difficult to install. In addition, multiprotocol management is a relatively new and misunderstood art. The system manager must be well aware of his/her responsibilities in supporting non-DOS workstations. The good news is that information and tools are growing rapidly in this arena.

When orchestrated well, the ODI model provides various benefits:

- Communication with various clients, servers, and mainframes concurrently via different protocol stacks

- Communication through any network board written to ODI specifications

- Few hardware components to support

- Flexible configurations

Let's take a closer look at the key components of the ODI architecture model.

## The ODI Architecture Model

The ODI model was developed jointly by Novell and Apple in 1989. It defines a set of standards in four layers:

- The MLID and LAN Adapter
- Link Support layer (LSL)
- Server Protocol Stacks
- NetWare Services

These four components work together to provide simultaneous support for various types of protocol (refer to Figure 11.2). The protocol stack layer works in conjunction with NetWare STREAMS to provide specific services to IPX, TCP/IP, OSI, or AppleTalk protocols. Let's take a closer look at each layer.

**MLID AND LAN ADAPTER LAYER**  The bottom layer of the ODI model consists of the physical LAN adapter and custom Multiple Link Interface Driver (MLID) driver. The LAN adapter is the physical component that communicates directly with the LAN media and provides connectivity between workstations and file servers. The MLID driver is a special type of NIC driver that

**FIGURE 11.2**
The ODI
architecture model

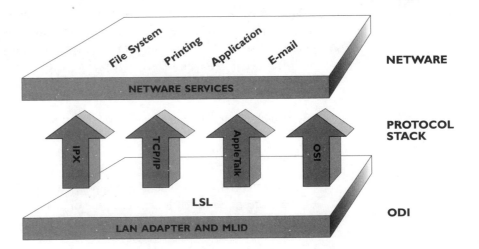

supports any type of packet. MLID packet support includes IPX, AppleTalk, and TCP/IP. Special NICs with MLID-supported drivers can simultaneously speak various languages. One critical component of the MLID layer is the frame type specified. As we discussed earlier, the frame type defines the architecture of the packet as it travels over the LAN media. Servers and workstations using different frame types cannot communicate because the packets arrive in different forms.

NetWare supports various frame types:

- ETHERNET_802.3, which is the default frame type for NetWare 2.2 and 3.11 networks

- ETHERNET_802.2, which is the default frame type for NetWare 3.12 and 4.1 systems

- ETHERNET_II for TCP/IP support

- ETHERNET_SNAP for AppleTalk support

- TOKEN RING for NetWare Token Ring networks

Because servers and workstations cannot communicate with different frame types, it's important to be specific about matching frame architectures. To define a frame type at the server, simply use the FRAME parameter with the LOAD NE2000 command. At the workstation, the frame type is established using a similar frame command in the NET.CFG file.

*Because the frame type is defining a unique architecture for the packets over the network, each bound LAN driver using a different frame type must have a different network number. Also, when you are assigning different frame types to the same NIC, the system will ask if you would like to perform the process "re-entrantly." This means that the system will use the same LAN driver for two frame types. This strategy is particularly important when your network is coexisting with NetWare 2.2, 3.11, 3.12, and 4.1 network servers.*

*Any smoothly functioning technology will have the appearance of true magic.*

*Arthur C. Clarke, IV*

**LINK SUPPORT LAYER** The Link Support layer (LSL) is the next layer in the ODI architecture model. It acts as a type of switchboard to route packets among the LAN adapter and protocol stacks. LSL identifies the type of packet it receives and then passes the packet to the appropriate protocol in the transport protocol stack layer. LSL implementation is built into the server.

**THE PROTOCOL STACK LAYER**  The Protocol Stack layer contains protocol stacks such as IPX, AppleTalk, and TCP/IP. A *stack* is a protocol-specific group of files used to translate and negotiate specific protocols. Once a packet arrives at the specified protocol stack, it either passes through and communicates with NetWare 3.1$x$ or is sent back down to the LSL layer. Once packets are sent down to the LSL layer, they are shuffled off through the MLID and NIC to another network. The protocol stack layer provides routing services for NetWare file servers. Routing involves two steps: interrogating NetWare packets and then deciding whether to keep the packet or send it to the next LAN. Protocol stack functionality is provided at the file server through an internal set of applications called NetWare STREAMS.

STREAMS provides a common interface between NetWare and communication protocols such as IPX/SPX, TCP/IP, and OSI. These protocols deliver data and user requests to NetWare for processing from various dissimilar systems. STREAMS makes the communication protocol transparent to the network operating system, therefore allowing the same set of services to be routed across the network regardless of whatever communications protocols are being used. NetWare STREAMS is implemented through six NLMs:

- STREAMS

- SNMP

- CLIB

- IPXS

- SPXS

- TLI

STREAMS.NLM includes the STREAMS interface, utility routines for STREAMS' modules, log device, and a driver for the ODI interface.

SNMP (Simple Network Management Protocol) is used to interface NetWare and the TCP/IP protocol suite. It lets TCP/IP-based network management clients exchange information about their configurations on a TCP/IP internetwork.

CLIB is a library of routines and functions that NLMs use to perform specific utility tasks.

IPXS is a protocol stack NLM that provides STREAMS-based IPX protocol services. IPXS requires STREAMS and CLIB.

SPXS is also a protocol stack NLM that provides SPX-based protocol services. SPXS has the same requirements as IPXS.

Finally, TLI (transport level interface) provides communications services among STREAMS and user applications. TLI requires STREAMS and CLIB to be loaded first.

*In order for the STREAMS-based NLMs to function properly, they must be loaded in the order listed.*

**NETWARE SERVICES** The top layer of the ODI model includes the NetWare services that clients are requesting. The brains behind the NetWare server architecture is NCP—the NetWare Core Protocol. NCP is a procedure that the NetWare operating system follows to accept and respond to client requests. Common requests handled by NCP include creating or destroying a service connection, manipulating directories/files, and printing. In addition to NCP, NetWare provides various other server-based multiprotocol services, including:

- IPX/SPX

- RIP

- SAP

- Packet Burst Protocol

*NetWare, by default, supports DOS clients running IPX. Additional workstations and additional protocols require some finagling. Although NetWare is extremely flexible in this area, the system administrator must be aware of the procedures and implications of supporting non-DOS clients.*

*IPX (Internetwork Packet Exchange)* defines the default protocol for NetWare servers. IPX provides addressing and routing functions for NetWare packets as they travel from workstation to server. As you'll learn in the next part, IPX uses a connectionless scheme for delivery of data packets. It relies on other protocols to perform acknowledgment and reliability services. One such reliability protocol is SPX. SPX (Sequence Packet Exchange) provides connection-oriented services to IPX packets. SPX ensures successful data delivery by requesting a verification that the data arrived at the destination. Some typical SPX applications include remote printing, RCONSOLE, and Netware SAA.

*RIP* is NetWare's Routing Information Protocol. RIP allows routers to exchange valuable network configuration information without the system manager's help. Servers and clients can use this information to determine the final destination of a packet and to predict the fastest route.

NetWare's *SAP (Service Advertising Protocol)* is used by all network devices to advertise their service, name, and address. NetWare servers and print servers use SAP to advertise configuration information, and clients use this protocol for initial server attachment and to find the nearest server. SAP and RIP work closely together to distribute valuable network information throughout the LAN. The system manager can use the TRACK ON console command to display the continuous flow of incoming and outgoing RIP and SAP information. For more discussion of NetWare services, see Chapter 19.

Other console commands that can be used to manage server communications include RESET ROUTER, DISPLAY NETWORKS, and DISPLAY SERVERS. All of these console commands were discussed in detail in Chapter 10.

That's enough ODI for now. Don't worry, you'll be seeing plenty of the ODI multiprotocol architecture model throughout this book. As a matter of fact, it reappears in the next section—Managing the NetWare Workstation. Speaking of workstations, let's take a look at NetWare server support for non-DOS clients.

*Give a small boy a hammer and he will find that everything he encounters needs pounding.*

*Abraham Kaplan*

## Non-DOS Support

NetWare, by default, supports DOS clients running IPX. Additional workstations and additional protocols require some finagling. Although NetWare is extremely flexible in this area, the system manager must be aware of the procedures and implications of supporting non-DOS clients. These clients fall into any of the following categories:

- Macintosh
- OS/2
- Unix
- GOSIP

**MACINTOSH** Macintosh connectivity is provided through the NetWare for Macintosh product. NetWare for Macintosh is an add-on product that has a group of NLMs and a workstation desk accessory. (It is included with NetWare 3.12 and 4.1.) The Macintosh server component provides a group of multipro-tocol NLMs that support the AppleTalk Filing Protocol (AFP). The NetWare for Macintosh product provides NetWare file, print, and routing services to Macintosh computers through AFP NLMs. Macintosh workstations load the NetWare desk accessory to provide common user tools through the native Macintosh interface. NetWare for Macintosh is an effective strategy for integrating DOS and Macintosh workstations on a NetWare 3.1x LAN.

**OS/2** OS/2 connectivity is provided through the NetWare Requester for OS/2. The Requester runs on the OS/2 workstation and is included with the NetWare 3.1x operating system. File server support for OS/2 is provided through NetWare's inherent IPX protocol stack. The workstation uses OS/2's high-performance file system (HPFS) to replace the file allocation table used by DOS. OS/2's HPFS supports long names and extended attri-butes. NetWare support for long names and extended attributes is provided through the OS/2 name space. This name space runs on the NetWare file server while the OS/2 workstations communicate using IPX protocol.

In addition, the NetWare Requester for OS/2 supports named pipes and NETBIOS so that OS/2 workstations can communicate directly with each other—without interfering with the IPX protocol stack on the NetWare server. The best thing about the NetWare Requester for OS/2 is that it's free.

**UNIX** Unix connectivity is the most complex of NetWare's non-DOS strate-gies. NetWare supports Unix connectivity in three ways:

First, there's TCP/IP routing—The Transmission Control Protocol/Internet Protocol (TCP/IP) was developed specifically to permit different types of computers to communicate over large internetworks. TCP/IP routing refers to NetWare's ability to aid in the communications between two Unix work-stations over a TCP/IP network. NetWare servers can coexist on TCP/IP internetworks while still speaking IPX with their workstations.

If the system manager loads the native TCP/IP NLMs in NetWare 3.1x, the file server can communicate packets from one Unix workstation to another but cannot process them. This option does not provide NetWare services to Unix workstations. This means that the protocol stack will accept the TCP/IP packet and then send it back down the protocol stack—off to another TCP/IP node. The NetWare 3.1x TCP/IP NLMs are stored in the SYS:SYSTEM directory when NetWare is installed. In addition, the ETC root directory is created to store additional database files that are needed for TCP/IP routing. If the system manager wishes to process TCP/IP packets and provide NetWare services to Unix clients, additional products are required: NetWare NFS or NetWare IP.

*Necessity is the mother of invention.*

*Jonathan Swift*

Second, there's NFS support on the NetWare server—NetWare NFS (Network File System) allows NetWare file servers to process TCP/IP packets from Unix clients. It is the de facto industry standard for Unix files. With NetWare NFS, NetWare file systems can be accessed using NFS and NetWare print queues can be used to view the Unix line printer commands. NetWare NFS allows Unix workstations to share files and print services with DOS clients.

And last, there are NetWare workstations attached to Unix hosts—the final approach toward Unix connectivity is attaching NetWare workstations to Unix hosts. Workstations running ODI drivers can attach directly to Unix hosts using an optional product called LAN Workplace for DOS. It loads a series of drivers and commands on the NetWare workstation to allow it to emulate a Unix client. The NetWare workstation can then communicate directly to the Unix host using Unix commands and proper syntax. LAN Workplace for DOS does not provide the facility for sharing files between DOS and Unix. NetWare workstations must use the Unix conventions.

*Novell provides three other interfaces for LAN Workplace: LAN Workplace for Windows, LAN Workplace for OS/2, and LAN Workplace for Macintosh.*

**GOSIP** NetWare 3.1*x* supports OSI GOSIP, Government OSI Profile through NetWare File Transfer Access Management (FTAM) and associated NLMs. FTAM is a standard protocol for OSI that deals with file handling in a diverse network environment.

In addition to support for multiple client workstation operating systems and protocols, NetWare server disks must be configured to support additional name spaces. Let's take a closer look.

### Name Space Support

In addition to communicating with non-DOS clients, NetWare file systems must support their unique naming habits. NetWare name space support accomplishes this task. Name space is activated on a volume-by-volume basis. Although adding name space to a volume increases client flexibility, it also increases server overhead.

The following two commands configure the SYS volume for the Macintosh name space:

```
LOAD MAC
```

loads the MAC.NAM name space module, and

```
ADD NAME SPACE MAC TO SYS:
```

activates Macintosh name space on the SYS volume.

The ADD NAME SPACE command is only required once, because it initializes the volume for the name space. Future support for a specific non-DOS naming scheme must be accomplished through loading the Name Space NLM each time the server boots. This is performed in the STARTUP.NCF server configuration file.

*To remove name space, you must load VREPAIR.NLM. This repairs the volume and strips away any unused name space. If you would like to run the VREPAIR NLM without stripping away name space, you must load specific V_NAMESPACE modules, such as V_OS2.NLM.*

*System managers can use the NDIR CLU to display extended file information for Mac and OS/2 files stored on NetWare volumes. Simply use the /MAC switch for displaying Macintosh files and directories with long names (up to thirty-one characters) or /LONG to view longer attributes for OS/2.*

That's it for multiprotocol management. As you can tell, it's not easy to incorporate various workstations into one cohesive LAN. Although NetWare provides the facility for transparent multiple protocols, it takes some massaging in order for them to work smoothly. The system manager welcomes multiple workstations into the LAN in the same way that the hotel manager opens Park Place's doors to various clients. It is extremely rewarding when all things come together and users become one big happy family. Speaking of happiness, I wonder how the workstations are doing. I'd hate to ignore the users just when I'm starting to understand them—*not!*

*Every advantage has its tax.*

Ralph Waldo Emerson

# Managing the NetWare Workstation

WELCOME TO THE WORKSTATION! A workstation is a stand-alone computer that uses a local operating system such as DOS to provide basic local services. The local operating system coordinates among local applications—word processing, spreadsheets, and databases, for example—and local devices that provide services such as file storage for local disks, screen display, printer access, and communications or modem access.

Various local operating systems provide various local services. Each has its own strengths and weaknesses. The strengths of DOS lie solely in its acceptance as the industry standard. There are faster, more reliable, more diverse operating systems, but DOS has been adopted by 85% of all local workstations. Other operating systems that improve on DOS are OS/2 with a more powerful GUI interface, Unix with much better connectivity, and System 7 for the friendly Macintosh.

NetWare prides itself on its ability to transparently support a multitude of workstation environments. NetWare 2.2 currently supports workstations running DOS, OS/2, and Macintosh operating systems. NetWare 3.1*x* includes these as well as Unix connectivity. Keep in mind, though, that NetWare was primarily designed to support the DOS workstation. DOS workstations can support DOS-like files on the NetWare-shared disk without any problem. Other workstation platforms must use name space modules to support non-DOS naming schemes. OS/2, for example, supports 255 characters and extended attributes in its naming scheme. Earlier in the chapter we discussed NetWare support for non-DOS workstation platforms.

*Because most of its customers are using DOS workstations, Novell has concentrated its workstation efforts on DOS-oriented shells. These shells use one of two strategies: IPX/NETx (older) or ODI/VLM (newer).*

NetWare services are provided to the workstation by two key devices:

- The internal NIC, a hardware device that provides communications between the local operating system and the NetWare server.

- Workstation connectivity software. This is a series of drivers, shells, and programs that translate and communicate among the local operating system and the network operating system, NetWare.

Because most of its customers are using DOS workstations, Novell has concentrated its workstation efforts on DOS-oriented shells. These shells use one of two strategies: IPX/NETx (older) or ODI/VLM (newer). The IPX/NETx strategy has been around since NetWare was first released. IPX/NETx uses two files, IPX.COM and NETx.EXE, for both protocol and requester communications. The second, newer strategy—ODI/VLM—employs a more modern modular approach toward protocols and requester facilities. ODI drivers and virtual loadable modules (VLMs) are much more flexible and allow for easy management and configuration.

*NetWare is moving toward full ODI compliance with NetWare 4.x and 3.12 shells. They use VLMs. VLMs are part of the NetWare DOS Requester, which provides full modular loading of workstation components.*

In this section, we will explore both workstation connectivity strategies. We will begin with the older IPX/NETx approach and then discuss ODI implementation at the workstation and the NetWare DOS Requester VLMs. In addition, we will discuss how workstation configuration files automate and customize the workstation connectivity environment. Finally, we'll discuss some workstation management strategies for the system manager.

As a CNA, you will spend just as much time managing the workstations as you do managing the server. In addition, managing the workstations can be more challenging because they encompass a much more diverse collection of users, applications, and operating systems. Let's start by looking at the older IPX/NETx connectivity strategy.

# The IPX/NETX Environment

IPX is a protocol utility that controls communications between NETx.EXE and the internal NIC. NETx.EXE is the NetWare shell that handles the communications between DOS and the IPX.COM protocol. If you think back for a moment to our earlier analogy of Play-Doh and Legos, the IPX/NETx strategy is like the Play-Doh option. It's older, like NetWare 2.2, and only supports one protocol. I guess it's safe to say it becomes hard and crusty once it's been configured. The ODI/VLM strategy, on the other hand, is much more like Legos. It's modular, advanced, and supports multiple protocols. Let's begin our discussion of IPX/NETx with a detailed look at IPX.COM.

### IPX.COM

IPX.COM is generated using the WSGEN utility and requires approximately 32KB of workstation RAM. IPX.COM comprises two key components:

- *.LAN. The LAN driver controls communications between the IPX object file and the internal workstation NIC. Each manufacturer-specific NIC has a unique driver. When creating IPX.COM, the system manager must ensure that the LAN driver explicitly matches the NIC settings.

- IPX.OBJ. The IPX object file controls all of the management applications of IPX.COM. IPX.OBJ is generic for all IPX.COM files, and it handles communications among IPX.COM, Windows, NETx, and other internal workstation components.

During the workstation generation (WSGEN), the system manager must specify the LAN driver and NIC configurations. The NIC configuration tells IPX.COM which interrupt, I/O address, and memory address to use. One of the most challenging aspects of using IPX.COM is ensuring that the correct IPX.COM is used with the correct LAN driver and the correct configuration settings matches the status of the NIC. In many cases, CNEs have felt the wrath of frustrated users who can't quite get the IPX.COM file to work.

*When you are troubleshooting IPX.COM problems, use the command IPX /I to view the LAN driver and configuration settings of the current IPX.COM file. In addition, rename IPX.COM to IPXINTEL.COM or IPXNE200.COM, for example, to differentiate NIC-specific IPX.COM files.*

### NETx

As we mentioned earlier, NETx.EXE is the NetWare shell that handles communications between DOS and IPX.COM. Unlike IPX, NETx.EXE is a generic file and is not specific to NICs or workstation settings. All DOS workstations in the world can use the same NETx.EXE file.

*The file NETx.EXE used to be NET3, NET4, and NET5; the number indicated which version of DOS it supported. After time, this system became confusing and difficult for system managers to track. In response, Novell created a DOS version-independent NET file and termed it NETx.*

The main purpose of the NETx file is redirection. The internal redirector handles user requests and decides whether they should be directed to the operating system, like DOS, or to the network. If the redirector determines that a request is destined for the network, it sends it off to IPX.COM. NetWare provides three versions of the NETx shell that accommodate different workstation environments:

- NETx.EXE, the basic NETx shell that loads in conventional memory. It supports any version of DOS from 2.1 to 7.00.

- EMSNETx.EXE, the EMS expanded memory specification version of NETx. EMSNETx runs in expanded memory and frees approximately 34KB of conventional RAM. EMSNETx.EXE requires the LIM 4.0 EMS specification. In most systems, this is accomplished by adding the line DEVICE=EMM386.EXE in the CONFIG.SYS file. On the downside, EMSNETx.EXE is slow.

- XMSNETx.EXE, the XMS, extended memory specification version of NETx. XMSNETx runs in extended memory and also frees approximately 34KB of conventional RAM. XMSNETx requires the LIM XMS 2.0 specification. This specification can be implemented by inserting the command DEVICE=HIMEM.SYS in the CONFIG.SYS file. On the downside, XMSNETx.EXE occupies the same 64KB of high memory as advanced versions of DOS. Therefore, DOS=HIGH and XMSNETx can't operate together; the user must choose one or the other.

Figure 11.3 illustrates these NetWare shell versions and how they impact workstation RAM.

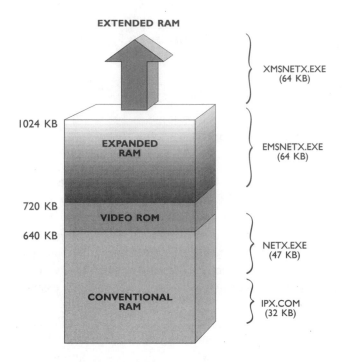

**F I G U R E  11.3**
Shells and
workstation RAM

*The workstation memory requirements for NetWare differ depending on the users' activities. Normal workstations require 512KB of RAM; workstations running WSGEN require the maximum conventional RAM of 640KB.*

IPX/NETx provides a stable strategy for workstation connectivity. IPX.COM initializes the NIC, and NETx completes the workstation connectivity by activating the DOS redirector and attaching to an available server. Keep in mind, though, that you're severely limited in using IPX/NETx. This strategy only supports the IPX protocol and, once configured, cannot easily be changed. A better solution for most newer, sophisticated operating systems is ODI/VLM.

*In this world of change, nothing which comes stays, and nothing which goes is lost.*

*Anne Swetchine*

*If I were you, I would focus on learning about ODI and the NetWare DOS Requester. This is where the NetWare workstation is going, and exactly where Novell expects you to be for the tests.*

# The ODI Environment

*ODI drivers and VLMs are relatively new additions to the NetWare puzzle. They are modular subcomponents that combine to enhance the functions of IPX.COM and NETx.EXE.*

ODI drivers and VLMs are relatively new additions to the NetWare puzzle. They are modular subcomponents that combine to enhance the functions of IPX.COM and NETx.EXE. We will begin our discussion of this superior workstation connectivity strategy with a detailed look at ODI implementation at the workstation.

Using ODI, your network can run multiple protocols on the same cabling system. ODI allows devices that use different communication protocols to coexist on one network, thus increasing your network's functionality and flexibility. For example, both IPX and TCP/IP can run on the same computer using the same NIC. This flexibility allows a user to concurrently access services from a NetWare server using IPX and a Unix host using TCP/IP on the same NIC. ODI provides maximum network flexibility transparently to various computing environments, preserving all the previous hardware and software investments. ODI currently supports the following platforms:

- AppleTalk (Macintosh)

- TCP/IP (Sun, NeXT, HP, and all Unix-based workstations)

- IPX/SPX (DOS, Microsoft Windows, and OS/2 clients)

Recall from our earlier discussion of ODI at the server that ODI's modular implementation consists of four layers. Refer again to Figure 11.2. Workstation ODI drivers operate at the bottom three layers, whereas the VLMs exist at the top layer—NetWare services. Each layer performs a specific function as user requests or packets travel from the client to the server and then back again. Let's take a look at the three modular layers of the ODI workstation model, as shown in Figure 11.4.

**FIGURE 11.4**
The workstation
ODI model

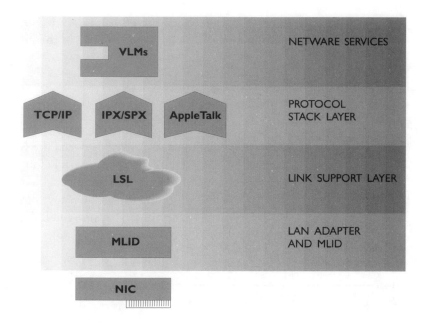

## LAN Adapter and MLID

The bottom layer of the ODI model consists of the physical LAN adapter and custom Multiple Link Interface Driver (MLID). MLIDs accept any type of packet: AppleTalk, TCP/IP, and IPX. Each physical LAN adapter has its own MLID driver. The MLID driver is analogous to the LAN driver that is used to create IPX.COM. Make sure you have the correct LAN driver for each of your workstation NICs.

*Recall from our discussion of IPX.COM that the LAN adapter is hard-coded into the IPX.COM file as the WSGEN creation utility is used. ODI is much more flexible. With ODI, the MLID driver exists as an independent .COM file. Configurations are established in the NET.CFG text file. If a user wishes to switch from one NIC to another, he/she simply runs a different MLID driver. This MLID flexibility is much simpler for the CNE, because it does not require the generation of a new IPX.COM file.*

ODI implementation at the workstation works a little bit differently from the way that the model shows it. Although the MLID layer is at the bottom and is the first point of contact for incoming or outgoing packets, it is not the first ODI driver loaded. The MLID driver, such as NE2000.COM, is loaded second. Again, MLID drivers can be loaded and unloaded as needed and their configuration settings are established in the NET.CFG file.

## Link Support Layer (LSL)

The Link Support Layer is the next layer in the ODI model. It acts as a type of switchboard to route packets between the MLID adapter and protocol stack. The LSL identifies the type of packet and then passes the packet to the appropriate protocol in the protocol stack layer. LSL.COM is implemented as the first ODI workstation file. A DOS client can use TCP/IP, IPX, or Apple-Talk services simultaneously, because the LSL will direct information to the appropriate protocol stack.

## Protocol Stack Layer

The Protocol Stack Layer contains protocol stacks, such as IPX, AppleTalk, and TCP/IP. Recall that a stack is a protocol-specific group of files used to translate and negotiate specific protocols. Once a packet arrives at the specified protocol stack, it either passes through and communicates with the Net-Ware DOS Requester or is sent back down to another network. Protocol stack implementation at the workstation is provided through a .COM or .EXE file that specifies the protocol type. The IPX file is IPXODI.COM. The TCP/IP implementation consists of TCPIP.EXE. The protocol stack file is loaded after the MLID driver that is loaded after the LSL driver at the workstation.

To summarize workstation implementation of the ODI model, each of the three files is loaded in the following order:

1. LSL.COM

2. LAN driver (NE2000.COM)

3. Protocol stack (IPXODI.COM or TCPIP.EXE)

Customization and configuration of the ODI strategy is implemented using NET.CFG. We will explore NET.CFG workstation parameters later in this section.

*Workstation ODI drivers can be unloaded. This feature is unavailable in the earlier IPX.COM implementation. To unload ODI drivers, simply type the name followed by a* /U . *Note: The drivers must be unloaded in reverse order.*

As you know from our earlier discussion, the ODI model provides numerous benefits:

- Communication with various workstations, servers, and mainframe computers that view different protocols concurrently

- Communication through any network board written to ODI specifications

- Fewer hardware components to support, meaning fewer NICs at the workstation

- Flexible configurations through use of the NET.CFG file

*There really isn't a reason not to use ODI drivers. ODI is flexible, reliable, and fast. In addition, Novell currently updates ODI drivers and protocol stacks several times a year. Support for IPX and NETx files has been less aggressive. The current version of IPX, ODI, and LAN drivers works extremely well with Windows and is fully supported by all NetWare applications. In addition, the ODI model is the future of LAN communications.*

*Ah, but a man's reach should exceed his grasp, or what's a heaven for?*

*Robert Browning*

*Novell is no longer officially supporting IPX and NETx. Eventually, your users are going to be forced to use ODI and the NetWare DOS Requester. I can't think of any better time than the present—especially since Version 2.0 seems to be an improvement over earlier versions of the VLMs.*

## The NetWare DOS Requester

The NetWare DOS Requester is a connection point between local software and network services. It lies between the workstation software and ODI to make transparent network communications attainable. Think of the NetWare

*The NetWare DOS Requester takes requests from the user and decides whether they should be redirected to the local operating system or to the NetWare server.*

DOS Requester as a traffic director that resides at the workstation. It takes requests from the user and decides whether they should be redirected to the local operating system or to the NetWare server. If a request is destined for the NetWare server, the Requester will send it down through the ODI layers. ODI and the Requester work closely together, and they're both completely modular and transparent to the user. ODI and VLMs, the DOS Requester, can be unloaded and reloaded without adversely affecting the performance of the workstation.

As you can see from Figure 11.5, the NetWare DOS Requester is software with a vise-like architecture that surrounds DOS. It shares drive table information with DOS, therefore reducing memory usage. The Requester performs tasks such as file and print redirection, connection maintenance, and packet handling. Application users can make calls to the Requester in one of three ways:

- Call the DOS requester before they call DOS.

- Call the DOS requester through DOS using the interrupt 2FH redirector.

- Call the DOS requester without going through DOS. Although the Requester shares drive tables with DOS, it does not have to go through DOS if it knows that a function is a network function. Bypassing DOS helps performance.

As you can see from the figure, the lower part of the Requester vise-like architecture handles workstation network services. The upper half of the

**FIGURE 11.5**
The NetWare DOS
Requester architecture

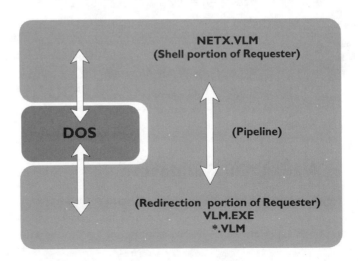

vise-like architecture is the shell portion and consists of only one module: NETx.VLM. This Requester shell is analogous to the NETx.EXE file used in the earlier connectivity strategy. Let's take a closer look at the Requester approach by understanding the many VLMs that operate at the lower half of the vise-like architecture.

### DOS Requester VLMs

The NetWare DOS Requester is made up of a number of VLMs. A VLM is a file that performs related functions. For example, PRINT.VLM performs or directs various printing functions such as CAPTURE from the workstation. Many modular VLMs are used to implement the various connectivity services provided by the Requester, including:

- Modularity—enables adopting third-party and future functionality, takes advantage of expanded and extended memory and (in the future) protected-mode DOS extenders.

- Memory swapping—enables efficient memory usage because the unnecessary items are not included.

- DOS redirection—eliminates the duplication of effort between the Shell and DOS; also allows for direct communications between workstation services and the Requester shell.

- System optimization—includes packet burst and large Internet packet support.

- Compatibility with other versions of NetWare—provides compatibility with previous versions of NetWare through NETx.VLM or with future versions of NetWare 4 through NDS.VLM.

Figure 11.6 diagrams the various VLMs implemented at the NetWare services layer of the Requester's vise-like architecture. These VLMs exist at three layers:

- The transport protocol layer

- Service protocol layer

- DOS redirection layer

**FIGURE 11.6**
The bottom-half services
of the NetWare
DOS Requester

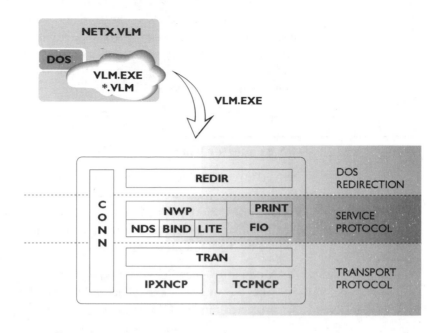

CONN.VLM is used for connectivity among these three layers. Let's take a closer look at the functions provided by each of the Requester layers.

*All change is a miracle to contemplate; but it is a miracle which is taking place every instant.*

*Henry David Thoreau*

**TRANSPORT PROTOCOL LAYER** The Transport Protocol layer maintains server connections and provides packet transmission and other transport-related services. The Transport Protocol layer and all other layers use two types of VLMs: parent and children. The parent VLMs route requests to the applicable children VLMs. Parent VLMs or multiplexers incorporate the services of multiple children VLMs. Children VLMs handle a particular implementation of a logical grouping of functions. For example, at the transport layer, the TRAN.VLM file is responsible for routing transport protocols to either IPXNCP.VLM for IPX services or TCPNCP.VLM for TCP/IP services. In this example, TRAN.VLM is the parent and IPXNCP.VLM and TCPNCP.VLM are children.

**SERVICE PROTOCOL LAYER**  Service Protocol VLMs handle requests for specific services such as broadcast messages, file reads and writes, and print redirection. The principal modules include:

- NWP.VLM—the NetWare multiplexer that establishes and maintains connections, logins, and logouts.

- NWP.VLM—also handles broadcasts and particular network server implementations through children including NDS, bindery (BIND.VLM), or Personal NetWare (LITE.VLM).

- FIO.VLM—the File Input/Output module implements the basic transfer protocol for files. This VLM handles cached or noncached reads and writes and burst mode reads and writes.

- PRINT.VLM—the print module provides printing services using FIO module for file writes. This process is analogous to the CAPTURE command redirecting print jobs from a local port off to a NetWare queue in the server file system. We'll explore this in much more detail in the next chapter.

**DOS REDIRECTION LAYER**  The REDIR.VLM is responsible for DOS redirection services. The Requester makes a NetWare server look like a DOS driver to the user by having REDIR.VLM provide the redirector level of client services. This function is analogous to the major function of NETx.EXE.

Now that you understand the many VLMs and how they operate within the Requester's vise-like architecture, let's take a closer look at the VLM manager and explore how the CNA implements the Requester at client workstations.

*If I were you, I wouldn't stress out over all the details of VLM architecture. Instead, focus on learning how it is implemented and all the VLM.EXE switches.*

### VLM Manager

The Requester's many VLMs are implemented at the workstation using the VLM manager. The VLM manager's major responsibilities include:

- Handling requests from applications and routing them to the proper VLM

- Managing communications between modules including child and multiplexer modules

- Controlling memory services, allocation, and management

When you run the VLM manager, it oversees the loading and sequencing of VLM files. VLMs are load-order dependent. The preferred NetWare protocol should be loaded first. Next, you load the security- and bindery-related services. Next are the multiplexer (NWP.VLM) and finally the VLM services. By default, VLM.EXE loads all the appropriate VLMs from the current directory in the correct order. To specify a different order for the loading of VLMs or to load only particular VLMs, you use the NET.CFG file with the command

```
USE DEFAULTS=OFF
```

Then you must specify which VLM is loaded and load each one in the correct order. Remember, you should always load children VLMs before their parents.

Table 11.2 lists all VLMs that are loaded by default, the order in which they're loaded, and whether they're required or optional.

In addition to the default VLMs in NetWare 3.12, NetWare 4.1 provides three more VLMs to enhance communications and workstation connectivity:

- NDS.VLM for NetWare Directory Services support

- AUTO.VLM for auto reconnect with the client

- RSA.VLM to support enhanced security and authentication services

The Requester supports DOS 3.1 and above and works with extended, expanded, and conventional memory. VLM.EXE by default tries to load all VLMs in extended memory first. Expanded memory is the second choice, and if extended or expanded memory are unavailable, conventional memory is used. VLM.EXE itself can be loaded in high memory but is not a built-in parameter. Many advanced users have been able to implement VLMs's memory advantages by loading VLM.EXE and all VLMs in extended memory using only 4KB of conventional memory. This is an astonishing feat compared with the clumsiness of IPX/NETx and memory management.

In addition to memory support, VLM.EXE has various switches that provide additional services:

- /? displays the help screen.

- /U unloads the VLM from memory.

- /C=*path* specifies a different configuration file other than NET.CFG.

- /MC loads VLMs in conventional memory.

- /ME loads VLMs in expanded memory.

- /MX loads VLMs in extended memory.

- /D displays file diagnostics, such as status information, memory type, current ID, and VLM manager functioning.

- /PS=*server* attaches to your preferred server.

- /PT=*tree* accesses your preferred tree in the NetWare 4.1 environment.

- /V helps determine which VLMs have been loaded and which VLM parameters in NET.CFG have been executed.

- /V*x* displays the detailed level of messaging where *x* runs from 0 to 4, 0 displays copyright and critical errors only, and 4 displays all diagnostic messages.

Well, that just about does it for the NetWare DOS Requester and ODI environment. Keep in mind that although ODI/VLMs are preferable, they're also much more complex. The system manager must be intimately familiar with all the switches and the files that need to be loaded in the correct order. Another important point is mixing the IPX/NETx and ODI/VLM environments. Although this is not recommended, it is possible to achieve with creativity.

*I find the great thing in this world is not so much where we stand, as in what direction we are moving.*

*Oliver Wendell Holmes, Sr.*

The first option has been heavily tested and is widely used in the 3.11 environment—that is, ODI and NETx.EXE. The ODI implementation will replace IPX.COM and provides a good solution for multiple protocols. NETx will operate properly with ODI.

The other option—IPX.COM with the VLMs—is technically not supported, although there is a NetWare 3.12 IPX.COM file that can operate with the DOS requester VLMs.

In either case, each of these workstation connectivity strategies requires specific configuration files to operate properly. These workstation configuration

| TABLE 11.2 NetWare DOS Requester VLMs | MODULE | REQUIRED/ OPTIONAL | WHAT IT DOES |
|---|---|---|---|
| | VLM=CONN.VLM | R | The connection table manager tracks and allocates connections. It supplies other modules with connection information. |
| | VLM=IPXNCP.VLM | R | The IPX/NCP transport module builds packets with the proper NCP header and hands the packet to ODI. |
| | VLM=TRAN.VLM | R | The transport protocol multiplexer is the parent for supported transport modules. |
| | VLM=SECURITY.VLM | R | The module provides additional packet security as needed including NCP packet signing. |
| | VLM=BIND.VLM | R | The module provides bindery services and compatibility with the NetWare bindery. |
| | VLM=NWP.VLM | R | The NetWare protocol multiplexer parent coordinates services with the bindery and security children. |
| | VLM=FIO.VLM | R | The file input/output module supports file access on the network. |
| | VLM=GENERAL.VLM | R | The general functions module provides generic administrative functions to all other VLMs. |
| | VLM=REDIR.VLM | R | The DOS redirector module works with DOS to handle redirection tasks. |
| | VLM=PRINT.VLM | O | The module handles print redirection from the workstation. |
| | VLM=NETx.VLM | R | The NetWare shell VLM provides compatibility with applications that use specific shell API calls. |

files include CONFIG.SYS, AUTOEXEC.BAT, and NET.CFG. Let's dive into them.

# Workstation Configuration Files

Both workstation connectivity strategies rely on workstation-specific configuration files for implementation and customization. The IPX/NETx strategy relies only on the NET.CFG file, whereas the ODI/VLM option requires customization of the CONFIG.SYS and AUTOEXEC.BAT as well as NET.CFG. Now we will explore these workstation configuration files and dissect some time-proven strategies for optimizing the NetWare workstation. Let's start with CONFIG.SYS.

## CONFIG.SYS

NetWare 3.12 and the NetWare DOS Requester require the last drive command to be used in CONFIG.SYS to identify the range of letters available to be used for network drives. CONFIG.SYS is a DOS configuration file used for registering devices, managing memory, and establishing local drives. The Requester reads the workstation hardware configuration and makes available all letters between the last known physical drive and the letter specified in the LASTDRIVE command.

For example, if the last physical drive on the workstation were C, the workstation CONFIG.SYS file would have to include a LASTDRIVE=Z command to make the letters D through Z available for the network. If the LASTDRIVE=Z command were not established, no drives would be available for NetWare connectivity. This no doubt sounds strange if you are used to working with the LASTDRIVE=Z command, but unfortunately that's the way it works.

*The NetWare DOS Requester can be used with NetWare 3.11 workstations, but remember to change the CONFIG.SYS file to support LASTDRIVE=Z. The reverse is also true. NETx.EXE can be used with NetWare 3.11 or 3.12, but if you use the LASTDRIVE=Z command with NETx, no drives will be available to the network. So, to recap, LASTDRIVE=Z, YES for DOS requester, NO for NETx.*

### AUTOEXEC.BAT

As a CNA, you can automate the NetWare connection by placing all of the connectivity commands in the AUTOEXEC.BAT file. The NetWare 3.1*x* client install program automatically creates a file called STARTNET.BAT that is loaded automatically from AUTOEXEC.BAT. The STARTNET.BAT configuration file contains the following:

```
C:
CD \NWCLIENT
LSL.COM
NE2000
```

(or other MLID driver)

```
IPXODI
VLM
F:
LOGIN username
```

That's it. By calling the STARTNET.BAT file from AUTOEXEC.BAT, you can automate the user login procedures. By default, the command

```
@CALL C:\NWCLIENT\STARTNET.BAT
```

is placed at the top of the user workstation AUTOEXEC.BAT file.

There is one problem with this strategy. Because the @CALL START-NET.BAT command is inserted at the top of the AUTOEXEC.BAT file, no other DOS parameters are activated until the user logs in. These parameters can include PATH statements, SET parameters, and the PROMPT command. Instead, you should place the STARTNET.BAT file last in AUTOEXEC.BAT, and remove the @CALL statement.

### NET.CFG

NET.CFG is a specialized configuration file that provides information to network connectivity shells. Values specified in NET.CFG adjust the operating parameters of the Requester or ODI. These values can revise client parameters for such activities as printing or file retrieval. In addition, NET.CFG can be used to customize the Requester environment.

You only need to create a NET.CFG file if you plan on deviating from the established defaults of ODI and the Requester. You can create NET.CFG with any DOS text editor and must follow the following general conventions:

- Left-justify section headings.

- Place options under each section heading and indent with a tab or at least one space.

- Use uppercase or lowercase for section headings and options.

- Precede comments with a semicolon (;) or pound (#) sign for documentation purposes.

- End each line with a hard return.

- Write all numbers in decimal notation except where noted.

The NET.CFG file is the key workstation connectivity configuration file. When creating a NET.CFG, the system manager must be aware of four categories of configuration:

- Old SHELL.CFG parameters

- Link driver

- Link support

- NetWare DOS Requester

Let's take a closer look at each of these configuration options and how the system manager can use them to customize and optimize workstation connectivity.

*There is no force so powerful as an idea whose time has come.*

*Everett Dirksen*

**OLDER SHELL.CFG PARAMETERS**  SHELL.CFG is a NetWare-specific configuration file that is loaded from the workstation. SHELL.CFG defines parameters for loading IPX and NETx. The SHELL.CFG file can be customized by the NetWare administrator to provide the facility for Windows support, COMSPEC, file handles, workstation buffers, and SPX connections. SHELL.CFG has been replaced by NET.CFG. NET.CFG supports all the same parameters as SHELL.CFG, plus some additional parameters for ODI workstations and the Requester. Following is a list of some of the most important SHELL.CFG parameters that can be implemented in the NET.CFG for IPX, NETx, or ODI implementation. These options are left-justified just as if they were separate section headings:

- **Cache buffers.** This SHELL.CFG parameter sets the number of buffers, or cache blocks, the shell will use for local caching of nonshared, nontransaction tracked files. Increasing the number of cache buffers can speed up the process of sequential reads and writes. This increase is analogous to an increase in file cache buffers in the CONFIG.SYS file. The default is 5.

- **File handles.** This parameter sets the number of files a workstation can have open on the network simultaneously. Some applications require more files open than the default number of forty. Increase this value if you receive the `No available files` error message.

- **IPX retry count.** IPX uses this parameter to recommend a number of times to resend packets. This setting should be increased for active networks that have heavy traffic and cover long distances. The IPX retry count parameter works in conjunction with SPX abort timeout.

- **SPX abort timeout.** This parameter adjusts the amount of time that SPX waits without receiving any response from the other side of the connection before it terminates the session. SPX abort timeout should be configured in conjunction with IPX retry count if this workstation is using RPRINTER over routers. The default SPX timeout should be increased from 540 to about 1080 in this case, and the IPX retry count should be doubled from 20 to 40.

- **Local printers.** This parameter overrides the number of local printers on the workstation. A 0 setting prevents the workstation from locking up when you attempt to use print screen and capture.

- **Long machine type.** This parameter tells the shell what type of machine is being used each time the %MACHINE login script variable is accessed. The default is IBM_PC. If the workstation is using Compaq DOS, the long machine type should be set to COMPAQ, for example.

- **Max tasks.** This parameter configures the maximum number of tasks that can be active at the same time. Certain multitasking applications such as Windows and Deskview require a higher setting than the default of 31.

- **Show dots.** This parameter allows the shell to emulate the "dot" and "double dot" in directory entries. The default is OFF and should be set to ON for Windows.

- **SPX connections.** This parameter must be set to at least 60 in order for a dedicated print server using PSERVER.EXE to work correctly. The default is 15. We will discuss the dedicated print server strategy in Chapter 12.

- **Printer header=72.** The printer header parameter is used to increase the buffer size for storing printer configuration information for print jobs traveling from the workstation to the server. The print header keeps formatting instructions, fonts, and special printer configuration files that are required for complex jobs. The default size of the print header buffer is 64 bytes, but it can be increased to 72 for complex jobs. The maximum is 255.

- **Print tail=24.** The print tail contains escape sequences that are used to reinitialize the printer. The default size of the print tail is 16 bytes, which is large enough for most jobs. If you're using the print header command for a complex print job from the workstation, increase the print tail as well.

*The relationship between the older SHELL.CFG and newer NET.CFG is interesting. The SHELL.CFG only allows for workstation customization parameters such as the ones we've described here. NET.CFG supports all SHELL.CFG commands plus some additional ODI and Requester parameters. If the SHELL.CFG file already exists and you create a NET.CFG that contains any SHELL.CFG commands, the SHELL.CFG file will be ignored. To alleviate this problem, simply copy all of the SHELL.CFG commands into the NET.CFG and do away with coexistence between SHELL.CFG and NET.CFG.*

**LINK DRIVER** LINK DRIVER is a section heading for ODI support. System managers use the link driver section to name the MLID driver and to specify hardware and software settings for this specific driver. This is probably the most important implementation of NET.CFG with respect to ODI. Recall that ODI, the MLID driver in ODI, specifies configuration settings in the

NET.CFG file. Well, this is where it happens. The format and some of the options are as follows:

```
LINK DRIVER driver
    INT interrupt number
    PORT I/O port address
    MEM memory address
    FRAME frame type
```

The LINK DRIVER heading in NET.CFG provides a modular and flexible approach for CNAs who must support different types of NIC and different types of workstation.

**LINK SUPPORT**  The LINK SUPPORT section heading is used for configuring receive buffers, the size of memory pools, and the number of boards and stacks. These options are used to customize LSL implementation in the ODI model. Remember that the LSL.COM file is a switchboard that handles communications between the MLID driver and corresponding protocol stack. The link support line in NET.CFG supports two main commands: BUFFERS and MEMPOOL. The BUFFERS option configures the number and size of received buffers that the LSL will maintain. The IPX protocol stack does not use LSL communication buffers. The TCP/IP protocol stack requires at least two buffers. The default is set to zero (0).

**NETWARE DOS REQUESTER**  The NET.CFG configuration file can be used in the ODI/VLM environment to customize default DOS Requester settings. You can also use the NET.CFG to establish default client environment parameters, such as preferred server and first network drive. A CNA will use NetWare DOS Requester as the section heading and insert any variety of NET.CFG parameters. Some of the most interesting include:

- **AUTO RECONNECT=ON.** A VLM.EXE parameter that supports auto reconnect so workstations can automatically reattach to a server with which they have lost a connection.

- **CONNECTIONS=8.** A CONN.VLM parameter that establishes how many connections the workstation can simultaneously support. You can set the parameter anywhere between 2 and 50; the default is 8.

- **FIRST NETWORK DRIVE=F.** A GENERAL.VLM parameter that establishes the first available NetWare drive for this particular workstation.

- **LARGE INTERNET PACKETS=ON.** An IPXNCP.VLM parameter used for workstation connectivity optimization.

- **LOAD CONN TABLE LOW=ON.** A CONN.VLM parameter used to load the connection table in low memory. This creates a more stable performance with the user's client configurations.

- **PB BUFFERS=3.** An FIO.VLM parameter used to establish buffers used for packet bursting. It is another workstation connectivity optimization parameter.

- **PREFERRED SERVER=*server*.** A BIND.VLM parameter used to establish which server the workstation will search for first.

- **SIGNATURE LEVEL=1.** An NWP.VLM parameter used for customizing NCP packet signing.

- **USE DEFAULTS=OFF.** A VLM.EXE parameter used in conjunction with the VLM=*.VLM statement to specify the loading of particular VLMs in a specific order.

*System managers can view the loading order of VLMs and their corresponding NET.CFG parameters using the VLM ( ) /V4 command.*

That completes our discussion of NET.CFG and all the configuration files for workstation management. As you can see, all the configuration files work together to automate and customize the user environment. The NET.CFG file is by far the most important, and the CNA should become intimately familiar with its parameters and customization scenarios. An exercise at the end of this chapter offers some practice at creating NET.CFG files.

*Some men see things as they are, and say "Why?" I dream of things that never were, and say "Why not?"*

*George Bernard Shaw*

# Workstation Management Strategies

*Vanilla strategies create a baseline for connectivity with 95% of NetWare workstations. Unfortunately, as you're going to learn over and over again, it's that other 5% that will jump up and bite you. Planning for every contingency, a CNA must be aware of other advanced strategies for workstation management.*

In our travels through the rooms of the NetWare hotel, we have focused on two straightforward strategies for workstation connectivity: IPX/NETx and ODI/VLM. These vanilla strategies create a baseline for connectivity with 95% of NetWare workstations. Unfortunately, as you're going to learn over and over again, it's that other 5% that will jump up and bite you. Planning for every contingency, a CNA must be aware of other advanced strategies for workstation management:

- Workstation updates

- Microsoft Windows support

- Virus prevention

- Diskless workstations

Don't underestimate the importance of polishing off each user's workstation. After all, this is the critical point of access to the LAN. After we discuss these final workstation management strategies, we can dive into the meat and potatoes of NetWare network management; that is, login scripts, user interface, NetWare backup, and the remote management facility. Let's start with a look at workstation updates.

### Workstation Updates

Imagine, if you will, that you are the system manager of a nine billion workstation LAN. You decide that it's about time you updated each workstation's VLM.EXE. Migrating from workstation to workstation, the first 1,000 or so, takes about a month and a half. At this point, you realize that by the time you finish the nine billionth workstation, there will be a whole new series of VLM.EXE files and, as a matter of fact, there'll probably be a whole new version of NetWare and probably a new planet. So you stop and think to yourself, "*Self, wouldn't it be nice if I could update all these workstation shells from one central location and have my users do it for me without knowing about it? Boy, wouldn't that be swell?*"

Well, today's your lucky day, because NetWare includes the WSUPDATE utility. This utility can update workstation shells and configuration files to all workstations from one central location. The WSUPDATE utility compares the date and time of all destination workstation files with a central source file. It then copies over existing shell files with the source file only if the source file is found to be newer than the workstation original.

A key to WSUPDATE is that it's not limited to network shell files. Although the DOS requester and NETx are the most common candidates for WSUPDATE, system managers can also use this utility to update workstation, CONFIG.SYS, AUTOEXEC.BAT, and NET.CFG files. The syntax for WSUPDATE is:

```
WSUPDATE source path destination drive:destination
    file /option
```

The source path is the full directory path, including the file name to the new centralized file. The destination drive must be a specific drive pointer; no paths are allowed. It also supports options ALL or ALL_LOCAL to search all local drives. The destination file name is the name of the file to be updated. For example, to update the VLM.EXE file on all workstation drives—including subdirectories from the Z:PUBLIC subdirectory central source on the file server—you would use the following command:

```
WSUPDATE Z:\PUBLIC\VLM.EXE ALL_LOCAL:VLM.EXE /S
```

In this case, the /S switch would search all subdirectories on all local drives. Your options are:

- **/C.** Copies the new file over the old one with no backup of the old file. This is the default.

- **/F.** Allows the system manager to set various WSUPDATE files in one text file and use that text file for reading and source and destination information.

- **/L.** Creates a log file and specifies a location and file name for the log file where WSUPDATE can store information.

- **/N.** Creates the file if it doesn't already exist.

- **/O.** Specifies that the WSUPDATE should update all files, even those flagged to read only.

- **/R.** Renames the existing file with a .OLD extension before copying the new file.

- **/S.** Updates subdirectories.

- **/V.** Adds the line LASTDRIVE=Z to the client CONFIG.SYS file.
- **/?.** Displays on-line help.

*You can use WSUPDATE to install VLMs to all local workstations by using the /F, /N, and /V options. This switch combination will copy all the new VLM files—including CONFIG.SYS and AUTOEXEC.BAT—and will update the CONFIG.SYS to all workstation files even though VLMs do not currently exist on those workstation drives.*

*If I were you, I would learn all the WSUPDATE switches. I know I sound like a broken record, but this is a really important utility.*

Now that you've gotten all excited about the use of WSUPDATE to automatically update all of your nine billion workstations, you should know there's one major drawback: WSUPDATE must be run from the client itself in order for it to work. This means that although it'll be simple to run, you'll still have to run the utility from every one of your nine billion workstations. I have a solution. Instead of running WSUPDATE yourself, why don't you allow the users to run WSUPDATE without knowing about it? Give up? The solution lies in login scripts.

As you're going to learn in the next section, login scripts are NetWare configuration files that are automatically executed when users log in. If you put the WSUPDATE command in the system login script, it will search all local drives for the specific configuration file and shell files and match the dates against a centrally updated file in the PUBLIC subdirectory. This stroke of brilliance will force every user to execute WSUPDATE each time he/she logs in. Remember, when using WSUPDATE from the login script, you must precede it with a pound (#) sign. We'll talk about this strategy later.

If WSUPDATE is updating many shell files and is run every time users log in, users might become frustrated in finding it takes up to five minutes to log in while WSUPDATE searches all local drives. One possible solution for this delay is to use an IF … THEN login script command to search only when the local shell file is not the newest version. The following command would help speed things up:

```
IF DOS_REQUESTER <> "V1.2" THEN BEGIN
 #WSUPDATE Z:\PUBLIC\VLM.EXE ALL_LOCAL:VLM.EXE
 /L=SYS:PUBLIC\WSUPDATE.LOG /s /r
END
```

With this code, the system checks for Requester types that are *not* 1.2 and prompts for an update.

### Microsoft Windows Support

Microsoft Windows is becoming a workstation standard. One of the key advancements in NetWare 3.12 is greatly improved Microsoft Windows support.

As the client software NetWare DOS Requester is installed, two sets of files are copied to the Microsoft Windows directories and one set of files is modified. As your friend, I urge you to allow the system to make these modifications. I can't think of anything worse than trying to manually modify Windows .INI configuration files.

Let's take a quick look at what NetWare does to Windows so that if it breaks, you'll know how to fix it.

**NEW NETWARE WINDOWS FILES**  The NetWare DOS Requester installation copies two sets of new NetWare Windows files to each of the \WINDOWS \SYSTEM subdirectory and \WINDOWS subdirectory. Let's take a quick look. The following set of files is copied to the \WINDOWS\SYSTEM subdirectory:

- NETWARE.DRV for accessing the network from a Windows application.

- NETWARE.HLP help text.

- NWPOPUP.EXE for displaying network messages within Windows.

- VIP.386 for running DOS applications in enhanced mode.

- VIPX.386, which is also NetWare's task switching file for enhanced mode. It synchronizes network calls and responses for DOS sessions.

- VNETWARE.386 for receiving broadcast messages. This file works in conjunction with NETWARE.DRV and NWPOPUP.EXE.

The next set of files is copied to the \WINDOWS subdirectory:

- NWADMIN.INI for setting options within Windows-based user tools.

- NETWARE.INI for customizing the Windows driver.

- ET.INI for initializing DynaText.

- NWUSER.EXE, which executes the file for NetWare Users Tools for Windows.

- NWUTILS.GRP, which creates a workgroup within Windows for the NetWare user tools.

Although I wouldn't lose any sleep over these files that end up sitting on the workstation, it is important as a CNA that you understand what the files do in case they become corrupted or lost.

*Since we cannot know all that is to be known of everything, we ought to know a little about everything.*

*Blaise Pascal*

**MODIFIED WINDOWS CONFIGURATION FILES** If you're a Windows user, I'm sure you've learned by now that Microsoft Windows relies heavily on configuration files. These files typically have the .INI extension. The NetWare installation modifies three such files: SYSTEM.INI, WIN.INI, and PROG-MAN.INI. Note that while these files are modified, a backup copy with the .BNW extension is created during installation. Let's take a closer look.
The SYSTEM.INI file gets the following three modifications:

- Under the [BOOT] option, `NETWORK.DRV=NETWARE.DRV`

- Under [BOOT.DES] option, `NETWORK.DRV=NETWARE.DRV`

- Under [386.ENH] option, `NETWORK.DRV=*VNETBIOS, VIPX.386, VNETWARE.386`

Next, the WIN.INI configuration file has one modification:

- `[WINDOWS], LOAD=NWPOPUP.EXE`

Finally, PROGMAN.INI has one modification:

- `[GROUPS], GROUPx=C:\WINDOWS\NWUTILS.GRP`

That does it for NetWare support for Windows. Bear in mind that the prettier software looks for the user, the more difficult it becomes for the system manager. Now let's take a look at keeping things running by using virus prevention and diskless workstations.

### Workstation Virus Prevention

Viruses can be playful and fun to talk about, but they quickly become the scourge of your life if they attack *your* network. It's paramount in network security to set standard procedures for protection against network viruses. The first approach in virus prevention is understanding how these little buggers work. Simply stated, computer viruses spread by exchanging and copying themselves, so the first strategy in virus prevention is to minimize the automated movement of files throughout the server disk. Ideally, of course, it's best to prevent the viruses from entering your system in the first place by blocking access points to the network. Major access points include floppy disk drives and modem connections.

In developing your workstation virus prevention strategy, consider some of the following guidelines:

- Limit logins under the supervisor account. This account is pinpointed by many network viruses.

- Grant only Read and File Scan rights whenever possible.

- Flag executable files as Read-Only and Execute-Only.

- Set the delete-inhibit and rename-inhibit attributes.

- Control modem use on the network.

- Use virus-scanning software.

- Use working copies of software for installations, not original diskettes.

- In case all else fails, back up the system frequently.

Finally, one of the most effective yet controversial strategies is diskless workstations. Let's see how they prevent viruses.

### Diskless Workstations

Diskless workstations are computers without a floppy or hard disk. Users don't take kindly to this limit to their storage capacity, but diskless workstations can dramatically improve the CNA's quality of life. Benefits of diskless workstations include virus prevention, cost savings, and, of course, better NetWare administrative control. If you're one of the lucky people who convinces management to install diskless workstations, you will need to set up the NetWare server for diskless workstation logins. As you learned in Chapter 1, the second stage of computer bootup sequence includes searching for critical DOS command files including COMMAND.COM, IBMBIO.COM and IBMDOS.COM. The system searches three places in the following order:

1. The floppy disk drive

2. A hard disk

3. Other addresses

A remote boot programmable read-only memory chip (PROM) can be placed on the NIC with an address that tells the system to search the F:\LOGIN> subdirectory for the information it needs to boot. This information is stored in the NET$DOS.SYS file. This booting configuration file is generated using the DOSGEN utility. It contains COMMAND.COM, IBMBIOS.COM, IBMDOS.COM, LSL.COM, the LAN driver, IPXODI.COM, the NetWare DOS Requester, and AUTOEXEC.BAT. In order for the remote boot PROM on the NIC to find the login subdirectory, RPL.LAN must be loaded on the server and bound to the server network board. Now, wasn't that simple?

To summarize, the CNA must install a remote boot PROM on the workstation NIC and use DOSGEN to create a NET$DOS.SYS file and put it in the login subdirectory. Finally, he/she must load RPL.LAN on the server and bind RPL.LAN to the network board.

*Most NetWare LANs contain workstations with different configuration files, so you have to be able to create various image files in the login directory for various users. DOSGEN enables you to create different remote boot image files with different names for each user. You then create a text file called BOOTCONF.SYS that tells the system which client should use which file. The BOOTCONF.SYS configuration file matches workstation NIC node addresses with remote image files.*

Well, that completes our discussion of managing the NetWare workstation. By now, our Park Place guests should be snug and cozy in their rooms with plenty of towels, cable TV, and a mint on their pillow. Remember, the workstation is the key interface point for NetWare users to the LAN. Now that the server has been configured and the workstations are connected, it's time to walk through the four main CNA management tasks:

- Login scripts

- User interface

- NetWare backup

- Remote management facility

It all starts with the login script. Once the server has been initialized and the workstation connected, the user logs in. This is NetWare registration. After a user logs in, the login scripts run and access certain user interface functions, such as menu systems, application software, and e-mail. To keep everybody happy, the system manager must perform routine maintenance tasks and a NetWare backup. Finally, the remote management facility enables the CNA to have a sick day once in a while and retain peace of mind, knowing that NetWare management is just a phone call away.

Let's start with login scripts.

# Login Scripts

T
AKE A MOMENT NOW to revisit NetWare registration and see how login scripts can please your frequent users, just as Park Place staff strives to please its frequently returning guests.

Once users have been authenticated with a valid username and password, the system greets them with login scripts. These are the mints on the user's pillow. NetWare provides various login scripts for system-wide and user-specific configurations. In addition, login scripts can establish important session-specific environments such as drive mappings. Think back for a moment to our discussion of drive mappings and remember that they are temporary user mappings that point to specific areas of the shared disk. Drive mappings are activated each time a user logs in and normally must be defined by the user each time. Login scripts enable the system to establish and define more permanent custom user configurations—transparent to the user.

*NetWare provides various login scripts (batch files for the network) for system-wide and user-specific configurations.*

Login scripts are batch files for the network. You are responsible for creating login scripts that are both productive and easy to maintain. Net-Ware accepts three types of login scripts—system, user, and default. The *system login script* provides user configurations and system-wide drive mappings for everybody who logs in to the network. The *user login script* is a user-specific script that provides user-customized configurations—each user executes his/her own script. The *default login script* executes if there is no user script. The default login script contains minimum drive mappings and system configurations.

*Although login scripts are not required, they are an affordable luxury. A well-designed and well-written system login script can save the system manager literally hours of individual workstation configuration. I recommend that you make use of this NetWare tool for decreasing your maintenance load and increasing your quality of worklife.*

In this section, we will explore the details of these three login script types. In addition, we will bolster our NetWare utility belt with a comprehensive understanding of NetWare login script commands and their syntax.

*Ability is of little account without opportunity.*

*Napoleon Bonaparte*

# Login Script Types

You just learned that there are three types of NetWare login scripts—system, user, and default. All three work in coordination to provide system-wide drive mappings and user-specific customization. Let's take a closer look.

### System Login Script

The system login script provides a facility for system-wide drive mappings. The system login script is executed by all users as soon as they log in. This script can only be created and edited by the supervisor (under the Supervisor

Options menu of SYSCON). The system login script is a special text file—NET$LOG.DAT. It is stored in the SYS:PUBLIC directory so all users can access it. The system login script file must consist of valid login script commands and be organized according to NetWare login script syntax and conventions.

### User Login Script

The user login script is a user-specific script. It provides customization at the user level. The supervisor can use this script to further customize user parameters beyond the system login script. The user login script typically contains user-definable drive mappings and commands that are customized for particular individuals.

Although the user script is a nice feature, it can quickly become a maintenance nightmare—imagine hundreds and hundreds of user login scripts to constantly maintain. The user login script is the text file LOGIN. in each user's unique SYS:MAIL\userid directory. In our discussion of directory structures, recall that there is a system-generated series of user directories under SYS:MAIL. This subdirectory stores user-specific configuration files such as the user login script.

*The intelligent system manager can create an effective system login script that makes user login scripts obsolete. Doing so provides the flexibility of user customization while retaining the ease of maintenance and centralization of one system script. Try hard to fit all of your login script commands into one system login script!*

### Default Login Script

The default login script is activated only when a user login script doesn't exist. The default login script contains some basic mappings for the system and a COMSPEC command that points to the appropriate network DOS directory. The default login script cannot be edited because it exists as part of the LOGIN.EXE system file. The default login script was created and is maintained by NetWare and therefore cannot be edited, modified, or deleted.

Earlier you learned that the ideal scenario is to have a system login script with no user login script. In this case, the default login script would execute after the system login script. The downside to this is that the default login script contains specific system-wide mappings that stomp all over the already created system login script mappings.

Various strategies can remedy this situation. One is to create a user login script with just one line. Although this strategy is effective, it defeats the purpose of having one centrally located login script—thus, you still have to manage a billion or so user scripts. The best strategy is to employ the EXIT command and bypass the user and default login scripts altogether. We will discuss this option a little later.

### Login Script Execution

*A NetWare login script—system, user, or default—must comprise valid login script commands and recognizable identifier variables.*

It is important to have a firm understanding of how login scripts relate to each other and how they are executed. The system script executes first and contains system-wide configurations. If a user login script exists, it will execute after the system login script. Once the user login script has been executed, the system will return to the NetWare prompt—at which point the user has control of the system. If a user login script does not exist, the system will automatically execute the default login script (part of the LOGIN.EXE file). The default login script will also execute when no system or user login script exists. This is typically when the system is first created.

Again, the ideal scenario is one system login script and no user or default script. We'll talk about how to do this in a moment.

*Consider the postage stamp, my son. It secures success through its ability to stick to one thing till it gets there.*

*Josh Billings*

## Login Script Commands

Login scripts consist of commands and identifiers just like any other program or batch file. A NetWare login script—system, user, or default—must comprise valid login script commands and recognizable identifier variables. In addition, the script must follow valid syntax conventions. The syntax for login script programming is quite simple—each line begins with a login script command and must contain either an identifier variable or a fixed value. For example, consider the following line:

```
MAP U:=SYS:USERS\%LOGIN_NAME
```

This uses proper login script syntax: It contains the login script command MAP and the login script identifier variable %LOGIN_NAME. Identifier variables are useful login script components that provide diverse customization. The idea is to establish one login script command that serves various users. For example, the %LOGIN_NAME identifier variable will return the value of each user's login name depending on who logs in. This is particularly useful for mapping user directories in a system login script. Remember, the ideal scenario is to have one login script that customizes both system-wide and user-specific environment variables. This is made possible through the use of identifier variables. Some of the more useful login script identifier variables are:

- MEMBER OF "*group*"
- DAY
- DAY_OF_WEEK
- YEAR
- GREETING_TIME
- FULL_NAME
- LOGIN_NAME
- USER_ID
- MACHINE
- OS
- OS_VERSION

Identifier variables (Figure 11.7) are preceded by a % sign and must be capitalized. So, where do we go from here? Well, to create a productive Net-Ware environment, you will need to have a firm understanding of all the login script commands and how they are used in each system, user, and default script. In the remainder of this section we will focus on the fourteen most recognizable NetWare login script commands. In addition, we will discuss how they are used to optimize the system and user environment. Remember,

| Identifier variable | Function |
|---|---|
| **CONDITIONAL** | |
| **ACCESS_SERVER** | Returns TRUE if Access Server is Functional, otherwise FALSE |
| **ERROR_LEVEL** | An Error Number, 0=No Errors |
| **MEMBER OF _"group"_** | Returns TRUE if member of group, otherwise FALSE |
| **DATE** | |
| **DAY** | Day number (01-31) |
| **DAY_OF_WEEK** | Day of week (Monday, Tuesday, etc.) |
| **MONTH** | Month number (01-12) |
| **MONTH_NAME** | Month name (January, June, etc.) |
| **NDAY_OF_WEEK** | Weekday number (1-7, Sunday=1) |
| **SHORT_YEAR** | Year in short format (88, 89, etc.) |
| **YEAR** | Year in full format (1988, 1989) |
| **DOS ENVIRONMENT** | |
| **< >** | Use any DOS environment variable as a string |
| **NETWORK** | |
| **NETWORK_ADDRESS** | Network number of the cabling system (8 hex digits) |
| **FILE_SERVER** | Name of the filer server |
| **TIME** | |
| **AM_PM** | Day or night (am or pm) |
| **GREETING_TIME** | Morning, afternoon, or evening |
| **HOUR** | Hour of day or night (1-12) |
| **HOUR24** | Hour (00-23, midnight = 00) |
| **MINUTE** | Minute (00-59) |
| **SECOND** | Second (00-59) |
| **USER** | |
| **FULL_NAME** | User's full name (from SYSCON files) |
| **LOGIN_NAME** | User's unique login name |
| **USER_ID** | Number assigned to each user |
| **WORKSTATION** | |
| **MACHINE** | The machine the shell was written for, e.g., IBMPC |
| **OS** | The workstation's operating system, e.g., MSDOS |
| **OS_VERSION** | The version of the workstation's DOS |
| **P_STATION** | Station number or node address (12 hex digits) |
| **SHELL_TYPE** | The workstation's shell version |
| **SMACHINE** | Short machine name, e.g., IBM |
| **STATION** | Connection number |

our focus here is to create _one_ system login script that can satisfy both our system-wide and user-specific needs.

Of course the world is full of weird exceptions. Identifier variables can be entered lowercase without a preceding % sign only if they are outside of quotes and separated by semicolons (;). In this case, the line:

```
WRITE "GOOD %GREETING_TIME, %LOGIN_NAME!"
```

would become really ugly:

```
WRITE "Good ";greeting_time;", ";login_name;"!"
```

Do yourself a favor and stick to the easy way—UPPERCASE with a percent sign (%).

*If I were you, I would focus on the following login script commands and how they can be combined with identifier variables to create a productive system login script. Some of the most important commands are MAP, WRITE, COMSPEC, REM, IF...THEN, DRIVE, and EXIT. See the Snouzer example at the end of this chapter.*

## COMSPEC

COMSPEC (COMmand SPECifier) is a crucial login script command. It redirects the DOS COMMAND.COM file to the appropriate NetWare DOS directory. This step is required because as applications load into workstation memory, they have a tendency to knock the COMMAND.COM file out of RAM. If an application loads itself and unloads the COMMAND.COM file, the system has to know where to go to find COMMAND.COM. That's where COMSPEC comes in—it tells NetWare where to find the command processor. Without it, users will receive one of these messages: `Invalid COMMAND.COM`, `COMMAND.COM cannot be found`, or `Insert boot disk in drive A`. These messages can be quite disruptive to users in a network environment.

COMSPEC tells the system where to search for the appropriate COMMAND.COM. Keep in mind that each version of DOS on each of your workstations supports a different type of COMMAND.COM. You must use the DOS directory structure discussed earlier to store the different COMMAND.COM files. In addition, use a drive mapping—typically S2—to make them easier to find.

Three identifier variables enable you to map the appropriate search drive to the appropriate DOS subdirectory based on which machine was used. This is an effective strategy when used in combination with the COMSPEC command. We will talk about these identifier variables and mapping DOS directories later when we get to the MAP command. At this point, it is important to note that COMSPEC is an important login script command that provides support for COMMAND.COM redirection. The syntax for COMSPEC is:

```
COMSPEC=S2:COMMAND.COM
```

Remember, this command line must follow the appropriate MAP S2 command. Refer to the MAP command later in this section for a discussion of S2, COMSPEC, and DOS.

### DISPLAY/FDISPLAY

You can use the DISPLAY and FDISPLAY login script commands to display a text file as soon as users reach a certain point in the login process. The text file is displayed on the screen in its simplest format, without any control codes or formatting characters. If a text file contains such characters, the DISPLAY command will display them as ASCII bullets. This can be quite distracting for users who see garbage all over the screen. The FDISPLAY command filters these types of text files and won't display control codes—the characters are filtered out and only the text is displayed. The syntax of DISPLAY and FDISPLAY are identical:

```
DISPLAY textfile
```

When the login script execution comes to this line, the script seeks out the selected text file and displays it. This particular command is useful when combined with the PAUSE command—the system pauses execution until a key is pressed. Without the PAUSE command, the text display will go by on the screen very quickly.

### DRIVE

The DRIVE command is used by the system manager to specify to what drive and directory NetWare should switch once login script execution has finished. By default, the system will leave the user at the first available network drive—typically F. Drive F is typically mapped to LOGIN, so the user may be confused and think, "Wow, I've already logged in. Why am I back here?" The DRIVE command is an effective strategy for system managers who want to leave users in their own home area—this is accomplished with:

```
DRIVE U:
```

Again, this strategy assumes that you've set up a home directory for each user and it specifies the U drive.

DRIVE can also be useful if you typically use the EXIT command to exit to a menu program or batch file at the end of login script execution. The menu program typically will be stored either in a public place—Z—or in each user's own subdirectory—U. The DRIVE command can be used preceding the EXIT command to switch to the directory where the menu is to be executed.

*When used in combination with the DRIVE command, EXIT can effectively create a transparent turnkey system whereby users log in and are automatically left within a menu system.*

### EXIT

The EXIT login script command provides a number of functions. EXIT terminates the login script and executes a specific network program. The network program can be any .EXE, .COM, or .BAT file and must reside in the default drive. When used in combination with the DRIVE command, EXIT can effectively create a transparent turnkey system whereby users log in and are left within a menu system. The syntax for the EXIT command is relatively simple:

```
EXIT "program"
```

*The program name inside the quotes can be a maximum of fourteen characters long. Some system managers find this a harsh limitation, because they want to execute a particular program name with several switches. To remedy this situation, you can create a batch file to enter the appropriate program commands and switches.*

*The key to proper use of the EXIT command is knowing that it will skip any other login script's execution. So, if you include the EXIT command in the system login script, it will skip the user and default login scripts.*

*Earlier you learned that the ideal circumstance is to have one system login script with no user login scripts to maintain. Also, I suggested skipping the execution of the default login script. The EXIT command enables you to do this by exiting the system login script to a menu program—thereby jumping over the user and default scripts. Although this is an effective strategy, it is also dangerous. Keep in mind that the EXIT statement in the system login script will bypass any user login scripts that have been created—past, present, or future.*

## FIRE PHASERS

FIRE PHASERS is a fun command that emits an ear-piercing, *Star Trek*-like phaser sound from the workstation. FIRE PHASERS is useful when you want to draw users' attention to a display. FIRE PHASERS can also be handy when you feel there is a breach in security. The syntax for FIRE PHASERS is simply:

```
FIRE n
```

The maximum number of phasers that can be fired in one command is nine—a one-digit number limitation. If you would like to fire phasers more than nine times, you can simply nest multiple FIRE commands one after another. There is no limit to the number of FIRE PHASERS commands you can have in a row, although they get quite annoying.

## IF...THEN...ELSE

The IF...THEN command is probably the most versatile login script command; it enables you to use script programming logic. IF...THEN checks a given condition and executes your command only if the condition is met. Otherwise, the IF...THEN skips the conditional command. In NetWare 3.1*x* you can add the ELSE statement to selectively execute a given command only when the condition is *not* met. For example, if you would like the system to display a message and fire phasers on each person's birthday, you can use the date identifier variables and the IF...THEN command to search for a specific date. Once the date is matched, the system will WRITE a friendly message. This command is also useful for displaying text messages on Fridays, Tuesdays, whenever there are staff meetings, or when a report is due on a set day.

IF...THEN is also useful in customizing group login scripts. Because there is no facility for group login scripts, the IF...THEN command can be used with the MEMBER_OF_GROUP identifier variable to configure specific drive mappings and configurations for groups of users. The IF...THEN command in combination with the many identifier variables enables the system manager to create one system login script that satisfies all user-specific customization needs.

*Experience is a comb that life gives you after you lose your hair.*

*Judith Stern*

If multiple activities depend on a condition, NetWare enables you to use the BEGIN and END commands in conjunction with IF...THEN. This command combination creates groups of conditional commands, for example:

```
IF DAY_OF_WEEK = "FRIDAY" THEN BEGIN
   WRITE "Welcome to Friday. Glad you could make it"
   DISPLAY Friday.txt
   MAP R:=SYS:DATA\REPORTS
END
```

*NetWare 3.1x supports nested IF...THEN statements to ten levels, whereas NetWare 2.2 doesn't support nested IF...THEN statements at all.*

### INCLUDE

The INCLUDE login script command is provided for cases in which one login script isn't enough. The INCLUDE statement branches to a DOS text file that is written using proper login script conventions. INCLUDE executes the text file as if it were a login script. Once the INCLUDE statement is finished, the original login script continues from the point of the INCLUDE statement. In combination with IF..., INCLUDE customizes the script for specific users and groups.

### MAP

MAP is the most widely used user-specific configuration. Mapping is essential to NetWare navigation and provides a facility for representing large directory paths as drive letters. The problem with mapping is that it's both session-specific (meaning drive pointers disappear when users log out) and user-specific (meaning they're unique for each user). The temporary nature of drive mappings makes them particularly annoying—the complex MAP commands must be entered each time a user logs in. Fortunately, NetWare provides a facility for mapping automation—the system login script.

MAP commands are entered at the beginning of the system login. Also, network mappings are typically activated before search drive mappings—search mappings are a lot more friendly in their acquisition of drive letters. All MAP commands work in login scripts except the MAP NEXT command, which can only be used at the NetWare prompt. The default login script includes two MAP commands:

```
MAP S1:=SYS:PUBLIC
MAP S2:=SYS:PUBLIC\%MACHINE\%OS\%OS_VERSION
```

Earlier we saw the importance of having different DOS versions in the network directory structure, to provide workstation access to the appropriate COMMAND.COM. The MAP S2 command, in conjunction with three identifier variables, enables us to intelligently MAP the appropriate DOS directory for the appropriate version of workstation DOS. The previous S2 command uses three identifier variables:

**%MACHINE**—identifies the machine type—IBM_PC for example

**%OS**—identifies the operating system—MS-DOS for example

**%OS_VERSION**—identifies the DOS version—v7.02 for example

*The %MACHINE variable can be customized with the LONG MACHINE TYPE statement in each workstation's NET.CFG file.*

This one command satisfies the COMSPEC requirement for all users on all workstations using all versions of DOS. Remember to put the correct COMMAND.COM file in each %OS_VERSION directory. Also, the directory structure that you created must match the parameters exactly.

### PAUSE

The PAUSE command pauses execution of the login script at a certain point and asks the workstation user to Press a key to continue. As you saw earlier, PAUSE is particularly useful when combined with the DISPLAY and FDISPLAY commands to display large messages one screenful at a time.

### REMARK

REMARK enables you to place comments and documentation in the login script without generating an error. Besides the word REMARK, NetWare supports three other uses of the REMARK command—REM, an asterisk (*), and a semicolon (;). Any text preceded by REMARK is ignored by the system. This strategy is effective for tracking script editing when you have multiple supervisors maintaining the system login script. Using REMARK is also a useful strategy for documenting large login scripts for system managers who follow you.

*When these system login scripts get large and complex, it is very hard to follow exactly what is going on. Novell, for example, in its international headquarters, has a login script that supports the whole organization—it exceeds seventeen pages. This system login script must be highly documented so that various system managers can follow exactly what's going on and how it's being implemented.*

### WRITE

The WRITE command is probably the most versatile login script command. It enables you to display any message on the screen. Any comment you enclose in quotes following the WRITE command displays at the appropriate point during login script execution. WRITE can display not only text but also identifier variable type information. For example, WRITE can display:

```
WRITE "Your username is %LOGIN_NAME"
WRITE "Your workstation number is %STATION"
WRITE "You DOS version is %OS_VERSION"
WRITE "Today is %DAY_OF_WEEK"
```

*Another interesting identifier variable that is used with WRITE is GREET-ING_TIME. GREETING_TIME will return a value of* Morning, Afternoon, *or* Evening, *depending on the time of day.* WRITE "Good %GREET-ING_TIME, %LOGIN_NAME" *provides a nice greeting to all users. Isn't that extra special?*

## # (DOS Executable)

*The DOS executable (#) command is ex-tremely detrimental in any login script.*

The DOS executable (#) command is extremely detrimental in *any* login script. It has been included by Novell in a last-ditch effort to support other commands outside of the login script—but it can cause more harm than good. Any nonlogin script command preceded by the # can be executed from within a login script. The problem is that while the command is running, the entire login script is stored in workstation RAM. Once the # command is fin-ished, NetWare reloads the login script from memory. The problem is that workstation TSRs do not completely free up the conventional RAM after it is released from use by the login script. In many cases, as much as 100KB of workstation RAM can be lost by using the #.

A more effective way to execute non-login script commands is the EXIT command. It is a good idea to use the EXIT command to execute a batch file at the end of the login script. This will remove the login script from memory and execute any list of non-login script commands from within a batch file.

*The CAPTURE command is a critical component in NetWare printing and needs to be executed at startup. This command can be launched from a system batch file upon exiting the system login script.*

## Required Components

At the beginning of this section, we described login scripts as a luxury. Although most of these login script commands are optional, there are three required components in a NetWare system login script:

- A search drive mapping to PUBLIC

- A search drive mapping to DOS

- COMSPEC to the DOS mapping

The search drive mapping to PUBLIC directory can be established by using the following command:

```
MAP INS S1:=SYS:PUBLIC
```

This should be the first search drive mapping and provide the facility for user and system manager access to common NetWare utilities.

The second required component is a search drive to the DOS directories. As you recall, the system manager should create a structure in which each of the DOS subdirectories will have the appropriate version of COM-MAND.COM for each of the workstation DOS types. The required drive mapping would read as follows:

```
MAP INS S2:=SYS:PUBLIC\%MACHINE\%OS\%OS_VERSION
```

This mapping statement would give users a means for finding their appropriate COMMAND.COM after they exited a network application.

The final required login script component is COMSPEC, which ensures that each workstation will reload the appropriate COMMAND.COM at the appropriate time. The syntax for COMSPEC is:

```
COMSPEC=S2:COMMAND.COM
```

These three required components will load whether or not a system or user login script exists, because they make up the fundamental components of the default login script.

That completes our discussion of NetWare login scripts. Keep in mind that login scripts are effective tools for customizing user workstation environments and providing system-wide drive mappings. A well-designed system login script can save you hours of maintenance. Once you have established an effective strategy for NetWare registration and have created a comfortable and productive environment for your users, it is time to move on to the user interface. User interfaces represent the marketing components of the system manager's job. There's nothing worse than grumbling users. A poorly designed user interface can destroy a LAN's productivity, but the flip side is true, too.

*When down in the mouth, remember Jonah. He came out all right.*

*Thomas Edison*

# User Interface

T HE MARKETING WORLD WOULD have you believe that "image is everything!" Well, the marketing types are not far off. The media onslaught of products during the late twentieth century has opened our eyes and emptied our pocketbooks. The goal of marketing is to associate products with positive feelings: a car with the open road, sneakers with athletic ability, a soft drink with beauty.

As the NetWare system manager, you must market the LAN to your users. Help them to associate their workstations with productivity and general peace-of-mind. The trick is to make your users *want* to be on the LAN. User interface is the key. It involves workstation connectivity, application software, menu systems, and e-mail. A well-designed user interface can make your users feel at home with the network. There is nothing worse than users who are apprehensive, intimidated, and threatened by the idea of logging in to a large, impersonal network.

There has been a lot of hyperactivity lately surrounding the Big Brother syndrome. As a result, many people are becoming LANphobic. They feel that becoming part of a larger electronic system will cost them their individuality. One of the most important cures for LANphobia is to provide user customization and individuality for each user. Even though users are part of a larger whole, they can feel as if they are a vital cog in the system's machine.

Another important aspect of user interface is productivity. The system manager's responsibilities revolve around setting up (and continually revamping

*As the NetWare system manager, you must market the LAN to your users. Help them to associate their workstations with productivity and general peace-of-mind.*

which software resides in) a productive software environment for each user. Then users can perform their tasks in synergy with the other LAN users while maintaining some unique job specialization. This strategy is accomplished by loading application software that is not only shared by everyone on the LAN but also customized for each user's needs.

In this section, we will explore the user interface responsibilities of the system manager. Its focus is the installation of application software for specific user productivity and the alleviation of LANphobia by installing a friendly custom menu environment. In addition, we will teach users how to communicate using e-mail. Throughout this discussion, think back to our earlier discussion of workstation connectivity. Remember the different strategies for workstation synergy. Oh, and look out for LAN marketeers—you never know what they're selling!

## Application Software

*It is important to determine whether the application software is NetWare compatible before you buy it.*

As you learned earlier, one important responsibility of the NetWare hotel manager is the development of a productive user environment—that is, a balance between custom user needs and global application synergy. This balance is accomplished through a seven-step approach to installing application software. In this section, we will explore this seven-step approach and learn how it optimizes application software in a NetWare environment.

Note that this is a general discussion. Most application software involves specific instructions for network installation and shared configurations. For the most part, these seven steps will help you to foster synergy between user productivity and shared application software.

*To be absolutely certain about something, one must know everything or nothing about it.*

*Olin Miller*

### Step 1: Making Sure Software Provides NetWare Compatibility

It is important to determine whether the application software is NetWare-compatible *before* you buy it. Approximately 7,000 software packages are compatible and registered with Novell. This compatibility information is important because NetWare makes demands on application software that can cause it to corrupt data or at least impede a productive work environment. NetWare compatibility information can be accessed on NetWire (Novell's electronic bulletin board) or from your local Novell sales and operations center. In addition, you can contact the software vendor for NetWare compatibility information.

### Step 2: Making Sure Software Is Truly Multiuser

For the best results and highest level of user productivity in a NetWare environment, it is critical that the application software support multiple users simultaneously. Many application packages are not multiuser and are designed to be used by one user at a time in a stand-alone environment. Most large software manufacturers now routinely create multiuser versions of popular software. Two signs of true multiuser capabilities are file sharing and multiuser access. Again, it is important to determine the level of multiuser compatibility of software *before* you purchase it so that you can be assured of the most productive user environment.

*Single-user software works in a NetWare environment. NetWare supports any DOS application, but these applications aren't very effective because they don't provide data- and application-sharing capabilities.*

### Step 3: Determining the Directory Structure

Before you can install the software or configure any of its components, have an intelligent organization directory structure in place. Such a structure supports not only the application software but also the data it will generate. Each application should have a specific subdirectory under the directory heading of APPS to avoid cluttering the root directory. This setup also organizes application software for easy, efficient security design. Some applications create their own directory structure during the installation process. Unfortunately, this directory structure is typically created off of the root directory. Although this strategy works fine in a local hard-disk environment, it does not work in a NetWare shared environment. Remember, networks have many more people accessing the shared disk. To fool the system into installing its directory structure in the appropriate place, you can map root the F drive to SYS:APPS. The system will then think that the APPS subdirectory is in fact the root and it will create its directory structure under APPS instead of under the real NetWare root. Tricky.

## Step 4: Installing Applications

The installation process is typically left up to the application. Most applications require you to run a setup or install program. The install program performs two functions: customization of network configurations and file decompression. It is not a good idea to just copy the programs off of the install disks. Instead, use the INSTALL program. If you must copy the disks to the NetWare drive, make sure to use NCOPY—not the DOS COPY command—because it both retains security and is a much more efficient command-line utility for file copying.

Once the network software has been installed, three more steps define special configurations.

## Step 5: Creating File Attributes

Application software must have the correct file attributes so programs can be shared without being destroyed. Application files are normally flagged sharable read-only, whereas data files are typically flagged nonsharable read/write. Most multiuser and NetWare-compatible application software provides information about specific file attributes and the flagging of files for the particular application's needs.

## Step 6: Creating User Rights

The second software configuration is user rights. It is very important to grant user access to network applications. By default, users have no rights to the new directory structure you've created. If you were to install the application and walk away, users would have no access to the applications and would be unable to run them.

Typically, if everyone is going to use all of the same applications, you can use the group EVERYONE to assign access rights and to the APPS directory.

As you recall, access rights flow down to all subdirectories of the parent directory. Typically, the RF (Read and File Scan) rights are sufficient for all files in an applications directory. In addition, all rights except SAM—Supervisory, Access Control, and Modify—are needed in data directories. Application data can be stored in various places depending on the type of data. User-specific data should be stored in the user's own home directory. Group-specific data should be stored in a GROUP subdirectory off of the root. Globally shared data should be stored in a DATA directory off of the root.

### Step 7: Configuring the Workstation

Many programs require special DOS configurations at the workstation in order to run properly. The most notable is CONFIG.SYS (which we talked about in Chapter 1), which customizes the DOS environment. For example, device drivers must be loaded for programs that use a mouse. There is also an environment space variable for large programs that use lots of workstation RAM. Environment space can be increased using the SHELL command. The syntax is:

```
SHELL = C:\COMMAND.COM /p /e:1024
```

*NetWare has a built-in menu system that provides custom, NetWare-looking menus.*

This command provides enough environment space for local DOS applications and NetWare drive mappings—1024 bytes (the default is 256). Chapter 1 gives a more detailed description of the DOS configuration files.

Once the application software has been installed and users have proper access rights, a friendly menu environment should be created to guide users from one application to another. In addition to making it easy for users to access network applications, a friendly environment also helps alleviate LANphobia. Let's take a look.

## Menu Software

NetWare has a built-in menu system that provides custom, NetWare-looking menus. This system uses a simple script file with which system managers create a batch-file menu system. Running this custom menu environment enables large groups to share the same menu file or each user to have his/her own file. In addition, NetWare 2.2 supports a customized color palette that allows each menu or submenu to have different colors and different characteristics—so it can be distinguished from previous menus.

The most appealing thing about NetWare's menu system is that it uses exactly the same function keys and has the same look and feel as all other menus, including SYSCON, FILER, SESSION, and so on. This similarity between menus makes NetWare's menu system easy for users and system managers to understand and maintain. NetWare's menu facility has specific syntax and rules for execution. Before we review them, let's take a moment to talk about how custom menus can be used to enhance transparent connectivity—it's called a *turnkey system*.

### The Turnkey World

A turnkey custom menu environment provides transparent user access from the point of turning on the computer to that of bringing up applications. The idea is to perform as many of the configuration functions and access activities as possible in the background so that the entire system is transparent to the user. The term *turnkey* comes from the notion that you can turn the key and everything takes care of itself. Although a turnkey system is a great environment for users and is simple to use, it is somewhat complex for the system manager to set up and maintain. A turnkey system consists of four components:

- **The workstation boot disk** should contain the hidden system files, COMMAND.COM, ODI files for accessing the NetWare protocol and for attaching to the server. Finally, the workstation boot disk should include an AUTOEXEC.BAT batch file that not only loads ODI and VLM but also moves to the F: prompt and logs in the user.

- **The system login script and user login script** should be maintained so they include an EXIT command that exits to a specific menu format. Whether the menu is user-specific or system-wide is not as important as the fact that the login script itself executes the menu.

- **The menu** must be easily executed and customized to the user's needs. The menu can be executed either from a user-specific directory where a customized menu resides or from a shared directory from which all users are accessing the same menu file.

▪ The fourth component of a turnkey system is the **menu execution options** from within the menu itself. It's necessary for users to have access to all of the applications, functions, and utilities they need. They should all originate from within one central menu program.

NetWare 2.2 and 3.1*x* differ dramatically in their approach toward custom menus—what a surprise! NetWare 2.2 and 3.11 use Novell's old, clumsy proprietary menu system. Granted it's simple, but the memory overhead and lack of performance leave much to be desired. So, Novell solicited some outside help and introduced a new menu system with 3.12—thanks to Saber, Inc. Let's start with a detailed look at the older system, and then explore the new and improved version.

### The NetWare 3.12 Menu System

Novell has revamped NetWare's menu system in NetWare 3.12—with a little help from Saber, Inc. The new menu structure is a "runtime" version of the successful Saber menu system. It follows the same simple Saber syntax and produces familiar NetWare-looking blue and gold menus (GO CAL BEARS!).

*If I were you, I would learn this new NetWare 3.12 menu system, even if you don't plan on using it. Who knows when you might need the knowledge? The good news is that you can sleep through the GETx discussion.*

NetWare 3.12 menu syntax is based on two simple command types: *organizational* and *control*. Organizational commands provide the menu's look and feel; control commands process internal menu instructions. Let's delve deeper.

**ORGANIZATIONAL COMMANDS** Organizational menu commands determine what the menu will look like. The two NetWare 3.12 organizational menu commands are:

▪ **MENU**—identifies the beginning of each menu screen

▪ **ITEM**—defines the options that appear on the screen

*The NetWare 3.12 menu system is only a partial version of Saber's own product. Therefore, NetWare menus cannot be fully customized. For example, system managers cannot specify the location of menus on the screen nor avoid the default color palette—blue and gold. In addition, NetWare's menu system is limited to eleven cascaded screens—one main menu and ten submenus.*

The MENU command is left-justified and followed by a number. A single NetWare 3.12 menu file can support 255 different menus—1 through 255. The menu number is followed by a comma and the title of the menu. Refer to the following sample for exact syntax. Options are listed under the menu command with the ITEM command. Each option is granted a letter (A–Z) and will appear in the exact order in which it is written. If you would like to force a different letter for a particular option, simply precede the text with a caret (^) and the desired letter—refer to the sample .SRC file you'll see in a moment. ITEMs can be customized using one of four built-in options:

- {BATCH}—shells the menu to disk and saves 32KB of the workstation's RAM.

- {CHDIR}—returns the user to the default directory upon completion of the item.

- {PAUSE}—temporarily stops menu execution and displays the message `Strike any key to continue.`

- {SHOW}—displays DOS commands in the upper left corner—only if they are executed.

*If you use the caret (^) for one option, you must use it for all ITEMs under a given MENU.*

**CONTROL COMMANDS** Control commands execute menu instructions. They are the workhorses of NetWare 3.12 menu commands. The six control commands are:

- EXEC—executes any internal or external program

- SHOW—branches to another menu within this menu file

- LOAD—branches to a different menu file

- GETO—gets optional user input

- **GETR**—gets required user input

- **GETP**—assigns user input to a DOS variable

*Although GET commands add power and flexibility to the NetWare 3.12 menu system, they are difficult to program and extremely finicky. Be careful.*

The EXEC command causes particular internal and external commands to be executed. The command can be an .EXE file, a .COM file, a DOS command, or any of the following internal commands: EXEC EXIT to exit the menu and return to the NetWare prompt; EXEC DOS to return to the Net-Ware prompt temporarily; and EXEC LOGOUT, which exits the menu and logs users out of the network. The SHOW and LOAD commands provide the same services from a slightly different angle. SHOW branches menu execution to a menu within the current menu file, whereas LOAD branches menu execution to a completely different menu file. Refer to the sample menu that follows shortly for an illustration of the SHOW and LOAD syntax.

The final three control commands allow for user input. This feature was previously not available in NetWare menus. GETO, GETR, and GETP are powerful commands, but their syntax is a little tricky. The format for these commands is:

```
GETx instruction {prepend} length,prefill, SECURE
{append}
```

*Instruction* is replaced by the message you want to display to the user, *prepend* attaches data to the front of the answer string, *length* is the maximum input window size, *prefill* provides a default response, SECURE displays asterisks in the user window, and *append* attaches data to the end of the answer string. Some rules to follow for GETx commands follow:

- Commands must be entered in uppercase.

- You can use a maximum of one hundred GETx commands per ITEM.

- There's a limit of one prompt per line.

- You can display ten prompts per dialog box— use a caret (^) to force one prompt per box.

*When you are using GETx commands, the Enter key accepts the input*
*but doesn't execute the command. To activate the corresponding EXEC*
*command, the user must press F10.*

The GETO command receives optional input from the user. The GETR command, on the other hand, *requires* input from the user. If the user does not respond, the menu will patiently wait until he/she does. The user can, however, press Esc to return to the previous menu. Both the GETO and GETR commands can only handle one piece of information at a time. The GETP command can handle many pieces of information at once. In addition, the GETP command stores user input as DOS variables—%1, %2, %3, %4, and so on. These variables are usable by other menu commands to further customize user menus.

Refer to the following sample .SRC file for a head-start on NetWare 3.12's new menu syntax:

```
MENU 01,TOM'S MAIN MENU
   ITEM ^AApplications
      SHOW 05
   ITEM ^UUtilities
      SHOW 10
   ITEM ^JJERRY's Main Menu
      LOAD U:\USERS\JERRY\JERRY.DAT
   ITEM ^DDOS Prompt
      EXEC DOS
   ITEM ^LLogout
      EXEC LOGOUT

MENU 05,Applications
   ITEM Word Processing
      EXEC wp
   ITEM Spreadsheet
      EXEC ss
   ITEM Windows
      EXEC win :

MENU 10,Utilities
   ITEM ^1NetWare Menu Utilities
      SHOW 12
```

```
          ITEM ^2NetWare Command-Line Utilities
             SHOW 14


      MENU 12,NetWare Menu Utilities
         ITEM System Configuration {BATCH}
            EXEC syscon
         ITEM FILER {BATCH}
            EXEC filer
         ITEM Network User Tools {BATCH}
            EXEC session


      MENU 14,NetWare Command-Line Utilities
         ITEM List Servers {SHOW}
            GETO Enter Server Name and Option: {} 25, {}
            EXEC SLIST
         ITEM Copy a File {PAUSE}
            GETP Enter Source {} 25, {}
            GETP Enter Destination {} 25, {}
            EXEC NCOPY %1 %2
         ITEM Display a MAP listing {SHOW CHDIR PAUSE}
            EXEC MAP
```

**MENU EXECUTION** NetWare 3.12 menu source files are created using any text editor; their names contain the .SRC extension. These files are then compiled using MENUMAKE.EXE into a .DAT file. The smaller, more flexible .DAT file is then executed using NMENU.BAT. In addition, NetWare 3.11 menu files (with the extension .MNU) can be converted into 3.12 source files (with the .SRC extension) using the MENUCNVT.EXE utility. See Figure 11.8.

*Spoken language is merely a series of squeaks.*

*Alfred North Whitehead*

The NMENU.BAT program is stored in the PUBLIC directory so it can be accessed from anywhere by any NetWare user. In addition, some security concerns affect the execution of NetWare menus, specifically:

- Users must have the Read and File Scan rights to the directory that holds the .DAT file—which is typically their own directory or a shared directory such as SYS:PUBLIC.

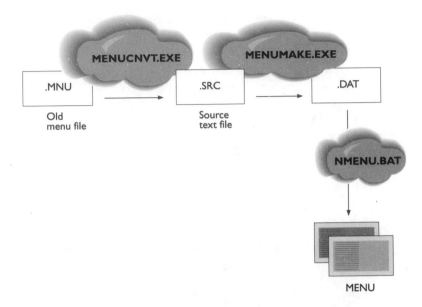

**FIGURE 11.8**
NetWare 3.1x
menu execution

- Users must have Write and Create rights in the directory to which they are currently logged in when they execute the MENU command, because the menu command creates temporary batch files in the current directory. You should have users accessing or running menus from their own directory whether or not they are executing a menu file that exists there.

- If a menu file is going to be used by multiple users, it should be flagged as sharable.

# E-Mail

NetWare 3.12 includes a sophisticated messaging system called the Basic Message Handling Service (Basic MHS). It provides electronic message delivery on a single server. Another product, Global MHS, provides more far-reaching e-mail message delivery. Both Basic and Global MHS are intended to be messaging engines—they aren't e-mail packages. Messages are created in an electronic mail application and delivered by Basic MHS. The e-mail package must comply with the Novell interface standard—SMF, Standard Message Format.

Novell has included Basic MHS with NetWare 3.12. Messaging has recently become one of the most productive features of local area networking. Novell has also included an entry-level e-mail application called First Mail. First Mail is a simple, MHS-compliant application that provides straightforward e-mail on a single server.

## Basic MHS

Basic MHS consists of an NLM at the server and an ADMIN utility at the workstation. To install Basic MHS, follow these simple steps:

1. Load INSTALL at the server and choose Product Options.

2. Add Basic MHS to the Currently Installed Products screen and enter the path to the Basic MHS files.

3. Enter a workgroup name and confirm SYS:MHS as the destination directory.

4. Let the system use your current bindery information to build a list of mail users. Also, choose "login names" instead of full names.

5. Let the installation program change your system login script and AUTOEXEC.NCF files. It will simply set MV= environment variables.

*Create all of your user accounts before you install Basic MHS, so you can let the system create your mail users from the bindery. Otherwise, you have to create them manually using ADMIN.EXE.*

Once Basic MHS has been installed, you can administer the system through the ADMIN.EXE utility in MHS\EXE. It enables you to create new user accounts, modify and delete existing accounts, manage distribution lists, register e-mail applications, and modify the Basic MHS system configuration. To run ADMIN.EXE at your workstation, you must first load the Btrieve Requester (BREQUEST.EXE).

### First Mail

Basic MHS provides the background service of managing user accounts and mail directories, but it doesn't provide a user interface for creating, sending, receiving, or deleting mail. Any e-mail package that uses SMF can use Basic MHS. One such application is First Mail—which is included with NetWare 3.12. First Mail provides basic messaging capabilities for a single server. It is a comprehensive e-mail application and supports both DOS and Macintosh clients. First Mail is installed automatically when you install Basic MHS, and it resides in the SYS:PUBLIC subdirectory as MAIL.EXE.

That completes our discussion of e-mail and user interface in general. Keep in mind that menus, application programs, and user configurations can provide a powerful strategy for warding off LANphobia. But I have found that the most effective strategy is a warm touch and a kind heart. Speaking of happiness, one sure way of maintaining a happy hotel family is to be prepared for emergencies. In the next section, we will discuss the hotel manager's contingency plan for natural and unnatural disasters. As they say, "Preparedness is the first step toward wisdom."

*It wasn't raining when Noah built the Ark.*

*Anonymous*

# NetWare Backup

As the old adage goes, "You never miss anything until it's gone." This saying holds especially true for NetWare data.

AS THE OLD ADAGE goes, "You never miss anything until it's gone." This saying holds especially true for NetWare data. The need to back up NetWare data files is often overlooked because they are not needed on a day-to-day basis. As soon as the data is lost, file backup is the first responsibility that the NetWare manager is reminded of. In many cases, having current backups can be the difference between a successful and prosperous career as a NetWare system manager and the unemployment line. *Never* neglect your NetWare backup duties.

Making backups using NetWare is not quite as simple as inserting a diskette and duplicating files with the DOS COPY *.* command. The complicated process of backing up data on a network involves the bindery, NetWare compatibility, reliability of backed up data, maintenance, and efficient restore procedures. In this section, we will briefly discuss the NetWare backup considerations and spend some time with NetWare 3.12's new Storage Management Services (SMS).

# Backup Considerations

In a stand-alone environment, a backup consists primarily of the data and directories. In a network environment, the backup consists of not only data and directories but also security, file attributes, the NetWare bindery, and users and groups. That is why one of the most important considerations of a NetWare backup system is NetWare compatibility. Many backup systems say that they work well with NetWare or that they are NetWare comfortable, but that doesn't mean that they're NetWare-compatible. The key component in NetWare compatibility is whether the system can recognize the bindery. Backing up the bindery is serious business, because it requires closing and reopening the bindery—you cannot back up a file that is currently open.

Few backup systems know how to access the NetWare bindery. They can't close and open it without bringing down the network. Most major brands of backup devices are, however, NetWare-compatible and provide facilities for backing up the NetWare bindery. Another important consideration is user interface—how easy it is to use? Another consideration is *who* performs the backup. In order to do a full NetWare backup, including the bindery, the user must be supervisor or supervisor equivalent. It's a good idea to perform the backup when no other users are logged in to the system, because the closing and opening of the bindery can create serious problems for users who are accessing the bindery at that moment. Also, it's difficult to back up data in open files. If users are currently logged in using data files or applications, those files will not be backed up.

This scenario brings up another consideration: unattended backup. It seems contrary to want to log in as a supervisor and yet have an unattended backup, because that leaves the system susceptible and vulnerable during non-working hours. The best strategy is to create a supervisor equivalent who logs in at a particular time and whose time restrictions lock the account after, let's say, 3:00 a.m.—so that the system stays logged in for a limited period of time.

*Some of the newest backup systems include a facility that logs the user in, performs the backup, and logs the user out—automatically.*

The final NetWare backup consideration is reliability. It is crucial to implement a schedule that provides complete data security, while at the same time not producing 365 tapes per year. The grandfather method, for example, uses 24 tapes and provides at least 4 or 5 years' worth of data integrity. It calls for recycling tapes every day, week, month, and year. Reliability is maintained by performing periodic restores to nonactive disks so that you can verify that the backup is truly good and that the restore functionality of the backup system works. One of the biggest problems with backup systems these days is that you spend your days, weeks, months, and years backing up data—and never actually restoring it. It could be disconcerting to find out that the system does not restore properly after you have years' worth of backup tapes.

NetWare 2.2 and 3.11 provide a rudimentary backup application called NBACKUP—it's not very powerful. NetWare 3.12 and 4.1, on the other hand, support a much more sophisticated NetWare-compatible backup engine: Storage Management Services (SMS).

## Storage Management Services

Storage Management Services (SMS) comprises a combination of related services that enable you to store and retrieve data from various targets—target service agents (TSAs). SMS is a backup engine that operates independently from the front end (application) and back end (devices). Many manufacturers are currently developing products that support NetWare 3.12's SMS engine. Figure 11.9 shows how five different TSAs can be backed up to three different backup devices.

NetWare 3.12 includes a rudimentary SMS application called SBACKUP. SBACKUP, an NLM that operates at the file server, is efficient because data files travel directly from the server to the attached backup device—hence, no network traffic. In addition, security and performance are enhanced. Finally, SBACKUP supports multiple protocols, internetworking, and four different name spaces. Let's take a closer look at the features and backup/restore rules of SBACKUP and SMS.

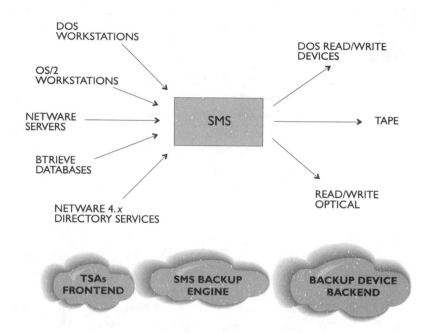

**FIGURE 11.9**
Storage Management
Services

*Novell's NetWare backup strategy has evolved rapidly. NetWare 2.2 supports only NBACKUP, which is a limited workstation product. NetWare 3.11 supports both NBACKUP and SBACKUP—but not SMS. NetWare 3.12 and NetWare 4.x support only SBACKUP and the new SMS implementation.*

## Features

*With the SMS SBACKUP process, the system manager can back up data from and restore data to NetWare 3.12 file servers and workstations.*

SBACKUP provides three main features beyond those of its NBACKUP cousin. First, it can support non-DOS name spaces including DOS, Macintosh, OS/2, and Unix. Second, NetWare 3.12 SBACKUP can be used to back up other NetWare 3.12 servers and workstations. SBACKUP relies on the concept of a host file server and target file server. The host file server runs the SBACKUP NLMs and has the tape backup drive attached. The target NetWare 3.12 file server loads target service agents (TSA) that provide the capabilities for a centralized backup of multiple remote file servers. SBACKUP, like all other facilities, supports multiple file server connections at one time. And, finally, SBACKUP has enhanced performance because it does not cause additional load on the network. The tape unit is connected directly to the file server and SBACKUP communicates directly with the internal shared disk.

In addition, SBACKUP supports a wider variety of backup devices in the form of independent .DSK device drivers. Hardware manufacturers can provide these drivers for any NetWare-compatible backup device. SBACKUP supports three backup strategies (see Table 11.3).

**FULL**   Completing a full backup each time is the most thorough option. It is, however, not practical. In Table 11.3, the Clear Modify Bit option is set to Yes and all other default SBACKUP options are chosen.

**INCREMENTAL**   The second option backs up only the files that have changed since the last backup. Although this choice offers a quick backup, restoring can be a nightmare—you restore one full and every incremental since the last backup. In Table 11.3, the Clear Modify Bit option is set to Yes and Exclude Files That Have Not Changed is set to Yes.

**DIFFERENTIAL**   The final, and most effective, strategy employs a combination of the first two. The differential strategy backs up only the files that have changed since the last *full* backup. This strategy makes for quick backups and easy restores—you restore one full and the latest differential. In Table 11.3, the Exclude Files That Have Changed option is set to Yes and all other SBACKUP defaults are used—including Clear Modify Bit at No.

### Components

SMS includes several modules that work together to perform backup and restore functions. These backup components fit into the SMS model as layers from the bottom device drivers up to the top target service agents (refer to Figure 11.10). As mentioned earlier, SMS relies on the host-target architecture. The SBACKUP host runs the SBACKUP.NLM and communication

| TABLE 11.3 Comparing Three SMS Backup Strategies | BACKUP STRATEGY | BACKUP | RESTORE | MODIFY BIT |
| --- | --- | --- | --- | --- |
| | Full | Slow | Easy | Cleared |
| | Incremental | Quick | Hard | Cleared |
| | Differential | Quick | Easy | Not Cleared |

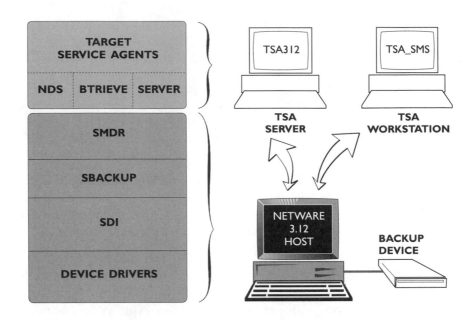

**FIGURE 11.10**
The SMS multilayered
backup/restore model

software, including device drivers and storage device interface. The target software runs on target service agents including file servers or workstations. The heart of this entire SMS strategy is the backup application. In NetWare 3.1*x*'s case, this is SBACKUP.NLM. Let's take a quick look at the SMS model and the different components that together provide reliable backup and restore functionality to NetWare servers.

**DEVICE DRIVERS** The device drivers are at the bottom of the SMS model. They control the mechanical operation of various storage devices and media such as read, write, forward, back, and stop. The device drivers must be specifically configured for each backup storage device that's attached to the host server. The backup application, SBACKUP, communicates with device drivers through SDI, the storage device interface.

Device drivers are loaded at the host server and include WANGTEK.NLM, AHA1640.DSK, ASPINTRAN.DSK, ADAPTEC.NLM, and so on. Device driver information and parameters are stored in the DIBI2$DV.DAT file in the SYS:SYSTEM\DIBI directory. This file contains information about all supported device drivers. As a system manager, you might need to edit this file to remove the lines for drivers you do not need and add lines for drivers that you might be using. You can edit the device driver data file using the following command:

```
LOAD EDIT SYS:SYSTEM\DIBI\DIBI2$DV.DAT
```

*Before you edit the DIBI2$DV.DAT file, change the file's flag to Normal. Then load EDIT and edit the file. After editing the file, change the flag back to Read-Only.*

**STORAGE DEVICE INTERFACE (SDI)**  The next layer in the SMS model is the storage device interface (SDI). SDI is loaded on the host server. It uses device drivers to pass commands and information among the backup application and storage devices.

**SBACKUP**  At the heart of the SMS model is the backup application. In our case, this is SBACKUP.NLM, which is included with NetWare 3.12. SBACKUP works within the SMS architecture to route data requests to the source and then route the returned information back to SDI. It reads and translates requests, determines the type of session being started, and decides which modules to activate. SBACKUP must load on the host server. Later in this section, we will follow the steps of backing up and restoring using the SBACKUP application.

**STORAGE MANAGEMENT DATA REQUESTER (SMDR)**  Moving toward the top of the SMS model is the SMDR requester layer. SMDR is located on the host server. It passes commands and information among the SBACKUP program, target service agents, and SDI. A sample SMDR file for 3.12 is SMDR31x.NLM. Once again, SMDR, like SBACKUP and the device driver, is required on the host server.

**NETWARE TARGET SERVICE AGENTS**  The final components in the SMS model are the target service agents (TSAs). TSAs must be loaded on target servers or workstations. Even if the host server is being backed up, it must also have valid TSA components loaded. TSAs communicate with the backup software using SMDR. SMS supports three main TSA types:

- **NetWare server target service agents.** The most common type of TSA is loaded on a NetWare server. The 3.12 TSA is TSA312.NLM. 4.1 uses TSA400.NLM.

- **Database target service agents.** Database TSAs are loaded on target servers to back up three types of NetWare database: BTRIEVE databases,

SQL databases, and NetWare 4.1 directory services. In the 4.1 environment, the TSA is TSANDS.NLM.

- **Workstation target service agents.** SMS finally supports the long-awaited facility for backing up workstations from a central server. Workstation TSAs are loaded at workstations and allow access to local drives. SMS supports access to both DOS and OS/2 workstations. Workstation TSAs require two components: the workstation TSA—TSA_SMS.COM, for example—and the workstation manager, TSA_DOS.NLM, which runs at the host server.

Although the SMS model can seem to be quite complex at first sight, it mellows with age. Most of these components are automatically loaded when the CNA activates device driver NLMs and SBACKUP.

*If I were you, I would focus on learning the SMS rules and Backup/Restore Steps. All of the other information is supplemental.*

### Rules

As mentioned earlier, SBACKUP relies on the host-target architecture. The SBACKUP host runs the SBACKUP.NLM communication software and device drivers. The target software runs target service agent NLMs or .COM files on workstations. To ensure a smooth and efficient backup, you should review preliminary backup checkpoints before beginning. You should use MONITOR.NLM to:

- Check the host memory and currently loaded NLMs

- Know the session description including the full path of the backed up data

- Know the password if a user has appropriate rights to the file server that's being backed up—whether it's a server or workstation

In addition to these simple checkpoints, make sure to follow these SBACKUP guidelines:

- Never mix SBACKUP and NBACKUP data formats. They are not compatible. Data backed up using NBACKUP must be restored with NBACKUP, and the same for SBACKUP.

- You must run SBACKUP.NLM from the file server. The backup device that you are using must also be attached to the host file server.

- Make sure you have enough disk space on the host server's SYS volume for temporary files and log files—1MB should be sufficient. Continue to monitor the size of these temporary files to make sure that SYS does not run out of space.

- Monitor the size of SBACKUP temporary files on the target server. These files can become quite large if you're using extended attributes or user's link Unix files. The file to monitor is SYS:SYSTEM:SYSTEM\ TSA$TMP.*.

- SBACKUP supports many non-DOS name spaces but the interface still supports only DOS-type file names. When you enter a file name that has a different format, use the DOS equivalent. For example, you would enter an OS/2 file with a thirty-two-character name as its eight-character truncated DOS equivalent.

- Make sure the designated medium has enough storage space when you perform delayed backups.

- Limit access to SBACKUP to maintain the security of your NetWare server and to ensure data integrity. I recommend that only users with supervisor or supervisor equivalent rights be allowed to access SBACKUP.

- Know the passwords assigned to servers and workstations.

- Never mount or dismount a volume during a backup or restore session. It could cause irreparable damage to the volume and NetWare bindery.

*Exit SBACKUP before you unload the support NLMs. Otherwise the server could ABEND—abnormally end.*

If you follow these simple backup guidelines, you should find the SBACKUP backup and restore steps to be straightforward. Let's elaborate on what goes on in each step.

### Backup Steps

SBACKUP backup tasks are more complex than NBACKUP back up tasks, because of the server requirements and support for target service agents. Here's a brief outline of what's involved:

1. **Load the required NLMs.** Before using SBACKUP, you must load the required NLMs. Load the TSA modules on the target file server by typing LOAD TSA at the file server console prompt. The program will automatically load the applicable modules and files. At the host server, the system manager must load the SBACKUP NLM. Even if the host server is the only server being backed up, the TSA module must be loaded as well. SBACKUP is loaded at the host server by typing LOAD SBACKUP. The system will prompt you for a username and password to ensure data integrity and NetWare security. Users accessing the SBACKUP facility can only back up files to which they have sufficient rights.

2. **Select a target for backup.** After you enter the username and password, a preliminary prompt asks you to choose the available device driver. After you select the driver, the main menu appears and you can select a target for backup or restoring. From the list of available target service agents, choose the file server you wish to back up. If it is different from the host server, you will be asked for your username and password on the target file server as well.

3. **Select the storage site using the File Server Backup menu.** The File Server Backup menu provides four choices. First, select Working Directory. The working directory defines a place where the SBACKUP facility can store session-specific log and error files. Next, choose Backup Selected Target. The Backup Selected Target option provides access to a detailed configuration menu.

4. **At the** proceed with backup **prompt, select YES.** The system will respond with a complex media ID. Write the media set ID on the tape cartridge to identify it for restore sessions. Incidentally, the media set ID consists of the medium's label, the cartridge number, and date and time of backup.

5. **At the** start backup **menu prompt, select one of two choices.** Select Now to back up now or Later to defer backup to a future date and/or time. The system manager will be asked to input the unattended backup time in the start backup timer window. The final two choices from the

backup menu allow the system manager to view the backup log and error log.

*I like work; it fascinates me. I can sit and look at it for hours.*

*Jerome K. Jerome*

*When you back up, be aware of rights security. To back up files, you must have Read and File Scan rights. You must have [RF] rights to SYS:SYSTEM to back up the supervisor utility files, for example.*

### Restore Steps

Before you restore data to the target file server, make sure the server has enough free disk space. The file server must have approximately 20% free disk space *more* than the amount needed to restore. The overhead space stores temporary files and additional name space information. Following is a brief outline of the SBACKUP restore steps:

1. **Load the TSA and SBACKUP NLMs.** Before using the SBACKUP restore function, the system manager must load the same NLMs he/she loaded during the SBACKUP backup session. These include the SBACKUP NLM and TSA NLMs on all target file servers. In addition, the system manager must enter his/her username and password.

2. **Select the target for the restore.** The system manager will then be provided with a list of available TSAs for SBACKUP restore. Select the appropriate TSA and enter the username and password.

3. **Use the Restore menu.** The SBACKUP Restore menu has five choices: Select Working Directory, Restore Session, Restore Without Session Files, View Backup Log, and View Error Log. The system manager uses the backup log to determine which data to restore and to identify the media ID for this set. In this step, the system manager can choose the select working directory option and input the same working directory that he/she used for the backup session. The system manager will then choose either Restore Session or Restore Without Session Files. The Restore Without Session Files option checks sequentially through backup entries on a tape to find a session to restore.

4. **When the system manager is prompted to** `proceed with restore,` **select YES.**

5. **When the system manager is asked to** `start restore,` **select YES.** Insert the media when prompted and the `mounting media` message is displayed. Just as for backups, when the restore session begins, the status window displays what data is being restored, what data has been restored, and how much time has elapsed in the restore window. To stop a restore session, press Esc and then Enter to confirm. The session stops as soon as the current data set is restored.

### Backup Management

Well, that wasn't so hard, was it? After all is said and done and you've completed the SBACKUP backup and restore steps, you will find a certain peace of mind that was lacking before you had these hot little tapes in your hands. In addition to the required steps just discussed, there are a few additional management strategies CNAs can use to improve backup performance and maintenance. Let's check them out.

**BACKUP PERFORMANCE ISSUES** The speed of SBACKUP varies depending on the configuration and location of the data being backed up. A file server backing up its own data runs about four times faster than a file server backing up data from a remote server, because communications are required between the host server and any target servers backing up. The communications speed over LAN topologies can dramatically decrease backup performance. To increase the speed of SBACKUP, you can add parameters to the LOAD SBACKUP command to change the number or size of cache buffers. Be aware, though, that if you have a device driver that uses low memory, NetWare could respond with the `Out of Memory` message. In this case, you will have to enter `SET RESERVED BUFFERS BELOW 16 MB=ON` to increase the number of low memory buffers available.

*If you change the number or size of buffers from the default, you must also change the total amount of memory allowed. Also be careful when you increase buffer size. If you are using either an 8-bit or 16-bit controller and you specify a buffer and size combination that exceeds 16MB of memory, corrupted data will be copied to the backup tape.*

You can also increase backup performance by allocating more packet receive buffers. To increase these buffers, add the following SET command to your STARTUP.NCF file:

```
SET MINIMUM PACKET RECEIVE BUFFERS=500
```

We will discuss these and many more performance optimization strategies in Chapter 13.

**MANAGING SESSION FILES**  Each time a backup or restore session is performed, session data is sent to files on the host server. SBACKUP puts these session files in the default SYS:SYSTEM\TSA\LOG subdirectory. Session files contain information that helps you effectively manage network backups. The information also facilitates the restore process and assists you in your trouble-shooting efforts. The two session files that are most relevant to the system manager are the backup log and the backup and restore error file. The backup log consists of all data backed up during the session. It also lists the media ID information, including the session date and time, session description, target from which the data was backed up, and location of data on the storage media. A backup log is created for every backup session.

In addition to the backup log, the system manager can manage the backup and restore error file. This error file is generated on the host server when a particular group of data is initially backed up. It contains the same header data as the backup log file but also contains additional error information, such as the names of files that were not backed up, files that were not restored, who accessed the bindery and when, and other valuable backup and restore information.

If the files for a session are deleted, the session can be restored without the session files. This is not the preferred scenario, but SBACKUP does enable you to re-create the session log and error files through the Restore Without Session Files option on the Restore menu.

# Workstation Backup

As if by some magical inspiration, NetWare finally supports workstation backup in 3.12. SMS uses SBACKUP to back up and restore information from local disks on DOS or OS/2 workstations. You can back up certain directories or the entire workstation, including floppy disks and hard drives.

The workstation backup and restore feature helps you provide additional protection and service to the network users. This is the ultimate in centralized peace of mind. The two main components for a DOS workstation backup are:

- TSA_DOS.NLM at the server
- TSA_SMS.COM at the workstation

The DOS TSA for the workstation is a terminate-and-stay-resident (TSR) program that you run at the workstation that you want to back up. There are various options that the DOS TSA can use to customize the target service agent. Let's take a closer look at some of the more important ones:

- /B=*n* enables you to change the number of buffers TSA will use to back up data. The default is 1KB. However, if you have workstations with 1MB of RAM or greater, the performance can be dramatically enhanced by increasing the default to ten or more. Note: The number of TSA buffers does not affect the performance of restores.

- /D=*x* permits the user to specify drives that are available for backup.

- /N=*name* enables you to give the workstation a name that will appear in the SBACKUP menu.

- /P=*password* enhances security by providing different passwords for each workstation.

- /SE=*server* specifies the name of the host server. This is a required component.

- /T allows the system manager to back up the workstation without knowing the password. In this case, *T* stands for trust.

- /U unloads the TSA from workstation memory.

The following is an example of the syntax used with DOS TSA:

```
TSA_SMS /SE=NIRVANA /P=RUMPELSTILTSKIN /D=C /B=30
```

Notice that we did not enter a colon (:) after the drive letter.

Workstation backup is a cool feature, but make sure that you use the correct parameters with the DOS TSA and that you remember to load the TSA_DOS.NLM at the server.

That completes our discussion of NetWare backup and most of network management in general. Keep in mind that network management is an extremely volatile part of your job. The many activities and responsibilities of the system manager are quite a puzzle. But once you get all of the puzzle pieces in place, the Novell picture is quite beautiful.

# Remote Management Facility

NOW THAT YOU'VE LEARNED about the many roles and responsibilities of the system manager, it's time to take a vacation to Bali. Bali can be quite beautiful this time of year—clear aqua oceans, sparkling sunshine, and incredibly exotic drinks with little umbrellas. Two days into your vacation, your cellular phone rings. It's the poor guy you left in charge of the LAN while you were gone. It seems as though he's having a horrible time getting the print server NLM to load on the server. In addition, he says that there are some memory problems with loading Macintosh name space. So what do you do? Well, you have two choices:

- Hop on a plane and fly back to the office, cutting your vacation short and fixing the problem in person.

- Implement NetWare's built-in Remote Management Facility (RMF). It enables you to hook up your notebook modem to the cellular phone and dial up the network from Bali.

In addition, RMF enables you to access the file server console from a remote workstation. Let's work out how you would implement RMF to fix the network problem—before your drink gets warm.

*Netware's remote management capability enables you to manage all your NetWare file servers from one location. Hence, a workstation can act as a file server console.*

## RMF Components

The remote management capability of NetWare enables you to manage all your NetWare file servers from one location. Hence, a workstation can act as a file server console. This ability is particularly useful because file server security states that the file server should be locked away in a cabinet with no monitor and no keyboard. This can be troublesome when you need to load and unload NLMs or use the MONITOR facility for routine network monitoring.

RMF supports both access from a workstation or access from a modem. The feature consists of two main components:

- The RMF NLMs

- The RMF console program

The RMF NLMs are broken into two parts: the REMOTE.NLM and connection NLM. The REMOTE.NLM manages the information exchange to and from the workstation and the server. REMOTE.NLM provides the facility for using RMF and defining an RMF password. The connection NLM provides communication support for remote workstations and the REMOTE.NLM.

When the system manager is accessing REMOTE.NLM from a modem, the connection NLM is RS232.NLM. In the other scenario, when the system manager is accessing REMOTE.NLM from a workstation on the LAN, the connection NLM is RSPX.NLM. In either case, the remote NLM must be loaded before the connection NLM.

*The REMOTE.NLM provides the facility for creating a user password by typing* LOAD REMOTE password*. This facility creates a security risk, because the system manager is tempted to put the* LOAD REMOTE password *command in the AUTOEXEC.NCF. The AUTOEXEC.NCF is a text file that can be viewed by any user on the LAN who has access to the SYSTEM subdirectory. NetWare solves this problem by making the supervisor's password a default password for remote management. The system manager can simply load REMOTE without a password, in which case the supervisor's password would be the remote management password.*

The second major component of remote management is the remote management program file. This program utility provides the capabilities to:

- Perform all tasks available at the file server console

- Scan directories

- Copy files to but not from directories on the server

If the system manager is accessing the remote console from a modem, the remote program utility is ACONSOLE.EXE. If the REMOTE.NLM is being

accessed from a workstation on the LAN, the remote management utility is
RCONSOLE.EXE. In either case, RCONSOLE or ACONSOLE is executed
from a remote workstation. Let's dive into deep water by exploring how
RCONSOLE and ACONSOLE work in the remote management environment.

# RCONSOLE

RCONSOLE provides the ability for system managers to remotely access
the file server console from a workstation attached to the same LAN. The
RCONSOLE utility is a supervisor utility, so it only resides in the SYSTEM
subdirectory. Once the system manager executes RCONSOLE.EXE, the preliminary remote management menu appears. This menu shows a list of all
available file servers. Each server on the network that is available to this
workstation and has the REMOTE NLM and RSPX.NLM loaded will appear on the list. The system manager simply chooses the file server and enters
the appropriate password. Then the system will automatically jump to the file
server console screen.

The console screen will appear as it was left during the previous session. It
could be in various states. That is to say, the MONITOR NLM could be running with the worm screen saver, the console prompt could appear with the
colon (:), or the TRACK ON or TRACK OFF facility could be activated, in
which case the screen would be displaying a list of file server routing activity. In
any case, the system manager now has direct access to the file server console
and can exercise any command at the console that could otherwise be
entered had the system manager actually been at the file server.

An additional list of available options can be activated by pressing the
asterisk key (*) on the numeric keypad. Doing so brings up the Available
Options menu for RCONSOLE (Figure 11.11), which has the following
six options:

- Select a screen to view

- Directory scan

- Transfer files to server

- Copy SYSTEM and PUBLIC files

**FIGURE 11.11**
The Available Options
menu of RCONSOLE

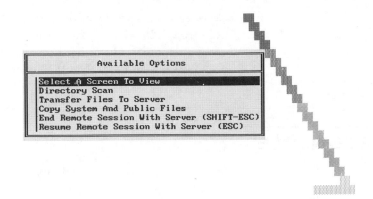

```
                    Available Options
 Select A Screen To View
 Directory Scan
 Transfer Files To Server
 Copy System And Public Files
 End Remote Session With Server (SHIFT-ESC)
 Resume Remote Session With Server (ESC)
```

*A CONSOLE is unique because it enables the system manager to access the file server console from a remote, remote, remote, remote workstation— such as Bali.*

▪ End remote session with server

▪ Resume remote session with server

The Select a Screen choice enables the system manager to move from one file server screen to another. The Directory Scan provides the facility for a scan of file server directories. Transfer Files to Server enables the system manager to transfer files from the local workstation to the file server hard disk. Copy SYSTEM and PUBLIC Files is a similar function that permits the supervisor to copy the SYSTEM and PUBLIC files from the diskettes located at the remote workstation. This choice would be used if the supervisor were using a remote workstation to install NetWare on an existing server. Pressing Shift-Esc will end the remote session with the server and pressing Esc will return to the file server console.

*Whenever a remote session is granted to either RCONSOLE or ACONSOLE, the file server broadcasts a message to the error log and console prompt, indicating that a remote session was attempted at a particular node address and that it was, in fact, granted at a particular node address. This information is particularly useful for system managers who are tracking who is trying to access the file server console using the RMF.*

# ACONSOLE

ACONSOLE is unique because it enables the system manager to access the file server console from a remote, remote, remote, remote workstation—such as Bali. This remote workstation is attached to the file server by modem. The modem must be attached directly to the file server and does not provide any facility beyond access to the file server console. This is not an option for system managers who are interested in providing remote access to the LAN for their users. Remote access for users would have to go through a communications gateway providing login security, and so on.

*Novell provides a gateway called the NetWare Access Server, which provides simultaneous login sessions from a single communications gateway.*

ACONSOLE permits a remote workstation with a modem to attach directly to the file server console and perform the same activities as RCONSOLE over modem lines. ACONSOLE relies on the REMOTE.NLM and the RS232 communications NLM. The ACONSOLE.EXE file also exists in the SYSTEM subdirectory, but it must be copied to a diskette or to the hard drive of the remote machine. The ACONSOLE main menu has two choices:

- Connect to remote location

- Configure modem

The Configure Modem option enables the system manager to configure the modem at the remote workstation and establish common parameters with the file server's modem, such as speed, parity, and stop bits. Configuration of the file server modem is performed using the RS232 NLM. Once the modem is configured, the system manager can use the Connect to Remote Location option to access the server console. At this point, the system manager must provide a phone number and appropriate communications protocols. Incidentally, the ACONSOLE remote location facility provides a built-in database for multiple locations using multiple phone numbers.

Once an ACONSOLE session has been activated, the system manager can use the asterisk key on the number pad to bring up the same remote console menu. Refer again to Figure 11.10. One interesting problem presents itself when upgrading or installing file servers from remote locations. Copying the SYSTEM and PUBLIC files can be quite cumbersome: The 15 to 20 megabytes worth of diskette files can take days if copied from a remote asynchronous connection. If the system manager is installing NetWare using the ACONSOLE facility, he/she must ship the SYSTEM and PUBLIC diskettes to the remote location and have somebody at that location insert the diskettes at the appropriate times at the physical file server. Doing so will expedite the remote installation procedures.

Let's review your actions in Bali. Well, you pulled up your ACONSOLE utility from your notebook computer, attached it to the cellular modem, and called up the office file server console. You activated the print server utility and loaded the appropriate name space modules for Macintosh. You performed all this simple network management from Bali and did it before your exotic drink got warm. Let this be a lesson to all of you that all work and no play makes Johnny and Jane dull kids!

*Great minds have purposes, others have wishes.*

*Washington Irving*

*Well, that's it for NetWare hotel management. You learned about the lobby, gift shops, pillow mints, registration, marketing, conventions, and emergency plans.*

Well, that's it for NetWare hotel management. You learned about the lobby, gift shops, pillow mints, registration, marketing, conventions, and emergency plans. In addition, you gained some valuable expertise on network management from Bali. The most important part of NetWare network management is to develop a management plan and stick to it like glue. This management plan can enable you to remain consistent and comprehensive in your management duties. In addition, the NetWare management plan can bail you out of some sticky network situations.

The next place to visit is the Park Place restaurants, where you'll learn all about how the chef prepares gourmet meals and monitors room service. As the NetWare chef, you will develop an effective and efficient printing philosophy. There is an art to NetWare printing just as there's an art to preparing fine cuisine. No cookbooks here!

# Exercise 11.1: Matching Server Startup Events

Server startup management is integral to the system manager's job. Place the following server startup events in the order in which they occur:

<table>
<tr><td>

Create AUTOEXEC.NCF

Load SERVER.EXE

Create SYS

Use FDISK

BIND IPX TO NE2000

Create NetWare Partition

Copy SYSTEM and PUBLIC files

IPX NETWORK NUMBER CAFE

LOAD ISADISK

Use FORMAT

Boot DOS

Load STARTUP.NCF

LOAD NE2000

Copy SERVER.EXE to C:\SERVER.312

</td><td>

HAPPENS EVERY TIME

1.

2.

3.

4.

5.

6.

7.

HAPPENS ONLY ONCE

1.

2.

3.

4.

5.

6.

7.

</td></tr>
</table>

## CASE STUDY IV

# Creating a NET.CFG File for Snouzer, Inc.

THROUGHOUT THIS BOOK, we've been working with Snouzer, Inc. to design, build, and manage that company's NetWare LAN. One of the most important CNA tasks is efficient workstation automation. To customize the Snouzer network at the workstations, you need to build a TEMPLATE.CFG file and copy it to all workstations. Let's review Snouzer's workstation requirements:

- Snouzer is using ODI drivers with the NE2000 NICs. Each workstation will be using interrupt 5, I/O port 320, and the 802.3 frame type.

- Staff will be using Microsoft Windows with up to sixty open files and many tasks.

- Most of the machines will be Compaq computers using Compaq DOS.

- The preferred server for most of the workstations in this LAN will be NIRVANA.

- Staff will be using RPRINTER over routers.

- Q should be the first network drive.

- Snouzer plans to use approximately fourteen servers.

- Some workstations will have to connect to all of the file servers simultaneously.

- The network managers would like to load the connection table in low memory for a more stable interaction between the NetWare connectivity files and their local configuration settings.

Now it's your turn to create NET.CFG for Snouzer's workstations. When you're done, check your answers against those in Appendix D.

# Exercise 11.2: Debugging Login Script Commands

Locate and correct the errors in the following login script:

**1.**   TURN MAP DISPLAY OFF

**2.**   MAP S1:SYS: PUBLIC

**3.**   MAP SEARCH 2:+PUBLIC\%MACHINE\%OS¦%OS VERSION

**4.**   COMPEC S2:COMMAND .COM

**5.**   MAP 1;=SYS;USERS\LOGIN NAME

**6.**   MAP 2: =SYS:USERS\LOGIN NAME\REPORTS

**7.**   MAP S3: =SYS:APPLIC\WP

**8.**   MAP S4: =SYS:APPLIC\DATABASE

**9.**   WRITE: "GOOD GREETING TIME, %LOGIN NAME

**10.**   WRITE "THE TIME IS"

**11.**   WRITE "TODAY IS% DAYOFWEEK, %MONTHNAME % DAY

**12.**   If %2 ="DATABASE" THEN BEGIN

**13.**   MAP 3; SYS\DBDATA

**14.**   END

**15.**   DISPLAY SYS:SUPERVISOR\MESSAGE.TXT

**16.**   TURN MAP DISPLAY ON

**17.**   MAP

See Appendix D to check your answers.

# CASE STUDY V

## Writing Login Scripts for Snouzer, Inc.

THE FIRST OF TWO procedures for implementing Snouzer, Inc.'s network management is login scripts. Although the company doesn't care how you implement these customizations, the managers would like them to be as user-specific as possible. In the login script section of this chapter, you learned that the system manager's responsibility is to create one system login script that satisfies all user needs. In this exercise, we will focus on designing a system login script for Snouzer, Inc., that satisfies users' needs while maintaining a single point of network management.

Sophy has made some straightforward requests with respect to the NetWare system login script. Following is a detailed list of the components as they should appear in the Snouzer, Inc. system login script. Use a login script worksheet to design your script on paper. Then use the SYSCON menu utility to implement the Snouzer, Inc. login script. Incidentally, the system login script choice is one of the Supervisor options of SYSCON. The script should contain:

- A system greeting that includes the username and date.

- Regular drive mappings as designed in Case Study II.

- Search drive mappings as designed in Case Study II. Keep in mind that some of the regular drive mappings are group-specific; to implement these in the system login script, you must use the IF…THEN login script commands.

- A COMSPEC to search drive 2.

- Sophy would like you to fire phasers and write a message stating that it's Friday for every Friday.

- Also, Sophy would like to display a large text file called PAY.TXT on the 20th of every month. It should display the information that today is payroll day and that employees should turn in all payroll information.

- You should input a PAUSE command after the FDISPLAY so that it will show on the screen.

- Sophy would like all users to jump directly into a user-specific menu from the login script. The user-specific menu will be defined in Case Study VI.

Once the system login script has been created according to Snouzer, Inc.'s specification, you can focus on the user interface. User interface requirements consists of a batch file for executing from the login script and a user-specific menu. Let's move onto Case Study VI, in which you'll build Snouzer's menu system.

# Building a Menu System for Snouzer, Inc.

THE SECOND COMPONENT in Snouzer, Inc.'s network management is the development of a transparent user interface. A transparent and friendly user interface is the most important component in defeating LAN-phobia. Snouzer, Inc.'s managers have little experience using networks and would appreciate a simple user interface. To develop a simple user interface, you must first program the login script to execute a user-specific menu. In addition, you must establish CAPTURE commands and other user-specific configurations before users execute the menu. In order to accomplish all of these, you will exit the system login script to a batch file called START.BAT. START.BAT will reside in each user's subdirectory and should consist of:

- CAPTURE commands
- User-specific configurations
- A menu command

The MENU command will specify a user-specific menu that resides in each user's subdirectory. This menu will be based on a system-wide menu but will contain minor modifications for each user. In this case study, we will concentrate on developing a system-wide template for the user menu and then you can customize it as needed. Snouzer is using NetWare 3.12.

The Snouzer, Inc. menu consists of some straightforward applications and a logout command. The title of the main menu is SNOUZER, INC. The four main title options are:

- Applications
- User Utilities
- File Management
- Logout

The Applications option will consist of a submenu that we'll talk about in just a moment. The User Utilities option consists of a branch to the SESSION NetWare user utility. The File Management option consists of a branching to the FILER user network utility. And, finally, the logout option will exit the menu and log the user out.

The Applications submenu lists all five of Snouzer, Inc.'s main applications. Three of these applications are particularly memory intensive: DBASE, WordPerfect, and 123. The five application options under Applications are:

- ACCT
- DBASE
- WP
- 123
- DESIGN

Furthermore, the ACCT option calls up another submenu with the following options:

- AP
- GL
- AR

The Snouzer, Inc. main menu should be friendly, easy, and productive. In addition, Sophy is concerned about users being confused when they exit the menu to the NetWare command line. To solve this problem, you will create a secure menu system that prevents users from escaping by using Esc. Refer to the answers in Appendix D for a discussion of this unique strategy.

Good luck and happy menu making!

# NetWare 3.12
# Printing

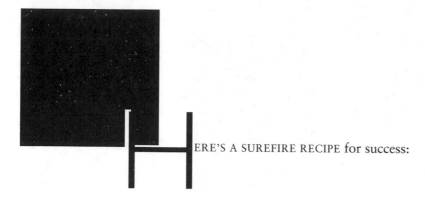

ERE'S A SUREFIRE RECIPE for success:

- 2 cups of technology

- 1 bushel of wisdom

- 7 ounces of creativity

- 1 liter of common sense

- 1 dollop of patience

*Mix the technology and the wisdom into a large bowl. Beat vigorously. Stir in common sense and let the mixture sit at room temperature for an hour. Add creativity and bake at an extremely high temperature for three hours.*

Mix the technology and the wisdom into a large bowl. Beat vigorously. Stir in common sense and let the mixture sit at room temperature for an hour. Add creativity and bake at an extremely high temperature for three hours. Remove from the oven and sprinkle with a little ability and patience. Now you have something.

Park Place owes a great deal of its success to its five-star restaurants. They are world renowned for providing the most exciting culinary treats. The Park Place chef is a master of the trade, responsible for shopping, prep work, baking, and presentation. As the restaurant's shopper, the chef must ensure the best quality foods without sacrificing price or freshness.

Once the chef purchases the raw ingredients, he prepares them for baking, broiling, or cooking. Prep work involves cutting vegetables, peeling potatoes, and so on. Once the ingredients have been prepared, baking, broiling, and cooking transforms the raw ingredients into delectable treats.

Finally, the chef must use his creativity to present the meal so that it's appetizing and pleasing to the eye. This is where the chef gets to show off by creating little animals out of rutabagas.

*It is better to create than to be learned; creating is the true essence of life.*

*Barthold Georg Niebuhr*

A well-designed printing system can be almost as exciting as visiting a five-star restaurant.

In addition to his main responsibilities, the chef must develop interesting restaurant menus and keep on top of the latest in food technology. After all, what would a five-star restaurant be without a robomixer?

As the chef of the NetWare Cafe, you set up and maintain a productive printing environment. A well-designed printing system can be almost as exciting as visiting a five-star restaurant. The NetWare chef is responsible for printing setup (shopping), performance optimization (prep work), printing maintenance (baking), and overseeing user printing operations (presentation).

In this chapter you will learn about the fundamentals of NetWare printing and explore the four roles and responsibilities of the NetWare chef. In addition, you will discover a few strategies for troubleshooting the printing system. Let's begin with a discussion of printing fundamentals and the NetWare Cafe.

*If I were you, I would concentrate on learning the three P's of NetWare printing: print queues, print servers, and printers. Also, notice the relationship among the three and how you set up and manage each component.*

# The Fundamentals of NetWare Printing

ONE OF THE MOST important shared resources in the LAN is the network printer. Printers produce quality hard-copy output for brochures, reports, memos, and general paperwork. Network printing is one of the most productive, useful functions of a NetWare LAN.

Superficially, NetWare printing appears to be easy, but don't be fooled—it is probably the most troublesome and mysterious management issue in the NetWare LAN. The fundamentals of NetWare printing are relatively straightforward, but the demands of the users can quickly frazzle the system manager. NetWare printing is designed around three components:

- The print queue

- The print server

- The printer

The print queue is a shared area on the file server that stores print jobs in the order in which they are received. The print queue lines up various user's print jobs and sends them to the printer in an organized, efficient manner. The print server directs the print jobs as they move from the queue to the network printer. The printer is the output device in a NetWare printing system (Figure 12.1) and it typically receives the jobs and prints them appropriately. Figure 12.1 shows the structure of NetWare's printing system and points out the relationships between print queues, print servers, and network printers.

In a transparent NetWare printing environment, users print directly from their network applications and the output magically appears in the printer

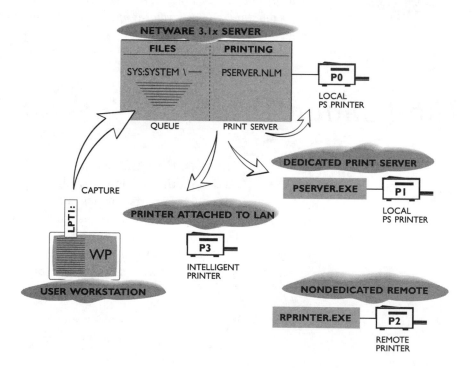

**FIGURE 12.1**
The NetWare printing system

down the hall. This type of sophistication might seem trivial to the user but is a source of great effort for the system manager.

In this section, we will discuss these three printing components in detail and provide an in-depth study of how they affect the NetWare printing system. The system manager must keep on top of these components and have a firm understanding of how they relate to each other. Let's start with print queues.

## Print Queues

*In a printing environment, print jobs stand in line and wait to be sent off to the network printer.*

The word *queue* means "to stand in line." In a printing environment, print jobs stand in line and wait to be sent off to the network printer. Because print jobs are simply data that is being translated by the printer, print queues must exist as directories on the NetWare file server. Print queues are stored as subdirectories under the SYS:SYSTEM directory and are given random, 8-digit hexadecimal names. As print jobs are sent from network workstations to the print queue, they are stored in the corresponding directory as files on the disk. The files are ordered by the print server and tracked on their way from the file server to the network printer.

> *The print server never stores the print job information; it only directs and controls it. All files are stored on the NetWare file server in the queue directory.*

Print jobs are sent directly to print queues in one of two ways: the NetWare CAPTURE command or network application printing. CAPTURE literally captures the local workstation's parallel port and redirects print jobs off to a NetWare queue. Printing from NetWare applications, on the other hand, is a little more sophisticated because those applications recognize NetWare print queues and print directly to them. In either case, the workstation NETx or VLM shell formats the print job so that the network can recognize it and place it in the correct queue.

When print queues are created, the system assigns print queue operators and print queue users. These are special NetWare managers who control and use NetWare print queues. The print queue operator has the ability to add, delete, or reorder the print jobs in a given print queue. By default, the supervisor user is assigned as the print queue operator on all NetWare print queues.

Print queue users can insert print jobs into NetWare queues. By default, the group EVERYONE is assigned as a queue user for all new print queues. You can control who accesses which printers by limiting print queue users.

## Print Servers

The NetWare print server is not so much a physical device as a logical process. The print server can exist as a dedicated workstation or as a process running on top of a NetWare file server. As a dedicated workstation, the print server process runs through a file called PSERVER.EXE that is included with NetWare. As a nondedicated process running on top of a NetWare file server, the print server exists as PSERVER.NLM—a NetWare 3.1$x$ loadable module, or PSERVER.VAP—a NetWare 2.2 value added process (VAP).

In either case, the print server's purpose is to control and redirect print jobs as they travel from NetWare workstations to file server print queues and ultimately to network printers. The print server constantly monitors the print queues and network printers and makes logical attachments from one to the other. When a job is inserted into the print queue, it works its way to the top of the line. At that point, the print server redirects it to the appropriate network printer. In addition, print servers monitor printers to make sure they are not out of paper, off-line, or jammed. If any of these situations occurs, the print server will notify the print server operator or supervisor.

Certain specifications restrict the functionality of the NetWare print server. The print server can have only up to five printers attached directly to it: LPT1, LPT2, LPT3, COM1, and COM2 (COM3 and COM4 are identical to 1 and 2). The print server can service print jobs from print queues on up to eight file servers. In addition, NetWare has provided an auxiliary functionality that expands the five-printer limitation: remote printing. Remote printing allows workstations with local printers to designate those printers as network devices. In NetWare, the print server supports a total of sixteen printers.

Print servers in NetWare can be installed on two devices: dedicated workstations or the file server. The creation of a dedicated print server on a workstation is made possible through the PSERVER.EXE file. In this particular case, the system manager must create a special NET.CFG file on the workstation that defines the command SPX CONNECTIONS = 60. This

*The NetWare print server is not so much a physical device as a logical process. The print server can exist as a dedicated workstation or as a process running on top of a NetWare file server.*

command is required to maintain communications with multiple users, queues, and file servers.

The nondedicated or internal print server is defined as PSERVER.NLM in NetWare 3.1*x* or PSERVER.VAP in NetWare 2.2. In both cases, the print server module runs in parallel to the operating system. NLMs do take up considerable file server resources, but they are well designed and coexist peacefully with the operating system functions. In addition to NetWare's print server functionality, some third-party products provide more tasks and detailed print job accounting. One of the most popular is Bitstream's Mosaic print server software.

*NetWare 2.2 supports PSERVER.VAP on the file server or an external ROUTER. NetWare 3.1x, on the other hand, only supports PSERVER.NLM on the server.*

Each of these two print server strategies has advantages and disadvantages. The advantage of running PSERVER.NLM on a file server is that it does not require additional hardware. The disadvantage is that it partially taxes the server's internal resources—the CPU and RAM. On the other hand, the main advantage of the workstation print server is that it is a dedicated device that doesn't share processes with any other server facility. The disadvantage of a dedicated workstation print server, however, is that it requires additional hardware.

Typically, the minimum configuration for a NetWare print server is an 8088 with a 20MB hard disk and 1MB RAM, although you may be able to get away with 640KB and no hard disk. In either case, these configurations have now been adopted as the industry doorstops. Let's take a closer look at these two NetWare print servers.

### File Server

As mentioned earlier, running the print server process on a NetWare file server requires a NetWare loadable module (NLM) or VAP. The NLM or VAP runs in parallel to the network operating system and shares the same server processor and RAM. Both PSERVERs operate from the SYS:SYSTEM subdirectory. The system manager can activate an NLM print server by typing `LOAD PSERVER print server`. Print server VAPs are automatically activated when the server is booted. In all cases, before the print server can be activated, it must be created and configured in the PCONSOLE utility. We will discuss this part of the NetWare print server setup process later in the chapter.

### Workstation

The process of installing the print server on a dedicated workstation is much more simple. The dedicated print server file exists as PSERVER.EXE. This file runs as any other application program and completely takes over the processor and memory of the workstation. Before PSERVER.EXE can be run, the system manager must attach the workstation to the network cabling by running IPX and NETx. The system manager does not have to log in to this workstation in order for the dedicated print server facility to operate. The facility only requires an attachment—so the system manager could run IPX/NETx or ODI/VLM, and PSERVER.EXE followed by a name for the print server.

*Nothing is really work unless you would rather be doing something else.*

*James Matthew Barrie*

PSERVER.EXE is not a large file, and it can be stored in the root directory of the workstation or on a diskette. Keep in mind that if you are going to run PSERVER.EXE on a dedicated workstation, you must include the NET.CFG file with one line: SPX CONNECTION = 60. This will open up enough connections so that the print server can communicate with multiple users, print servers, and file servers.

To review, print servers are required for a variety of reasons:

- When the number of printers exceeds five

- When printers must be distributed throughout the LAN for location reasons

- When the system manager would like to support intelligent printing devices

- When the printing system supports other file servers from newer versions of NetWare including 3.12 and 4.1

## Printers

The real star of this show is the network printer—the shared device that provides hard-copy output to multiple NetWare users. Shared printers can be attached to the print server, the file server, or local workstations using the remote printing facility. Printers attached directly to the file server use NetWare internal printing functionality—PSERVER.NLM or PSERVER.VAP.

Printers attached directly to print servers are controlled by a dedicated print server and can service users on up to eight file servers. Printers attached directly to local workstations and shared as network devices must use the remote printing facility. Remote printing is handled through a terminate-and-stay-resident (TSR) program called RPRINTER.EXE that runs in workstation RAM. RPRINTER communicates directly with the print server and makes the printer available through the workstation NetWare shell.

In addition to these traditional printing configurations, the industry is providing some new, exciting, *intelligent printers* that are capable of communicating directly with the print server. Intelligent printers have internal network interface cards (NICs) that allow them to attach directly to the LAN trunk. These printers act as print servers. Some examples of intelligent printers include the Hewlett-Packard LaserJet 4si and the LaserJet 5.

Print jobs find their way to network printers through print queues and print servers. The NetWare printing model provides various configurations: one queue per printer, multiple queues per printer, and multiple printers per queue. The system manager must be well versed on NetWare's many printing management issues in order to optimize the printing environment. Printing management is a difficult but rewarding proposition.

*In addition to the hot new printers with internal NICs, some manufacturers are providing little print server boxes that connect any printer directly to LAN cabling. These boxes, like Intel's NETPORT, use a combination of internal processing and firmware to provide distributed alternatives to RPRINTER.EXE.*

## Printing Management

Printing management is at the heart of the NetWare chef's craft. Printing management defines the roles for printing setup, optimization, and maintenance.

In addition, printing management can define certain strategies for approaching printing troubleshooting. Printing setup involves the procedures for creating print queues and print servers, and defining NetWare printers. In addition, during the setup procedure, the system manager must assign queues to printers. Performance optimization involves the organization of printing components to maximize speed and reliability. Printing maintenance allows the system manager to control queues, print servers, and printers on a daily basis. The development of a good printing maintenance strategy will increase the quality of user output.

Let's take a brief look at the four components responsible for NetWare printing management.

### Setup

Printing setup is defined by four steps:

1. Creating print queues

2. Creating print servers

3. Defining printers

4. Assigning queues to printers

The NetWare system manager can implement NetWare printing by using one utility: PCONSOLE. It creates and manages certain aspects of print queues and print servers. In addition, PCONSOLE provides the facility for activating print job configurations. The four steps in setup provide a good framework for vanilla LANs—networks with less sophisticated printing needs. More sophisticated LANs require additional setup considerations: remote printing, multiple file servers, queue design, and custom printer parameters. We will discuss printing setup in depth later in this chapter.

### Performance Optimization

Optimization of the printing environment can spell the difference between a two-star and a five-star LAN. The NetWare system manager must be aware of a variety of performance issues including printing capacity, queue priority, multiple queues per printer, and multiple printers per queue. In addition, the system manager must be well versed in the detailed steps of the printing process. These steps define the print job's path from workstation to queue to print server and finally to printer.

### Maintenance

Printing maintenance monopolizes the NetWare chef's day. Printing maintenance involves the daily routine of controlling and managing print queues, print servers, and NetWare printers. Queue maintenance is performed using the PCONSOLE utility. PCONSOLE provides a print job configuration window that the chef uses to view and prioritize current print jobs—much as orders for a dining party must be prioritized and balanced so all the party's diners get their food at the same time. Print server control involves access to the print server itself—through PCONSOLE or the PSC command-line utility (CLU). The PSC printing maintenance tool provides a wide range of maintenance options. We will discuss printing maintenance and the use of PSC later in this chapter.

### Troubleshooting

Unfortunately, things don't always go as planned in the NetWare kitchen, and the system manager must be light on his/her feet in case operations start falling apart. The good news is that NetWare has a built-in resiliency against printing disasters. The system manager has a wealth of tools available for battling print jobs that don't print properly or print servers that don't load properly. Later in this chapter we will discuss some of the most common printing troubleshooting problems and suggested courses of action. I guess this particular section falls under the category of "if you can't stand the heat, get out of the kitchen."

## Printing Customization

Remember the beginning of this chapter, when printing was called "the most troublesome and mysterious management issue in the NetWare LAN." Know why that is? Because the NetWare printing architecture is so incredibly complex? *Not!* No, it's because there are sooo many users printing sooo many types of print jobs to sooo many kinds of printers from sooo many types of applications.

The incredible variety of printing components puts a dramatic strain on NetWare's straightforward, easy printing architecture. It's similar to what the NetWare chef goes through when faced with ninety-seven zillion types of spices. How does he find just the "right" combination? The trick is, he doesn't! The NetWare chef uses a simple, generic base and then builds on that as needed, like a generic chicken soup stock to which anything from gumbo to matzo balls can be added.

NetWare provides a simple, generic stock upon which to create your particular NetWare printing system. If all goes well, you can spend the rest of your life using NetWare's simple printing architecture and relying on application print drivers for fancy fonts and printing spice. Unfortunately, life doesn't always work that way, and sometimes you are forced to support COMPRESSED, ITALIC, LANDSCAPED, and ENVELOPES from "Joe's Word Processor." In this case, NetWare provides print forms, print modes, and print job configurations. Using PRINTDEF, PRINTCON, and CAPTURE, you can be the hero and support any print job customization "Joe" could possibly ever want!

NetWare printing customization is a great thing but hard to figure out and not well understood. So be forewarned—life is much better without having to customize NetWare print jobs manually. Don't worry, we'll explore these strategies in greater depth later in the chapter.

*So what does all this mean? The real goal in NetWare printing is to magically transform electronic data into a beautiful combination of ink and paper.*

## Printing

So what does all this mean? The real goal in NetWare printing is to magically transform electronic data into a beautiful combination of ink and paper. NetWare provides three ways to do this:

- NetWare-aware applications
- CAPTURE
- PCONSOLE/NPRINT

NetWare-aware applications communicate directly with file server queues. These applications are intelligent enough to understand the sophistication of NetWare printing. NetWare-aware applications, such as Windows and Word-Perfect, print directly to NetWare queues and require no intervention from the system manager. Applications that aren't aware of NetWare queues require a printing facility known as CAPTURE. CAPTURE literally hijacks the local workstation port and redirects print jobs to NetWare queues.

Finally, the user or system manager has the choice of inserting a job directly into a NetWare queue by using the PCONSOLE menu utility or NPRINT CLU. PCONSOLE enables users to choose print job files and insert them into valid NetWare queues. The NPRINT command performs the same function from the command line. When print jobs finally reach the NetWare printer, they contain various customized configurations. These print job configurations can be defined by the NetWare system manager using the PRINTCON menu utility. We will discuss the actual process of printing toward the end of this chapter.

*As machines get to be more and more like men, men will come to be more like machines.*

*Joseph Wood Krutch*

As you can see, NetWare printing is a sophisticated, complex system. NetWare provides various components for reliably moving print jobs from workstation A to printer B. In this chapter, we will explore the four major components of NetWare printing management—printing setup, printing performance optimization, printing maintenance, and general user printing. In addition, you will learn about some common printing problems and possible courses of action—the delights of troubleshooting.

# Printing Setup

T
HE FIRST STEP OF culinary excellence is shopping for the finest ingredients. Similarly, the system manager must get printing started by collecting all the best and necessary resources. Printing setup involves the acquisition of printers, the setup of print servers, and the definition of the NetWare printing environment.

*Printing setup involves the acquisition of printers, the setup of print servers, and the definition of the NetWare printing environment.*

Printing setup is a relatively straightforward task involving four simple steps:

1. Creating print queues

2. Creating print servers

3. Defining printers

4. Assigning queues to printers

*If I were you, I would remember PCONSOLE and focus on the creation of printers—Print Server Information. Also, don't forget the fourth startup step—attaching queues to printers.*

During step 1, the system manager creates the print queues on the system and assigns print queue operators and users. During step 2, the system manager creates the print server and gives the print server a unique name and password. In step 3, the system manager continues with print server definition by defining the printers, assigning names to the printers, and configuring their internal parameters. These parameters include, among other things, port type, interrupt, and serial configurations. The final step in print server setup is assigning the queues to printers. This step is required so that print jobs can find their way from specific queues to appropriate printers.

As discussed earlier, these four steps provide adequate functionality for most vanilla LANs. Unfortunately, just as some restaurant patrons insist on substitutions, some NetWare Cafes insist on pushing the envelope of NetWare printing. For these LANs, NetWare provides some additional setup configurations. In this section, we will explore these considerations, including multiple file servers, queue design, and custom printer parameters. Let's begin by exploring the four standard setup steps in some depth.

## Step 1: Creating Print Queues

Print queues are the central component of NetWare printing, because they provide the link between NetWare workstations and shared printers. Print queues are created using the PCONSOLE menu utility that is stored in the SYS:PUBLIC directory (Figure 12.2).

To create a print queue in PCONSOLE, simply choose Print Queue Information from the Available Options menu of PCONSOLE and press Ins at the Queue Name box. Next, type in a queue name of up to forty-seven characters and press Enter. At this point, the print queue name will appear in the queue names box.

Once a print queue has been created, the system will assign it an eight-digit hexadecimal number and a subdirectory under the SYSTEM root directory. Incidentally, the subdirectory gets a .QDR extension. Using PCONSOLE, the system manager can define other print queue parameters:

**The Current Print Job Entries** screen provides a list of all print jobs that are currently held in this queue. This screen is a central point for queue management and job reordering.

**FIGURE 12.2**
Creating print queues

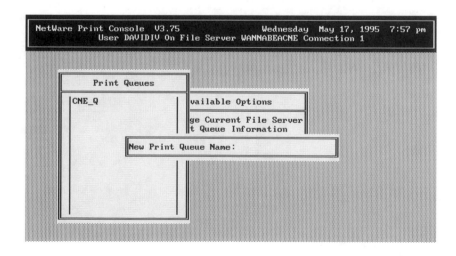

**Current Queue Status** displays the status of the queue with respect to the number of entries in the queue and the number of servers being serviced by this queue and operator flags.

**Currently Attached Servers** is a list of print servers that can service this queue. Those print servers keep track of which network printers are also servicing this queue.

**Print Queue ID** is the 8-digit random number that is assigned to this particular print queue and it matches the subdirectory under SYSTEM.

**Queue Operators** is a list of users who have been assigned queue operator status. By default, the supervisor is the only queue operator.

**Queue Servers** is a list of print servers that can service this queue. It does not mean they are currently attached. The system manager can add or delete print servers from this list.

**Queue Users** includes a list of all users who can add jobs to this queue. By default, the group EVERYONE is assigned as a queue user for all new print queues. Once the print queue has been created, the system manager can move on to defining and creating the print server and attaching a link between the two.

Figure 12.3 illustrates the Print Queue Information screen in PCONSOLE.

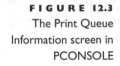

**FIGURE 12.3**
The Print Queue Information screen in PCONSOLE

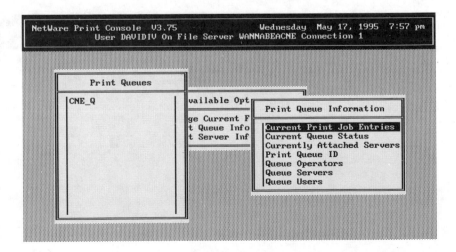

## Step 2: Creating Print Servers

Print server creation consists of two steps: setup and installation. The setup step involves creating a print server in PCONSOLE. The print server installation step involves choosing a print server type and activating appropriate print server files—for a print server on the file server the file is PSERVER.NLM; and for a print server on a dedicated workstation it's PSERVER.EXE.

You set up a print server with the PCONSOLE utility using the Print Server Information menu from Available Options (Figure 12.4). The system manager simply presses Ins at the print server's menu screen and enters the name of a print server.

*I recommend that the system manager use the file server name followed by
_PS to show the relationship between print servers and file servers they
service.*

Once a print server has been created, the system manager can customize the print server configurations through the Print Server Information screen (Figure 12.5). This screen includes the following options:

- Change Password

- Full Name

- Print Server Configuration

**FIGURE 12.4**
Step 2: Creating
print servers

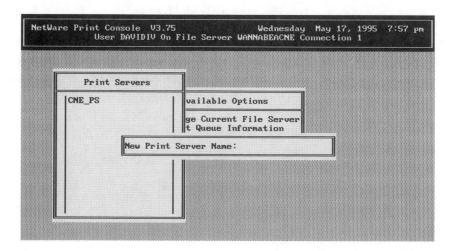

**FIGURE 12.5**
The Print Server
Information screen
in PCONSOLE

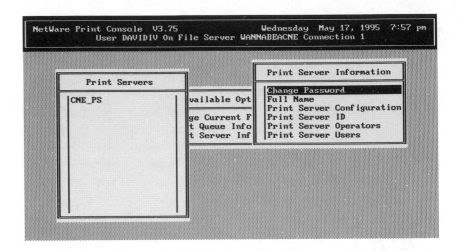

- Print Server ID
- Print Server Operators
- Print Server Users

The Change Password option enables the system manager to assign a password to the print server so that not just anybody can activate it. The Full Name option provides more information about this particular print server and what queues and file servers it services. Print Server Configuration is used for steps 3 and 4 in print server installation. Print Server ID defines the object ID of the print server. This information is not particularly useful because it is not used by any other NetWare configuration. Print Server Operator displays the list of the users and groups who have been assigned as operators for the print server. Print Server Users is a list of users or groups who can send print jobs to printers that are defined using this print server. By default, the Supervisor is assigned as a print server operator and the group EVERYONE is defined as print server users for all newly created print servers.

Once the print server has been defined, the system manager must activate it. Print servers are activated by simply typing PSERVER followed by the name of the server:

At File Server—LOAD PSERVER print server

At Workstation—PSERVER print server

*Before the print server can be properly activated, you must complete setup steps 3 and 4.*

Once the print server has been configured and activated, a seventh choice will appear in the Print Server Information menu—Print Server Status/Control. It enables you to view the status of the print server and provides valuable information about print servers that are currently running. This option is unavailable to the system manager if the print server is not activated. Once the print server has been created and before the print server is activated, the system manager must move on to step 3.

## Step 3: Defining Printers

Printer definition is accomplished through the PCONSOLE utility under Print Server Information. The Print Server Configuration menu provides a list of four choices that involve printer definition:

- File Servers to be Serviced
- Notify List for Printer
- Printer Configuration
- Queues Served by Printer

The printer definition choice is Printer Configuration. Using this option, the system manager defines up to sixteen printers for this print server and customizes their ports and configurations. By default, the sixteen print server printers are assigned numbers 0 through 15, in order. The system manager also has the flexibility of assigning a name to printers so they can be tracked for management and queue assignment.

To define a NetWare printer, choose the printer number from the top of the list (which is typically 0 for the first printer) and press Enter. The printer 0 configuration option, which gives various options for defining, naming, and configuring NetWare printers, appears (Figure 12.6). The first option is Name. The printer name will again define it for printing management and queue assignment. The Type parameter is handy because it enables the system manager to define not only serial or parallel but whether this printer is going to be attached to a remote workstation. The printer types option appears

**FIGURE 12.6**

Step 3: Defining printers

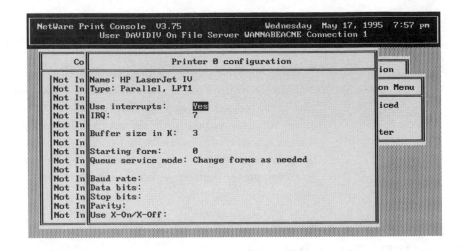

```
NetWare Print Console  V3.75                Wednesday  May 17, 1995  7:57 pm
                User DAVIDIV On File Server WANNABEACNE Connection 1
```

|        | Printer 0 configuration                        |
|--------|------------------------------------------------|
| Not In | Name: HP LaserJet IV                           |
| Not In | Type: Parallel, LPT1                           |
| Not In |                                                |
| Not In | Use interrupts:      Yes                        |
| Not In | IRQ:                 7                           |
| Not In |                                                |
| Not In | Buffer size in K:    3                           |
| Not In |                                                |
| Not In | Starting form:       0                           |
| Not In | Queue service mode: Change forms as needed      |
| Not In |                                                |
| Not In | Baud rate:                                      |
| Not In | Data bits:                                      |
| Not In | Stop bits:                                      |
| Not In | Parity:                                         |
| Not In | Use X-On/X-Off:                                 |

*Once the print queues have been created, the printers have been defined, and the queue has been assigned to the printer, users are ready to print. Although print servers at first glance seem complex, they really aren't—they're just sophisticated!*

with nineteen choices. The first seven are local definitions used by printers that are attached directly to the print server: LPT1, LPT2, LPT3, COM1, COM2, COM3, and COM4.

The next seven type options are assigned to remote printers (parallel and serial) that are attached to local workstations running remote printing. The final two are Other/Unknown and Defined Elsewhere. Other Unknown is used by intelligent printers with internal NICs. Defined Elsewhere is for printers that are being serviced by other print servers on other file servers. We will discuss this option in more depth in a few minutes.

Once the printer type parameter has been set, the system manager can choose interrupts for parallel printing or baud rate, data bit, stop bits, parity, and XON/XOFF for serial printing.

## Step 4: Assigning Queues to Printers

Assigning queues to printers provides a path from the NetWare file server queue to the appropriate printer. If the system manager forgets this step, users become quite miffed. The symptom is that print jobs are sent off to the NetWare queue and they sit there forever waiting to be serviced by the print server. It is typical for up to one hundred or so print jobs to gather in the print queue without one of them being serviced by the printer. If this is the case, the first place to check is the assignment from queue to printer.

Queue assignments are accomplished using the Print Server Configuration menu and the Queues Serviced by Printer option. When you choose this option, the system responds with a list of defined printers. Choose the printer that is going to be serviced and press Enter. The system responds with the queue list. If this is the first queue that is to be assigned to this printer, the queue list will be empty. The system manager presses <Ins> and the system responds with a list of available queues. Choose the appropriate queue and assign a priority number that establishes the queue assignments with the printer (Figure 12.7).

Once a print queue has been assigned to the appropriate printer and all other steps have been accomplished, users can now print directly to the queue and their jobs will be forwarded to the appropriate printer.

That's it for the printing setup process. Once the print queues have been created, the printers have been defined, and the queue has been assigned to the printer, users are ready to print. Although print servers at first glance seem complex, they really aren't—they're just sophisticated!

*The light at the end of the tunnel has a train attached.*

*Anonymous*

The standard printing setup just described works well with most vanilla LANs. But vanilla is boring. Most NetWare cafes strive for more—more variety, more customization, more sophistication. NetWare provides additional facilities

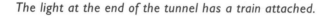

**FIGURE 12.7**
Step 4: Assigning queues
to printers

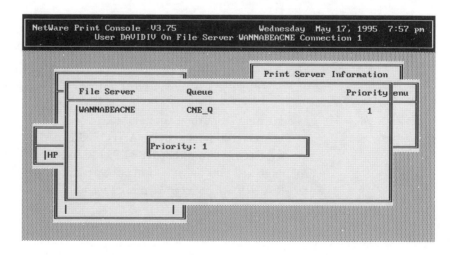

for supporting nonvanilla LANs. Let's explore some of its unique printing setup features.

# Additional Setup Considerations

NetWare's built-in printing facility is quite sophisticated. It supports a multitude of print types and user requirements. In addition, NetWare's printing setup design has been adopted as a standard for network type applications. Besides the four setup steps, NetWare helps you handle additional setup considerations: remote printing, multiple file servers, unique queue design, and customized printer parameters. This discussion expands on NetWare's standard printing setup by exploring the additional setup considerations. Let's begin with remote printing.

### Remote Printing

*Remote printing enables system managers to distribute network printers throughout the LAN. Remote printing defines local workstation printers as shared network devices.*

Remote printing enables system managers to distribute network printers throughout the LAN. Remote printing defines local workstation printers as shared network devices. The RPRINTER command is the workstation utility that provides the remote printing facility. RPRINTER is a terminate-and-stay-resident program that runs in workstation RAM and controls the movement of print jobs from queues to the local workstation. The RPRINTER syntax is simply

```
RPRINTER
```

to bring up the RPRINTER menu or

```
RPRINTER PS=print server P=printer number
```

to activate it from the command line.

The second command in the AUTOEXEC.BAT file activates the RPRINTER facility. Keep in mind that RPRINTER consumes some workstation RAM and communicates directly with local printer ports. RPRINTER can be unloaded using the -R switch, which removes it from memory.

*Two commands can prevent local printers from operating as shared network devices: NET.CFG and PSC. The NET.CFG file can be configured to include the* LOCAL PRINTERS = 0 *command. This command will block communications between workstations and attached printers. The PSC command can be used with the /PRI switch to activate PRIVATE mode. The PRIVATE printer mode switches the local printer's function from shared to private. This condition may be reversed by using the /SH (shared) switch.*

*RPRINTER does not require that the user actually be logged in to the network—but simply attached. An RPRINTER attachment can be accomplished by issuing an IPX or IPXODI. Once the workstation has been attached to the network, RPRINTER can be issued.*

### Multiple File Servers

Earlier you learned that NetWare supports print queues on up to eight file servers. The print server is a separate process from the file server, so one print server can support multiple file servers. However, the file servers on which the queues reside *must* be connected on an internetwork. To support queues on multiple file servers, the system manager must specify which file servers the print server will service. This substep is done as part of the print server installation, step 2 of the four steps. The multiple file servers setup process enables users on multiple file servers to print to the same printer. This process requires a few additional setup steps:

*If I were you, I would learn printing from multiple file servers. Who knows when this information will come in handy in your life?!*

1. The system manager must define an identically named print server on each of the file servers to be serviced by this print server. In other words, the print server is given exactly the same name for each file server.

2. The system manager must go to step 3, defining printers, and configure printers with exactly the same numbers on the new print servers. The difference is that these printers will be defined in the type field as Defined Elsewhere instead of LPT1. This type tells the phony print server that the real printers are defined on another file server. The system is intelligent enough to know which file server it needs to go to for the printer definitions.

3. The system manager assigns each of the defined printers to a print queue located on the host file server.

4. Finally, the system manager must go to the Print Server Configuration of the real print server and highlight file servers to be serviced from the print server configuration screen. The system manager presses Ins to display a list of available file servers. He/she highlights the proper one and presses Enter on each of the file servers that have phony print servers defined on them. They will be sharing the services of this single print server. Then repeat the step on "phony" print server configurations.

Here's an example. The system manager creates a print server called Print Server A. In Print Server A, he/she defines all of the printers and the appropriate assignments from queues to printers. The system manager has a few users and a queue on File Server B that need to access printers on Print Server A. The system manager goes to File Server B and defines a phony Print Server A on File Server B with identical printers and Defined Elsewhere in the Type field. Next, the system manager assigns each of the phony printers to real queues on File Server B. Lastly, the system manager inserts File Server B as a File Server to Be Serviced on the actual print server A, and then defines them in a standard way.

## Queue Design

*The NetWare system manager can optimize printing performance by planning efficient queues.*

The NetWare system manager can optimize printing performance by planning efficient queues. To achieve an efficient queue design, he/she can rearrange workgroups, set queue priorities, add or delete queues, assign queue operators, or remove print servers. The supervisor is automatically assigned as a queue operator during print server setup, so the supervisor can efficiently design and maintain NetWare print queues. Print queues are subdirectories residing on file servers so they cannot easily be moved.

When you create queues, remember that you can only assign queues to printers that have already been created. The Current Queue Status option in PCONSOLE can display the number of entries in a queue and the number of print servers attached to the queue. The system manager can monitor the queue's status to track queues that are being overloaded and queues that are not being used to their potential. In addition, the system manager can use queue priorities to rearrange the printing order of various queues.

The simplest design defines one print queue per printer. Although this design is ideal in most circumstances, some LANs require multiple queues per printer. In such cases, make sure to pay close attention to the queue priorities.

*Novell provides an additional utility for monitoring queue efficiencies: QueueScan. It provides detailed information about print queues and how they are being used by appropriate print servers. QueueScan is currently available on NetWire.*

## Printer Parameters

Most of our discussion so far has focused on the optimization and development of efficient print servers and print queues. Let's not forget that the real workhorse of network printing is the printer itself. NetWare enables you to configure custom printer parameters in three categories: forms, notifications, and queue servicing.

*Forms* are printing definitions that detail the width and length of the printer's current paper. NetWare enables the system manager to define up to 256 different forms. The default form (Form 0) calls for an $8.5 \times 11$" piece of white paper. The system manager can use the PRINTDEF utility to define other forms and mount them as needed. *Notification* is extremely important in the printing environment; it allows NetWare managers to configure alerts for job completion or problem notification.

Job Completion Notification is a print job configuration that the user can define during the job customization process. Problem Notification is defined by the system manager during the setup process. The Notify List for Problem Alerts is created under the Print Server Configuration menu of PCONSOLE. By default, the supervisor, as a print server operator, is added to the problem notification list, even though the supervisor doesn't appear on the menu.

Finally, *Queue Servicing* defines how the printer will react to mounting multiple forms. By default, the printer calls for various forms as they are needed. The NetWare system manager can configure queue servicing so that the printer services only the mounted form or minimizes form changes across or within queues. Minimizing form changes is a more efficient approach that instructs the printer to ask for form changes across all queues or within queues only when all jobs using the current form have been completed.

Printing setup can be as simple or complex as you like. NetWare provides a wide range of facilities for satisfying your every printing need. The standard four steps of printing setup accommodate 95% of NetWare printing needs. For those LANs with unique printing needs, NetWare provides additional setup considerations and facilities. Once printing setup has been established and the users are actively involved in NetWare printing, the system manager can shift his/her attention to optimizing the process. Printing performance optimization involves a detailed understanding of the printing process and issues that affect it.

In the next section we will take a closer look at the detailed events of the printing process and how these events can be optimized.

# Printing Performance Optimization

IMAGINE HOW DIFFICULT IT would be to create a gourmet meal if the assistant chefs did not prepare the food beforehand. Printing performance optimization is the process of preparing the printing components so that the actual process of printing operates smoothly. This is where the NetWare chef peels the potatoes and chops up the vegetables. But before you can dive into printing optimization issues, you must have a detailed understanding of the events involved in the printing process. Let's explore the process of printing from Workstation A to Printer B. Then we will move on to the more pressing issues of performance optimization.

## The Printing Process

Fortunately, NetWare printing is transparent to the user. It's hard to imagine the chaos that would result if users truly understood what was going on as print jobs were moving from their workstation off to the network printer. As the system manager, you do not have the luxury of closing your eyes to these details. The details for the NetWare printing process are illustrated in Figure 12.8, which shows four main components: the workstation shell, print queue, print server, and NetWare printer.

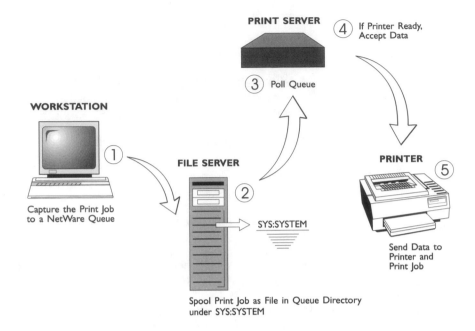

**FIGURE 12.8**

The printing process

---

*One machine can do the work of fifty ordinary men. No machine can do the work of one extraordinary man.*

*Elbert Hubbard*

*Printing performance optimization is the process of preparing the printing components so that the actual process of printing operates smoothly. This is where the NetWare chef peels the potatoes and chops up the vegetables.*

Let's take a close look at the steps as the print job is sent from a non-network-aware application to a central, shared printer.

1. The CAPTURE command activates the printing components of the NetWare shell and tells the system to redirect any jobs destined for the local LPT1 port off to a NetWare queue.

2. The shell places the CAPTURE parameters into a buffer in NETx or VLM.

3. The user uses the non-network-aware application to print a job to the local LPT1 port. The system recognizes the job as destined for LPT1 and redirects it to a NetWare queue. The shell adds the printer-specific information to the print header and print tail.

4. The print job is sent off to the file server as a NetWare file.

5. The file server accepts the file and recognizes that it is indeed a print job. It reads the print header information and redirects it to the appropriate queue subdirectory on the shared hard disk.

6. When the print job is redirected during step 3, the print job finds its way to the correct queue, and the shell appends the parameters to the SYS file in the queue. The .SRV file holds print server information.

7. The print job is affected by a variety of performance optimization parameters: the printing capacity of the printer, the queue priority, whether there are multiple queues per printer, or whether there are multiple printers for this queue.

8. The print job moves up the queue priority ladder and is eventually serviced by the print server.

9. The print server then routes the print job file from the NetWare queue and off to the appropriate printer.

10. Finally, the print job is printed at the NetWare printer. Once the print server recognizes that the printing is completed, the print server will issue a command to the file server to delete the print job file from the shared queue directory.

As you can see, a lot goes on when a user sends a print job to the printer down the hall. The user thinks it is all magic, because he/she presses the print button and a few seconds later the job begins printing out of a shared printer. Somewhere in the middle of all this, the print queue is subject to a variety of optimization issues. These issues affect the print job's ability to move up the priority ladder.

## Performance Issues

Let's look closer at some of the more dominant performance issues. The print job's ability to be serviced by the print server can be affected by various events. These events include issues controlling the capacity of the printer, the priority of the queue, and the number of types of queues per printer. The system manager should have a firm grasp on how these performance issues are balanced in his/her printing system. If the system manager monitors a particular performance problem, he/she can alter the printer or queue's ability to get the job done.

### Printing Capacity

Printing capacity defines the number and size of jobs that each printer can handle, just as the reservation station in the NetWare restaurant determines the seating of diners to minimize their waiting. If jobs overlap in the queue, print time is affected. Printing performance is not only affected by a printer's capacity but also by the size of the jobs ahead of a particular print job in the queue. For example, if a 1-page memo is sitting behind a 500-page manuscript, the memo writer will have a long wait before seeing hard copy. It is important to monitor the printing load. If large documents are printed on a regular basis, the system manager can explore alternatives such as using temporary printers, deferring printing to nonoffice hours, or changing priorities for specific jobs. After all, even the NetWare restaurants offer discounts for diners who order before 5:00!

### Queue Priority

One option for alleviating printing traffic jams is changing the queue priority. Each queue has a priority that is established during the printing setup phase. A queue's priority defines when its jobs are serviced by the print server. A queue with priority 1, for example, will have the highest priority in sending jobs to a queue printer. A print job in a queue with priority 2 will not be serviced until all jobs in the priority 1 queue have been completed. This heirarchy is effective for differentiating the priority of workgroups throughout the LAN. For example, month end reports should not be sent to queues with a lower priority than administrative faxes or memos. Queue priority also provides a strategy for isolating key users and providing them with the best printing performance.

### Multiple Queues per Printer

The number and types of queues per printer will also affect printing performance. The simplest setup is one queue per printer. However, for complex printing environments, printers often have more than one queue assigned to them. When multiple queues are serviced by one printer, the print server determines order according to criteria. The first criterion is queue priority. If the print server comes across two queues with the same priority, it will use the first-come, first-served criterion. Sometimes queues become quite overloaded. In these cases, the system manager can consider having multiple printers per queue.

### Multiple Printers per Queue

Using multiple printers per queue is ideal for high-load environments such as typing pools, just as hiring assistant chefs for peak mealtimes helps the Park Place chef serve all luncheon and dinner guests promptly. All printers should be grouped in one area. In addition, all the printers serviced by one queue should be identical in all configurations—type, memory capacity, and so on.

*If you are going to use multiple printers per queue, you must manually assign the one queue to each of the NetWare printers. Having multiple printers per queue can dramatically increase printing performance in high-load environments.*

*Printing mainte-nance is the periodic monitoring and management of NetWare print queues, print servers, and printers.*

As you can see, just as the Park Place chef must handle peak lunch and dinner schedules, the system manager must handle a LAN's printing performance optimization—not a simple proposition! It involves various components and their interrelationships. The relationships of queues to printers and print server priorities play an important role in how quickly print jobs are processed. The system manager should periodically monitor the printing environment to determine the best course of action. After all, NetWare printing is like serving a ten-course meal.

# *Printing Maintenance*

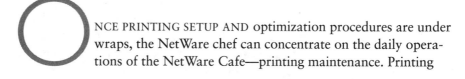

ONCE PRINTING SETUP AND optimization procedures are under wraps, the NetWare chef can concentrate on the daily operations of the NetWare Cafe—printing maintenance. Printing maintenance is the periodic monitoring and management of NetWare print queues, print servers, and printers. Printing maintenance tasks include:

- Print job customization
- Print job prioritization
- General queue maintenance
- Checking the printer's status
- Mounting forms
- Monitoring printer definitions

Printing maintenance is accomplished using two NetWare printing utilities: PCONSOLE and PSC. PCONSOLE is the mother of all printing utilities. It provides the facility for management and maintenance of print queues, print servers, and NetWare printers. As you recall, PCONSOLE enabled the system manager to access real-time printing information.

The PSC (Print Server Control) command is used to issue instructions directly to printers and print servers from the NetWare command line. The NetWare chef can use the PCONSOLE and PSC utilities to enhance the presentation of the printing meal. In many cases, printing maintenance determines the daily reliability of the printing operation.

*Those who work most for the world's advancement are the ones who demand least.*

*Henry Doherty*

In this section, we will learn how to implement NetWare printing maintenance through the use of PCONSOLE and PSC. In addition, we will discover some routine maintenance tasks that can proactively prevent printing problems. Let's begin with a discussion of queue control.

*In addition to these critical printing maintenance tasks, the system manager needs to be aware of one hidden little time-bomb—mixing printer languages. Today's more advanced users are printing to more advanced printers with multiple printing languages. NetWare 3.1x supports a variety of printer types: AppleTalk, Unix, Extended Network Protocol (XNP), Asynchronous Input/Output protocol (AIO), and of course PostScript and PCL (Printer Control Language). Pay careful attention to what your users are trying to do,*

*because many of these auxiliary languages require additional third-party printing components.*

## Queue Control

The first line of attack for NetWare printing maintenance is queue management. Queue management involves monitoring print jobs and changing their print job parameters. This information is detailed in the current print job entry screen of PCONSOLE. Figure 12.9 illustrates the Print Queue Entry Information window in PCONSOLE.

This queue management screen displays various parameters that can be monitored and maintained by the NetWare system manager. An explanation of some of the more interesting parameters follows:

**Print job**—a random number assigned by NetWare for each print job that enters the queue. The print job number is used to track print jobs as they move up the priority ladder and off to NetWare printers.

**File size**—an indication of the size of the file as its exists in the print queue. The size is listed in bytes.

**Description**—an identification string detailing the type of file the print job is. LPT1 catch shows it was a CAPTURE command redirected from the workstation's local LPT1 port.

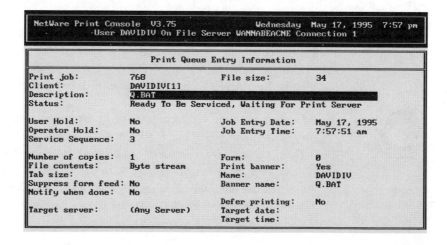

**Status**—an indication of the current status of this particular print job. Status indicates that the print job is ready and waiting to be serviced by the print server, being added to the queue, or currently being printed.

**User hold and operator hold**—two facilities for putting a hold on the print job. Print jobs on hold will be paused in the print queue until the hold flag is removed. A user hold can be set by a user or a print queue operator and can be removed by either. An operator hold can only be set by a print queue operator and cannot be removed by the user.

**Service sequence**—an indication of where the particular job currently resides in the queue priority list. A service sequence of 1 means that the job is currently at the top of the ladder and waiting to be serviced by the print server.

**File contents**—specifies which mode the printer should use in processing tabs and control characters. Text mode replaces all tabs with spaces while byte stream allows an application to use formatting commands to print the document. Byte stream is the default and works for most print jobs adequately.

**Form**—an indication of the form number that this job needs to be printed.

**Notify when done**—allows the user to change the flags so that the system notifies them when the print job has been completed. Print job completion notifications are broadcast as one line commands at the bottom of the workstation screen.

**Print banner**—a one-page title screen that appears at the beginning of each print job. The banner lists the name of the user and a descriptive banner name string.

**Deferred printing**—enables system managers and users to delay jobs to be printed until a later date. The target date and target time parameters allow the system manager or print queue operator to schedule unattended printing. Only the operator can defer someone else's print job. The default listing for deferred printing is 2:00 AM the following morning. The assumption is that jobs that are deferred are typically large and should be printed during off hours.

*The current print job entry screen can be accessed by highlighting a print job from the particular queue and pressing Enter. Once changes have been made to the entry information window, the system manager or user can insert the job back into the queue by pressing Esc. It will retain its appropriate place in the ladder.*

In addition to queue management, NetWare provides the PSC command to control and maintain NetWare print servers. The print server's primary function is routing information from appropriate queues to appropriate printers. In addition to the PSC command, the system manager can use PCONSOLE to view the current status of printers and print servers.

*If I were you, I would pay special attention to Print Server Control, especially the Print Server Status/Control menu in PCONSOLE.*

## Print Server and Printer Control

The PSC command is a useful printer and print server control utility. System administrators use it to manage and maintain NetWare print servers. PSC provides similar functionality to PCONSOLE, except PSC performs its operations from the command line and issues commands directly to the printer or print server. You can perform the following PCONSOLE tasks with PSC:

- View the status of printers
- Pause the printer temporarily
- Stop printing the current job
- Start the printer
- Mark the top of form
- Advance printer to top of next page
- Mount a new form

The syntax for PSC is:

```
PSC PS[=]printserver P[=]printer
```

where [ ] encloses optional input.

*You can use the DOS SET command to set a default print server and printer number for PSC so that you do not have to specify this information at the command line every time. Try this:* SET PSC = "PS printserver P#" *(where # is the printer number).*

The system manager is responsible for various print server and printer maintenance tasks. The following is a brief list of these tasks, along with some insight into how they can be executed using the PCONSOLE or PSC utilities:

**View the Status of Printers.** The system manager can check printer status in PCONSOLE by accessing the Print Server Status and Control option from Print Server Information. This type of information can also be viewed from the command line using the STAT flag with PSC.

**Stop Jobs.** The system manager or print server operator can stop the current job using PCONSOLE or PSC. PCONSOLE provides this option from the Status of Printer box. There the system manager can highlight Printer Control and select Abort Print Job. This action stops the current print job and continues to the next job in the queue. The system manager can also choose the Stop Printer choice that will abort the current job but not continue to the next print job in the queue until the system manager chooses to resume printing by using the Start Printer option.

Similar functions can be managed from the command line using PSC. The system manager can abort print jobs using the AB flag or stop the printer using the STO flag. In addition, the system manager will have to use the STAR or start flag to restart the printer if the STO flag switch is used.

*When print jobs are stopped or aborted, NetWare automatically deletes their corresponding files from the queue directory. If the system manager would not like the print job to be deleted, he/she can issue the K flag, which will keep the job and resubmit it at the top of the queue.*

**Mount Forms.** The system manager can mount forms for printers using PCONSOLE or PSC. The PCONSOLE utility provides the Mounted Form option under Printer Status and Control. The system manager can simply type in the form number as assigned with the PRINTDEF utility. Mounting forms with PSC is performed using the MO F=*number* flag. The number parameter indicates the form number as defined by PRINTDEF.

**Change to Private Setting.** Print server operators or system managers can prevent other network users from accessing remote printers by issuing the PRI (private) flag with PSC. Doing so will break communications between the print server and the local workstation printer. Remote printers can be reinstigated as shared printers by issuing the SHAR (share) flag.

**Cancel Down.** NetWare provides two facilities for downing the NetWare print server. Both of these choices are accessed from the print server status control option in PCONSOLE. The two choices are Going Down After Current Jobs or DOWN. If the system manager chooses Going Down After Current Jobs, the system will pause the queue and continue finishing all active print jobs. New print jobs added to the queue will continue to line up but will not be printed.

The system manager has the capability to cancel the DOWN command if he/she chooses Going Down After Current Jobs, because a lag occurs between the time the down command is issued and the time the printer actually comes down. The cancel down command can only be issued using the PSC utility and the CD flag. The other option for downing a print server is to select DOWN from the Print Server Status/Control menu. The DOWN command immediately downs the print server and is not cancellable.

*Downing the print server does not delete any jobs from the queue; it simply stops the print server from servicing queues and printers.*

**Rewind Printer.** Because NetWare print jobs are files in the queue directory, NetWare provides the facility for rewinding print jobs if an error occurs. If the printer jams in the middle of a 100-page job, the system manager can pause the job and fix the printer. Once the printer has been fixed, the system manager can use PCONSOLE to rewind the print job back a few pages and start on page 70, for example, instead of on page 1. The Rewind Printer facility is available in the Print Server Status/Control menu.

Other print server or printer maintenance options that can be implemented using PCONSOLE or PSC include:

- Form Feed
- Mark Top of Form
- Pause Printer

It is important for the system manager to pay very close attention to printing maintenance. He/she should routinely check these components weekly or monthly. Routine maintenance of the print queue, print server, and printer can dramatically improve printing quality, performance, and reliability. Speaking of reliability, the next topic of discussion is troubleshooting.

*If I were you, I would study the following troubleshooting discussion. You can never learn too much about NetWare printing problems.*

# Printing Troubleshooting

*No matter how many precautions the NetWare chef takes, he's going to burn some toast sooner or later. It is not a perfect world— yet! NetWare printing is riddled with LAN mines and pitfalls.*

NO MATTER HOW MANY precautions the NetWare chef takes, he's going to burn some toast sooner or later. It is not a perfect world—yet. NetWare printing is riddled with LAN mines and pitfalls. The best way to avoid them is to be prepared and take a proactive stance toward printing maintenance. But once in a while, some simple little problem is going to fall through the cracks. In that case, we have a few suggestions for you:

- Check network interface cards and printing cables before you go too far with troubleshooting. Many printing problems are the results of conflicting interrupts or faulty hardware.

- Use PCONSOLE to review the setup of print queues, print servers, and printers. In addition, investigate the printer configurations used in the third stage for defined printers.

- If the user is using CAPTURE to redirect print jobs from local ports to NetWare queues, ensure that the CAPTURE command is in fact activated. Also check the parameters that the CAPTURE command is using.

- Finally, check the print queue itself. Make sure the queue is reliable and has not been corrupted. If all else fails, delete and re-create the print queues and print servers.

Although this advice provides some general guidance in printing troubleshooting, most NetWare printing problems fall into one of four categories. In this section, we will explore these four categories and provide some suggested avenues of redress. Let's begin with print jobs that make it to the queue but not to the printer.

# Print Jobs That Go to Queue But Not to Printer

The system manager checks the print queue information box in PCONSOLE and finds that print jobs are piling up in line waiting to be serviced by the print server. This circumstance occurs for a variety of reasons, and there are almost as many solutions. As you recall, the print server is responsible for routing print jobs from queues to printers. The main area to focus on for this particular problem is the print server itself. Let's review the three possible causes and solutions.

### Printer Definition

The first cause could be that the printer definition was established incorrectly for this printer. The system manager can check the Print Server Information screen in PCONSOLE to ensure that the configuration for this printer in fact matches its location. Thus, if it is a remote printer, is the machine defined as remote? If it is a printer attached directly to the print server, is it in fact defined as an LPT or COM1 printer?

Also, the printer could be off-line, jammed, or out of paper. In such a case, print jobs would wait and queue up in the print queue because the print server would recognize the printer as not being capable of processing them.

*Give us the fortitude to endure the things which cannot be changed, and the courage to change the things which should be changed, and the wisdom to know one from the other.*

*Oliver J. Hart*

### NET.CFG

The NET.CFG or SHELL.CFG file could have the line Local Printers = 0. This line is particularly serious if the local printer is attached to a workstation that is running RPRINTER. RPRINTER allows the local workstation printer to act as a shared network device. If the `Local Printers = 0` command has been issued at the NET.CFG for this workstation, the system will not recognize the local printer as a network device.

### Private

The final possible cause is the use of the PSC private flag. The private flag breaks communications between remote printers and the print server. To solve this problem, the system manager must issue the PSC /SHAR command flag to reestablish the local printer as a shared device.

*The best indication that the print server is performing normally is the* `Waiting for Job` *message at the print server screen. Each printer that is defined and currently waiting for a job should have this message displayed at the print server screen.*

## Print Jobs That Don't Print Properly

*In many cases, when the print server indicates that the printer is out of paper or off-line, the printer is in fact not attached to any port or the correct port on the print server.*

The next printing problem is that print jobs go to the printer but do not print properly. One possible cause is a mismatch between the printing configuration and the current printer status. For example, PostScript jobs being sent to a non-PostScript printer will print garbled characters. In addition, a byte stream print job sent in text mode will also cause the same effect.

A more common problem is with interrupt mismatch. The Printer Definition screen defines hardware interrupts for shared network printers. If the interrupt listed in the Print Server Setup screen is different from the interrupt that the printer is using, printing will be slow and erratic.

Finally, one culprit for common printing problems is the RPRINTER remote printing facility. RPRINTER has been known to interact unfavorably with complex memory workstations or enhanced Windows setups. The best course of action is to move the remote printer to another workstation and try

RPRINTER there. Also, upload the newest RPRINTER fix from Novell's Net-Wire or World Wire. If all else fails, try setting the RPRINTER to "polled" mode. Doing so will eliminate any possible problems with workstation interrupts. Granted it's a little slower, but in many cases it's the only fix:

```
RPRINTER [PS=]print server [P=]printer -P
```

## Printer Is Out of Paper or Off-Line

One of the most common printing error notifications is that the printer is out of paper or off-line. In this case, you can't always believe your eyes. In many cases, when the print server indicates that the printer is out of paper or off-line, the printer is in fact not attached to any port or the correct port on the print server. A more accurate message would be that the printer is *out of printer*, not out of paper.

If you receive the message that the printer is out of paper or off-line, the first thing to check is the printer definition screen. Check which port the printer has been defined for and make sure that the suspect printer is in fact attached to that port. If the printer is in the correct location, check the hardware interrupts that have been defined. One way to isolate an interrupt problem is to create a dummy print server and queue and define the local printer as no interrupts. If this works fine, then the problem is certainly interrupt oriented.

## Print Server Password Prompt Appears

One of the most annoying printing problems is the print server password prompt. In many cases, the print server will prompt you for a password even when no password exists. This prompt can delay the automatic loading of the PSERVER.NLM from AUTOEXEC.NCF. There are various reasons this problem could happen. Let's explore some of those causes now.

### PSERVER

PSERVER.NLM or PSERVER.EXE may have been loaded without specifying a print server name. In this case, the system will try to load without a name. A print server without a name will be prompted for a password. Another possibility is that when PSERVER was loaded, the print server name was typed incorrectly. To test this theory, simply unload the print server and try again.

### Bindery

The bindery may have become slightly corrupted and lost track of the print server name information. This corruption is actually the most common cause of the password error. To solve bindery problems, simply decorrupt the bindery by running BINDFIX from the SYSTEM subdirectory. Incidentally, the BINDFIX CLU can be used to solve many NetWare bindery-oriented errors.

### New File Server

Finally, the print server password prompt will erroneously appear if a new file server has been added but a print server was not defined on it. In this case, the print server looks to all attached file servers for print queue information and notices a new file server with an attached queue. The attached queue is mapped to this print server, but the print server itself has not been defined on the new file server. In this case, the print server will load but assume an erroneous name. This is the same type of situation as loading PSERVER without specifying a name.

Although NetWare printing can be troublesome and mysterious, a good proactive maintenance strategy will solve many of these problems. In addition, a few notes in the NetWare log book can help present and future NetWare system managers troubleshoot common printing problems. Remember, even the best chefs in the world drop a soufflé once in a while.

# *Printing Customization*

*Many of your problematic users will force you to bend the rules and venture far beyond the reaches of normal printing—to a galaxy far, far away!*

As I MENTIONED EARLIER, the incredible variety of printing components puts a dramatic strain on NetWare's straightforward, easy printing architecture. Many of your problematic users will force you to bend the rules and venture far beyond the reaches of normal printing—to a galaxy far, far away! Printing customization is required when:

- Users don't have an application print driver of their own.

- Users want to print COMPRESSED, ITALIC, or LANDSCAPED on special 3 × 7 ENVELOPES.

In this case, NetWare provides print FORMS, print MODES, and print JOB CONFIGURATIONS. Using PRINTDEF, PRINTCON, and CAPTURE, you can be the hero and support any print job customization any user could possibly come up with. This is when you earn that CNA badge and all the faith your users have put in you.

This is how it works. When a user requests something unusual, such as a special font or compressed envelopes, the printer needs to know about it. In addition, the printer needs to be specifically told *how* to fulfill these requests. Users inform their printers about such requests using a special set of printer strings called escape codes. *Escape codes* are printer-specific programming sequences that instruct the printer how to print fonts, landscaped, compressed, and so on. Pages full of escape codes can be found in the back of almost all printer manuals. Okay, now back to the story. Fortunately, most applications have escape codes and special formatting built into their printer drivers. Each printer's driver contains its specific set of escape codes, so users need to tell the system—Windows NT, for example—which printer they are using during installation. So when the user prints a compressed-type address on an envelope, the application print driver attaches the correct set of escape codes to the print job and sends it off to the NetWare printer. *No problema!*

*If I were you, I would totally forget about printer customization...Just kidding! Even though you probably won't ever use this information, you should definitely learn it, especially PRINTDEF and PRINTCON.*

The problem occurs when the application can't attach the correct codes to the print job, and the user asks *you* to do it. Yuck! Well, fortunately, printing customization can be broken down into three simple steps:

1. Establishing printer definitions with PRINTDEF—during this step you create the custom forms and printer-specific modes.

2. Configuring print jobs with PRINTCON—next, you incorporate these printer definitions into a print job configuration with other settings such as number of copies, no tabs, and so on.

3. Printing with the /J parameter—and finally, you print using the special printer configuration with CAPTURE /J=job config.

Let's take a closer look at these three printing customization steps and help Joe print his compressed, landscaped, italic envelopes.

## Printer Definitions with **PRINTDEF**

It all starts with printer definitions. In this step, we focus on creating custom forms and printer-specific modes. A MODE is a collection of "printer functions" that perform some specific tasks—such as compressed, italic, or landscaped settings. *Functions* are printer-specific escape sequences that instruct the printer how to print. For example, the italic function for the HP_LASER-JET_IV printer is defined as ESC {s1S}. Each printer (or DEVICE) can have hundreds of functions that are combined into thousands of modes.

*Fortunately, we don't have to manually input all of the escape sequences for the many functions for each of our printers. This would literally take months! Novell is kind enough to provide a large collection of already configured devices through printer definition files (PDFs). You will find many *.PDF files in the SYS:PUBLIC subdirectory that can be imported into PRINTDEF. Also, if you create a fancy little device of your own, you can EXPORT it from PRINTDEF into a custom PDF file. Cool running.*

All of these devices, modes, and functions are kept in a global LAN database called NET$PRN.DAT. NET$PRN.DAT is stored in the SYS:PUBLIC subdirectory and it defines the supported printer types, modes, and forms. We will begin our little journey by creating an ENVELOPE form. From the

PrintDef Options menu in PRINTDEF, choose Forms. Press Ins to add a new form and enter the Forms Definition Form window (see Figure 12.10). Here you name the form—ENV in our case—and provide the length (in lines per page, 1–255) and width (in characters per line, 1–999) parameters. We are going to use a length of 18 and width of 70 (roughly 3 × 7). To save these changes, press Esc and choose Yes from the Save Changes confirmation box. It's that easy.

Next, we will define the COmpressed, ITalic, LANDscaped mode—or COITLAND as I have dubbed it. Return to the PrintDef Options menu and choose Print Devices. At this point, we haven't imported the HP LaserJet IV functions. To do so, choose Import Print Device and specify the SYS:PUBLIC subdirectory. There you will see a long list of available .PDF files. Choose HPLJ4.PDF and press Enter. Suddenly all the HP LaserJet IV print functions will appear in our NET$PRN.DAT database. Believe me, this automation is a lot easier than entering them by hand. Next, highlight Edit Print Devices from the Print Devices Options box and press Enter. Then, choose Device Modes. Here you will see a list of existing modes for the HP LaserJet IV printer. Go ahead and scan the list, but I bet there's no COITLAND mode there (see Figure 12.11). To create your own custom mode, press Ins and type COIT-LAND in the names box. Next, highlight the three functions that will make up our special mode. Use the F5 key to highlight COMPRESSED, ITALIC, and LANDSCAPED. Then press Enter. Notice the complex escape sequences. Don't look too long or you'll grow a pocket protector!

Now that we've defined printer forms, devices, and modes, it's time to move onto something a little more "real"—print job configurations.

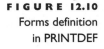

**FIGURE 12.10**
Forms definition
in PRINTDEF

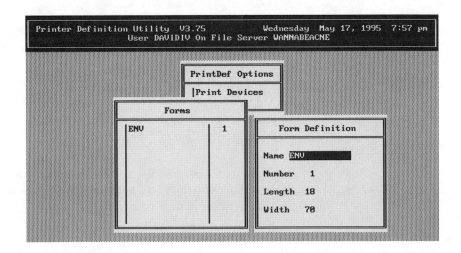

FIGURE 12.11
Device modes
in PRINTDEF

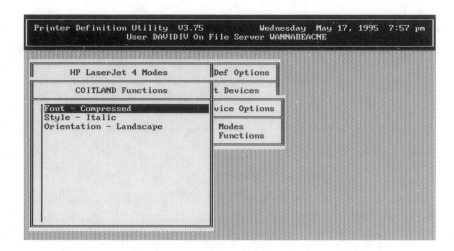

FIGURE 12.11
Device modes
in PRINTDEF

# Print Job Configurations with **PRINTCON**

The second step in printing customization is print job configurations. The farther we move away from PRINTDEF, the easier it gets. In this section, we are only dealing with one menu—the Edit Print Job Configuration menu (see Figure 12.12). Here we can specify various printing parameters and lump them together into one printing configuration—COENV in our example.

COENV calls for a specific series of printing parameters, including the HP LaserJet IV Device, ENV form, and COITLAND mode. In addition, it uses seven copies, no print banner, a timeout of 10 seconds, and notification when done (see Figure 12.12). All of these parameters are stored in a configuration called COENV in a database called PRINTCON.DAT. Unfortunately, PRINTCON.DAT is user-specific, not global as is the printer definition database. Each user stores his/her own PRINTCON.DAT in the SYS:MAIL\*userid* subdirectory. This can be a drag when multiple users want to share the same printer configuration file. Fortunately, NetWare enables you to COPY printer configurations from one user to another.

*PRINTCON configurations are user specific. They exist as the file PRINTCON.DAT in the user's SYS:MAIL\userid subdirectory. The system manager must define these parameters for each user. PRINTCON offers the facility to copy printing configurations from one user to another. Ah, but there's another solution.*

**FIGURE 12.12**
Print job configurations
in PRINTCON

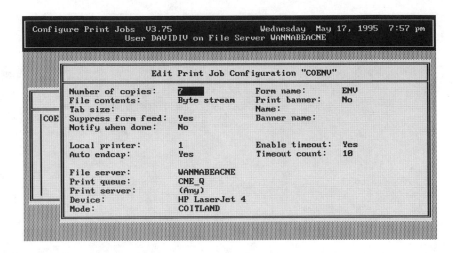

```
Configure Print Jobs  V3.75                Wednesday  May 17, 1995  7:57 pm
                    User DAVIDIV on File Server WANNABEACNE

                        Edit Print Job Configuration "COENV"

         Number of copies:     7          Form name:        ENV
COE      File contents:        Byte stream    Print banner:     No
         Tab size:                         Name:
         Suppress form feed:   Yes        Banner name:
         Notify when done:     No

         Local printer:        1          Enable timeout:   Yes
         Auto endcap:          Yes        Timeout count:    10

         File server:          WANNABEACNE
         Print queue:          CNE_Q
         Print server:         (Any)
         Device:               HP LaserJet 4
         Mode:                 COITLAND
```

Now that we've defined a print job configuration (COENV) that includes the custom printer definition, all that's left is to PRINT a file using the new configurations. I can't wait.

## Printing with the /J Parameter

Here we are: It's printing time. So let's summarize using Figure 12.13. Joe wanted to print COMPRESSED, ITALIC, LANDSCAPED ENVELOPES to the HP LaserJet IV down the hall. Unfortunately, his word processing application didn't have a smart enough print driver to handle the special codes for him. So he turned to you. Being the clever CNA that you are, you said "*No problema*" and proceeded to PRINTDEF. While you were using PRINTDEF, you imported the HP LaserJet IV print device and created a custom mode (COITLAND) using the COMPRESSED, ITALIC, and LANDSCAPED functions. In addition, you created an envelope form called ENV. So far so good. Next, you left PRINTDEF and entered PRINTCON. You created the COENV print job configuration with all the parameters Joe requested, including the new form, mode, and device. Then, you copied the configuration over to Joe because it is user specific.

All that is left is printing. This is the easiest step. Simply use the following CAPTURE command:

```
CAPTURE /J=COENV
```

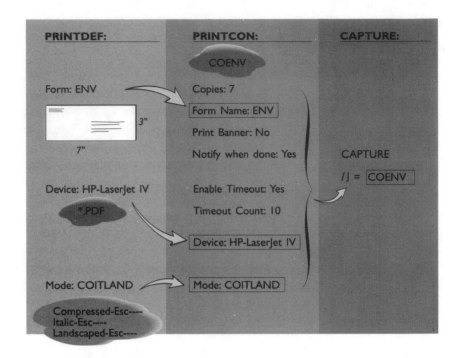

**FIGURE 12.13**
Printing customization summary

This command will cause every print job to print COMPRESSED, ITALIC, LANDSCAPED on the ENVELOPE form. Remember, the system will ask you to mount the correct form before it actually prints. Do you remember how to do that? It's PSC /MO F=*form*. To return Joe back to normal printing, simply ENDCAP and reCAPTURE with default settings.

Now that wasn't so bad, was it? I'm sorry I asked. Let's just say, you'll probably lead a happy, successful life without ever having to fool around with PRINTDEF and PRINTCON. Let's finish the chapter with a more detailed discussion of general user printing.

# Printing

NOW THAT THE PREPARATION is over, it's time for the big event. The chef has purchased all the raw materials, prepared the vegetables, and slaved over a hot stove. The plate has been garnished and it's time to serve the meal.

## Three Ways to Print

*The ultimate goal of all this setup, optimization, maintenance, and customization is the movement of a print job from Workstation A to Printer B. NetWare provides three different ways to do this: NetWare-aware applications, CAPTURE, and PCONSOLE/NPRINT.*

The ultimate goal of all of this setup, optimization, maintenance, and customization is the movement of a print job from Workstation A to Printer B. NetWare provides three ways to do this:

- Printing from NetWare-aware applications

- Using CAPTURE to redirect local ports

- Using PCONSOLE/NPRINT to insert print jobs directly into NetWare queues

Users can use one or many of these three approaches toward NetWare printing. The bottom line is that the user presses the print button and the job magically appears in the printer down the hall. If the system manager has done his/her job correctly, NetWare printing is completely transparent to the user. But don't be fooled—this level of printing transparency is difficult to install and a bear to maintain. In the end, it's worth the effort when the system manager sees the smile on his/her user's face. We can only imagine it is the same feeling a chef enjoys when a guest raves about the restaurant's meal.

*Every action of our lives touches on some chord that will vibrate into eternity.*

*Edwin Hubbel Chapin*

Let's take a look at the three ways to print in a NetWare printing system.

### NetWare-Aware Applications

A few special applications exist that fully understand NetWare printing. These applications are aware of NetWare queues and can print directly from workstations to centralized queues and shared printers. Two of the most popular NetWare-aware (and compatible) applications are WordPerfect and Microsoft Windows. The WordPerfect word-processing program prints directly to NetWare queues through the printer edit facility. The system manager can define the NetWare queue name as an auxiliary printing device. Microsoft Windows works in much the same way, except it relies on its internal Print Manager. The Windows Print Manager is aware of local ports as well as NetWare queues. Printing directly from any Windows application to a NetWare queue is seamless and transparent.

These two NetWare-aware applications and their printing sophistication have created a groundswell around NetWare printing intelligence. More and more applications are exploring the concept of printing directly to NetWare queues, thus solving some common problems with local port redirection. Most of your non-NetWare-aware applications currently pose difficulties for system managers. These applications can be obtrusive and uncooperative in redirecting from local ports to NetWare queues. Unfortunately, most other NetWare applications aren't aware of NetWare queues. These non-NetWare-aware applications print directly to local ports as if a local workstation were attached.

*If I were you, I would spend most of my time working on understanding CAPTURE. It is the most practical and popular printing strategy. Also, learn those switches—they are your friends!*

### CAPTURE

The CAPTURE command is a printing utility that provides flexibility for the workstation so that printing can be done from non-NetWare applications. CAPTURE literally hijacks the local printer port and redirects all print jobs destined for that port off to a NetWare queue. The syntax is:

```
CAPTURE /QUEUE=name of queue /switch
```

There is a plethora of additional parameters that can be used with the CAPTURE command to customize the way that print jobs are printed. Some of the more interesting CAPTURE switches include:

**/B** for banner name.

**/C** for copies.

**/CR=***path* to print to a file.

**/F=***form* to use a specific type of form for this print job.

**/FF** for form feed.

**/J** for print job name (from printing customization).

**/L=***number* for the local port that needs to be CAPTUREd by default. Without /L=*number*, CAPTURE will capture the LPT1 parallel port.

**/NFF** for no form feed.

**/NT** for no tabs.

**/SH** for show, which will display the current status of the CAPTURE command.

**/T** for Tabs=*number* to replace all tab characters with spaces if you specify.

**/TI** for timeout, which is important for certain misbehaving non-network applications.

**/EC** for Endcap in NetWare 3.12 and above.

Here's a sample CAPTURE command that works well in most environments:

```
CAPTURE QUEUE=queuename /NB /NT /TI=10 /NFF
```

Once CAPTURE has been loaded into memory, it cannot be unloaded or stopped unless you issue an ENDCAP command. ENDCAP is particularly useful because it allows the flexibility to capture to specific queues for specific applications and then end that capture session and recapture for another queue in another application. Incidentally, all of this can be accomplished using batch files.

In addition to CAPTURE, the NetWare 3.1*x* user can redirect local ports to NetWare queues using the GUI-based User Tools for Windows. Simply access User Tools from within Windows and click on the Printer Icon. A list of available local ports appears on the left with a list of available NetWare queues on the right. Simply highlight a port and connect it to an available queue using the CAPTURE button in the bottom right-hand corner. Sometimes life can be so easy!

*Just when you thought things were getting easy, along comes the SPOOL command. SPOOL is a console command that must be used in two cases: To establish default print queues for NPRINT and CAPTURE, and to support earlier NetWare printing environments—NetWare 2.0a and before. In the second case, many earlier NetWare versions printed directly to printer numbers instead of queues. The SPOOL console command* SPOOL printer # TO QUEUE queue name *will redirect printers back to queues and then back to printers. Oh, it's really simple; not!*

## PCONSOLE/NPRINT

NetWare provides a third method for access to shared printers. This method involves one menu utility and one CLU. The menu utility PCONSOLE provides the facility for inserting print jobs directly into NetWare queues. The system manager can highlight the pre-queue information screen for PCONSOLE and highlight an appropriate queue. The system manager can then move into the current job entry screen and press the Ins key. Pressing Ins at the Current Job Entry screen displays an input box into which the system manager puts a NetWare file. This file will be inserted directly into the queue using the default print job configurations. This strategy is effective for system managers who need to quickly print text files directly from the shared disk. This strategy is not good for printing files with complex control codes and application-specific formatting.

NPRINT is a workstation CLU that sends a text file directly to a NetWare queue. NPRINT's syntax is NPRINT file /Q queuename and it uses the same parameters as CAPTURE. In this case, instead of capturing from a local port, NPRINT prints a text file from the command line directly to a NetWare queue. There's no port involved.

Wow, wasn't that fun!? In this chapter, we explored the NetWare Cafe from the system manager's printing point of view. You learned about the fundamentals of NetWare printing and explored the relationships between printer servers and printers. We went through the four steps of setting up vanilla printing systems and then moved on to setup considerations for

*I wish there were a cookbook you could follow in setting up the most reliable and efficient NetWare printing system. Unfortunately, NetWare printing seems to be more trial by fire.*

unique printing systems. You learned about how to optimize printing performance through printing capacity, queue priority, and multiple queues and printers. Printing maintenance focused on the print queue, the print server, and the printer using PCONSOLE and the PSC CLU. We explored some serious printing problems and discovered possible courses of action, and finally we defined the three ways that NetWare users can send print jobs from their workstation to shared NetWare printers.

I wish there were a cookbook you could follow in setting up the most reliable and efficient NetWare printing system. Unfortunately, NetWare printing seems to be more trial by fire. The good news is that you have a good printing education under your belt and some Novell resources to rely on—much more than Julia Child ever had.

# NetWare 3.12
# Performance
# Management

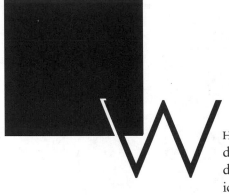

WHAT WOULD A LUXURY hotel be without interior decorating? How appealing would it be without fancy drapes and interior fountains, beautiful paintings, and ice sculptures?

The interior decorator is responsible for the subtle nuances that make the difference between ultimate comfort and just a place to stay. The Park Place decorator spends hours each day walking the halls and examining the interior luxuries of the hotel. She inspects the rooms, examines the restaurants, and monitors the interior artwork. When the decorator finds any small detail that could be improved upon, she acts quickly. Interior decorating at a luxury resort is a 24-hour-a-day job.

As the system manager you are the interior decorator of your LAN. You are responsible for examining the LAN's furnishings and making improvements wherever possible. The goal of NetWare interior decorating is performance optimization. The system manager must be 100% committed to optimizing file server and communication performance.

Performance revolves around two key functions: monitoring and optimization. NetWare monitoring involves the examination of key file server resources and determination of possible discrepancies. File server optimization is the continuation of NetWare decorating—redecorating the hotel/network, as it were. This function involves correcting the discrepancies found in the monitoring stage. Diligent monitoring and effective optimization can make the difference between LAN success and failure.

As the NetWare interior decorator, the system manager focuses his/her performance management efforts on various components. These components affect shared disk usage, file server communications, memory, security access, and processor utilization. In this chapter, we will explore the file server performance management components so you can understand their role in monitoring and optimization. We will explore the file server memory pools in depth and learn how they combine to provide an efficient, effective memory management strategy.

*As the NetWare system manager you are the interior decorator of your LAN. You are responsible for examining the LAN's furnishings and making improvements wherever possible.*

Once you understand the performance management components and file server memory pools, we will move on to monitoring and optimization. File server monitoring is performed using the MONITOR.NLM utility. We will explore its features. File server optimization is performed using the SET console command, and we will explore its nine optimization categories.

Performance management is as important to your NetWare LAN as water fountains and ice sculptures are to Park Place. It is one of your most important responsibilities and, as we mentioned earlier, can determine the success or failure of your LAN.

*Science does not know its debt to imagination.*

*Ralph Waldo Emerson*

# Performance Management Components

*NetWare incorporates two main performance management components: tables and allocation units. Tables control shared disk organization and hold properties of NetWare files and directories. Allocation units define logical groups of data as they reside in memory and on the disk.*

PERFORMANCE MANAGEMENT COMPONENTS determine how Net-Ware file servers interact with shared resources. They control communications, shared disk access, and memory management. NetWare incorporates two main performance management components: tables and allocation units. Tables control shared disk organization and hold properties of NetWare files and directories. Allocation units define logical groups of data as they reside in memory and on the disk. In addition, NetWare employs a performance optimization strategy called *caching,* which increases file server disk access by an amazing 10,000%. Caching is explained in detail later in the chapter. Tables and allocation units are analogous to the artwork and fabric that the Park Place interior decorator uses to improve the quality of the hotel rooms and lobby.

In this section, we will explore tables, caching, and allocation units. We will discover their relationship to memory management and optimization. Let's begin with NetWare drive tables.

*If I were you, I would jump into performance management components with both feet! This is where NetWare optimization starts. Focus on blocks, FATs, and PRBs.*

# Tables

NetWare drive tables are the phonebooks of the LAN. They record information about where files are located and what kind of information resides in shared NetWare disks. There are two types of NetWare drive tables: the directory entry table (DET) and file allocation table (FAT). The DET maintains information about file names, trustees, security, and ownership. The NetWare FAT performs the same function as it does in DOS; that is, to provide a master index of file names and physical locations on the shared disk. DETs and FATs work together to provide an organized and efficient method of indexing, retrieving, and storing shared network data.

### Directory Entry Table

The directory entry table is unique to NetWare—it doesn't even exist in DOS. The DET contains information that is unnecessary in a stand-alone environment. The network-specific type data includes ownership, rights, attributes, and shared name space. NetWare's DET maintains a basic list of directory entries. Directory entries include files and directories. The DET stores valuable information about directory entries such as:

- Name of files
- Ownership
- Date of last update
- The first block of the network hard disk in which the file is stored
- Trustees of files and trustees of directories
- A pointer to the FAT

The FAT contains the actual physical address of each block of a shared network file.

*The file server does not cache the entire DET. It only caches directory blocks that are being used or areas of the DET that are being used. Earlier versions of NetWare did, in fact, cache the entire DET. DETs are stored for each volume on the disk.*

### File Allocation Table

The FAT in NetWare performs exactly the same function as it does in DOS: It maintains a list of all files on the shared disk and their physical track, sector, and cylinder addresses. The FAT works closely with the DET to provide files to NetWare clients. When a user requests a file from the central shared disk, the DET matches that user's trustee assignments against the properties of the file. If the two match, a pointer is sent off to the FAT. The system then searches the FAT for all corresponding addresses for this file and returns the values to the disk controller. The disk controller then returns the data to the network interface card (NIC), from whence it is sent off to the user. Unlike the DET, the entire FAT is cached in file server memory.

*NetWare provides a facility for more efficient and faster access to large files. Files that exceed 64 blocks or 64 FAT entries are turbo-indexed. Turbo FAT indexing provides a facility for grouping these blocks together in the FAT. This makes access of large files much more efficient and lightning fast.*

*NetWare FATs theoretically support 536,870,912 FAT entries and 2,097,152 DET entries.*

NetWare stores DETs, FATs, and files on the shared internal disk. As you learned from Chapter 1, disk storage is much slower than memory storage. Temporary RAM storage can be used to increase the performance of accessing and retrieving shared data through caching.

# Caching

*Caching* means storing frequently used files and tables in memory rather than on the disk. NetWare 3.1*x* provides three built-in performance features that relate to caching:

- Directory caching

- Directory hashing

- File caching

*Directory caching* is the process of copying the DET and FAT into file server RAM and accessing them from there. Accessing these tables from memory instead of disk is one hundred times faster. Directory caching substantially increases file server performance because the DETs and FATs are accessed every time a user requests a file. As mentioned earlier, NetWare 3.1*x* only copies the most recently used DET portions into file server RAM.

*Directory hashing* indexes the memory stored DET. This process in effect alphabetizes the NetWare phone book. Searches of indexed DETs are performed 30% faster than nonhashed directory entry tables.

Finally, *file caching* is the automatic process of storing frequently used files in server RAM. When a file is first requested by a user, it is accessed from disk and a copy is stored in RAM. Subsequent requests from users are then accessed from RAM one hundred times faster than they would be from disk. NetWare 3.1*x* uses all available memory beyond the operating system and other resources for file caching.

*A*llocation units are the most important performance management components because they define areas of file server storage that are reserved for files and tables. NetWare defines two types of allocation units: blocks and buffers.

*The more file caching memory that is available, the faster file server performance is. One of the most important strategies for performance management is increasing the amount of memory available for file caching on the server.*

# Allocation Units

*Allocation units* are the most important performance management components because they define areas of file server storage that are reserved for files and tables. NetWare defines two types of allocation units: blocks and buffers. *Blocks* are data storage areas on the hard disk. *Buffers* are data storage areas in file server memory. Blocks and buffers have a dramatic impact on file server performance. They determine the speed and efficiency of the file server disk's read and write operations. In addition, buffers control directory and file caching. Let's take a closer look at NetWare's performance management allocation units.

### Blocks

Blocks are data storage areas on the disk. NetWare divides the file server disk into small allocation units—blocks. Typically, the default block size in NetWare is 4KB. For example, a 100MB hard disk is allocated into 25,000 blocks. These blocks are organized into one of two types: disk allocation blocks and directory entry blocks.

**DISK ALLOCATION BLOCKS**   Disk allocation blocks store NetWare data. NetWare divides each volume into several disk allocation blocks that provide the smallest common denominator for storing network data. These allocation blocks can be configured in 4, 8, 16, 32, or 64KB increments. The default size is 4KB. As files are stored on the NetWare disk, they are broken down into multiple blocks. Because a file can consist of more than one block, it is important for the FAT to link these blocks together. Files that contain more than 64 blocks are turbo FAT indexed, meaning that NetWare has a built-in algorithm for faster access of these types of files.

   The advantage of having large block sizes is that they provide more efficient disk access because the read/write head doesn't have to work as hard to access the data. The disadvantage of large block sizes is that they waste a lot of disk space. For example, a 4KB file would use an entire 64KB block if the block size were set to 64KB.

*If the block size is set to 64KB, it's possible to run out of disk space on an 80MB file server disk by loading just the SYSTEM and PUBLIC files. Many of the files are much smaller than 64KB and the block size is wasted.*

   The advantage of small block sizes is that they store files more efficiently than large block sizes. Thus, less disk space is wasted. The disadvantage to small block sizes is that they require a great deal more read/write head activity and can cause wear and tear on the disk. In addition, volumes with small block sizes have slower file access times for large files.

**DIRECTORY ENTRY BLOCKS** Directory entry blocks store NetWare DETs. Directory entry blocks are special allocation units that are reserved for storing the DET. Directory entry blocks are a default 4KB in size and cannot be changed. Each DET is divided into one or more directory blocks that store directory entries. By default, NetWare reserves six directory entry blocks to store the early DETs. This number will rise as needed and can reach as many as 65,536 blocks.

Each volume has its own DET and therefore reserves its own directory entry blocks. A directory entry block can accommodate thirty-two 128-byte entries. Keeping in mind the maximum number of directory blocks, we get a total number of directory entries of 2,097,152. Bear in mind that the main difference between directory entry blocks and disk allocation blocks is that directory entry blocks are always 4KB. Disk allocation blocks can be made larger or smaller as needed.

*If I were you, I would focus on disk allocation blocks and file cache buffers. These are the foundations of MONITOR.NLM and internal SET parameters. Learn the max, min, and suggested settings for each component, because you will see them again someday.*

### Buffers

The next allocation unit type is buffers, which are storage areas in file server RAM. Buffers are important to file server performance because they are the areas to which directory entries and files are cached. Each buffer corresponds with a particular type of block on the disk. For example, disk allocation blocks are stored in file cache buffers, whereas directory entry blocks are stored in directory cache buffers. The third type of buffer, packet receive buffers, defines communication holding cells for user requests (Figure 13.1).

*File cache buffers impact file server performance more than any other buffer type. File cache buffers reside in RAM and temporarily store disk allocation blocks.*

**FILE CACHE BUFFERS** File cache buffers impact file server performance more than any other buffer type. File cache buffers reside in RAM and temporarily store disk allocation blocks. Because these buffers store blocks, they are sometimes referred to as *cache blocks*—an extremely confusing term. Figure 13.1 shows how the disk allocation blocks are stored on disk. These blocks then correspond to file cache buffers. The file cache buffers can also be configured for differing sizes, but they have a smaller range. 4KB is the default, but they can be configured for 8KB or 16KB sizes as well.

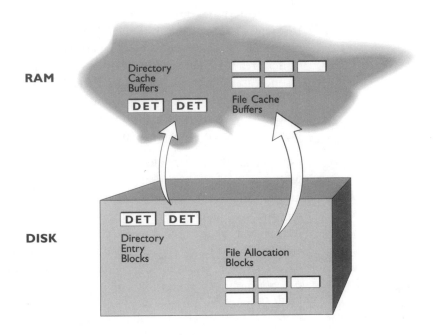

Earlier you saw that file caching improves disk performance by 10,000%. Because file caching is such a vital component in performance management, cache buffers are an extremely important component in increasing server performance. File cache buffers and disk allocation blocks have a 1:1 relationship (as Figure 13.1 shows). That is, each disk allocation block is cached in memory in one file cache buffer. If the cache buffer size exceeded the block size, server RAM would be wasted. If, for example, the cache buffer size was 8KB and the disk allocation block size was 4KB, each 4KB block would take 8KB of memory!

*If the cache buffer size is larger than the smallest disk allocation block size on any volume, the file server will not mount the volume, because the cache buffer services all blocks on all volumes. If multiple volumes on the server have different disk allocation block sizes, the cache buffer size must match the smallest allocation block size.*

**DIRECTORY CACHE BUFFERS** Directory cache buffers are areas of server RAM that hold the DET blocks. Figure 13.1 shows the 1:1 relationship between directory entry blocks and directory cache buffers. By default, the directory cache buffer size matches the directory entry block size, which is 4KB.

NetWare allocates directory cache buffers as needed for caching the most frequently used portions of the DET. As more directory entries are added to the system, directory entry blocks increase and the system allocates file cache buffer area for directory cache buffers. As the number of directory cache buffers increases, file cache buffers decrease. This relationship can make it tough to balance performance versus storage organization. Later in this chapter, you will learn how to monitor the number of directory cache buffers and use SET parameters to optimize server performance.

**PACKET RECEIVE BUFFERS** The final server buffer type has nothing to do with disk storage. Packet receive buffers (PRBs) describe an area in server memory that is set aside or reserved to temporarily hold user requests while they are waiting to be serviced by NetWare. These user requests arrive at the file server as packets. *Packets* are communication components that include, among other things, user requests for data or processing information. These packet requests are handled by file service processes (FSPs). FSPs are built-in subroutines that respond to incoming user requests. NetWare treats FSPs and PRBs in much the same way a bank treats its clients.

In Figure 13.2, you can see that the file service processes are like bank tellers. These tellers service clients one at a time as they come in for requests to withdraw or deposit money (packets). Clients who are waiting to be serviced by the tellers wait in the bank lobby—large enough to hold 50 to 100 important clients. The bank lobby is analogous to the PRB. Packets wait in the buffer until an FSP becomes available. Once one becomes available, they are serviced accordingly and their request is acknowledged.

If there are too few tellers to service all of the clients, the lobby can become quite full. And if it overflows, clients are forced to wait outside. Much the same thing happens in the NetWare environment if the number of FSPs is not enough to service all of the packets waiting in the buffer. If a client or a packet user request is forced out of the PRB, the user will receive the following message: `Error sending on the network`.

Efficient network performance then becomes a balance between having a large number of FSPs and the right size PRB. Both the FSP and PRB components can be optimized using MONITOR and SET parameters.

*Nothing is impossible for the man who doesn't have to do it himself.*

*A. H. Weiler*

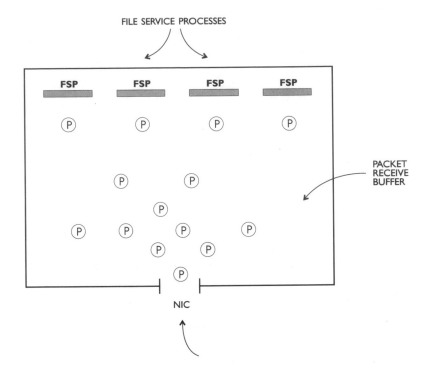

**F I G U R E  13.2**
The NetWare bank

FILE SERVICE PROCESSES

FSP    FSP    FSP    FSP

PACKET
RECEIVE
BUFFER

NIC

That completes our discussion of performance management components. In this section we have seen the uses of the DET and FAT, focusing on their functions in organizing network data. We then discussed the caching features that provide efficient and high performance access to network data. Finally, we explored allocation units that provide areas of disk and server memory for storage of DETs and user data.

Next we will discuss server memory management and how NetWare allocates particular areas of RAM for performance management components, resources, and operating system requests.

# Server Memory Management

M
EMORY MAKES THE WORLD go 'round in the NetWare server. It is the life blood that provides a storage area for user instructions, file caching, applications, directory caching, hashing, and a conduit for LAN communications and packet processing.

NetWare 2.2 and 3.1*x* differ dramatically in their approach toward server memory, but both operating systems use it for the same things: caching, file service processes, and buffering incoming user requests. Let's begin with a look at NetWare 2.2's memory architecture, and then spend the rest of the section on NetWare 3.1*x*'s sophisticated "memory pool" strategy. In later sections, we will take this knowledge and apply it toward our advanced CNA performance monitoring and optimization techniques.

## NetWare 3.1*x* Memory Pools

*N*etWare 3.1*x* uses memory for many functions. The dynamic configuration of NetWare 3.1*x* and its 32-bit processing capabilities allow the server to allocate memory according to need and availability.

Now, let's take a closer look at the NetWare 3.1*x* memory architecture and how its memory pools interact with OS performance management components.

NetWare 3.1*x* uses memory for many functions. The minimum memory of 4MB is required for the operating system just to function—not to function well! NetWare supports (addresses) memory up to 4GB. The dynamic configuration of NetWare 3.1*x* and its 32-bit processing capabilities allow the server to allocate memory according to need and availability. The many resources, components, and functions that require server RAM can be served efficiently and dynamically.

In order for NetWare to dynamically service all of the many resources that need server RAM, memory has been allocated into logical pools. These pools do not physically exist within the NetWare RAM but are used as logical pointers to areas of available RAM. Figure 13.3 graphically shows all available server RAM. The most RAM occupied by one large pool is in file cache buffers. Earlier we mentioned that NetWare makes all available RAM available for file caching. Memory not available for file caching is reserved for operating system requirements such as the SERVER.EXE operating system

**FIGURE 13.3**
Server RAM in
NetWare 3.1x

file, COMMAND.COM that is running in the background, the ROM BIOS, and so on.

*Memory is the cabinet of imagination, the treasury of reason, the registry of conscience, and the council chamber of thought.*

*Saint Basil*

The file cache buffer pool handles all of the server's file caching needs. In addition, this pool services the other five memory pools that provide allocated areas of RAM for specific file server resources and functions. Some common functions for memory pooling include NetWare loadable module (NLM) loading, DETs and FATs, turbo FAT, drive mappings, PRBs, disk and LAN drivers, and so on. In this section, we will discuss the file cache buffer pool and the other five pools that provide logical extensions of server RAM. In addition, you will learn how to optimize server memory by controlling the size and dynamic allocation of these pools.

Let's begin with file cache buffers.

*If I were you, I would send out for pizza. This is going to be a long, hard night. NetWare 3.1x server memory pools are the most important, and potentially challenging, performance management components. Also, check out MONITOR.NLM while you're reading this section.*

### File Cache Buffers

NetWare uses file cache buffers to speed access to shared disk storage. When the server boots, it loads SERVER.EXE, COMMAND.COM, and a few other files that eat into server RAM. All other available file server memory is automatically added to one pool: file cache buffers. The operating system uses cache buffers for various functions, including:

*W*hen the server boots, it loads SERVER.EXE, COM-MAND.COM, and a few other files that eat into server RAM. All other available file server memory is automatically added to one pool: file cache buffers.

- Caching frequently used files

- Loading NLMs

- Caching the DET

- Housing the FAT

- Building hash tables for directory hashing

- Handling Turbo FAT indexing

- Servicing other memory pools

As the five other memory pools draw from file cache buffers, the user's ability to cache frequently used files decreases. Keep in mind that all other memory pools draw originally from file cache buffers. Two of these pools reside directly in the file cache buffer area—they are the cache-nonmovable and cache-movable subpools.

### Cache Nonmovable

The cache-nonmovable memory pool resides directly in the cache buffer area. In Figure 13.4, this pool is shown as a door. The cache-nonmovable memory pool can be thought of as a door to file cache buffers—it provides a port for NLMs to load into server RAM. Cache nonmovable is so named because, as a port, it cannot move its location in RAM.

*This analogy holds true, because most doors would be fairly useless if they were able to move their locations randomly. It would be funny, though.*

The cache-nonmovable door borrows memory temporarily from file cache buffers and returns it when not needed. This is indicated by the double arrow

FIGURE 13.4
The cache-nonmovable
memory pool

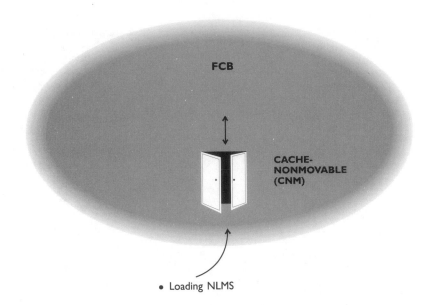

that resides above the door. Once NLMs enter the cache-nonmovable door, they continue through server memory and grab RAM from other pools.

## Cache Movable

The second subpool that resides directly in the file cache buffer area is cache-movable. The cache-movable pool is so named because it contains components that are flexible enough to move their address throughout RAM. This flexibility optimizes memory usage and avoids fragmentation of the file cache buffer pool. This pool is used by system tables that grow dynamically, such as DETs and FATs. Directory hashing is also performed within the cache-movable pool. Figure 13.5 shows the cache-movable pool with wings to illustrate that it can move throughout the file cache buffer area. The double arrows above cache-movable show that this pool works the same as cache-nonmovable—it returns memory to file cache buffers when it is finished.

## Permanent

Another subpool that draws from file cache buffer is the permanent memory pool. The permanent memory pool is not as cooperative in its returning of

**FIGURE 13.5**
The cache-movable
memory pool

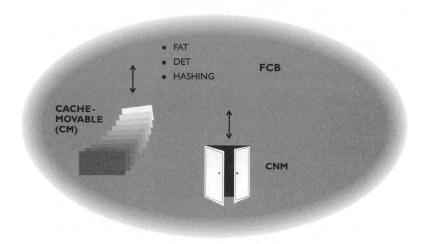

memory as cache-movable and cache-nonmovable. As a matter of fact, as you can tell from Figure 13.6, there is a one-way arrow that indicates that the permanent memory pool draws memory from file cache buffers and *does not return it.* This attitude on behalf of permanent memory can cause the pool to grow quite large, diminishing the amount of memory available for file caching.

NetWare uses the permanent memory pool for long-term memory needs and permanent resources. These resources include permanent tables and

**FIGURE 13.6**
The permanent
memory pool

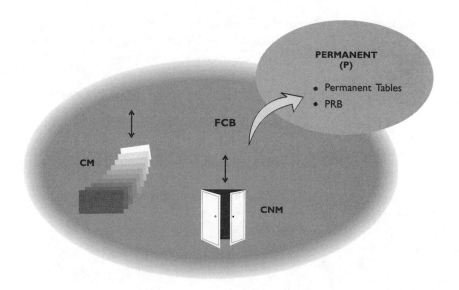

PRBs. If you return to our analogy of the packet receive buffers being the lobby of a bank, it is quite difficult for that lobby to grow dynamically once it has been established in concrete. The process of changing the size of the PRB, for example, involves the downing and reinitializing of the server—serious stuff.

Because of their permanent nature, permanent memory pools do not provide memory to loadable modules. NetWare loadable modules can be loaded and unloaded and therefore change dynamically. Permanent memory, once it is allocated, cannot be changed.

*If I were you, I would get out my highlighter. Especially focus your studies on the part about permanent, semipermanent, and alloc short-term memory.*

### Semipermanent

There are, however, a few types of loadable modules that are semipermanent in their function—that is, they are loaded and rarely unloaded. These loadable modules are serviced from a subpool of permanent memory called the *semipermanent memory pool*. Semipermanent memory is a subpool of permanent memory. This pool draws from permanent memory as needed and returns unused RAM. It is used for small amounts of memory that loadable modules use for a long period of time.

*NLMs enter through the cache-nonmovable memory door and spread their wings throughout server RAM.*

Two common types of semipermanent NLMS are LAN drivers and disk drivers. LAN driver NLMs are loaded at the server to initialize communications between NetWare and the NIC. Disk drivers are similar loadable modules that control communications between the shared disk and the NetWare operating system. Figure 13.7 illustrates the semipermanent memory pool as an amoeba with a double-lined arrow. The graphic illustrates that the semipermanent memory pool can in fact change in size and does migrate throughout the permanent pool.

### Alloc Short-Term

Earlier we mentioned that NLMs enter through the cache-nonmovable memory door and spread their wings throughout server RAM. File cache buffers themselves do not service NLMs; neither do permanent memory pools. So

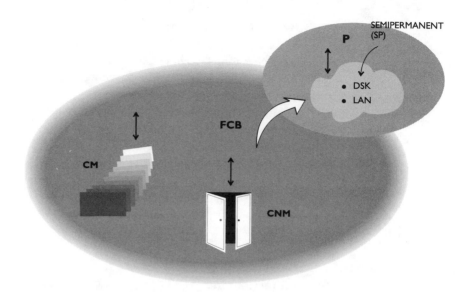

where do loadable modules go? There is one last memory pool that feeds off permanent memory; it's called *alloc short-term memory.*

Alloc short-term memory is used for short-term memory requests and loadable module menus. Figure 13.8 demonstrates that the alloc short-term memory pool indeed feeds off permanent memory in the same way that permanent memory feeds off file cache buffers—that is, a one-way arrow. Memory is not returned once it is finished, so alloc short-term memory can grow quite large as multiple NLMs are loaded. Once the NLMs are unloaded, the alloc short-term memory pool retains its size even though it is not using 100% of the memory.

Other short-term resources and functions include drive mappings, menu programs, service advertising packets, and queue manager tables. One of the best examples of the use of alloc short-term memory is pop-up windows in NLMs. MONITOR's pop-up windows, for example, provide a facility for navigating from one menu to another. As users move through the MONI-TOR utility, the previous menu information is stored in alloc short-term memory until the user returns, at which time it is released. As the system manager moves through the MONITOR utility—popping up more and more windows—alloc short-term memory grows larger and larger. Once the NLM is unloaded, all of this memory becomes unused—but it is *not* returned to permanent memory.

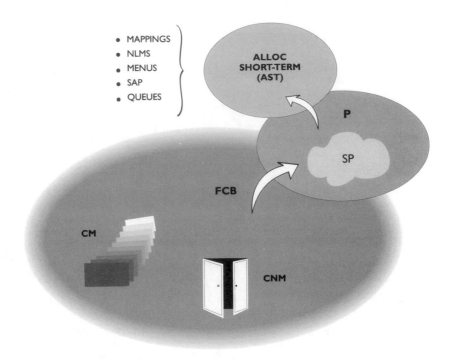

**FIGURE 13.8**
The alloc short-term
memory pool

*The system man-
ager can monitor
inefficiencies in mem-
ory pools using
MONITOR.NLM and
control their sizes us-
ing SET parameters.*

Figure 13.9 illustrates how, when the NLM is loaded, alloc short-term memory and permanent memory grow larger and larger (see the upper illustration). They take memory away from file cache buffers and when the NLM is unloaded, the pool itself stays large while its usage shrinks (see the loser illustration). This growth is an efficiency problem, because it decreases the amount of memory available for file cache buffers. In our earlier discussions you saw that file caching is one of the most important performance optimization tools available in NetWare.

*The willingness to take risks is our grasp of faith.*

*George E. Woodberry*

Later in this chapter, we will discuss how you can monitor these memory pools using MONITOR and control their sizes using SET parameters. The only way to return these memory pools to their default state is to down the server, turn off the file server machine, and reboot the NetWare operating system.

**FIGURE 13.9**
The memory effects
of loading and
unloading NLMs

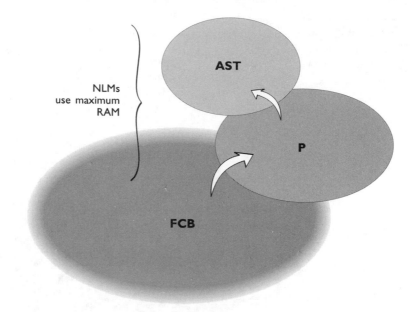

NLMs
use maximum
RAM

WITH NLMs LOADED

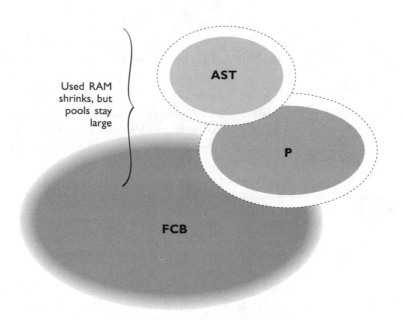

Used RAM
shrinks, but
pools stay
large

AS NLMs ARE UNLOADED

*Although downing the server might seem like a good idea for memory effi-
ciency, it is a bad idea for a lot of other reasons—error tracking, communications reliability, and so on. You should only down the server when all other
courses of action have been exhausted, or it has been active for more than
one hundred days.*

*Think of NetWare memory inefficiencies as being like milking a cow. In the
analogy, the cow would be file cache buffers and the pail would be alloc
short-term memory. The farmer squirts milk into the pail until the pail is full.
Say he's using a medium-sized pail and one morning Betsy decides to give it
her all. Suddenly, the pail is not large enough for all the milk. So the farmer
goes out and buys a larger pail. Well, the next day, Betsy has a bad day and
her milk fills only half the pail. Well, the farmer cannot take the pail back and
is therefore forced to use the larger pail for the rest of his life, whether or
not Betsy ever fills it again. In NetWare, the alloc short-term memory pail
will grow large and never shrink in size.*

Now you can see that memory pools play an important role in NetWare
performance management. These pools can provide a dynamic link for file
caching and other performance features, but at the same time they create
large inefficiencies through alloc short-term memory pools.

In the next section, you will learn how to use the MONITOR NLM to
track these memory pools and use SET parameters to optimize their use.
But before we move on to the MONITOR NLM, take a moment to explore
the memory requirements of NetWare and learn how to calculate minimum
memory needs.

## Memory Requirements

Many resources and functions of the operating system are granted memory as
needed from various pools. Although NetWare is dynamic and effective in its
allocation of memory, it is important to consider the minimum memory requirements when you are using this operating system. Some resources to consider when you calculate minimum memory include:

- Minimum memory to run NetWare, which is 4MB

- Memory required by NLMs

- Memory required by drivers

- Memory required by communication products

- Memory required by hard disk and volume for directory caching

- Block size, which affects the buffer size

- DETs, FATs, and memory needed for file caching

Although file caching is certainly the most important memory requirement, all of the previous operating system functions must be considered as well. The following is a simple formula that can be used to balance all of these resources in determining how much memory is required.

- For a DOS volume, the memory requirement calculation is memory = .023 × the volume size in megabytes ÷ the block size. The requirement for each volume is calculated and then added together. The minimum to run NetWare—4MB—is incorporated in the number so the total memory calculation then becomes memory for all volumes plus 4MB rounded to the highest number.

    Suppose your file server disk has two volumes. Volume I is 80MB and Volume II is 100MB. The memory requirement for Volume I is .023 × 80 ÷ 4 (the default block size). This calculation gives us a value of .46MB. The memory requirement for Volume II is .023 × 100 ÷ 4, which is .575. These two together give us a value of 1.045. Add 1.045 to the 4MB minimum and round to the next whole number—6MB.

- Another calculation is required for volumes that have name space added. Name space is the facility built into NetWare that allows for files using name conventions other than DOS. These file name conventions can include OS/2, Unix, and Macintosh. Volumes that require name space use the formula .032 × volume size in megabytes ÷ block size. Incidentally, notice that the .032 and .023 are simple reversals of each other.

Volumes with name spaces are treated in exactly the same way as DOS volumes. The following is a sample calculation. We have a file server with three volumes: one DOS volume, one Unix volume, and one Macintosh volume. The DOS volume is 80MB, the Unix volume is 300MB, and the Macintosh volume is 100MB. The memory requirement for this server would consist of the following calculations: the DOS volume would be .023 × 80 ÷ 4, which gives us .46MB. The Unix volume calculation would be .032 × 300 ÷ 4, which gives us 2.4MB. The Macintosh volume calculation would consist of

.032 × 100 ÷ 4, or .8MB. Therefore, the final memory requirement for this server would consist of .46 + 2.4 + .8 and then + 4 rounded to the higher value, or a memory requirement of 8MB.

*Memory requirements are the absolute minimum for supporting the disk as well as the name space and block sizes. The optimal environment would consist of double this number making more file server RAM available for file caching. Remember the old rule: the more you can cache, the better off you are. Do yourself a favor: Start with 16MB.*

That's it for server memory management. We discussed the memory pools and how they allocate server RAM to NetWare resources and operating system functions. Then we discussed the memory requirements and how to calculate minimum memory for given situations.

The rest of this chapter will be dedicated to monitoring these components and memory pools, and to using SET parameters to optimize the balance. Keep in mind that as the NetWare interior decorator, it is your responsibility to balance resources and components to create the most beautiful, effective, and productive environment for your users. The moral of the story is that you better watch out where you hang that painting.

# Monitoring Server Performance with MONITOR

S O FAR YOU HAVE learned about the resources that are available to the hotel interior decorator. She must be concerned with various components in optimizing the design and layout of Park Place. The interior decorator is responsible for:

- Hanging paintings
- Arranging flowers
- Dressing windows

- Buying furniture

- Choosing fabric

- Designing color schemes

- Overseeing the general maintenance of hotel amenities

The NetWare interior decorator is also responsible for the optimization of LAN resources. The focus of your interior decorating efforts and LAN optimization is at the file server. The file server houses all shared resources, including disk, printing, memory, and communications. As the NetWare interior decorator, you are responsible for:

- Hanging hard disks

- Arranging memory pools

- Designing internal NICs

- Buying more memory

- Choosing NLMs

- Designing server configurations

- Overseeing the general maintenance of LAN amenities

The NetWare interior decorator has two tools available for her use: MONITOR and SET. The MONITOR server NLM is used for monitoring the server components; the SET parameters allow for proactive configuration of optimal settings. In this section you will learn about monitoring server performance with the MONITOR.NLM utility and move on to optimizing server performance with SET in the next section. Let's begin with the main screen of MONITOR.

*The MONITOR server NLM is used for monitoring the server components; the SET parameters allow for proactive configuration of optimal settings.*

## Main Screen

MONITOR.NLM is the major tool used by NetWare to check information on memory and resource utilization. The main screen in MONITOR (Figure 13.10) provides a snapshot of current resource settings. This screen is dynamic; it changes as NetWare services user requests.

**FIGURE 13.10**
The main screen
of MONITOR.NLM

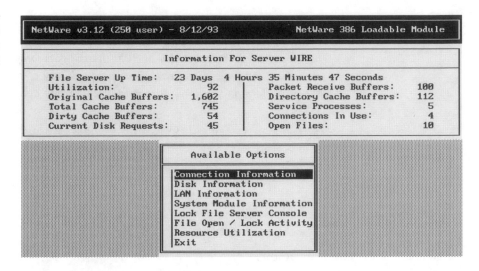

```
NetWare v3.12 (250 user) - 8/12/93          NetWare 386 Loadable Module

                    Information For Server WIRE

    File Server Up Time:   23 Days  4 Hours 35 Minutes 47 Seconds
    Utilization:                92      Packet Receive Buffers:    100
    Original Cache Buffers:  1,602      Directory Cache Buffers:   112
    Total Cache Buffers:       745      Service Processes:           5
    Dirty Cache Buffers:        54      Connections In Use:          4
    Current Disk Requests:      45      Open Files:                 10

                        Available Options
                    ┌────────────────────────────┐
                    │ Connection Information      │
                    │ Disk Information            │
                    │ LAN Information             │
                    │ System Module Information   │
                    │ Lock File Server Console    │
                    │ File Open / Lock Activity   │
                    │ Resource Utilization        │
                    │ Exit                        │
                    └────────────────────────────┘
```

The Available Options menu in MONITOR provides nine choices that can be broken up into four categories:

**Resource utilization,** which provides information on tracking resources and server memory statistics

**Processor utilization,** which is a histogram of internal file server processes

**Information screens,** which provide information-only windows for connections, disks, LAN, and system module information

**Other available options,** which include facilities for locking the file server console, viewing file lock activity, and exiting the system

You can load MONITOR.NLM from the file server console prompt by typing LOAD MONITOR. MONITOR supports three switches:

**NS**—loads MONITOR without issuing the screen-saver worm

**NH**—does not load MONITOR help, which saves approximately 10–15KB of file server RAM

**P**—loads MONITOR with the Processor Utilization menu choice available

*Once MONITOR loads, it has a built-in screen saver that has a dual function. Affectionately known as the worm, the screen saver consists of a box that travels around the screen in a random pattern with a tail following it.*

---

*O*nce MONITOR loads, it has a built-in screen saver that has a dual function. Affectionately known as the worm, the screen saver consists of a box that travels around the screen in a random pattern with a tail that indicates processor utilization.

TIP

*Although it's amusing to look at, the tail actually has a performance utilization function; i.e, the length of the tail indicates utilization. So, for example, as utilization rises above 25% or 30%, the tail gets longer, and the worm moves around the screen faster. This is a quick way of monitoring file server performance without having to dive into any detailed screens.*

The main screen in MONITOR provides information on the following four categories:

- Utilization
- Buffers
- Service processes
- Other

In addition, the main screen provides the server name and an indication of file server uptime detailing for how many days, hours, minutes, and seconds this particular file server has been active. Let's take a quick look at the four types of information provided by the MONITOR main screen.

*If I were you, I would learn the three most important MONITOR.NLM choices: Main Screen, Resource Utilization, and Processor Utilization. These areas are where you will spend most of your time as a NetWare 3.1x optimizer.*

### Utilization

Utilization is a measurement of how busy or active the file server processor is. The utilization percentage from 0 to 100 indicates the percentage of time the processor is busy. As user requests are stored in the PRB and FSPs continue to process these requests, utilization will climb. Typically, utilization jumps from 4% or 5% to 20% or 30% rather quickly and then back down to 5%. The processor is rarely used above 25% for an extended period of time.

### Buffers

As you recall, buffers are storage areas in file server RAM. In our discussion of performance management components, we learned about three types of buffers: file cache, directory cache, and packet receive. The main screen in MONITOR provides valuable information about the status of these buffers in addition to original cache buffers and dirty cache buffers.

*People are very open-minded about new things—as long as they're exactly like the old ones.*

*Charles F. Kettering*

**ORIGINAL CACHE BUFFERS**  Original cache buffers indicate the number of cache buffers available when the file server is first booted. This is the number of buffers installed in your server minus the operating system components such as SERVER.EXE, COMMAND.COM, and so on. The default buffer size is 4KB, so the actual memory is calculated as $4 \times$ the number of original cache buffers. In Figure 13.10, you saw $1602 \times 4$, or 6,408,000 bytes. This file server has 8MB of memory, so roughly 1.5MB is required by the operating system components.

**TOTAL CACHE BUFFERS**  Total cache buffers indicate the number of buffers currently available for file caching. The difference between original cache buffers and total cache buffers is the memory allocated to permanent, semipermanent, and alloc short-term memory pools.

Total cache buffers decrease as other server modules are added and memory pools draw from the central cache pool. Total cache buffers are extremely important for memory and performance because they provide the number one file access feature in NetWare: file caching. You should constantly monitor the availability of total cache buffers and track other pools as they are drawing from this central pool. An alarm clock should go off in your head as soon as the total cache buffers reach half the original number. At this point, only 50% of your original cache memory is available for file caching. If this occurs, you should move to the Server Memory Statistics screen, where you can get a more accurate description of the percentage of total cache buffers available. If the percentage in the Server Memory Statistics-window drops to 20%, you have a real crisis situation.

*T*otal cache buffers decrease as other server modules are added and memory pools draw from the central cache pool.

During a memory caching emergency, the system administrator has two courses of action:

- You can add more memory immediately.

- You can down the file server and reboot the machine to regain memory from inefficient permanent and alloc memory pools.

The bottom line is: If total cache buffers reaches 20%, action must be taken immediately.

**DIRTY CACHE BUFFERS**  Dirty cache buffers are an interesting anomaly. They are areas of cache memory that contain files that have not yet been written to disk. Recall from our discussion of file caching that file caching stores frequently used files in memory so users can perform read and write operations much more quickly. If a user saves a cached file, it will be stored in cache before it is written to disk. If the hard disk or processor is busy, this information will be stored in the cache temporarily, waiting to be written to disk. The problem with dirty cache buffers is that if a lot of changes are made and this information is kept in memory before it is written to disk and the power goes out, the users will lose all of their edits or changes.

The ideal situation is for dirty cache buffers to be at or near zero. If the number of dirty cache buffers rises and reaches 70% of the total number of cache buffers, this is a serious situation. 70% of your total cache memory has not yet been written to disk and is vulnerable in the case of a power outage. The percentage of dirty cache buffers can be calculated by dividing the number of total cache buffers into the number of dirty cache buffers.

A possible cause for an increase in dirty cache buffers is a slow hard disk or busy processor. The action the system manager should take in increasing the speed of writes from dirty cache buffers is to alter the maximum concurrent disk cache write set parameter. Increasing the value of this SET parameter will improve the performance of writing from cache memory to the hard disk. Incidentally, increasing the concurrent disk cache write parameter will slow the performance of disk cache reading. Refer to the optimization section under the SET parameter for a discussion of the maximum concurrent disk cache write parameter.

**PACKET RECEIVE BUFFERS**  PRBs are, as you know, the lobby of our NetWare bank—a holding cell for user requests that are waiting to be serviced by file service processes. The PRBs item in the main screen of MONITOR indicates how many buffers are currently reserved for incoming user requests.

The minimum default value is 100, and this number will not change in most docile networks. As user requests increase and the need for a larger lobby occurs, NetWare will automatically assign PRBs from the permanent memory pool. Keep in mind that the PRBs use memory drawn from cache RAM.

PRBs and FSPs are closely linked. They rely on each other for optimal performance of the NetWare server. As PRBs increase, the need for FSPs decreases, because more requests can wait in RAM. On the other hand, as FSPs become more busy, a need for large PRBs can be decreased by adding FSPs. Both of these parameters are setable using SET parameters and can be dynamically increased and decreased as needed by NetWare.

If the number of PRBs approaches 100, there are not enough FSPs to service all of the user requests. It could also be the case that user requests are coming in faster than the PRBs can keep up. Overall, the largest number of PRBs is 1,000. If the number reaches the minimum of 100 and cannot go any further, dramatic pressure is placed on the FSPs. If both the PRBs and FSPs are maxed out, the system will begin to drop packets and eventually crash. The system manager can increase the maximum number of PRBs allowed using the SET parameter, discussed in the next section.

**DIRECTORY CACHE BUFFERS**  DCBs cache commonly used portions of the DET. The default minimum number of directory cache buffers is 20, which is typically enough to store 640 directory entries. This is only a start. Most busy servers with large numbers of files and directories will quickly reach 100 DCBs. One hundred DCBs can cache 3,200 directory entries. But remember that the entire DET is not cached; only the most recently used portions are.

The maximum number of DCBs is 4,000 (500 by default), but Novell suggests that if the number of DCBs exceeds 100, the minimum number should be increased to 200 or 300. Increasing the minimum number of DCBs will speed up directory searches, because the system does not have to dynamically allocate DCBs as users need them. Reserving a large number of cache buffers makes that memory immediately available and increases the speed of directory searches. The SET parameters relating to DCBs will be discussed in the next section.

That completes our discussion of buffer tracking. Now let's take a look at some of the other, related parameters from the main screen of MONITOR.

### Service Processes

Service processes are the tellers of our NetWare bank. These task handlers are internal subroutines that service user requests. NetWare dynamically allocates service processes as needed for incoming packets. As we mentioned earlier, service processes are dynamically linked to the PRBs that are the lobby of our NetWare bank.

In Figure 13.10 you saw service processes set at 5 and the PRBs set at the minimum 100. Although this system has 92% utilization, there are only 4 connections in use and it is not busy. A busy network with 50 or so users and 70 to 80% utilization will max out PRBs at 400 and max out service processes at 20. The service processes maximum can be increased to 40 using the SET parameter. Incidentally, it is suggested that you increase the maximum service processes parameter by increments of five.

Also, increasing the number of service processes does take up a dramatic amount of server RAM. If file cache buffers are low or memory caching is a concern, service processes should be increased cautiously. The optimization section gives a more thorough discussion of the relationship between PRBs and service processes.

### Other Information

The final information options available from the main screen of MONITOR include general types of system information. The Current Disk Request option shows the number of disk requests that are waiting in a line to be serviced by the NetWare server. These are dirty cache buffers that have been sent to the disk. The Connections in Use option is an indication of how many stations are currently attached to the file server. The Available Options menu provides further choices for viewing details about these two connections. Finally, Open Files is the number of files currently being accessed by the server that are open on network workstations. The Available Options menu also provides a choice for viewing detailed information about currently opened files.

The main screen in MONITOR provides a snapshot that freezes the current, valuable statistics concerning performance management components. It is a good place to start for the system manager to track and identify components that need further attention. The Available Options menu in MONITOR provides a great deal more detail in analyzing the sources and destination of server memory and resource utilization. Let's take a closer look at some of the more useful Available Options choices, starting with Resource Utilization.

# Resource Utilization

*The system manager should routinely use the Resource Utilization option for viewing detailed information about memory pools and tracking suspect NLMs and internal resources.*

Resource Utilization is the most important performance monitoring menu. It logs server memory pool utilization. In addition, Resource Utilization provides a method for tracking resources and discovering how server resources are using internal memory pools. The system manager should routinely use the Resource Utilization option for viewing detailed information about memory pools and tracking suspect NLMs and internal resources. Discoveries made here can go a long way toward optimizing file service performance using SET parameters.

The Resource Utilization menu provides two types of information: Server Memory Statistics and Tracked Resources. Server Memory Statistics is a summary screen that provides detailed information and percentages for the five main NetWare 3.1*x* memory pools (the semipermanent pool is combined with the permanent memory pool statistics). Tracked Resources information is a detailed navigation of screens that allows the system manager to zero in on NLMs and internal routines that are using various pools of server RAM.

*Vision: the art of seeing things invisible.*

*Jonathan Swift*

Let's explore server memory statistics and tracked resources in detail.

### Server Memory Statistics

The Server Memory Statistics submenu of Resource Utilization is shown in Figure 13.11. This menu lists the five main memory pools on the left and their current size in bytes on the right. In addition, server memory statistics provides the percentage of total server work memory each pool is occupying. In the cases of permanent and alloc memory pools, this screen indicates how much of their maximum size is currently being used.

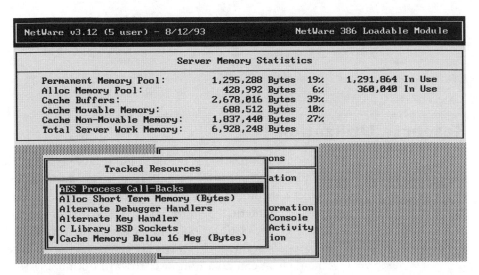

Total server work memory is an indication of how much memory is currently available to file cache buffers and the other pools. Total server work memory is the total amount of memory installed minus SERVER.EXE, DOS, and ROM BIOS. This number should closely match the number calculated for original cache buffers. The small discrepancy between the two can be attributed to auxiliary operating system memory requirements. In this case, the number 6,928,248 bytes is 500,000 or so more than the original cache buffers. That means that 500KB has been reserved by auxiliary operating system routines. They are available as server work memory but not available for caching.

Notice in Figure 13.11 that the permanent and alloc memory pools show a value of memory In Use. Recall from our earlier discussion that these two memory pools draw memory from file cache buffers but do not return it. Refer to the dotted line in Figure 13.9, which indicates the actual growth size of these pools; note that the shaded area is considerably less. The shaded area would be the in-use value of the Server Memory Statistics screen.

Cache buffers should always represent the largest percentage of total server work memory. In this case, 39% is a little low for file caching. Cache-movable and cache-nonmovable pools should roughly match the permanent memory pool, but in this case they don't. Alloc memory is typically a lot smaller. Remember from our earlier discussions that cache-nonmovable is the door through which NLMs enter the file cache buffers and then move on to alloc short-term memory. Keep in mind that most of the memory requirements made by NLMs are provided from cache-nonmovable memory.

## Tracked Resources

Detailed information about which resources are using the memory pool can be viewed through the Tracked Resources menu. MONITOR's Tracked Resources facility lists operating system components that make demands for server RAM. Figure 13.11 showed the alphabetic listing of tracked resources, starting with AES process callbacks and continuing from there.

The system manager can use this menu to track resources and gain valuable information about how they are using server RAM. If you highlight a resource—alloc short-term memory, for example—and press Enter, the system will return a list of resource tags. Resources tags are NLMs that are associated with this particular resource. The NLMs or server applications are using this resource to access server memory. For example, you could select the alloc short-term memory resource to provide a list of resource tags. These tags include INSTALL.NLM, MONITOR.NLM, REMOTE.NLM, SERVER.NLM, and so on.

By highlighting the MONITOR.NLM resource tag, you gain valuable information about how much alloc short-term memory MONITOR is using. Figure 13.12 shows the resulting screen from highlighting the MONITOR.NLM resource tag. This graphic tells us that of the 365,776 bytes of

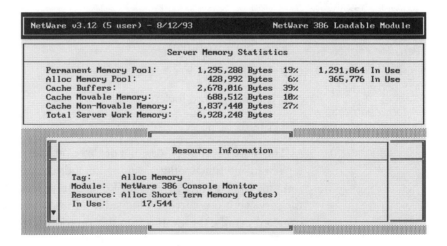

**FIGURE 13.12**
Monitoring NetWare
3.1x resources

memory currently being used in alloc short-term, 17,544 are being used by MONITOR.NLM.

This strategy is particularly useful if certain NLMs or resources are monopolizing file server RAM. If the server memory statistics screen shows an abnormally high amount of permanent or alloc memory, the system manager can use resource tracking to identify the greedy NLM culprit.

# Information Screens

Other information screens provided through MONITOR's Available Options menu offer the system manager a chance to gain valuable information about shared server resources. These information screens include Connection Information, Disk Information, LAN Information, and System Module Information.

### Connection Information

*Other information screens provided through MONITOR's Available Options menu include screens for: connection information, disk information, LAN information, and system module information.*

The Connection Information screen in MONITOR provides detailed information about active connections. The system manager can view connection-oriented details including:

- Connection time

- Network node address

- Number of requests made by this connection

- Kilobytes written

- Kilobytes read

- Logical record locks

- Status

The Status field provides one of three options: Normal (connection is logged in and functioning), Waiting (an indication that the connection is waiting for a file to be unlocked) or Not Logged In (the connection is attached to the file server but not currently logged in). In addition to listing connection-oriented details, the Connection Information screen lists all open files that are currently in use by this connection. This information is particularly useful for system managers who are tracking shared files, databases, record locking, and user performance. The initial Connection Information screen lists all active connections with their connection number and user login name. This information is also useful because it provides a facility not only for connection-oriented but login name-oriented details.

### Disk Information

The Disk Information option in MONITOR (Figure 13.13) provides details about the internal shared hard disk. It provides a summary list of valuable disk statistics. Some of the more interesting statistics are in:

- Driver
- Disk Size
- Mirror Status
- Data Blocks
- Redirection Blocks

The Redirection Blocks show how many blocks have been reserved for hot fix internal dynamic bad block remapping. The Redirected Blocks show how many blocks have been used. It is a good idea for the system manager to track the number of redirected blocks to see whether the redirection area is

**FIGURE 13.13**
Disk Information option in MONITOR.NLM

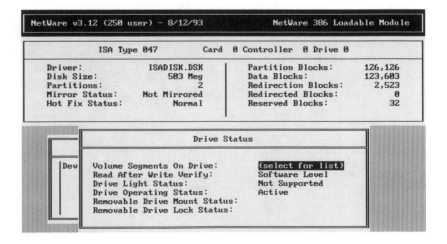

being used. If the hot fix redirection area is being filled up quickly, the server disk is about to fail and any number exceeding 50% is a point for concern. If the redirected blocks exceed 50% of the reserved redirection blocks, the system manager should either replace the hard disk or reformat it and reinstall NetWare.

The Disk Information option also provides a supplementary window called Drive Status that provides information about read-after-write verification, the drive operating status, and volume segments that have been assigned to this drive.

### LAN Information

The LAN Information option in MONITOR provides details about internal server NICs. The initial LAN driver information screen provides a list of all internal NICs and their configurations, including port, interrupt, and frame type. The system manager can highlight the appropriate NIC name and press Enter to view a much more detailed list of custom NIC statistics. These statistics include node address, bound protocols, the network address, and generic communication statistics. Figure 13.14 illustrates the generic statistics for the 200E NIC. These statistics include total packets sent and total packets received. In addition, the system manager can view information about collisions and possible lost packets.

The LAN Information option in MONITOR is a valuable tool for isolating and troubleshooting network communication problems.

*The LAN Information option in MONITOR is a valuable tool for isolating and troubleshooting network communication problems.*

**FIGURE 13.14**
LAN Information option in MONITOR.NLM

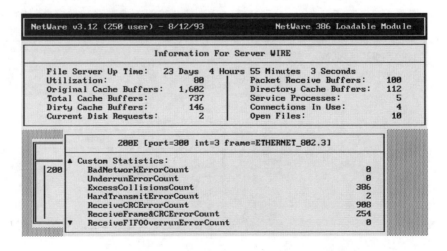

```
NetWare v3.12 (250 user) - 8/12/93          NetWare 386 Loadable Module

                         Information For Server WIRE

   File Server Up Time:   23 Days  4 Hours 55 Minutes  3 Seconds
   Utilization:                 80    Packet Receive Buffers:     100
   Original Cache Buffers:   1,602    Directory Cache Buffers:    112
   Total Cache Buffers:        737    Service Processes:            5
   Dirty Cache Buffers:        146    Connections In Use:           4
   Current Disk Requests:        2    Open Files:                  10


                  200E [port=300 int=3 frame=ETHERNET_802.3]

            ▲ Custom Statistics:
      200       BadNetworkErrorCount                    0
                UnderrunErrorCount                      0
                ExcessCollisionsCount                 386
                HardTransmitErrorCount                  2
                ReceiveCRCErrorCount                  908
                ReceiveFrame&CRCErrorCount            254
            ▼   ReceiveFIFOOverrunErrorCount            0
```

### System Module Information

The System Module Information option in MONITOR provides a detailed listing of internal operating system modules and their corresponding resource tags. This menu provides the same type of information as does Resource Utilization, except that System Module Information is module-specific rather than resource-specific.

You can highlight the appropriate system module and press Enter to display a window of resource tags. You can then get a feel for what type of resource a particular module is using and how much of what type of memory is currently being used. Figure 13.15 illustrates the type of details for the SERVER.NLM module. SERVER.NLM is the operating system itself as it resides in module form. Bear in mind that there is no such thing as SERVER.NLM—this is SERVER.EXE, but as a module it appears to the system as an NLM.

*Get your facts first, then you can distort them as you please.*

*Mark Twain*

Highlighting the NetWare operating system provides a supplemental menu of the resource tags that SERVER.NLM is using. As you can see from Figure 13.15, SERVER.NLM is using almost 935KB of memory. The system manager can view more detailed information about how SERVER.NLM is using resources such as DCBs, connection user information, DETs, disk cache buffers, extended attributes, file locks, IPX protocol stacks, sockets, semipermanent

**FIGURE 13.15**
The System Module Information option in MONITOR.NLM

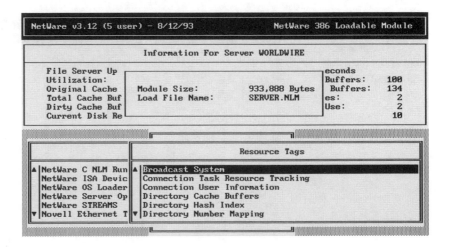

memory, NCP tables, print queues, routing information, TTS, and user disk space restrictions.

It is evident that the System Module Information facility is quite detailed in scope and provides a great deal of information for tracking problematic NetWare modules.

# Processor Utilization

*The Processor Utilization menu choice becomes available if the system manager loads MONITOR with the /P switch. Processor utilization provides a histogram of internal NetWare processes and the type of load they are putting on the server CPU.*

The final MONITOR tool available to system managers is processor utilization. The Processor Utilization menu choice becomes available if the system manager loads MONITOR with the /P switch. Processor utilization provides a histogram of internal NetWare processes and the type of load they are putting on the server CPU. The transitional Utilization screen lists available processes and interrupts. These processes and interrupts are competing for CPU resources. The system manager can press F5 to highlight each process he/she is willing to track, and then press Enter or F3 to view *all* resources. The system will respond with a histogram similar to the one in Figure 13.16.

The processor utilization histogram provides three different types of information: time, count, and load. The time parameter shows the amount of time the CPU has spent working on this particular process. The count is the number of times the process ran during the sample period. The load is the most important statistic of all. It indicates the percentage of processor use per second. Notice from Figure 13.16 that the majority of the processor's time

**FIGURE 13.16**
The processor utilization histogram in MONITOR.NLM

| | Name | Time | Count | Load | |
|---|---|---|---|---|---|
| Fi ▲ | FAT Update Process | 4,182 | 11 | 0.37 % | |
| Ut | Instal Process | 0 | 0 | 0.00 % | 00 |
| Or | Media Manager Process | 0 | 0 | 0.00 % | 12 |
| To | Monitor Main Process | 0 | 0 | 0.00 % | 5 |
| Di | Polling Process | 414,916 | 554 | 37.63 % | 4 |
| Cu | Remote Process | 16,410 | 20 | 1.48 % | 9 |
| | RSPX Process | 0 | 0 | 0.00 % | |
| | Server 01 Process | 125,217 | 164 | 11.35 % | |
| | Server 02 Process | 58,950 | 59 | 5.34 % | |
| | Server 03 Process | 0 | 0 | 0.00 % | |
| | STREAMS Q Runner Process | 0 | 0 | 0.00 % | |
| | TTS Finish Process | 0 | 0 | 0.00 % | |
| | Interrupt  3 | 210,131 | 410 | 19.06 % | |
| | Interrupt 14 | 194,943 | 339 | 17.68 % | |

NetWare v3.12 (250 user) – 8/12/93          NetWare 386 Loadable Module

Total Sample Time:          1,190,508
Histogram Overhead Time:       88,108    ( 7.40 %)
Adjusted Sample Time:       1,102,400

is spent in the polling process. This is the processor waiting idly by for processes to come by and bother it. The most aggressive processes in this graphic are the remote process and the cache update process.

The Processor Utilization histogram can be used by system managers to monitor and track how active the file server processor truly is. If server responses tend to be a bit sluggish, the system manager can open this screen and monitor how different processes are accessing the CPU. A detailed help screen is available within Processor Utilization by pressing F1.

That completes our discussion of performance monitoring using the built-in NetWare MONITOR.NLM utility. As you can see from this discussion, MONITOR.NLM is a highly extensive facility with a great deal of detailed information for CNAs. It is a good idea for you to set up a schedule of daily or weekly perusals of MONITOR, focusing on specific areas. Some of the most common areas are Server Memory Statistics in Resource Utilization, the main menu, and disk and LAN statistics.

So far in this chapter we have focused on what to look for and how to look for it. Now that you have learned the different strategies the system manager can use for performance management, it is time to roll up our sleeves and focus on exactly what kind of actions can be taken when problems are found.

# Optimizing Server Performance with SET

T HE SET CONSOLE COMMAND provides the facility for customizing the SERVER.EXE program and optimizing its various parameters. The SET command defines nine areas of customization:

- Communications
- Memory
- File caching
- Directory caching

*The SET parameters are customizing the SERVER.EXE program while the server is running. This is like trying to tune up a moving car. Be cautious as you use the SET parameters.*

- Miscellaneous
- File system
- Locks
- Transaction tracking
- Disk

NetWare 3.1$x$ provides almost one hundred different SET parameters for proactive performance optimization. In this section, we will discuss the twenty most effective SET parameters.

The SET parameters are customizing the SERVER.EXE program while the server is running. This is like trying to tune up a moving car. It is extremely important that you realize that a lot of damage can be done by setting the wrong parameters. Be cautious as you use the SET parameters. Also, focus on where the SET parameters need to be set. Some parameters that relate to communications, caching, and disk, for example, must be set in the STARTUP.NCF and will not take effect until the server is downed and brought back up. All other SET parameters can be set at the console prompt or in the AUTOEXEC.NCF file. Six SET parameters must be set in the STARTUP.NCF:

- Auto register memory above 16MB
- Auto TTS backout flag
- Cache buffer size
- Maximum physical receive packet size
- Maximum subdirectory tree depth
- Minimum PRBs

*If I were you, I would make special note of where certain SET parameters are stored: STARTUP.NCF or AUTOEXEC.NCF or either.*

Keep in mind that any parameters installed in the AUTOEXEC.NCF or STARTUP.NCF files will not take effect until the file server is downed and rebooted. Current SET parameter values can be viewed by typing SET at the console prompt and pressing Enter. The system will respond with a list of the nine different categories, numbered 1 through 9. You then enter a number and the system asks whether you would like to see advanced settings. Advanced settings are SET parameters that configure detailed and advanced operating system parameters. If you choose Yes, the system will respond by listing all SET parameters and values for that particular group. By the way, the advanced parameters show automatically in NetWare 3.12.

To configure a specific SET parameter, you must type SET and the name of the parameter followed by an equal (=) sign and a value. For example, to change the subdirectory tree depth, the system manager would type:

```
SET MAXIMUM SUBDIRECTORY TREE DEPTH = 25
```

Throughout the chapter we have discussed the need for SET parameters and optimizing file server performance. Earlier we talked about the different components that affect file server performance, and in the last section we used the MONITOR.NLM to track resources utilization and performance management components. In the remaining sections of this chapter, we will discuss the twenty most popular set parameters and how they are used to implement maximum file server performance. Let's begin with the communications parameters.

## Communications

*The communications SET parameters control communications among the server, NIC, and incoming and outgoing packets.*

The communications SET parameters control communications among the server, NIC, and incoming and outgoing packets. Communication SET parameters focus on two different areas of server communications: PRBs and watchdog packets. PRBs are the waiting area in server RAM where user requests are held until FSPs are available—the lobby of our NetWare bank. Watchdog packets, on the other hand, are NetWare sentries that patrol the LAN cabling for inactive workstations. The watchdog packet will disconnect or drop a connection for a workstation that does not respond after a specific number of tries. Let's take a closer look at these two types of communication SET parameters.

### Packet Receive Buffers

PRBs are closely linked to FSPs in that they provide a waiting area for incoming packets. If NetWare does not allocate enough FSPs, the PRB can become quite full. In addition, busy file servers require large PRBs. NetWare provides two SET parameters that configure or customize the PRBs: maximum and minimum settings.

Another communication parameter that relates to PRBs is maximum physical packet size. The PRBs are 4KB by default and contain four 1KB packets per buffer. If the LAN communications protocol can support larger or smaller packets, the system manager must configure this setting to accommodate. In our earlier analogy, the maximum physical packet size would represent the number of people waiting in line. Obviously, the larger the number of people, the larger the lobby needs to be. Let's take a closer look at the PRB settings.

**MAXIMUM PACKET RECEIVE BUFFERS**  The maximum packet receive buffers parameter determines the maximum number of PRBs the operating system can allocate. The default setting is 400. This setting is much too low for busy servers. As mentioned earlier, the system will dynamically allocate PRBs as needed. If the number reaches 400 and this is not adequate, packets will get lost and the system will eventually crash. A setting between 500 and 1000 is ideal for busy servers.

**MINIMUM PACKET RECEIVE BUFFERS**  The minimum packet receive buffers parameter determines the minimum number of PRBs the operating system can allocate. The default is 100. The minimum setting is important because the operating system will reserve this many buffers as soon as the server boots. This is a much faster way to allocate PRBs than waiting for the dynamic allocation. Dynamic allocation of PRBs decreases system performance. If your LAN is extremely busy and you find communications a little sluggish, it is a good idea to increase the minimum packet receive buffers in intervals of ten. NetWare supports up to 1,000 minimum packet receive buffers.

*The minimum packet receive buffers parameter can only be changed in the STARTUP.NCF file, because the minimum number must be set when the file server is booted. Therefore, the minimum packet receive buffers SET parameter cannot be issued at the console prompt.*

*Our life is frittered away by detail. Simplicity, simplicity, simplicity!*

*Henry David Thoreau*

### Maximum Physical Receive Packet Size

Maximum physical receive packet size determines the maximum size of packets that can be transmitted on any of the file server's networks. The default is 4202, including the packet header. The default setting is ideal for most token ring or Ethernet LANs. If you have high-end Token Ring NICs that are capable of transmitting larger packets, increasing the maximum physical receive packet size will increase communications performance up to 24,682 bytes. Keep in mind that increasing the maximum physical receive packet size will dramatically affect the performance of PRBs. The system manager will have to increase the minimum and maximum number of PRBs if the maximum physical receive packet size is increased.

*This parameter must be set and can only be set in the STARTUP. NCF file. That file defines the communications tolerance of the internal NIC. Maximum physical receive packet size parameters cannot be set at the console prompt.*

### Watchdog

The next type of communications SET parameter is watchdog. Watchdog is a built-in NetWare facility for patrolling active connections. If a workstation is occupying a valid connection from the file server and not responding to routine watchdog packets, the system will disconnect the workstation. This is a built-in efficiency feature that is designed to drop inactive connections. There are two watchdog SET parameters that specifically affect the performance of NetWare communications:

- The number
- The delay

Let's take a closer look.

**NUMBER OF WATCHDOG PACKETS** The number of watchdog packets parameter defines how many packets the server will send without receiving a reply from a workstation. The default is 10. This means that NetWare will send out ten watchdog packets to all workstations. If a particular workstation does not respond after the tenth packet, its connection will be dropped.

**DELAY BEFORE FIRST WATCHDOG PACKET** The next parameter is delay before first watchdog Packet. This option determines how long to wait before sending out the first of ten watchdog packets. The default is 4 minutes and 56.6 seconds. You can choose any time period between 15.7 seconds and 20 minutes and 52.3 seconds.

**DELAY BETWEEN WATCHDOG PACKETS** The delay between watchdog packets parameter defines how long the server waits between sending watchdog packets. The default is 59.3 seconds. The range is 9.9 seconds to a maximum of 10 minutes and 26.2 seconds. A system manager who is concerned about inactive connections can set the number of watchdog packets to 5 and set the delay between watchdog packets to 10 or 12 seconds. The system will drop workstations that don't respond after a minute's worth of polling.

## Memory

*Memory SET parameters control the size of dynamic memory pools, block sizes of cache buffers, and the automatic registering of memory on EISA bus computers.*

The next type of SET parameter is associated with memory. Memory SET parameters control the size of the dynamic memory pools, block sizes of cache buffers, and the automatic registering of memory on EISA bus computers. These parameters do not specifically apply to file or directory caching—those parameters have their own particular groupings.

The system manager should focus his/her memory SET parameters on the following three factors that are associated with performance management:

- Maximum alloc short-term memory

- Auto register memory above 16MB

- Cache buffer size

Let's take a quick look.

### Maximum Alloc Short-Term Memory

The maximum alloc short-term memory parameter controls how much memory the operating system will allocate to alloc short-term memory. The default is 8MB, and NetWare supports a value of up to 32MB. The smallest maximum setting is 50K. Recall from our earlier discussions that the alloc memory pool grows in size and does not return memory to file caching. The maximum alloc short-term memory parameter can be used to limit the size to which alloc short-term memory can grow. Keep in mind, though, that if the alloc short-term memory pool reaches its default maximum of 8MB, the system will not allow the loading of NLMs or additional drive mappings.

This scenario could also have a dramatic effect on user connections, queue management, and the opening of locked files. If the system manager is not concerned about the growth of alloc short-term memory, he/she can increase the maximum in increments of 1 million bytes.

*Many NetWare 3.1x features draw heavily on alloc short-term memory, including GUI utilities, disk drivers, and drive mappings.*

### Auto Register Memory Above 16 Megabytes

The auto register memory above 16MB parameter is used to automatically register memory in excess of 16MB. This parameter only works for EISA computers. You learned in our earlier discussion of console commands that NetWare does not automatically register memory above 16MB for ISA or Micro Channel machines. It does, however, automatically register memory for EISA computers. This is only the case if the auto register memory above 16MB SET parameter is set to ON (the default setting).

*This particular parameter must be set and can only be set in the STARTUP.NCF file, because it defines the operating system configuration and identification of internal RAM.*

*It's a good idea to set the auto register memory above 16MB parameter to OFF if you installed a network board or disk adapter that uses on-line direct memory access (DMA). These boards use 24-bit address lines and can only address 16MB of memory without crashing.*

### Cache Buffers Size

The cache buffers size parameter controls the block size of the cache buffer. By default, all cache buffers are 4KB. As mentioned earlier, NetWare provides the facility for having 4, 8, or 16KB buffer size. This parameter is directly linked to the disk allocation block size (which is 4KB by default). If disk allocation block sizes are larger on all volumes, the cache buffer size can be increased, thus increasing file service performance and the efficiency of file cache buffer RAM. Remember, if you increase the cache buffer size parameter without increasing the disk allocation block size, the system will recognize this as a huge inefficiency. NetWare takes action against people with buffer sizes larger than their smallest block size: NetWare will not mount any volumes in which this is the case.

*The cache buffers size parameter can only be set in the STARTUP.NCF file because it defines the smallest allocation unit of server RAM. Also, remember from our earlier discussion how to set it at server startup:*
SERVER -C 16384.

*Common sense is instinct, and enough of it is genius.*

*Josh Billings*

## File Caching

Two of the most important functions of file server memory are file caching and directory caching. File caching increases the server's disk performance by up to 10,000%. Directory caching caches most commonly used portions of the DET. NetWare provides three SET parameters for both file caching and directory caching that dramatically improve server performance. The file caching parameters are:

*NetWare provides three SET parameters for both file caching and directory caching that dramatically improve server performance.*

- Minimum file cache buffers
- Minimum file cache buffer report threshold
- Maximum concurrent disk cache writes

The system manager is responsible for balancing these settings with cache buffer size and other directory caching parameters. Settings here will impact the system manager's ability to react when caching is becoming a problem.

### Minimum File Cache Buffers

The minimum file cache buffers parameter sets the minimum number of cache buffers the operating system can allow for file caching. This is the minimum level the system manager is willing to accept. As you recall from our earlier discussions, all memory not allocated for operating system processes is given to file caching. As memory is requested from other pools, it is drawn from the file cache buffer pool. The default setting of 20 buffers is equivalent to 80KB of file cache RAM. A number this low is almost inconsequential because the file server will probably lock up or crash before it reaches as low as 20 file cache buffers.

The range is 20 to 1,000. That is to say, the maximum minimum file cache buffers the system will support is 1,000. If the system manager sets the minimum file cache buffers setting too high, let's say to 1,000, then the other five supplemental memory pools will have difficulty acquiring needed RAM. If the minimum file cache buffer size is set to 1,000, most NLMs will not be able to load, because alloc short-term memory is restricted and cannot allocate memory to NLMs for loading. The key to the minimum file cache buffer is balance. A setting too small will not allow the system to protect itself against losing all of its file cache buffers, whereas a setting too large will reserve too many file cache buffers and not allow for the allocation of memory to supplemental pools.

### Minimum File Cache Buffer Report Threshold

The minimum file cache buffer report threshold is an advanced parameter that sets a threshold for notifying the system manager when file cache buffers are getting too low. The threshold specifies a range in excess of the minimum. The default is 20, so if all defaults are set, the system will display a console message when file cache buffers reach within 20 of the minimum (which is 40). So if all but 40 cache buffers have been allocated, the system will respond with `Number of cache buffers is getting too low`. Again, even 40 file cache buffers is not enough to operate NetWare on an effective basis.

Regardless of where the threshold is set, the system will respond when file cache buffers fall below the minimum. The following console message will be displayed: `Cache memory allocator exceeded minimum cache buffer left limit`. Bear in mind that the system manager will probably see some auxiliary symptoms of low cache limits before he/she ever sees the console message.

### Maximum Concurrent Disk Cache Writes

The maximum concurrent disk cache writes parameter sways the balance of disk performance to favor writing. This advanced parameter determines how many write requests from dirty cache are put in the elevator before the disk head begins a sweep across the disk. The default is 50, meaning that 50 requests are sent to the disk all at one time. If the number of dirty cache buffers on the main screen of MONITOR is more than 50% or 70% of the total cache buffers, this parameter must be increased. Increasing the maximum concurrent disk cache writes increases the number of requests that can be taken from the dirty cache buffers and sent to the disk simultaneously. The maximum value for this setting is 1000.

*Increasing the number of concurrent disk cache writes decreases the performance of reading, because the system spends more time and more effort writing and buffering write requests and does not prioritize the access of reads. The good news is this setting is transparent to most users.*

## Directory Caching

Directory caching allows fast access to frequently used directories. The directory cache buffer holds directory entries in it as long as they are being accessed frequently. The default is every 33 seconds. When a particular directory entry is not being accessed every 33 seconds, it can be overwritten by a more frequently accessed entry.

Three SET parameters directly relate to directory caching:

- Maximum directory cache buffers
- Minimum directory cache buffers
- Maximum concurrent directory cache writes

Directory cache buffers are permanent reserved areas of memory that are allocated by the permanent memory pool. As directory cache buffers increase, file cache buffers decrease, thus creating a tradeoff between directory caching and file caching. Let's explore the three directory caching SET parameters in more detail.

## Maximum Directory Cache Buffers

The maximum directory cache buffers parameter sets the maximum number of cache buffers used for directory entries. The default is 500; the system will tolerate values from 20 to 4,000. Allocation of directory cache buffers is dynamic, and NetWare assigns them as needed. If the server disk is populated by a very large amount of file and directory entries, the DET and directory cache buffers can increase quite rapidly.

Once all these files are deleted, the permanent memory pool maintains its size and the directory cache buffers remain high. Keep in mind that directory cache buffers, once allocated, do not go away until the file server is rebooted.

When the maximum number of directory cache buffers is reached, directory entries are dropped from memory and accessed from disk. This will slow down directory searches. Users will begin to notice that directory and file searches become quite sluggish. The system manager can increase the maximum directory cache buffer size if the file server is responding slowly to directory searches. Keep in mind, though, that as the maximum is increased and directory cache buffers are allocated, the permanent memory pool continues to grow and draw from file caching.

*For people who like peace and quiet: a phoneless cord.*

*Anonymous*

## Minimum Directory Cache Buffers

The minimum directory cache buffer parameter determines the number of cache buffers that the operating system will allocate immediately for directory caching (the default is 20, but it can be set as high as 2,000). When the minimum number of directory cache buffers has been allocated and another one is needed, the operating system will wait a specified amount of time (the default is 1.1 seconds) before allocating another buffer. Users will see noticeable decreases in directory and file search performances as new directory cache buffers are allocated.

Increasing the minimum directory cache buffer setting automatically sets a reserved number of buffers at file server bootup, thus allowing user file and directory searches to be performed much more quickly. On the downside, a high level of minimum directory cache buffers causes the permanent memory pool to grow—whether or not the unneeded portions are used.

### Maximum Concurrent Directory Cache Writes

The maximum concurrent directory cache writes parameter functions identically to the maximum concurrent disk cache writes parameter. This advanced parameter determines how many write requests the directory cache buffers can put in the elevator before the disk head begins a sweep across the disk. The default is 10, and the range is from 5 to 50. If you increase the maximum concurrent directory cache writes, the system will favor writing directory entries from directory cache buffers to the disk. If you decrease the number, the system will favor reading directory entry tables from the disk and allocating them to directory cache buffers.

*NetWare does not provide a facility for viewing the number of dirty directory cache buffers.*

## Miscellaneous

The miscellaneous grouping of SET parameters describes two different areas with which the system manager should be concerned:

- Maximum service processes

- Alerts

The maximum service processes parameter is used to define the number of tellers in the NetWare bank. Various alert parameters can be used to broadcast system messages in cases of minor emergency. Let's take a look at some of these valuable miscellaneous parameters.

## Maximum Service Processes

The maximum service processes parameter determines the maximum number of service processes that the operating system will use. The default is 20 and the range is from 5 to 40. If you remember from our earlier analogy, the FSPs are task handlers or tellers that service user requests. FSPs are linked closely with PRBs, wherein the user requests wait. If the packet receive buffer lobby is too small, the number of FSPs needs to be increased so user requests can be processed more quickly.

The number of FSPs currently available can be viewed in the main screen of MONITOR. If this number approaches 20, the maximum should be increased in increments of 5. Increasing the maximum number of FSPs makes more tellers available to process user requests. Increasing this number decreases the amount of available file cache buffers. Incidentally, NetWare dynamically allocates FSPs as needed. It starts at 1 or 2 and increases to the maximum.

## Alerts

Alert parameters control the broadcast of messages on the server console when particular conditions or emergencies occur. The system manager can use the alert SET parameters to control which alerts are broadcast. Here's a list of the four file console alerts and their default values:

| | |
|---|---|
| Display Spurious Interrupt Alerts | ON |
| Display Lost Interrupt Alerts | ON |
| Display Disk Device Alerts | OFF |
| Display Relinquish Control Alerts | OFF |

Each of these alerts can be used to notify the NetWare system manager when serious operating system problems are evident. Incidentally, most of these alerts are not fatal, and the system will continue although it will make lots and lots of noise.

That completes our discussion of the performance management SET parameters and various strategies for optimizing file server performance. SET parameters are serious operating system tools and should be used extremely cautiously. A few SET parameters don't directly apply to file server performance but do affect the ability of the file server to perform its duties. These other SET parameters fall into four categories:

- File system

- Locks

- Transaction tracking

- Disk

# Other SET Parameters

In the remainder of this section, we will look at these four different groups and some possible SET parameters that can increase the system manager's quality of life. Think of these as the little details that provide that special touch beyond ordinary interiors.

### File System Parameters

File system parameters control how NetWare interfaces with the shared file system. Three file system parameters control warnings about volumes, four parameters control file purging, and one advanced parameter controls the reuse of turbo FATs. Of these eight parameters, three jump out at you as useful NetWare tools:

- Volume low warning threshold

- Maximum percent of volume used by directory

- Maximum subdirectory tree depth

Take a quick look now at these file system SET parameters.

**VOLUME LOW WARNING THRESHOLD** The volume low warning threshold controls how little free disk space can remain on a volume before the operating system issues a console warning. The default is 256 blocks. The supported values are 0 to 100,000 blocks. Using the default values, NetWare will send a broadcast message as soon as the available disk space on the volume falls below 1MB. If you increase the disk allocation unit or block size on each volume, the 1MB threshold will change accordingly. For example, a volume with a 64KB block size will issue this warning once available disk space falls below 16MB.

*The volume low warning threshold also is sent to each workstation as a broadcast console message.*

**MAXIMUM PERCENT OF VOLUME USED BY DIRECTORY** The maximum percent of volume used by directory parameter limits the portion that may be used as directory space. By default, 13% of the volume space can be used for directory entries. This number becomes important when you are working with small server disks and many directory entries. Incidentally, in earlier versions of NetWare, this number was not a setable parameter. It was a complex calculation of volume space and directory entries. If the system manager has a small disk with multiple volumes, he/she can increase the maximum percentage of volume space used by a directory.

*ock parameters control how many open files each station can have and how many total open files the operating system will handle.*

**MAXIMUM SUBDIRECTORY TREE DEPTH** The maximum subdirectory tree depth parameter determines how many levels of subdirectories the operating system will support. The default value is 25 and the value can go as high as 100. By default NetWare's file system supports 25 subdirectories underneath each other from the root.

*The maximum subdirectory tree depth parameter must be set in the STARTUP.NCF file and will not take effect until the file server is rebooted, because the parameter redefines the structure of the file system at bootup time.*

*Periods of tranquillity are seldom prolific of creative achievement. Mankind has to be stirred up.*

*Alfred North Whitehead*

---

### Locks

Lock parameters control how many open files each station can have and how many total open files the operating system will handle. They also control how many record locks each connection can have and how many total record locks the operating system will handle. Lock parameters control three different types of locks: file, physical, and logical.

A file lock secures the entire file and prevents other stations from accessing it. A physical record lock controls data access by multiple users. It prevents other users from accessing or changing a range of bytes or a record in a file. A logical record lock also controls data access by multiple users except that in this case it relies on the application to assign the range of bytes or record. NetWare provides four SET parameters for customizing record lock activity.

### Transaction Tracking

The transaction tracking parameters control NetWare's internal transaction tracking system. TTS provides a guarantee that a transaction will either be written to disk in its complete form or backed out in case of a fault. This ensures database integrity and provides general peace of mind to users of large database files. NetWare provides five different SET parameters that control its internal TTS function.

### Disk

The disk SET parameters control one facet of the shared NetWare environment—hot fix redirection. One disk parameter controls read-after-write verification: Enable Disk Read After Write Verify. By default, read-after-write verification is set ON. The system manager has the flexibility to switch it to OFF. The OFF parameter is only useful when disks are mirrored and the speed of disk writes is a problem. Turning read-after-write verification OFF will almost double the speed of disk writes if mirroring and duplexing have been activated.

Disabling read-after-write verification does not disable hot fixing but it does decrease its effectiveness. With read-after-write verification turned off, hot fixing relies on write redirection and read redirection during actual reading and writing operations.

That completes our discussion of NetWare optimization using SET parameters. This section gave you a proactive strategy for acknowledging MONITOR problems and fixing them. In this chapter, we have explored the wealth of performance management components, and you have learned how their interrelationships affect file server management. In addition, we used

MONITOR.NLM to track resources and their effect on memory pools. You gained valuable information about disks, LANs, NICs, and file server memory.

The SET parameters enabled us to configure and optimize the operating system in areas such as communications, memory, file caching, directory caching, and service processes. You learned about a large variety of parameters, components, and MONITOR statistics and how to correct situations with SET parameters. Table 13.1 provides a review of these actions and the SET

| TABLE 13.1 Summary Actions | COMPO-NENT | MONITOR | SET |
|---|---|---|---|
| | File Cache Buffers | Check that total cache buffers does fall below 20% of original cache buffers. If that is the case, then... | Add more memory or unload NLMs. |
| | Dirty Cache Buffers | Make sure they don't reach 70% of total cache buffers. If so... | Set Maximum Concurrent Disk Cache Writes = 100. |
| | Directory Cache Buffers | If directory cache buffers reach 100, then... | Set Minimum Directory Cache Buffers = 200 and Maximum Directory Cache Buffers = 1000. |
| | Packet Receive Buffers | If packet receive buffers grow beyond 100, then... | Set the Minimum Packet Receive Buffers = 200 and the Maximum Packet Receive Buffers = 500 parameters. |
| | File Service Processes | Check the file service processes in MONITOR and if they are approaching 20... | Increase the number to 25 or 30 in increments of 5. |
| | Alloc Short Term Memory | If alloc short-term memory approaches 8 megabytes,... | Set maximum alloc short-term memory = 9,000,000, increasing in 1,000,000 increments. |
| | Packet Size | Under LAN information, you're using a network interface card capable of larger packet sizes, then... | Increase the Maximum Physical Receive Packet Size to 8404 and increase the Minimum Packet Receive Buffer to 500 and the Maximum Packet Receive Buffer to 1,000. |

parameters that need to be set to solve certain problems. Keep in mind that NetWare interior decorating is not an exact science. It requires diligence, patience, and creativity—not to mention some NetWare taste.

*If I were you, I would memorize Table 13.1. This summary will help you decide when and where to apply MONITOR.NLM and internal SET parameters. You might even want to photocopy this page and hang it on your refrigerator door.*

# Alternative Performance Management Strategies

TO FINISH OFF THE performance management chapter, let's take a look at some additional performance management techniques including large Internet packets and packet bursts.

As you have seen throughout the chapter, NetWare 2.2 and 3.1*x* provide three main facilities for managing and optimizing the server:

- MONITOR.NLM for monitoring key NetWare 3.1*x* performance management components

- SET parameters to actively customize the core NetWare 3.1*x* operating system

- FCONSOLE as the NetWare 2.2 performance management tool

In addition to these tools, NetWare 3.1*x* supports two more performance management strategies: Packet Burst Protocol and large Internet packets. The Packet Burst Protocol speeds LAN transmissions significantly by sending multiple packets with a single reply. In conjunction, large Internet packets enhance communications over routers by increasing the packet size eight-fold. Let's finish off this chapter with a brief look at these two alternative performance management strategies.

*If I were you, I would get a firm grasp on how packet bursting and LIP can increase network performance, and on when to use either or both.*

## Packet Burst Protocol

Packet Burst Protocol improves performance of NetWare Core Protocol (NCP) reads and writes by speeding the transfer of multiple packet requests. Packet burst is automatically used in NetWare 3.1*x* when an application makes a read or write request that requires more than one data packet.

*Any given data request has a maximum of 64KB at one time.*

Here's how it works:

1. When a client makes an NCP read or write request without the benefit of packet burst, each packet is followed by an acknowledgment. This process takes time and energy.

2. Packet burst increases LAN communications speed by sending multiple packets with only one acknowledgment.

3. In order to implement packet burst, the system manager must enable it at both the server and workstation. If only one station has packet burst enabled, it will not operate properly and every packet will be acknowledged in a one-to-one relationship.

4. Packet burst implementation can be customized at the server with special SET parameters and at the workstation using the NET.CFG file.

*In some independent tests, packet bursting increased network throughput by 10% to 300%.*

Finally, packet burst is especially useful within networks in which high bandwidths exist on the media and wide area links are being used, such as:

- Fast Asynchronous Digital Links (T-1)
- Multiple routes (X.25)
- Multiple hops over routers or bridges

Packet burst also helps in LAN situations as long as the media bandwidth is high enough. A low bandwidth can actually decrease network performance with packet burst.

*Although packet burst is built into NetWare 3.12, NetWare 3.11 LANs must use special workstation and server files to implement this performance management feature. At the server, you run PBURST.NLM, and at the workstation, BNETX.COM.*

## Large Internet Packets

Large Internet packets (LIPs) are another factor in enhancing network performance. LIPs work by increasing the speed of data transmission when communications occur over routers:

1. Clients and servers always negotiate packet size when they attach to each other.

2. Without LIPs, if the server identified a router between itself and the client, the packet size would be automatically set to 576 bytes.

*The 576-byte packet size contains 512 bytes of data and 64 bytes worth of header information. Refer to the "Networking Technologies" part of this book for more details.*

3. LIP allows the client and server to negotiate a much higher packet size when communications occur over a router. In some cases, the size grows as high as 4202 bytes. Of course, the final packet size depends on the physical packet size supported by the server.

4. LIP implementation is automatically activated at both the client and server. To disable LIP at the server, use the following SET parameter: SET ALLOW LIP = OFF.

Well, that just about does it for packet burst, LIP, and NetWare performance management in general. This has been a very exciting and important ride.

As the NetWare interior decorator, you can see it's extremely important to create a comfortable environment for the users that is both productive and

*Performance management is one of the most important NetWare system management responsibilities and should be taken seriously. As a CNA, your duty is to continually monitor file server performance using the MONITOR and SET parameters.*

pleasant to use. Performance management is one of the most important NetWare system management responsibilities and should be taken seriously. As a CNA, your duty is to continually monitor file server performance using the MONITOR and SET parameters. The performance management duties are the final responsibilities of the NetWare system manager.

That's it for NetWare 3.1*x* and the many hats of the CNA. In this part, you have learned what it's like to be the NetWare architect, house detective, handyman, hotel manager, chef, and interior decorator. I hope the analogy of Park Place has helped you to understand the varying responsibilities that fill up a day in the life of the CNA. If you take these responsibilities to heart and treat the network as a valuable resource for your users, you will become and remain a successful CNA. I trust this book will be the beginning of your journey and I wish you the best of luck in attaining your life's goal. Live long and prosper! Onward and upward!

# Exercise 13.1: Performance Management Components

| | | |
|---|---|---|
| _____ | **1.** FAT | **A.** Can be configured in 4KB, 8KB, 16KB, 32KB, or 64KB sizes |
| _____ | **2.** DET | **B.** This table is only partially cached in NetWare 3.1x |
| _____ | **3.** Directory caching | **C.** Increases disk I/O one hundred times |
| _____ | **4.** Directory hashing | **D.** Stores the DETs in memory |
| _____ | **5.** File caching | **E.** The lobby of the NetWare bank |
| _____ | **6.** Disk allocation blocks | **F.** Speeds file access by caching DET and FAT |
| _____ | **7.** Directory entry blocks | **G.** Must match disk allocation block size in order for volume to mount |
| _____ | **8.** File cache buffers | **H.** Special reserved area that stores DETs on disk |
| _____ | **9.** Directory cache buffers | **I.** Keeps track of physical locations of files on disk |
| _____ | **10.** Packet receive buffers | **J.** Increases disk performance by 30% |

## Exercise 13.2: Memory Pools

\_\_\_\_\_ **1.** Total server memory outside the memory pools

\_\_\_\_\_ **2.** File cache buffers

\_\_\_\_\_ **3.** Cache-nonmovable memory

\_\_\_\_\_ **4.** Cache-movable memory

\_\_\_\_\_ **5.** Permanent memory

\_\_\_\_\_ **6.** Semipermanent memory

\_\_\_\_\_ **7.** Alloc short-term memory

**A.** Used to store PRBs

**B.** Used by loadable modules with pop-up windows

**C.** Acts as a door for the entrance of NLMs

**D.** Used by system tables that grow dynamically, such as DETs and FATs

**E.** Cannot be used by NLMs

**F.** Provides memory for LAN drivers and disk drivers

**G.** Provides memory for both semipermanent and alloc short-term memory

**H.** Stores information such as mappings, user connection information, and temporary messages

**I.** Where SERVER.EXE resides

**J.** Used as an original source for all other memory pools

**C A S E  S T U D Y  V I I**

# Performance Management for Snouzer, Inc.

The final step in implementing the Snouzer, Inc. NetWare LAN is performance optimization. Sophy has come to you and voiced some concerns about intermittent problems she and her managers are having on the LAN. Of course, it has nothing to do with how you set up the LAN—it's just a manifestation of daily operations. She has asked whether you could monitor these problem areas and fix them. Of course, from what you've learned in this chapter, you know that your monitoring duties will be performed using MONITOR.NLM and optimization will be performed using the SET parameters. Here are some of Sophy's performance concerns:

- File access has been slow.
- The message `Error sending on network` has appeared for some users.
- The server is slow to respond when it is rebooted.
- Directory searches are sluggish.
- Certain NLMs won't load.

As the Snouzer, Inc. system manager, it is your responsibility to address each of these issues and suggest some possible courses of action. For each issue ask yourself these two questions:

- What MONITOR statistics would you check?

- How would you remedy the situation?

**1.** File access has been slow. The users have been experiencing slow file access and sluggish applications.

**2.** Some users are experiencing the message `Error sending on network` and losing their connection. This message occurs at random intervals when users are trying to access the file server.

**3.** The server is slow to respond when it is rebooted. Whenever Sophy turns on the server, it takes a great deal of time for it to come back up. This problem has caused some concern because the system is vulnerable and down during that time period.

**4.** Users are experiencing sluggish directory searches. In addition, some users are losing their connection during directory searches.

**5.** NLMs won't load. Sophy has been trying to load some network management NLMs at the server and has found that NLMs that require pop-up menus will not load. She receives an error message to the effect that the appropriate memory pool is out of space.

Once you have completed your performance management design and suggested some possible courses of action, you can use SET parameters and other tools to implement Snouzer, Inc.'s performance optimization.

Congratulations! You have designed, installed, and managed a NetWare LAN for Snouzer, Inc. You have completed directory structures, drive mapping, security, server startup, NET.CFG, login scripts, user interface, and performance management. You took a barely functioning system and breathed life into it. As a NetWare system manager and CNA, you should be proud of your efforts and use this experience to gain momentum in your next project. Good luck and happy LANning!

# Part 3—NetWare 3.12 Administration

**ACROSS**

1. Checking out RIPS and SAPs
6. SRC to DAT
8. Back me up, please
9. Workstation's all washed up
10. Server optimization
12. Bottom of the ODI totem pole
16. "Anybody out there?"
17. Required for dedicated print servers
19. The GOAL
20. Server post office
22. Counting hops and ticks
24. Global printer definitions
27. "The End"
29. NetWare 3.1x Legos
30. Workstation switchboard
31. Workstation Legos

33. SMS compromise strategy

**DOWN**

2. "We don't need no stinkin' DOS"
3. NetWare shell with a face lift
4. NetWare 3.12 OS file
5. User post office
7. Supervisor "back door"
11. Multiple protocols at the server
13. Plug and play
14. Remote access on the LAN
15. "Greedy" NLM pool
17. Mother of all NetWare utilities
18. Multiple protocols at the workstation
21. Guarding workstation connections
23. The birth of a printing system
24. "Brains" of the server
25. "Virtual" console
26. SMS controller configuration with an attitude
28. Rights make a stand
32. Changing files one at a time

APPENDICES

# Overview
# of Novell
# Education

APPENDIX

A

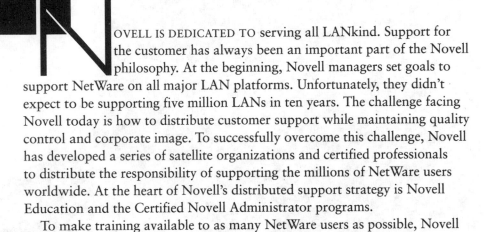

OVELL IS DEDICATED TO serving all LANkind. Support for the customer has always been an important part of the Novell philosophy. At the beginning, Novell managers set goals to support NetWare on all major LAN platforms. Unfortunately, they didn't expect to be supporting five million LANs in ten years. The challenge facing Novell today is how to distribute customer support while maintaining quality control and corporate image. To successfully overcome this challenge, Novell has developed a series of satellite organizations and certified professionals to distribute the responsibility of supporting the millions of NetWare users worldwide. At the heart of Novell's distributed support strategy is Novell Education and the Certified Novell Administrator programs.

To make training available to as many NetWare users as possible, Novell has developed a worldwide network of more than 1,500 authorized education partners, including colleges and universities. Only organizations that meet Novell's stringent educational standards are authorized to teach Novell-developed courses. These courses must be taught by Certified Novell Instructors (CNIs), who are qualified through an extensive training and testing program conducted by Novell. Novell authorized courses are intended to train and certify consultants, independent service organizations, technicians, support professionals, system managers, and users.

*The education of the soul is the object of our existence.*

*Ralph Waldo Emerson*

The goal of Novell education is to provide high-quality NetWare education to potential NetWare support engineers, so that Novell can distribute the support of its five million LANs to qualified independent professionals. Currently there are approximately 60,000 certified Novell professionals supporting five million NetWare LANs. That's roughly ninety-five LANs per professional—plenty of work!

This discussion gives you a comprehensive overview of Novell's educational strategy by exploring the implementation of Novell's authorized education programs, the certification programs, and testing. In addition, we will briefly discuss the varied NetWare courses and alternative education methods. Let's begin with a brief discussion of Novell's educational philosophy.

# Novell's Education Philosophy

NOVELL'S MISSION IS TO "accelerate the growth of the network computing industry." To achieve this goal, Novell puts a great deal of effort into the education of distributed support professionals. Novell's educational philosophy is at the heart of its resounding success. According to Novell, market leadership is perpetuated through product diversification and education. After all, it is difficult to implement and support a product that nobody understands.

Novell Education is the leading training provider in the network computing industry. Through the years, Novell Education has provided NetWare-oriented training to more than two million users. Novell Education is designed to help industry professionals develop network design, installation, and management skills. Novell-authorized courses provide comprehensive training in network performance, network functionality, and user productivity.

Novell's worldwide network of more than 1,500 authorized education partners can be categorized into two groups: NAECs and NEAPs. *Novell Authorized Education Centers (NAECs)* are private independent training organizations that meet Novell's strict quality standards. *Novell Education Academic Partners (NEAPs)* are colleges or universities that meet the same strict guidelines. In addition, NEAPs provide Novell-authorized courses in a normal semester- or quarter-length format.

These Novell authorized education partners offer more than fifty NetWare-oriented courses. Students can simply drop in for one or two courses or complete a rigorous NetWare certification program. Novell offers the following four certification programs:

- CNA
- CNE
- Master CNE
- CNI

The *Certified Novell Administrator (CNA)* program is designed for users or administrators who are responsible for the day-to-day operations of the LAN. The *Certified Novell Engineer (CNE)* program certifies service technicians or consultants to provide quality support for Novell networks, including system design, installation, and maintenance. CNEs can focus on either NetWare, UnixWare, or GroupWare objectives. The *Master Certified Novell Engineer (Master CNE)* program is designed to give CNEs an opportunity to achieve a higher level of certification, focusing on the support of enterprise-wide networks, Unix connectivity, or GroupWare. Finally, the *Certified Novell Instructor (CNI)* program is a comprehensive training program for advanced Novell engineers who want to teach Novell-authorized courses. CNI candidates are required to attend courses, pass high-level tests, and perform satisfactorily at a rigorous performance-evaluation course.

Candidates who are interested in attaining any of these certifications must pass comprehensive Novell-authorized exams. These exams are designed to provide an accurate and efficient measurement of a candidate's skill level. Novell currently offers three types of certification testing through Drake Authorized Testing Centers: form, adaptive, and performance-based. All tests are administered on a personal computer. They are "closed-book" and are graded on a pass/fail basis. We will discuss CNA and CNE testing later in this appendix.

At the heart of Novell's educational philosophy are the courses. Novell Education currently offers more than fifty courses in four different categories:

- core courses
- administration courses
- services courses
- product courses

Novell Education's *core courses* focus on fundamental and advanced issues in NetWare LAN management. Topics include microcomputer/DOS basics, networking technologies, and service and support. *Administration courses* highlight the roles, responsibilities, and tools available to NetWare managers in any of the five Novell product lines—NetWare-2, NetWare-3, NetWare-4, UnixWare, and GroupWare. *Services courses* are designed to add specialized functionality to the basic core and administration courses. Services courses supplement NetWare products by providing detailed information on key issues. Topics include NetWare 4 Design and Implementation, NetWare internetworking products, and NetWare programming: basic services. Finally, *product courses* provide in-depth training on new and proven Novell products. Topics include NetWare NFS, NetWare for Macintosh, UnixWare, and NetWare for SAA.

In addition to these instructor-led courses, Novell offers a variety of educational alternatives, including self-study workbooks and technology-based training (TBT). These self-study materials diversify the delivery method of Novell-based education. Because these products are self-paced, you can focus on information you are unfamiliar with and reduce training time. You can also review course materials as often as necessary and refer to them as needed to learn specific skills. Additional education alternatives include user groups, conferences, on-line universities, multi-media learning systems, NetWare Users International (NUI), and free seminars routinely provided by the Network Professional Association (NPA).

As you can tell, Novell's education philosophy is quite comprehensive. Whether you are interested in becoming a NetWare expert or just want to learn the basics, you can count on Novell Education to meet your training needs.

This discussion provides detailed information about how you can benefit from Novell Education. It's an excellent way to learn the ins and outs of NetWare, UnixWare, and GroupWare.

# *Education Centers*

ORE THAN 1,500 NOVELL authorized training partners worldwide offer instructor-led courses and self-study education products to give you convenient access to a Novell-authorized education. You can count on the classes to be topnotch. Furthermore, Novell guarantees complete customer satisfaction for all Novell courses when they are taught at Novell-authorized training partners that meet four strict education guidelines:

- The facility must use Novell-developed course materials.

- The course must be taught within a recommended time frame.

- The facility must be Novell authorized. Authorization is based on a strict set of standards for equipment, instructional soundness, and student comfort.

- The course must be taught by a Certified Novell Instructor who is certified to teach the specific course.

To ensure training quality, Novell routinely inspects education partner facilities. In addition, students are provided with an opportunity to evaluate the course material, the instructor, and the facility at the end of each course. These evaluation forms are forwarded immediately to Novell for review. Facilities that do not adhere to these strict standards are subject to being removed from the program. Novell-authorized training partners fall into two categories:

- NAECs

- NEAPs

Let's take a quick look.

# NAEC

Novell Authorized Education Centers are private training organizations that provide Novell-authorized courses. Most NAECs are solely in the business of training. The advantage of attending an NAEC is that these organizations typically have a great deal of experience in technology training and are driven to provide quality education. You can be assured that because the success of the NAEC is dictated by the quality of the training, all courses are accurate, timely, and comprehensive. In order to become an NAEC, the private training organization must submit an extensive application to Novell Education. In addition, they pay an initiation fee and annual licensing fees. NAECs are required to offer a variety of courses in a consistent and timely manner.

*The things taught in colleges and schools are not an education, but the means of education.*

*Ralph Waldo Emerson*

For a list of NAECs in your area and the courses they are authorized to teach, call 1-800-233-EDUC in the U.S. and Canada. In all other areas, call 1-801-429-5508 or contact your nearest Novell office.

# NEAP

NEAP stands for Novell Education Academic Partner. The NEAP program was recently created to provide quality Novell-authorized education through participating technical schools, colleges, and universities. NEAP implementation was driven by students who wanted to participate in Novell-authorized courses in a traditional education format and by colleges and universities that saw the value of NetWare-oriented training. NEAPs must follow the same strict guidelines as NAECs and provide Novell courses as part of their standard curriculum. Currently there are more than 125 colleges and universities authorized to teach NEAP courses—and the number is quickly growing. For a list of participating schools, call 1-800-233-EDUC in the U.S. and Canada. In all other areas, call 1-801-429-5508 or contact your nearest Novell office.

# Certification Programs

NOVELL EDUCATION USES A two-pronged approach to Novell-oriented training. On the one hand, each course is designed to offer education on a specific topic. Each course's focus is clearly outlined and completed in a one- to five-day format. On the other hand, Novell Education courses can be combined to provide a comprehensive certification. Novell Education's certification programs are designed to develop a high level of expertise in the management implementation of Novell-oriented products. To ensure the availability of quality NetWare, UnixWare, and GroupWare administrative and technical support professionals, Novell has developed the following four certification programs:

- Certified Novell Administrator, CNA program

- Certified Novell Engineer, CNE program

- Master Certified Novell Engineer, Master CNE program

- Certified Novell Instructor, CNI program

Those who certify are recognized by others in the network computing industry as competent, knowledgeable resources for network management, technical support, and training. Novell's instructor-led courses and self-study materials can help candidates prepare for the required certification tests. These tests are currently offered at Drake Authorized Testing Centers, or DATCs, throughout the world.

Novell does not currently require that certification candidates attend any courses—the CNE program is test-based. CNEs who have successfully passed all of the required exams have varying degrees of hands-on experience with Novell products. The purpose of Novell's CNE program is to establish a baseline standard of network support knowledge in the industry. Obviously, a CNE with practical experience is more valuable to the industry than a CNE with only academic knowledge. Novell strongly recommends that candidates seek as much hands-on experience with Novell products as they can before and during the certification process. In addition to on-the-job experience, candidates can gain valuable practice by attending hands-on training at Novell-authorized facilities. In fact, with the recent introduction of Novell's performance-based Service and Support test, CNE candidates will find it difficult to complete their certification without hands-on experience obtained on the job or by attending Novell's lab-intensive 801 Service and Support course.

Let's take a brief look at the four different certification programs.

# CNA

The CNA program is designed for users who are responsible for the day-to-day operation of a network. System managers typically perform tasks such as adding and deleting user accounts, backing up the server, loading applications, and maintaining security. CNA candidates may currently choose to specialize in NetWare-2, NetWare-3, NetWare-4, UnixWare, or GroupWise. CNAs are certified by passing one CNA test for the operating system they choose. Make sure to use the correct test numbers:

- NetWare-2 CNA (50-115)
- NetWare-3 CNA (50-390)
- NetWare-4 CNA (50-394)
- UnixWare CNA (50-135)
- GroupWise CNA (50-395)

Successful completion of the certification test identifies CNAs as knowledgeable and trained Novell administrators. It also serves as a valuable credential in the networking industry. CNA program objectives are covered in the system manager and advanced system manager courses for NetWare 2.2 and the administration courses for the other four technologies. These objectives are identical to the CNE objectives in most areas. The only difference is that some of the advanced CNE objectives are not required for CNA certification. This book, for example, covers all of the CNA program objectives for both NetWare 2.2 and 3.1$x$.

Candidates who pass the CNA test receive a certificate from Novell identifying them as Certified Novell Administrators. If a CNA decides to go on to become a CNE, the knowledge gained in the courses will be useful and applicable. Also, NetWare-3, NetWare-4, UnixWare, and GroupWise CNAs can apply their test credits toward CNE certification. Contact Drake Training & Technologies for more details (1-800-REDEXAM).

CNA candidates should learn the CNA program objectives that are covered in the administration courses. In addition, CNA candidates should gain the prerequisite knowledge included in the *DOS for NetWare Users* and *Microcomputer Concepts for NetWare Users* workbooks. The objectives in these workbooks, however, are not tested in the CNA certification exams. If you have any more questions about Novell's CNA program, contact Novell Education at 1-800-233-EDUC in the U.S. and Canada. In all other locations, contact your local Novell office or call 1-801-429-5508.

# CNE

The CNE program certifies service technicians and consultants to provide quality support for Novell networks. This support includes NetWare, Unix-Ware, and GroupWare design, installation, and maintenance. Once certification requirements are met, Novell stands behind its CNEs with technical support and up-to-date product benefits. To earn CNE certification, candidates must demonstrate mastery of networking concepts by passing a series of seven tests. CNE certification consists of nineteen credits, and tests are worth from two to five credits. Each credit is roughly equivalent to one day at a Novell-authorized Education Center. Requirements for CNE certification are organized into four different groupings:

- Prerequisites

- Core Requirements

- Target Requirements

- CNE Elective Requirements

*Major changes are currently being made to the CNE program. Novell education continues to evolve the CNE requirements to ensure compatibility with changing technology. The "old" program includes students who passed their first exam before Sepetember 30, 1995. These students may either transfer their credits to the "new" program or complete certification before June 30, 1996 using the "old" requirements. This discussion features the "new" program, beginning on September 30, 1995.*

### Prerequisites—2 Credits

The CNE Prerequsites are designed to bring all candidates to an equal starting point, and ensure quality students. You must sign a CNE Agreement form after taking your first test. You can receive this form by calling 1-800-233-EDUC.

### Core Requirements—8 Credits

The CNE Core Requirements are designed to provide candidates with the fundamentals of networking technology, troubleshooting, and optimization. The Core Requirements provide 8 credits toward the 19 needed for the CNE credential. The two Core Requirement courses are as follows:

| Course No. | Course Name | Credits | Test No. |
|---|---|---|---|
| 801 | NetWare Service and Support | 5 | 50-153 |
| 200 | Networking Technologies | 3 | 50-147 |

*You don't have to take these courses in the order shown here. It's best to start with the Target courses and then move on to NetWare Service and Support, and finally, Networking Technologies.*

### Target Requirements—9 credits

The CNE Target Requirements are designed to make sure that Certified Novell Engineers understand the details of one of the four main CNE specializations: NetWare-3, NetWare-4, UnixWare, and GroupWare. The Target Requirements provide 9 credits of the 19 needed for the CNE credential. The following is a list of the courses that satisfy the Target Requirements in each of the four areas of specialization.

NetWare-3 (CNE-3)

| Course No. | Course Name | Credits | Test No. |
|---|---|---|---|
| 508 | NetWare 3.1*x* Administration | 3 | 50-130 |

### NetWare-3 (CNE-3)

| Course No. | Course Name | Credits | Test No. |
|---|---|---|---|
| 518 | NetWare 3.1x Advanced Administration | 2 | 50-131 |
| 802 | NetWare 3.1x Installation and Configuration Workshop | 2 | 50-132 |
| 526 | NetWare 3 to NetWare 4.1 Update | 2 | 50-162 |

### NetWare-4 (CNE-4)

| Course No. | Course Name | Credits | Test No. |
|---|---|---|---|
| 520 | NetWare 4.1 Administration | 3 | 50-152 |
| 525 | NetWare 4.1 Advanced Administration | 2 | 50-161 |
| 804 | NetWare 4.1 Installation and Configuration Workshop | 2 | 50-163 |
| 532 | NetWare 4 Design & Implementation | 2 | 50-601 |

### UnixWare (CNE-U)

| Course No. | Course Name | Credits | Test No. |
|---|---|---|---|
| 220 | Unix OS Fundamentals | 2 | 50-107 |
| 680 | UnixWare System Administration | 3 | 50-150 |
| 685 | UnixWare Advanced System Administration | 2 | 50-151 |
| 678 | UnixWare Installation and Configuration Workshop | 2 | 50-149 |

### GroupWare (CNE-GW)

| Course No. | Course Name | Credits | Test No. |
|---|---|---|---|
| 325 | GroupWise 4 Administration | 3 | 50-154 |
| 328 | GroupWise 4 Advanced Administration | 2 | 50-604 |

### GroupWare (CNE-GW)

| Course No. | Course Name | Credits | Test No. |
|---|---|---|---|
| 326 | GroupWise 4 Asynchronous Gateway and Remote Client Support | 1 | 50-155 |
| 520 | NetWare 4 Administration | 3 | 50-152 |

---

### CNE Elective Requirements—2 Credits

CNE Elective Requirements are designed to provide candidates with more specialization in a variety of Novell-oriented topics. Candidates can choose among numerous elective tests worth from 1 to 3 credits. Remember, you only need 2 elective credits. CNE-3, CNE-4, and CNE-Unix (CNE-U) candidates have two electives pools: "Network Management" and "Infrastructure and Advanced Access." CNE-GroupWare (CNE-GW) candidates have only one pool: "GroupWare Integration."

Let's take a closer look.

### Network Management Elective Pool (CNE-3, CNE-4, CNE-U)

| Course No. | Course Name | Credits | Test No. |
|---|---|---|---|
| 535 | Printing with NetWare | 2 | 50-137 |
| 550 | NetWare Navigator | 2 | 50-138 |
| 730C | NetWare Expert for NMS | 2 | 50-205 |
| 1125 | LANalyzer for Windows | 1 | 50-105 |

### Infrastructure and Advanced Access Elective Pool (CNE-3, CNE-4, CNE-U)

| Course No. | Course Name | Credits | Test No. |
|---|---|---|---|
| 601 | LAN WorkPlace for DOS 4 | 2 | 50-104 |
| 605 | NetWare TCP/IP Transport | 2 | 50-86 |
| 610 | NetWare NFS | 2 | 50-87 |
| 625 | NetWare NFS Gateway | 1 | 50-119 |

### Infrastructure and Advanced Access Elective Pool (CNE-3, CNE-4, CNE-U)

| Course No. | Course Name | Credits | Test No. |
| --- | --- | --- | --- |
| 630 | NetWare IP | 1 | 50-139 |
| 640 | NetWare NFS Services: Management and Printing | 2 | 50-160 |
| 645 | NetWare NFS Services: File Sharing | 2 | 50-160 |
| 718 | NetWare Connect | 2 | 50-114 |
| 720 | NetWare for SAA | 3 | 50-148 |
| 725 | NetWare for LAT | 2 | 50-140 |
| 750 | NetWare Global MHS | 2 | 50-108 |

### GroupWare Integration Elective Pool (CNE-GW)

| Course No. | Course Name | Credits | Test No. |
| --- | --- | --- | --- |
| 345 | SoftSolutions 4 Administration | 3 | 50-158 |
| 348 | SoftSolutions 4 Advanced Administration | 2 | 50-159 |
| 335 | InForms 4 Administration & Form Design | 3 | 50-156 |
| 338 | InForms 4 Advanced Administration & Form Design | 2 | 50-157 |

Novell's CNE program is growing rapidly. There are currently more than 60,000 CNEs worldwide supporting more than five million NetWare LANs. That's approximately eighty-five LANs per CNE. Novell Education is exploring alternatives for providing NetWare-oriented training to a larger variety of engineers. Finally, it is important to note that gold and platinum Novell-authorized resellers are required to have a number of CNEs on staff.

Remember, Novell certification requirements are changing every day. So, make sure to get the latest scoop from Novell Education at 1-800-233-EDUC in the U.S. and Canada, or 1-801-429-5508 internationally.

# Master CNE

The Master Certified Novell Engineer (Master CNE) program is designed to give CNEs an opportunity to achieve a higher level of certification, focusing on the support of enterprise-wide networks. Master CNE candidates must demonstrate proficiency in specialized networking technologies. At the least, Master CNE candidates must begin with a CNE certification, and then complete an additional 19 certification credits.

The Master CNE program is viewed by many as the Ph.D. of Novell certification. Candidates must complete 19 elective credits in three groups: Core Requirements, Target Requirements, and Master CNE Elective Requirements.

### Core Requirements—CNE plus 6 Credits

The first Core Requirement for the Master CNE certification is a valid CNE credential—either CNE-3, CNE-4, or CNE-U. If you plan to explore GroupWare Integration, you must first become a CNE-GW. Next, you must pass the following three tests:

- NetWare 4 Design and Implementation

- Fundamentals of Network Management

- Fundamentals of Internetworking

### Target Requirements—2 Credits

The Master CNE Target Requirements are designed to ensure that these advanced professionals have an in-depth understanding of NetWare, UnixWare, or GroupWare. You can choose one of three tracks for satisfying your Master CNE Target requirements:

#### Network Management (CNE-3, CNE-4, or CNE-U)

| Course No. | Course Name | Credits | Test No. |
| --- | --- | --- | --- |
| none | Network Management Using NetWare ManageWise | 2 | none |

**Infrastructure and Advanced Access (CNE-3, CNE-4, or CNE-U)**

| Course No. | Course Name | Credits | Test No. |
|---|---|---|---|
| 740 | Internetworking with NetWare MultiProtocol Router | 2 | 50-142 |

**GroupWare Integration (CNE-GW)**

*No Target Requirements*

Four Elective credits needed

---

### Master CNE Elective Requirements—2 Credits

Master CNE Elective Requirements are included to provide a variety of specialization areas for CNE Ph.D. candidates. Candidates are free to choose any variety of electives but they must fall within their given area of specialization:

- Network Management—2 credits from list shown in CNE section.

- Infrastructure and Advanced Access—2 credits from list shown in CNE section.

- GroupWare Integration—4 credits for CNE-GW only. Choose from the list shown in the CNE section.

*Elective credits used to gain your CNE certification cannot be used toward becoming a Master CNE.*

---

# CNI

The Certified Novell Instructor (CNI) program is a comprehensive training and testing program for people who want to teach Novell-authorized courses. Candidates who have been accepted into the program are required to attend courses, pass tests, and satisfy a rigorous performance evaluation. Novell Education recognizes that CNIs are the heart of its educational philosophy.

CNIs are the delivery mechanism for NetWare-oriented training and Novell-authorized courses. Novell Education views the CNI's role as a partnership with the Novell-authorized Education Center and Novell Education itself. Novell feels that CNIs share a common mission—"to broaden the availability of quality Novell product training in the marketplace."

CNI responsibilities include:

- Completing required update training and passing required competency tests.

- Staying up-to-date on current technology and communicating this knowledge to students.

- Teaching Novell-authorized courses at NAEC or NEAP facilities.

- Making sure Novell course objectives are met, using original Novell course materials. In addition, they must ensure that student course evaluations are completed after each Novell class and that everybody has a good time learning NetWare-oriented topics.

*The teacher is like the candle which lights others in consuming itself.*

*Giovanni Ruffini*

To become a CNI, the candidate must meet four requirements:

1. The application must be approved.

2. The student must attend all the courses he/she wants to teach.

3. The student must achieve higher scores than he/she did for the other certifications.

4. The student must satisfactorily pass an instructor performance evaluation (IPE).

The CNI program is constantly evolving. Please call Novell Education for the latest information and a CNI application form. They can be reached at 1-800-233-EDUC in the U.S. and Canada, or 1-801-429-5508 elsewhere.

# *Testing*

NOVELL PROVIDES TESTING FOR certification through Drake Authorized Testing Centers—or DATCs. Drake Training & Technologies is a third-party organization that has been licensed to provide testing to Novell certification candidates. Drake Authorized Testing Centers are located worldwide. To register for a Drake test, candidates must call 1-800-RED-EXAM. Candidates are required to provide two forms of ID before taking a Novell-authorized test.

CNE certification tests are administered on a personal computer using a proprietary Windows-based interface. They are "closed-book" and are graded on a pass/fail basis. You receive immediate results once the test is complete. Each test has a moderate price tag associated with it. These prices vary around the world.

Novell Education currently utilizes three types of certification tests:

- Form tests

- Adaptive tests

- Performance-based tests

Let's take a closer look.

## Form Testing

Some CNE proficiency tests use standard computerized testing methods. These traditional *form* tests contain 59 to 94 questions and take approximately 60 to 120 minutes to complete. Exams are graded on the percentage of questions answered correctly. You can navigate through the test, answering questions in any order you choose.

Almost ALL tests are form tests when they are first introduced. Novell Education uses data collected from form tests to build complex question weighting tables. These tables are then used to create *adaptive tests* (see below). Not all form tests become adaptive tests, because the tranformation process is very time-consuming. Only the most popular core certification tests are eventually altered. Now, let's take a look at the process of transforming form caterpillars into adaptive butterflies.

## Adaptive Testing

In November 1991 the Novell testing program began using computerized adaptive testing technology. This technology is currently used to deliver many of Novell's certification tests. Although adaptive testing has been used by various government agencies, professional organizations, and school districts for more than a decade, it is still an unfamiliar concept to most people.

Traditional paper-and-pencil or computerized tests deliver the same set of questions to every examinee regardless of the examinee's level of knowledge or proficiency. Your score on a traditional test depends on the number of questions you answer correctly. Traditional tests have a long history and have proven useful. Nevertheless, a traditional test is not the most efficient way to measure a candidate's knowledge or proficiency. Adaptive testing, on the other hand, works more like a testing conversation. It begins by giving you a question of moderate difficulty. After you respond, the test scores your response and estimates your level of ability. It then looks for a question whose difficulty matches your presumed ability. It presents that question, you respond and the program scores your response and revises its estimate of your ability on the basis of the two questions given thus far. This process continues, with the program revising its estimate of your ability following each response.

As you can imagine, the estimate becomes more and more accurate with each question. The test concludes when your ability is estimated with sufficient accuracy.

Because an adaptive test tailors itself to your ability, it does not base your score on the number of correct answers. Adaptive testing scores are based on the difficulty of the questions you answer correctly and incorrectly. In other words, the score is based on your ability rather than simply the number of items you get right. Novell Education has adopted an ability score scale that has a minimum value of 200 and a maximum value of 800. For each test, a passing score will be established somewhere on the scale. You will pass the test if your ability scores are equal to or greater than the passing score.

*My greatest strength as a consultant is to be ignorant and ask a few questions.*

*Peter F. Drucker*

The two main advantages of adaptive testing over traditional testing are accuracy and efficiency. Questions that are too easy or too difficult provide little information about your true ability. By minimizing the number of such questions, adaptive testing can accurately measure your ability with fewer questions—saving you valuable time. Another benefit is saving you from the boredom or intimidation of questions that are too easy or too hard. You should find that most of the items you receive are moderately challenging, helping to make the testing sessions more interesting and less stressful—that is, if you can imagine an unstressful test.

## Performance-Based Testing

With the release of the NEW Service and Support test (50-153), Novell Education has introduced a radical new testing system—performance-based testing. Performance-based tests are designed to more accurately measure your problem-solving ability. Performance-based testing is designed to test your ability to deal with these realistic situations. It's more than just a bunch of multiple-choice questions. Here are some key differences between performance-based testing and form/adaptive tests:

- Measures problem-solving ability instead of memorization.

- More than 95% of the questions are presented in the context of a case study or problem/solution format.

- Questions are grouped into "testlets" covering a specific topic and are presented in a group.

- Heavy use of graphics.

- Tests take considerably longer (3 hours) because each question requires more effort (there are approximately 70 questions).

- They challenge the "closed book" concept by making real-world reference tools available (namely NSEPro and MHTL).

- Test is strictly aligned to course materials and exercises.

- Orientation frames between testlets prepare candidates for subsequent questions and provide a "big picture" view.

As you can see, performance-based testing is a totally new and potentially exciting improvement to Novell's certification programs. It represents a quantum leap in education and testing philosophy. Performance-based testing could be the single most important change in the history of the CNE program. Good luck, and enjoy the test.

*The greatest mistake you can make in life is to be continually fearing you will make one.*

*Elbert Hubbar*

For a complete list of Novell-authorized courses and the corresponding test numbers for CNAs, CNEs, and Master CNEs, refer to the list in the following section. In addition, a vast collection of sample CNA test questions has been included with this book. Check out the new Interactive Learning System. Please avail yourself of this valuable opportunity!

Testing is tricky business, and although nobody enjoys taking a test, Novell has done everything they can to make the experience quick, painless, and accurate.

# Instructor-Led Courses

THE GOAL OF INSTRUCTOR-LED courses is to deliver well-designed courses with technically accurate information from talented CNIs in a superior, comfortable facility. Novell courses are recognized as the best in the technical training industry. In addition, the courses continue to evolve. For example, the current Service and Support and Networking Technologies courses are quantum leaps ahead of earlier versions. Also, feedback from the NetWare 4.1 courses shows that the introduction of new concepts and techniques has made the education materials even more productive. As I mentioned earlier, Novell Education offers more than fifty instructor-led courses. Following is a list of the courses that we haven't discussed yet. For a more thorough list, consult Novell Education at 1-800-233-EDUC in the U.S. and Canada, or 1-801-429-5508 elsewhere.

| Course No. | Course Name | Credits | Test No. |
| --- | --- | --- | --- |
| 105 | Introduction to Networking | none | none |
| 205 | Fundamentals of Internetwork and Management Design | 1 | 50-106 |
| 321 | GroupWise 4.1 | none | none |
| 501 | NetWare 2.2 System Manager | 3 | 50-20 |
| 502 | NetWare 2.2 Advanced System Manager | 2 | 50-44 |
| 507 | NetWare 3.11 to NetWare 3.12 Update Seminar | none | none |
| 611 | NetWare FLeX/IP | none | none |
| 760 | NetWare Telephony Services | none | none |
| 930 | NetWare Programming: NLM Development | none | none |
| 940 | NetWare Programming: Basic Services | none | none |
| 941 | NetWare Programming: Directory Services | none | none |
| 945 | NetWare Programming: Protocol Support | none | none |
| 950 | AppWare Programming: Visual AppBuilder | none | 50-146 |
| 954 | AppWare Programming: ALM Development | none | none |
| 960 | NetWare Client-Server Programming | none | none |

Keep in mind that Novell is constantly upgrading and evolving courses, so make sure to call 1-800-233-EDUC in the U.S. and Canada, or 1-801-429-5508 internationally. Of course, you could always contact your local Novell office to verify course numbers, test numbers, and credit values.

In addition to the obvious value of gaining knowledge and advancing toward Novell certification, Novell instructor-led courses have the additional advantage of being recognized by the International Association for Continuing Education and Training. Anyone who completes a Novell course may apply for continuing education units (CEUs) by sending in the CEU application card enclosed in each student kit. As required by the association, Novell maintains permanent records of students requesting CEUs for Novell course completion and issues a transcript of records at the request of the participant.

# Education Alternatives

I N ADDITION TO THE instructor-led courses, Novell provides alternative education methodologies such as workbooks and technology-based training. Education alternatives have been included so that professionals can train at their own pace in a more convenient manner. Alternative education materials can be purchased through authorized NAECs and resellers through Novell After Market Products. Following is a brief discussion of the most popular Novell Education alternatives.

## Workbooks

Novell Education provides a series of self-study workbooks. These workbooks are designed to supplement existing instructor-led courses or provide additional details in areas of specialty that do not warrant an instructor-led course. Novell-authorized workbooks are intended to be completed at the student's own pace. Each section within the workbook includes objectives, a list of terms, and review questions. Following is a list of currently available Novell Education workbooks:

- DOS for NetWare Users
- Microcomputer Concepts for NetWare Users

- NetWare 2.15 to 2.2 Update

- LANalyzer for Windows

- NetWare SFT III 3.11

- Administering NetWare for Macintosh 3.12

- Administering NetWare for Macintosh 4.01

- Administering SNAD for NetWare Global MHS

- Administering SMTP for NetWare Global MHS

## Technology-Based Training

A sophisticated series of technology-based training courses augments the existing Novell Education materials. These courses are fully graphical and interactive. They are based on the Microsoft Windows interface. In addition to providing the technical information in an easy-to-understand format, the technology-based training courses include mastery tests and review questions. Novell has currently limited the number of computer-based training (CBT) and video-based training (VBT) courses because they're extremely difficult and expensive to create. However, there are five existing technology-based training courses:

- NetWare User Basics

- Introduction to Networking

- NetWare 3.1$x$ Administration

- NetWare 4 Administration

- NetWare Expert for NMS

Make sure to take a look at this wonderful, interactive, graphical format. Once you start one, you won't be able to quit!

## Other Alternatives

In addition to Novell Education, other organizations provide alternatives for NetWare-oriented training. These organizations are primarily concerned with developing and distributing accurate technical information. The serious NetWare professional can dramatically improve his/her understanding of NetWare-related topics by dabbling in any of the following three educational alternatives:

- NetWare Users International
- LearningWare
- Cyber State University

Let's take a closer look.

### NetWare Users International

NetWare Users International (NUI) is an organization that was created in conjunction with Novell to provide support to distributed NetWare users groups. These users groups meet monthly to discuss critical technology issues and provide short training seminars. Through NUI, users present a united voice to Novell, giving vital feedback on improving products and services. In addition, NUI provides a supplemental education program to its members through regional NetWare users conferences, *NetWare Connection* magazine, and NUI-sponsored videos, products, and services. For more information about these resources or to join NUI, call Novell at 1-800-228-4NUI.

### LearningWare

LearningWare and I have banded together to create an exciting new way to learn—*The Clarke Tests v2.0*. This CD-ROM is a next-generation interactive learning system. It combines a colorful Windows-based interface with valuable text, 3-D graphics, sound clips, clues, and interactive answers. *The Clarke Tests v2.0* includes seventy tests covering nine CNE courses and over three thousand study sessions. Each study session combines a variety of question types with interactive graphics, sounds, and clues. But the real stars of the show are the interactive answers. Each answer includes a full page or more of explanation and study material—plus page references to Novell-Authorized Courseware, NetWare Documentation, and NUI's "So You Wanna Be A CNE?!" video series. For more information, please call LearningWare at 1-800-684-8858.

## Cyber State University

One of the most exciting ways to learn is *on-line*. Now this exciting new education alternative is available to CNA and CNE candidates. You can become a CNA in only 6 weeks from the comfort of your own sofa, or a CNE in 20 weeks. Cyber State University has a state-of-the-art on-line CNE program that includes interactive instructors, classroom chats, Q&A, hands-on exercises, tests, and even a virtual graduation ceremony. In addition to the on-line lessons, students enjoy a variety of other learning tools to enhance the program:

- *The CNA Study Guide*
- *The CNE Study Guide*
- The Clarke Tests v2.0
- "So You Wanna Be A CNE?!" video series
- World Wire on-line labs

For more information and to register for a class starting next week, call Cyber State University at 1-800-253-TREK.

*Experience is a hard teacher because she gives the test first, the lesson afterwards.*

*Vernon S. Law*

In this appendix, we have explored Novell's educational strategy and learned of the many facets of Novell-authorized courseware and certification programs. As you can see, there's a huge variety and diversity to Novell's educational approach. And it's safe to say that Novell Education is successful in "accelerating the growth of the network computing industry." As networking technology evolves in complexity and sophistication, the need for NetWare-oriented education will grow even larger. Fortunately, NetWare offers a wide base upon which to build the future of network computing.

# NetWare 2.2
# Worksheets

**FIGURE B.I**

External Hard Disk
Worksheet

## External Hard Disk Worksheet

Controller Type: _____ Controller: _____ Drive: _____  Ref #:
    Controller type: _____

Mfg. Model #/ Name: _____ Type #: _____
Removable Media: _____

ZTEST  ☐ Yes ☐ No      Interleave  ☐ 1   ☐ 2   ☐ Other____
Physical size: _____   Logical size: _____   Hot Fix size: _____

**Mirror Status:**  ☐ Primary   ☐ Secondary   w/ Reference #
**Capacity** (MB):_____   **Netware partition** (MB): _____  bootable ☐      **Other** (MB): _____

---

Controller Type: _____ Controller: _____ Drive: _____  Ref #:
    Controller type: _____

Mfg. Model #/ Name: _____ Type #: _____
Removable Media: _____

ZTEST  ☐ Yes ☐ No      Interleave  ☐ 1   ☐ 2   ☐ Other____
Physical size: _____   Logical size: _____   Hot Fix size: _____

**Mirror Status:**  ☐ Primary   ☐ Secondary   w/ Reference #
**Capacity** (MB):_____   **Netware partition** (MB): _____  bootable ☐      **Other** (MB): _____

---

Controller Type: _____ Controller: _____ Drive: _____  Ref #:
    Controller type: _____

Mfg. Model #/ Name: _____ Type #: _____
Removable Media: _____

ZTEST  ☐ Yes ☐ No      Interleave  ☐ 1   ☐ 2   ☐ Other____
Physical size: _____   Logical size: _____   Hot Fix size: _____

**Mirror Status:**  ☐ Primary   ☐ Secondary   w/ Reference #
**Capacity** (MB):_____   **Netware partition** (MB): _____  bootable ☐      **Other** (MB): _____

**Notes:**

For use with the NetWare v2.2 Installation manual.

**FIGURE B.2**
File Server Definition
Worksheet

# File Server Definition Worksheet

File server name: _____

Maximum number of open files: _____

Maximum number of open indexed files: _____

TTS backout volume: _____

Maximum number of TTS transactions: _____

Limit disk space: ☐ Yes ☐ No   If yes, number of bindery objects: _____

Install Mac VAP: ☐ Yes ☐ No

**Channel 0, controller 0, drive 0** (Internal Hard Disk)          Ref #:

Mfg. Model #/ Name: _____  Type #: _____
Removable Media: _____

**ZTEST**     ☐ Yes ☐ No          Interleave  ☐ 1   ☐ 2   ☐ Other_____
Physical size:                Logical size:                Hot Fix size:

**Mirror Status:**  ☐ Primary   ☐ Secondary     w/ Reference #
**Capacity** (MB):_____   **Netware partition** (MB): _____  bootable ☐      **Other** (MB): _____

**Channel 0, controller 0, drive 0** (Internal Hard Disk)          Ref #:

Mfg. Model #/ Name: _____  Type #: _____
Removable Media: _____

**ZTEST**     ☐ Yes ☐ No          Interleave  ☐ 1   ☐ 2   ☐ Other_____
Physical size:                Logical size:                Hot Fix size:

**Mirror Status:**  ☐ Primary   ☐ Secondary     w/ Reference #
**Capacity** (MB):_____   **Netware partition** (MB): _____  bootable ☐      **Other** (MB): _____

**File server hardware type:** _____   **Installer:** _____

**Floppy diskette drives:**      **Drive A:**              **Drive B:**
                                 ☐ 5.25"  1.2MB           ☐ 5.25"  1.2MB
                                 ☐ 5.25"  360KB           ☐ 5.25"  360KB
                                 ☐ 3.5"   1.44MB          ☐ 3.5"   1.44MB
                                 ☐ 3.5"   720KB           ☐ 3.5"   720KB

For use with NetWare v2.2 Installation manual.

FIGURE B.3
DOS Workstation
Configuration Worksheet

## DOS Workstation Configuration Worksheet

| Location: | | Installed By: | |
|---|---|---|---|

**Type of computer:**

| Floppy Diskette Drives: | Drive A: | Drive B: |
|---|---|---|
| | ❏ 5.25"  1.2MB | ❏ 5.25"  1.2MB |
| | ❏ 5.25"  360KB | ❏ 5.25"  360KB |
| | ❏ 3.5"   1.44MB | ❏ 3.5"   1.44MB |
| | ❏ 3.5"   720KB | ❏ 3.5"   720KB |

**Internal Hard Drives:**    Drive C: _____ MB   Drive D: _____ MB

**Memory:**  Standard _____ KB    Expanded _____ KB    Extended _____ KB

**LAN Driver:**

| Name | Option No. | Interrupt (IRQ) | Station Addresses | I/O Base Address | DMA Channel | RAM/ROM Addresses |
|---|---|---|---|---|---|---|
| | | | | | | |

**Boot Information:**         — **Additional Information for Remote Boot Workstations Only**

❏ Boot from hard disk          Remote reset enabled ❏ Yes ❏ No

❏ Boot from diskette           ❏ Remote reset PROM (s) _____

❏ Remote boot ——              Installed on LAN board _____

❏ LAN board set to configuraiton option 0

Network address _____

Node number ❏ Hex ❏ Decimal _____

Remote boot filename _____

**Files contained on the Master Shell Diskette:**

**DOS**  w/ Standard Drivers                          **ODI**  DOS w/ ODI Drivers

❏ DOS System Files    DOS version: _____        ❏ DOS System Files  DOS Version: _____

❏ IPX.COM                                           ❏ LSL

❏ NET4.COM or ❏ NET3.COM or ❏ NET2.COM              ❏ NE2   ❏ NE2000   ❏ 3C523   ❏ 3C503

❏ NETBIOS.EXE and INT2F.COM                                 ❏ NE1000   ❏ NE2-32 ❏ LANSUP

❏ EMS or ❏ XMS                                      ❏ IPXODI

❏ SHELL.CFG options (see *Using the Network* )      ❏ Net x.COM

                                                    ❏ EMS or ❏ XMS

                                                    ❏ SHELL.CFG options

                                                      (see *Using the Network* )

For use with the NetWare v2.2 Installation manual.

*Copy this worksheet for each workstation on your network.*

**FIGURE B.4**
Router Configuration
Worksheet

## Router Configuration Worksheet

| Location: | | Installed by: |
|---|---|---|

**Type of computer:**  File server name:

**Software generated from:** ❑ Floppy disk —❑ 5.25"-1.2MB  ❑ 3.5"-1.44MB

❑ Hard disk

❑ Network drive

**Memory:** Standard _____ KB  Expanded_____ KB  Extended _____ KB

**Operating system mode:**  ❑ Dedicated real mode
*(routing software)*
❑ Dedicated protected mode

❑ Nondedicated protected mode

**Nondedicated network address:** _____

**Communication buffers:** ❑ 500 (default)  ❑ _____ (specified)

**Network boards:**

| LAN | Name | Option No. | Interrupt (IRQ) | I/O Base Address | DMA Channel | Network Addresses |
|---|---|---|---|---|---|---|
| A | | | | | | |
| B | | | | | | |
| C | | | | | | |
| D | | | | | | |

**Notes:**

For use with the NetWare v2.2 Installation manual.

## Volume Configuration Worksheet

| Volume Name | Disk Ref. No. | Size (MB) | Directory Cached? | Directory Entries(#) | Notes: |
|---|---|---|---|---|---|
| SYS | | | | | |
| | | | | | |
| | | | | | |
| | | | | | |
| | | | | | |
| | | | | | |
| | | | | | |
| | | | | | |
| | | | | | |
| | | | | | |
| | | | | | |
| | | | | | |
| | | | | | |
| | | | | | |
| | | | | | |

For use with the NetWare v2.2 Installation manual.

## Operating System Generation Worksheet

**Operating System mode:** ☐ dedicated   ☐ nondedicated

**Nondedicated network address:** _____

**Number of communication buffers:** _____

**Will this machine be the server?** ☐ Yes   ☐ No

**Include core printing services?** ☐ Yes   ☐ No

**Network boards:** _____

| LAN | Name | Option No. | Hardware Settings | | | |
|-----|------|------------|-------------------|---|---|---|
| | | | Interrupt (IRQ) | I/O Base Address | DMA Channel | Network Addresses |
| A | | | | | | |
| B | | | | | | |
| C | | | | | | |
| D | | | | | | |
| | | | | | | |

**Disk drivers:** _____

| Channel | Disk Driver (HBA/Controller Type) | Option No. | Hardware Settings |
|---------|-----------------------------------|------------|-------------------|
| 0 | | | |
| 1 | | | |
| 2 | | | |
| 3 | | | |
| 4 | | | |
| | | | |

**Notes:**

For use with the NetWare v2.2 Installation manual.

**F I G U R E B.7**
Printer Configuration
Worksheet

## Printer Configuration Worksheet

**Printing Option**

    Core   ☐

    Print Server  ☐   (see *Print Server* for setup instructions)

**Serial Printers**

| Port | Printer No. | Printer Manufacturer/Model No. | Baud Rate | Word Size | Stop Bits | Parity | XON/ XOFF | Poll | Int |
|------|------------|-------------------------------|-----------|-----------|-----------|--------|-----------|------|-----|
| COM1 |            |                               |           |           |           |        |           |      | 4   |
| COM2 |            |                               |           |           |           |        |           |      | 3   |

**Parallel Printers**

| Port | Printer No. | Printer Manufacturer/Model No. | Poll | Int |
|------|------------|-------------------------------|------|-----|
| LPT1 |            |                               |      | 7   |
| LPT2 |            |                               |      | 5   |
| LPT3 |            |                               |      |     |

**Notes:**

For use with *NetWare v2.2 Installation.*

# NetWare 3.12 Worksheets

## File Server Worksheet

File server name: _____ Installed by: _____

File server make/model: _____

Memory: Base: _____ Extended: _____ Total: _____ **Server boot method:**
❑ Diskette
Internal network number: _____ ❑ Hard disk

Non-network board information: _____
_____
_____

**Network boards** (Fill in columns that apply to each network board.)

| Name | LAN driver | I/O port | Memory address | Interrupt (IRQ) | DMA channel | Station/Node address | Slot number | Network number |
|------|-----------|----------|----------------|-----------------|-------------|----------------------|-------------|----------------|
|      |           |          |                |                 |             |                      |             |                |
|      |           |          |                |                 |             |                      |             |                |
|      |           |          |                |                 |             |                      |             |                |
|      |           |          |                |                 |             |                      |             |                |
|      |           |          |                |                 |             |                      |             |                |

**Floppy Diskette Drives:** A Drive:                 B Drive:
❑ 5.25"  1.2MB      ❑ 5.25"  1.2MB
❑ 5.25"  360KB      ❑ 5.25"  360KB
❑ 3.5"   1.44MB     ❑ 3.5"   1.44MB
❑ 3.5"   720KB      ❑ 3.5"   720KB

**Internal hard drives:**     C Drive:  Make/Model: _____ Size: _____
DOS partition size: _____ NetWare partition: _____
Controller Type: _____
D Drive:  Make/Model: _____ Size: _____

**Disk coprocessor boards:**

| Name | Disk driver | I/O port | Interrupt |
|------|-------------|----------|-----------|
|      |             |          |           |
|      |             |          |           |
|      |             |          |           |
|      |             |          |           |

**Disk subsystems:**     Total number of devices: _____
Number of mirrored drives: _____

1. Drive Make/Model: _____ Size: _____ Heads: _____ Cylinders: _____ Mirrored with #: _____
2. Drive Make/Model: _____ Size: _____ Heads: _____ Cylinders: _____ Mirrored with #: _____
3. Drive Make/Model: _____ Size: _____ Heads: _____ Cylinders: _____ Mirrored with #: _____
4. Drive Make/Model: _____ Size: _____ Heads: _____ Cylinders: _____ Mirrored with #: _____
5. Drive Make/Model: _____ Size: _____ Heads: _____ Cylinders: _____ Mirrored with #: _____
6. Drive Make/Model: _____ Size: _____ Heads: _____ Cylinders: _____ Mirrored with #: _____
7. Drive Make/Model: _____ Size: _____ Heads: _____ Cylinders: _____ Mirrored with #: _____
8. Drive Make/Model: _____ Size: _____ Heads: _____ Cylinders: _____ Mirrored with #: _____
9. Drive Make/Model: _____ Size: _____ Heads: _____ Cylinders: _____ Mirrored with #: _____
10. Drive Make/Model: _____ Size: _____ Heads: _____ Cylinders: _____ Mirrored with #: _____
11. Drive Make/Model: _____ Size: _____ Heads: _____ Cylinders: _____ Mirrored with #: _____
12. Drive Make/Model: _____ Size: _____ Heads: _____ Cylinders: _____ Mirrored with #: _____

**F I G U R E   C.2**

Workstation
Configuration Worksheet

# Workstation Configuration Worksheet

**Current workstation owner:** _____ **Serial #:** _____
**Network address for board A:** _____ **Installed by:** _____
**Network address for board B:** _____ **Type of workstation:** _____

**Floppy Diskette Drives:**　　**A Drive:**　　　**B Drive:**
　　　　　　　　　　　　　　❏ 5.25"  1.2MB　❏ 5.25"  1.2MB
　　　　　　　　　　　　　　❏ 5.25"  360KB　❏ 5.25"  360KB
　　　　　　　　　　　　　　❏ 3.5"  1.44MB　❏ 3.5"  1.44MB
　　　　　　　　　　　　　　❏ 3.5"  720KB　❏ 3.5"  720KB

**Memory:**  Base: _____ Extended: _____ Expanded: _____ Total: _____
**Internal hard disks:** _____ Memory: _____ Driver type: _____

**Network board**　(Fill in columns that apply to each network board.)

| Name | Option number | I/O address | Memory address | Interrupt (IRQ) | DMA channel | Station/Node address | Slot number |
|---|---|---|---|---|---|---|---|
|  |  |  |  |  |  |  |  |
|  |  |  |  |  |  |  |  |
|  |  |  |  |  |  |  |  |
|  |  |  |  |  |  |  |  |
|  |  |  |  |  |  |  |  |

**LAN driver**

| | | | | | | | |
|---|---|---|---|---|---|---|---|
| LAN A |  |  |  |  |  |  |  |
| LAN B |  |  |  |  |  |  |  |

**Boot information:**
❏ Boot from hard disk
❏ Boot from diskette
❏ Boot by Remote Reset

DOS version _____

**Remote Reset checklist:**
❏ Network board set to configuration option 0
❏ Remote Reset PROM(s) installed on LAN board
❏ Remote Reset enabled on network board

Remote boot filename: _____

**Files needed to connect to the network:**
❏ IPX.COM
❏ NET4.COM or ❏ NET3.COM or ❏ EMSNET or ❏ XMSNET
❏ NETBIOS.EXE and INT2F.COM
❏ Others _____
❏ SHELL.CFG options _____

*Copy one page for each workstation*

**FIGURE C.3**
Directories Worksheet

## Directories Worksheet for File Server

| Volume: SYS | Directory Structure | | | | Files (Source) | File Attributes | Inherited Rights Mask (Applies only to the contents of this directory) | Directory Attributes (None automatically flagged) |
|---|---|---|---|---|---|---|---|---|
| | Directory | /Subdirectory | /Subdirectory | /Subdirectory | | | | |
| | LOGIN | OS_2 | | | login files (copied in at installation) | automatically flagged | [S R W C E M F A] | |
| | MAIL | subdirectory for each user created automatically | | | | automatically flagged | [S R W C E M F A] | |
| | SYSTEM | subdirectory for queue-print server -automatically | | | system files (copied in at installation) | automatically flagged | [S R W C E M F A] | |
| | PUBLIC | | | | public files (copied in at installation) | automatically flagged | [S R W C E M F A] | |
| | HOME | user name created automatically if you use RDEF | | | user created | user defined | [S  ] | |
| | | Machine name | DOS Directories — Operating system MSDOS | DOS version | copied files from DOS diskettes | [R F] | [S R W C E M F A] | |
| | | | | | | | | |
| | | | | | | | | |
| | | | | | | | | |
| | | | | | | | | |
| | | | | | | | | |
| | | | | | | | | |
| | | | | | | | | |
| | | | | | | | | |
| | | | | | | | | |

FIGURE C.4
Users Worksheet

**Users Worksheet** for File Server

| Full Name | Username | Application Used | Groups | Access to Directories (Specify) | Time Restrictions (If not default) | Station Restrictions (Specify network and node address) | Managed by | Operator or Manager (Specify) |
|---|---|---|---|---|---|---|---|---|
| | | | | | | | | |
| | | | | | | | | |
| | | | | | | | | |
| | | | | | | | | |

**FIGURE C.5**
Group Worksheet

## Group Worksheet for File Server _____ for Workgroup _____

| Group Name | Basis of Group | Access to Directories | Trustee Directory Assignments | Access to Files | Trustee File Assignments |
|---|---|---|---|---|---|
| | | | | | |
| Full Name | Managed by | | | | |
| | | | | | |
| Usernames of Members | (NetWare utilities list names alphabetically) | | | | |
| | | | | | |
| | | | | | |
| | | | | | |
| | | | | | |
| | | | | | |
| | | | | | |
| | | | | | |
| | | | | | |
| | | | | | |

**FIGURE C.6**
User Defaults

# User Defaults for File Server _____ Workgroup _____

☐ **YES** ☐ **NO** Account has expiration date?
Date account expires: _____

☐ **YES** ☐ **NO** Allow unlimited credit?
Low balance limit: _____

☐ **YES** ☐ **NO** Limit concurrent connections?
Maximum concurrent connections: _____

☐ **YES** ☐ **NO** Intruder Detection/Lockout?

Intruder Detection Threshold
*(number of incorrect login attempts permitted):* _____

Bad login count retention time
*(how long after last incorrect login):* Days:___ Hours:___ Min:___

☐ **YES** ☐ **NO** Lock account after detection? How long? Days:___ Hours:___ Min:___

☐ **YES** ☐ **NO** Require password?
Minimum password length: _____

☐ **YES** ☐ **NO** Force periodic password changes?
Days between forced changes: _____

☐ **YES** ☐ **NO** Limit grace logins?
Grace logins allowed: _____

☐ **YES** ☐ **NO** Require unique password?

☐ **YES** ☐ **NO** Install Accounting?

Initial Account Balance: _____

Time Restrictions

| | | | | | | | | |
|---|---|---|---|---|---|---|---|---|
| SUN | | | | | | | | |
| MON | | | | | | | | |
| TUE | | | | | | | | |
| WED | | | | | | | | |
| THU | | | | | | | | |
| FRI | | | | | | | | |
| SAT | | | | | | | | |

**FIGURE C.7**
Trustee Directory
Security Worksheet

## Trustee Directory Security Worksheet for File Server

Trustee Directory Rights to Be Assigned to Groups or Individual Users
(Possible trustee rights: Supervisory, Read, Write, Create, Erase, Modify, File Scan, Access Control)

| Directories (To be used in conjunction with Directories Worksheet) | USER OR GROUP NAME → | | | | | | | | | | | | | | | | |
|---|---|---|---|---|---|---|---|---|---|---|---|---|---|---|---|---|---|
| | EVERYONE | | | | | | | | | | | | | | | | |
| SYS:LOGIN | [ ] | | | | | | | | | | | | | | | | |
| MAIL | automatically assigned [W C] | | | | | | | | | | | | | | | | |
| SYSTEM | no rights | | | | | | | | | | | | | | | | |
| PUBLIC | automatically assigned [R F] | | | | | | | | | | | | | | | | |
| PUBLIC    DOS Directories | [R F] | | | | | | | | | | | | | | | | |

**FIGURE C.8**
Trustee File Security
Worksheet

## Trustee File Security Worksheet for File Server _____

Use only if you need to redefine
trustee rights for individual files

**Trustee File Rights to Be Assigned to Groups or Individual Users**
(Possible trustee rights: Supervisory, Read, Write, Create, Erase, Modify, File Scan, Access Control)

| Directory Path | USER OR GROUP NAME Filename | EVERYONE | | | | | | | | | | | | | |
|---|---|---|---|---|---|---|---|---|---|---|---|---|---|---|
| SYS:LOGIN | | / / | | | | | | | | | | | | | |
| MAIL | | automatically assigned [W C] | | | | | | | | | | | | | |
| SYSTEM | | no rights | | | | | | | | | | | | | |
| PUBLIC | | automatically assigned [R F] | | | | | | | | | | | | | |

**FIGURE C.9**

Login Scripts Worksheet

**Login Scripts Worksheet** for File Server _____

**System Login Script**

**rem** *preliminary commands (optional)*

**rem** *greeting (optional)*

**rem** *display login messages (optional)*

**rem** *attach to other file servers (optional)*

**rem** *NetWare utilities mappings*

   MAP INS S1:=SYS:PUBLIC

**rem** *DOS directory mapping and COMSPEC*

   MAP INS S2: =
   COMSPEC   = S2:COMMAND.COM

**rem** *application directory mappings*

**rem** *miscellaneous search drives (optional)*

**rem** *supervisor mappings*

**rem** *preliminary commands (optional)*

   IF "%LOGIN_NAME" = "SUPERVISOR" THEN

**FIGURE C.9**
Login Scripts Worksheet
(continued)

> **rem** *home or username directory mapping*

> **rem** *work directory mapping (optional)*

> **rem** *default printer mappings or printing batch files (optional)*

> **rem** *display directory path at prompt*
> SET PROMPT = "$P$G"

> **rem** *display all current drive settings (optional)*
> MAP DISPLAY ON
> MAP

> **rem** *run miscellaneous programs*

**Basic User Login Script** for_____ Group_____ Workgroup _____
**rem** *set environmental variables*

**rem** *individual drive mappings*

**Basic User Login Script** for_____ Group_____ Workgroup _____
**rem** *set environmental variables*

**rem** *individual drive mappings*

# Answers to
# CNA Exercises

# Exercise 1.1: Microcomputer Concepts

1. E
2. F
3. A
4. T
5. P
6. J
7. S
8. G
9. N
10. L
11. B
12. Q
13. O
14. H
15. M
16. C
17. K
18. D
19. I
20. R

# Exercise 2.1: Understanding NetWare Basics

1. G
2. M
3. K
4. C
5. D
6. A
7. B
8. E
9. F
10. J
11. P
12. L
13. O
14. N
15. I
16. Q
17. H

**PART I**
CNA Fundamentals—
Crossword Puzzle
Answers

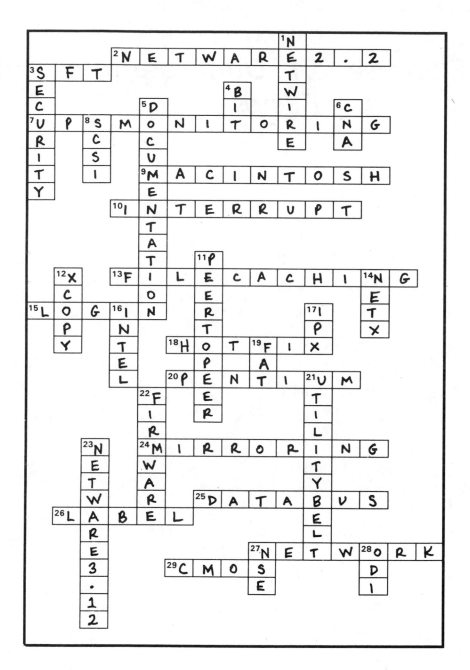

# Exercise 2.2: Using NetWare 3.12 DynaText

**4.** 3 instances of the word CNA appear in the catalog.

**6.** The word Supervisor appears 104 times in the Concepts manual and 631 times in the entire NetWare 3.12 library.

**8.** The subtopic Viewer Features appears under Novell DynaText. The Quick Access Guide is not available on-line.

**10.** A figure that describes the printing procedure screen appears when you double-click on the green camera icon. The book *NetWare 3.12 System Administration* appears in the outline.

# Exercise 3.1: Using the MAP Command

**1.** `MAP U:=JERRY/SYS:USERS\OPUS`

**2.** `MAP S1:=JERRY/SYS:PUBLIC`

**3.** `MAP S16:=JERRY/SYS:PUBLIC\%MACHINE\%OS\%OS_VERSION`

**4.** `MAP NEXT TOM/ACCT:GL\DATA`

**5.** `MAP S16:=TOM/ACCT:AP`

**6.** `MAP INSERT S3:=JERRY/APPS:DBASE`

**7.** `MAP ROOT R:=JERRY/SYS:USERS\BILL\REPORTS`

# Exercise 3.2: The Effects of CD on MAP

5.  *Type MAP and press Enter. What happened and why?*
    The system responds with `Bad Command or File Name` and the
    MAP command does not execute, because the `CD` command at the Z:
    drive remapped the PUBLIC subdirectory to the root. By doing so, the
    user no longer has a search mapping to the PUBLIC subdirectory and
    the MAP utility, which resides in PUBLIC, cannot be executed from
    this point.

7.  *Now that your Z drive has been remapped to the PUBLIC subdirectory,
    type MAP and press Enter. What happens and why?*
    The MAP command is executed and displayed on the screen, because
    the CD command returned Z: to PUBLIC. The new search drive finds
    and executes the MAP utility.

13. *Type MAP and press Enter. What happened and why?*
    The system responded with `Bad Command or File Name` and
    the MAP command did not execute. Once again, the `CD` command
    remapped the Z: drive to root and the search drive 1 to PUBLIC no
    longer exists; it now points to the root. Therefore, when we go to the
    F: drive and type the `MAP` command, the system cannot find MAP.EXE.

16. *Now type MAP and press Enter. What happened and why?*
    The MAP command executes and appears on the screen, because the
    CD command was used to remap search drive 1 or the Z: drive from
    the root back to PUBLIC. This way, no matter where we are, even from
    the F: drive, the MAP command will execute because the system will
    use the search drive 1 to find the utility in the PUBLIC subdirectory.

22. *Now type MAP and press Enter. What happened and why?*
    The system will respond with `Bad Command or File Name` and the
    MAP command will not execute, because you have mapped a network
    drive rather than a search drive to the PUBLIC subdirectory. Remember,
    network drive mappings do not search through the directory tree for
    applications or .COM files.

24. *Now type* MAP *and press Enter. What happened and why?*
    The MAP command executes and appears on the screen, because a search drive mapping was inserted for the PUBLIC subdirectory.

# Exercise 4.1: Calculating Effective Rights

Refer to Figure D.1 for an illustration of calculating effective rights.

1. Effective rights = R, W, C, F.

2. Effective rights = R and F.

3. Effective rights = None.

4. Combined rights = R, W, C, F.
   Effective rights = R, W, F.

5. The MRM restricts Read and File Scan. These are the default user rights. Therefore, the MRM should be set to W, C, E, M, A.

**FIGURE D.1**
Calculating effective
rights for NetWare 2.2

|  | R | W | C | E | M | F | A |
|---|---|---|---|---|---|---|---|
| USER RIGHTS | R | W | C |  |  | F |  |
| MRM | R | W | C | E | M | F | A |
| EFFECTIVE RIGHTS | R | W | C |  |  | F |  |

CASE 1

|  | R | W | C | E | M | F | A |
|---|---|---|---|---|---|---|---|
| USER RIGHTS | R | W | C |  |  | F |  |
| MRM | R |  |  |  |  | F |  |
| EFFECTIVE RIGHTS | R |  |  |  |  | F |  |

CASE 2

|  | R | W | C | E | M | F | A |
|---|---|---|---|---|---|---|---|
| USER RIGHTS | R |  | C | E |  | F |  |
| MRM |  | W |  |  | M |  | A |
| EFFECTIVE RIGHTS |  |  |  |  |  |  |  |

CASE 3

|  | R | W | C | E | M | F | A |
|---|---|---|---|---|---|---|---|
| COMBINED RIGHTS | R | W | C |  |  | F |  |
| MRM | R | W |  | E |  | F |  |
| EFFECTIVE RIGHTS | R | W |  |  |  | F |  |

CASE 4

**FIGURE D.1**
Calculating effective
rights for NetWare 2.2
(continued)

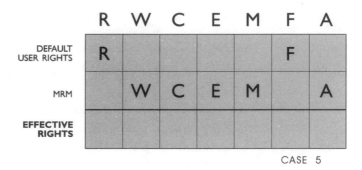

CASE 5

# *Exercise 6.1: Configuring NetWare Restrictions*

**7.** *Login as your supervisor equivalent account once again and change FRED's expiration date to yesterday's date. Exit SYSCON once again and attempt to login as FRED. Explain what happened.*
The system will respond with an error message saying `This Account has expired or been disabled by the Supervisor`. The system will not allow FRED to log in, because FRED's expiration date has passed and the account has been locked.

**9.** *Log in as your supervisor equivalent account and enter FRED's account restrictions once again. Change the date the password expires to yesterday's date. Log in once again as FRED and note the changes below.*
The system allows FRED to log in but displays the following message: `Password for user FRED on Server CNA has expired. You have NO grace logins left to change your password. This is your last chance to change it. Enter your new password`. The system freezes at the input screen asking for a new password to be entered.

**13.** *Enlarge the file by typing COPY WILMA.TXT + Z:MAIN.MENU NEW.TXT and press Enter. Note what happens below and check the limitations in SYSCON once again for WILMA.*
During the copy procedure, the system responds with `Insufficient disk space; 0 files copied` and returns to the PUBLIC

subdirectory. The disk space restriction in SYSCON states that the volume space limit is 4K and the volume space in use is also 4K; therefore, WILMA cannot copy or write any more files to the NetWare volume.

15. *Enter SYSCON and choose FRED from the User Name window. In FRED's user information box, select Station Restrictions. Restrict FRED to the network number and node address that you wrote down for your workstation. Exit SYSCON and move to another workstation. Attempt to log in as FRED. Make note of what happens.*
The system responds with an error message CNA/FRED:Attempting to login from an unapproved station. The supervisor has limited the stations that you are allowed to login on and the systems logs FRED out and responds with the F:\LOGIN> subdirectory.

16. *... Make note below of what happens as the system approaches the half hour that is restricted.*
Five minutes before the half hour period, the system warns you that WILMA's account is approaching an unrestricted period. It asks that you please save your files and log out. At the half hour point, the system responds with another error message and clears the connections. The workstation receives the message Error Sending on the Network. The system does not log out the user and close open files; it simply clears the connection.

18. *Enter DINO's User Information window and create a password for him. Exit SYSCON and log in as DINO twice, using the wrong password. Finally, the third time, note what happens.*
Each time you log in as DINO with the incorrect password, the system responds with CNA/DINO: Access to server denied. You are attached to server CNA. The final time when you attempt to log in as DINO, the system responds with the following error message: CNA/DINO: Intruder Detection/Lockout has disabled this account. At this point, DINO cannot log in until the supervisor unlocks his intruder detection.

# *Exercise 6.2: Writing Login Scripts*

```
REMARK **** Drive Mappings ***
MAP ROOT U:=SYS:USERS\%LOGIN_NAME
MAP G:=SYS:DATA
MAP NEXT SYS:LOGIN

MAP S1:=SYS:PUBLIC
MAP S2:=SYS:PUBLIC\%MACHINE\%OS\%OS_VERSION
MAP S3:=SYS:APPS\WP
MAP S16:=SYS:APPS\DBASE
MAP INSERT S3:=SYS:ACCT

REMARK **** COMSPEC ***
COMSPEC = S2:COMMAND.COM

REMARK **** Greetings ***
WRITE "Good %GREETING_TIME, %LOGIN_NAME!"
WRITE "Today is %DAY_OF_WEEK %MONTH_NAME %DAY.
Have a Nice Day!"

**** Informational ***
IF DAY_OF_WEEK = "Friday" THEN BEGIN
    WRITE "Congratulations, you made it through
      the week!"
    WRITE "Welcome to your Friday."
END

IF MONTH_NAME = "May" AND DAY = "3" THEN BEGIN
    FIRE 9
    FIRE 9
    FIRE 9
    WRITE "Happy Birthday to you, happy birthday
      to you, you live in a zoo."
END
```

```
WRITE "Today is %DAY_OF_WEEK, %MONTH_NAME %DAY,
%YEAR"
WRITE "The Time is %HOUR:%MINUTE %AM_PM."
WRITE "You are running %OS %OS_VERSION."

IF MEMBER OF "Sales" THEN BEGIN
     DISPLAY SYS:GROUP\SALES\SALES.TXT
END

REMARK **** The END ***
DRIVE U:
EXIT "Start"
```

# Exercise 6.3: Building Menus

**BOB.MNU**

```
%Bob's Personal Menu,12,40,1
Applications
     %Applications
Utilities
     %Utilities
System Configuration
     Z:SYSCON
File Management
     Z:FILER
Logout
     !LOGOUT
%Applications,1,1,2
Word Processing
     %Word Processing
Spreadsheet
     F:
     CD\APPS\LOTUS
     123
```

```
Windows
     F:
     CD\APPS\WINDOWS
     WIN : -- executes Windows without displaying
        the title screen.
Dbase
     F:
     CD\APPS\PARADOX
     PARADOX
%Word Processing,1,79,3
WordPerfect
     F:
     CD\APPS\WP51
     WP
Microsoft Word
     F:
     CD\APPS\WORD
     WORD
WordStar
     F:
     CD\APPS\WORDSTAR
     WS
%Utilities,24,79,4
Session
     Z:SESSION
Norton Utilities
     F:
     CD\APPS\UTILS
     NU
Print Management
     Z:PCONSOLE
```

**Extracurricular**

To stop users from escaping your menu, make a minor modification to your START.BAT file. Create an endless "loop" that brings users back to the menu when they try to escape. Here are the modifications:

```
ECHO OFF
CLS
CAPTURE Q=LASER /NB NFF TI=10
:TOP
MENU BOB
GOTO TOP
```

The only way to exit the menu is to press Ctrl+Break. Note: Ctrl+Break can also be deactivated with the BREAK OFF login command.

# Exercise 7.1: Using the CAPTURE Command

1. ```
   CAPTURE Q=REPORTS TI=7 C=4 NFF NAM=USERNAME
   B=FILENAME
   ```

2. ```
   CAPTURE S=SALES Q=GRAPHICS NT NB L=2 FF
   ```

3. ```
   CAPTURE L=3 CR=SYS:PLOTTER\FILENAME
   ```

4. ```
   CAPTURE SH
   ```

5. ```
   CAPTURE J=ACCOUNT
   ```

6. ```
   CAPTURE NB NFF NT TI=10
   ```

7. ```
   ENDCAP L=2
   ```
   ```

**PART 2**
The NetWare 2.2 CNA
Program—Crossword
Puzzle Answers

# Exercise 8.1: Understanding Directory Structure

1. *How many volumes have been defined in this directory structure?*
   Four

2. *Assuming that this is a NetWare 3.12 directory structure, which default system directories are missing?*
   ETC, DELETED.SAV, and DOC directories

3. *How is the volume structure organized in the accompanying graphic? What are the benefits of this structure? What are the possible pitfalls of this structure?*
   The volume structure is organized according to the separation of network applications. In addition, users have been organized under their own specific USERS directory. The benefits of this structure are that users can be organized according to one directory structure and applications can be branched off into their own volume. This organization scheme makes backup and fault tolerance extremely easy. The disadvantage of this structure is that the APPS volume can grow quite large and fill up independently of the available space in the SYS: volume. The same goes for the ACCT volume. Keeping data in one volume gives you the flexibility to better manage available disk space.

4. *Draw the path to each of the following directories:*

   A. The REPORTS directory under BILL.  `JERRY/SYS:USERS\BILL\REPORTS`

   B. MS-DOS v7.00.  `JERRY/SYS:PUBLIC\IBM_PC\MS-DOS\V7.00`

   C. The user directory for OPUS.  `JERRY/SYS:USERS\OPUS`

   D. The data directory for GL.  `TOM/ACCT:GL\DATA`

5. *How would you communicate or copy files from one subdirectory to another? Indicate the NetWare command you would use to copy a file from STIMPY's user directory to the data directory under GL.*
   The easiest way to communicate between volumes and servers is to set drive mappings to destination subdirectories. To copy a file from STIMPY's user directory to the data directory under GL would be a two-step process.

   A. Type `MAP NEXT TOM/ACCT:GL\DATA (G:)`.

   B. From STIMPY's subdirectory, type `NCOPY filename G:`.

6. *What NetWare command would you use to view a graphical tree of the JERRY/SYS: directory structure?*
   From the root of the JERRY/SYS: volume, type `LISTDIR /s`.

7. *What NetWare directory command would you use to view the space available on the TOM/ACCT: volume?*
   From the TOM/ACCT: volume root subdirectory, type `CHKVOL` for a command line listing and `VOLINFO` for a menu listing.

# *Case Study I: Creating a Directory Structure for Snouzer, Inc.*

See Figure D.2 for an illustration of the SNOUZER, INC. directory structure.

**FIGURE D.2**
The directory structure
for SNOUZER, INC.

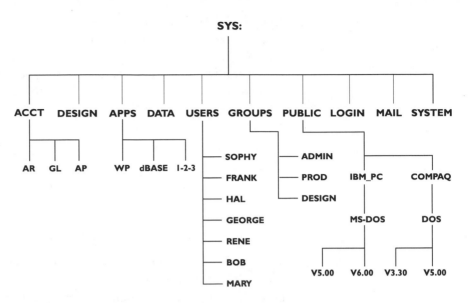

# Exercise 8.2: Using the MAP Command

**1.** MAP ROOT G:=SYS:DATA

**2.** MAP U:=SYS:USERS\JACK

**3.** MAP S16:=SYS:APPS\WP
MAP S16:=SYS:APPS\APPS\WP
MAP S16:=SYS:APPS\DBASE

**4.** *How does the system indicate a map root drive?*

Within the MAP display in NetWare, the system will indicate a MAP ROOT by placing a backslash after the directory path.

**5.** MAP DEL U:
MAP U:=SYS:USERS\JILL

**6.** MAP INSERT S3:=SYS:APPS\WINDOWS

7. *Move to the G drive. Now type* CD \ *to return to the SYS: volume root. What happens?*
Nothing! The system does not allow the user to move back to the volume root from the DATA subdirectory, because the MAP ROOT indicates to NetWare that this is a pseudo root. Therefore, users who exist in drives that are MAP ROOTed cannot move back in the directory structure.

8. MAP NEXT SYS:DATA

10. *How does the system execute the MAP command from the U drive?*
The system executes the MAP command from the U: drive because MAP.EXE is a NetWare utility that exists in the PUBLIC subdirectory. By default, the PUBLIC subdirectory is defined as search drive 1 and therefore allows users to execute files from within the PUBLIC subdirectory without having to physically be located there.

14. *Type* MAP *once again to verify your drive mappings. What happened and why?*
The system responded with the message Bad Command or File Name and the MAP command did not execute, because the search drive to PUBLIC that existed as Z: has been remapped to the root. This remapping occurred when the user used the CD command while at the Z drive.

16. *Now type* MAP *and notice what happens.*
The MAP command executes and the system responds with a display of drive mappings on the screen. This occurred because the search drive 1 (Z) was remapped to the PUBLIC subdirectory.

# Case Study II: Drive Mappings for Snouzer, Inc.

## Regular Drive Mappings

```
MAP U:=SYS:USERS\[username]
MAP G:=SYS:GROUPS\[groupname]
MAP H:=SYS:DATA
```

## Search Drive Mappings

```
MAP INSERT S1:=SYS:PUBLIC
MAP INSERT S2:=SYS:PUBLIC\%MACHINE\%OS\%OS_VERSION
MAP INSERT S3:=SYS:APPS\WP
MAP INSERT S4:=SYS:DESIGN
MAP INSERT S5:=SYS:ACCT
MAP INSERT S6:=SYS:APPS\dBASE
MAP INSERT S7:=SYS:APPS\123
```

# Exercise 9.1: Understanding Special User Accounts

See Table D.1 for the answers to the Special User Accounts matrix.

| TABLE D.1 Understanding Special User Accounts | S | SE | WGM | UAM | CO | PQO | PSO |
|---|---|---|---|---|---|---|---|
| Create supervisor equivalence | X | X | | | | | |
| Automatically acquire all rights to dir/file | X | X | | | | | |
| Create other users/groups | X | X | X | | | | |
| Manage all user accounts | X | X | | | | | |
| Manage special user accounts | X | X | X | X | | | |
| Manager/operator type can be user or group | X | X | X | | | | |
| Create WGM | X | X | | | | | |
| Assign managed users as UAMs | X | X | X | X | | | |
| Delete any user account | X | X | | | | | |
| Delete special user accounts | X | X | X | X | | | |
| User/supervisor functions of FCONSOLE | X | X | | | X | | |
| Create print queues | X | X | | | | | |
| Manipulate print queues | X | X | | | | X | |
| Delete print queue entries | X | X | | | | X | |
| Create print servers | X | X | | | | | |
| Manage print server | X | X | | | | | X |

# Exercise 9.2: Calculating NetWare 3.12 Effective Rights

See Figure D.3 for an illustration of calculating NetWare 3.12 effective rights.

1. Effective rights = R, W, C, F. The Explicit assignment overrides the IRM.

2. Effective rights = S, R, W, C, E, M, F, A. The Supervisory right includes all other rights, and it cannot be revoked by the IRM.

3. Effective rights = S, R, W, C, E, M, F, A. The Supervisory right cannot be revoked by the IRM, even when it is inherited.

4. Effective rights = W, M. The IRM only allows the W and M inherited rights to flow through.

5. Effective rights = None. The IRM blocks all inherited rights from flowing through.

6. Combined rights = R, W, C, E, F in SYS:PUBLIC. These rights are the combination of user and group assignments.
   Effective rights = C, F in SYS:PUBLIC\DOS. The IRM only allows the C and F inherited rights to flow from the SYS:PUBLIC parent directory.

7. Combined rights = R, W, C, M, F, A. These rights are the combination of explicit group rights and inherited user rights. Hint: keep track of which rights are explicit and which are inherited.
   Effective rights = R, C, F, A. The R and F explicit rights override the IRM. The C and A inherited rights are allowed to pass through by the IRM. The M and W inherited rights are blocked by the IRM.

**FIGURE D.3**
Calculating effective rights for NetWare 3.12

|  | S | R | W | C | E | M | F | A |
|---|---|---|---|---|---|---|---|---|
| EXPLICIT TRUSTEE RIGHTS |  | R | W | C |  |  | F |  |
| IRM | S | R |  |  |  |  | F |  |
| **EFFECTIVE RIGHTS** |  | R | W | C |  |  | F |  |

CASE 1

|  | S | R | W | C | E | M | F | A |
|---|---|---|---|---|---|---|---|---|
| EXPLICIT TRUSTEE RIGHTS | S | R |  |  |  |  | F |  |
| IRM |  | R | W | C |  |  | F |  |
| **EFFECTIVE RIGHTS** | S | R | W | C | E | M | F | A |

CASE 2

|  | S | R | W | C | E | M | F | A |
|---|---|---|---|---|---|---|---|---|
| EXPLICIT TRUSTEE ASSIGNMENTS |  |  |  |  |  |  |  |  |
| INHERITED TRUSTEE ASSIGNMENTS | S | R | W | C | E | M | F | A |
| IRM |  | R | W |  |  | M |  |  |
| **EFFECTIVE RIGHTS** | S | R | W | C | E | M | F | A |

CASE 3

**FIGURE D.3**
Calculating effective rights for NetWare 3.12 (continued)

| | S | R | W | C | E | M | F | A |
|---|---|---|---|---|---|---|---|---|
| EXPLICIT TRUSTEE ASSIGNMENTS | | | | | | | | |
| INHERITED TRUSTEE ASSIGNMENTS | | R | W | | E | M | | |
| IRM | | | W | C | | M | | A |
| **EFFECTIVE RIGHTS** | | | W | | | M | | |

CASE 4

| | S | R | W | C | E | M | F | A |
|---|---|---|---|---|---|---|---|---|
| EXPLICIT TRUSTEE ASSIGNMENTS | | | | | | | | |
| INHERITED TRUSTEE ASSIGNMENTS | | R | W | C | | M | F | |
| IRM | S | | | | E | | | A |
| **EFFECTIVE RIGHTS** | | | | | | | | |

CASE 5

| | S | R | W | C | E | M | F | A |
|---|---|---|---|---|---|---|---|---|
| EXPLICIT GROUP RIGHTS | | R | | | | | F | |
| EXPLICIT USER RIGHTS | | | W | C | E | | | |
| COMBINED | | R | W | C | E | | F | |
| IRM | S | | | C | | | F | A |
| **EFFECTIVE RIGHTS** (Public\DOS) | | | | C | | | F | |

CASE 6

|  | S | R | W | C | E | M | F | A |
|---|---|---|---|---|---|---|---|---|
| **EXPLICIT GROUP RIGHTS** |  | R |  |  |  |  | F |  |
| **EXPLICIT USER RIGHTS** |  |  | W | C |  | M |  | A |
| **COMBINED** |  | R | W | C |  | M | F | A |
| **IRM** | S |  |  | C | E |  |  | A |
| **EFFECTIVE RIGHTS** (Public\DOS) |  | R |  | C |  |  | F | A |

CASE 7

# Exercise 11.1: Matching Server Startup Events

## Happens Every Time

1. Boot DOS.

2. Load SERVER.EXE.

3. Set up IPX NETWORK NUMBER CAFE.

4. Load STARTUP.NCF.

5. Load ISADISK.

6. Load NE2000.

7. BIND IPX TO NE2000.

## Happens Only Once

1. Run FORMAT.

2. Run FDISK.

3. Copy SERVER.EXE to C:\SERVER.312.

4. Create NetWare partition.

5. Create SYS volume.

6. Copy SYSTEM and PUBLIC files.

7. Create AUTOEXEC.NCF.

# Case Study IV: Creating a NET.CFG File for Snouzer, Inc.

Here is Snouzer's template NET.CFG file:

```
IPX RETRY COUNT=50
SPX ABORT TIMEOUT=1000
LINK DRIVER NE2000
    INT 5
    PORT 320
    FRAME Ethernet_802.3
NETWARE DOS REQUESTER
    FIRST NETWORK DRIVE=Q
    SHOW DOTS=ON
    FILE HANDLES=60
    CACHE BUFFERS=20
    MAX TASKS=50
    LONG MACHINE TYPE=COMPAQ
    PREFERRED SERVER=NIRVANA
    CONNECTIONS=14
    LOAD CONN TABLE LOW=ON
```

# Exercise 11.2: Debugging Login Script Commands

1. TURN MAP should be written as MAP. TURN is not a valid login script command.

2. An = sign is missing between the S1: and the SYS and there should not be a space between the colon and PUBLIC.

3. SEARCH 2—there should not be a space between SEARCH and 2. The + sign should be an = sign. The vertical bar after %OS should be a \. There should be an underscore between OS and VERSION.

4. COMPEC should be COMSPEC. There should be an = between COM-SPEC and S2 and there should be no space between COMMAND and .COM.

5. MAP 1 should read MAP *1. The semicolon should be a colon both after the 1 and after the SYS. There should be a % in front of LOGIN and there should be an underscore between LOGIN and NAME.

6. There should be an * in front of the 2. There should not be a space between the colon and the =. LOGIN NAME again should appear as %LOGIN_NAME.

7. There should not be a space between the : and the =.

8. Again, there should not be a space between the : and the =.

9. There should not be a colon after the WRITE command. There should be a % before GREETING and there should be an underscore between GREETING and TIME. There should also be an underscore between LOGIN and NAME and there should be a quote at the beginning and at the end of the whole LOGIN_NAME line.

10. The WRITE command is missing the parameters for the time. It should read WRITE "The Time is %HOUR:%MINUTE %AM_PM."

11. There should be a space between IS and %. There should not be a space between the % and DAY_OF_WEEK. There should be an underscore between DAY and OF and WEEK. There should be an underscore between MONTH and NAME. There should not be a space between % and DAY and it should all end with quotes.

12. It's okay.

13. There should be an * in front of 3 and an = after. The semicolon should be a colon and the SYS\ should be SYS:.

14. It's okay.

15. It's okay.

16. TURN should be removed. Again, TURN is not a valid login script command.

17. It's okay.

## Corrected Version:

1. `MAP DISPLAY OFF`

2. `MAP S1:=SYS:PUBLIC`

3. `MAP SEARCH2:=PUBLIC\%MACHINE\%OS\%OS_VERSION`

4. `COMSPEC=S2:COMMAND.COM`

5. `MAP *1:=SYS:USERS\%LOGIN_NAME`

6. `MAP *2:=SYS:USERS\%LOGIN_NAME\REPORTS`

7. `MAP S3:=SYS:APPLIC\WP`

8. `MAP S4:=SYS:APPLIC\DATABASE`

9. `WRITE "GOOD %GREETING_TIME, %LOGIN_NAME"`

10. `WRITE "THE TIME IS %HOUR:%MINUTE %AM_PM"`

11. `WRITE "TODAY IS %DAY_OF_WEEK, %MONTH_NAME %DAY"`

12. `If %2=DATABASE THEN BEGIN`

**13.** MAP *3:=SYS:DBDATA

**14.** END

**15.** DISPLAY SYS:SUPERVISOR\MESSAGE.TXT

**16.** MAP DISPLAY ON

**17.** MAP

# *Case Study V: Writing Login Scripts for Snouzer, Inc.*

```
REMARK **** Greetings ***
WRITE "Welcome to SNOUZER, INC. -- The home of
   world famous doggy doos!!"
WRITE "Good %GREETING_TIME, %LOGIN_NAME!"
WRITE "Today is %DAY_OF_WEEK %MONTH_NAME %DAY.
   Have a Nice Day!"

REMARK **** Drive Mappings ***
MAP U:=SYS:USERS\%LOGIN_NAME
IF MEMBER OF "ADMIN" THEN MAP Q:=SYS:GROUPS\ADMIN
IF MEMBER OF "PROD" THEN MAP Q:=SYS:GROUPS\PROD
IF MEMBER OF "DESIGN" THEN MAP Q:=SYS:GROUPS\DESIGN
MAP H:=SYS:DATA

MAP INSERT S1:=SYS:PUBLIC
MAP INSERT S2:=SYS:PUBLIC\%MACHINE\%OS\%OS_VERSION
MAP INSERT S3:=SYS:APPS\WP
MAP INSERT S4:=SYS:DESIGN
MAP INSERT S5:=SYS:ACCT
MAP INSERT S6:=SYS:APPS\dBASE
MAP INSERT S7:=SYS:APPS\123
```

```
REMARK **** COMSPEC ***
COMSPEC = S2:COMMAND.COM

REMARK **** Informational ***
IF DAY_OF_WEEK = "Friday" THEN BEGIN
    WRITE "Congratulations, you made it through
       the week!
    WRITE "Welcome to your Friday."
    FIRE 9
    FIRE 8
END

IF DAY = "20" THEN BEGIN
    FDISPLAY SYS:PUBLIC\PAY.TXT
    FIRE 9
    PAUSE
END

REMARK **** The END ***
DRIVE U:
EXIT "Start"
```

# *Case Study VI: Building a Menu System for Snouzer, Inc.*

## USERNAME.SRC

(Note: USERNAME.SRC must be compiled into USERNAME.DAT using MENUMAKE.EXE)

```
MENU 01,SNOUZER, INC.
   ITEM Applications
      SHOW 02
   ITEM User Utilities
      EXEC Session
   ITEM File Management
      EXEC Filer
   ITEM Logout
      EXEC Logout

MENU 02,Applications
   ITEM ACCT
      SHOW 03
   ITEM DBASE {Batch}
      EXEC DBase
   ITEM WP {Batch}
      EXEC WP
   ITEM 123 {Batch}
      EXEC 123
   ITEM DESIGN
      EXEC Design

MENU 03,ACCT
   ITEM A/P
      EXEC AP
   ITEM G/L
      EXEC GL
   ITEM A/R
      EXEC AR
```

---

## START.BAT

Use the following START.BAT to create a secure menu system:

```
ECHO OFF
CLS
CAPTURE Q=SNOUZER_Q /NB TI=10 NT NFF
:TOP—creates a loop so users can't "escape" the
menu
NMENU username
GOTO TOP—points to the beginning of the loop
```

# Exercise 13.1: Performance Management Components

1. I
2. B
3. F
4. J
5. C
6. A
7. H
8. G
9. D
10. E

# Exercise 13.2: Memory Pools

1. I
2. J
3. C
4. D
5. A, E, G
6. F
7. B, H

# Case Study VII: Performance Management for Snouzer, Inc.

1.  *File access has been slow. The users have been experiencing slow file access and sluggish applications. What MONITOR statistics would you check?*

    Compare the number of "Total Cache Buffers" with "Original Cache Buffers" in the Main Screen of MONITOR. Calculate the percentage of "Total Cache Buffers."

    *How would you remedy the situation?*

    File caching is the key NetWare 3.12 performance management component. If the percentage of Total Cache Buffers approaches 20%, add more memory *immediately!* Ideally, it should never drop below 50%. Also, consider unloading NLMs, or downing the server to regain lost permanent or alloc memory.

2. *Error sending on network. Some users are experiencing the message* `Error sending on network` *and losing their connection. This problem occurs at random intervals when users are trying to access the file server. What MONITOR statistics would you check?* Check "Packet Receive Buffers" in the Main Screen of MONITOR. *How would you remedy the situation?* Users are experiencing the problems because there are not enough packet receive buffers to store their incoming requests. If the number approaches 400, consider increasing the maximum to 1000—`SET Maximum Packet Receive Buffers = 1000`. Also, consider increasing the minimum to 200 so that PRBs become immediately allocated—`SET Minimum Packet Receive Buffers = 200`. This parameter must be set in the STARTUP.NCF file. You will need to reboot the file server for the changes to take effect.

3. *The server is slow to respond when it is rebooted. Whenever Sophy turns on the server, it takes a great deal of time for it to come back up. This problem has caused some concern because the system is vulnerable and down during that time period.* *What MONITOR statistic would you check?* Check "Packet Receive Buffers" in the Main Screen of MONITOR. *How would you remedy the situation?* The server is slow in responding because the minimum packet receive buffers are set too low. Consider increasing the minimum to 200 so that PRBs become immediately allocated—`SET Minimum Packet Receive Buffers = 200`. This parameter must be set in the STARTUP.NCF file. You will need to reboot the file server for the changes to take affect.

4. *Users are experiencing very sluggish directory searches. In addition, some users are losing their connection during directory searches. What MONITOR statistics would you check?* Check "Directory Cache Buffers" in the Main Screen of MONITOR. *How would you remedy the situation?* Directory cache buffers improve the performance of directory searches by caching the DET and FAT tables. If the number of Directory Cache Buffers approaches or exceeds 100, consider increasing the minimum—`SET Minimum Directory Cache Buffers = 200`. Also, consider increasing the maximum—`SET Maximum Directory Cache Buffers = 500`.

5. *NLMs won't load. Sophy has been trying to load some network management NLMs at the server and has found that NLMs that require pop-up menus will not load. She receives an error message to the effect that the appropriate memory pool is out of space.*
*Which MONITOR statistic would you check?*
Check "Alloc Memory Pool" in the Server Memory Statistics screen under Resource Utilization of MONITOR. Compare the "total bytes" value with the number of bytes "in use."
*How do you remedy the situation?*
Most NLMs, especially the programs with pop-up menus, require large amounts of Alloc Short Term memory. If the total number of bytes of Alloc Short Term memory approaches 8,000,000, NLMs do not have enough memory to load. Consider increasing the maximum value to 9 million in 1,000,000 byte increments—SET Maximum Alloc Short Term Memory = 9,000,000.

**PART 3**
The NetWare 3.12 CNA
Program—Crossword
Puzzle Answers

# Acronyms

| | |
|---|---|
| AFP | AppleTalk Filing Protocol |
| ALU | Arithmetic Logic Unit |
| ANSI | American National Standards Institute |
| ASCII | American Symbolic Code for Information Interchange |
| AT | Advanced Technology |
| AUI | Auxiliary Unit Interface |
| BIOS | Basic Input/Output System |
| BIT | Binary Digit |
| BNC | Bayonet Navy Connector |
| CBT | Computer Based Training |
| CD | Change Directory |
| CD-ROM | Compact Disk-Read Only Memory |
| CGA | Color Graphics Adapter |
| CI | Copy Inhibit |
| CIM | CompuServe Information Manager |
| CIS | CompuServe Information Service |
| CLS | Clear Screen |
| CLU | Command Line Utility |
| CMOS | Complementary Metal Oxide Semiconductor |
| CNA | Certified Novell Administrator |
| CNE | Certified Novell Engineer |
| CNI | Certified Novell Instructor |
| COMSPEC | Command Specifier |
| CPU | Central Processing Unit |
| CRT | Cathode Ray Tube |
| DA | Desk Accessory |
| DCB | Directory Cache Buffer |
| DCB | Disk Coprocessor Board |
| DCE | Data Communications Equipment |
| DEB | Directory Entry Blocks |
| DET | Directory Entry Table |
| DI | Delete Inhibit |
| DIP | Dual In-line Package |
| DIX | Digit Intel Xerox |
| DMA | Direct Memory Access |
| DOS | Disk Operating System |
| DPI | Dots Per Inch |
| DRAM | Dynamic Random Access Memory |

| | |
|---|---|
| .DSK | Server Disk Driver |
| DTE | Data Terminal Equipment |
| ECNE | Enterprise Certified NetWare Engineer (now called Master CNE) |
| EGA | Enhanced Graphics Adapter |
| EISA | Extended Industry Standard Architecture |
| EMI | Electromagnetic Interference |
| EMS | Expanded Memory Specification |
| EPROM | Erasable Programmable Read Only Memory |
| ESDI | Enhanced Small Device Interface |
| ETLA | Extended Three Letter Acronym |
| FAT | File Allocation Table |
| FCB | File Cache Buffer |
| FPU | Floating Point Unit |
| FTAM | File Transfer Access Management |
| GB | Gigabytes |
| HMA | High Memory Area |
| HPFS | High Performance File System |
| IBM | International Business Machines |
| IDE | Intelligent Drive Electronics |
| INT | Interrupt |
| I/O | Input/Output |
| IPX | Internetwork Packet Exchange |
| IRM | Inherited Rights Mask |
| IRQ | Interrupt Request Line |
| ISA | Industry Standard Architecture |
| KB | Kilobytes |
| .LAN | LAN Disk Driver |
| LAN | Local Area Network |
| LIM | Lotus Intel Microsoft |
| LSL | Link Support Layer |
| MAN | Metropolitan Area Network |
| MB | Megabytes |
| MB/S | Megabits per Second |
| MCA | Micro Channel Architecture |
| MD | Make Directory |
| MFM | Modified Frequency Modulation |
| MHZ | Megahertz |
| MIPS | Million Instructions Per Second |

| | |
|---|---|
| MLID | Multiple Link Interface Driver |
| MRM | Maximum Rights Mask |
| MSAU | Multistation Access Unit |
| N | Normal |
| NAEC | Novell Authorized Education Center |
| .NAM | Name Space Module |
| NCP | NetWare Core Protocol |
| NEAP | Novell Education Academic Partner |
| NFF | No Form Feed |
| NFS | Network File System |
| NIC | Network Interface Card |
| NLM | NetWare Loadable Module |
| NOS | Network Operating System |
| NSE | Network Support Encyclopedia |
| NT | New Technology |
| NT | No Tabs |
| ODI | Open Datalink Interface |
| OS | Operating System |
| OS/2 | Operating System/2 |
| OSI | Open System Interconnection |
| PC | Personal Computer |
| PDF | Printer Definition File |
| PDS | Processor Direct Slot |
| PIXELS | Picture Elements |
| PRB | Packet Receive Buffer |
| PROM | Programmable Read Only Memory |
| PS/2 | Personal System 2 |
| PS | Print Server |
| PSC | Print Server Control |
| Q | Queue |
| RA | Read Audit |
| RAM | Random Access Memory |
| RD | Remove Directory |
| REM | Remark |
| RETLA | Really Extended Three Letter Acronym |
| RGB | Red Green Blue |
| RI | Rename Inhibit |
| RISC | Reduced Instruction Set Computing |

| | |
|---|---|
| RLL | Run Length Limited |
| RMF | Remote Management Facility |
| RO | Read-Only |
| ROM | Read Only Memory |
| RPM | Revolutions Per Minute |
| RSPX | Remote SPX |
| RW | Read-Write |
| S | Shareable |
| SCSI | Small Computer System Interface |
| SFT | System Fault Tolerance |
| SH | Shared |
| SH | Show |
| SIMMS | Single In-line Memory Modules |
| SMSP | Storage Management Services Protocol |
| SNA | System Network Architecture |
| SPX | Sequenced Packet Exchange |
| SRAM | Static Random Access Memory |
| SYSCON | System Configuration |
| TB | Terabytes |
| TCP/IP | Transmission Control Protocol/Internet Protocol |
| TI | Time Out |
| TLA | Three Letter Acronym |
| TLI | Transport Level Interface |
| TSA | Target Service Agent |
| TSR | Terminate-and-Stay Resident |
| TTS | Transactional Tracking System |
| UMB | Upper Memory Block |
| UPS | Uninterruptible Power Supply |
| VAP | Value Added Process |
| VGA | Video Graphics Array |
| VINES | Virtual Network System |
| WA | Write Audit |
| WAN | Wide Area Network |
| WORMFACE | Write Read Modify File-Scan Access-Control Create Erase |
| WOS | Workstation Operation System |
| WSGEN | Workstation Shell Generation |
| XMS | Extended Memory Specification |

# Index

**Note to the Reader: Boldfaced** numbers indicate pages on which you will find the principal discussion of a topic or the definition of a term. *Italic* numbers indicate pages on which a topic is illustrated in a figure.

## Numbers and Symbols

\# (pound sign)
  DOS executable command to allow commands to be executed in login script, 241, 546
  to identify key words for MAKEUSER utility, 196, 444

\$ (dollar sign) to designate important NetWare system files, 118, 307

% (percent sign)
  preceding identifier variables in login scripts, 233, 537, 539
  preceding menu title, 250
  preceding submenu name, 250

\* (asterisk) as DOS wildcard character, 49, 50

. (period) to separate file name or directory name from extension, 49

.. to denote parent directory, 182, 429

/ (forward slash)
  to identify DOS command switches, 49
  after network address in DISPLAY NETWORKS command, 206, 462
  to separate file server name from volume, 121, 313

: (colon)
  for console prompt in RCONSOLE, 577
  to identify devices and ports, 49
  to identify a drive letter, 48
  to identify the root of a volume, 121, 313

< (less than sign) to redirect data in DOS command lines, 49

> (greater than sign)
  in DOS prompt, 47
  to redirect data in DOS command lines, 49

? (question mark)
  as DOS wildcard character, 49, 50–51
  supported by NCOPY NetWare 2.2 command, 165

\ (backslash)
  to identify DOS directories, 49, 51, 121, 313
  to represent the root directory, 182, 429

^ (caret) to force a letter for an option in the NetWare 3.12 MENU command, 555

_ (underscore) to represent a space in the file server name, 208, 463

## A

Access Control (A) access right
  in NetWare 2.2, 145, 147
  in NetWare 3.12, 371–373

access rights
  in NetWare 2.2, *141*, 142, **144–153**
    applied to directories, 372
    assigning, 247
    directory rights for, 150–152, *151*
    effective rights for, 152–153, *153*
    functions of, 145, 371
    list of, 145–146
    required for common activities, 147
    trustee assignments for, 147–150
  in NetWare 3.12, 340, *341*, 342, **370–382**

## M

# Get the
# Best Connections

with

# Network Press

from  SYBEX

**A** full spectrum of Network Press books fill the following

section. You'll find that each has top-quality contents and

timeliness—everything you need to stay ahead in today's

fast-moving networking environment.

**SYBEX, Inc.**   2021 Challenger Drive   Alameda, CA  94501   800-227-2346   510-523-8233

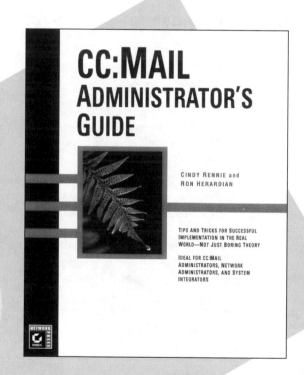

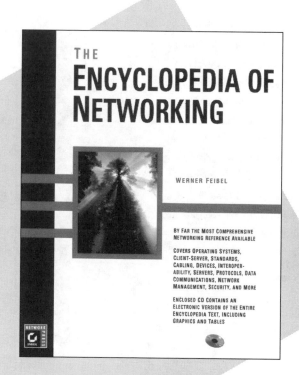

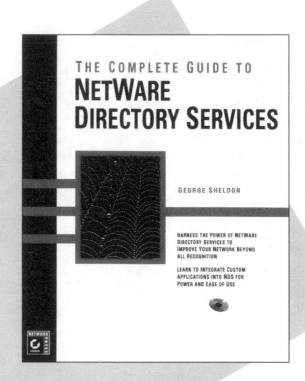

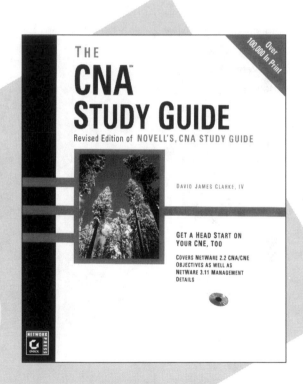

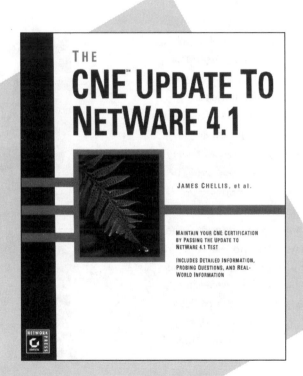

# Let us hear from you.

 **T** alk to SYBEX authors, editors and fellow forum members.

 **G** et tips, hints and advice online.

 **D** ownload magazine articles, book art, and shareware.

## Join the SYBEX Forum on CompuServe®

If you're already a CompuServe user, just type **GO SYBEX** to join the SYBEX Forum. If not, try CompuServe for free by calling 1-800-848-8199 and ask for Representative 560. You'll get one free month of basic service and a $15 credit for CompuServe extended services—a $23.95 value. Your personal ID number and password will be activated when you sign up.

 Join us online today. Type **GO SYBEX** on CompuServe. If you're not a CompuServe member, call Representative 560 at **1-800-848-8199**.

**SYBEX** (outside U.S./Canada call 614-457-0802)

*[1819-4] The CNA Study Guide*

# GET A FREE CATALOG JUST FOR EXPRESSING YOUR OPINION.

Help us improve our books and get a *FREE* full-color catalog in the bargain. Please complete this form, pull out this page and send it in today. The address is on the reverse side.

Name _____  Company _____

Address _____  City _____ State ____ Zip _____

Phone ( ) _____

**1. How would you rate the overall quality of this book?**

❑ Excellent
❑ Very Good
❑ Good
❑ Fair
❑ Below Average
❑ Poor

**2. What were the things you liked most about the book? (Check all that apply)**

❑ Pace
❑ Format
❑ Writing Style
❑ Examples
❑ Table of Contents
❑ Index
❑ Price
❑ Illustrations
❑ Type Style
❑ Cover
❑ Depth of Coverage
❑ Fast Track Notes

**3. What were the things you liked *least* about the book? (Check all that apply)**

❑ Pace
❑ Format
❑ Writing Style
❑ Examples
❑ Table of Contents
❑ Index
❑ Price
❑ Illustrations
❑ Type Style
❑ Cover
❑ Depth of Coverage
❑ Fast Track Notes

**4. Where did you buy this book?**

❑ Bookstore chain
❑ Small independent bookstore
❑ Computer store
❑ Wholesale club
❑ College bookstore
❑ Technical bookstore
❑ Other _____

**5. How did you decide to buy this particular book?**

❑ Recommended by friend
❑ Recommended by store personnel
❑ Author's reputation
❑ Sybex's reputation
❑ Read book review in _____
❑ Other _____

**6. How did you pay for this book?**

❑ Used own funds
❑ Reimbursed by company
❑ Received book as a gift

**7. What is your level of experience with the subject covered in this book?**

❑ Beginner
❑ Intermediate
❑ Advanced

**8. How long have you been using a computer?**

years _____
months _____

**9. Where do you most often use your computer?**

❑ Home
❑ Work

❑ Both
❑ Other _____

**10. What kind of computer equipment do you have? (Check all that apply)**

❑ PC Compatible Desktop Computer
❑ PC Compatible Laptop Computer
❑ Apple/Mac Computer
❑ Apple/Mac Laptop Computer
❑ CD ROM
❑ Fax Modem
❑ Data Modem
❑ Scanner
❑ Sound Card
❑ Other _____

**11. What other kinds of software packages do you ordinarily use?**

❑ Accounting
❑ Databases
❑ Networks
❑ Apple/Mac
❑ Desktop Publishing
❑ Spreadsheets
❑ CAD
❑ Games
❑ Word Processing
❑ Communications
❑ Money Management
❑ Other _____

**12. What operating systems do you ordinarily use?**

❑ DOS
❑ OS/2
❑ Windows
❑ Apple/Mac
❑ Windows NT
❑ Other _____

**13.** On what computer-related subject(s) would you like to see more books?

_____

_____

_____

**14.** Do you have any other comments about this book? (Please feel free to use a separate piece of paper if you need more room)

_____

_____

_____

- - - - - - - - - - PLEASE FOLD, SEAL, AND MAIL TO SYBEX - - - - - - - - - -

**SYBEX INC.**
Department M
2021 Challenger Drive
Alameda, CA
94501

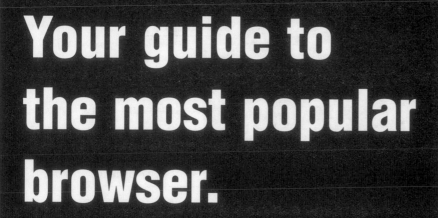

# NetWare 2.2 CNA Tasks